MW01055430

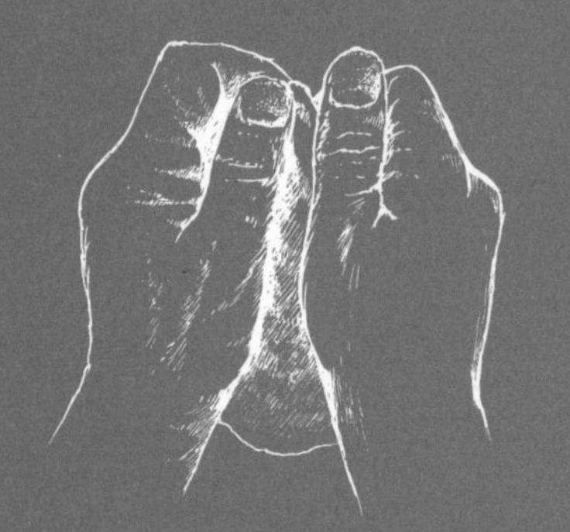

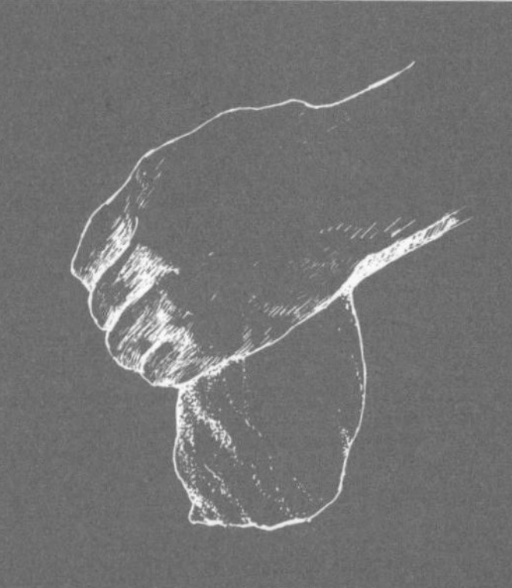

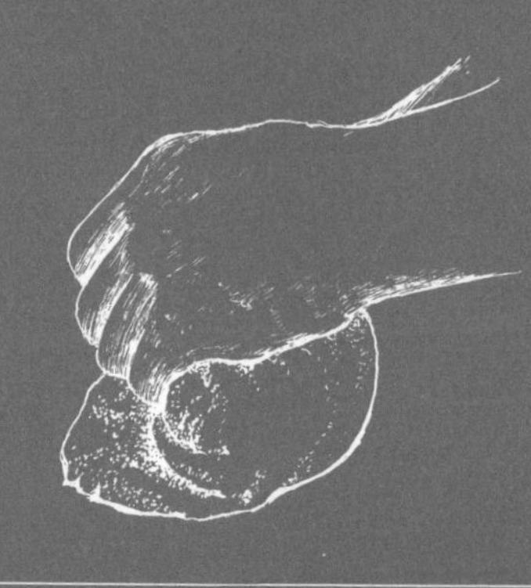

BREAD

A BAKER'S BOOK OF TECHNIQUES AND RECIPES

BREAD

A BAKER'S BOOK OF TECHNIQUES AND RECIPES

Jeffrey Hamelman

John Wiley & Sons, Inc.

This book is printed on acid-free paper. ♾

Published by John Wiley & Sons, Inc., Hoboken, New Jersey
Published simultaneously in Canada

Design by Vertigo Design, NYC
www.vertigodesignnyc.com

LIBRARY OF CONGRESS CATALOGING-IN-PUBLICATION DATA:

Hamelman, Jeffrey.
Bread : a baker's book of techniques and recipes / Jeffrey Hamelman.
p. cm.
Includes bibliographical references and index.
ISBN-13: 978-0-471-16857-7 (acid-free paper)
ISBN-10: 0-471-16857-2 (acid-free paper)
1. Cookery (Bread) 2. Bread. I. Title.
TX769 .H235 2004
641.8'15--dc22

2003022086

Printed in the United States of America

10 9 8

I DEDICATE THIS BOOK TO ALL MY TEACHERS.

THE SCOPE AND RANGE OF YOUR SKILLS HAVE HAD

AN IMMEASURABLE IMPACT ON MY LIFE.

THE BEST THANKS I CAN OFFER YOU IS TO PRESENT

A BOOK THAT IS BENEFICIAL TO OTHER BAKERS.

AND IF I ACHIEVE THAT GOAL,

I WILL HAVE SUCCEEDED COMPLETELY.

Cont

ents

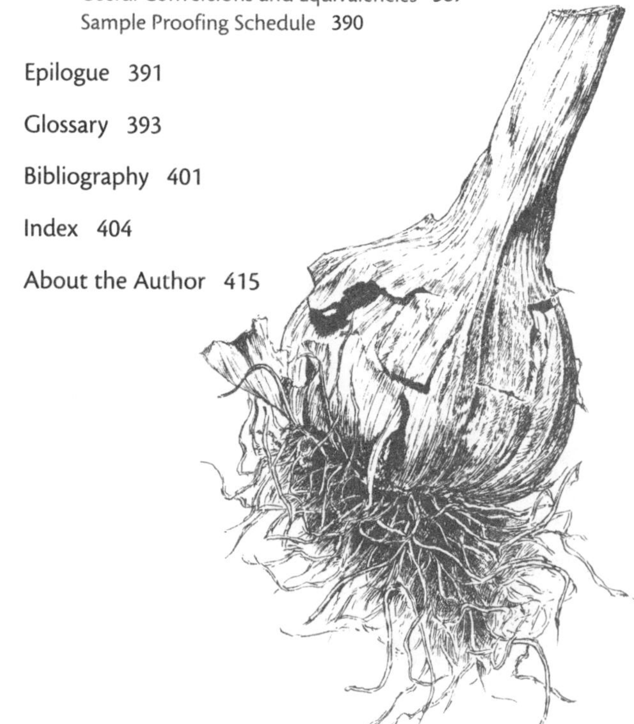

Recipes

CHAPTER FOUR

Breads Made with Yeasted Pre-Ferments

CHAPTER FIVE

Levain Breads

CHAPTER SIX

Sourdough Rye Breads

CHAPTER SEVEN

Straight Doughs

CHAPTER EIGHT

Miscellaneous Breads

CHAPTER NINE

Braiding Techniques

CHAPTER TEN

Decorative and Display Projects

Acknowledgments

I have the immense good fortune of being a baker. For me, the baker's life has always been one of work and reward. What begins as tangible—the work—has often over the years been transformed into something less tangible, because the rewards of baking are not just financial. The rewards can take the form of community service, personal growth, and often social and spiritual development. It may be commonplace these days for people to romanticize the life of a baker, but it would be wrong to underestimate the amount of work the baker is required to perform daily. Coupled as it is with early and often long hours, the baking trade is a strenuous one that requires physical dexterity, finesse, and stamina. Years of determined focus and commitment to hard work are necessary in order to achieve mastery.

When I began baking professionally in the mid-1970s, I was attracted by both the manual nature of the work and the anonymity of being a baker. What has become an explosion of "artisan" bakeries in the last couple of decades was then barely nascent. Where once there was anonymity, we now have bakers enjoying celebrity status. Regardless of the lights and clamor surrounding baking today, the bread itself is still the most important thing. A baker has the potential to make breads that are enriching, delicious, and memorable. This, I hope, remains our steadfast goal.

What a wonderful feeling it is to turn and look behind us at the hundreds of generations who have baked before us, and realize that we have inherited the accumulation of their experience. When we turn and look forward to the innumerable generations of bakers to come, we realize that we are at the fulcrum of this great balance, imbued with a deep responsibility to the future, and hopefully equally imbued with gratitude to our colleagues from the past.

James MacGuire of Montreal has been a colleague for many years. He is a true master, and I thank him for his friendship and help.

I would like to offer a final thanks to Frank and Brinna Sands, and to the employee-owners of the King Arthur Flour Company for the support and encouragement they have given me during this project.

Foreword

I have taken pleasure in reading *Bread* and being asked to give my impressions. It was for me a most agreeable surprise to find that such a book exists in English and I must add that I find it most difficult to adequately express the joy that this has brought me.

Everything about good bread is covered: how it is made, it's role in gastronomy, and as with good bread itself, one can hardly resist indulging in the pure and simple pleasure of partaking in it and savoring it.

I, who have written so much about bread, and so steadfastly maintained that well-made bread must both look good and be good to eat, see something of myself in these pages, and often, a better version of myself.

I can only hope that those whose mission it is to make good bread seize the opportunity to read our colleague Jeffrey Hamelman's book, heed his advice, and adopt his methods using due care and respect.

I should also say that it is clear that he has read my writings and often shares my opinions. I thank him for this.

As I read I sensed his great experience, which to me is such a precious thing, and therefore, in conclusion, I can only say *bravo* and once again, thanks.

Raymond Calvel

Preface

Bread. The process of bread baking is at once a simple endeavor, yet at the same time it can be one of enormous complexity.

The merest of ingredients are required, and these few are easily procured, requiring little intricacy in their preparation. And since so few ingredients are needed or necessary to the bread baker, from one bake to the next not much seems to change. One style of mixer suffices and can mix a full range of doughs. Some *couche* linens, a few stacks of proofing baskets, a decent scale, a durable work table, a couple of razor blades stuck on slender *lames,* and a sturdy oven: The needs are few. And yet from the time the grain is planted until baked bread is on the table, the hands and skills of dozens of people have been engaged. Farmers in the field plow, plant, cultivate, and harvest. Grain is transported to the mill to be tempered, ground, sifted, analyzed, and bagged—brought from berry to flour. Flour in the bag is trucked and hefted to the domain of the baker. Here the final magic is performed, for the flour is nothing by itself—it needs the baker to bring it to fulfillment, to coax all the flavor he or she can from the inert grain. The flour, unable to sustain life on its own, is transformed by the hands of the baker into wondrous bread, nurturing and nourishing. What we hold in our hands, months after the original planting of the seed, is the final resolution of the labor of many: a loaf of bread—ephemeral, fragrant, alive.

It is difficult, albeit tempting, to generalize about the quality of life enjoyed by bakers. The style of work varies so widely from one shop to another that no accurate generalization is possible. There are bakers who work in hard hats, using machinery on a scale that produces tons and tons of bread. There are bakers who work in factories larger than four football fields, and whose breads travel thousands of miles in a frozen state before reaching the final consumer. There are bakers who are not bakers at all, but simply specialized human cogs in a production plan that keeps them separate and oblivious to the labor of others in the same bakery. In these conditions, some are mixers mixing, some are shapers shaping, and some are oven workers involved in the actual bake. A shaper leaves and applies for work in another bakery. "Can you mix?" asks the owner. "No, I can't, but I sure can shape," comes the reply. In this sort of bakery, the segregation of labor ensures that no one person knows all of the owner's "secrets" of production. I would contend that the cogs-in-a-wheel approach has, at first, a deskilling effect on the workers; when the situation is prolonged, it degenerates into a dehumanizing effect.

I like to think of a more traditional sort of bakery when I think of the quality of life possible for a baker. This baker has earned, through hard work, perseverance, and dedication, the ability to perform all the tasks associated with bread production. The subtleties of the mix, the complexities and variations involved in fermentation, the strong hands and the delicate touch needed for shaping, and the finesse in scoring and baking the golden loaves are all skills he or she has developed during years of focus and growth. Problems and mishaps occur in the bakeshop, as they do everywhere, and years of experiencing the vagaries of the bake enable the baker to overcome obstacles and proceed.

In the traditional bakery, in all likelihood the baker knows a good portion of his customers, at least well enough to offer a smile and a hello. He surely has heard many a story of how his breads are enjoyed by toddlers and children, by the elderly, and by adults in their prime. It may be difficult to sort out who owns the place—is it the baker, who provides nourishment and pleasure to the community, or is it the community, which provides income and a livelihood to the baker? There is a mutual need and a mutual benefit to this relationship. The baker is a proud, valued, and essential person in the life of the community.

The work is demanding, ongoing, and manual—no need to romanticize it. The perishable nature of bread requires a constant presence and connection to its life cycle on the part of the baker. The sourdough cultures are daily links in an old chain, and each day they must be carefully fed, nurtured, ripened. Each day, their living contents are dispersed into the loaves, suffusing them with enlivening aromas and delicate, distinct flavors. Each day, the *bannetons* and *couches* give up their fragile contents, and the oven is loaded, again and again, and the bread racks are filled with golden crackling loaves. At day's end, the baker's pores have become permeated with a mingling of sweat and the fragrance of bread. And each morning, the bread racks are again empty, with yesterday's breads now in hundreds and hundreds of bellies. The bakery is quiet, the cycle of labor ready to begin again.

The baker's life may be more aligned with that of the dairy farmer—milking the cows on Christmas day, just as the baker must set the poolish and sourdough that day—than to the work life of most other members of society. Is this baking life then a drudgery? I have worn an apron and been involved with the work of bread for more than a quarter of a century. In my experience, baking has not been a segmented job, where I have been a mixer for a decade and then a shaper for another. For one whose work entails the *all* of baking, there is no confusing the natural repetitiveness of the work with drudgery. I believe that, in the lives of many bakers, an immense inner dignity develops from the daily immersion in the labor of the bake. John Ruskin, in the nineteenth century, said "*Laborare est orare,*" that is, "Labor is prayer." The baker who has constructed a life around the wholeness of bread making might justifiably feel that Ruskin was speaking about him.

PART ONE

INGREDIENTS and TECHNIQUES

It's really quite simple to make a loaf of bread: Take some flour, a measure of water, a bit of salt and yeast. Mix for a while, knead for a while, ferment for a while, then shape, proof, and finally bake for a while. Not much to it, really. It's a little more intricate if we want to make a dozen loaves, but still pretty straightforward. Making fifty loaves, or a hundred, or five hundred, or a thousand or more—now, even though the principles are the same, the stakes are higher, the repercussions from a failed batch are more resounding. But if we acquire the skill to make a dozen or a hundred or a thousand loaves, the next level of proficiency is to be able to make them *consistently.* And that, for both the professional and the home baker, is probably the greatest challenge: to be able, day after day, to adjust to the specific needs of the day's doughs, to factor in and accommodate the slight changes in ambient temperature and humidity, as well as the degree of ripeness of the poolish or biga or sourdough and the tolerance of the dough during fermentation, and to be constantly mindful of the interrelationship among all the steps in production and what small changes might be required on any given day in order to attain consistency. In short, to be successful, the baker must be able to think like a yeast spore, and sense things like lactobacilli.

If consistency is the goal, then a foremost principle of baking is that whatever we do to a loaf of bread, at any point in its production, will affect the bread throughout the rest of its trajectory from raw ingredients to baked bread; each step of the bread-making process is intricately and ineluctably connected to each subsequent step.

I like to think that a loaf of bread in one's hands is the result of a thousand factors that went into its making. In a sense, the bread always seems to be one micro step ahead of us, and our daily endeavor is to come to terms with as many of the subtleties as we can. Those who wish to conquer bread making, then, are sooner or later sure to be disillusioned. In fact, just befriending the bread is reward enough, and a much worthier aspiration.

Once the grains have been sown and grown, tended and harvested, milled and bagged, the baker has the opportunity to do his or her work. I used to marvel at my ability to make acceptable loaves one day, while the next day I would make bread that I wanted to hide. How could there be such a variation of results? Since I was not the beneficiary of a standardized apprenticeship program, my early baking years were characterized much more by empirical, practical, and intuitive experience rather than formal academic and technical training. I would never wish to forego the learning and lessons I garnered from those early years; nothing of equal value can substitute for years of in-depth, hands-on focus at the bench. As my academic understanding increased, however, so did the consistency of my baking endeavors. Reading books about baking will never be a substitute for time spent with your hands immersed in the dough, yet the quality of the baker's work can be immensely improved if he or she has an understanding of what takes place from the time a bag of flour is opened until fragrant finished loaves are pulled from the oven.

THE BREAD-MAKING PROCESS from MIXING through BAKING

1

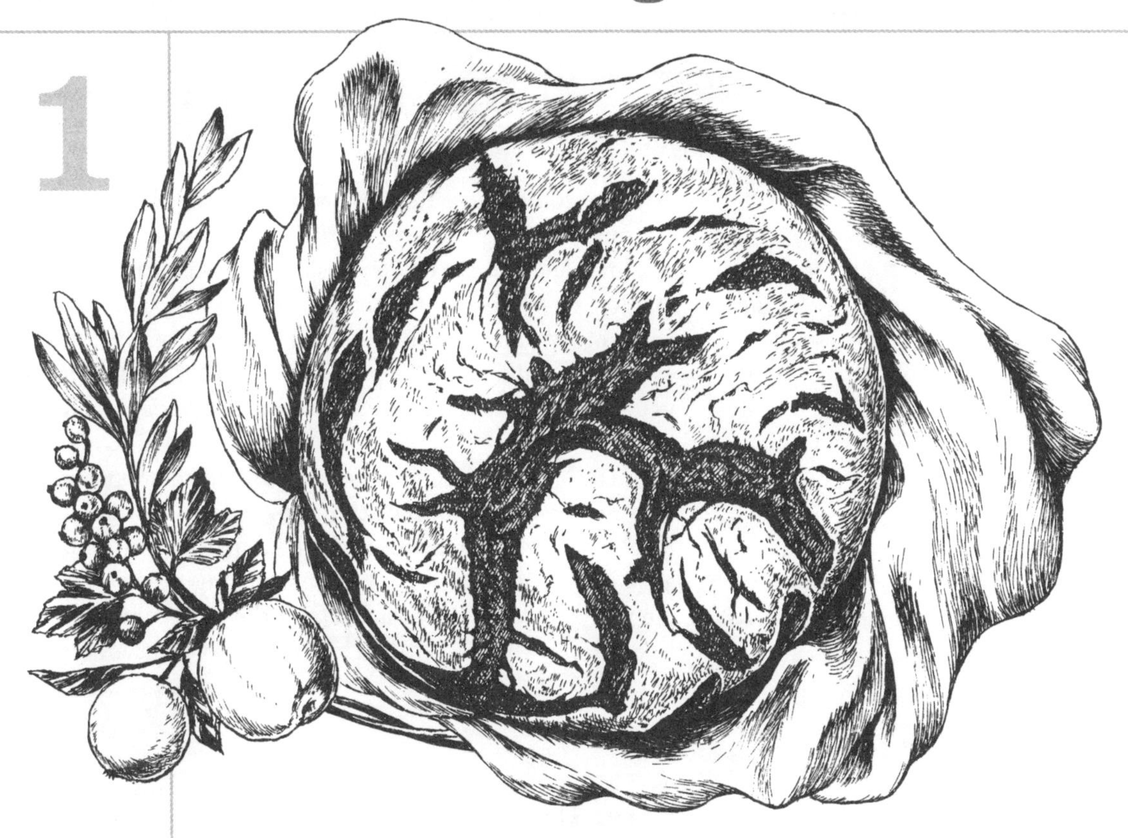

From the womb of the Earth to the mill—and beyond—the seed that makes bread is a living creature.

—H. E. JACOB, FROM *SIX THOUSAND YEARS OF BREAD*

In the discussion that follows, we will look at each phase of the bread-making process, from the scaling of ingredients through the cooling of the baked loaves. Each step of the way we will examine not only the importance of the individual step, but also try to see how each step affects the ensuing steps.

Volumes could be written on many of these individual steps, but for our present purposes, we will endeavor to present a clear overview and confine the discussion to those aspects of bread production that have a direct impact on the daily life of the baker. Some of the information presented will be scientific; I am, however, a baker and not a scientist, and the goal is to undertake explanations that are useful and applicable to the daily reality of the baker.

The bread-making process can be divided into twelve separate steps. Occasionally, one of the steps, such as folding, might be eliminated. Some steps, like bench resting or final fermentation, are fairly straightforward; others, like mixing and baking, are enormously complex. Bear in mind from the outset that whatever the baker does to his or her dough will have an impact on every step in the rest of the process.

Step One: Scaling

The first step in bread making is the scaling of ingredients. Correct and accurate scaling is necessary in order to achieve consistency and uniformity of production. When scaling, we are also calculating the final dough yield, and accuracy will prevent under- or overproduction. Therefore, cost control is a small but significant aspect of scaling. Measuring ingredients by weight and not by volume is the only way to ensure accuracy, and a reliable scale is an invaluable tool for every baker.

At Gram's House

My earliest food memories may be of bread. One of my grandmothers was Polish or Russian, depending on where the ever-changing boundary line happened to be drawn at a given time. As a boy, I visited or was visited by my grandparents most every weekend. If we went to Gram's house, there was sure to be a boundless array of home-cooked foods, which fit effortlessly into my seemingly bottomless belly. If my grandparents visited us, there was less food, but food was still the hub of the visit. No matter where the visit took place, Gram always had bread. The funny thing was, I never saw an entire loaf. In those days, people still bought bread by the pound. Gram would order a few pounds, which were then dutifully hacked off some endless loaf and wrapped in paper. The bread was crusty, dense, and fragrant. At times, we would get the end portion of this mother lode of loaves, which had a paper union stamp. We'd rip the stamp off, but usually some paper remained on the loaf. We didn't care; we ate and ate.

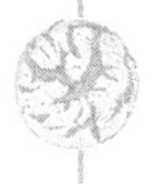

Step Two: Mixing

The first step in proper mixing has nothing to do with actual mixing at all: It involves the simple determination of the water temperature required for the mix, which is calculated by computing the desired dough temperature (described fully beginning on page 382). Consistent baking results require many things, not the least of which is consistent temperature control. The importance of spending a few moments calculating water temperature in order to achieve mixed dough in a correct temperature zone cannot be overstressed. Once we have the correct water temperature, the actual mixing can proceed.

Life in the mixing bowl is complex indeed, and it begins the moment the flour and water come together and mixing ensues. Mixing accomplishes a number of important goals. Most simply, it brings about a uniform distribution of ingredients so they are evenly dispersed throughout the dough. Other aspects of mixing are far more complex. During mixing, gluten is formed. At first, the gluten molecules in flour are randomly bunched, haphazardly oriented in all directions. During mixing, the molecules are stretched and become aligned in more or less straight lines, and it is this stretching and aligning of the gluten strands that develops the dough's strength. Mixing the dough so that the gluten is adequately developed enables the dough to stretch well, to resist ripping, and to hold trapped carbon dioxide gases that are produced during yeast fermentation, which in turn enables bread to emerge from the oven with good volume and lightness. It's a bit more complicated than that, however. There are, in fact, two proteins in flour that combine to form gluten—glutenin and gliadin—and they have seemingly opposite natures. (Rye flour has gliadin but very little glutenin, and therefore the mixing requirements as well as the dough properties for rye breads are very different than those for wheat bread. The method for mixing rye breads is discussed in detail beginning on page 189). Glutenin helps develop dough structure and the elastic quality of the dough, that is, the dough's resistance to stretching. Gliadin provides dough with its extensible characteristic, that is, its ability to be stretched. Both are necessary, and proper mixing is required to develop the potential for both elasticity and extensibility. These two qualities, in balance with each other, enable the dough both to resist stretching (elasticity) and to be stretched without tearing (extensibility). And the balance between these discrete aspects continues to be important throughout the entire bread-production process.

Here's an example: Imagine that you are shaping a baguette, and the small 12- or 14-ounce dough piece is about to be rolled to 22 inches long, with an even diameter along its entire length. If there is an excess of elasticity (this could be caused by either insufficient bench rest after preshaping, or by using a very-high-protein flour and mixing to too high a development), the dough will be fighting you throughout the rolling process—and in all likelihood it will win! Ripping and tearing, resisting and defying, by the time it is at full length it will look like it needs a hospital or a lawyer. (Now, imagine having a hundred of these pieces to roll!) At the other extreme, the dough on the bench has too much extensibility (from a weak flour insufficiently mixed, or from too long a rest after preshaping). It doesn't feel like dough at all; it's a body with no bone structure, it's a worm, a mollusk! It offers no resistance whatsoever as you roll it out, and it's flat and misshapen, and will remain so through the bake.

It's one thing to talk about gluten molecules, but I've never seen a baker mix with a microscope in hand as the dough spins. We mustn't neglect the actual hands-on aspect of mixing and the visual and tactile changes that occur. Once we put the dough ingredients into the mixer and turn it on, we begin to hydrate the flour. It is important, regardless of what style of mixer is used, that the initial process of mixing takes place on first speed. During this period of the mix, the outer surface of the starch granules become moistened, the ingredients take on cohesion, and the dough begins to form. Once the ingredients are incorporated, generally from 2 to 3 minutes after mixing begins, turn off the mixer and feel the dough (this is also a good time to taste a piece of dough to make sure salt was added). It will be sticky, shaggy, and loose, lacking in strength, smoothness, or elasticity. Pull on a handful—it will shred away from the bulk of the dough, offering little resistance. And so it should, for at this stage of mixing we are concerned above all with the *consistency* of the dough, not its *strength*.

It is woefully common at this point in the mix for inexperienced bakers to conclude that the dough is too wet and to add flour. What seems to be excessively loose dough early in the mix, however, will soon transform once the second phase of mixing—gluten development—is accomplished. Extra flour added early on has ruined many a dough. Only by feeling the dough throughout the mixing process can we understand—through our hands—the considerable change from loose and shaggy to firm, elastic, and developed.

Oxidizing and Overoxidizing

We read and hear about the need to oxidize flour before using it in bread production and, which seems somewhat contradictory, the need not to overoxidize dough in the mixer. An explanation of the needs and precautions for oxidizing flour may serve to clarify the topic.

When flour is first milled, it must be oxidized before it is used in baking. During this period of oxidization, and later when the flour is mixed with water in the mixer, things happen on a molecular level that have an important impact on the flour's baking quality. (As a baker and not, distinctly not, as a scientist, I give this miniature explanation to bakers and distinctly not to scientists.) At that misty molecular level of things, what are known as thiol groups and sulfide bonds interact with each other in the presence of oxygen. As the thiol groups oxidize, they donate a hydrogen molecule to the sulfides, creating disulfides. These disulfide bonds strengthen the gluten bonds inherent in wheat flour. Without sufficient oxidation, the disulfide bonds will only partially form, gluten strands will not develop fully as the dough is mixed, and the quality of the finished bread will suffer from poor volume and weak structure.

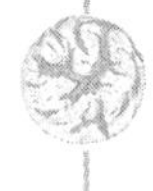

This oxidizing of the flour is best achieved simply by letting it age, from roughly three to four weeks, before baking with it. Oxygen gently penetrates the flour during this natural form of aging, stabilizing the flour and improving its baking quality. (In earlier days, flour was stored in wooden barrels or cloth sacks, both of which allowed oxygen to enter and age the flour. Double-walled bags are the norm in bakeries today, so natural aging may be a bit slower than when flour was stored in wood or cloth; nevertheless, modern bags are an improvement over cloth sacks, since the droppings of nocturnal mice on the cloth did not provide a desirable addition to the flour within.) It is only when flour has sufficiently aged that it attains its optimum baking potential. Flour that is unaged or underaged is known as "green flour." Breads made with green flour have poor elasticity, poor oven spring and loaf volume, coarse crumb texture, and a thick, unpleasant crust. Here's a dilemma: Many modern mills produce well over a million pounds of flour each day—can you imagine the miller's reaction if you asked him to store a three weeks' supply of flour so that it was properly aged before leaving the mill? An alternative to the natural aging of flour is to chemically treat it and thereby *artificially* oxidize it. In spite of the considerable negative effects on flour and baked breads, chemical aging by the addition of bleach or other artificial oxidants is common throughout the United States (see "Flour Additives," beginning on page 373, for a lengthier treatment of bleach and its consequences).

When flour is placed in the mixer and dough is mixed, oxygen is incorporated, which assists in the development of the gluten bonds. The action of the dough hook or mixing arm is adequate to provide this oxidizing of the dough. Overoxidizing the dough from overmixing, however, has negative consequences for a number of reasons. First, when overmixed, the gluten structure breaks down and the dough weakens in strength, loses elasticity, and becomes shiny and sticky as dough water, at first absorbed during mixing, is released. Second, the carotenoid pigments, which are naturally present in unbleached flour and help to impart the creamy color to it along with the wheaty aroma necessary for ultimate bread flavor, are destroyed by excessive mixing. Just as egg whites, which have a slight yellow hue, become snowy white when mixed into meringue—simply by the addition of oxygen from the mixer whip—so too will bread dough in the bowl transform from a subtle creamy color to toothpaste white when it suffers from overmixing. One further consideration is that a warm dough oxidizes more quickly than a cool dough; careful attention to dough temperatures is imperative.

Once the consistency of the dough has been checked and corrected as necessary, the gluten-development phase of mixing proceeds. Usually, the mixer is turned to second speed and the dough mixes to its appropriate development. Reach in and yank on the dough again. A well-mixed dough will resist your pulling; it will have strength and muscle, and at the same time be supple and have some swing to it. Some bakers pull off a small piece of dough and look at the "gluten window" by gently stretching the dough to the thinnest sheet possible (sometimes called the "windowpane test"). This is one way to gauge gluten development, but be careful: If the window is completely clear and the gluten totally developed, the dough has almost certainly been overmixed. *Appropriate* development does not necessarily mean *full* gluten development, and as we shall see, many factors affect the amount of time a dough mixes on second speed, and consequently how fully we should develop the gluten in the mixing bowl. If our only goal is dough volume, a lot of yeast and maximum gluten development in the mixer is the method of choice. Maximum *volume* is one thing, however, and maximum *flavor* is another, and a mixing technique that favors the utmost volume will also compromise optimum flavor.

With each revolution of the mixing arm, oxygen is incorporated into the dough and a new portion of the dough is mixed by the arm. The incorporation of oxygen is important, as it contributes to the strengthening of the gluten network. An excess of oxygen, however, has a devastating effect on dough. Carried to an extreme, the dough becomes overmixed, and the gluten bonds, after first stretching and developing elasticity, begin to break down; the dough becomes shiny and sticky as water is released back into the dough, elasticity decreases, and the entire structure of the dough unknits. Even before reaching that point of breakdown, an excess of oxidation can occur, reducing flavor and therefore bread quality.

What, then, are the considerations regarding dough development that the baker should be aware of during the mixing phase? At one extreme we have the following: The dough is mixed on high speed to maximum gluten development, and it reaches a state of maturity in the mixer, due to the excess incorporation of oxygen as well as to the dough's high level of physical development. Dough strength is at a peak, and bulk fermentation consequently must be all but eliminated. Flavor components in the flour, known as carotenoids (which also give unbleached flour its creamy color), are oxidized out of the dough due to the excessive mixing. The development of full bread flavor, which is always a lengthy process, is not possible. At the other extreme, imagine that the dough is mixed very slowly, on low speed only (or by hands or even feet, as was the case for many centuries). Gluten development is at a minimum, as is oxidation of the dough. Bulk fermentation lasts for many hours, punctuated by a number of folds, and the dough slowly reaches maturity. The carotenoids are not oxidized out of the dough, and the bread flavor is superb. Loaf volume, however, is comparatively small, because of the relative lack of physical dough development.

Autolyse

The autolyse technique was developed by Professor Raymond Calvel, the foremost expert on French bread production, and author of the important and invaluable book *Le Goût du Pain* (*The Taste of Bread*). It is an effective technique in French bread production, as well as in many naturally leavened sourdough breads. The technique involves the slow-speed mixing of just the flour and water of a formula. Salt, yeast, and pre-ferments are not included in this phase (with the exception of a liquid-levain culture or a poolish, as detailed below). Once the flour and water are incorporated, the mixer is turned off, and the dough is covered and left to rest for twenty minutes to an hour. During the rest period, the flour fully hydrates, and the gluten bonds, in spite of the lack of active mixing, continue to develop. After the rest period, the remaining dough ingredients are added, and mixing resumes, usually on second speed. Much less mixing time is required to develop the dough (in fact, the dough will develop rather rapidly, and also can break down quite quickly—you must keep a close eye on it as it mixes). The autolyse method reduces the overall mixing time (and therefore minimizes dough oxidation and loss of carotenoids) and increases the dough's extensibility. The baked loaves have a greater volume, a better flavor, a creamier and more open crumb structure, and more pronounced cuts.

Salt is not added to an autolyse, because its tightening effect on the gluten network acts against the development of the gluten bonds that the autolyse is trying to achieve. Yeast is not added to the autolyse, because if it were, fermentation would occur, and with it the beginning development of acidity and the strengthening of the dough, neither of which is desired during this phase. Pre-ferments are generally not added because of the presence of both yeast activity and acidity. The exceptions to this are when a liquid levain or a poolish is used. In these cases, the high percentage of water that is present in the pre-ferment is enough that, if the remaining flour and water were mixed without including the pre-ferment, there would be insufficient water to hydrate the flour; small pebbles of unhydrated flour would persist in the dough, right through to the end of the bake. Since the percentage of yeast is quite small in both poolish and liquid levain, however, the inclusion of either of these does not significantly affect the eventual autolyse benefits.

In levain bread production, the autolyse technique can be a great benefit: The levain contributes a considerable amount of acidity, one effect of which is the reduction of extensibility. The autolyse, by increasing extensibility, helps to offset the effects of the levain's acidity. Dough work-up is easier, and bread volume improves.

Then there is the middle ground: The dough is mixed to moderate gluten development in the bowl. Physical development is furthered both by time—sufficient bulk fermentation—and appropriate folding. The carotenoids have not suffered from overoxidation in the mixer, and contribute their part to bread flavor. Bread volume is good. What has been achieved by this method is a balance that respects both the need for gentle mixing in order to preserve the fragile carotenoids, as well as the need for adequate bulk fermentation to encourage the fullest possible bread flavor, dough strength, and keeping quality.

There is no doubt that dough of proper strength is necessary for the best bread. There are alternatives, however, to achieving complete development of the dough in the mixer, with its attendant consequences of excess oxidation and too-speedy dough maturation. Long fermentation times and the use of pre-ferments both increase the acidity of the dough through the development of organic acids; one benefit of this increased acidity is the strengthening of dough structure. Another effective method of increasing strength is to fold the dough, which has an immediate and considerable effect. The concept of the relationship among the degree of mixing, the resulting dough strength, and the fermentation requirements of that dough is an important one. Like so many parts of bread production, it is difficult to precisely quantify the parameters, for the boundaries seem amorphous and ever shifting. With careful attention to mixing and careful observation of the results (that is, dough performance), the baker can arrive at a practical, empirical understanding of cause and effect.

Mixing Time

Many other factors affect mixing time. Here is a brief discussion of some of them.

The type of mixer. Spiral mixers, oblique (axis) mixers, and planetary mixers are the most common types used by professional bakers in the United States, and stand mixers (similar in action to planetary mixers) predominate among home bakers. Not only are the revolutions per minute different in each speed for each mixer, the mixing arms affect the dough differently. Spiral mixers are highly efficient, and develop the dough comparatively quickly without an excess of oxidation. Being so efficient, they also have the ability to overmix a dough quite quickly, and so require careful timing. Oblique mixers are slower and gentler (seeing them spin, I have always believed they

Mixing Guidelines:

Different mixers and their mixing times

One of the most common defects in bread is overmixing and the consequent loss of color and flavor. Once the mixer is switched on, the bread's destiny is underway. With few exceptions, moderate mixing in the bowl—as opposed to mixing to maximum gluten development—is preferred. The dough strength that is not developed during mixing can be built into the dough through correct folding during bulk fermentation. It is in fact quite startling to see a dough that leaves the mixer as a weak sticky mass become transformed by something as simple as a few folds into a cohesive, well-structured dough, bearing little resemblance to its former self.

When bread dough is mixed slowly, on first speed only, little physical dough strength is developed by the mechanical action of the mixer. This lack of strength is compensated for by a lengthy bulk fermentation (the acidity produced during the fermentation strengthens the dough) and a few folds along the way. On the other hand, when dough is mixed intensively on high speed until the gluten is developed to its maximum, the dough is so highly developed at the end of the mix that it will not support a lengthy bulk fermentation. The dough has become overoxidized, and the fragile carotenoid pigments have been mixed to oblivion. In this case, the bread will come out of the oven sooner, but at the inevitable expense of flavor, texture, and keeping quality. For most breads then, the preferred method is the middle ground: moderate gluten development in the bowl, and folding as needed to increase dough strength.

It is hard to generalize about mixing times, because there are so many factors that affect them. Some breads are made with sourdough or some other pre-ferment, some are high in butter and eggs, others are made with soaked grains, and all these factors affect mixing time. Further, on some mixers the bowl turns, while on others it does not. One useful guideline is knowing how many rpms a mixer makes in each speed, and then to mix doughs to a certain number of rpms. Generally speaking, moderate gluten development can be accomplished by mixing to about 900 to 1,000 revolutions (doughs high in rye flour, those like brioche that are high in butter, and those that are intentionally mixed only lightly on first speed have different needs, which are detailed in the individual formulas). The following chart gives approximate mixing times to achieve 900 to 1,000 revolutions for the four styles of mixers, including home-style stand mixers. Note that rpms vary not only between different mixer styles, but also between different manufacturers' models of the same type mixer. Make a call, write a letter, but somehow—know your rpms!

For better or worse, it is true that if you mix the same dough four times, once each using one of the four different-style mixers, four different doughs would result. In other words, even if the dough is mixed to about 1,000 revolutions total, the mixing arms of the different mixers have a different action and a different effect on the dough. A stand-type mixer in particular has difficulty developing the strength of the dough, and while 3 minutes on first and 3 minutes on second speed is usually sufficient with a spiral mixer, in a stand mixer the dough will be comparatively undermixed at that point, and more second-speed mixing will be required. Without a doubt, the length of mix time is very important, but you should always factor in the feel of the dough and its degree of gluten development when mixing.

MIXER	FIRST-SPEED MIXING	SECOND-SPEED MIXING
Spiral	3 minutes	3 to 3 1/2 minutes
Planetary	3 minutes	6 1/2 to 7 1/2 minutes
Oblique	5 minutes	8 1/2 to 10 minutes
Stand Mixer (such as a KitchenAid-type mixer)	2 1/2 minutes	4 to 5 minutes

were designed to simulate the kneading performed in former times by two bakers standing opposite each other at a dough trough, literally up to their elbows in dough as they mixed). As with spiral mixers, the bowl in an oblique mixer rotates along with the mixing arm. Because of the action of the mixing arm, oblique mixers, in spite of their gentleness, incorporate a greater amount of oxygen into the dough than spiral mixers do, and overoxidation can potentially be more of a problem. Planetary mixers operate with the mixing arm descending vertically from above the bowl, which does not rotate. They are highly regarded (and rightfully so) as all-purpose mixers, since, unlike spiral or oblique mixers, they can accommodate not only dough hooks, but paddles and whips as well, and therefore can mix a great variety of products, from sponge cakes to cookie doughs. Although they are fairly inefficient as bread mixers, great bread can nevertheless be made using them. With any mixer, knowing the rpms at different mixer speeds is important. Calculating the friction factor of the machine is equally important (this is discussed in "Desired Dough Temperature," beginning on page 382).

The amount of dough in the bowl. I used to believe that when the mixer was three-fourths rather than half full, the dough developed more quickly. I was mistaken. It's true that with more dough, the greater mass means that the dough ferments more quickly once mixed, but gluten development actually takes place more quickly when there is less dough in the bowl. Envision a mixer that can hold 150 pounds of dough. Two doughs are mixed: first a 50-pound batch of dough, followed by a 120-pound batch. As the 50-pound batch mixes, a greater proportion of the overall dough is worked with each revolution of the mixing arm than when the 120-pound batch mixes. Gluten development, therefore, occurs more quickly with the smaller batch.

Hydration. Hydration is the percentage of water in a dough relative to the flour. Wet dough, dry dough—which develops more quickly? With a very dry dough (roughly 60 percent or less hydration), there is barely sufficient moisture to properly hydrate the flour, and it takes a long while to develop the gluten. With a very wet dough (roughly 72 percent or more hydration), the gluten develops more slowly too—the high percentage of water makes development more difficult. Therefore, if 3 minutes of second-speed mixing is appropriate for a dough of 66 percent hydration, more will be necessary to achieve similar gluten development as hydration heads toward the extremes.

The types of flours in the dough. Rye flour has little of the structure-forming properties of wheat flour, and you can mix it all day and not approach the kind of physical gluten development typical of wheat flour. In fact, mixing requirements are quite different with rye (they are discussed in depth beginning on page 189). When mixing whole-wheat bread, the comparatively coarse and sharp particles of the wheat tend to have a puncturing effect on the gluten network, which in turn necessitates somewhat longer mixing for dough development. White flours have their own considerations. A high-gluten white flour will require more mix time than a white flour with a lower gluten content, because it simply takes longer to develop the gluten in high-gluten flour. Soft-wheat flours, such as pastry flour, barely develop at all, and once they do, are often subject to quick breakdown if overmixed. While there are some effective methods for improving the performance of poor flour (for example, a higher percentage of preferment, more folds, or longer bulk fermentation), careful and appropriate flour choice at the outset is always recommended.

The presence of other ingredients. When fats are added in the form of butter, oil, eggs, and so on, the lipids coat the gluten strands and delay their development. As fat content increases, so too does the mixing time required to develop the dough. It is for this reason that doughs such as brioche, which typically have from 40 percent to as much as 70 percent butter in relation to flour, are fully mixed before the butter is added. Sugar also softens gluten structure, and as the sugar content in a dough increases, so too does necessary mixing time. Last, when seeds or grains, either toasted, raw, or in the form of a soaker, are added to dough, they will have a puncturing effect on the gluten, and therefore the dough will require more mixing.

Step Three: Bulk (Primary) Fermentation

As soon as the mixer is turned off, dough fermentation begins. Whatever oxygen is in the dough at the end of mixing is consumed within minutes by the yeast, and fermentation proceeds in an anaerobic state, that is, in the absence of oxygen. As a rule, fermentation is initiated either by the use of a natural sourdough, elaborated from a pure culture that the baker maintains, and added to the dough at the time of mixing in order to generate the fermentation; the use of a yeast-generated pre-ferment such as a poolish, biga, or *pâte fermentée;* the addition of commercial baker's yeast to the dough; or the combined use of two or more of these. It is during primary fermentation that the majority of the dough's flavor develops. (Needless to say, artificially speeding up this phase by using dough conditioners, powdered sourdough, or no-time dough mixes will have consequences that emphatically detract from bread quality.)

Of great importance for the development of bread flavor is the production of organic acids during fermentation. Not only do these organic acids contribute significantly to bread flavor, they also have a strengthening effect on dough structure and therefore are a major contributor to dough development. Since the organic acids develop quite slowly—it takes hours before they are sufficiently present to benefit bread flavor—the use of pre-ferments, which mature over the span of many hours and are replete with developed organic acids, is a highly effective way of augmenting bread flavor. Another result of dough fermentation is the production of carbon dioxide gas, a by-product of the yeast's activity. The carbon dioxide exists in a dissolved state in the liquid portion of the dough, where it

The Stages of Fermentation

There are four distinct, interconnected stages of fermentation in bread doughs, with a fifth that is common. Bulk (or primary) fermentation is the first stage, and it begins the moment the mixer is turned off. The dough may be folded once, twice, or even three times before dividing, but these all take place within the bulk fermentation phase. After dividing and preshaping, the second phase of fermentation begins: bench rest. Once the loaves are shaped, the third phase, known as final proofing or fermentation, begins. The final phase takes place once the dough is loaded into the oven. This phase, known as oven spring, is accelerated, since yeast activity increases dramatically in the presence of oven heat; however, it is of short duration, since the yeast dies at about 138°F. Once this "thermal death point" is reached, all fermentation ceases. An optional phase of fermentation takes place when pre-ferments are used. The hours of yeast activity that occur as the pre-ferment ripens are a distinct phase of fermentation.

THE STAGES OF FERMENTATION

Pre-Ferment	Bulk (Primary) Fermentation		Bench Rest	Final Fermentation	Oven Spring	138°F
(optional)	Fold	Fold				

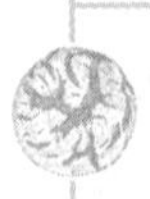

remains until the bread temperature rises during baking, at which point it becomes gaseous, expands, contributes to oven spring, and eventually evaporates.

While fermentation can occur at temperatures anywhere from 30°F to 130°F, there is an optimum range. For wheat-based breads, the range is between 75° and 78°F, while for rye breads it is 5°F higher at least. From the narrow perspective of yeast activity and gas production, maximum activity occurs at temperatures somewhat higher—over 80°F, in fact. However, gas production is not the only goal: Flavor development must also be considered, and generally speaking the flavor components in the dough prefer temperatures lower than that required for maximum gas production. For wheat breads the 75° to 78°F range encourages both flavor and volume to develop in a balanced fashion, without favoring one characteristic at the expense of the other.

Step Four: Folding

Until quite recently, most American bakers were taught to punch down the dough once or twice while it rose. While this accomplished an important need, it was at best only partially effective. Folding the dough, as opposed to punching it down, is much more effective, and is, in fact, a baker's technique that is as important as it is overlooked. Proper folding, at the right time, can make the difference between mediocre bread and exceptional bread. Why?

First of all, how to fold: Flour the work surface, using somewhat more flour than you think is necessary. Excess flour will not be incorporated into the dough because it will all be brushed off. If there is a lack of flour on the work surface, the dough will stick to it as it is folded, with an accompanying ripping of the dough's surface. This, needless to say, is not a desirable sight. Next, turn the dough out onto the work surface, so that the top of the dough is neatly turned over and spread onto the floured work surface. Now take one side, say, the left side of the dough, and lift up about one-third of the bulk and turn it vigorously onto the body of the dough. With spread fingers, use both hands to pat down the dough and degas it. Don't attempt to drive out every bit of fermentation gas; just press enough to expel the major portion of the gases. Now take about one-third of the dough from the right side and fold it in toward the center, overlapping the first fold. Again press to degas. Be sure, before that second folding and prior to all folds, that any raw flour on the top surface of the dough is brushed away. Make every effort to avoid incorporating raw flour into the dough; otherwise, gray streaks will show in the baked loaf, and the seam of baked raw flour will give a bad visual as well as eating impression. After folding the right-hand third of the dough into the center, reach over to the far side of the dough, bring about one-third toward you, and fold this portion. Finish by taking the dough closest to you and folding that portion away from you and into the center. When this fourth side has been folded, turn the dough over on the work surface so the seams are underneath, bring your arms under the dough from the left and right sides, pick it up in a mass, and replace it in the dough container. It is not unusual or particularly difficult to fold a container of 50, 60, or even 70 pounds of dough; it can, however, be a bit tricky to transfer the dough back to the container when it gets much heavier than that; in this case, a second person is helpful, or you can simply use more containers with less dough in each.

Once the dough has been folded, there is a top portion that is seamless and smooth, more or less the outer surface skin of the dough. And there is also an underside where the seams from the folding action come together. From the time of the first fold throughout the rest of the dough's journey to baked bread, the smooth top and seamed bottom remain in the same orientation. If there are further folds, the top remains the top and the bottom the bottom; when the dough is divided and preshaped, the orientation continues, as it does once the dough is shaped. Think of the dough—both in bulk and then when divided into individual loaves—as having an axis, not unlike the North and South Poles of that giant round loaf we all live on.

By folding the dough correctly, we accomplish three important things. First, we degas the dough. If the excess of carbon dioxide gas that is generated by the yeast is not periodically expelled, fermentation can be impaired. The degassing function can in fact be achieved by the old "punching down" method; however, it is more effective when the dough is folded, and other benefits are derived as well. A second benefit is the equalization of dough temperature. Although this is not always a factor, it can be helpful. If we have a cool dough in a warm room, the outside of the dough warms more rapidly than the inside; by folding, we tend to equalize the temperature by bringing the warmer outside into the center of the dough. Conversely, if we have a warm dough in a cool room, in a similar fashion correct folding helps to equalize the temperature of the dough. A third benefit of correct folding is an increase in dough strength, and this can have an enormous impact on the dough. When we fold the dough, the gluten strands are again being stretched and aligned, and we instantly feel a dramatic strengthening of the dough.

When to Fold

The third consideration when we discuss folding is when to fold, and this is the most complex aspect of the three. As we have seen, in order to preserve the flavor components of the dough and to avoid overoxidizing it, we intentionally mix to less than full gluten development. We make up for this slight undermixing by folding correctly and thereby increasing dough strength. But how often should a dough be folded? This depends on the type of dough, its desired strength, and the length of fermentation prior to dividing. Here are some considerations:

- **DOUGHS (PARTICULARLY THOSE MADE WITH BAKER'S YEAST)** that ferment for more than about 1½ hours should receive at least one fold if for no other reason than to degas them.
- **DOUGHS MADE WITH A HIGH PERCENTAGE OF PRE-FERMENTED FLOUR** (35 percent or more) tend to have good strength (because of the strength-inducing properties of the acids that develop in the pre-fermented flour), and too many folds can be detrimental to the finished bread. If an excess of strength is built into the dough, extensibility suffers, and the too-strong dough will have difficulty achieving a full rise in the oven. This is directly counter to the notion that the only thing that matters in flour and dough is protein and strength, but without a doubt when a dough is too strong its expansion is impaired.
- **DOUGHS MADE WITH WEAK FLOUR** benefit from extra folds.
- **DOUGHS WITH A HIGH HYDRATION** benefit from extra folds. Ciabatta dough, with its typically high hydration rates of 75 percent up to even 85 percent (really macho bakers go for the 90s, and more's the pity), is a great example of the benefits of folding. As more folds are incorporated, the resulting breads are progressively more voluminous.

Benefits of Pre-Ferments

A pre-ferment is made by taking a portion of a bread dough's overall ingredients, mixing them together, and allowing them to slowly ferment for several hours before mixing the final dough. Typically, pre-ferments ripen between roughly 6 and 18 hours, although there are instances where they ripen for a longer or shorter duration. Although not every type of bread dough requires or necessarily benefits from the presence of a pre-ferment, the correct use of pre-ferments has important benefits, which result from the gradual, slow fermentation that occurs during the maturing of the pre-ferment. Chapters 4 through 6 contain a thorough examination of the major pre-ferments and their individual characteristics. In this section we will take a quick glance at the main benefits derived from their use:

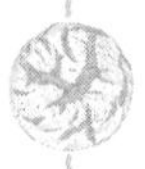

- **DOUGH STRUCTURE IS STRENGTHENED.** A characteristic of all pre-ferments is the development of acidity as a result of fermentation activity, and this acidity has a strengthening effect on the gluten structure.
- **BREADS DEVELOP A SUPERIOR FLAVOR.** Breads made with pre-ferments tend to possess a subtle wheaty aroma (or a robust rye flavor, as the case may be), delicate flavor, a pleasing aromatic tang, and a long finish. Organic acids and esters (aromatic compounds produced by the yeast) are a natural product of pre-ferments, and they contribute to superior bread flavor.
- **KEEPING QUALITY IMPROVES.** There is a relationship between a bread's acidity and its keeping quality. As the pH of a bread decreases (that is, as acidity increases), there is a concomitant increase in the keeping quality of the bread. Historically, Europeans, particularly those in rural areas, baked once every two, three, or even four weeks. The only breads that could keep that long were breads with high acidity, that is, levain or sourdough breads.
- **OVERALL PRODUCTION TIME IS REDUCED.** Above all, to attain the best bread we must allow sufficient time for its development. Straight dough that is mixed and 2 or 3 hours later is in the oven will always lack character when compared with bread that contains a well-developed pre-ferment. By taking 5 or 10 minutes today to scale and mix a sourdough, a poolish, or some other pre-ferment, we significantly reduce the length of the bulk fermentation time required tomorrow. The ripe pre-ferment immediately incorporates acidity and organic acids into the final dough, serving to reduce required bulk fermentation time after mixing. As a result, the baker can bring bread from the mixer to the oven in substantially less time than when using a straight dough.

- **DOUGHS WITH A SHORT BULK FERMENTATION**, such as sourdough rye breads, do not require any folding, nor do they benefit from it, since there is little in the way of glutenin, and dough structure will not be improved by folding.
- **DOUGHS THAT ARE BY NATURE STIFF**, such as challah, do not require folding, since they tend to have adequate dough strength at the completion of mixing. Thorough degassing may be indicated, however, when bulk fermentation is longer than an hour or so.

Step Five: Dividing

Bulk fermentation ends when the dough is divided. There are numerous mechanical methods of dividing dough, from hydraulic dough dividers that tend to drive an inordinate amount of fermentation gas from the dough, to the new generation of much gentler, and very expensive, dividers that treat the dough more kindly. Mechanical dividing is considerably speedier than hand dividing. At the same time, it can be argued that the gentleness inherent in hand dividing gives bread a better potential for excellence. A metal dough cutter, a scale, and good hands are all that is necessary to perform the task. Speed is important, particularly when dividing dozens of pieces at once, in order to avoid overaging the dough. Frequently dusting the plate of the scale and the hands with flour keeps things dry, and the work goes quickly and smoothly. If the dough sticks to either the hand or the scale, speed suffers, and so does the surface of the dough, which in all likelihood will rip. Once a dough piece has been divided at the correct weight, it is helpful to cut successive pieces as close to that size as possible. Small corrections—either adding on or taking off a small piece of dough—are almost always necessary. However, try to avoid having a dough piece that consists of lots of little chunks of dough; one cohesive dough piece is preferable to one made up of numerous small chopped bits.

Step Six: Preshaping

Once divided, the dough is preshaped in order to change the randomly shaped pieces into more consistent shapes. Preshaping organizes the dough pieces, making final shaping easier and more effective. A light rounding suffices for most breads. Final shaping must wait until the dough has relaxed sufficiently after the preshaping; therefore, the tightness to which a loaf is preshaped will determine when the final shaping can occur, and the baker can use this to his or her advantage. For example, if, because of other aspects of the production schedule, the bread needs final shaping in a relatively short time, a light preshaping is sufficient; if, on the other hand, other doughs must be divided, mixed, or loaded into the oven before the preshaped dough gets its final shaping, then a tighter preshaping is indicated, since the dough will require more time to relax before final shaping.

Preshaped loaves should be placed on a floured work surface or floured bread boards. Lay the dough pieces down sequentially, with the same number of pieces in each row. It is then an easy matter to calculate the dough yield (it is easier to calculate 10 rows with 6 loaves in each row than it is to count 60 individual pieces of dough). Further, an orderly placement of the dough means that the loaves receive final shaping in the order in which they were preshaped, so their length of bench rest will be similar.

Some bakers place the preshaped loaves onto the work surface with the seams down, while others put the good side down and the seam side up. Although it isn't exactly a raging controversy, it's worth discussing the two approaches. Those who place the seams down do so in order to keep the dough more concise, and it's true that a preshaped loaf will hold its shape better when the seams are underneath; when the seams are on top, they tend to spread somewhat. I have never found the slight spreading of the seams to be a problem, and prefer placing the good side down. Here is my reasoning: In a typical situation, I work with hundreds of loaves each day—that's a fair bit of dividing, preshaping, and shaping. Flour is spread onto the work surface prior to receiving the preshaped loaves, and in fact sometimes it is a little on the light side, sometimes a little on the heavy side. By keeping the seams up and the good side down, I avoid any incorporation of raw flour into the loaf, because none of the work surface flour becomes incorporated into the dough during shaping. All too often, when preshaped loaves are placed seams down, some work surface flour finds its way into the loaf during the final shaping, resulting in seams of raw flour in the baked bread.

Step Seven: Bench Rest

This passive step is for the dough, not the baker. The baker has many more hours to go before it's time for rest. The preshaped loaves are covered with a sheet of plastic to prevent a surface crust from forming, or vinyl covers are zipped down if the bread rests on wooden bread boards in rolling racks. As mentioned above, the duration of bench rest is directly determined by how loosely or tightly the loaves have been preshaped.

Step Eight: Shaping

Round or *boule*-shaped loaves, oblong or *bâtard*-shaped loaves, baguette-shaped loaves, and some of the less common shapes, such as *fendu* loaves where the dough is impressed with a rolling pin, tri-

The Festival of Fornicalia

On the ancient Roman calendar, February 17 was the day of Fornicalia, the Festival of the Ovens, dedicated to Fornax, the goddess of ovens. Bakers draped garlands of flowers above the hearth of their ovens, gifts were offered to the oven goddess, and prayers were made for the success of the wheat crop, which was typically sown around this time.

There is an obvious association of the words *Fornicalia* and *fornication,* and two theories exist about the connection between them. The first theory: The prostitutes in Rome were forced to ply their trade outside the city walls, and the city walls were built with an arch shape that simulated the arch of the baker's oven. Although this is plausible, I am personally more inclined toward a second interpretation of the connection: In the womb of the oven, bread comes to life, and there has always been an association of the baker's oven with the generation of life. After all, haven't we all heard the oft-repeated expression about a pregnant woman that "she has a bun in the oven"? Further, the inside of the back walls of the vagina is called the fornix. The similarity of *fornix* and *Fornax* is such that it is hard to ignore the possibility of a connection.

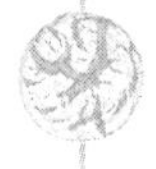

angular shaped loaves, and all the variations on the shaping theme, proceed toward their destiny as the baker takes the pre-shaped loaves and gives them a final shaping (the specifics of how to make some of the various shapes are detailed beginning on page 66). Once shaped, the loaves go into *bannetons* or between folds of baker's linen, or into metal loaf pans or onto sheet pans. Once again, they are covered to prevent dehydration of the surface. Temperature- and humidity-controlled environments, such as retarder-proofers, are excellent for this purpose, but lacking that, choosing an area in the bakery that is either warmer or cooler as appropriate, and covering the loaves with baker's linen and plastic, is adequate.

Step Nine: Final Fermentation

Final fermentation (final proofing) is the phase between shaping and loading the loaves into the oven. While bread flavor is largely determined by the correct mixing technique, the use of a pre-ferment if appropriate, the duration of the bulk fermentation, and the quality of the bake, the major goal of the final fermentation is to raise the bread to the desired degree. If the bread is either overrisen or underrisen, the eventual eating quality, as well as its visual aspect, will suffer. As a rule, bread should not be 100 percent risen at the time of the bake. Just as we will fall onto our noses if we lean over 100 percent, so too will the loaves tend to collapse if they receive a full 100 percent proofing before the bake. It is difficult to quantify with unvarying certainty the perfect degree of rise, since there are so many variables involved; however, 85 to 90 percent rising is a fair approximation to begin with. With careful and consistent observation of each bread, the baker's eyes and hands will soon learn the parameters that work best.

Step Ten: Scoring

Some breads, like braided loaves, ciabattas, *fendu*-shaped loaves, and some pan loaves, go into the oven with no scoring. Most breads, however, are scored with a razor before baking. By scoring the bread, we intentionally create a weak section on the surface of the loaf in order to encourage a controlled expansion of the bread. Left unscored, bread has difficulty expanding to its fullness; it will burst out through any weak spots on the surface (like the tube on a bicycle that breaks through a weak spot on the tire) and generally will have a distorted and tortured shape. Breads like baguettes

Baking and the Five Senses

There is a lot to be said for learning the technical aspects of bread baking, and in no way do I mean to diminish them. As we learn the academics of bread, we become better bakers: more knowledgeable, more consistent, more confident. But bread baking is about much more than just academic information—it is a pursuit that truly involves all the senses.

HEARING. As the dough spins in the mixer, the sound changes, and as it begins to develop we hear a slap, slap, slap against the side of the bowl, a popping sound as the dough strengthens. Train yourself to listen for those sounds; they are guides to the way the mixing dough is developing.

TOUCHING. So much of baking is about the sense of touch. We feel the dough as it mixes, in order to learn to understand in a tactile sense the changes it goes through from the beginning of the mix to the end. Every dough should be squeezed and tugged and examined with the fingers. As the bulk mass of dough rises, feel it; as the shaped loaves are rising, feel them—we slowly train ourselves to understand what is happening *inside* the dough simply by feeling the *outside* of the dough. How do we know when the bread is sufficiently baked? Until quite recently, no one plunged a thermometer into the nether regions of the bread. Ascertaining doneness has always been a function of touch. Just by giving the bread a good squeeze and a thump on its bottom, your fingers gradually gain the knowledge of "doneness."

SMELLING. The sense of smell is crucial! Smell the poolish or sourdough, inhaling deeply—is it wheaty and ripe, with a nice sweet tang, or bland and weak, stuck in neutral? There is a magic time once the bread is in the oven, when the first faint risings of aroma—almost timid!—waft into the air; and even when you are running around with a dozen things to do, a small smile comes to your face as you breathe in the first fragrances of the baking bread.

SEEING. Our eyes guide us at every stage, from the mix right through to the end of the bake. If "the books" say to let the loaves rise for an hour and a half, but your eyes (in conjunction with your fingers) say the bread is ready to bake after an hour and a quarter—get rid of the book and go with your senses! Our eyes divide the loaf into sections as we glide the *lame* over the dough's surface, helping us to score the bread with symmetry; our eyes guide us in determining doneness—if the bread is still too pale at the base of the cuts, give it another few minutes.

TASTING. There is so much to taste from start to finish. Always taste the sourdough when it is ripe—after all, we want to keep our sourdough healthy and vigorous for years and years, and by tasting it each time it ripens we will know if it is properly matured with a balanced acidity, or if it is showing signs of imbalance and needs some special treatment. Taste the dough as soon as the ingredients have come together—is the salt in there, and is it the correct amount? Roll a bit of the dough around in the front of your mouth once the mix is done—you will slowly learn to pick up the flavor of the pre-ferment in the raw dough. When the bake is done and the bread cool, taste it and taste it again. First with a critical mouth to determine how today's efforts went. But then for the pleasure and fulfillment of eating bread.

Hearing, touching, smelling, seeing, and tasting—bread is about all of these. The bread is always talking to us, and only when we open ourselves fully—mind and senses together—do we slowly begin to learn the subtle, but quite articulate, language of bread.

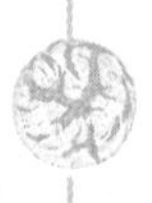

have a traditional scoring that rarely varies; other breads are scored in an infinite variety of ways, which not only give a certain distinctiveness to their appearance, but also, in a sense, become the signature of the baker.

There are, of course, no rules that dictate how to score bread. Experimentation will soon show how great an impact different scoring methods have on different breads. If a bread is weak, either from overrising or due to its nature (for example, breads with a high proportion of rye flour), light scoring is indicated: Since the lateral structure of the loaf is already somewhat compromised, deep scoring with a razor makes the bread tend to flatten out rather than rise upward. On the other hand, breads that have good strength and are at the optimum degree of rising at the time of the bake can handle more vigorous scoring, and their cuts will expand beautifully in the oven.

Step Eleven: Baking

It's unlikely that the stalk of wheat, inclining sunward, bathed with breezes and light (and ravenous bugs and withering fungi and pummeling hail and frost), is merrily awaiting the day it will become a loaf of bread. And yet I can't help but regard the baked loaf as the ultimate fulfillment of a grain's long journey from the field to the oven. So much of human culture, civilization, and history are interwoven with the story of grain, for so many centuries humans have relied (often almost solely) on grain for their sustenance, and so much of the labor of lives has been directed toward the raising, procuring, and transforming of grain into edible nourishment that it is difficult to imagine life as we know it without this food. It is true that there are rice cultures and corn cultures and manioc cultures, but wheat culture runs as deep or deeper than any in the physical and psychic realms of humans. In any event, leaving aside culture, myth, and even the bare needs of sustenance, it is only when the baker has consigned his or her loaves to the vagaries of the oven that the final transformation occurs—behold, the baked loaf.

Generally, bread dough is in the 70° to 80°F range at the time of loading into the oven, and when it enters the hot environment of the oven, it undergoes enormous physical, biological, and enzymatic changes. The first visible change to the observer is the dramatic phenomenon known as "oven spring," the last phase of fermentation. During the initial phase of the bake, there is an intensive yeast fermentation, accompanied with the production of carbon dioxide and ethyl alcohol gases. These gases expand as the dough heats up, and result in the initial phase of oven spring. This quickly ceases, however, since the yeast is killed at about 140°F. These same gases have been produced by the yeast throughout the entire fermentation of the dough, remaining dissolved in the liquid portion of the dough. A second, more pronounced, phase of oven spring occurs as these trapped gases heat up and expand. As they do, there is a prominent increase in loaf volume. Enzymes are highly active at this early stage, particularly on the surface of the dough, where they convert starches into sugarlike compounds called dextrins, which will contribute to crust coloration later in the bake. Bacteria die when the internal dough temperature reaches about 122°F; also at about that temperature, the starch in rye flour begins to gelatinize (the potentially disastrous consequences—the starch attack—are described on page 47).

During the outset of the baking process, the flour starches absorb water, swell, and become glossy (when bread dough is mixed, only the outer surface of the starch granules is moistened; later, under the influence of the heat of the oven, the water is able to penetrate into the granules). As temperatures increase from 140°

TEMPERATURE INFLUENCES ON BREAD AS IT BAKES	
77° to 122°F (25° to 50°C):	**Rapid increase in yeast fermentation; increase in enzymatic activity; beginning of crust formation; starch swelling; accelerated gas production and expansion contributing to oven spring.**
122° to 140°F (50° to 60°C):	**Rye starch begins to gelatinize; bacteria die; enzymes in yeast are inactivated; yeast reaches "thermal death point" (at about 140°F).**
140° to 158°F (60° to 70°C):	**Wheat starch begins to gelatinize; loaf expansion slows; coagulation of gluten begins; amylase enzymes reach maximum activity.**
158° to 176°F (70° to 80°C):	**Gluten coagulation is complete and dough structure is formed; enzyme activity decreases; rye starch gelatinization ends.**
176° to 194°F (80° to 90°C):	**Wheat starch gelatinization is complete; enzyme activity ceases.**
194° to 212°F (90° to 100°C):	**Maximum internal loaf temperature is reached; crust coloration begins.**
212° to 350°F (100° to 177°C):	**Maillard reaction develops crust color; ketones and aldehydes form, eventually contributing to flavor and aroma.**
300° to 400°F (149° to 204°C):	**Further crust color and flavor development through caramelization.**

to 158°F, swollen wheat starch granules begin to gelatinize and contribute to the formation of the crumb. Loaf expansion slows down at around 140°F, at which temperature all the carbon dioxide in the dough has been released. Amylase enzyme activity increases to its maximum during this period. Also at this time (about 145°F), the gluten, initially soft and with no firm structure at the time of the load, begins to stretch and expand until, at approximately 167°F, its coagulation is complete and the loaf structure is set. As internal dough temperatures continue to increase, enzyme activity as well as starch gelatinization slow correspondingly, until, at around 194°F, they cease.

The crust of the bread is the only part of the loaf that exceeds 212°F; the internal temperature of baked bread reaches a maximum of about 210°F. When surface dough temperatures reach 212°F, crust formation and coloration begin, due to the process known as the Maillard reaction, a complex chemical change that causes a rich browning of the bread's crust (or the surface of a grilled steak) and contributes significantly to the flavor of baked bread. The Maillard reaction occurs in the presence of heat, moisture, protein, and reducing sugars, all of which coexist when properly made bread is loaded and steamed. Substances called aldehydes and ketones are formed in this temperature range, and they too contribute to the aroma and flavor of baked bread. At surface temperatures of approximately 350°F, the Maillard reaction is complete. A further contributor to crust color and flavor is caramelization, which occurs at temperatures between 300° and 400°F.

Moisture Loss in Baked Bread

A baked loaf never weighs as much as an unbaked one. The water evaporation in dough can be as much as 10 to 20 percent. Some of the various factors that affect the amount of moisture loss in baked bread are:

- **LOAF WEIGHT.** Larger pieces tend to lose a lower proportion of their initial weight.

- **DOUGH SHAPE AND CRUST-TO-CRUMB RATIO.** Long, skinny loaves such as baguettes are characterized by a high crust-to-crumb ratio, and lose a considerably higher percentage of moisture than the same dough weight shaped into a round or oblong loaf. Pan breads have less evaporation than hearth-baked loaves of the same weight.

Steam

Anyone who bakes with a steam-injected oven knows the virtues of steam. With the exception of breads that receive an egg wash prior to baking and therefore do not require steam, every bread benefits from steam. Just prior to loading the oven, steam is injected into it so that the loaves enter a moist environment. Once loaded, a second steaming is applied. If the oven's steam injection is effective, approximately 4 to 6 seconds of overall steaming is normally appropriate. It is, unfortunately, quite commonplace to see over-steamed bread (if a little is good, more must be better, and besides, that oven cost $45,000 and I want to get my money's worth from the steam injection); the consequences are flattened loaves with a thick, chewy crust and cuts that don't spring open. If bread is slightly underrisen, a little extra steam ensures that the surface of the loaf remains moist longer, so the bread can rise more. If bread is slightly overrisen, somewhat less steam is necessary, since it is important to have the crust firm more quickly to prevent the bread from flattening out. Proper steaming has a profound effect on bread for a number of reasons: It promotes a rich color to the crust and a surface shine on the loaf, and it also increases the volume of the bread. Let's look at the details of each of these.

Crust color is enhanced when steam is injected into the oven. This is because during the early stages of baking, there is a rapid increase in enzymatic activity on the surface of a loaf. These enzymes break down the starches in the dough into dextrins and other simple sugars called "reducing sugars"; these substances eventually contribute to crust color. Steaming the oven has a cooling effect on the dough, and this enables the enzymes to remain active for a longer period of time, yielding richer color. In an unsteamed oven, the surface of the loaf quickly becomes too hot for these enzymes to function, and the resulting bread will have a pale, lusterless crust.

A properly steamed oven promotes a crust with a good sheen to it. This is because steam at the initial stages of baking provides moisture that gelatinizes the starches on the surface of the loaf. The starches swell and become glossy, resulting in a shining crust. In an oven without steam, the crust undergoes a process called pyrolisis. In this case, instead of gelatinizing, the starches and the crust of the bread remain dull.

A properly steamed oven results in bread with better volume. As the bread enters the hot environment of the oven, there is a rapid increase in volume due to oven spring. When we load an oven without steam, the surface of the loaf quickly heats up, and as a crust forms on the surface, oven spring is reduced and the bread's ability to attain further volume is impeded. On the other hand, in a steamed oven, the surface of the

- **LENGTH OF BAKE.** There will obviously be a greater weight loss the longer bread bakes. A full bake yields a richer bread flavor, a fact too often underestimated.
- **HEAT.** A hotter oven will bake bread more quickly, and overall evaporation and weight loss will be less than if the same dough weight and shape were baked in a lower oven.

dough remains moist longer, enabling greater oven spring to occur before the formation of a surface crust, and the result is bread with superior volume.

The benefits of steam occur only during the first third or so of the baking cycle. If the baker neglects to inject steam at the time of bread loading, he or she cannot compensate by steaming the oven several minutes later. In order to ensure that the crust remains thin and crisp, it is important to finish the bake in a dry oven. For this reason, the oven should be vented or the doors notched partially open for the last portion of the bake. As a general rule, once the bread begins to show color, the vents can be opened for the duration of the bake. In the home oven, venting can be accomplished by cracking open the oven door slightly with a metal spoon.

When baking naturally leavened breads, that is, breads made with no commercial yeast, the proper steaming technique is slightly different. In order to assure that the breads have the opportunity to reach their optimum rise, it is first necessary to give the oven a full steaming just prior to loading the breads. Once loaded, steam again, slightly longer than you would for a yeast-leavened bread. And once that steam has subsided (perhaps 1 to 2 minutes after the steaming), give the oven one more hit of steam. The effect of the extra steam is to ensure that the loaves remain moist on the surface long enough to rise fully, a process that takes longer with naturally leavened breads than with their yeasted kin. As with any bread, once a surface skin has formed, it is difficult for the loaf to break through to further expansion. Since naturally leavened breads spring more slowly in the oven, the extra steaming delays the formation of the surface skin, and loftier loaves are the result.

Even in the home oven, a reasonable amount of steam can be created. First of all, a preheated baking stone of some sort should be used for most bread. As the stone is pre heating, a sturdy cast-iron pan should be placed in the oven. When the oven is good and hot, and the bread ready to load, bring a cup of water to the boil. As it is heating, throw a couple of ice cubes onto the bottom of the oven (or, as this could warp the oven floor, into a small loaf pan on the bottom of the oven). The ice will serve to moisten the oven, which is quite different from steaming the oven. Next, place your bread on a peel, score the bread and mist it lightly, open the oven door, load the bread onto the stone, pour the boiling water into the superheated cast-iron pan, and shut the oven door right away. I keep honeybees, and always wear my beekeeper's gloves, which go up to the elbow, when I steam the oven this way at home. Be sure to wear a long-sleeved shirt and gloves of some sort to avoid a steam burn.

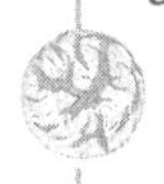

- **TYPE OF OVEN.** Wood-burning brick ovens, steam-injected deck ovens, rotary rack ovens, and unsteamed pizza-style ovens can each affect the rate of moisture evaporation, although the heat of the baking chamber, the size and shape of the loaves, and the degree of baking combine to have more of an impact than the type of oven used.

Old Bread

I was in the midst of a week of teaching a professional bread class at King Arthur Flour's Baking Education Center, when I had an unexpected visit from a dear friend, the great Austrian baker, pastry chef, and chocolatier Markus Färbinger. As we chatted, he kept taking chunks from a loaf of sourdough that had been cut for evaluation purposes quite some time earlier. "Markus," I said. "Let me get you another loaf; that one is way too hard." Markus looked up from his munching, his eyes half amused and half admonishing. "Old bread isn't hard," he said. "No bread is hard."

Step Twelve: Cooling

In a technical sense, a loaf of bread begins to stale the moment it is removed from the oven. This is true, as it is also true that we humans and other living creatures begin to die the moment we are born. In fact, the quality of a loaf is never at its best when first pulled from the oven. While really bad bread may only be palatable when eaten warm (if at all), well-made breads never possess their finest aroma or flavor until they have cooled completely. While warm, the crumb remains doughy and the aroma flat. Some types of breads, for instance sourdough breads, don't come into their own until they have had a few hours or more for their flavors to settle and mingle after cooling. In the case of rye breads made with a high proportion of rye flour, 24 to 48 hours of resting after the bake is necessary for the crumb to stabilize and full flavor to develop. The crumb then loses its threat of gumminess and the flavors meld and mingle beautifully. The eating quality can increase for days.

Delaying Staling

There is, somehow, a distinction between old bread and stale bread. Old bread (well made) can, like old people, improve in character. The wonderful crust of the fresh loaf may be gone, but there is a subtle complexity that accompanies the bread as the days go by. Nevertheless, bread does eventually age and deteriorate. This process of staling is called "starch retrogradation." Prior to baking, starch is in a crystalline state; during baking, the starch gelatinizes as it swells with water. As the baked bread begins to cool, the starch begins to revert to its former crystalline structure and the crumb of the bread hardens. While eventual retrogradation and staling cannot be eliminated, there are ways to prolong the onset and somewhat delay the effects:

- **COOL THE LOAVES CAREFULLY AFTER BAKING.** Air currents on bread hasten the evaporation of moisture from the crumb and cause a premature crust to form on the surface of the loaf (in humid environments, some airflow can help to pull moisture away from the loaves, helping the crust to remain crisp).
- **BAKED BREADS WILL STALE MOST QUICKLY** at temperatures between 32° and 50°F. Clearly, the worst environment for bread is in the refrigerator.

- **WHEN COOLED BREAD IS WRAPPED TIGHTLY** in plastic and frozen to 0°F or lower (particularly if the freezing is done very rapidly), the rate of staling is slowed. However, the bread then goes through the danger zone of 32° to 50°F twice—once as it cools, and again as it is thawed. Even in the best of freezers and with the best possible wrapping, long, skinny loaves like baguettes tend to dry out after a few days; larger round or oblong loaves will keep longer, as will breads that contain a portion of fat. Nevertheless, freezing should not be considered a long-term solution or technique.

- **ONE OF THE GREAT BENEFITS OF USING PRE-FERMENTS** or having a long bulk fermentation is that the organic acids developed in the pre-ferment phase or during the lengthy fermentation assist in lengthening the shelf life of bread. The appropriate use of pre-ferments can always be recommended as a way to, among other benefits, add some hours to the fresh life of bread. It is fairly common to read that adding sugar is a good way to extend a bread's shelf life. Although this is technically true, it can rarely if ever be considered an intelligent or skillful way to accomplish that goal. The addition of sugar may increase shelf life, but texture and flavor will certainly be compromised in breads that do not ordinarily contain sugar.

- **STALE BREAD CAN REGAIN SOME OF ITS FORMER EATING QUALITY** if reheated right to the core, which allows the starches to once again gelatinize and the loaf to take on some of its former characteristics. However, it quickly reverts to stale, and should be eaten soon after reheating.

Tasting Bread

It might seem odd to think in terms of learning how to taste bread, but I confess that for years—most of my baking life, in fact—I did not eat bread with an eye toward critical assessment. True, we don't want to sanitize or negate the wonderful pleasure of savoring a slice of well-made bread by confining it to "objective" criteria in an attempt to critically evaluate it. On the other hand, the baker must have standards of judgment, and must be able to appraise the relative merits of today's bread, if for no other reason than to be able to compare it with the breads of yesterday and tomorrow. One of the more alluring aspects of bread baking is the very fact of its variability: The same amount of flour, water, salt, and yeast that made bread today can make a bread with subtle but perceptible differences tomorrow. In fact, sometimes the results one day are sublime, and the next day disastrous. The baker keeps returning to the bench, ever striving to redeem the mistakes of yesterday, ever seeking to improve the bread.

In any case, developing a language to assess our products allows

(continued)

us to monitor our daily efforts, which in turn can be beneficial in achieving breads that stay within certain quality parameters. Where do we begin? In 1996, I was chosen as one of three Americans to represent the United States in the Coupe du Monde de la Boulangerie (the World Cup of Baking, held in Paris every three years). Bread was one of three areas of competition (Viennoiserie and Artistic Showpiece were the other two). It was in preparation for the competition, and then at the competition itself, that I initially began learning how to evaluate bread with a certain degree of objectivity. Each of the twelve countries that competed in Paris was required to make five different breads, and each bread was judged based on several criteria: weight, volume, taste, and aspect. Weight was a completely objective matter. For example, the baguettes were to weigh 250 grams. If they were within 5 grams of that, they received full score, with 1 point being lost the further the weight strayed from 250. Volume was gauged in relation to weight. In other words, if the baguette weighed 250 grams, was it a voluminous pillow of dough? Was it a truncated, dense stick of a loaf? Or was the volume appropriate to the weight? This too was a relatively objective aspect of the judging.

Taste was the third criteria considered by the judges, and here some of the lines did blur. After all, what one person deems fine is poor by another's standard. Nevertheless, one would expect that there would be reasonable commonality among the judges. The final category considered by the judges was that of "aspect." Aspect, a slightly vague and subjective consideration, included a multitude of assessments. For instance, were the cuts evenly spaced on the baguettes? Were they of equal length and depth? Did they cover the entire surface of the loaf symmetrically? How was the shaping? Was there a nice balance along the entire loaf? The inside of the loaf held other clues to quality. Was there a random, open cell structure? Was the interior of the baguettes tight and devoid of holes? Were there holes big enough to hide a mouse? How about the color of the crumb, was it snowy white or creamy? And were thin, translucent cell walls evident in the interior?

Characteristics such as creamy color, random cell structure, and translucency of the cell walls in the crumb of a white flour loaf are all suggestions of quality. They are not, however, guarantees of quality. Many a loaf looks great, but doesn't meet the ultimate standard of aroma and flavor, and these are the final arbiters. When we assess breads from this perspective, we look for a wheaty aroma. It may be subtle because, after all, the ingredients are few, and these few do not shout. Further, we want to smell the inimitable aroma of fermented flour. So, when you taste bread, do so without butter, or cheese, mayonnaise, meat, or anything at all. First, eat the bread, taking a bite that includes both crust and crumb. Chew slowly and conscientiously. The tongue picks up salt, sour, sweet, and bitter, so at first just a few sensations will be prominent. Keep chewing. As you inhale and exhale, your nose will register a myriad of subtle flavor notes. And at last, swallow. Did you enjoy a delicate nuttiness in the flavor? A suffusing sense of wheat and fermentation? And finally, is there a long and lingering finish? Did you still taste the bread several minutes after swallowing? If we train ourselves to taste with care and give consideration to what we are experiencing, our vocabulary of bread assessment will grow, and along with it our discernment.

It is interesting to see words like *subtlety, delicacy,* and *long finish* being used in relation to the taste of bread. But really it is not so unusual. Bread, after all, holds its place with wine and cheese as one of the three great fermented foods of Western culture, and these terms apply as much to bread as they do to the finest wines.

INGREDIENTS and THEIR FUNCTION

2

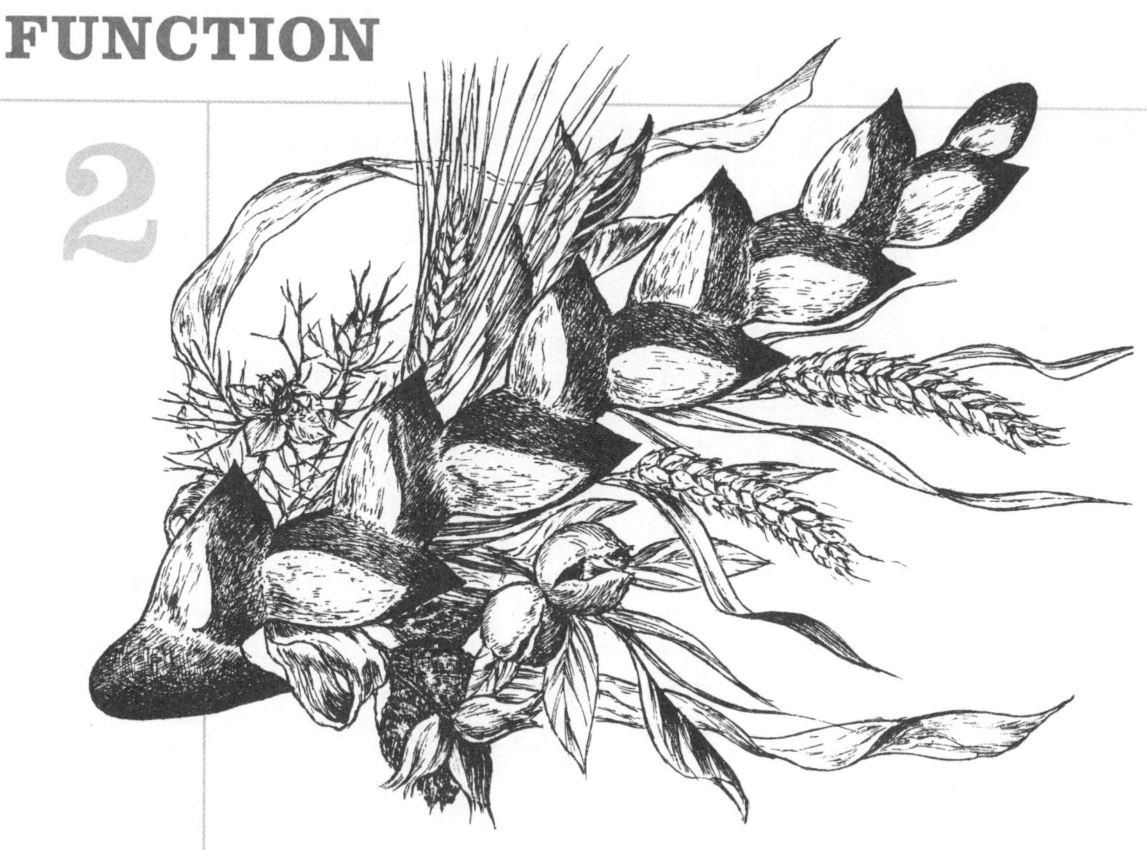

Bread is made from just flour, water, salt, and yeast. Just as the earth is made from just earth, air, fire, and water.

—CAROL FIELD, AUTHOR

To make bread with consistent high quality requires the mastery of many skills: tactile, physical, technical, academic, and, I might even suggest, intuitive. Understanding the role played by the ingredients used in bread production is one way the baker maintains consistency in the outcome of his or her labors.

In an endeavor such as bread baking, where a comparatively small number of ingredients are used, a change in one can have a significant impact on the results. For example, if a baker decides to increase the percentage of rye flour in a formula for naturally leavened bread from 10 to 20 percent, not only will the final taste of the bread be altered, but the dough's rate of fermentation as well as its final volume will also be impacted by the increase. It is not so much a matter of one formula being "better" than another; rather, changes in ingredients produce changes in all aspects of the dough's development, and therefore a thorough understanding of the function and effect of the major bread ingredients will be a large benefit to achieving consistent production results, whether for a few loaves baked in a kitchen oven, or a few hundred baked in a big hearth oven. In this chapter, we will first look at the Big Four—flour, water, salt, and yeast—and then at some of the other ingredients used in bread baking.

Flour

The topic of flour is enormous. Hundreds of pages could be devoted to a discussion of it, and once written, hundreds more could be added. Civilizations have risen around wheat-growing regions; governments have fallen when their ability to guarantee the availability of bread faltered; individuals have made fortunes from manipulations of the grain trade; social injustice stemming from the grain trade has kept thousands of people impoverished. For centuries, in many parts of the world it was bread alone that provided people with the strength to live and to labor. During difficult times, for example in England at the end of the eighteenth century, it took more than 100 percent of the breadwinner's salary simply to purchase the family's bread (baker and anthropologist Jules Rabin of Vermont told me in conversation that bread functioned during that era as oil does in our own times, that is, as the fuel that did the work for society; bread was the *literal* fuel, and humans the machines). Hunger, that is to say, the lack of bread, was used as a tool to control the workforce (as the English Reverend Joseph Townsend wrote in 1786, speaking of the poor: "It is only hunger which can spur them on to labour. Hunger will tame the fiercest animal, it will teach decency and civility, obedience and subjection, to the most brutish, the most obstinate, and the most perverse."). There were periodic failures of the wheat crop, or harvests too small to guarantee enough bread for all. Lack of bread led directly to civil unrest and rioting, as it has even to this day in parts of the world where bread remains a primary food source.

In the 1770s, the French investigated ways of combining other grains and vegetables with wheat in order to make palatable and nutritious bread during times of wheat shortages or famine. Similarly, the English looked into alternative grains as a way of ensuring sufficient bread for the masses. *The Annals of Agriculture,* published in London in 1796, gave a detailed account of experiments in making seventy different breads using various ingredients: "The following were the species pitched upon, viz. Wheat, rye, rice, barley, buck wheat, maize, oats, pease, beans, and also potatoes." The results appear to have been mixed. On the one hand, it was opined that "at first a change may prove disagreeable, yet the practice of a few days will soon reconcile the stomach to almost any species of food." Yet in spite of this hopeful pronouncement, not everyone enjoyed these hybrids: "In Nottinghamshire, opulent farmers consume one-third wheat, one-third rye, and one-third barley; but their labourers do not relish it, and have lost their *rye teeth* [taste for rye]."

The preeminence of wheat as a foodstuff is centuries old. Archeological evidence provides us with a fascinating insight into the origins of wheat cultivation. More than eighteen thousand years ago, in the area from the eastern shores of the Mediterranean to the Persian Gulf, in what is now Iraq and Syria, wild grains such as emmer and einkorn ("one seed") were being harvested by humans. By chewing the grains, soaking and pounding them, or parching or simmering them, people received life-sustaining nour-

Wheat Harvest

There is something about the wheat harvest that invariably inspires one to stop and take note. Until the 19th century it was done by people who worked together and gathered the wheat essentially by hand. Those sheaves of wheat, carefully gathered and tied together, standing like sentinels in a field, symbolize the annual rhythm of civilization in a way that nothing else can.

Today the harvest is accomplished quite differently, but it's still somewhat awe-inspiring. In America it starts in late May in the southern plains states, when the annual migration of the great wheat combines begins. Over the next few months, like great beasts they graze their way north into Canada, consuming each crop as it reaches its apogee. Although these machines represent twentieth-century "high technology," they have an archetypal model in the massive migrations of animal herds that have occurred annually for thousands of years, giving this event a very primordial implication.

—Brinna Sands,
The King Arthur Flour Company,
Norwich, Vermont

ishment. Gradually, it was discovered that by intentionally planting some of the seeds, a crop could be cultivated. This led to the establishment of settled cultures, as people changed from a hunting-and-gathering lifestyle to one of cereal farming, and later, animal husbandry. These early civilizations learned that by planting the seeds that were the largest, or most resistant to insect infestation, or those that held firmly to the plant during rain or wind, they could improve the quality of the grain they harvested. Since those ancient days, what was originally a primitive pursuit has become today a complex science, and yet the goal has remained the same: to manipulate grains in order to have a measure of control over their characteristics. (Looming ominously on the near horizon is the possible commercial introduction of genetically modifed wheat in the United States.)

Wheat

Today, there are six classes of wheat cultivated, within which there are some thirty thousand varieties. (There is an immense amount of acreage planted to wheat in North America—over 60 million acres in 2001—and it would be easy to conclude that wheat as we know it has always grown on the continent, but in fact wheat is not indigenous to North America, and was originally brought by farm immigrants from Europe.) The six classes of wheat are hard red winter, hard red spring, hard white winter, durum, soft white winter, and soft white spring. It is the first four that are of primary interest to the bread baker (the soft wheats have a lower proportion of protein and a higher proportion of starch than the hard wheats, and are more applicable to the production of pastries and other baked goods that don't require a highly developed gluten structure). For our discussion, we will focus on the first four classes of wheat.

Winter wheat (both red and white) is grown in areas of comparatively gentle winters. Northern Texas, eastern Colorado, Nebraska, and Kansas are the primary winter-wheat-growing regions in the United States, with Kansas being the nation's highest producer. The grain is sown in September and October; it sprouts and grows four or five inches before winter arrives. It spends the winter in a dormant phase, hopefully protected by a covering of snow. In spring, it resumes its growth, and harvest of the wheat begins in May, continuing until early to mid July.

Hard red spring wheat has a different growing culture. In North America, it is sown in areas with fierce winters, such as the

Dakotas, Minnesota, Montana, Alberta, Saskatchewan, and Manitoba. The seed is planted in spring, goes through its entire growth cycle during spring and summer, and is harvested in mid- to late summer.

Hard white wheat differs genetically from red wheat in that it contains a recessive gene for bran color, resulting in a lighter appearance to the grain. Further, the bran flavor is milder than that of red wheat, so breads and other baked goods made with whole-wheat flour milled from white wheat are lighter in color and more subdued in taste than those made with red whole-wheat flour. It is easy to be confused by the term *white whole wheat,* which after all sounds somewhat contradictory. Since the bran is "white," the flour milled from the entire kernel is therefore "white whole wheat." As with red wheat, typically the germ and bran are removed from white wheat, and although whole-wheat flour is available for both red and white wheat, almost all of it is milled into white flour.

White flour made from hard white wheat has been preferred for many years in some overseas markets for two reasons: First, the lighter bran particles present when the grain is milled into white flour yield whiter products, considered more desirable in foods such as Chinese-style noodles; second, since the bran is lighter than in red wheat, even at higher extraction levels (80 percent and above), the flour remains comparatively white. Much of the reluctance of North American farmers to grow white wheat was due to its tendency to sprout in the field during wet weather. When this occurs, both farmer and baker can have difficulties. The farmer may have grain with poor storage quality, while the baker may find that advanced levels of amylase activity resulting from the sprouting of the grain can negatively impact dough performance. New varieties of white wheat were developed in the 1980s and '90s, mostly at Kansas State University, and the sprouting tendency has been corrected. In some countries, for example Australia, white wheat is the dominant class grown; in the United States, Kansas has the most acreage of white wheat under cultivation. Analysis shows little nutritional or compositional differences between red and white wheat.

Durum wheat, cultivated mostly in North Dakota, is grown primarily for use in pasta production, but it does have an application in bread baking. It is interesting to note that while durum flour has a higher percentage of protein than either winter or spring wheat, the protein is by no means all usable in the forma-

Winter Wheat Way Up North

Often, things I have accepted as true for years turn out to be not quite as I imagined. An example comes to mind: the growing culture of winter wheat.

I had an interesting meeting with Robert Beauchemin, the owner of an organic flour mill in Québec, La Meunerie Milanese. He mentioned that he tries to visit the farmers who grow the wheat that he mills, and had recently been to northern Saskatchewan for that purpose.

"Must be all spring wheat they grow up there," I said.

"No, actually they plant winter wheat."

I was startled to hear this. "How can they grow winter wheat in such a harsh climate?"

"The grain is planted in August before the ground freezes, and spends the long winter under a cover of snow. When the ground finally thaws in May, the wheat resumes its growth. It is so far north that there are over twenty hours of daylight each day, and this allows the wheat to reach maturity." What a wonderful example, not only of the adaptability of wheat, but even more so, the skill and ingenuity of humans in growing food.

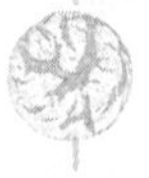

tion of the gluten matrix. There is a tendency for doughs containing a high proportion of durum to break down during mixing, and the baker must keep a careful eye on the degree of development in the mixer. With most all breads it is recommended to bring strength to the dough not just through mixing but through fermentation time, the use of pre-ferments, and proper folding; this certainly holds true in the production of breads made with durum. Semolina is made from durum, the difference being that durum flour has a lovely golden softness; when the grain is milled into semolina it has a sandy coarseness. As a rule, durum flour is preferred over semolina for bread making. The coarse grains in semolina have a puncturing effect on the dough, adversely affecting dough strength and bread volume.

It is the spring wheats that provide the baker with high-gluten flour, with protein levels typically between 13 and 15 percent. Although winter wheats have lower levels of protein (11 to 12 percent is average) than spring wheats, there is evidence that the quality of the protein in winter wheats is superior to that of spring wheats in the manufacture of certain breads. Specifically, hearth breads, which are characterized by the use of pre-ferments, that have long, slow fermentations, and are hand shaped, proofed in *bannetons* or between folds of baker's linen, and baked directly on the hearth or baking stone, benefit from the use of winter-wheat flour. High-gluten flours in general do not support the kind of long fermentation associated with hearth-bread production. Although the protein content is higher, the doughs tend to lose structure and stability over the course of the fermentation, and the breads are likely to flatten. On the other hand, there are ways that the higher level of protein in high-gluten flour can benefit the baker. For example, when making breads that contain a lot of heavy grains, the elevated protein in high-gluten flour helps provide extra lift to the bread. High-gluten flours can also be beneficial in the production of pan breads, where the volume of the finished loaves is often considered to be a foremost measure of quality.

Winter wheat spends several months in the ground, much longer than spring wheat. Although it is dormant for much of the time, it would be interesting to know if the lengthy growing cycle of winter wheat has a beneficial effect on its nutritional qualities and its flavor component. One could surmise that the plant's ability to absorb elements from the soil for so long a time might yield nutritionally superior wheat.

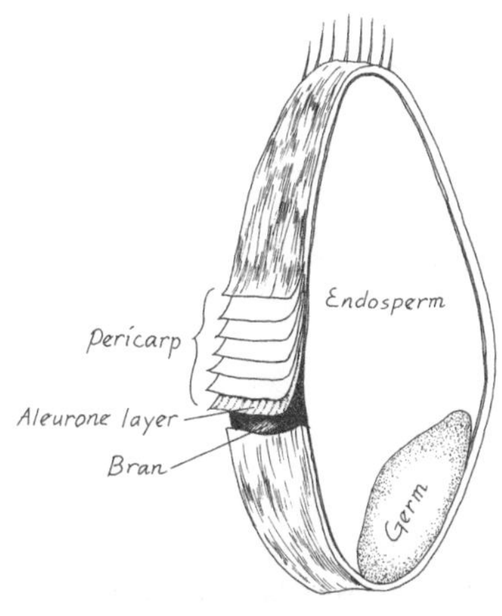

Wheat kernel

Bran, Germ, and Endosperm

When we consider any of the component parts of the wheat kernel, we should remember that the wheat is not growing in the field thinking how nice it will be to turn into a loaf of bread one fine day. As for all biological creatures, reproduction, self-protection, and nourishment are foremost necessities for grain. The bran, germ, and endosperm are three separate but completely interdependent components of the grain, which function as one entity to ensure perpetuation.

The wheat kernel is enclosed by several outer husk layers known as the pericarp (fruit coat). These layers serve as the protective coating of the germ and endosperm. The innermost of these layers is known as the aleurone layer. Although it is technically the outer surface of the endosperm, it is considered by the miller to be part of the bran coating, and is removed with the entire pericarp prior to milling. The bran layers constitute about 14 percent of the wheat kernel, and are comprised of cellulose and minerals.

The germ of the kernel is the embryonic heart. Although it comprises only 2.5 to 3.5 percent of the kernel, it is packed with vitamins, minerals, and fats. If the kernel is planted, it is from the germ that the rudimentary root and shoot of the new plant emanate. The highly nutritious germ provides a concentrated food source to the developing plant in its initial phases of growth. Because of the high proportion of fats, the germ has a tendency to become rancid, a consideration for the baker using whole-wheat flour (freezing or refrigerating whole-wheat flour delays rancidity in the germ. For most bakers, however, it is impractical to store large quantities of flour under refrigeration, and the baker therefore should scrupulously rotate his or her stock). Along with the bran, the germ is entirely removed prior to milling white flour.

The endosperm serves as the storehouse for starch and protein in flour. For the developing kernel, it is the endosperm that provides long-term nutrition. Protein levels in white bread flour are generally in the range of 10 to 14 percent, with starch coexisting in inverse proportion (from 70 to 73 percent of the weight of the entire kernel). That is, a flour that is higher in protein is lower in starch, and vice versa. Water is the last component of the endosperm, comprising about 14 percent. When we hold flour in our hand we don't, of course, see drops of water in the flour. The water in the endosperm is in the form of moisture in the starch.

Water Absorption

As a general rule, the higher the protein level in flour, the larger the amount of water it absorbs. From the perspective of the baker, this can mean many things. For example, let's assume a baker is accustomed to making French bread with 66 percent hydration (that is, for each 100 parts of flour in the dough, there are 66 parts water), using flour with 11.5 percent protein. He is familiar, day in and day out, with the consistency of his dough, and there is little variation other than that caused by changes in ambient humidity. One day, his flour delivery is delayed, and he has on hand only 12.5 percent protein flour, which he uses. The higher protein in this flour increases water absorption, and the 66 percent hydration dough feels rather stiff by comparison with his usual 11.5 percent flour; the addition of more water is necessary to achieve the proper dough consistency. When working with any bread formula, it is important to know what kind of flour is used, and its protein level. When making substitutions, or when trying out new flours, adjustments in hydration are very often necessary.

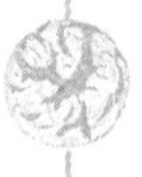

It is within the endosperm of the wheat kernel that we find a fascinating, almost magical attribute. Here reside glutenin and gliadin, two proteins that combine to form gluten. When wheat flour is mixed with water, dough is formed. The gluten that develops during dough mixing is responsible not only for the cohesive structure of the dough, but it is also the gluten that has the ability to retain the carbon dioxide gases that are produced by the yeast during fermentation, and expand as the gases accumulate in the gluten network. Once baked, there is a lightness of structure in wheat doughs that cannot be duplicated with any other grain. Glutenin and gliadin do exist in other grains, but the amount is either insignificant, or the proportion is not balanced. Certainly delicious breads are made with rye and other gluten-deficient grains, but none of these can have the characteristic lightness and openness that is possible with wheat breads.

To look a bit closer, it is the glutenin in flour that gives bread dough its elasticity, that is, its ability to resist extension. This elasticity supports the structure of the dough as it rises. On the bench, as the baker works up the loaves, the glutenin provides the resistance necessary to achieve good shaping. Without resistance, the dough would simply sag into place and not be able to keep its shape. Gliadin, the other protein in gluten, gives the dough its property of extensibility, that is, the ability to extend the loaf into the desired shape. Combined and in balance, the attributes of both glutenin and gliadin allow the baker to shape loaves that are both durable and strong, and at the same time can be manipulated to the desired length and shape without tearing.

A Short Look at Milling

Once the wheat has been harvested, and before milling, it undergoes a resting phase called "sweating." During this time, which generally lasts about six weeks, a number of subtle metabolic changes occur that will improve the milling quality of the grain, as well as slightly reduce the moisture in the wheat. Moisture in the field may be as high as 17 percent or more; once the grain is milled, the moisture level is close to 14 percent.

Once the sweating phase is complete, barges, trucks, or freight trains transport the wheat to the mill. It now goes through a series of steps to remove any iron or steel particles, stones, sticks, stray grains such as rye or oats (which are considered to be "weeds" by wheat farmers), and any other foreign matter that

Damaged Starch

The length of tempering at the mill is one of many factors that have a direct influence on the degree of what is known as "damaged starch." It's not easy being a grain of wheat. The rigors of growing in the field are merely the beginning of a long and arduous process that continues with the ruthless treatment incurred when the combine devours the field, followed by the grain being shot through chutes, shoved through augers, and dumped at the mill—all this before the tempering, stripping, cracking, grinding, sifting, and the entire harsh process of the actual milling. It's a tough life indeed, and along the way, it's no surprise that some of the starch granules, particularly in the hard wheats used in bread baking, get banged around and split open. These martyrs are the damaged starch particles.

During the fermentation phase of bread production, the amylase enzymes present in the flour perform one noble task: They convert starch into sugar, which is then consumed by the yeast to generate fermentation. The amylases focus their activity on the damaged starch particles, which, unlike the intact, undamaged particles, allow easy access.

Shorter tempering times and comparatively rough milling practices in North America increase the amount of damaged starch relative to that of European flours. In the United States, starch damage levels of 8 to 9 percent are typical, while in Europe levels around 7 percent are more common. Above 10 percent starch damage in flour will have a definite negative effect on dough properties.

While damaged starch is quite beneficial for bread fermentation, too much damaged starch presents the baker with serious problems. Practical problems that arise from excess starch damage in flour include:

- Overabsorption of water (since the damaged starch particles absorb more water than undamaged). The water is gradually released, and dough structure weakens.
- The dough becomes slack at the end of mixing.
- The dough becomes more and more sticky during bulk fermentation.
- Once shaped, the loaves tend to flatten out.
- In the oven, the cuts on the loaf open poorly or not at all.
- An excess of crust color may be noted, due to the increased level of enzyme activity.
- Once baked, the crust on the finished loaves softens.

could impair the purity of the milled flour. Once this phase is completed, the wheat berries go through the process called "tempering." During tempering, moisture is added to the wheat, usually in the form of chlorinated water, to prevent microbial growth. This moisture toughens the outer bran layers (the aleurone layers, which serve as protective skins to the interior portion of the berry) and softens the endosperm. The result is an easier separation of the bran from the endosperm during milling. How long to temper the wheat? In the United States, around 6 hours is a typical tempering time. In Europe, tempering might last 24 to 48 hours.

Stone-Ground Flour

The term *stone-ground flour* conjures up images of small mills, perhaps water powered, milling small quantities of wheat that are transported to the mill by a farmer leading a horse that pulls a cart mounded with newly harvested grain. And it may have been just like that once—long ago. Today in the United States, if wheat goes through just one pass of stone grinding at the mill, it can be labeled stone ground, even if the rest of the milling is done by steel rollers. So it is rare indeed in this country to eat bread made with fully stone-ground flour. And if we could compare bread made from stone-ground flour to the same bread made with roller-milled flour, would we find one distinctly superior?

I can't presume to know the answer to that question, although a fond recollection on the topic comes to mind. Several years ago I was honored to be invited to a meeting in Paris of L'Amicale des Anciens Élèves et des Amis du Professeur Calvel, Fidèle au Bon Pain—The Association of Elder Students and Friends of Professor Calvel, Faithful to Good Bread. There was hot debate on the subject of stone-ground versus roller-milled flour. This august group of French bakers had strong opinions, backed up with impassioned voices, wagging fingers, and photos. The conclusion, by no means unanimous, seemed to be that stone-ground flour produced bread with better flavor, while bread made with roller-milled flour had better volume.

It is logical, if not ultimately of the greatest benefit to the baker, for the miller to reduce the amount of overall milling time required to take wheat berries and convert them into flour. The tendency for more than a century in U.S. mills has been toward consolidation and increased levels of production (there were 23,000 mills in the United States in 1873, fewer than 300 a century later in 1973, and barely 200 in 1993). As milling capacity gets larger—modern mills typically produce in excess of two million pounds of flour each day—there is a concomitant effort to reduce milling time as much as possible. This in turn tempts the miller to reduce tempering time as much as possible.

Once tempering is complete, the grain is ready to be milled into flour. Corrugated steel rollers "break" the grain, which is then sifted or "bolted." A series of further breaks known as "reductions" remove the bran and germ from the endosperm, and reduce particle size (generally there are five or six reductions; the number of reductions can have an effect on the amount of starch damage present in the flour). As the size of the grain becomes increasingly smaller, more and more flour is obtained from the continued siftings. What becomes of the bran and germ? Since the miller makes more money from the flour than from the bran or germ, it is in his or her best interest to extract as much of the endosperm as possible. Each 100 pounds of grain yields between 72 and 75 percent flour, with the remainder being "mill feed," that is, it is used to feed animals. It is common, in fact, to see animal-feed plants adjacent to flour mills; the germ and bran require almost no transportation, and are taken right from the mill and processed into pet or stock feed.

Straight, Patent, and Clear Flour

Once the grindings and siftings are complete and the maximum amount of flour has been obtained from the grain, the various streams of flour are either blended or kept separate, depending on the desired flour to be bagged. If all the sifted flour is reblended, and therefore the entire endosperm is recombined, the result is called "straight flour." "Patent flour" is flour milled from the part of the kernel closest to the center of the endosperm, and for bread baking it is generally considered to be the best. "Extra short" or "fancy patent" is the designation for flour milled from the very heart of the endosperm, with short, medium, and long patent slightly farther from the center. Flour milled from the outer periphery of the wheat kernel is known as "clear flour"; it is darker in color due to the higher level of minerals present toward the periphery, and higher in protein than patent flour, although not all of the protein is usable in the sense of being beneficial to bread volume. Typically, clear flour is used in the production of American-style rye breads; the darker color of the clear flour is not considered a negative factor in these breads.

We have noted that modern mills generally obtain 72 to 75 pounds of flour from 100 pounds of wheat berries. This is expressed as an extraction rate of 72 to 75 percent. As extraction rates rise above 75 percent, the flour is increasingly flecked with bran particles, until, at 100 percent extraction, we have whole-wheat flour. In earlier years, when mills were unable to completely separate the germ and bran from the endosperm, it was normal to have flour of higher extraction, with more color. Today, there is something of a trend in the production of breads made with high-extraction flour. These breads are not quite white breads, but neither are they whole-wheat breads. Breads skillfully made from high-extraction flours can be as beautiful to look at as they are to eat (the Miche, Pointe-à-Callière on page 164 is one such example). If high-extraction flour is unobtainable, it is not difficult for the baker to add a portion of white flour to whole-wheat flour in order to make a blend that simulates the flours of old. We will note here that as extraction increases, the resulting flours have an increase in the percentage of ash. A full discussion of ash content and its importance to the baker appears on page 366.

Alternative Wheats

There are several wheats of either quite ancient or quite current origin that play a small part in bread production today.

Einkorn and Emmer

Einkorn ("one seed") is the original wild wheat that grew in the area known as the Fertile Crescent, in present-day Iraq and Syria. The wild grain was harvested as long ago as 16,000 B.C., with cultivated einkorn dating from about 10,000 B.C. Its production today is limited and isolated, with small plantings found in Turkey, India, Italy, France, and Yugoslavia. Emmer, another wild wheat, had a similar and contemporaneous origin to that of einkorn, and by around 4000 B.C. it surpassed einkorn as a cultivated crop. Today, the production of emmer is quite limited. Both of these grains produce well in adverse conditions, with yields surpassing those of other cereals such as barley and oats, and even common wheat. Nutritionally, they are also comparable or superior to other cereals. A drawback in their cultivation arises from the weakness of the stalk and the tendency of the grain head to split open and shed its seed. This of course was how its survival was ensured throughout the centuries, but from the perspective of modern wheat harvesting, these characteristics are considered detrimental. The use of einkorn and emmer in bread making remains negligible. There is, however, an indication that flour from einkorn may be nontoxic to people suffering from celiac disease, in which case there is a definite benefit to its continued production.

Spelt

Spelt appeared later than did einkorn or emmer, and evidence suggests the area of present-day Iran as its place of origin, sometime around 6000 B.C. Unlike those two earlier grains, spelt has continued to be an important, albeit secondary, grain. In Germany and Italy, it continues to be highly cultivated, and is known in those countries as *dinkel* and *farro* respectively. It has attributes similar to regular wheat in bread baking, such as a high protein level and sufficient gluten to produce breads with reasonable volume. It is nutritionally similar if not superior to regular wheat. Another important benefit of spelt is that it can be tolerated by people with certain wheat allergies. Along with einkorn and emmer, spelt is one of the "covered wheats." The kernels of these wheats are enclosed on the plant in a way that makes dehulling at harvest more difficult than for common wheat. This adds time and expense to the harvest, which in turn have contributed to low interest in the United States for the growing of these grains.

Kamut

A registered grain, originally from Egypt, kamut has been grown for approximately forty years in the United States. Its protein level is high and its gluten quality low. It is also a grain that can be tolerated by certain people for whom common wheat is toxic.

Triticale

In Scotland in 1875, rye and wheat were intentionally crossed in an effort to develop a grain with the ryelike virtues of thriving in cool and wet conditions, and the wheatlike characteristics of high yields and acceptable bread-making quality. The resulting cross was named triticale. The yields in fact are higher than those of wheat or rye, but the relatively low gluten level produces breads considered inferior to wheat breads. Presently, the majority of triticale grown in the United States is harvested as livestock feed. Since part of its parentage is wheat, triticale is toxic to people who are wheat intolerant.

Rye

Rye is a grain of immense importance in many parts of Europe: In Russia, Poland, Germany, Austria (northern and eastern Europe in general), and Scandinavia as well, rye breads have always enjoyed special significance. It is curious that, in spite of the large number of Americans whose ancestors emigrated from these countries, rye breads have never had the popularity in the United States that they have in Europe. This is distinctly unfortunate, because properly made rye breads have a rich fullness of aroma, a unique and bold flavor, excellent keeping quality, and a delicious eating quality quite different from wheat breads. Perhaps the reason rye breads have not ascended to a level of acceptance in North America as they have in many parts of Europe is that they are so often made with white rye flour, yielding a bland and insipid bread, or worse, they are made with no clear understanding of the special requirements of rye bread, and the result is bread with an aggressive and unpleasant sourness. Well-made rye breads have a depth of character provided in part by an appropriate sour flavor; in no case is the assault of excess sourness a desirable characteristic. Another lamentable practice seen in North American rye bread production is the overuse of caraway seeds (rarely seen in European rye breads). While a small proportion of caraway can give another flavor note, an excess masks the flavor of the rye flour, completely distorting its taste.

An even more egregious insult to rye bread is the inappropriate use of caramel color to make something erroneously called pumpernickel bread. How could such a practice have arisen, and does it have any connection whatsoever to European rye bread? In point of fact, for centuries bread was baked in wood-burning ovens. A well-constructed oven would have great mass, hence great insulating properties. It took hours to reach full temperature, and it retained heat for many hours after the bake. Bakers were not rich men, and wood was a costly commodity. It was quite natural for the baker to utilize as much of the oven's residual heat as possible. One way this was accomplished was to put bread into the oven at the end of the bake day in loaf pans that had tight-fitting covered lids and bake it in the gentle, receding heat of the oven throughout the night. For years, I baked this style of bread (although in a modern deck oven, not a wood-fired oven). In the wee hours of the morning, the smell of the bread, even though it was still in the oven, would completely suffuse the bakery with a wondrous dark sweetness. Once it was removed from the pans, the bread was a rich dark brown, almost black. Over the course of the long, slow bake, the starches in the rye were converted to sugars, which provided the intensity of aroma and color. These breads, true pumpernickels, have long been considered in Europe to be highly beneficial to infants and old folks, because their starches have undergone so much of a transformation that they are quite easily digested. In any case, how did this time-honored method of bread production become bastardized in the United States, and why? I think that few bakers were willing to take the time to produce what at first glance appears to be a fragrant brick. Rather than make the effort to bake using the traditional overnight technique, American bakers found they could get even blacker bread by the simple addition of caramel color. Apparently, the complete lack of taste was not deemed sufficient reason to consider abandoning this style of baking. And once gullible consumers were trained to view these ersatz loaves as something vaguely "European," there was no turning back. Then some enterprising baker came along with the baffling idea of braiding together a couple of strands of this tasteless black dough with a couple of strands of equally bland white dough, and a new genre of artistic bread was formed: marble rye. These loaves still abound in some parts of the United States, an insult to bakers and consumers alike.

One reason that rye bread has been the bread of peasants for centuries is that rye grows in areas inhospitable to wheat cultivation. It thrives in comparatively poor soils, does well in cool environments, and yields a good crop in areas of high humidity. These conditions prevail in many parts of northern and eastern Europe, and rye became the grain of life for many of the poor folk there (the German Christmas specialty *Lebkuchen,* from a dough traditionally made with rye flour and honey and matured for several months in wooden troughs or barrels, translates as "life cake").

Requirements of Rye Flour

Rye flour is significantly different from wheat flour; in fact, from the growing culture of the grains, to the mixing, fermenting, proofing, steaming, baking, and even in the eating, rye differs from wheat. In order to produce rye breads of a consistent high quality, a thorough understanding of rye's unique requirements is necessary:

- **THE GLUTEN-FORMING PROTEINS GLUTENIN AND GLIADIN** exist in sufficient quantity in wheat flour to produce doughs that are at once extensible (this is an attribute of gliadin), and at the same time elastic (an attribute of glutenin). Combined, the glutenin and gliadin help provide structure to dough, and in combination they capture the carbon dioxide gases produced by the yeast fermentation, allowing the dough to expand to full leavened volume. Rye flour will not form a gluten web of similar strength; although there is gluten in rye, there is considerably less than there is in wheat, hence rye breads will always have a denser structure.

- **RYE FLOUR IS HIGHER IN BRAN AND FIBER THAN WHEAT,** which means rye breads have higher water absorption. A poolish made with 10 pounds of water and 10 pounds of white flour will be as loose as pancake batter. A similar mixture of 10 pounds of water and 10 pounds of whole rye flour will be considerably thicker. Since rye holds more water, the dough yield from rye breads is higher. While this can be of economic benefit to the baker, the extra water-holding capacity will produce bread with a moist and pasty crumb unless proper care is taken.

- **THE HIGHER LEVEL OF BRAN AND MINERALS IN RYE** has another impact on the bread: As the mineral content of the flour increases, there is a corresponding decrease in bread volume. This is caused because the sharp shape of the bran pieces cuts the gluten network. This is least evidenced when white rye is used, and most visible as more and more dark rye is present in the formula. This cutting property of the bran has an identical effect on wheat breads, which is why the volume of whole-wheat bread is less than that of white bread.

- **RYE HAS MORE SOLUBLE SUGARS THAN WHEAT,** and therefore rye doughs ferment more quickly than wheat doughs. This trait, coupled with rye's inability to form a wheatlike dough structure, means that rye doughs can quickly overferment and collapse.

- **RYE IS HIGH IN A SUBSTANCE CALLED PENTOSANS,** a polysaccharide substance found in plants. The pentosan content is higher in rye flour (about 8 percent) than in any other flour. The pentosans contribute to the high water absorption of rye breads, and at the same time compete with the glutenin and gliadin in the flour for moisture. This serves to undermine the gluten's already limited ability to develop in rye breads. Further, the pentosans are fragile and easily broken, with a resulting potential for rye doughs to become sticky as the flour unknits. As a consequence of this characteristic, rye doughs must be gently mixed (a standard rye bread mixer in Germany, called a *Langsamenkneter,* or slow-speed mixer, rotates at only 25 to 40 rpms, roughly 25 percent of the rpms in a spiral mixer).

- **RYE IS A GRAIN HIGH IN AMYLASE ENZYMES** (during humid growing seasons, the amylases can be in an advanced state of activity even before the time of harvest). A thorough understanding of the characteristics of amylases, and their potential to damage crumb structure, is essential for the baker of rye breads.

Enzymes have one specific activity, and in the case of amylase, the activity it performs is the conversion of starch into sugar. Starches swell with water during the bake, and eventually form the crumb of the bread. Sugars, on the other hand, do not contribute to the formation of crumb structure; in fact, if they exist in too high a proportion in the dough, they have the effect of causing gumminess in the crumb. During the bake, when the internal dough temperatures are between 122° and 140°F, the starches in the rye begin to expand, absorb water, and gelatinize, and the crumb structure of the loaf begins to form. The amylases, however, are in a state of accelerated activity at these temperatures, and are not destroyed by heat until about 176°F. Therefore, they have an opportunity to wreak considerable havoc by breaking down the starch into sugar, and preventing the starch from forming a well-structured crumb. This is the dreaded "starch attack." The result (unless the baker uses his or her skill) is bread with a gummy, pasty crumb. Wheat flour is exempt from these problems, first because wheat has less amylase than rye, and second because wheat starch gelatinizes at higher temperatures (beginning at about 158°F and ending at about 194°F), giving the enzymes less opportunity to damage crumb structure. The baker of rye breads has one great tool at his disposal to inhibit the decomposing activity of the amylase, and that tool is sourdough. In the presence of acid, the activity of the amylases is slowed down. Therefore, by using sourdough, the baker stabilizes the baking ability of the bread by inhibiting the enzymatic activity that would otherwise result in bread with a gummy crumb.

There are many advantages associated with the use of sourdough in rye breads. Certainly one is that the presence of sourdough inhibits the starch attack and allows the baker to obtain good characteristics in the finished loaf. Another pertains to phytic acid, a substance found in bran that inhibits the minerals in the bran from being absorbed by the human body. The natural bacterial action in a sourdough environment neutralizes the phytic acid, resulting in more nutritious whole-grain breads. Breads—either wheat or rye based—made by the sourdough process eliminate all the phytic acid, while in straight, yeasted, whole-grain breads, about 90 percent of the phytic acid remains. Other benefits connected with the use of sourdough include the leavening power of a healthy sourdough culture, and the vastly increased storing ability of breads made with sourdough. This last is due to the correlation between the pH of a bread and its keeping quality. That is, as the pH decreases, the level of acidity increases, and the higher acidity in turn contributes to the increased life span of the loaf. Sourdough therefore provides the benefits of good eating quality, increased nutrition, good leavening ability, and good keeping quality. This commonplace miracle of nature has been of incalculable value over the centuries in lands where bread was the primary foodstuff and, being baked but once every three or four weeks, needed to be stored for lengthy periods.

Rye flour in Germany is categorized by its ash content. That is, a sample of flour is incinerated, the charred remains, or "ash," is weighed, and the flour is labeled according to the percentage of ash it contains. The ash is almost all minerals, and the higher the percentage, the more whole is the flour. In this way, Type 610 rye flour contains .61 percent ash (in the United States, Type 610 would be labeled white rye), while Type 1740 has 1.74 percent ash (whole rye in the United States); in between are numerous gradations, each signifying ash content and the relative lightness or darkness of the flour. The amount of ash correlates to the degree of extraction; Type 610 is about 60 percent extraction, with Type 1740 being close to 95 percent extraction. Beyond these gradations of rye flour, there is another German category called *Schrot,* which is a form of chopped grain. It is available in a number of degrees of coarseness, referred to as *fein, mittel,* or *gross* (fine, medium, or coarse).

In the United States, the baker has access to quite a diminished array of rye flours, usually sold only as white, medium, dark, and whole. Extraction rates, ash content, and protein quantity are lowest in white rye and highest in whole rye. White rye flour has little in the way of flavor or color, and is generally a poor choice in bread making. Medium rye is substantially better, producing breads with better nutritional value and more flavor. And whole-rye flour is better yet in terms of flavor and food value (it is the rye flour of choice for most of the formulas in this book). Dark rye is the flour milled from the periphery of the grain, similar to the clear flour produced during the milling of wheat. It tends to be coarse and sandy, to absorb quite a lot of water, and in general is difficult to work with.

Pumpernickel rye, often called rye meal, is just that: a coarse meal rather than a flour; it is made by milling the entire rye berry. It can substitute for whole-rye flour, the main difference being the mealy consistency of pumpernickel. In any event, pumpernickel means that the entire berry has been ground, and from a milling perspective does not have anything to do with the artificially black breads known in the United States as pumpernickel. Filling out the rye list are rye chops (similar to the German *Schrot* in that the rye berry is chopped rather than ground), cracked rye, and whole rye berries. Although the rye spectrum available to American bakers is not quite as broad as that enjoyed by European bakers, we nevertheless have sufficient variety at our disposal to make breads of first-class character and quality.

Chapter 6, "Sourdough Rye Breads," has more information on the unique requirements of rye, from mixing and handling through baking and eating.

Grains and Seeds

There are a number of seeds and grains that are cousins to wheat, and whose use can enhance the flavor profile of bread. Seeds such as sunflower, sesame, and flax, and grains such as millet, oats, roasted barley, cracked rye and wheat, whole rye and wheat berries, and cornmeal are all flavorful and nutritious additions to breads. For the most part, these grains and seeds are soaked before being added to the mix. When using sunflower and sesame seeds, however, a lovely nutty flavor note can be added to the bread by toasting rather than soaking the raw seeds. Small changes like this provide the baker with additional ways to produce breads with subtle, individualized differences. Keep in mind that when seeds are used to cover the outer surface of a loaf, they should always be applied raw. If toasted, the additional cooking they undergo once the bread is in the oven will result in an unpleasant bitterness.

A number of packaged grain mixes are available today. These can save the baker the step of scaling several grains and seeds, but may also give his or her breads something of a generic character if the same mix is used in each grain bread. Of course, the cost per pound of the grain mix will always be more than that of the individual ingredients purchased by the baker.

Water

Water is an ingredient of considerable importance in bread dough. Although it is easy to overlook—after all, turn on the tap and it is there—it helps to be aware of the effects water has in bread baking. The most important attributes are the following:

Soakers

Generally, when using whole or cracked grains and seeds, they are first made into what is known as a "soaker"; that is, they are left to soak for a number of hours in at least an equal weight of water. The water, of course, is part of the overall dough water, and its presence in the soaker is accounted for in the overall formulation of the bread. The water for grains such as cracked or whole rye and wheat must be boiled, and the grains steeped overnight. This allows them to absorb water, soften, and become palatable once the bread is baked. Other seeds and grains, such as raw sunflower seeds, sesame seeds, flaxseeds, and cornmeal, can be prepared with cold water since they soften more readily. In both cases, since the grains have absorbed water prior to dough mixing, they will not rob water from the dough. A common flaw in the production of grain breads is the inclusion of unsoaked grains in the mix, which not only give the sense of "eating the beach," but also result in a significant drying of the crumb, as the grains suck up dough water.

Frequently, part or all of the salt in the formula is added to the soaker. There is good sense to this practice: Once the grains have become hydrated, enzymatic activity commences, especially when adding boiled water to grains to make a hot soaker. During the warmer months particularly, the enzymatic activity can give an unpleasant sourness to the grains when the soaker is left at room temperature overnight. By adding the dough salt to the soaker, the enzymatic activity is reduced and the development of off flavors avoided.

When to add the soaker to the dough? There are two schools of thought about this. One school advocates adding the soaker at the end of the mix. Using this technique, the dough is mixed to full gluten development, after which the soaker is added and incorporated on first speed until it is fully and evenly distributed throughout the dough. Considering the fact that the comparatively sharp grains in a soaker have a puncturing effect on the dough, and that therefore the gluten matrix develops more slowly in the presence of

- It is in the presence of water that gluten forms.
- Water serves as a solvent and dispersing agent (for salt, sugar, and yeast).
- Water is necessary for yeast fermentation and reproduction (and softer doughs will ferment more quickly than dry doughs).
- Water is responsible for the consistency of bread dough.
- The temperature of water can be varied in order to obtain dough of the correct temperature.

The degree of hardness in water is an indication of the amount of calcium and magnesium ions present, expressed in parts per million (ppm). Soft water has less than 50 ppm, while hard water has more than 200 ppm. Generally, water of medium hardness, with about 100 to 150 ppm of minerals, is best suited to bread baking.

a soaker, it makes sense to add the soaker at the end of the mix. Although this approach is sound from a technical perspective, in a practical sense there may be advantages to the second method. In the second method, all the ingredients, including the soaker, are placed in the mixer at the outset and the dough is mixed until it is properly developed. The line of thought supporting this method goes like this: It is preferable to be able to correct the dough hydration early on in the mix than it is to mix the dough without the soaker and not be sure how the final consistency will be until the soaker has been incorporated. And the reason it's difficult to forecast the final consistency of the dough is because the absorption of the grains in the soaker can be quite variable. For instance, in a soaker made with boiling water, some water may have evaporated before being poured on the grains. Also, older grains absorb more water than freshly milled ones. It follows to reason that if the soaker is added at the beginning of the mix, the baker can correct the dough's hydration within the first 2 or 3 minutes of mixing. It is true that more overall mixing time may be needed to develop sufficient dough strength (the friction factor may need to be increased in this case when calculating desired dough temperature), but at least the baker knows that the dough is mixing at the correct hydration. When the soaker is added at the end, dough hydration may need adjustment after it has been incorporated. And it can be difficult indeed for the dough to accept added water once it has been fully mixed. Adding water to a fully developed dough can be a woeful sight, as the added water makes a sloppy paste that smears around the outer surface of the dough. Only reluctantly does the dough incorporate this additional water.

Regardless of when it is added, breads made with a soaker tend to have a lovely whole-grain aspect, but at the same time they are comparatively light textured, especially when the base of the dough is made with all or mostly all white flour. Another worthy aspect to these breads is their high moisture retention, which prolongs keeping quality.

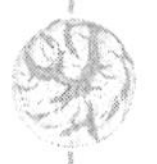

These minerals provide food for the yeast, and therefore can benefit fermentation. If water is excessively hard, however, there is a tightening effect on the gluten, as well as a decrease in the fermentation rate (the minerals make water absorption more difficult for the proteins in the flour). On the other hand, if water is excessively soft, the lack of minerals results in sticky, slack dough. Generally speaking, most water is not extreme in either direction, and if water is potable, it is suitable for bread baking.

In the creation of a sourdough or levain culture, there is another consideration. If the water used is highly chlorinated, the chlorine can have a negative impact on the culture by inhibiting the metabolism of the developing microorganisms. In this case, simply leave a bucket or jar of water out overnight, uncovered. By the next day, most all the chlorine will have dissipated. Alternatively, filtered water can be used.

The amount of acidity in water, expressed as pH (potential hydrogen), also has an effect on fermentation. Hard water is generally more alkaline than soft water, and can decrease the activity of yeast. Water that is slightly acid (pH a little below 7) is preferred for bread baking.

Salt

For centuries, salt was a rare and expensive commodity; the cause of wars and strife, it enriched some and impoverished others. Towns were named after it (Salzburg, for example, means "salt town"). Bread and salt have long implied welcome and hospitality; words like "salary" have their root in the word *salt*. Taxes on it over the centuries have many times resulted in riots and massacres.

Prior to the 1700s, salt was rarely used in bread production. Although there are still areas where salt is used in either very small quantities or not at all (Tuscany being an example), people today almost universally consider bread to be of the highest quality only when salt is used in appropriate quantities. Although it is quite insignificant in terms of the weight it contributes to a loaf of bread, salt is nevertheless a major component in bread, and performs several important functions.

Salt provides flavor. Bread baked without salt will have a flat and insipid taste. On the other hand, bread made with an excess of salt will be unpalatable. Generally, the correct amount of salt in bread dough is 1.8 to 2 percent of salt based on flour weight (that is, 1.8 to 2 pounds of salt per 100 pounds of flour). Bakers who lack the ability to coax fermentation flavor from flour sometimes resort to an excessive use of salt. This dubious tactic of oversalting foods that have little intrinsic flavor is pervasive in the fast-food industry, and commonplace as well in canned, frozen, and microwave foods. But while salt provides flavor, it is not a substitute for the fine flavor of well-fermented flour. The role of salt is to enhance, not take the place of, true bread flavor.

Salt tightens the gluten structure. The tightening gives strength to the gluten, enabling the dough to efficiently hold carbon dioxide, which is released into the dough as a by-product of the yeast fermentation. When salt is left out, the resulting dough is slack and sticky in texture, work-up is difficult, and bread volume is poor.

Salt has a retarding effect on the activity of yeast. The cell wall of yeast is semipermeable, and by osmosis it absorbs oxygen and nutrients as it gives off enzymes and other substances to the dough environment. Water is essential for these yeast activities. Salt by its nature is hygroscopic, that is, it attracts moisture. In the presence of salt, yeast releases some of its water through its cell walls, and since yeast cells require a certain degree of hydration in order to function, the water that has been released from the cells causes the yeast's fermentation, or reproductive activities, to slow down. If there is an excess of salt in a bread dough, the yeast is retarded to the point where there is a marked reduction in volume. If there is no salt, the yeast will ferment too quickly. So the salt, in a sense, aids the baker in controlling the pace of fermentation. Nevertheless, careful use of yeast, control of dough temperature, and the type, maturity, and amount of pre-ferment used are better ways to control fermentation.

Salt indirectly contributes to crust coloring. This attribute is a result of the salt's characteristic of retarding fermentation. Flour starch is converted into simple sugars by amylase enzymes, and the yeast consumes these sugars in order to generate fermentation. Since salt slows the rate of sugar consumption, more of what is known as "residual sugar" is available at the time of the bake for crust coloration. In the absence of salt, the yeast quickly consumes the available sugars, and the crust on the baked bread will be pale and dull.

Salt helps preserve the color and flavor of flour. The carotenoid pigments naturally present in unbleached wheat flour are responsible for giving flour its creamy color and wheaty aroma. Salt has a positive effect on the preservation of carotenoids, because dough oxidation is delayed in the presence of salt. For this reason, it is preferable to add salt at the beginning of the mix. In this way, salt benefits the eventual flavor of the bread by helping to preserve the carotenoids during the mixing of the dough. When salt is added during the later stages of dough mixing, it is detrimental to the carotenoids, which become more oxidized, yielding bread with a whiter crumb and less aroma.

As stated, the parameters of salt in bread dough are from 1.8 to 2 percent based on flour weight. In sourdough production, 1.8 percent is usually adequate. The acidity in the dough, while not providing any saltiness to the flavor, does contribute its own strength of flavor, which allows for the lower use of salt.

When making certain types of *viennoiserie,* such as croissant, danish, or brioche, it is common to see the overall salt content at 2.5 percent of the flour weight. This is an appropriate amount, because the high proportion of butter in these doughs requires salt to obtain a correct balance of flavor. Similarly, when seeds or grains are added to breads, they too need salt. For this reason, when making a multigrain bread, salt use should be 1.8 to 2 percent based on the total combined weight of the flour and the seeds or grains.

One other use of salt is useful to note. It is common to include a portion of salt in a levain culture during warmer and more humid months. This addition of salt, at a rate of .2 to .3 percent, retards the action of the wild yeasts, and thus prevents the overmaturing of the culture. In the preparation of German-style rye bread, there is a similar technique that is occasionally employed, called the salt-sour method, in which a portion of the overall dough salt is used in the sourdough phase. The result is to slow the activity of the sourdough yeast cells (allowing the sourdough to be used up to forty-eight hours after the initial mixing), to reduce the production of acidity, and to strengthen the gluten structure.

The most common salts used in bread production are noniodized granular salt, sea salt (mineral salt), kosher salt, and, occasionally, iodized salt. While iodized salt may impart some off flavor to bread, it is quite difficult to detect any flavor differences among noniodized granular, sea, or kosher salt when they are used in breads. As with other bread ingredients, salt should be weighed. Since the granular structure of different salts varies so much, measuring with teaspoons or cups results in inaccurate weights. In other words, the same weights of kosher salt and noniodized granular salt provide essentially identical saltiness in bread, but a tablespoon of granular salt provides much more saltiness than a tablespoon of kosher salt because of the difference in grain size.

Yeast

Yeast is a single-celled microorganism that is neither a plant nor an animal — it is a member of the fungus kingdom — and it requires suitable conditions to thrive. These conditions include moisture, oxygen, food, and appropriate temperatures, and when they are provided, the life cycle of the yeast will become activated, resulting in both reproduction and alcoholic fermentation. Fermentation is the conversion of sugars into alcohol and carbon dioxide, by yeast and bacteria, and it is primarily this attribute of yeast that pertains to the bread baker.

In nature, there are dozens of genera of yeast, hundreds of species, and thousands of subspecies or strains. For thousands of years, bakers made use of wild yeasts in order to bake leavened bread. Later, yeasts derived from beer brewing were utilized, alone or along with wild yeasts. Although there are hundreds of yeast species that can ferment sugar into carbon dioxide and alcohol, today *Saccharomyces cerevisiae* is the strain used for commercial yeast production, primarily because of its characteristic of rapid gas production. Commercial yeast is available in a number of forms, from cream yeast (a liquid form of compressed yeast, usually delivered in tank trucks to storage bins and used in very large operations), to compressed yeast (also called cake yeast or fresh yeast), and finally dry yeast.

Requirements of Yeast

As noted, yeast requires moisture, oxygen, a suitable temperature, and food in order to reproduce and generate fermentation. Generally speaking, bread dough is an ideal environment for yeast, providing all the necessary conditions for its needs.

Moisture. Once water is added to the other ingredients in bread dough, the metabolic activity of the yeast commences. The cell membrane of yeast is semipermeable. Oxygen and nutrients are absorbed through the cell membrane, and enzymes and other substances are given off to the environment. Yeast can only absorb nutrients in a dissolved state, and it requires water in order to absorb these nutrients. Further, yeast can only absorb small-molecule nutrients, such as simple sugars, through the cell membrane, and it releases enzymes in order to break down large-molecule nutrients in the dough. Salt retards the activity of yeast fermentation due to the osmotic pressure it exerts on yeast cells. Salt, being hygroscopic (attracting moisture), draws water out of the semipermeable yeast cell, reducing the amount available to the yeast, and this is why there is a decrease in fermentation due to the presence of salt.

Oxygen. Oxygen is obtained mostly by the mixing of the dough, enabling the yeast to metabolize nutrients and to reproduce. However, although yeast requires oxygen for its reproduction, there is virtually no reproduction of yeast occurring in bread dough, and the rise we see is almost entirely due to gas production during fermentation. It takes several hours for yeast to begin its reproductive cycle, and there is insufficient time between mixing and baking for reproduction to begin. Available oxygen is used up within a matter of minutes after dough mixing, and fermentation occurs in an anaerobic environment. There is an exception to this: When bread is made using a pre-ferment, there is enough time during the maturing of the pre-ferment for yeast reproduction to occur. When yeast reproduction is necessary, as in a yeast manufacturing plant, oxygen is extremely important, and the machines that provide oxygen to the yeast can be among the most expensive ones in the facility.

Temperature. Correct dough temperature is crucial for yeast activity. For commercial yeast, the optimum temperature range for fermentation is between 86° and 95°F, but it is important to note that dough temperatures in this range are inappropriate; fermentation would be favored at these high temperatures, but it would occur at the expense of flavor development, which requires lower temperatures. (Wild yeasts, such as those in a sourdough culture, prefer a narrower temperature zone than commercial yeast, and in general perform better at slightly lower temperatures than commercial yeast.) As temperatures get higher or lower, yeast activity is reduced. Between 32° and 50°F and between 116° and 131°F there is very little activity. At about 138° to 140°F, yeast reaches what is known as "thermal death point" and dies. Bakers often ask about freezing fresh yeast. When frozen, yeast cells (whether in a packet of compressed yeast, a frozen raw dough, or a sourdough culture) begin to die within a matter of days. Although fresh yeast can survive for a few weeks at temperatures as low as –4°F, it gradually loses its fermentation ability. Dry yeast, being dehydrated, is less affected by freezer temperatures and can be safely frozen for several months.

Food. Food is provided to yeast during fermentation by the conversion of starches into sugar. Yeast cannot directly ferment starch and requires the amylase enzymes naturally present in flour, and also added at the mill or in the bakeshop, to convert the starches into fermentable sugars (see the discussion on malt on page 364). The small amount of sugar naturally present in flour is initially metabolized for fermentation. After this has been converted and consumed by the yeast, the amylases utilize the damaged starch particles. It is these damaged starch particles that provide almost the entire food source for the yeast's fermentation. Whole, undamaged starch particles remain intact in the dough until it reaches the oven, at which time they become available to the amylases. The fermentation enzyme zymase separates dextrose into carbon dioxide gas and ethyl alcohol, which are the principal by-products of fermentation. The carbon dioxide is trapped by the gluten network in the dough, and provides volume to the baked loaf. The alcohol is largely evaporated during the baking of the bread; what alcohol does remain contributes to aroma and flavor. One other by-product of fermentation is heat.

The forms of yeast most commonly used by the baker are fresh yeast (also known as cake yeast or compressed yeast), active dry yeast, and instant dry yeast. Fresh yeast has a moisture content of about 70 percent. During the production of dry yeast, the percentage of moisture is reduced to about 5 to 7 percent. There is tremendous stress put on yeast cells when they are dehydrated to these levels, and this stress makes dry yeast more sensitive than fresh yeast to high sugar or highly acidic dough environments. Yeast manufacturers have responded to this by developing different strains of yeast that, when dried, are more tolerant of sweet and acidic conditions.

Converting from Fresh to Dry Yeast

When converting from fresh yeast to dry, it is necessary to adjust the weight of the yeast. Although it is best to follow the conversion ratio provided by the manufacturer, there are general conversion guidelines that may be helpful.

- **TO CONVERT FROM FRESH YEAST TO ACTIVE DRY YEAST,** multiply the weight of the fresh yeast by .4. Active dry yeast must be dissolved in warm water before being incorporated into a dough.
- **TO CONVERT FROM FRESH YEAST TO INSTANT DRY YEAST,** multiply the weight of the fresh yeast by .33. Instant yeast can be incorporated into the dough without first dissolving it; however, it is sensitive to ice-cold temperatures, and if the water temperature of the dough is cold, it is best to mix the dough for a minute or two before adding the yeast. In order to maintain dough yield, most manufacturers suggest making up the weight difference between dry yeast and fresh with additional water.

People occasionally refer to the flavor of bread as "yeasty." In fact, yeast cannot be tasted in bread, unless the bread is poorly

The Subtle Balance of a Sourdough Environment

There is an interesting relationship in what we call San Francisco sourdough between the wild yeast *Candida milleri* and the dominant lactobacillus strain *Lactobacillus sanfranciscensis*. *C. milleri* cannot utilize maltose during fermentation, while *L. sanfranciscensis* is happy to use it. And once it does, it excretes glucose. This is fortunate for *C. milleri*, because it is fond of glucose, and ferments this simple sugar readily. At the same time, competing bacterial species are inhibited by the presence of so much glucose, and this is to the benefit of *L. sanfranciscensis*, whose development is therefore favored. A last factor in this relationship pertains to acidity. *L. sanfranciscensis* produces a lot of acetic acid, and *C. milleri* is more tolerant of an acidic environment than many yeast varieties. The high level of acidity prevents competing yeasts from dominating the culture, much to the benefit of *C. milleri*. What we see in this relationship is the commonplace perfection so often seen in the unimpeded world of nature. In this case, both *L. sanfranciscensis* and *C. milleri* work to create a symbiotic environment that protects the other while ensuring conditions favorable for their own growth and perpetuation.

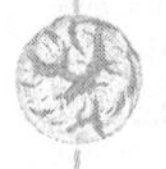

made, with way too much yeast, in which case a bitter flavor from an abundance of amino acids is evident. The "yeasty" flavor some people associate with bread is actually the aroma of fermentation, and in the case of freshly baked bread that is cut open, the aroma of residual alcohol.

As previously mentioned, yeast reproduction is almost completely nonexistent during the development of bread doughs. There are, however, a few noteworthy aspects of yeast reproduction that may be of interest. Under favorable conditions, yeast multiplies by a process called "budding," where individual cells divide and thereby create new cells. When conditions are adverse, and nutrients and water are absent, the yeast undergoes a process called "sporulation." The spores created in this instance are not only impervious to heat or cold, but in the absence of moisture they are also able to survive for hundreds of years. When conditions again become suitable for the yeast, it resumes its life cycle, unperturbed by an interruption of a few centuries.

Sugar

Sugar (as well as honey and malt syrup), although not used often as an ingredient in bread making, has some important characteristics worthy of note. Beyond simply providing sweetness to the finished loaves, sugar also imparts more crust color to the finished loaves. Therefore, the bake temperature is lower than for doughs made without sugar. When levels are low, 5 percent or less, there is little extra crust coloration; as sugar levels increase, so too does crust coloration. Hearth loaves baked directly on the floor of the oven may darken excessively on the bottom unless precautions are taken. Although inefficient, it may be necessary to finish baking on sheet pans once loaves have baked about halfway. Breads like challah, which contain not only sugar but other crust-darkening ingredients as well (oil and eggs), bake entirely on sheet pans, at much lower temperatures.

When sugar levels reach 10 percent, as in the production of certain *viennoiserie* goods, the level of yeast activity decreases. Sugar (like salt) is by nature hygroscopic, that is, it attracts moisture. As the percentage of sugar increases, it claims moisture that would otherwise be absorbed through the outer membrane of the yeast cells and applied to the fermentation. The lack of moisture available to the yeast reduces its activity. Yeast levels are comparatively high in *viennoiserie* production in order to offset the effect of higher sugar levels in the doughs.

Eggs

Eggs also impart color to the crust of baked goods, due to the lipids in the yolk. Therefore, baking temperatures must be reduced to prevent an excess of coloration. Eggs also provide flavor, again from the yolk (there is relatively little flavor in egg whites). When eggs are present, the protein, calcium, iron, and potassium they contain increases the nutritional value of the baked goods. Finally, the coagulating property of eggs gives an even texture and grain to the finished product.

Milk

Lactose, a sugar that is present in milk, caramelizes on the surface of baked goods, imparting a rich color, and also necessitating baking precautions similar to those for eggs and granulated sugar. Although the lactic acid in milk tightens the gluten structure, the fats present soften the structure, and the result is baked products that have less elasticity and an even grain. The food value of milk is significant, providing proteins and minerals. When milk is used in yeast breads, it should be heated to about 190°F, a temperature higher than pasteurization, in order to denature the serum protein. Unheated, the serum is active and has a weakening effect on the structure of the gluten. Bakers often replace whole milk in formulas with dried milk, first for convenience, and second because the serum protein is deactivated in dry milk. Four ounces of dry milk replace 1 quart of whole milk, with the liquid being made up with water.

Fats

Fats used in baking coat the gluten strands during mixing, making baked goods more tender. Cell structure in the baked products is more close-grained. The presence of fats also increases shelf life. Fats are derived from either animal or vegetable sources. Those produced from animal sources include butter and lard. Butter is of course the preeminent fat used in baking, and is unsurpassed for the aroma, rich color, delectable mouth feel, and exceptional taste it provides. Solid at room temperature, butter melts at temperatures lower than body temperature, and this contributes to the smooth mouth feel imparted to baked goods made with butter. Unsalted butter is always recommended. For one reason, it gives the baker thorough control of the amount of salt used in his or her formulas. Even more importantly, salt is used as a preservative in butter, and typically salted butter is older, often carrying off flavors. The perishable nature of unsalted butter makes it more expensive than salted butter, but the additional cost should in no way tempt the baker or cook to settle for inferior, salted butter. For those who prefer to eat less butter, my advice is not to alter properly proportioned formulas, but instead to have a thinner slice of the product.

Fats derived from vegetable sources are either natural or, as in the case of shortening and margarine, hydrogenated. Natural oils, such as olive, soy, and canola, are liquid at room temperature. When used in bread doughs, these oils are liquifiers, and as such their weight is included with that of the water when computing dough hydration.

Liquid oils are susceptible to oxidation, and therefore subject to rancidity. Science developed the process of hydrogenation to prolong shelf life and curtail rancidity. During hydrogenation, a hydrogen atom is added to the liquid oil, the result being the formation of a new form of fat, called a trans unsaturated fat. These hydrogenated fats are in fact solid at room temperature, with melt-

A Bakery Story

I was talking with an equipment salesman not long ago. He grew up in a baking family, and he told me an interesting story. We go through life only once, as far as I can tell. We make choices and don't always stop to realize that they can affect everything in our lives. Sometimes the way we die is a reflection of how we have lived. Here is the story as it was told to me. . . .

The salesman is French, and he has lived in the United States for many years. He was born and raised in Paris; his parents were bakers. As a boy in the '50s, his parents bought a bakery in one of the outer *arrondissements* of the city. The owner was an old woman, a widow who had run the bakery for years after the death of her husband. For a baker, she was unusually prosperous; in fact, she was rich. Although these days we hear from time to time about a baker becoming wealthy, usually as a result of attaining some measure of celebrity status, throughout most of history, and right up until almost the end of the twentieth century, a rich baker was practically unheard of. How had this old woman amassed her considerable wealth?

During World War II, Paris was occupied by the Nazis, and the people were hungry, as they were all over Europe. Bread became more important in people's daily diet. As it became more scarce, it became more important still. Meat vanished, and so too vegetables and cheese and most of the foods that had once been abundant. But the bread, the bread—please let us have the bread! Gradually, money too became scarce. What would people do now? For hundreds of years, bakers in France had sold their bread on credit to their customers (using a system called *taille,* the baker would notch a wooden stick in order to keep track of the number of loaves for which a customer owed; normally between forty and one hundred loaves would be accounted for on the *taille* stick). During this time of extremity, bakers again offered their bread on credit. The widow, though, refused to do this, and as people became more desperate, and as she continued to insist on payment, her customers began to bring in their valuables. Gold, silver, jewelry, family heirlooms and treasures—all these found their way into her till. Gold for bread. When faced with the hunger of one's children or parents or spouse, who would not trade gold for bread? By the time the war ended, the widow had accumulated a considerable fortune.

The widow sold the bakery to the parents of my acquaintance in the early '50s, and moved to a fashionable *quartier* in central Paris to enjoy her retirement. Even after the purchase of a fine home, the fruits of her greed had left her with a great deal of remaining gold and jewelry and other valuables. These she would not put in the bank, for fear they would be lost or stolen. Instead, she put them in boxes in her cellar. Every day, she would walk down the cellar stairs to look at her wealth. She did this daily, the daily walk down the stairs to gaze at her riches. One day she slipped, fell down the stairs, and was found dead at the bottom.

This is the story as it was told to me by my acquaintance. It isn't necessarily a story with a moral, but it could be. There may not have been any connection between the glitter of the jewels in the dark basement and the manner of the widow's death. But when he told it, it made me pause for a moment. The lives we lead; the choices we make.

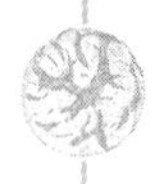

ing temperatures of 115°F or higher. Since this is above body temperature, the eating quality of products made with these fats is not as smooth and melting as those made with butter. Although there is no cholesterol in these plant-based shortenings, the human body has difficulty recognizing hydrogenated fats, and one alarming characteristic of them is that they wreak havoc on the body's ability to regulate cholesterol. This in turn can lead to serious health side effects.

HAND TECHNIQUES

3

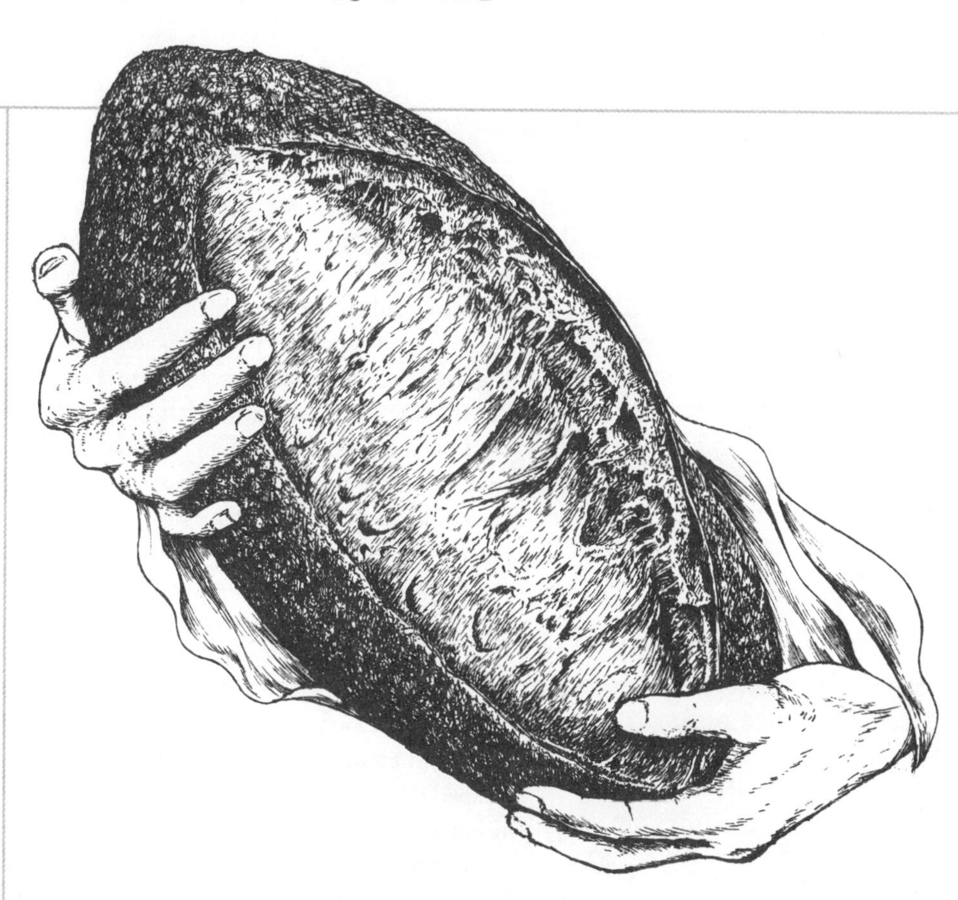

Tools were made, and born were hands.

—WILLIAM BLAKE, FROM "AUGURIES OF INNOCENCE"

There are a relatively small number of techniques that the baker must learn in order to be competent at the trade. In this way, the baker shares a similarity with the potter, the mason, and the woodworker. And as is the case with these other artisans, it is of paramount importance that the techniques are learned thoroughly.

Although modern equipment seeks to duplicate, and thereby nullify, the hand work of the baker, in the actual bakery setting there is no true substitute for skilled hands. Dividing and shaping equipment is vastly speedier than laborious hand scaling and hand forming, yet the mechanical equipment can never be as subtle and considerate of the dough as can the hand. In many bakeries, production requirements make it mandatory that equipment is relied on more than hand work. However, for someone aspiring to be an artisan in the historical sense of the word, that is, a skilled manual worker whose hands are integral to the creation of the product, a firm mastery of hand technique is required.

From a personal perspective, I can say that in my more than twenty-five years of professional baking experience, the finest breads I have made and eaten are those where, other than the mixer and the oven, no mechanical equipment was used. Why is this? Advances in equipment design now enable doughs to be divided and shaped with much more gentleness than before, but in spite of this no machine has yet been devised that can equal the sensitivity of the baker's hand. If the dough is slightly underdeveloped, or slightly stiffer than usual, the baker can make subtle handling adjustments. Machinery, programmed simply to divide a hopper full of dough at so many ounces or grams, or to shape it to some certain length, cannot make the slight alterations necessary to accommodate dough variations. So although machine-made bread can be very good, it can never surpass the finest efforts of the well-trained baker.

It is becoming increasingly common for bakeries to segregate the different aspects of production, so that one person is a mixer, one a shaper, and yet another the steward of the oven. Ultimately, this distorts the sense of pride in an individual's work, since the shaper sees little or nothing of the oven work, and the mixer has no connection to the shaping. To be a baker in the fullest sense, a person must become competent in all aspects of production, fitting fluidly into any area.

Each technique described in this section accomplishes the task in question well. There are, however, different methods possible in each instance. If the baker competently learns one method, and at a later time sees another, a few criteria will help determine if the new method is superior. If the new method can accomplish the task with no punishment to the dough (for example, ripping the surface, or incorporating large inner air chasms in the interior of the loaf), can be done in equal or less time as the method normally used, and yields results that have the desired visible qualities, both internal and external, then the new method is suitable. Numerous methods for forming shapes are startlingly fast; for the most part they sacrifice gentleness for speed, and the resulting loaf is inferior. Above all, the baker should learn methods that respect the needs of the dough. Learning new hand tech-

The Baker's Hands

The baker is lucky, lucky indeed, to have this life of the hands. Walk into a bakery and watch. The shaped loaves are enclosed in their snug linen *couches;* the master touches the surface of one and says to the aspiring young worker, "We'll load them in six minutes." How does the master know? A loaf is pulled from the oven, golden and crackling. A quick squeeze from the master, who says, "Give them another half minute." How does the master know?

For thousands of years, most of the world's work—the "days of hands," as T. S. Eliot called it—was manual and required the ineffable sensitivity of the human hand. To be sure, there were people of wealth and power whose hands had little purpose. But for the bulk of humanity, the hands were the conduit between effort and result. Then, perhaps 90 percent or more of the population was engaged directly in hand work of some form. And now, perhaps the number is reversed. Today, increasingly, the primary use of the hand seems to be for computer and telephone.

The life of the hands has characterized the work of the baker for dozens of centuries. Machines have been devised to divide and to shape bread, and even to score the fragile loaves at the moment of the load. More machines will surely follow. None will replace the confident knowledge of the skilled hand.

It's true that the machines of today can with certainty guarantee a consistency of output, and breads can be produced of predictable good quality. On the other hand, the baker who relies on his hands will surely have mishaps, and at times his efforts might yield only a 75 percent level of quality. But at other times he will coax loaves of incredible beauty and taste, and score a 95 percent! He lives for this, and the memory of these surpassing loaves lingers. He strives for perfection, for the perfect loaf, secretly hoping never to attain it—for where would he go from there?

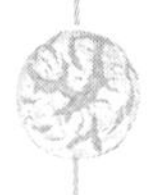

niques can be quite challenging, and patience pays off in the long run. If falling belongs to the bravery of running, then in the same way some ripped loaves and questionable cuts belong to the demanding process of learning new skills. By first working slowly and carefully to attain proficiency in these techniques, speed will naturally follow. When desire for speed precedes attention to accuracy, the results are almost guaranteed to be less than perfect.

Shaping a Round Roll

A piece of dough weighing up to 4 or 5 ounces can be comfortably shaped with one hand. Place the dough piece on the work surface, with seams down and the good side up. Start by cupping your hand, with all the fingers together, and putting the palm of the hand directly on top of the dough piece. Throughout the shaping process it is important to keep your thumb and pinky finger on the work surface. These will provide a sort of cage for the dough, within which it will take shape. With firm downward pressure, the hand is rotated, the dough is compressed in the area bounded by the pinky and the thumb, and the palm remains firmly atop the dough. The left hand rotates in a clockwise direction, and the right counterclockwise. With each rotation of the hand, smaller rolls (those weighing up to about 3 ounces) will be passed back and forth between the pinky and the thumb. Larger rolls will remain in contact with both pinky and thumb throughout the procedure. As the roll begins to take shape, you will feel it tightening beneath your hand.

If the dough rips during formation, it is a sign that there is too much pressure being applied by the hand, or that the hand is tacky. If the dough simply slides along the bench, flat and wrinkly on its underside, there is insufficient downward and inward pressure from the

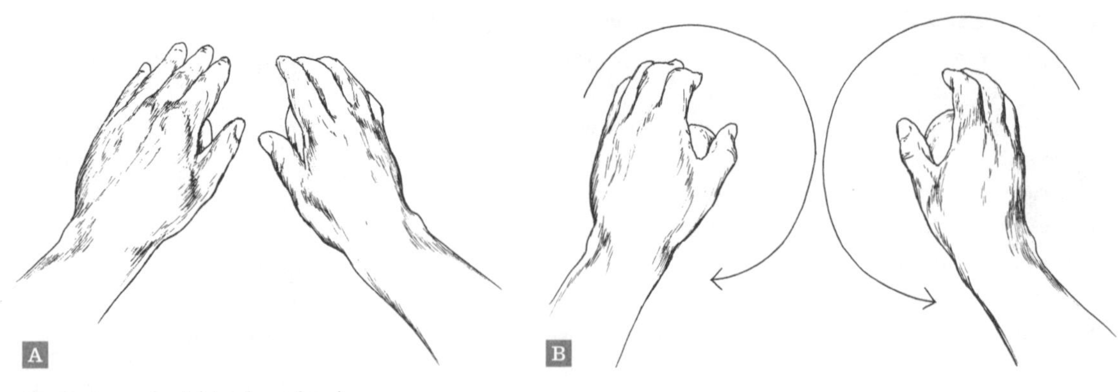

Shaping a round roll (view from above)

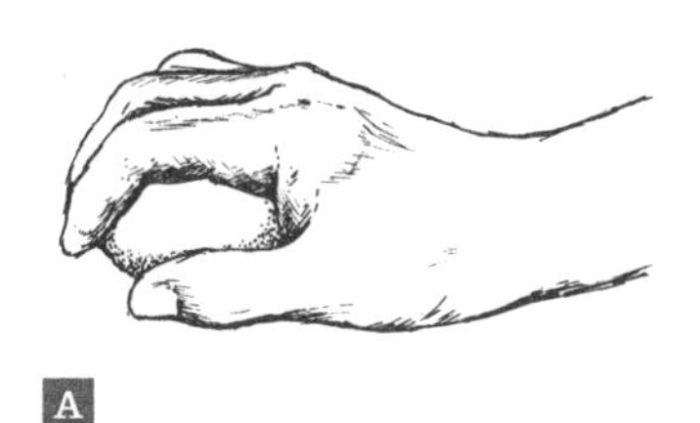

A

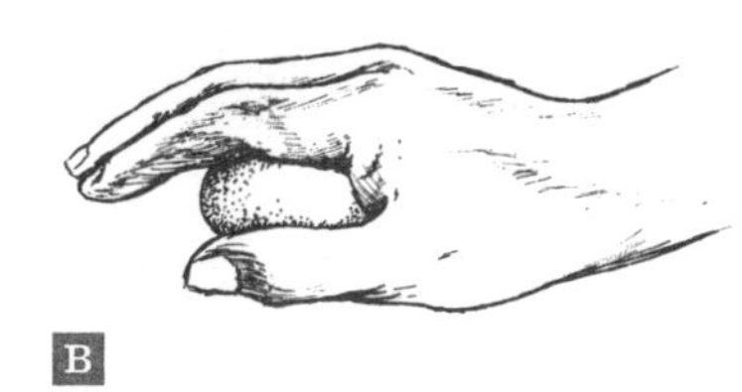

B

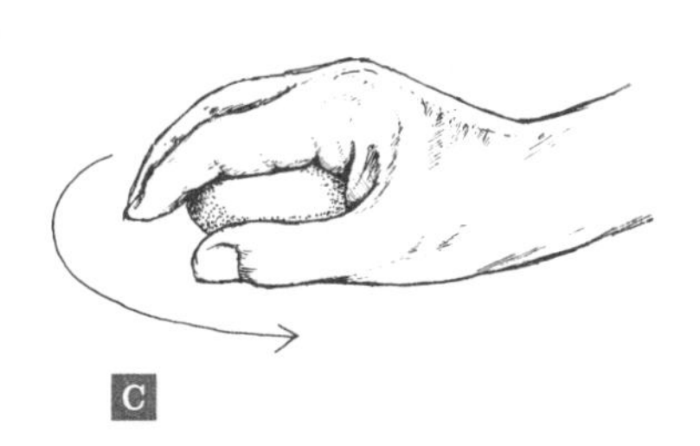

C

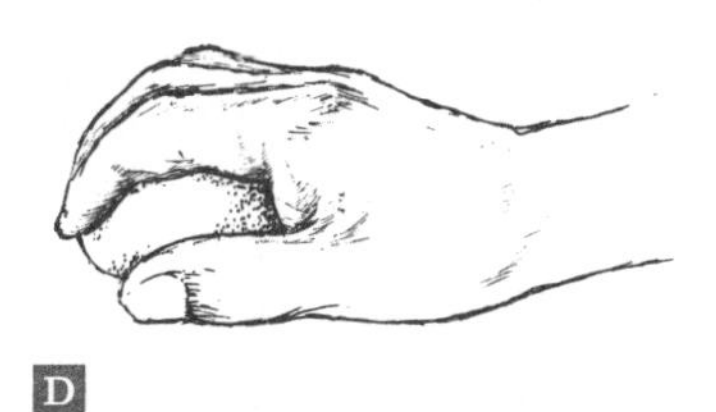

D

Shaping a round roll (view from the side)

hand, or there is an excess of flour on the bench. One thing to keep in mind when making rolls (and round loaves) is the importance of the relationship of the dough to the hand and to the bench. The baker's hands should be dry, so a quick patting in flour will prevent the dough from sticking to the palm. If it does stick, the surface of the dough will in all likelihood rip, and the final roll will be less than perfect. If, as the roll is being formed, you feel it becoming tacky on your palm, quickly run your hand along the bench. That should be sufficient to dry the hand and prevent tearing. While the hand must remain dry throughout the shaping, the bench should not. A very slight tackiness will give the dough something to "grip" during formation. The combination of a dry hand, to prevent surface tearing of the dough, and traction between dough and bench, gives the best results. If, after making several rolls, there is a buildup of dough on the bench, slightly more flour is needed. On the other hand, if the bench has too much flour on it, the rolls cannot be formed because they will just slide along the bench.

Preshaping

Generally speaking, round loaves, oblong loaves, loaves baked in pans, and baguettes are preshaped after scaling, and after a period of rest, the final shaping is performed. Once divided, the dough is in an irregular, disorderly condition, and the purpose of preshaping is to take the scaled-out dough piece and lightly bring it to roundness, from which state it will be much easier to accomplish the final shaping.

To preshape, the scaled-out dough is placed on the bench, which has a very slight film of flour covering it. If there are any small scrap pieces of dough resulting from the scaling, these should be on the top of the dough. As the preshaping proceeds, the scrap will be incorporated into the body of the dough. We will refer to the side of the dough that has the scrap as the "seam side," since the seams of the shaped loaf will eventually be on this side; the bottom side of the dough piece will be referred to as the "good side"; that is, it is the seamless outer surface of the dough, intact and unbroken. This good side will remain the good side throughout the entire preshaping and final shaping process, and will eventually become the top of the baked loaf.

To begin the preshaping, pat out any large air pockets in the dough with a few quick strokes, using a flat hand. Do not knead the dough with the fingers, or dimple it. Keeping the hand flat will quickly and effectively achieve the necessary degassing. Next, fold

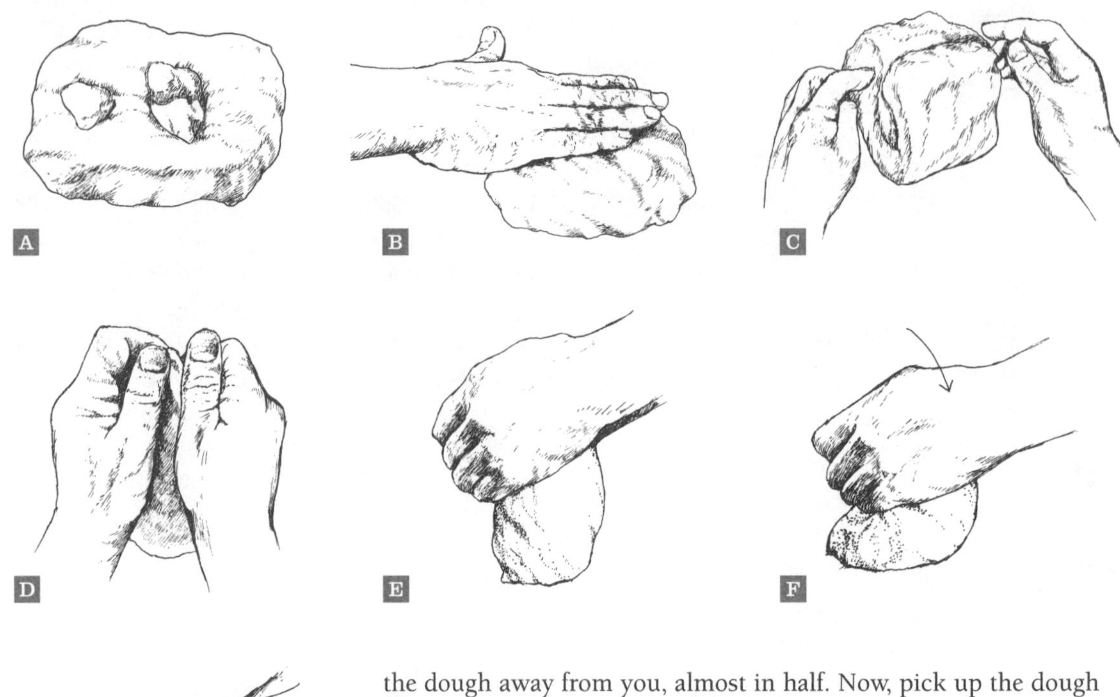

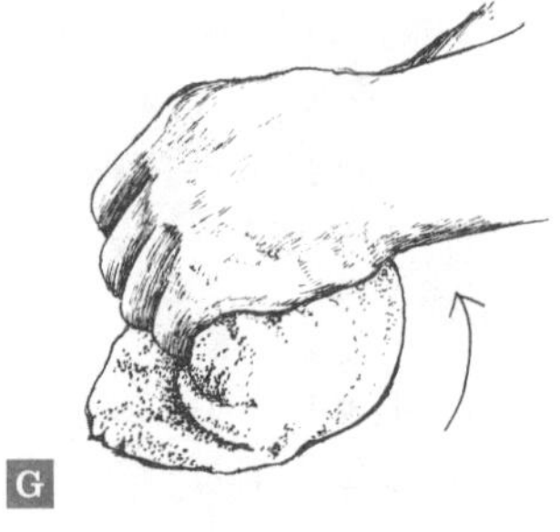

Preshaping

the dough away from you, almost in half. Now, pick up the dough with both hands, with the seam side away from you and the bottom side (the good side) facing you. Your thumbs should be facing up, and all fingers should be in contact with the seam side. Lay the portion of the good side that is farthest from your fingers onto the bench. Now, commence a process that incorporates two actions at the same time: As your fingers begin to tuck the seam side of the dough in on itself, roll the dough piece toward you. This rolling will stretch the outer skin (you may notice flecks of flour stretching on the outer skin of the dough); the tucking will help consolidate the dough into a more rounded form. Once the dough has been rolled and tucked in this manner and is again on the bench, pick it up at a point a quarter or a third of the way to one side (this enables you to work a new quadrant of the dough) and repeat the rolling and tucking. A light hand is all that is needed, and any surface tearing of the dough indicates handling that is too harsh. Repeat the above steps, and after 3 or 4 sequences of rolling and tucking, the loaf should be somewhat rounded. Remember, at this point you are only preshaping, so avoid overworking the dough. More exertion and more thorough tightening will occur during the final shaping. Once the loaf is preshaped, lay it good side down, on a slight film of flour and cover lightly with plastic.

A

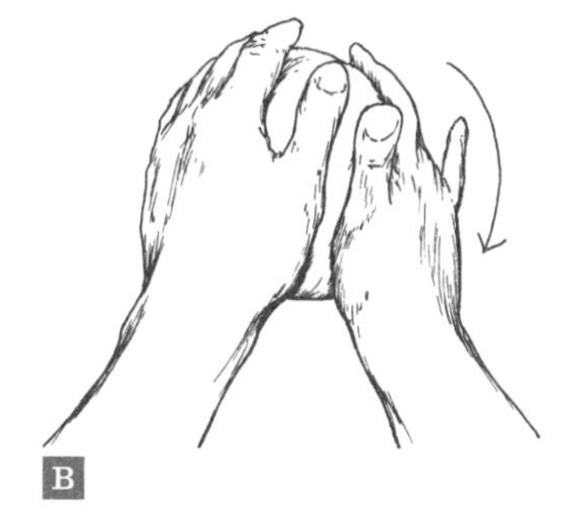

B

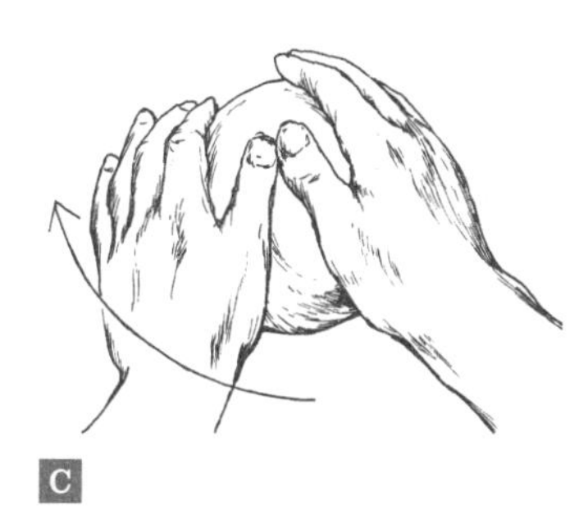

C

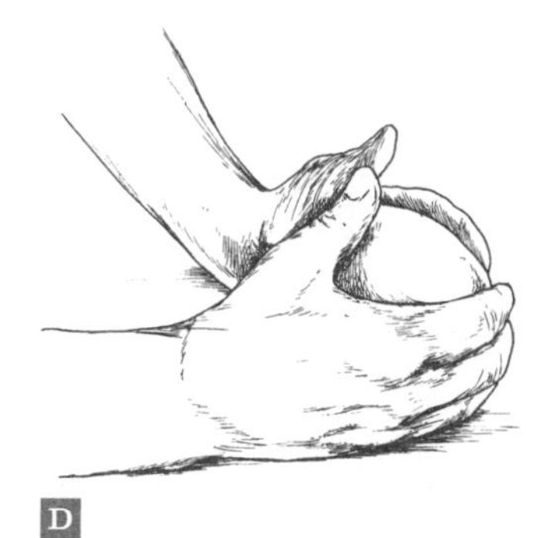

D

Shaping a round loaf

Shaping a Round Loaf

The final shaping of a round loaf begins once the dough piece has relaxed sufficiently to be worked again. This rest time, called "bench rest," typically lasts between 5 and 30 minutes, depending on the type of bread and the tightness of the preshaping. The more tightly the dough is preshaped, the longer the time needed to rest it before beginning the final shaping. If the dough rests too long on the work surface, it will become overaged and difficult to shape, excessively slack and gassy, and its final color and appearance could be impaired. If it is not sufficiently relaxed, there is a risk of tearing the outer surface of the dough because the dough is still too tight to accept further working. This too, of course, impairs the final appearance of the loaf. It is difficult to verbalize the exact time requirements for the bench rest phase; however, with experience the baker learns to ascertain when the dough is sufficiently relaxed and final shaping can begin. Remember, the dough shouldn't be too tight or too slack, and should accept the final shaping with fair ease.

Lightly flour the work surface, pick up the dough, and place it in front of you, good side down. Repeat the initial steps of the preshaping, from the patting out of the air with a flat hand to the folding of the dough to the tucking and folding. Since you are now performing the final shaping, more exertion is helpful as long as there is no tearing of the outer skin.

Once you have achieved a more-or-less round loaf, place it seam side down. Now the good side of the loaf is on top. Lightly dust both hands, either by running them along the work surface or patting them quickly in flour. Place both hands over the loaf in such a way that the sides of each hand, from the tip of the pinky all the way to the base of the palm, are on the work surface. Loosely overlap your thumbs on top of the loaf (if the loaf weighs more than about 2 pounds, or if your hands are small, the thumbs may not overlap completely). Your hands will form a sort of cage, within which the loaf will rotate and tighten. Keep the sides of your hands on the work surface and begin to rotate your hands in a clockwise direction. As your hands move through the circular motion, they should remain approximately parallel to each other, moving as a single unit. As the loaf is rounded, the pinkies of both hands help to tighten and form the base of the loaf, and the pressure from the thumbs and other fingers helps to tighten the structure of the loaf. The finished loaf should be a round, tight, and seamless ball, with no perceptible inner chasms, and with no rips on the surface skin of the loaf. Just as there is an axis to the earth, so there is one to the round loaf: the "North Pole" of the loaf should remain essentially in the same spot throughout the rounding process.

There are two common obstacles to shaping round loaves. The first is the dough sticking to the hands, which at the least slows down shaping progress, and at the worst results in a ripped dough surface. Preventing this is simple: Pat your hands in flour or run them along the work surface. It may be necessary to repeat this drying 2 or 3 times as the loaf is being rounded. The second obstacle occurs when an excess of flour is on the work surface and the dough slides along without taking shape. When making a round loaf, avoid flouring the work surface unless the dough is actually sticking to it and the underside is ripping, in which case a very light dusting of flour is all that is needed to correct things. The combination for success is dry hands to prevent surface tearing, and a work surface with just the slightest amount of tackiness, to provide a little traction to the dough as it takes on its final shape.

Forming Two Round Loaves at the Same Time

The technique of forming 2 round loaves at the same time is common in Germany, and seems less so in France. A skilled baker can form 2 round loaves, 1 in each hand, in about the time it takes to form 1 round loaf. Clearly, from the perspective of speed, it is a skill worth developing.

Begin by having 2 preshaped loaves on the work surface, good sides down. The fingers of each hand are responsible for folding over a new flap of dough, while the heel of each hand has the job of kneading and rotating the dough piece. Place 4 fingers of each hand on the back side of the dough piece; the thumb remains in front. The fingers fold approximately 20 to 25 percent of the dough over into the center. The heel of the hand then rolls the dough away from you, kneading the folded flap of dough. During this stroke, the heel of the hand also makes a slight rotation of the dough (the dough in the right hand rotates counterclockwise, and the dough in the left clockwise). Once rolled and kneaded, the fingers, still behind the dough piece, fold another flap of dough forward, and the heel of the hand repeats the rolling and kneading stroke. By continuing the rotation of the dough piece, the heel of the hand enables the fingers to fold a new portion of dough to the center. In this way, the entire piece gets evenly worked. Just as

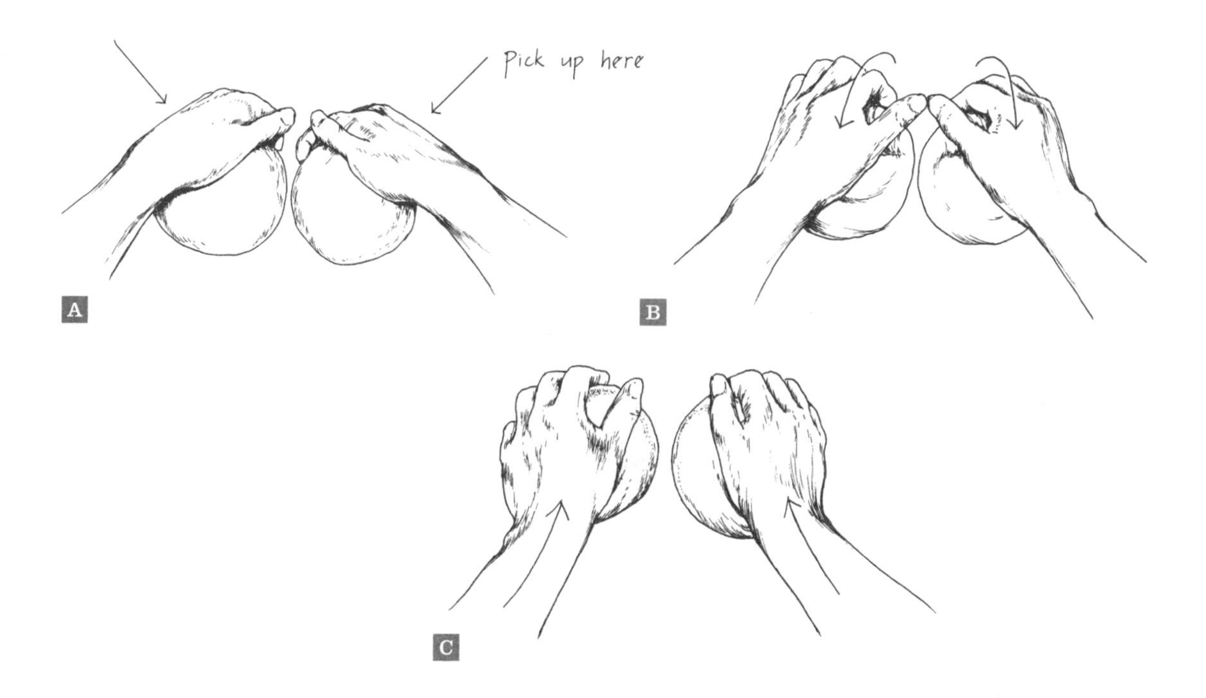

Forming two round loaves simultaneously

there is an axis to the dough when forming one round loaf, so too there is an axis to the loaves when forming two at once. While it is possible to form the loaves completely with this method, it is generally preferable to bring the loaves to about 80 to 90 percent completion, and then to finish the rounding in the same manner that one loaf is finished, with a few quick strokes to tighten each loaf completely.

Forming an Oval (Bâtard) Loaf

Forming an oval or oblong loaf begins with a dough piece that has been scaled and preshaped. After resting, the dough is lifted from the work surface, and placed, seam side up, on a lightly floured surface. With the fingers and palm of one hand, excess gas is gently patted out. At this point, if the dough is oblong in shape rather than round, the long portion is facing "north and south," as in the diagram. Fold one-third of the dough toward you so that it rests on itself, and pat out the air. Now take the 2 squared-off corners at the farthest part of the dough and bring them in toward the center of the dough piece. Pat out the air. Turn the dough piece around 180 degrees and again fold one-third of the piece toward you. Again, bring the 2 squared-off corners in toward the center

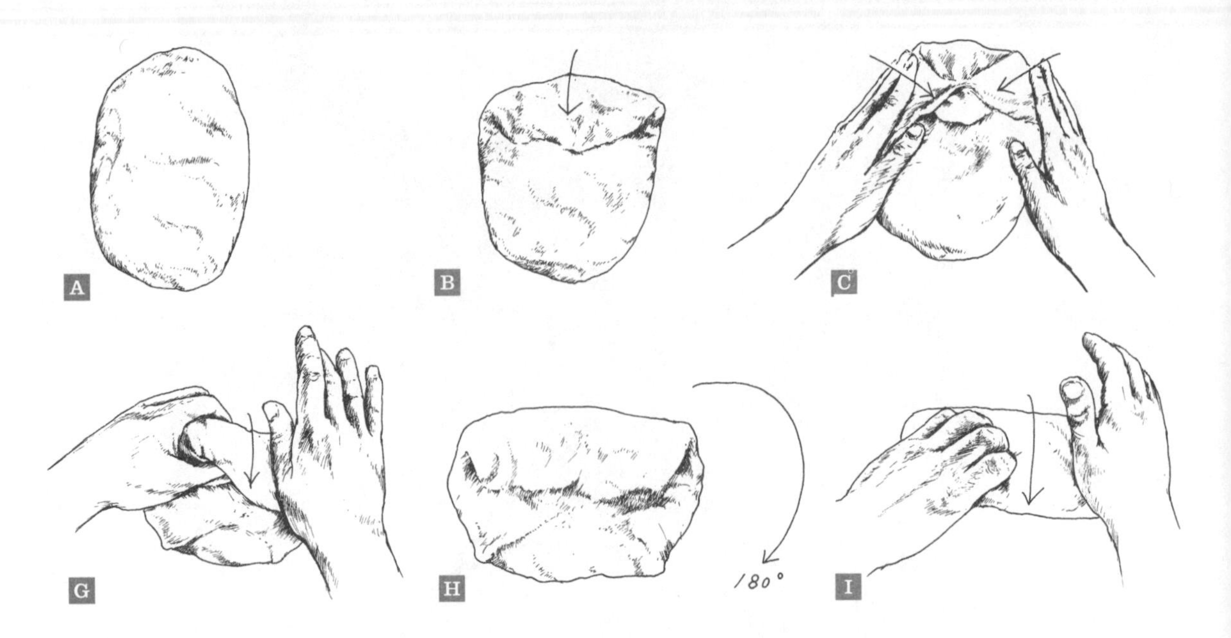

Forming an oval loaf

and pat out the air. At this point, you should have a tight piece of dough with a solid density. If insufficient hand pressure has been applied, there may be internal air pockets that will make further shaping difficult. If too much pressure has been applied, the outer surface of the dough may rip.

Beginning at the right side of the dough (for right-handed people), fold and press the dough down its length until you have reached the left side of the dough. To do this step, place your left thumb at the top of the dough, and the fingers of your left hand out of sight around the back of the dough. The fingers fold a small flap of dough over, burying the thumb. Then, using the heel of your right hand, press the folded flap of dough to seal it. Continue with this folding and pressing motion until you have covered the entire length of the dough. There are two things to note: Make sure the heel of your right hand stays flat, so that entire portion of the hand is pressing into the loaf. Using the side of the hand will result in a lumpy seam. Second, when this phase of the shaping is done, there should be a small lip at the base of the dough, as in illustration H.

Turn the dough piece around 180 degrees and repeat the folding and pressing motions. Again, right-handers begin at the right side of the dough and work across the entire length. This time, however, rather than leaving a lip of dough at the base, take the fold all the way, so that the seam is made right at the work surface. The seam should be tight along its entire length, and reasonably straight.

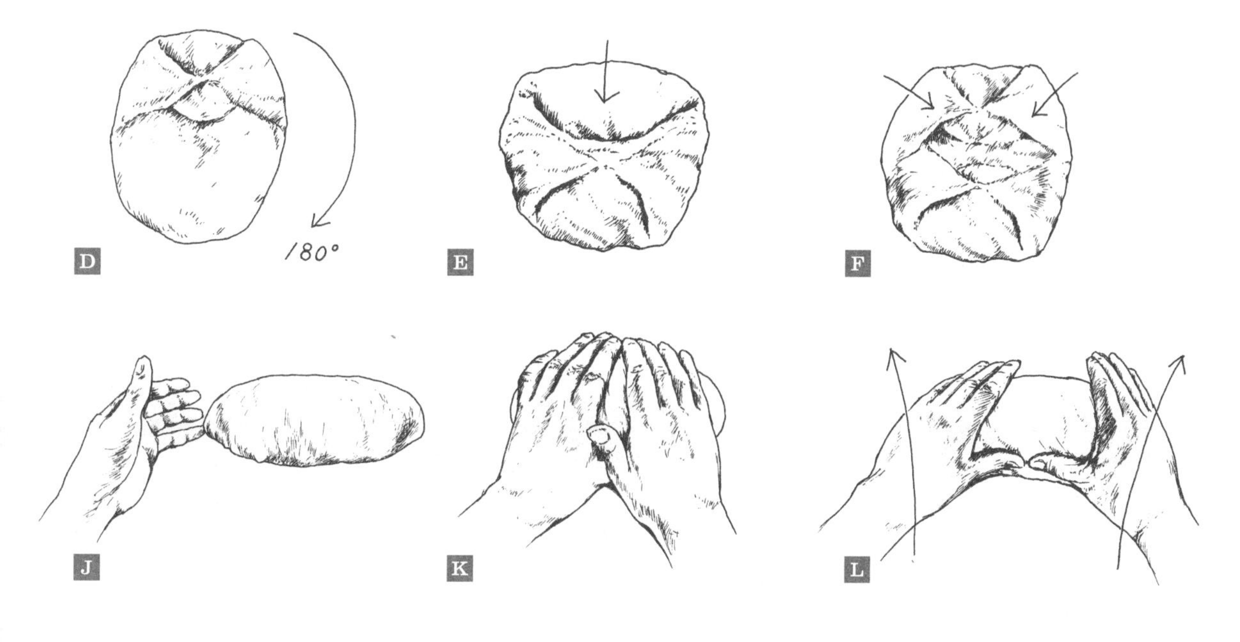

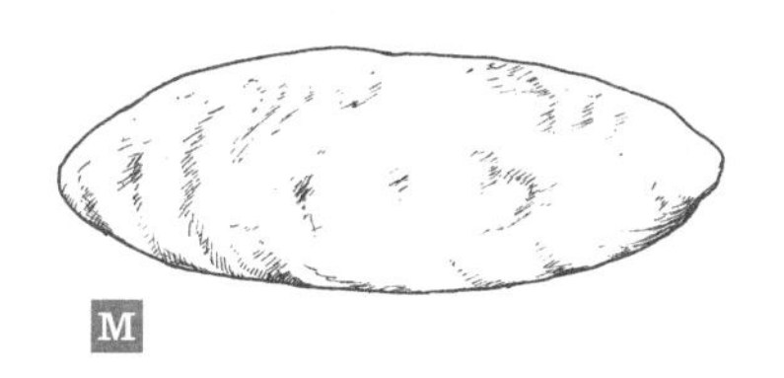

Turn the loaf over so that the seam is directly underneath. Place both hands on top of the loaf, with your index fingers touching at the center of the loaf. Gently curve your hands so that the fingertips and the heels of your hands rest on the work surface. The palm of each hand should be curved around the dough surface. Begin to roll the dough back and forth, with firm softness, working your hands toward the ends of the dough. When your hands have worked the entire length of dough, look over the piece: Is the shape adequate in terms of length and evenness, or does it need further working? It is usually necessary to repeat the motion once or twice in order to streamline the shape and fine-tune the length. Whether the loaf is blunt or pointy at the ends (a personal preference), the objective is the same: to give a final shaping that yields a loaf that is symmetrical, with its high point at the center and a gradual taper to the ends.

Again, keep in mind throughout the forming the need for dry hands. If at any time the dough begins to stick—even the slightest bit—immediately dust your hands with a minimum of flour. The work surface should be dry as well during the final shaping, and if the dough shows any sign of sticking to it, pick up the dough, dust a light sheen of flour onto the work surface, and proceed (the slight tackiness of the work surface that allows the dough to grip during the formation of round loaves is not desired when shaping ovals and baguettes). This brief moment of drying the work surface or your hands prevents ripped surfaces on the bread.

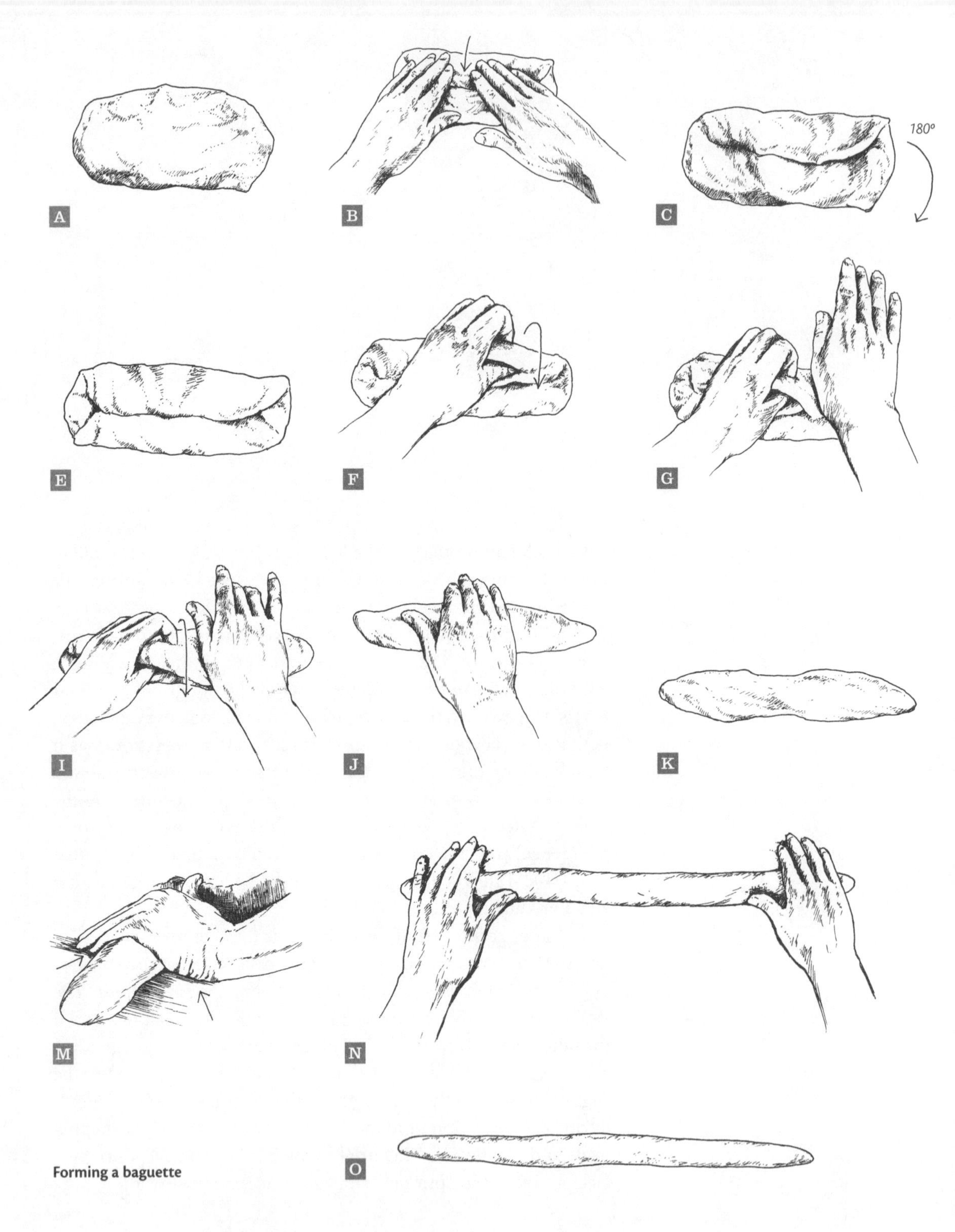

Forming a baguette

Forming a Baguette

D

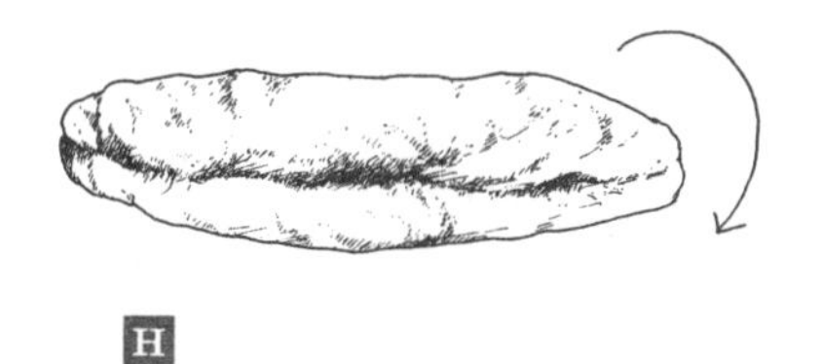

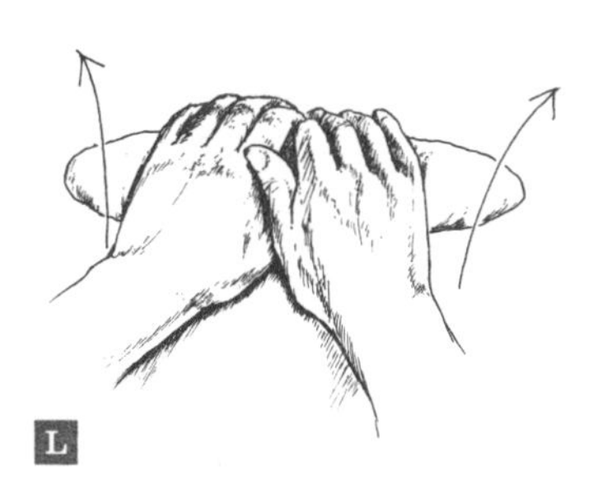

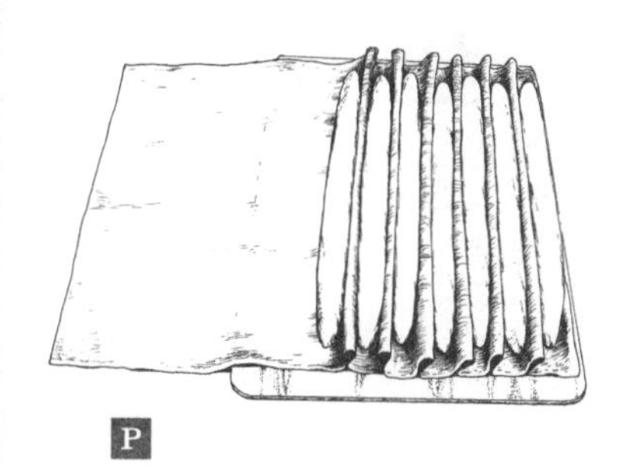

The final forming of a baguette begins in the same manner as that of an oval loaf. Take the preshaped dough and, on a lightly floured work surface, place the good side down. Using gentle pressure with the flat of one hand, flatten the piece into an oblong shape of even thickness. The eventual length of the baguette will be almost 2 feet, and you should begin by having the dough piece oriented in an "east-west" manner, not "north-south" as in shaping an oval.

Fold one-third of the dough piece toward you so that it rests on itself, and gently pat out the air. Turn the dough piece around 180 degrees, and again fold one-third of the dough toward you. Again, gently pat out the air. The dough should now be approximately rectangular, and of even thickness.

Beginning at the right side of the dough piece (for right-handed bakers), begin the folding and pressing procedure: The left thumb rests at the top of the dough with the fingers of the left hand holding the loaf from behind. The fingers fold a flap of dough over, covering the thumb, and the heel of the right hand presses the folded flap of dough to seal it. This folding and pressing is repeated down the entire length of the dough. As with the oval loaf, the seam should be tight, and there should be a lip of dough along the bottom length. Turn the dough piece around 180 degrees and repeat the folding and pressing process, this time bringing the seam right to the work surface. Again, the seam should be tight and more or less straight along the entire length.

Turn the dough over so that the seam is directly on the bottom. Place your right hand in the center of the dough, contouring your hand so that your fingertips and the heel of your hand are on the work surface, and the palm of your hand is in contact with the dough. Roll the dough gently back and forth 3 or 4 times, in a manner more caressing than harsh, so that you slightly flatten the center of the dough. Then, take both hands and place them side by side on top of the dough, with your index fingers touching and the fingertips and the heel of each hand on the work surface. Begin to roll the dough back and forth, and at the same time, begin to elongate the dough. It is easy to see your hands rolling the dough back and forth; the outward pressure exerted by the hands is less visible, but very important. When your hands have reached the ends of the dough, check the symmetry, proportion, and length of the baguette. If the dough is not yet long enough, bring both hands to the center of the loaf again, and roll the dough back and forth and outward once more to continue lengthening the baguette. Refine the shape by working directly on any areas that need attention: If there are areas that are too thick, work to thin them; if one end is bulbous, roll it back and forth until it has a similarity with the shape of the other end. Above all, the purpose of these refining strokes is to finish with a baguette that has a graceful appearance and harmonious taper. The high point should be in the center, with a symmetrical tapering to the ends. Throughout the shaping process, take the precaution, as with shaping an oval, that the dough does not stick to either your hands or the work surface.

Once baguettes are shaped, their final fermentation typically takes place on perforated screens, sheet pans, or *couches,* between folds of baker's linen. Since the best volume (and arguably the best flavor) is achieved when baking is done directly on the floor of the oven, without sheet pans or perforated screens as an intermediary layer, the use of linen *couches* is commonly considered to be the best method for rising the shaped loaves. At the same time, the method is highly labor-intensive and requires a deck oven or baking stone, so different methods are often used for the final fermentation and the bake. In any case, when proofing the baguettes on linen, the shaped dough is placed seam side down. As each baguette is placed on the *couche,* pull up a fold of baker's linen so that the adjacent baguette will not join with it during final proofing. As subsequent baguettes are formed, be sure each one is sufficiently spaced from the preceding one on the *couche* so that it can rise properly. An alternative method of using the baker's linen is as follows: Sift a light but thorough covering of flour onto the *couche.* Place the shaped baguettes onto the *couche* with the seam side up and the good side down on the flour. When the risen baguettes are transferred to the loading conveyor or baker's peel, they will be placed with the floured side up. The surface skin will be just a bit thicker (this makes scoring easier and can help the "ears," or thin flaps of dough, open nicely, particularly in very humid weather), and the baked loaves will have a pleasing rustic aspect.

Forming a Strand for Braiding

Beautifully formed braids begin with beautifully formed strands. There are examples of braiding techniques in this book that utilize just one strand of dough up to as many as 70 strands. Regardless of the number, the technique used to form them is the same.

Most doughs used for braiding are comparatively stiff, and the pieces should remain covered with plastic at all times. Also, due to their stiffness, any excess of flour on the work surface will impede

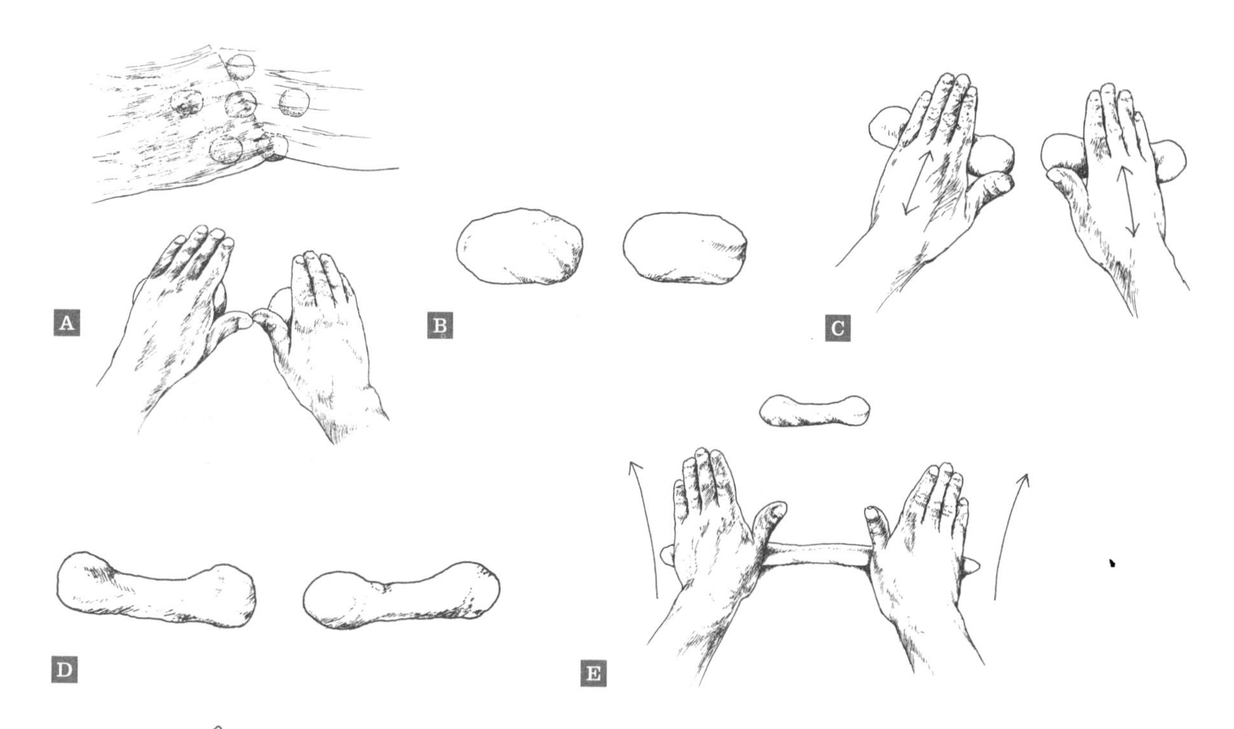

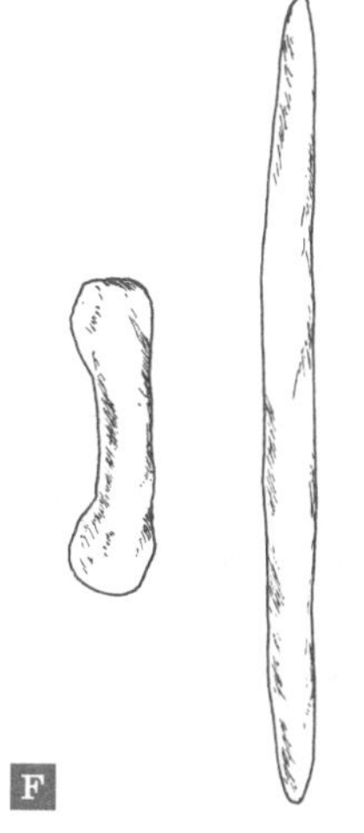

Forming a strand for braiding

shaping, as the dough will tend to slide and not roll. Once scaled, the small dough pieces should be preshaped in either a round or oval form. When sufficiently relaxed, take a piece from under the plastic and place it on the work surface in front of you, seam side down. It is unlikely that flour will be necessary on the work surface, but lightly floured hands will help during the shaping process. Begin by placing the flat part of one hand on top of the dough. Press firmly into the dough while rolling it back and forth 3 or 4 times. The goal is to form a sort of dog-bone shape, with a narrow center and bulbous ends. Once this is accomplished, place both hands onto the dough, with the index fingers of each hand touching. Roll the dough back and forth with good downward pressure from your hands, and at the same time extend your hands outward in order to elongate the strand. The stroke is finished when each hand has worked all the way out to the end portion of the dough. If the strand is not long enough, return your hands to the center of the dough and repeat the motion. Depending on how relaxed the dough is when the shaping began, and the final length needed for the strand, you may have to return to the center and repeat the rolling motion 3 or 4 times. Often, the strand is almost at its finished length, but it is not symmetrical. When this occurs, do not continue to bring both hands to the center and roll outward in an equal fashion—this simply exacerbates the irregularity of the shape. Instead, bring one or both hands to the area that needs tapering, and work only on that area of the dough. The strand is finished when it is both long enough and has an even, gradual, symmetrical taper.

As the individual strands are finished, it helps to roll them in a very slight, almost invisible coating of flour. When the braid is formed, this slight coating of flour buffers each strand from the next, and when the loaf is baked, the strands tend to keep a lovely distinctness, rather than merging into each other.

When a braid is made using more than 1 strand of dough, it is important that all the strands are of the same length and taper. Unevenness in the strands tends to stand out prominently in the finished loaf, and developing the skill to control both the length and the evenness of the taper will reward the baker with braided loaves that are beautiful to look at.

Scoring Bread

Since we strive for a measure of visual consistency with our loaves, proper scoring is an important skill to develop. As bread encounters the fierce heat of the oven, it undergoes enormous expansion during the first few minutes of oven spring. By slicing the dough with a razor or cutting it with scissors to intentionally create weak spots in the dough, the baker attempts to control the final shape of the loaf. Bread that is unscored will pop rather indelicately any place it finds weakness along the surface. Loaf volume also increases when the bread is properly scored; by enabling the loaf to expand in certain areas, maximum loaf volume is encouraged. Conversely, unscored or improperly scored bread often has a somewhat distressed and truncated appearance.

Visual appeal is another reason we score bread. While a baguette has a recognized and established technique for scoring, there is a great deal of latitude in how we score round and oval loaves. With a skillful use of blade or scissors, the baker brings visual variety to his or her loaves. People do eat with their eyes, and it is exciting to see a bread rack filled with an array of shapes and cuts, patterns and styles. This brings us to a fourth reason we score our loaves: It becomes the signature of the baker. It's a pleasure to look at a loaf that has been skillfully scored and to recognize it as your own. I have often felt that if ten of the world's finest bakers got together, and each made a few dozen baguettes using the same equipment and ingredients, and each scored his own baguettes, each one of those ten bakers would know exactly which were his breads when they came out of the oven. How we hold the blade, the depth and angle of the cut, and the length and overlap of each cut all contribute to making our personal technique our personal signature.

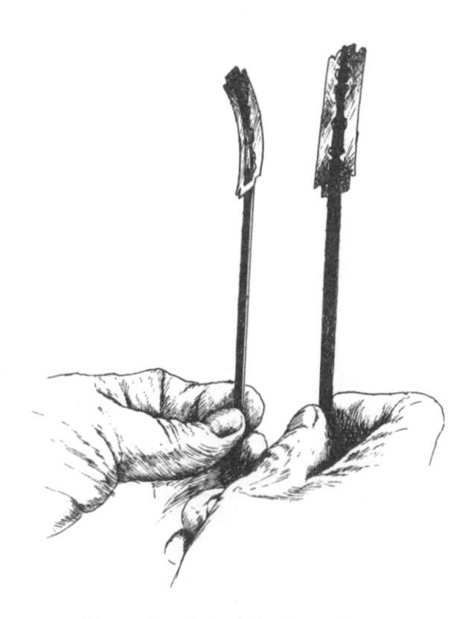

Curved and straight *lames* for scoring bread

Two types of blades (or *lames*) are used to score bread: curved and straight. The curved is appropriate for cutting "ears" in baguettes and oval loaves; the straight blade is used when vertical cuts are made on round or oval loaves. Properly scoring a baguette begins by holding the *lame* at the extreme left end of the dough (for right-handed bakers). The *lame* is held so that the razor is at about a 30-degree angle to horizontal. Keeping the wrist rigid, a swift, straight, slice is made toward the far end of the loaf. The goal is to slice a thin flap of dough, and the curved *lame* facilitates this. The second cut (and each subsequent cut) overlaps the prior cut by 25 to 30 percent of the length of the cut. Generally, 5 to 7 cuts are sufficient for a baguette, with the final cut ending at the far end of the loaf, correlating with the place the first cut commenced. All the cuts remain in the top center portion of the baguette.

There are a few common problems in baguette scoring. One is incorrect direction of the cuts. Avoid cutting on a bias, from the far side of the baguette over to the near side. Be sure the blade stays only in the top center portion of the loaf. Another common fault is incorrect depth of cut. To score baguettes so that they have pleasing "ears," only a thin flap is opened with the blade. If the blade cuts too deeply, the tendency is for the sheer weight of the cut to simply collapse back onto the loaf, resulting in little or no opening of the cuts. A third problem is incorrect angle of the blade. When the blade is held upright and vertical to the dough, the cuts tend to seal up during the bake, and the resulting loaf will not have the pleasing open scoring we associate with baguettes.

Scoring an oval loaf can be done using either a curved or straight blade, depending on the desired appearance of the fin-

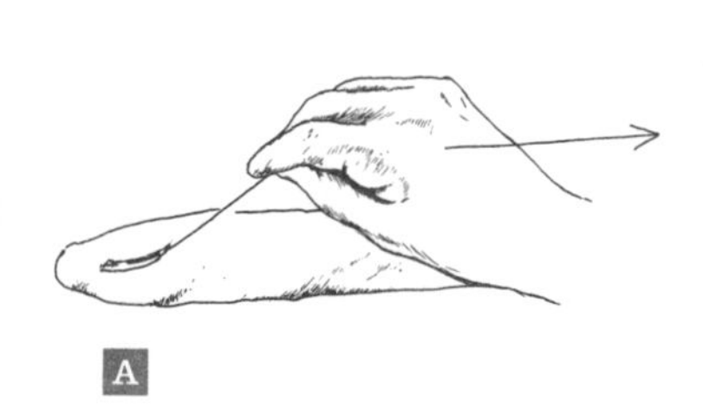

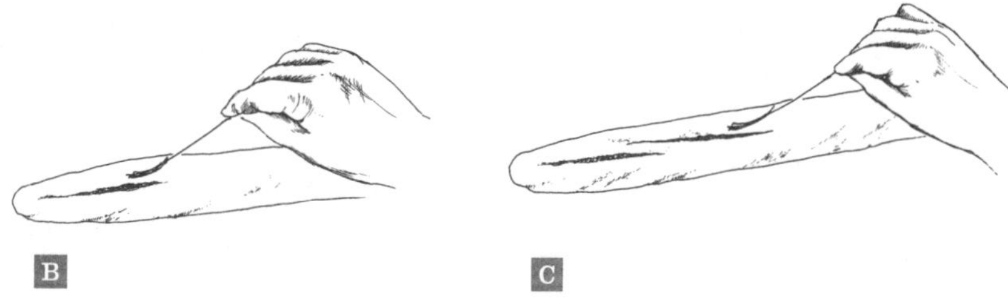

Scoring a baguette

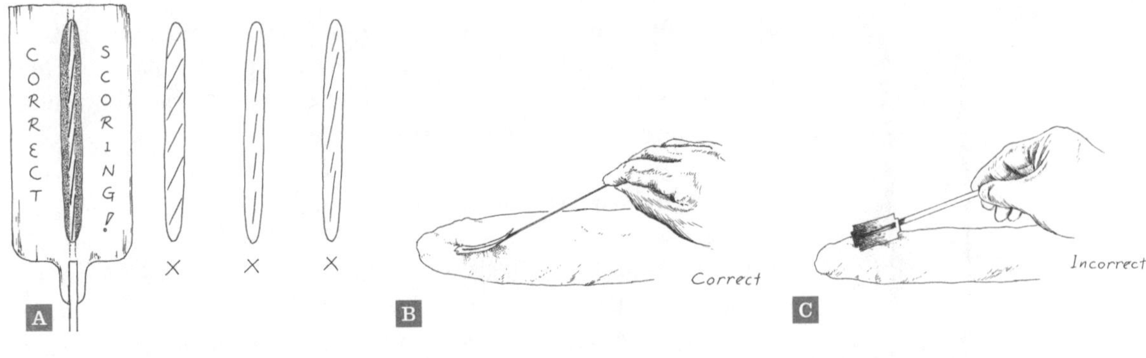

Correct scoring technique

ished loaf. The straight blade is used to make repetitive vertical scorings along the dough's surface, either lengthwise, crosswise, crosshatched, or at an angle to the length of the loaf. To create a loaf with one proud end-to-end opening, use the curved blade. Hold it as in scoring a baguette, that is, with the blade concave and at about a 30-degree angle. Begin at the top of the extreme left side of the loaf (for right-handed bakers) and, keeping the wrist rigid, slice swiftly straight to the other end of the loaf. The cut should be straight, and, as in scoring the baguette, only a slight piercing of the surface skin is necessary. It may seem that a straight and shallow cut will not be sufficient to open the loaf. Once in the oven, though, the loaf will expand and the cut will open beautifully. It may also seem that if a shallow cut gives a good opening, a deep cut will result in a more prominent opening. More is not better, though, and a deep cut will simply collapse from its own weight.

Using a straight blade to cut round or oval loaves offers the baker (and consumer) a wide variety of visual possibilities. The straight blade is held perpendicular to the loaf; in this way, it differs from the flat cutting angle used with the curved blade. Incisions with the straight blade are generally slightly deeper than those made with the curved blade, in order to encourage maximum expansion in the oven, and because the baker is not attempting to

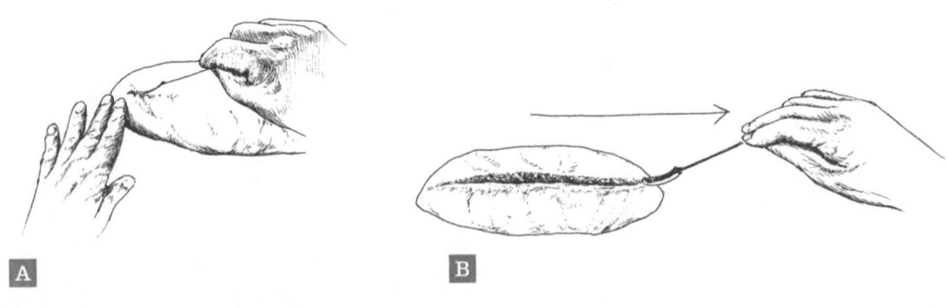

Scoring an oval loaf with a curved *lame*

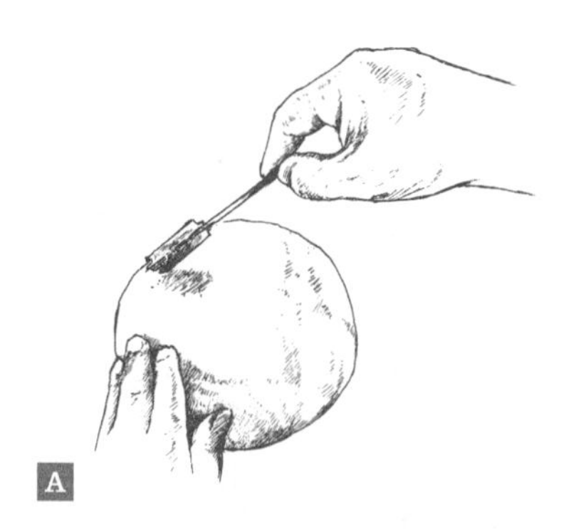
A

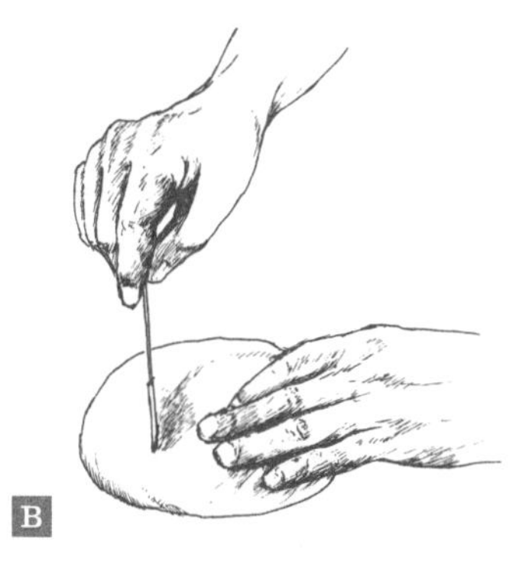
B

C

D

Scoring a round loaf with a straight *lame*

develop the kind of "ear" associated with baguettes. Again, strive for symmetry, evenness of line length and depth, and a balanced pattern that not only is pleasing to the eye, but that also encourages good dough expansion.

Scissors can be used to cut rolls, as well as round, oblong, and pan loaves, giving a different effect than that achieved when cutting with a blade. When cutting bread in a loaf pan, begin at the end closest to you, keeping the scissors perpendicular to the dough, and walk it down the loaf, snipping at regular intervals along the length. Round loaves can be cut around the shoulder or in the center of the loaf. Use both hands when cutting with scissors. The top hand, of course, holds the scissors through the loops. The thumb and index finger of the bottom hand hold the scissors by the shaft. Two hands are used rather than just one for a couple of reasons: First, the bottom hand acts as a sort of depth gauge, helping to ensure that each snip is at the same depth. Second, the bottom hand is actively engaged with the work of

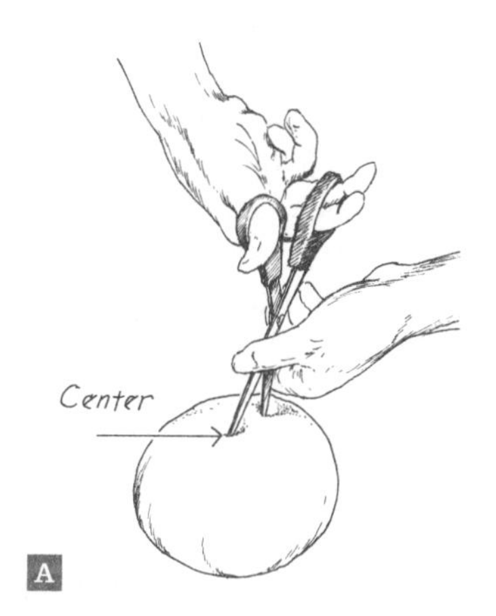

A

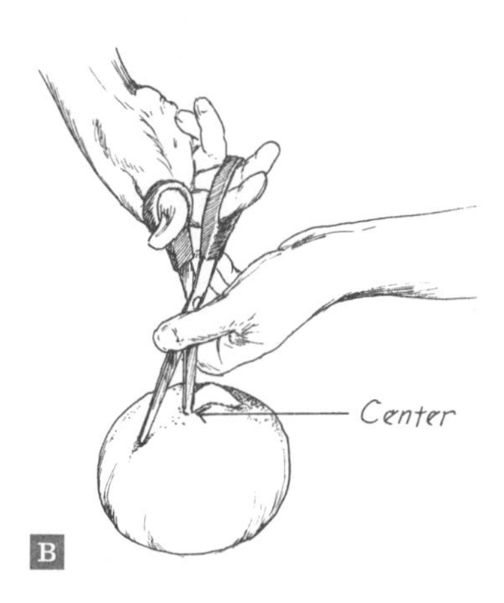

B

C

Cutting a round loaf with scissors

closing the scissors at each snip. Cutting a few dozen breads or innumerable dozens of rolls with scissors is tiring work; by using the bottom hand to share some of the burden, the baker lessens what would otherwise be quite a demanding task.

Cutting a round roll with scissors

A baguette of slightly longer and slightly more slender shape is preferred for the *épi de blé* ("sheaf of wheat"). Hold the scissors at a shallow angle in relation to the baguette, as shown in the diagram. Open the blades of the scissors so they are wider than the width of the bread. Cut briskly to get a crisp and clean cut and, using the fingers of the other hand, place the cut piece to one side of the loaf. Move the scissors down the loaf and make a second cut, this time placing the cut piece of dough to the other side of the loaf. Continue to work down the length of the dough, alternating the placement of the cut dough pieces, first to one side and then to the other. The most graceful *épis* are ones where the scissors cut deepest and leave a thin core of dough. These are also, however, the most fragile. Conversely, while an *épi* cut with a thick core is sturdy, it lacks gracefulness. After the bake, be sure the *épis* are thoroughly cooled in a flat position before being stood up on a bread rack. If displayed while still warm, they will almost certainly slump into a bent shape, or worse, break at a thin spot in the core.

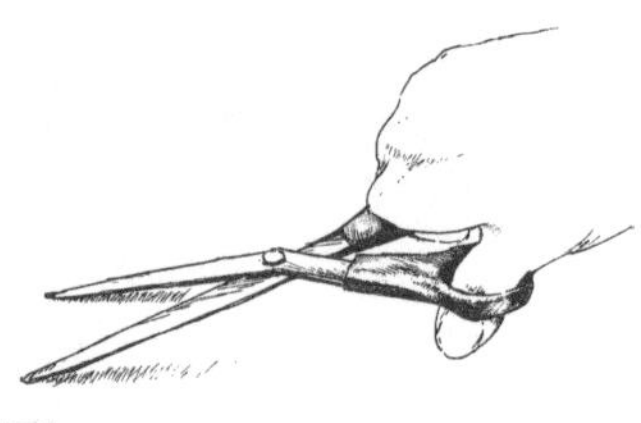
A correct

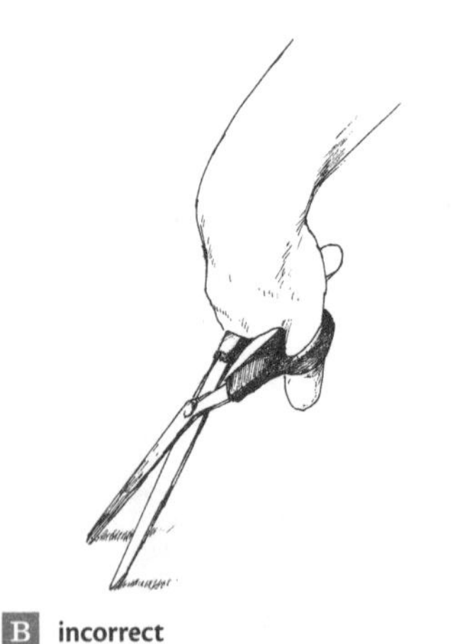
B incorrect

Scissor position for cutting *épis de blé*

A final method of scoring bread is with a rolling pin. There is a lovely shape called *pain fendu,* or "split bread," used on round or oval loaves, and on rolls. Use a rolling pin of narrow diameter (perhaps 1½ to 2 inches thick for loaves, 1 inch or less for rolls or decorative pieces). The dough should be divided, preshaped, and given its final shaping. Liberally flour the top surface of the dough (any excess will be shaken off). When the dough has relaxed, place the rolling pin in the center of the loaf and push down into the loaf. Once the pin is at the bottom, roll it slightly back and forth to create an open valley, with equal mountains of dough on each side. There should be enough flour beneath the loaf so that it does not stick to the work surface during the pinning. Remove the pin, lift the loaf, and shake off the excess flour. Now hold the loaf from the back side, lightly squeeze the sides of the loaf so that the valley is a deep seam with the walls of dough on each side of it touching each other, and place the loaf into a floured *banneton* or on a length of baker's linen. The loaves are proofed upside down, then inverted at the time of loading into the oven. If the technique is performed correctly, the loaf will expand so that there are 2 even sides of dough separated by the narrow seam of the valley, giving the appearance of a loaf that is split down the center.

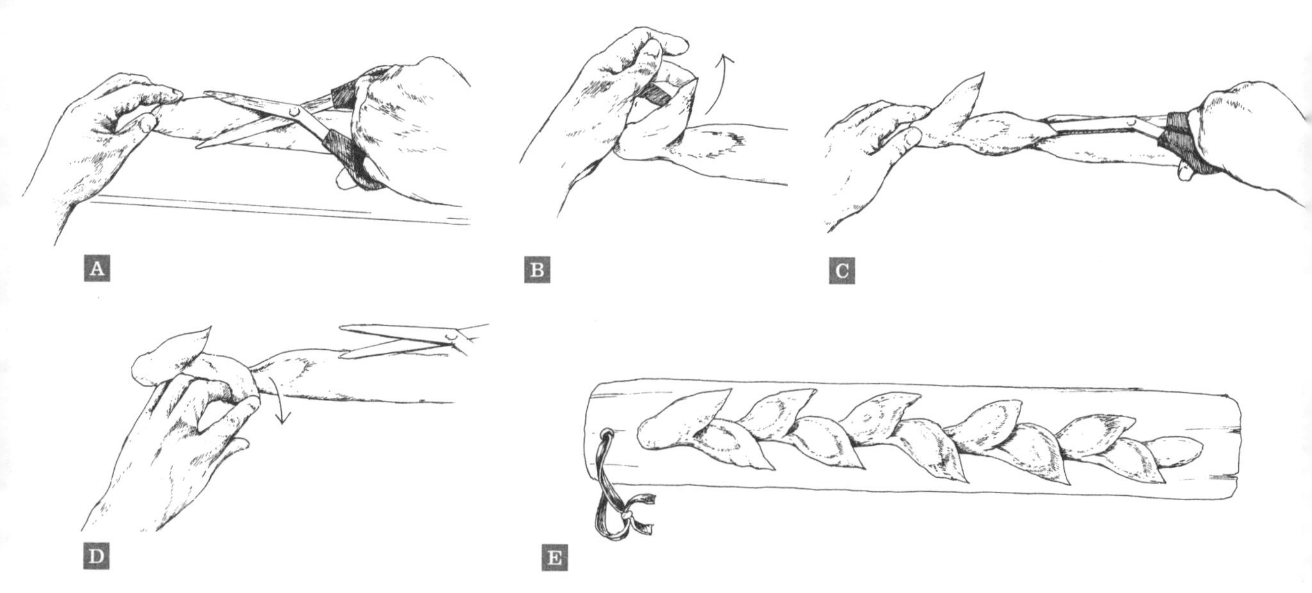

Cutting *épis de blé*

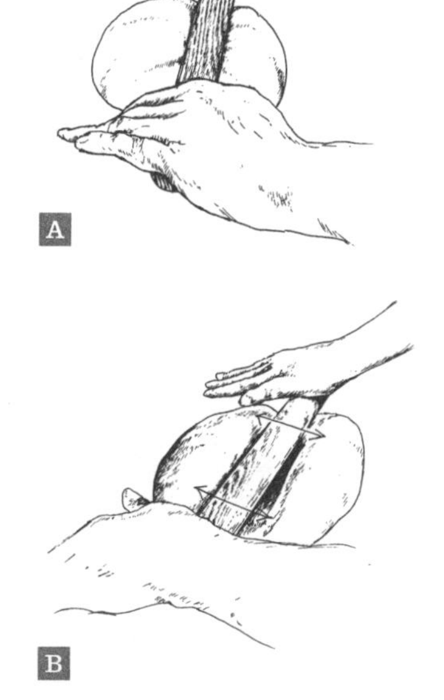

We will assume that the baker is making not one split loaf, but dozens, and therefore the way the rolling pin is used is important. When the pin is placed on the center of the loaf, the baker's shoulders should be directly above it. This way, all the strength of the upper body is involved in the work, and not just the arms and hands. The loaves are then formed with the least exertion and the greatest speed. For the same reasons, it is also advisable to use a rolling pin that is long enough to form 2 loaves at once (usually a pin of about 20 inches is sufficient, unless the loaves are scaled at more than a couple of pounds). Keep the 2 loaves separated by a few inches, so that during the pinning motion they do not join in the center. This technique will work for round loaves and rolls, but not for oval loaves, which are too long to allow working on two simultaneously.

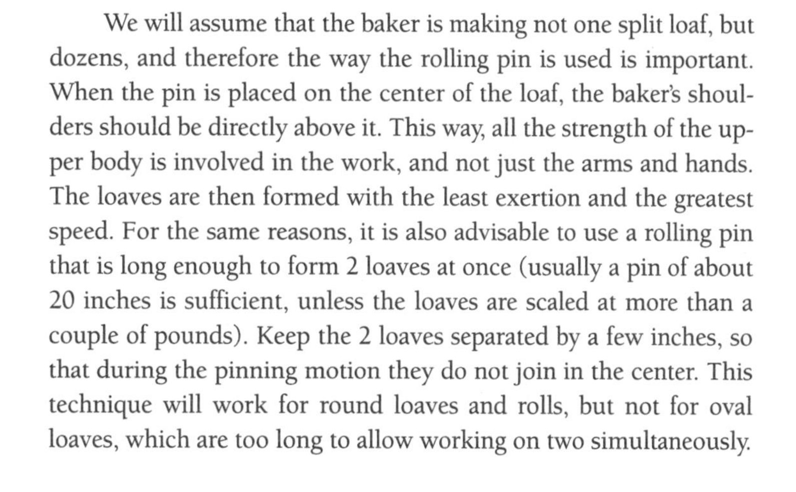
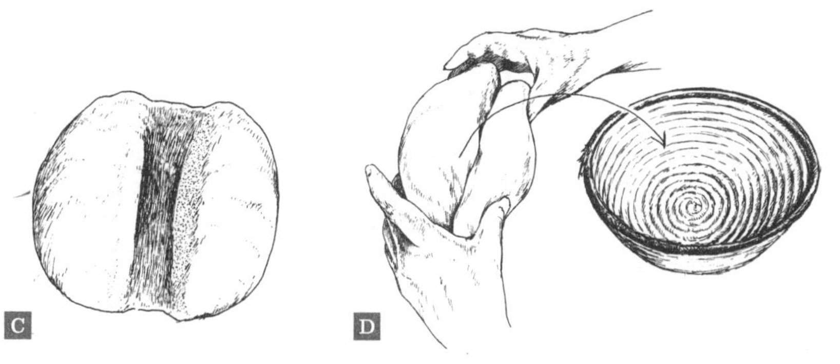

Scoring *pain fendu* with a rolling pin

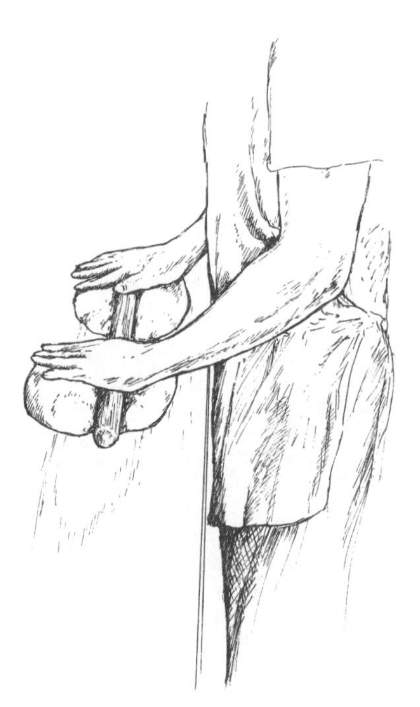

Scoring two loaves simultaneously with a rolling pin

Standing and Lifting

When I first began baking as a profession, I was more fit than I had ever been. A few years of farming, with all its manual intensity, had brought my body to a high level of stamina and strength. I was in my mid-twenties, the springtime of my life. I entered the bakery with enormous enthusiasm, ardor, and excitement. I was working with skilled Frenchmen and Germans, who had learned through the apprentice system of their respective countries. Before the end of the first week, the head pastry chef was teaching me how to stand! It would be an understatement to say I was mildly put off to have anyone tell me, in all the strength of my youth, how to stand. Fortunately, my wish to learn all I could superseded my feeling that I had no need to learn anything about standing at the bench. Now, as I look back, I realize I have taught correct standing posture to hundreds of students and many people new to baking. Correct bench height is important. Typically, the bench for dividing or shaping bread is 36 inches high. This is suitable for anyone of average height, between 5 feet 4 inches and 6 feet. A slight elevation may be necessary for taller individuals, and some kind of low platform on the floor will benefit shorter bakers (having two benches at different heights is a sensible solution, albeit impractical in many shops). Stand with your legs placed squarely, separated shoulder width. Your knees should be slightly bent. Your shoulders should be in line with your waist and feet, or at most inclined slightly forward over the bench. Avoid working in a position that causes you to lean over too far, as this will put an unnecessary strain on your lower back. That said, keep the scale close to the near edge of the bench when dividing dough, and when shaping, keep the dough close to you; in this way the distance you lean forward will be minimized.

Improper standing at the bench will take a heavy toll over the years. Improper lifting can cause damage to the body in seconds. The majority of lifting injuries seem to occur from lifting dough tubs and flour bags from the floor to the bench. Proper body posture can eliminate these injuries. Begin by keeping your back straight. Bend at the knees, so the flour or tub can be lifted with the strength of your legs. When the weight is at waist level, there may still be several more inches of lifting required to get it onto the bench. One useful technique is to use one knee to assist in the final hoisting. Lift one leg, bending the knee, and when it contacts the bottom of the flour bag or the tub, use the strength of the leg combined with the upper body to finish the lifting procedure.

Unloading with a Peel

A baker's peel with a 7- or 8-foot handle weighs upwards of ten pounds. Unloading 6 or 8 loaves of bread at a time from the oven increases the weight considerably. Like most other aspects of baking, this work can be done in a way to minimize exertion and maximize the baker's efficiency. It may matter little if you are making just a few loaves, but most bakers make many dozens or hundreds each day, and cumulatively these seemingly small tasks can be rather strenuous. Even though the peel weighs less than 10 pounds, if I try to pick it up by the end of the handle, I am unable to do so, even with both hands! The closer I get to the center of gravity, or the balance point of the peel, the easier it is to hold it. At the place of balance, I can hold it with two fingers. Therefore, to minimize the unnecessary expenditure of energy, hold the peel with your lead hand, gripping it at the point where the peel and the handle meet. Not only will this require the least strength, it also provides the maximum stability. A peel full of bread is heavy, and often has a propensity to wobble due to the random distribution of the bread on the peel. By grasping the base of the peel with your forward hand, swaying is less likely to cause those fresh loaves to hit the floor before they make it to the cooling rack.

Lifting a dough tub

A note is in order: I like to think that if we use our bodies with the highest level of efficiency, we minimize excess exertion and can enjoy the wonderful baking life for decades. How we stand, how we balance our weight, and how we use our arms and legs will all have an impact on how much energy and strength we exert. Baking is always manual work, but by training ourselves to

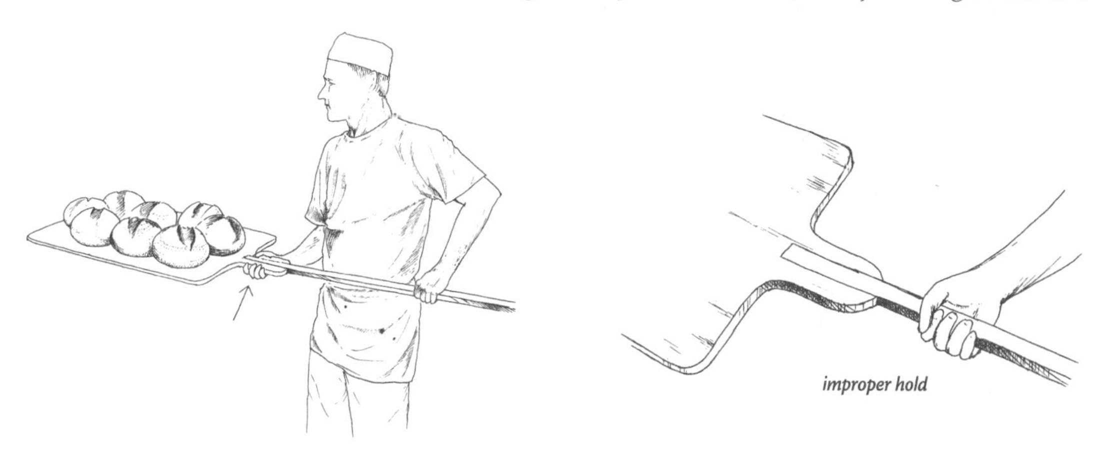

Holding a peel

work with the least strain, we minimize wearing down our bodies. Not only do we remain productive for a longer time in our baking work, but we also can take a bit more energy home with us at the end of the day. After all, the truly successful baker is one who not only performs the good work of baking in a way that keeps him fit and nimble, but who also has a life outside of work, and sufficient energy to enjoy that life.

Artist or Artisan?

One asks, Is the baker an artist? An artisan? These days *artisan* and *baker* are often combined into one term, as if the unadorned noun *baker* needs further enhancement. To me, the baker is certainly no artist, for an artist creates something new: This is the domain of poets and painters. The skilled baker, working with his hands, doing the same work each day, takes his place with the artisans of history: the potters, coopers, carpenters, and smiths. His work may excel and reach toward perfection, but there is little, really, that is new for the bread baker to invent. The pastry chef and the hot-food chef can devote themselves to discovering the next great food combination, the next winning flavor, the new pairing or presentation that brings the light of celebrity to their names. The baker has no such aspiration, and the glamour of fame is not a goal, because the nature of the work is different. The baker, each day, tries to perfect something that was worked out hundreds of years ago. Mastering the art of fermentation is the ultimate aspiration of the bread baker, and the secrets of fermentation, though not scientifically enumerated until quite recently, have been understood for hundreds of generations. When it all goes just right (which it rarely does), and the day's breads have attained more than just good taste, but are, for that day, memorable and charismatic, then the baker knows again why he sets his alarm for that challenging hour. And when all has not come out of the oven just as he had wished or expected, he gets another chance tomorrow—each day we have the opportunity to redeem the setbacks of yesterday.

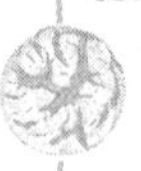

PART TWO

FORMULAS and DECORATIVE BREADS

All the formulas in this volume are written with the hope that they can be easily visualized, scaled, and used in a baking situation. In almost every case (with the exception of the formulas presented in Chapter 10, "Decorative and Display Projects," and some of those used in Chapter 8, "Miscellaneous Breads"), the formulas are all based on 20 pounds, 10 kilograms, or 2 pounds of flour. Although 10 kilograms is clearly not the exact equivalent of 20 pounds, by using these weights the overall proportion of ingredients can be readily assessed. For example, when 7.5 kilograms of water are used with 10 kilograms of flour, we see instantly that we have a dough hydration of 75 percent. Further, with these flour weights most dough yields in the book are between 34 and 40 pounds (15 and 18 kilograms), a fairly baker-friendly weight when trying out new doughs. For home use, an additional column is included that yields one-tenth the weight of the American column—roughly 3½ to 4 pounds of dough—a good quantity for a home mixer or for hand kneading.

(continued on page 90)

Baking at Home

Baking hundreds of loaves of bread a day has always been a deeply enriching experience for me—the world of bread is not merely beautiful, it also seems to connect me to some deeper truths about life. On the other hand, those times when I have baked just two or three loaves, quietly focused in the kitchen at home, have had their own measure of satisfaction—each loaf a real birth. The baker of hundreds of loaves has quite a set of challenges, because the overall choreography of the production, from the mixing to the end of the bake, can be somewhat unforgiving—when the bread says "Now!" it means just that, and the oven better be empty and hot. But in many ways, it is the home baker who faces the greater challenges. Lucky the production baker who refreshes and bakes with his sourdough culture 5, 6, or 7 times each week—it stays vigorous and enthusiastic with all that attention. The home baker has to make a concerted commitment to keeping the starter fed and happy on a continual basis, even when it is not going to be used for days at a time. Then there is the equipment: The professional baker has mixers and ovens that almost always surpass those of the home baker in terms of quality and durability—the equipment most of us have at home just can't begin to compete (most of us would have to remortgage the house just to buy a good professional oven). And this brings me to a specific point.

I have often maintained that few people in the United States bake bread at home through motives of subsistence or necessity; people bake at home because they love the process, love to be connected to this very instinctive and fundamental work, and love to share their results with friends and family—the delicious breads of their labors. That said, the home baker should do everything possible to achieve consistency in his or her endeavors, and work to overcome the challenges of small batches and somewhat deficient mixers and ovens. I have a small list of ways that I think the home baker can do this:

- **RESPECT TIME AND TEMPERATURE AS THE FOREMOST TOOLS FOR PRODUCING CONSISTENT BREADS.** The yeast is alive, and if dough temperatures are too cool or too warm, everything suffers. Always use a thermometer, and learn the simple calculation needed to achieve the desired dough temperature (see page 382 for a full discussion). Never force the bread—above all bread needs *time* in order for it to develop its full potential. An excessive use of yeast will always be to the detriment of the finished product.
- **WEIGH INGREDIENTS RATHER THAN MEASURE THEM.** An electronic scale is a huge ally in the quest for consistency. When you buy a bag of flour from the supermarket, if the flour has been stacked on the shelf standing up, a cup of flour from the top of the bag will weigh less than a cup scooped from the bottom, where more of it has settled and become compacted. An ounce of coarse salt brings as much saltiness to bread as an ounce of fine granular salt, but a tablespoon of coarse salt contributes less saltiness than a tablespoon of fine salt, simply because of the difference in particle size. These and other variables make measuring a dicey affair.
- **AVOID THE TEMPTATION OF ADDING FLOUR TO THE DOUGH AS IT MIXES.** This is a common mistake, and often re-

sults in doughs that are sluggish, dense, and deficient in volume, flavor, and keeping quality. Of course, there will be times when some small addition is necessary, and some doughs (challah, for instance) are by nature dry, but in general, most doughs should have perceptible dough strength but a moderate looseness to the tug. At the other extreme, superhydrated doughs are in fashion these days, and some, like ciabatta, make quite delicious loaves, but beyond those breads that rightly fall into the genre of wet and slack, there is no special virtue to adding water for water's sake.

- **GIVE AN EXTRA FOLD IF NEED BE.** It's difficult to mix doughs to optimum gluten development using a home stand mixer. If you feel that there is insufficient dough strength after mixing, don't hesitate to add an extra fold during bulk fermentation. Something as simple as that can have a significant effect on increasing dough strength and, later, loaf volume. So if a formula in the book calls for 1 fold during a 2-hour bulk fermentation, and you sense that the dough has inadequate gluten development, fold it 2 or even 3 times (spread the folds evenly throughout the duration of the bulk fermentation). And always make a point of trying to ascertain the effect of your actions. Did the extra fold give you favorable results? If it did, remember that the next time you make bread, and now you will be joining experience with intuition—a good combination!
- **DEVELOP A METHOD FOR STEAMING YOUR BREAD.** One method that works well is described on page 27. Other methods may work just as well, but use them only if they give your breads good shine and color, and much better volume.
- **FOR HEARTH BREADS, BAKE ON A PREHEATED BAKING STONE AND BAKE HOT.** When bread is baked on a sheet pan, the pan must first heat up before the bottom of the bread does, and the loaf will never be as full and expanded as it would if baked directly on the hearth. You might lower the oven temperature partway through the bake, but you will make breads with much better volume and much more flavorful crust if you start them in a hot oven. Remember that the bread that you just loaded is at room temperature, sucking away lots of oven heat, and if the initial bake temperature isn't hot enough, both volume and crust color will be meager. All the breads in this book should be loaded into an oven that has been thoroughly preheated. Expect the preheating of a home oven to take a minimum of 30 minutes. If you are using a baking stone, begin to preheat the oven 45 minutes before loading your bread. For most breads in this book, that means no more than 5 or 10 minutes after shaping the loaves.
- **IF YOU KEEP A SOURDOUGH STARTER, LOVE IT.** Do you have a pet? That's just a single being, but think how much care and consideration it gets. One minuscule gram of sourdough has billions of beings—they need attention too if they are going to be happy for years. Your sourdough will feel very reassured if you feed it often.
- **A LAST WAY TO BAKE CONSISTENTLY IS SIMPLY TO BAKE OFTEN.** There is a definite language to bread, and it takes practice and lots of patience to learn it, but if you are attentive and receptive, you will see that the language is clear and accessible. I hope that this book in time comes to smell of bread.

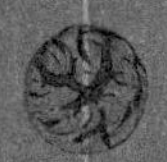

Cups and tablespoons are inherently inaccurate, and serious home bakers should buy a good scale. Nevertheless, in the Home column cups and tablespoons have been entered in parentheses adjacent to the corresponding weights of the ingredients. If you are making the formulas in this book using cup measures, however, note that the cup measurements in the Home column have been rounded either up or down as necessary, so please take extra care when checking the consistency of the dough.

Most of the formulas have a section titled Overall Formula, which lists the total percentage of each ingredient in the bread. This enables the baker who is fluent in baker's math to determine at a glance different aspects of the dough, for example the proportion of yeast and salt, the amount of other grains present in the dough, the percentages of nuts or dried fruits, and so on. (For an explanation of baker's percentage, see page 376.) If the dough has a pre-ferment, the baker's percentages for it are also included. Although seeing the percentages for a pre-ferment is not as important as seeing them for the overall formula, it can help the baker see if the pre-ferment is stiff—is it 50 percent hydration? 55 percent? 60 percent—or is it liquid—100 percent? 125 percent? Using a baker's-percentage column for the final dough does not give much useful information to the baker, and in fact can be downright confusing, so none is offered in the formulas in this book.

Fresh yeast continues to be the standard among professional bakers, and for that reason it is used in the present formulas, except in the Home column, where instant dry yeast is called for. If you are making one of the formulas using 10 kilograms or 20 pounds of flour and don't have access to reliable fresh yeast, don't be deterred. If using active dry yeast (the kind that must first be dissolved in water before using), convert from fresh to active by multiplying the weight of fresh yeast by .4. With instant dry yeast, convert from fresh by multiplying the weight of the fresh yeast by .33 (refer to page 57).

Occasionally, some doughs may seem to have an elevated percentage of salt in the Overall Formula section. For the most part, these breads contain an abundant portion of various grains or seeds (or in the case of brioche, a considerable amount of unsalted butter). Since these added grains or butter also need salt to balance the bread's flavor, the seemingly elevated salt percentage is appropriate in these formulas.

With the same goal of providing a baker-friendly format, the percentage of pre-fermented flour is listed in all the formulas where sourdoughs or some other pre-ferment is used. It should be an easy matter for a baker conversant in the language of baker's math to adjust a formula to suit either his individual taste or that of his clientele. For example, a bread presented here may be made with 25 percent pre-fermented flour; with little effort, that formula can be altered to increase or decrease the percentage of pre-fermented flour, thereby accommodating the tastes of each baker. Similarly, a baker might decide to alter, say, the percentage of whole wheat or soaked grains, or the hydration of a dough, changes that are easily accomplished when he is fluent in baker's math.

A comparison of approximate mixing times for different style mixers can be found on page 11.

One last note: Flour absorption varies considerably, from one season to the next and from one part of the country to the next. So, even though the liquid percentage in the formulas seems so inflexibly precise, the baker should always check the dough as soon as the ingredients have come together, in order to ascertain that dough consistency is correct for that particular mix. A formula with 66 percent hydration might need 68 percent or even more water in the dry Southwest, and the same formula might only need 64 percent water in a humid climate. Hydrations are approximations; the hand of the baker, experience, and final dough performance are the surer guides.

BREADS MADE with YEASTED PRE-FERMENTS

4

Wheat seed is received by the earth as it is preparing to hibernate. The shoots sprout slowly, feeling the warmth underneath the snow and preserving the evanescence of dreams as they grow.

—GIANCARLO CONSONNI, AUTHOR

In this chapter, we will look at a selection of breads made with yeasted pre-ferments. The benefits of using pre-ferments are undeniable, from the perspective of flavor, dough strength, keeping quality, and reduced production time (see Chapter 1, "The Bread-Making Process from Mixing through Baking," for a full explanation of the benefits of pre-ferments).

Yeasted Pre-Ferments

Before discussing the specifics of bread production, we will clarify the basic types of yeasted pre-ferments and explain their predominant characteristics.

Pâte Fermentée

Pâte fermentée, or simply "old dough," is just that: a piece of white-flour dough that is reserved after mixing and incorporated into the next batch of bread. Although the name is French, the practice exists wherever bread is made. (If your customers ask why your baguettes taste so good, you can probably charge an extra quarter if you tell them it's because you use *pâte fermentée;* telling them you put "old dough" into the mix just doesn't sound as good!) Aside from the flavor benefits of using some old dough in the new mix, it is obvious that using it is economically preferable to throwing it away. Of the major yeasted pre-ferments, this is the only one that contains salt.

Like other yeasted pre-ferments such as poolish and biga, *pâte fermentée* has a limited life expectancy, unlike natural sourdough cultures, which can be perpetuated for years. Refrigerated, *pâte fermentée* will last at most 48 hours before its leavening potential is expended. With ample freezer space, it can be frozen, although within a week the yeast spores in it will begin to die off and the *pâte fermentée* will suffer a loss of vigor. For the home baker who bakes once a week or so, freezing may be an option. The effort required to make a *pâte fermentée* the night before a bake day is minimal, however, and is justified by the superior bread that will result.

Poolish

Poolish is a mixture of equal weights flour and water, with a very small portion of yeast added (in the .08 to 1 percent range, depending on how long the poolish will ripen before the final dough is mixed, and the temperature of the room in which the poolish will ripen). Being of equal weight in flour and water, it has 100 percent hydration—more like a batter than a dough. Salt is not included in poolish. Protease is an enzyme whose function is to denature protein, and in a loose mixture like poolish, protease activity is relatively high. It has the effect of increasing the extensibility of bread dough, which not only makes shaping easier (though perhaps harder during the early stages of hand-skill development), but also results in increased loaf volume. The aroma of a bowl of ripe poolish is intoxicating—sweet and nutty with a delicate hint of acidity—and the texture of the dough is beautifully silken, a true delight for the hands. As the name suggests, poolish is of Polish origin. Originally used in pastry production, it eventually found a place in bread making, and today is used by bakers around the world.

Biga

Biga is a generic Italian term for "pre-ferment." It can be stiff textured at 50 to 60 percent hydration, or it can be essentially the same as a poolish when made with 100 percent hydration and a small portion of yeast. In either case, there is no salt in a biga, just flour, water, and a bit of yeast. The yeast quantity is determined by ambient temperature, and by the length of time it will be left to ripen before the final dough is mixed. As with poolish, the yeast in a biga is generally in the .08 to 1 percent range.

Production Notes for the Formulas in This Chapter

Preparing the Pre-Ferment. The pre-ferment is made at least 6 hours or up to 16 hours before the final dough is mixed (*pâte* *fermentée* is usually an exception to this, as it is simply dough removed from the prior batch, but it too, of course, can be mixed on its own). The flour, water, and yeast are mixed for about 3 minutes on first speed. Gluten development is not the goal at this point, so first speed is all that is required. Be certain that all the flour has been hydrated, turn off the mixer, and cover the pre-ferment with plastic to prevent a crust from forming on the surface. The pre-ferment will ripen at room temperature.

Knowing the signs of ripeness is very important: When the poolish is ripe, the surface will be covered with small bubbles—in fact, you should see bubbles breaking through to the surface, indicating the continuing activity of the yeast. If there is evidence that the poolish has risen and then collapsed (you may see a "high-water" mark on the sides of the bowl), then the poolish is past its prime. A stiff-textured biga and a *pâte fermentée* are ripe when they have domed and are just beginning to recede in the center. The goal is to have the pre-ferment at its full ripeness when you are ready to use it, and therefore the correct yeast quantities will increase and decrease as the seasons come and go. The amount of yeast necessary for a poolish to ripen in 16 hours at 80°F might be .08 percent of the poolish flour weight, but the same poolish might need .25 percent yeast at 65°F. The other factor determining yeast quantity is the duration of the ripening phase, with longer ripenings needing less yeast. Below is a general guideline, based on a room temperature of 70° to 75°F: The percentage of yeast is based on the weight of the flour used in the pre-ferment, not the flour in the overall formula. The percentages given are for fresh yeast.

LENGTH OF RIPENING	% YEAST
Up to 8 hours	.7 to 1%
Up to 12 hours	.3 to .6%
Up to 16 hours	.1 to .25%

When a portion of a fully mixed batch of bread is removed for use as *pâte fermentée* in a subsequent mix, this portion is fully yeasted, as is of course the rest of the dough from which it has been removed, and is therefore in a special category. If the *pâte fermentée* will not be used within about 6 hours, it must be refrigerated—if it stays at room temperature for too long, it will completely lose its vigor because it contains a full proportion of yeast. Let it stand at room temperature for an hour or so in order for it to begin fermenting, then degas and refrigerate it. It should be cooled as quickly as possible, and degassed once or twice more over the next few hours. When it is used in the new mix, its temperature must be accounted for when computing the correct water temperature for the final dough.

The amount of fresh yeast used in the pre-ferments for all the formulas in this chapter is .2 percent. This often amounts to little more than .1 ounce. Further, for the sake of consistency, the yeast in the pre-ferments is expressed in units of pounds and kilograms, even though this means there are weights like .007 kg or .013 lb, as in the Baguettes with Poolish formula. A review of kilogram-to-gram and pound-to-ounce conversions will be helpful here; let's do it using the Baguettes with Poolish formula (more metric-to-U.S. conversions are given in the Appendix on page 387). To convert kilograms to grams, multiply the portion of a kilogram by 1,000 (the .007 kg needed for the pre-ferment in the Baguettes with Poolish formula converts to .007 × 1,000 = 7 grams). To convert from pounds to ounces, multiply the portion of a pound by 16 (the .013 lb of yeast in the formula converts to .013 × 16 = .2 ounces). The biggest difficulty arises with the Home column: Since baking is not usually done in quantities that justify the use of fresh yeast for most home bakers, instant dry yeast is called for in the formulas. In the Home column of the Baguettes with Poolish formula, the amount of instant yeast needed for the poolish is .0067 ounces. Clearly, this can't be accurately scaled. The solution: Use a speck of instant yeast in the pre-ferment, pay careful attention to temperature and to time duration, and closely observe the signs of ripeness. If, for instance, the pre-ferment ripens in 10 hours and you had hoped it would need 16 hours, use a smaller speck or a cooler ripening temperature next time. And conversely, if you want to ripen the pre-ferment in 12 hours and it seems not to have budged after that time, your speck should be a bit bigger next time, or the ripening room warmer.

Preparing the Soaker. A few of the formulas in this chapter use soakers. The soaking makes hard grains palatable, reduces their tendency to break the developing gluten network during mixing, and also reduces their tendency to "rob" moisture from the dough once it has finished mixing. Cold soakers are made by simply pouring water over the grains, mixing everything together, and covering the container with plastic to prevent evaporation. Hot soakers are made when any of the soaker grains are particularly hard and won't soften sufficiently in cold water (for example, cracked wheat and millet). In this case, bring the water to the boil and pour it over the grains. Stir and cover, as for a cold soaker. Salt is sometimes incorporated into the soaker in order to lessen enzymatic activity that might otherwise develop, with the potential of bringing some off flavors to the soaker. It's easiest to make a soaker when the pre-ferment is mixed. Both can then be left at room temperature until the time of the final mix.

Mixing the Final Dough. All the ingredients are placed in the mixing bowl. (There are some exceptions, for instance when ingredients like raisins or nuts are part of the formula; these are added at the end of the mix. Another exception is when dough is mixed using the autolyse technique. In that case, the salt and *pâte fermentée,* if used, are not incorporated at the beginning of the mix. There is a full discussion of the autolyse technique on page 9.) If using a spiral mixer, mix on first speed for about 3 minutes to thoroughly incorporate the ingredients (mixing guidelines for other kinds of mixers are given on page 11). Check the dough's hydration and make corrections as necessary, adding small amounts of water or flour as needed. (The formulas are balanced, but minor adjustments may be necessary; for instance, in very humid months it is a good practice to hold back a small portion of the dough water to compensate for the extra moisture held by the flour. It is best not to add flour if possible, since it would alter the overall proportion of salt in the formula.) It is also a good practice to taste for salt at this time to be certain it has not inadvertently been left out. Once satisfied that dough consistency is good, turn the mixer to second speed and mix for approximately 3 minutes, until a moderate gluten development has been achieved. Full gluten development in the mixer would mean overoxidizing the carotenoid pigments and loss of both the wheaty flavor of the flour and the creamy color we see in well-made breads. Rather than mixing fully, effective folding of the dough during bulk fermentation will complete the process of building dough strength, with no loss of color or flavor. There are a few exceptions to the 3-minute mix on second speed: First, when mixing doughs with soakers, another 30 to 60 seconds of mixing may be necessary, since the dough develops a bit more slowly in the presence of soaker grains; second, when using the autolyse technique, only 1½ to 2 minutes of second-speed mixing will be necessary. The dough develops miraculously well during the autolyse, in spite of the lack of mechanical action, and surprisingly little time is needed on second speed to finish the mix. It will, in fact, break down rather quickly if overmixed. Since flour absorption rates can vary significantly from season to season and from mill run to mill run, and since soakers lose sometimes more and sometimes less water to evaporation, it isn't possible to be exact about water quantities in the formulas. It should be noted, however, that looser doughs tend to ferment better and have better volume and better flavor. For the most part, the doughs in this chapter should have a moderately loose feel to them. Each formula's hydration percentage will serve as a guide initially; your hands and experience will ultimately be the best guide.

Bulk Fermentation. Ripe pre-ferments contribute acidity to the finished mix, which in turn helps mature the dough and strengthen it. Bulk fermentation time can therefore be reduced. For the most part, 1 to 2 hours is long enough to fully mature the dough. As the percentage of pre-ferment increases, bulk fermentation time can be accordingly reduced. Some doughs, such as ciabatta, favor a lengthy bulk fermentation and seem to attain their fullest potential with as much as a 3-hour fermentation.

Folding is a fundamental requirement, and is a topic that is not without complexity. See page 15 for a full discussion of folding.

Dividing and Shaping. Breads like baguettes are typically divided into 12- to 16-ounce pieces, while other breads might weigh up to a few pounds. Once divided, all the doughs are preshaped round and left to relax, seams up, on a floured work surface, covered in plastic to prevent crust formation on the surface. Depending on the tightness of the preshaping and the nature of the individual dough, the pieces may need to relax from 10 to 30 minutes before the final shaping. For the most part, the breads in this chapter can be shaped round or oval (exceptions being breads like baguettes or ciabatta), and are suitable as well for pan loaves and rolls. The shaped breads take their final proofing in floured *bannetons* or between folds of baker's linen (or in loaf pans, as the case may be). Cover the loaves with baker's linen and plastic for the final proofing to prevent a surface skin from forming. When making rolls, proof them on sheet pans that have been sprinkled with coarse cornmeal or semolina, and later bake them on the sheet pans or directly on the hearth or baking stone.

Final Fermentation. For the most part, breads made with pre-ferments need about 1 to 1½ hours of final fermentation at 75°F. They should look well risen and feel light. Loading the breads when they are about 90 percent risen gives them the opportunity to spring proudly once exposed to the fierce heat of the oven.

Steaming and Baking. The proofed loaves are transferred to the loading conveyor or baker's peel and placed with their seams down. Breads like baguettes or oval-shaped loaves that are scored like baguettes (that is, so that only thin flaps of dough are cut on the surface) should be slashed with a curved blade held at about a 30-degree angle to the surface of the bread. Round and oval loaves that receive non-baguette-style scoring should be slashed with a straight blade, held vertically to the surface. The oven is then steamed prior to the load, the bread loaded, and the oven steamed again. From 4 to 6 seconds of steam is ample. Temperatures in the vicinity of 460°F are suitable for most of the breads, with variations noted in the individual formulas. Once the bread shows color, open the oven vents and allow the bread to finish the bake in a drying environment (this promotes a thin, crispy crust). In a home oven, you may open the oven door very slightly with a metal spoon. Bake times given for the individual bread formulas are for round loaves weighing 1½ pounds, except where otherwise noted. A full bake coaxes full flavor from the bread.

Eating. Like all well-made breads, these breads should cool fully before eating. Because they have pre-ferments, they tend to keep fairly well—not as well, perhaps, as sourdough breads, but better than straight doughs. Once sliced, store the loaves cut side down on a wooden cutting board. If the bread won't be eaten for a few days, a better storage technique is to wrap the bread tightly in a paper bag, then put the paper bag inside a plastic bag. Leave the plastic bag partially open; the slight air circulation will allow the crust to remain distinct from the crumb, while the plastic will help prevent the loaf from drying out.

Baguettes with Poolish

PRE-FERMENTED FLOUR: 33%

DOUGH YIELD | U.S.: About 38 baguettes at 14 oz each | Metric: About 42 baguettes at .4 kg each | Home: 4 baguettes

OVERALL FORMULA

	U.S.	METRIC	HOME	BAKER'S %
Bread flour	20 lb	10 kg	2 lb	100%
Water	13.2 lb	6.6 kg	1 lb, 5.2 oz	66%
Salt	.4 lb	.2 kg	.6 oz	2%
Yeast	.22 lb, fresh	.11 kg, fresh	.13 oz, instant dry	1.1%
TOTAL YIELD	**33.82 lb**	**16.91 kg**	**3 lb, 5.9 oz**	**169.1%**

POOLISH

	U.S.	METRIC	HOME	BAKER'S %
Bread flour	6.6 lb	3.3 kg	10.6 oz (2⅜ cups)	100%
Water	6.6 lb	3.3 kg	10.6 oz (1⅜ cups)	100%
Yeast	.013 lb, fresh	.007 kg, fresh	(⅛ tsp, instant dry)	.2%
TOTAL	**13.213 lb**	**6.607 kg**	**1 lb, 5.2 oz**	

FINAL DOUGH

	U.S.	METRIC	HOME
Bread flour	13.4 lb	6.7 kg	1 lb, 5.4 oz (4⅞ cups)
Water	6.6 lb	3.3 kg	10.6 oz (1⅜ cups)
Salt	.4 lb	.2 kg	.6 oz (1 T)
Yeast	.207 lb, fresh	.104 kg, fresh	.13 oz, instant dry (1¼ tsp)
Poolish	13.213 lb	6.067 kg	1 lb, 5.2 oz (all of above)
TOTAL	**33.82 lb**	**16.91 kg**	**3 lb, 5.8 oz**

The simplest breads are the most difficult to produce, and the baguette is high on the list of "simple" breads: simple, in that it is made with a minimum of ingredients; there are no strong flavors that dominate, and it is above all the flavor of the flour that prevails. Properly made, it is magnificent; poorly made, it is bland and insipid. One of the more beautiful aspects of the

1. **POOLISH:** Disperse the yeast in the water, add the flour, and mix until smooth. Cover the bowl with plastic and let stand for 12 to 16 hours at about 70°F.

2. **MIXING:** Add all the ingredients to the mixing bowl, including the poolish. In a spiral mixer, mix on first speed for 3 minutes in order to incorporate the ingredients. If necessary, correct the hydration by adding water or flour in small amounts. Finish mixing on second speed for 3 to 3½ minutes. The dough should be supple and moderately loose. Desired dough temperature: 76°F.

3. **BULK FERMENTATION:** 2 hours.

4. **FOLDING:** Fold the dough once after 1 hour.

baguette is the amount of crust it has. A finished baguette should have a rich, russet crust, crackling and fragrant—don't underestimate the virtue of a bold bake. At the same time, the crumb should be creamy and aromatic, with a cell structure characterized by lots of random-sized holes, with translucent cell walls (if the holes are big enough to hide a mouse, though, your shaping skills need some attention).

Production time can be reduced by 30 to 60 minutes, but the most superior results are obtained with a full 2-hour bulk fermentation. As with all breads, careful attention to detail throughout production is the best method to achieve consistently tasty results. Round loaves (*boules*), oval loaves (*bâtards*), and rolls can be made with this dough. Round and oval loaves of 1 to 1.5 pounds, and rolls scaled at 2.5 to 3.25 ounces give nice results.

5. DIVIDING AND SHAPING: Divide the dough into 12- to 16-ounce pieces. Preshape lightly into rounds and leave on a lightly floured work surface, seams up, covered with plastic. Once the dough has relaxed sufficiently (10 to 30 minutes, depending on how tightly it was preshaped), shape into long, slender, and graceful baguettes. Place them between folds of baker's linen, leaving enough space between each baguette so they can expand without tearing during final fermentation. Cover the loaves with baker's linen and plastic to protect them from air currents and prevent the formation of a crust on the surface of the loaves.

6. FINAL FERMENTATION: 1 to 1½ hours at 76°F.

7. BAKING: With normal steam, 460°F for 24 to 26 minutes for baguettes, depending on dough weight. Round and oval loaves: about 30 minutes for a 1-pound loaf, with round loaves taking slightly longer than oval ones.

Baker's Notes

Around 1840, Baron August Zang brought the poolish style of bread making to Paris from Vienna. A great deal of flavor was enticed from the bread thanks to the presence of the poolish, and only a small amount of yeast was required, which suited the bakers of the day, who had little access to reliable fresh baker's yeast. Further, the new breads lacked the acidity that chararcterized traditional levain-based breads, and this contributed to their popularity. *Pain viennois*, as the breads were called, became immensely successful, as did *viennoiserie*—lightly sweetened yeasted goods whose production fell under the domain of the bread baker. Gradually, a complete genre of breads developed that used yeasted preferments in place of, or along with, sourdough, and today we are the fortunate recipients of those advances made almost two centuries ago.

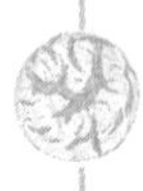

Baguettes with Pâte Fermentée

PRE-FERMENTED FLOUR: 25%

DOUGH YIELD | U.S.: About 38 baguettes at 14 oz each | Metric: About 42 baguettes at .4 kg each | Home: 4 baguettes

OVERALL FORMULA

	U.S.	METRIC	HOME	BAKER'S %
Bread flour	**20 lb**	**10 kg**	**2 lb**	**100%**
Water	**13.2 lb**	**6.6 kg**	**1 lb, 5.1 oz**	**66%**
Salt	**.4 lb**	**.2 kg**	**.6 oz**	**2%**
Yeast	**.25 lb, fresh**	**.125 kg, fresh**	**.13 oz, instant dry**	**1.25%**
TOTAL YIELD	**33.85 lb**	**16.93 kg**	**3 lb, 5.8 oz**	**169.25%**

PÂTE FERMENTÉE

	U.S.	METRIC	HOME	BAKER'S %
Bread flour	5 lb	2.5 kg	8 oz (1¾ cups)	100%
Water	3.3 lb	1.65 kg	5.3 oz (⅝ cup)	66%
Salt	.1 lb	.05 kg	.2 oz (1 tsp)	2%
Yeast	.01 lb, fresh	.005 kg, fresh	(⅛ tsp, instant dry)	.2%
TOTAL	**8.41 lb**	**4.21 kg**	**13.5 oz**	

FINAL DOUGH

	U.S.	METRIC	HOME
Bread flour	15 lb	7.5 kg	1 lb, 8 oz (5½ cups)
Water	9.9 lb	4.95 kg	15.8 oz (2 cups)
Salt	.3 lb	.15 kg	.4 oz (2 tsp)
Yeast	.24 lb, fresh	.12 kg, fresh	.13 oz, instant dry (1¼ tsp)
Pâte fermentée	8.41 lb	4.21 kg	13.5 oz (all of above)
TOTAL	**33.85 lb**	**16.93 kg**	**3 lb, 5.8 oz**

1. **PÂTE FERMENTÉE:** Disperse the yeast in the water, add the flour and salt, and mix until just smooth. Cover the bowl with plastic and let stand for 12 to 16 hours at about 70°F. Alternatively, remove a portion from a previous mix for use as *pâte fermentée.* In this case, refer to "Preparing the Pre-Ferment" (page 96), for correct handling of the pre-ferment.

2. **MIXING:** Add all the ingredients to the mixing bowl except the *pâte fermentée.* In a spiral mixer, mix on first speed for 3 minutes in order to incorporate the ingredients. As the dough is coming together, add the *pâte fermentée* in chunks. If necessary, correct the hydration by adding water or flour in small amounts. Finish mix-

Baguettes produced with *pâte fermentée* share certain qualities with those made with poolish: rich crust color, creamy crumb, subtle nutty fragrance. The cell structure tends to be slightly more open with poolish baguettes due to the higher proportion of the protease enzyme in poolish, which also results in a more extensible bread. Nevertheless, production can be simplified when the *pâte fermentée* comes from a previous mix, and the overall bread quality can be of the highest quality. Round loaves (*boules*), oval loaves (*bâtards*), pan loaves, and rolls can be made with this dough. Scale the round and oval loaves at 1 to 1.5 pounds, and the rolls at 2.5 to 3.25 ounces.

ing on second speed for 3 to 3½ minutes. The dough should be supple and moderately loose. Desired dough temperature: 76°F.

3. **BULK FERMENTATION:** 2 hours.

4. **FOLDING:** Fold the dough once after 1 hour.

5. **DIVIDING AND SHAPING:** Divide the dough into 12- to 16-ounce pieces. Preshape lightly into rounds and let stand on a lightly floured work surface, seams up, covered with plastic. Once the dough has relaxed sufficiently (10 to 30 minutes, depending on how tightly it was preshaped), shape into baguettes. Place them between folds of baker's linen, leaving sufficient space between each baguette so they can expand without tearing during final fermentation. Cover the loaves with baker's linen and plastic to protect them from air currents and prevent the formation of a crust on the surface of the loaves.

6. **FINAL FERMENTATION:** 1 to 1½ hours at 76°F.

7. **BAKING:** With normal steam, 460°F for 24 to 26 minutes for baguettes, depending on dough weight. Round and oval loaves: about 30 minutes for a 1-pound loaf, with round loaves taking slightly longer than oval ones.

Ciabatta with Stiff Biga

PRE-FERMENTED FLOUR: 20%

DOUGH YIELD | U.S.: About 31 loaves at 1 lb, 2 oz each | Metric: About 34 loaves at .51 kg each | Home: 3 loaves

OVERALL FORMULA

	U.S.	METRIC	HOME	BAKER'S %
Bread flour	20 lb	10 kg	2 lb	100%
Water	14.6 lb	7.3 kg	1 lb, 7.4 oz	73%
Salt	.4 lb	.2 kg	.6 oz	2%
Yeast	.24 lb, fresh	.12 kg, fresh	.13 oz, instant dry	1.2%
TOTAL YIELD	**35.24 lb**	**17.62 kg**	**3 lb, 8.1 oz**	**176.2%**

BIGA

	U.S.	METRIC	HOME	BAKER'S %
Bread flour	4 lb	2 kg	6.4 oz (1½ cups)	100%
Water	2.4 lb	1.2 kg	3.8 oz (½ cup)	60%
Yeast	.008 lb, fresh	.004 kg, fresh	(⅛ tsp, instant dry)	.2%
TOTAL	**6.408 lb**	**3.204 kg**	**10.2 oz**	

FINAL DOUGH

	U.S.	METRIC	HOME
Bread flour	16 lb	8 kg	1 lb, 9.6 oz (5¾ cups)
Water	12.2 lb	6.1 kg	1 lb, 3.6 oz (2½ cups)
Salt	.4 lb	.2 kg	.6 oz (1 T)
Yeast	.232 lb, fresh	.116 kg, fresh	.13 oz, instant dry (1¼ tsp)
Biga	6.408 lb	3.204 kg	10.2 oz (all of above)
TOTAL	**35.24 lb**	**17.62 kg**	**3 lb, 8.1 oz**

Ciabatta is a bread that America has learned to love dearly. Its domestic popularity rose quickly after it was chosen as one of the five breads that were baked in 1996 in Paris, at the Coupe du Monde de la Boulangerie, the World Cup of Baking. The exceptional quality of the ciabatta helped earn the United States first prize for breads at that memorable competition.

1. **BIGA:** Disperse the yeast in the water, add the flour, and mix until just smooth. The biga should be stiff and dense, but add a few drops of water if it is so stiff that it can't "breathe." Cover the bowl with plastic and leave for 12 to 16 hours at about 70°F. When ripe, the biga will be domed and just beginning to recede in the center.

2. **MIXING:** Add all the ingredients to the mixing bowl except the biga. In a spiral mixer, mix on first speed for 3 minutes in order to incorporate the ingredients. As the dough is coming together, add the biga in chunks. If necessary, correct the hydration by adding water or flour in small amounts. The dough will be quite sticky and slack at this point. Finish mixing on second speed for 3½ to 4 minutes. Wetter doughs develop more slowly in the bowl than dry

Ciabatta dough is unique in many ways: First, it is a very wet and sticky dough, with often upwards of 80 percent or even higher hydration. This requires some special handling (like locking all the doors so the bakers can't run for the exits). Further, there is no preshaping or final shaping—once divided, the dough is simply placed onto a floured work surface for its final proofing. And last of all, ciabatta dough is left unscored when loaded into the oven. The ciabatta formulas printed here all have a deep, suffusing wheaty aroma; large air holes due to both the high hydration and lack of degassing that occurs when breads are shaped; and a thin, blistered crust. When well made, it yields splintered crumbs when cut, and a long and memorable flavor, as the bread vanishes into happy bellies.

In the formulas, the ciabatta dough is scaled at 18 ounces. Other possibilities are little rolls—ciabattini—weighing 2 or 3 ounces each, large round loaves of a few pounds (these are sometimes called "pugliese"), or slender loaves weighing a few pounds that are 4 or 5 feet long. I call these impressive sights "Vermont cordwood."

ones, and the extra mixing helps to develop the dough structure a little more. The dough will be rather loose and sticky, but when tugged on, some definite dough strength will be noted—there should be some "muscle" to the dough. Desired dough temperature: 75°F.

3. BULK FERMENTATION: 3 hours.

4. FOLDING: Folding the ciabatta dough has an enormous impact on strengthening it. Fold the dough twice, after 1 hour of bulk fermentation and again after 2 hours. Spread a considerable amount of flour on the work surface for the folds, and fold quickly and assertively. Be sure no extra flour is incorporated into the dough as it is folded. Good folding is essential to eventual bread volume, and since there will be no final shaping to the dough, the folding represents the baker's last chance to increase dough strength.

5. DIVIDING AND SHAPING: Flour the work surface copiously. Invert the dough onto the work surface and gently pat out the larger air bubbles—but remember that for the most part the fermentation gases and the associated interior holes and pockets in the dough should remain intact. Lightly flour the top surface of the dough. Have ready a sufficient number of bread boards that are thoroughly (but not too thickly) covered with sifted bread flour. Cut a narrow strip, about 4 inches wide, down the length of the dough. Then cut the strip into rectangles weighing 18 ounces. If the dough is too light, place the additional bits of dough needed to correct the weight onto the top of the main dough piece. Place the dough piece onto the floured bread board, with the scrap on top. If it is more square than rectangular, give a gentle stretch, but be careful not to tear the dough. When all the dough has been scaled, cover the boards with baker's linen and then plastic.

6. FINAL FERMENTATION: Approximately 1½ hours at 75°F.

7. BAKING: The dough will be very light and fragile when risen (don't sneeze in its vicinity—it may collapse). To transfer the proofed ciabatta dough to the loading conveyor or baker's peel, spread the fingers of both your hands wide. Bring them alongside the long length of the dough and, with a quick, deft stroke, invert the dough piece so that the side that was touching the bread board is now on top. Now, place one hand at each end of the dough piece, bring your fingers underneath, and pick it up. Here you will slightly bunch the dough for easier transport; there should be wrinkles in the center of the loaf as you transfer it to the conveyor or peel. Carefully place the loaf onto the conveyor and, as you do so, unbunch your hands so the loaf is again at its full length. Take care to place the loaf exactly where you want it on the conveyor or peel—it is so fragile that you must minimize any excess moving of the loaves. Fill the oven with steam, load the trembling ciabattas, steam again, and bake at 460°F for 34 to 38 minutes. An important note: One of the greatest attributes of ciabatta is its crisp crust. As hydration increases, so too does baking time. If the ciabatta is taking on too much color in the oven too soon, lower the oven temperature by 10° or 20°F. But by all means give a full bake—if taken out too soon, the considerable internal moisture in the bread will soften the crust, greatly impairing eating quality.

Ciabatta with Poolish

PRE-FERMENTED FLOUR: 30%

DOUGH YIELD | U.S.: About 31 loaves at 1 lb, 2 oz each | Metric: About 34 loaves at .51 kg each | Home: 3 loaves

OVERALL FORMULA

	U.S.	METRIC	HOME	BAKER'S %
Bread flour	**20 lb**	**10 kg**	**2 lb**	**100%**
Water	**14.6 lb**	**7.3 kg**	**1 lb, 7.4 oz**	**73%**
Salt	**.4 lb**	**.2 kg**	**.6 oz**	**2%**
Yeast	**.22 lb, fresh**	**.11 kg, fresh**	**.13 oz, instant dry**	**1.1%**
TOTAL YIELD	**35.22 lb**	**17.61 kg**	**3 lb, 8.2 oz**	**176.1%**

POOLISH

Bread flour	6 lb	3 kg	9.6 oz (2¼ cups)	100%
Water	6 lb	3 kg	9.6 oz (1¼ cups)	100%
Yeast	.012 lb, fresh	.006 kg, fresh	(⅛ tsp, instant dry)	.2%
TOTAL	**12.012 lb**	**6.006 kg**	**1 lb, 3.2 oz**	

FINAL DOUGH

Bread flour	14 lb	7 kg	1 lb, 6.4 oz (5⅛ cups)
Water	8.6 lb	4.3 kg	13.8 oz (1¾ cups)
Salt	.4 lb	.2 kg	.6 oz (1 T)
Yeast	.208 lb, fresh	.104 kg, fresh	.13 oz, instant dry (1¼ tsp)
Poolish	12.012 lb	6.006 kg	1 lb, 3.2 oz (all of above)
TOTAL	**35.22 lb**	**17.61 kg**	**3 lb, 8.1 oz**

Although the percentages in the Overall Formula section in this formula are virtually identical to the preceding one, there are some distinct differences between the two breads. In the present formula, 30 percent of the flour is pre-fermented, compared to 20 percent in the Ciabatta with Stiff Biga, and an increase in aroma may be noted. With the extra pre-fermented flour in the Ciabatta with Poolish, the slight reduction of yeast to 1.1 percent is appropriate. Because of the high level of protease activity in the poolish, the consistency of the present formula's dough may seem just slightly looser, even though the overall water percentage is identical.

1. **POOLISH:** Disperse the yeast in the water, add the flour, and mix until smooth. Cover the bowl with plastic and let stand for 12 to 16 hours at about 70°F.

2. **MIXING:** Add all the ingredients to the mixing bowl, including the poolish. In a spiral mixer, mix on first speed for 3 minutes in order to incorporate the ingredients. If necessary, correct the hydration by adding water or flour in small amounts. Finish mixing on second speed for 3½ to 4 minutes, until gluten development is evident. The dough will be rather loose and sticky, but when tugged on, some definite dough strength should be noted—there should be some "muscle" to the dough. Desired dough temperature: 75°F.

3. **BULK FERMENTATION:** 3 hours.

4. **FOLDING:** Fold the dough twice, after 1 hour of bulk fermentation and again after 2 hours. The folds will give a final strengthening to the dough.

5. **DIVIDING AND SHAPING:** Flour the work surface copiously. Invert the dough onto the work surface and gently pat out the larger air bubbles—but remember that for the most part the fermentation gases and the associated interior holes and pockets in the dough should remain intact. Lightly flour the top surface of the dough. Have ready a sufficient number of bread boards that are thoroughly (but not too thickly) covered with sifted bread flour. Cut a narrow strip, about 4 inches wide, down the length of the dough. Then cut the strip into rectangles, each weighing 18 ounces. If the dough is too light, place the additional bits of dough needed to correct the weight onto the top of each dough piece. Place the dough pieces on the floured bread boards, with the scrap on top. If they are more square than rectangular, give a gentle stretch, but be careful not to tear the dough. When all the dough has been scaled, cover the boards with baker's linen and then plastic.

6. **FINAL FERMENTATION:** About 1½ hours at 75°F.

7. **BAKING:** With normal steam, 460°F for 34 to 38 minutes for a loaf scaled at 18 ounces. (Refer to step 7 in Ciabatta with Stiff Biga, page 106.) If the ciabatta is taking on too much color in the oven too soon, lower the oven temperature by 10° or 20°F. Be sure to bake fully.

Ciabatta with Olive Oil and Wheat Germ

PRE-FERMENTED FLOUR: 30%

DOUGH YIELD | U.S.: About 31 loaves at 1 lb, 2 oz each | Metric: About 35 loaves at .51 kg each | Home: 3 loaves

OVERALL FORMULA

	U.S.	METRIC	HOME	BAKER'S %
Bread flour	19 lb	9.5 kg	1 lb, 14.4 oz	95%
Wheat germ, toasted	1 lb	.5 kg	1.6 oz	5%
Water	14.4 lb	7.2 kg	1 lb, 7 oz	72%
Extra-virgin olive oil	.6 lb	.3 kg	1 oz	3%
Salt	.4 lb	.2 kg	.6 oz	2%
Yeast	.24 lb, fresh	.12 kg, fresh	.13 oz, instant dry	1.2%
TOTAL YIELD	**35.63 lb**	**17.82 kg**	**3 lb, 7 oz**	**178.2%**

POOLISH

Bread flour	6 lb	3 kg	9.6 oz (2¼ cups)	100%
Water	6 lb	3 kg	9.6 oz (1¼ cups)	100%
Yeast	.012 lb, fresh	.006 kg, fresh	(⅛ tsp, instant dry)	.2%
TOTAL	**12.012 lb**	**6.006 kg**	**1 lb, 3.2 oz**	

FINAL DOUGH

Bread flour	13 lb	6.5 kg	1 lb, 4.8 oz (4¾ cups)
Wheat germ, toasted	1 lb	.5 kg	1.6 oz (⅜ cup)
Water	8.4 lb	4.2 kg	13.4 oz (1⅝ cups)
Salt	.4 lb	.2 kg	.6 oz (1 T)
Yeast	.228 lb, fresh	.114 kg, fresh	.13 oz, instant dry (1¼ tsp)
Poolish	12.012 lb	6.006 kg	1 lb, 3.2 oz (all of above)
Extra-virgin olive oil	.6 lb	.3 kg	1 oz (2 T)
TOTAL	**35.64 lb**	**17.82 kg**	**3 lb, 7 oz**

1. **POOLISH:** Disperse the yeast in the water, add the flour, and mix until smooth. Cover the bowl with plastic and let stand for 12 to 16 hours at about 70°F.

2. **MIXING:** Add all the ingredients to the mixing bowl, including the poolish and the toasted wheat germ, but not the olive oil. In a spiral mixer, mix on first speed for 3 minutes in order to incorporate the ingredients. If necessary, correct the hydration by adding water or flour in small amounts. Turn the mixer to second speed and be-

What might seem to be an insignificant addition of olive oil and wheat germ here results in a distinct change of flavor. The oil lends a smooth but almost slightly bitter quality to the bread, and the presence of the toasted wheat germ adds a subtle nutty note to the flavor. Combined, this bread stands apart from the two preceding ciabattas. There is a slight improvement in keeping quality, albeit at the slight expense of crust vigor, due to the olive oil in the dough.

gin to add the olive oil in a slow, steady stream. Mix on second speed for 3½ to 4 minutes, until gluten development is evident. The dough will be rather loose and sticky, but when tugged on, some definite dough strength should be noted—there should be some "muscle" to the dough. Notice the nice flecks of wheat germ spread throughout the dough. Desired dough temperature: 75°F.

3. BULK FERMENTATION: 3 hours.

4. FOLDING: Fold the dough twice, after 1 hour of bulk fermentation and again after 2 hours. The folds will give a final strengthening to the dough.

5. DIVIDING AND SHAPING: Flour the work surface copiously. Invert the dough onto the work surface and gently pat out the larger air bubbles—but remember that for the most part the fermentation gases and the associated interior holes and pockets in the dough should remain intact. Lightly flour the top surface of the dough. Have ready a sufficient number of bread boards that are thoroughly (but not too thickly) covered with sifted bread flour. Cut a narrow strip, about 4 inches wide, down the length of the dough. Cut the strip into rectangles, each weighing 18 ounces. If the dough is too light, place the additional bits of dough needed to correct the weight on top of the dough pieces. Place each dough piece on a floured bread board, with the scrap on top. If they are more square than rectangular, give a gentle stretch, but be careful not to tear the dough. When all the dough has been scaled, cover the boards with baker's linen and then plastic.

6. FINAL FERMENTATION: Approximately 1½ hours at 75°F.

7. BAKING: For a loaf scaled at 18 ounces, with normal steam, 460°F for 20 minutes, then, because of the olive oil in the dough, lower the oven temperature to 440°F and bake 16 to 20 minutes longer. This prevents the loaves from getting too dark. (Refer to step 7 in Ciabatta with Stiff Biga, page 106.)

Pain Rustique

PRE-FERMENTED FLOUR: 50%

DOUGH YIELD | U.S.: About 30 loaves at 1 lb, 2 oz each | Metric: About 33 loaves at .51 kg each | Home: 3 medium loaves

OVERALL FORMULA

	U.S.	METRIC	HOME	BAKER'S %
Bread flour	20 lb	10 kg	2 lb	100%
Water	13.8 lb	6.9 kg	1 lb, 6.1 oz	69%
Salt	.4 lb	.2 kg	.6 oz	2%
Yeast	.3 lb, fresh	.15 kg, fresh	.17 oz, instant dry	1.5%
TOTAL YIELD	**34.5 lb**	**17.25 kg**	**3 lb, 6.9 oz**	**172.5%**

POOLISH

	U.S.	METRIC	HOME	BAKER'S %
Bread flour	10 lb	5 kg	1 lb (3⅝ cups)	100%
Water	10 lb	5 kg	1 lb (2 cups)	100%
Yeast	.02 lb, fresh	.01 kg, fresh	(⅛ tsp, instant dry)	.2%
TOTAL	**20.02 lb**	**10.01 kg**	**2 lb**	

FINAL DOUGH

	U.S.	METRIC	HOME
Bread flour	10 lb	5 kg	1 lb (3⅝ cups)
Water	3.8 lb	1.9 kg	6.1 oz (¾ cup)
Poolish	20.02 lb	10.01 kg	2 lb (all of above)
Salt	.4 lb	.2 kg	.6 oz (1 T)
Yeast	.28 lb, fresh	.14 kg, fresh	.17 oz, instant dry (1½ tsp)
TOTAL	**34.5 lb**	**17.25 kg**	**3 lb, 6.9 oz**

Pain Rustique, or Rustic Bread, is unique in its own way. After bulk fermentation, the dough receives no preshaping or final shaping, so in that respect it is similar to ciabatta dough. The cell structure of Pain Rustique is open and airy, the crumb is delightfully creamy, and this humble bread, while a good companion to a wide assortment of foods, is also flavorful enough to be

1. **POOLISH:** Disperse the yeast in the water, add the flour, and mix until smooth. Cover the bowl with plastic and let stand for 12 to 16 hours at about 70°F.

2. **MIXING:** Pain Rustique is mixed with an autolyse: Add the Final Dough flour, water, and the ripe poolish to the mixing bowl. Do not add the salt or yeast. In a spiral mixer, mix on first speed just until the ingredients come together in a shaggy mass. Cover the mixing bowl with a sheet of plastic and let this rough dough rest for 20 to 30 minutes. At the end of the rest period, sprinkle the salt and yeast over the dough and turn the mixer to second speed. Mix until the dough is fairly well developed, 1½ to 2 minutes (adjust the mixing time accordingly for other types of mixers).

eaten alone. Half the flour in the formula is pre-fermented, which enables the baker to produce good bread in less than 3 hours, not including the ripening time for the poolish. The bread's origin is attributed to Professor Raymond Calvel, author of *Le Goût du pain* and widely considered the world's foremost expert on French breads. The present formula is the work of James MacGuire of Montreal, with a couple of changes I've made through work at the bench.

The dough should be supple and moderately loose. Desired dough temperature: 76°F.

3. BULK FERMENTATION: 70 minutes.

4. FOLDING: Give a quick fold to the dough twice, once after 25 minutes of bulk fermentation, and again after 50 minutes.

5. DIVIDING: Gently divide the rectangles into even pieces, also rectangular, weighing 1 pound, 2 ounces (larger or smaller pieces can be cut too, with good results). Place scrap pieces of dough on top (on the unfloured side of the dough). Place the weighed-out pieces onto lightly floured baker's linen, with the floured side of the dough still down and the scrap side up, and cover with plastic.

6. FINAL FERMENTATION: The dough will only need 20 to 25 minutes of final proofing at 76°F.

7. BAKING: Invert the dough onto the loading conveyor or peel so that the floured side is up. Slash the bread with one quick stroke of the blade. Lightly presteam the oven, load the bread, and steam again. Bake at 460°F for about 35 minutes, opening the oven vents about halfway through the bake in order to finish the bake in a drying oven.

Country Bread

PRE-FERMENTED FLOUR: 50%

DOUGH YIELD | U.S.: About 22 loaves at 1.5 lb each | Metric: About 25 loaves at .68 kg each | Home: 2 large loaves

OVERALL FORMULA

	U.S.	METRIC	HOME	BAKER'S %
Bread flour	20 lb	10 kg	2 lb	100%
Water	13.6 lb	6.8 kg	1 lb, 5.8 oz	68%
Salt	.36 lb	.18 kg	.6 oz	1.8%
Yeast	.12 lb, fresh	.06 kg, fresh	.06 oz, instant dry	.6%
TOTAL YIELD	**34.08 lb**	**17.04 kg**	**3 lb, 6.4 oz**	**170.4%**

PRE-FERMENT

	U.S.	METRIC	HOME	BAKER'S %
Bread flour	10 lb	5 kg	1 lb (3⅝ cups)	100%
Water	6 lb	3 kg	9.6 oz (1¼ cups)	60%
Salt	.18 lb	.09 kg	.3 oz (½ T)	1.8%
Yeast	.05 lb, fresh	.025 kg, fresh	(⅛ tsp, instant dry)	.5%
TOTAL	**16.23 lb**	**8.115 kg**	**1 lb, 10 oz**	

FINAL DOUGH

	U.S.	METRIC	HOME
Bread flour	10 lb	5 kg	1 lb (3⅝ cups)
Water	7.6 lb	3.8 kg	12.2 oz (1½ cups)
Salt	.18 lb	.09 kg	.3 oz (½ T)
Yeast	.07 lb, fresh	.035 kg, fresh	.06 oz, instant dry (½ tsp)
Pre-ferment	16.23 lb	8.115 kg	1 lb, 10 oz (all of above)
TOTAL	**34.08 lb**	**17.04 kg**	**3 lb, 6.4 oz**

1. **PRE-FERMENT:** Disperse the yeast in the water, add the flour and salt, and mix until just smooth. At 60 percent hydration, it will be stiff and dense. Add a few drops of water if the pre-ferment seems too stiff to move. Cover the bowl with plastic and let stand for 12 to 16 hours at about 70°F. When ripe, the pre-ferment will be domed and just beginning to recede in the center.

2. **MIXING:** Add all the ingredients to the mixing bowl except the pre-ferment. In a spiral mixer, mix on first speed for 3 minutes in order to incorporate the ingredients. As the dough is coming together, add the pre-ferment in chunks. If necessary, correct the hydration by adding water or flour in small amounts. Finish mix-

A small percentage of yeast, a high percentage of pre-fermented flour, and long fermentation characterize Country Bread. It keeps well due to the high level of pre-ferment, and has a good clean flavor that supports many different foods. It is an attractive bread, with its floured surface and confident scoring pattern. Ovals or rounds are the shapes of choice, although small crusty rolls or large, substantial *boules* can also be made.

ing on second speed for about 2½ minutes. The dough should be supple and moderately loose, with moderate gluten development. Desired dough temperature: 75°F.

3. BULK FERMENTATION: 2½ hours.

4. FOLDING: Fold the dough twice, once after 50 minutes of bulk fermentation and again 50 minutes later.

5. DIVIDING AND SHAPING: Divide the dough into 1.5-pound pieces. Preshape lightly into rounds and place on a floured work surface, seams up. Cover the rounds with plastic. When the dough has relaxed sufficiently (10 to 20 minutes), shape into round or oval loaves, place them either into floured *bannetons* or between folds of floured baker's linen, and cover with plastic.

6. FINAL FERMENTATION: Approximately 1¼ to 1½ hours at 75°F.

7. BAKING: Transfer the risen loaves onto the loading conveyor or peel. Slash the desired scoring pattern with a blade. Presteam the oven, load the bread, and steam again. Bake at 450°F. Open the oven vents after the loaves show color, in order to finish the bake in a drying oven. Loaves scaled at 1.5 pounds will bake in approximately 35 minutes.

Rustic Bread

PRE-FERMENTED FLOUR: 50%

DOUGH YIELD | U.S.: About 22 loaves at 1.5 lb each | Metric: About 25 loaves at .68 kg each | Home: 2 large loaves

OVERALL FORMULA

	U.S.	METRIC	HOME	BAKER'S %
Bread flour	16 lb	8 kg	1 lb, 9.6 oz	80%
Whole-rye flour	2 lb	1 kg	3.2 oz	10%
Whole-wheat flour	2 lb	1 kg	3.2 oz	10%
Water	13.8 lb	6.9 kg	1 lb, 6.1 oz	69%
Salt	.36 lb	.18 kg	.6 oz	1.8%
Yeast	.12 lb, fresh	.06 kg, fresh	.06 oz, instant dry	.6%
TOTAL YIELD	**34.28 lb**	**17.14 kg**	**3 lb, 6.7 oz**	**171.4%**

PRE-FERMENT

Bread flour	10 lb	5 kg	1 lb (3 5/8 cups)	100%
Water	6 lb	3 kg	9.6 oz (1 1/4 cups)	60%
Salt	.18 lb	.09 kg	.3 oz (1/2 T)	1.8%
Yeast	.05 lb, fresh	.025 kg, fresh	(1/8 tsp, instant dry)	.5%
TOTAL	**16.23 lb**	**8.115 kg**	**1 lb, 10 oz**	

FINAL DOUGH

Bread flour	6 lb	3 kg	9.6 oz (2 1/4 cups)
Whole-rye flour	2 lb	1 kg	3.2 oz (7/8 cup)
Whole-wheat flour	2 lb	1 kg	3.2 oz (3/4 cup)
Water	7.8 lb	3.9 kg	12.5 oz (1 1/2 cups)
Salt	.18 lb	.09 kg	.3 oz (1/2 T)
Yeast	.07 lb, fresh	.035 kg, fresh	.06 oz, instant dry (1/2 tsp)
Pre-ferment	16.23 lb	8.115 kg	1 lb, 10 oz (all of above)
TOTAL	**34.28 lb**	**17.14 kg**	**3 lb, 6.7 oz**

1. **PRE-FERMENT:** Disperse the yeast in the water, add the flour and salt, and mix until just smooth. At 60 percent hydration, it will be stiff and dense, but add water if necessary to correct the hydration. Cover the bowl with plastic and let stand for 12 to 16 hours at about 70°F. When ripe, the pre-ferment will be domed and just beginning to recede in the center.

Rustic Bread shares many of the visual and flavor attributes as the preceding Country Bread. With the inclusion of 20 percent whole-grain flour, however, it has a more robust and distinctive flavor. Since absorption levels vary considerably with whole-grain flour, check the dough carefully once the ingredients are incorporated and make adjustments to hydration as necessary. As with Country Bread, ovals or rounds are the shapes of choice, although small crusty rolls or sizeable *boules* can also be made.

2. MIXING: Add all the ingredients to the mixing bowl except the pre-ferment. In a spiral mixer, mix on first speed for 3 minutes in order to incorporate the ingredients. As the dough is coming together, add the pre-ferment in chunks. If necessary, correct the hydration by adding water or flour in small amounts. Finish mixing on second speed for about 2½ minutes. The dough should be supple and moderately loose, with moderate gluten development. Desired dough temperature: 75°F.

3. BULK FERMENTATION: 2½ hours.

4. FOLDING: Fold the dough twice, once after 50 minutes of bulk fermentation and again 50 minutes later.

5. DIVIDING AND SHAPING: Divide the dough into 1.5-pound pieces. Preshape lightly into rounds and place on a lightly floured work surface, seams up. Cover the rounds with plastic. When the dough has relaxed sufficiently (10 to 20 minutes), shape into round or oval loaves, place them either into floured *bannetons* or between folds of floured baker's linen, and cover with plastic.

6. FINAL FERMENTATION: Approximately 1¼ to 1½ hours at 75°F.

7. BAKING: Invert the risen loaves onto the loading conveyor or peel. Slash the desired scoring pattern with a blade. Presteam the oven, load the bread, and steam again. Bake at 450°F. Open the oven vents after the loaves show color, in order to finish the bake in a drying oven. Loaves scaled at 1.5 pounds should bake for 35 to 38 minutes.

Roasted-Potato Bread

PRE-FERMENTED FLOUR: 30%

DOUGH YIELD | U.S.: About 25 loaves at 1.5 lb each | Metric: About 27 loaves at .68 kg each | Home: 2 large loaves

OVERALL FORMULA

	U.S.	METRIC	HOME	BAKER'S %
Bread flour	17 lb	8.5 kg	1 lb, 11.2 oz	85%
Whole-wheat flour	3 lb	1.5 kg	4.8 oz	15%
Water	12.2 lb	6.1 kg	1 lb, 3.5 oz	61%
Salt	.48 lb	.24 kg	.8 oz	2.4%
Yeast	.25 lb, fresh	.125 kg, fresh	.13 oz, instant dry	1.25%
Potatoes, roasted	5 lb	2.5 kg	8 oz (1¹/₄ cups, packed)	25%
TOTAL YIELD	**37.93 lb**	**18.965 kg**	**3 lb, 12.4 oz**	**189.65%**

PÂTE FERMENTÉE

Bread flour	6 lb	3 kg	9.6 oz (2¹/₄ cups)	100%
Water	3.9 lb	1.95 kg	6.2 oz (³/₄ cup)	65%
Salt	.12 lb	.06 kg	.2 oz (1 tsp)	2%
Yeast	.012 lb, fresh	.006 kg, fresh	(¹/₈ tsp, instant dry)	.2%
TOTAL	**10.032 lb**	**5.016 kg**	**1 lb**	

FINAL DOUGH

Bread flour	11 lb	5.5 kg	1 lb, 1.6 oz (4 cups)
Whole-wheat flour	3 lb	1.5 kg	4.8 oz (1 cup)
Water	8.3 lb	4.15 kg	13.3 oz (1⁵/₈ cups)
Salt	.36 lb	.18 kg	.6 oz (1 T)
Yeast	.238 lb, fresh	.119 kg, fresh	.13 oz, instant dry (1¹/₄ tsp)
Potatoes, roasted (see headnote)	5 lb	2.5 kg	8 oz (1 cup)
Pâte fermentée	10.032 lb	5.016 kg	1 lb (all of above)
TOTAL	**37.93 lb**	**18.965 kg**	**3 lb, 12.4 oz**

1. **PÂTE FERMENTÉE:** Disperse the yeast in the water, add the flour and salt, and mix until just smooth. Cover the bowl with plastic and let stand for 12 to 16 hours at about 70°F. Alternatively, remove a portion from a previous mix for use as *pâte fermentée*. In this case, refer to "Preparing the Pre-Ferment," page 96, for correct handling of the pre-ferment.

Toward the end of the eighteenth century, numerous grain failures had taken a devastating toll on the populations of Europe. People were hungry, civil unrest lurked in the poorer classes of society, and governments were scared. In an effort to fill bellies and keep the peace, attempts were made to develop breads that included other ingredients, from barley and oats to peas to potatoes. Most of those experiments amounted to little, but somehow potato bread found a place of acceptance among bread bakers and consumers alike.

Flavorful potatoes such as Yukon Gold or Yellow Finn are best for this bread. I find that oven roasting them concentrates the flavor in a way that boiling them does not. Once roasted, they can be chopped with a knife or dough cutter into small pieces. Leaving the skins on saves time, and the dark skin bits contrast nicely with the crumb color once the bread is sliced. I am very fond of the taste of potato bread, and eating it makes me think of how tenuous the food supply always is, and how hunger has always been a fact of life for so many people at all times.

2. MIXING: Add all the ingredients to the mixing bowl, including the potatoes, but not the *pâte fermentée*. In a spiral mixer, mix on first speed for 3 minutes in order to incorporate the ingredients. As the dough is coming together, add the *pâte fermentée* in chunks. If necessary, correct the hydration by adding water or flour in small amounts. The dough should feel slightly stiff, but since the potatoes hold a fair amount of moisture, which they will eventually contribute to the dough, be careful not to add much extra water as the dough mixes. Finish mixing on second speed for 3 to 3½ minutes. The dough should be supple and the gluten moderately developed. Desired dough temperature: 75°F.

3. BULK FERMENTATION: 1½ hours.

4. FOLDING: Fold the dough after 45 minutes of bulk fermentation.

5. DIVIDING AND SHAPING: Divide the dough into 1.5-pound pieces. Preshape lightly into rounds and place on a lightly floured work surface, seams up. Cover the rounds with plastic. When the dough has relaxed sufficiently (10 to 20 minutes), shape into round or oval loaves, place them either into floured *bannetons* or between folds of floured baker's linen, and cover with plastic wrap. A nice effect for potato bread is to shape it in the *fendu* style, by pressing deeply into the dough with a rolling pin to bisect it (see page 82). Proof these loaves top side down. The bread can also be baked in loaf pans.

6. FINAL FERMENTATION: Approximately 1¼ hours at 75°F.

7. BAKING: Transfer the risen loaves onto the loading conveyor or peel. Slash the desired scoring pattern with a blade; *fendu*-style loaves do not require slashing. Presteam the oven, load the bread, and steam again. Bake at 450°F. Open the oven vents after the loaves show color, in order to finish the bake in a drying oven. Loaves scaled at 1.5 pounds will bake in approximately 40 minutes. The potatoes will bring a great deal of color to the bread, so if the loaves are darkening too quickly, lower the oven temperature by 10° or 20°F. A comparatively long bake is necessary due to the moisture in the potatoes.

HERBED POTATO BREAD: Different herbs can be used to bring a subtle alteration to the flavor of potato bread. Rosemary is a common addition. Being quite strong, it is best used with restraint. About 1 percent of fresh rosemary based on the overall weight of the flour is a good starting point. Chives add a bit of color and a slight bite to the bread. They can be chopped and added at the rate of about 1.5 to 2 percent of the flour weight. Last, chopped dill is occasionally added to the bread. About 1.5 percent of the flour weight is a good starting point. With all of these herbs, add them at the outset of mixing. Adjust the percentage used based on personal preferences, keeping in mind that the bread should be adaptable to a variety of foods, and this is best achieved if the herbs are not too potent a flavor in the bread.

ROASTED GARLIC POTATO BREAD: Garlic is another possible addition to potato bread. Use about 3 percent garlic based on the overall flour weight. To prepare the garlic, cut about ½ inch off the top of whole bulbs, and place them right side up on a sheet pan. There is no need to peel the bulbs. Sprinkle a light coat of olive oil on the exposed cloves. Cover the sheet pan with aluminum foil and bake at about 350°F until the garlic is soft. Remove the garlic from its husk by squeezing the individual cloves. Add the garlic to the dough at the beginning of the mix. Brushed with olive oil and grilled, or simply toasted and buttered, potato bread with garlic is a special treat. Any of the herbs listed above can of course be added in conjunction with the garlic.

Potato Bread with Roasted Onions

PRE-FERMENTED FLOUR: 30%

DOUGH YIELD | U.S.: About 29 loaves at 1.5 lb each | Metric: About 32 loaves at .68 kg each | Home: 3 medium loaves

OVERALL FORMULA

	U.S.	METRIC	HOME	BAKER'S %
Bread flour	**17 lb**	**8.5 kg**	**1 lb, 11.2 oz**	**85%**
Whole-wheat flour	**3 lb**	**1.5 kg**	**4.8 oz**	**15%**
Water	**12 lb**	**6 kg**	**1 lb, 3.2 oz**	**60%**
Salt	**.48 lb**	**.24 kg**	**.8 oz**	**2.4%**
Yeast	**.25 lb, fresh**	**.125 kg, fresh**	**.13 oz, instant dry**	**1.25%**
Onions, roasted	**6 lb**	**3 kg**	**9.6 oz**	**30%**
Olive oil, as needed				
Potatoes, roasted	**5 lb**	**2.5 kg**	**8 oz**	**25%**
TOTAL YIELD	**43.73 lb**	**21.865 kg**	**4 lb, 3 oz**	**218.65%**

PÂTE FERMENTÉE

	U.S.	METRIC	HOME	BAKER'S %
Bread flour	6 lb	3 kg	9.6 oz (2¹⁄₄ cups)	100%
Water	3.9 lb	1.95 kg	6.2 oz (³⁄₄ cup)	65%
Salt	.12 lb	.06 kg	.2 oz (1 tsp)	2%
Yeast	.012 lb, fresh	.006 kg, fresh	(¹⁄₈ tsp, instant dry)	.2%
TOTAL	**10.032 lb**	**5.016 kg**	**1 lb**	

FINAL DOUGH

	U.S.	METRIC	HOME
Bread flour	11 lb	5.5 kg	1 lb, 1.6 oz (4 cups)
Whole-wheat flour	3 lb	1.5 kg	4.8 oz (1 cup)
Water	8.1 lb	4.05 kg	13 oz (1⁵⁄₈ cups)
Salt	.36 lb	.18 kg	.6 oz (1 T)
Yeast	.238 lb, fresh	.119 kg, fresh	.13 oz, instant dry (1 ¹⁄₄ tsp)
Onions, roasted (see headnote)	6 lb	3 kg	9.6 oz (1¹⁄₄ cups)
Potatoes, roasted (see headnote, page 118)	5 lb	2.5 kg	8 oz (1 cup)
Pâte fermentée	10.032 lb	5.016 kg	1 lb (all of above)
TOTAL	**43.73 lb**	**21.865 kg**	**4 lb, 3 oz**

1. **PÂTE FERMENTÉE:** Disperse the yeast in the water, add the flour and salt, and mix until just smooth. Cover the bowl with plastic and let stand for 12 to 16 hours at about 70°F. Alternatively, remove

By adding richly roasted onions to the preceding formula for Roasted Potato Bread, the result is a bread that is both sweet from the full cooking of the onions, and rich in flavor from both the onions and the olive oil in which they are coated.

The bread is handled in the same manner as Roasted Potato Bread, with a couple of adjustments. First, thinly slice the onions, toss them in the minimum amount of olive oil needed to coat them thoroughly, place in a baking pan with aluminum foil or a lid on top, and place them in a 350° to 400°F oven. Stir occasionally, and roast them until they are wilted and brown. They will be fragrant and sweet. Allow them to cool before adding to the bread dough (this step is best done a day ahead). One small note: The hydration in the present bread is 60 percent, while in the preceding one it is 61 percent. The onions and the oil in which they are roasted compensate for the slight reduction of overall water in the dough.

a portion from a previous mix for use as *pâte fermentée*. In this case, refer to "Preparing the Pre-Ferment," page 96, for correct handling of the pre-ferment.

2. MIXING: Add all the ingredients except the *pâte fermentée* and onions to the mixing bowl. In a spiral mixer, mix on first speed for 3 minutes in order to incorporate the ingredients. As the dough is coming together, add the *pâte fermentée* in chunks. If necessary, correct the hydration by adding water or flour in small amounts. The dough should feel slightly stiff, but since the potatoes hold a fair amount of moisture, which they will eventually contribute to the dough, be careful not to add much extra water as the dough mixes. Finish mixing on second speed for 3 to 3½ minutes. The dough should be supple and the gluten moderately developed. Finally, add the onions and mix on first speed until they are evenly incorporated. Desired dough temperature: 75°F.

3. BULK FERMENTATION: 1½ hours.

4. FOLDING: Fold the dough after 45 minutes of bulk fermentation.

5. DIVIDING AND SHAPING: Divide the dough into 1.5-pound pieces. Preshape lightly into rounds and place on a lightly floured work surface, seams up. Cover the rounds with plastic. When the dough has relaxed sufficiently (10 to 20 minutes), shape into round or oval loaves, place them either into floured *bannetons* or between folds of floured baker's linen, and cover with plastic. A nice effect for potato bread is to shape it in the *fendu* style, by pressing deeply into the dough with a rolling pin to bisect it (see page 82). Proof these loaves top side down. The bread can also be baked in loaf pans.

6. FINAL FERMENTATION: Approximately 1¼ hours at 75°F.

7. BAKING: Transfer the risen loaves onto the loading conveyor or peel. Slash the desired scoring pattern with a blade; *fendu*-style loaves do not require slashing. Presteam the oven, load the bread, and steam again. Bake at 450°F. Open the oven vents after the loaves show color, in order to finish the bake in a drying oven. Loaves scaled at 1.5 pounds will bake in approximately 40 minutes. The potatoes will bring a great deal of color to the bread, so if the loaves are darkening too quickly, lower the oven temperature by 10° or 20°F. A comparatively long bake is necessary due to the moisture in the potatoes.

Whole-Wheat Bread

PRE-FERMENTED FLOUR: 25%

DOUGH YIELD | U.S.: About 23 loaves at 1.5 lb each | Metric: About 25 loaves at .68 kg each | Home: 2 large loaves

OVERALL FORMULA

	U.S.	METRIC	HOME	BAKER'S %
Whole-wheat flour	10 lb	5 kg	1 lb	50%
Bread flour	10 lb	5 kg	1 lb	50%
Water	13.6 lb	6.8 kg	1 lb, 5.8 oz	68%
Salt	.4 lb	.2 kg	.6 oz	2%
Yeast	.22 lb, fresh	.11 kg, fresh	.13 oz, instant dry	1.1%
Honey	.6 lb	.3 kg	1 oz	3%
TOTAL YIELD	**34.82 lb**	**17.41 kg**	**3 lb, 7.5 oz**	**174.1%**

PÂTE FERMENTÉE

	U.S.	METRIC	HOME	BAKER'S %
Bread flour	5 lb	2.5 kg	8 oz (1¾ cups)	100%
Water	3.25 lb	1.625 kg	5.2 oz (⅝ cup)	65%
Salt	.1 lb	.05 kg	.2 oz (1 tsp)	2%
Yeast	.01 lb, fresh	.005 kg, fresh	(⅛ tsp, instant dry)	.2%
TOTAL	**8.36 lb**	**4.18 kg**	**13.4 oz**	

FINAL DOUGH

	U.S.	METRIC	HOME
Whole-wheat flour	10 lb	5 kg	1 lb (3⅝ cups)
Bread flour	5 lb	2.5 kg	8 oz (1¾ cups)
Water	10.35 lb	5.175 kg	1 lb, .6 oz (2 cups)
Salt	.3 lb	.15 kg	.4 oz (2 tsp)
Yeast	.21 lb, fresh	.105 kg, fresh	.13 oz, instant dry (1¼ tsp)
Honey	.6 lb	.3 kg	1 oz (1 T + 1 tsp)
Pâte fermentée	8.36 lb	4.18 kg	13.4 oz (all of above)
TOTAL	**34.82 lb**	**17.41 kg**	**3 lb, 7.5 oz**

1. **PÂTE FERMENTÉE:** Disperse the yeast in the water, add the flour and salt, and mix until just smooth. Cover the bowl with plastic and let stand for 12 to 16 hours at about 70°F. Alternatively, remove a portion from a previous mix for use as *pâte fermentée*. In this case, refer to "Preparing the Pre-Ferment," page 96, for correct handling of the pre-ferment.

This whole-wheat bread is clean-flavored and light. The comparatively long fermentation and low percentage of yeast help bring out the intrinsic wheat flavor of the flour. Using a small amount of honey helps balance the flavor. The bread has just the slightest sense of sweetness, a nice balance to the strong flavor of the whole-wheat flour.

2. MIXING: Place all the ingredients except the *pâte fermentée* in the mixing bowl. In a spiral mixer, mix on first speed for 3 minutes in order to incorporate the ingredients. As the dough is coming together, add the *pâte fermentée* in chunks. If necessary, correct the hydration by adding water or flour in small amounts (the absorption of whole-wheat flour varies considerably; don't hesitate to add a fair bit of water if the dough seems dry). Finish mixing on second speed for 3 minutes. The dough should be supple and slightly loose, and the gluten should be moderately developed. Desired dough temperature: 75°F.

3. BULK FERMENTATION: 2 hours.

4. FOLDING: Fold the dough after 1 hour of bulk fermentation.

5. DIVIDING AND SHAPING: Divide the dough into 1.5-pound pieces. Preshape lightly into rounds and place on a lightly floured work surface, seams up. Cover the rounds with plastic. When the dough has relaxed sufficiently (10 to 15 minutes), shape into round or oval loaves, place them either into floured *bannetons* or between folds of floured baker's linen, and cover with plastic. The bread can also be baked in loaf pans or shaped into rolls.

6. FINAL FERMENTATION: 1 to 1½ hours at 75°F.

7. BAKING: Transfer the risen loaves onto the loading conveyor or peel. Slash the desired scoring pattern with a blade. Presteam the oven, load the bread, and steam again. Bake at 450°F. Open the oven vents after the loaves show color, in order to finish the bake in a drying oven. Loaves scaled at 1.5 pounds will bake in approximately 40 minutes. The honey contributes color to the bread, so if the loaves are darkening too quickly, lower the oven temperature by 10° or 20°F.

Whole-Wheat Bread with Hazelnuts and Currants

PRE-FERMENTED FLOUR: 25%

DOUGH YIELD | U.S.: About 28 loaves at 1.5 lb each | Metric: About 31 loaves at .68 kg each | Home: 3 medium loaves

OVERALL FORMULA

	U.S.	METRIC	HOME	BAKER'S %
Whole-wheat flour	10 lb	5 kg	1 lb	50%
Bread flour	10 lb	5 kg	1 lb	50%
Water	14.6 lb	7.3 kg	1 lb, 7.4 oz	73%
Salt	.4 lb	.2 kg	.6 oz	2%
Yeast	.25 lb, fresh	.125 kg, fresh	.13 oz, instant dry	1.25%
Honey	.6 lb	.3 kg	1 oz	3%
Hazelnuts, roasted and skinned	3.2 lb	1.6 kg	5.1 oz	16%
Dried currants	3.2 lb	1.6 kg	5.1 oz	16%
TOTAL YIELD	**42.25 lb**	**21.125 kg**	**4 lb, 3.3 oz**	**211.25%**

PÂTE FERMENTÉE

	U.S.	METRIC	HOME	BAKER'S %
Bread flour	5 lb	2.5 kg	8 oz (1¾ cups)	100%
Water	3.25 lb	1.625 kg	5.2 oz (⅝ cup)	65%
Salt	.1 lb	.05 kg	.2 oz (1 tsp)	2%
Yeast	.01 lb, fresh	.005 kg, fresh	(⅛ tsp, instant dry)	.2%
TOTAL	**8.36 lb**	**4.18 kg**	**13.4 oz**	

FINAL DOUGH

	U.S.	METRIC	HOME
Whole-wheat flour	10 lb	5 kg	1 lb (3⅝ cups)
Bread flour	5 lb	2.5 kg	8 oz (1¾ cups)
Water	11.35 lb	5.675 kg	1 lb, 2.2 oz (2¼ cups)
Salt	.3 lb	.15 kg	.4 oz (2 tsp)
Yeast	.24 lb, fresh	.12 kg, fresh	.13oz, instant dry (1¼ tsp)
Honey	.6 lb	.3 kg	1 oz (1 T + 1 tsp)
Pâte fermentée	8.36 lb	4.18 kg	13.4 oz (all of above)
Hazelnuts	3.2 lb	1.6 kg	5.1 oz (1⅛ cups)
Dried currants	3.2 lb	1.6 kg	5.1 oz (1 cup, packed)
TOTAL	**42.25 lb**	**21.125 kg**	**4 lb, 3.3 oz**

This tasty variation on whole-wheat bread incorporates two ingredients—roasted hazelnuts and dried currants—whose flavors provide both a contrast and a complement, not only to each other, but to the overall flavor of the bread as well. The hazelnuts can be left whole or chopped slightly before being added to the dough.

1. PREPARING THE HAZELNUTS AND CURRANTS: Roast the hazelnuts in a medium oven, about 375°F, shaking the pan back and forth once or twice, for 12 to 15 minutes, until the nuts have turned light brown. Let cool. Rub the nuts vigorously between your hands to skin them, and set aside. Break up the currants so they are separated. If they are very moist, toss them with a small amount of flour in order to keep them separated.

2. PÂTE FERMENTÉE: Disperse the yeast in the water, add the flour and salt, and mix until just smooth. Cover the bowl with plastic and let stand for 12 to 16 hours at about 70°F. Alternatively, remove a portion from a previous mix for use as *pâte fermentée*. In this case, refer to "Preparing the Pre-Ferment," page 96, for correct handling of the pre-ferment.

3. MIXING: Add all the ingredients except the *pâte fermentée,* hazelnuts, and currants to the mixing bowl. In a spiral mixer, mix on first speed for 3 minutes in order to incorporate the ingredients. As the dough is coming together, add the *pâte fermentée* in chunks. If necessary, correct the hydration by adding water or flour in small amounts. The dough will firm up a bit once the nuts and currants are added, so be sure it is slightly loose at the early stages of mixing. Turn the mixer to second speed and mix for 3 minutes. The dough should be supple and somewhat loose, and the gluten should be moderately developed. Now add the hazelnuts and currants all at once, and mix on first speed just until they are evenly incorporated. In a spiral mixer, the reverse function of the bowl can be used to encourage speedy incorporation. Desired dough temperature: 75°F.

4. BULK FERMENTATION: 2 hours.

5. FOLDING: Fold the dough after 1 hour of bulk fermentation.

6. DIVIDING AND SHAPING: Divide the dough into 1.5-pound pieces. Preshape lightly into rounds and place on a lightly floured work surface, seams up. Cover the rounds with plastic. When the dough has relaxed sufficiently (10 to 15 minutes), shape into round or oval loaves, place them either into floured *bannetons* or between folds of lightly floured baker's linen, and cover with plastic. Very nice rolls can also be made with the dough. If you are making just a few loaves, take a few moments and pick out the currants on the surface. This prevents them from overbaking and becoming bitter. This is not practical for large production.

7. FINAL FERMENTATION: Approximately 1 to 1½ hours at 75°F.

8. BAKING: Transfer the risen loaves onto the loading conveyor or peel. A simple scoring pattern is best, as the blade will be running into hazelnuts and currants as you slash the surface. Presteam the oven, load the bread, and steam again. Bake at 450°F. Lower the oven temperature by 10° to 20°F after about 20 minutes to prevent the extra sugars in the dough from coloring the bread too quickly. Open the oven vents after the loaves show color, in order to finish the bake in a drying oven. Loaves scaled at 1.5 pounds will bake in approximately 40 minutes.

Whole-Wheat Bread with a Multigrain Soaker

PRE-FERMENTED FLOUR: 35%

DOUGH YIELD | U.S.: About 27 loaves at 1.5 lb each | Metric: About 30 loaves at .68 kg each | Home: 3 medium loaves

OVERALL FORMULA

	U.S.	METRIC	HOME	BAKER'S %
Whole-wheat flour	10 lb	5 kg	1 lb	50%
Bread flour	10 lb	5 kg	1 lb	50%
Cracked wheat	1 lb	.5 kg	1.6 oz	5%
Coarse cornmeal	1 lb	.5 kg	1.6 oz	5%
Millet	1 lb	.5 kg	1.6 oz	5%
Oats	1 lb	.5 kg	1.6 oz	5%
Water	15.6 lb	7.8 kg	1 lb, 9 oz	78%
Salt	.48 lb	.24 kg	.8 oz	2.4%
Yeast	.26 lb, fresh	.13 kg, fresh	.13 oz, instant dry	1.3%
Honey	1 lb	.5 kg	1.6 oz	5%
TOTAL YIELD	**41.34 lb**	**20.67 kg**	**4 lb, 1.9 oz**	**206.7%**

SOAKER

Cracked wheat	1 lb	.5 kg	1.6 oz (3/8 cup)	25%
Coarse cornmeal	1 lb	.5 kg	1.6 oz (3/8 cup)	25%
Millet	1 lb	.5 kg	1.6 oz (1/4 cup)	25%
Oats	1 lb	.5 kg	1.6 oz (1/2 cup)	25%
Water, boiling	5 lb	2.5 kg	8 oz (1 cup)	125%
TOTAL	**9 lb**	**4.5 kg**	**14.4 oz**	

PÂTE FERMENTÉE

Bread flour	7 lb	3.5 kg	11.2 oz (2½ cups)	100%
Water	4.55 lb	2.275 kg	7.3 oz (⅞ cup)	65%
Salt	.14 lb	.07 kg	.2 oz (1 tsp)	2%
Yeast	.014 lb, fresh	.007 kg, fresh	(⅛ tsp, instant dry)	.2%
TOTAL	**11.704 lb**	**5.852 kg**	**1 lb, 2.7 oz**	

FINAL DOUGH

Whole-wheat flour	10 lb	5 kg	1 lb (3⅝ cups)
Bread flour	3 lb	1.5 kg	4.8 oz (1 cup)
Water	6.05 lb	3.025 kg	9.7 oz (1¼ cups)
Salt	.34 lb	.17 kg	.6 oz (1 T)
Yeast	.246 lb, fresh	.123 kg, fresh	.13 oz, instant dry (1¼ tsp)
Honey	1 lb	.5 kg	1.6 oz (2 T)
Soaker	9 lb	4.5 kg	14.4 oz (all of above)
Pâte fermentée	11.704 lb	5.852 kg	1 lb, 2.7 oz (all of above)
TOTAL	**41.34 lb**	**20.67 kg**	**4 lb, 1.9 oz**

This version of whole-wheat bread is more robust than its soakerless cousins, and keeps quite well because of the high moisture level. By pre-fermenting 35 percent of the flour, the dough has an extra boost of not only flavor but leavening potential as well. What may seem at first glance like a high percentage of salt is in fact a balanced measure, since the soaker grains need salt in order for the bread to be balanced. Other grains and seeds, such as flax, sesame, sunflower, and cracked rye, can be used in lieu of or in addition to the grains used in the present formula.

1. SOAKER: Prepare the soaker by measuring the grains into a bowl and pouring the boiling water over them. Stir to incorporate, then cover the bowl with a sheet of plastic. In hot weather, the dough's overall salt can be used to prevent enzymatic activity from commencing. Make the soaker at least 4 hours before mixing the final dough so the grains have enough time to absorb the water and soften. A finer-textured bread can be made if the soaker ingredients are ground in a food processor before adding the water.

2. PÂTE FERMENTÉE: Disperse the yeast in the water, add the flour and salt, and mix until just smooth. Cover the bowl with plastic and let stand for 12 to 16 hours at about 70°F. Alternatively, remove a portion from a previous mix for use as *pâte fermentée*. In this case, refer to "Preparing the Pre-Ferment," page 96, for correct handling of the pre-ferment.

3. MIXING: Place all the ingredients, including the soaker but not the *pâte fermentée*, in the mixing bowl. In a spiral mixer, mix on first speed for 3 minutes in order to incorporate the ingredients. As the dough is coming together, add the *pâte fermentée* in chunks. If necessary, correct the hydration by adding water or flour in small amounts. Soakers tend to have quite a range of water absorption; don't hesitate to add a fair amount of water if the dough seems too dry. Turn the mixer to second speed and mix for

3 to 3½ minutes. The dough should be supple and lively to the pull, and the gluten moderately developed. Desired dough temperature: 75°F.

4. BULK FERMENTATION: 2 hours.

5. FOLDING: Fold the dough after 1 hour of bulk fermentation.

6. DIVIDING AND SHAPING: Divide the dough into 1.5-pound pieces (or make rolls with smaller pieces). Preshape lightly into rounds and place on a lightly floured work surface, seams up. Cover the rounds with plastic. When the dough has relaxed sufficiently (10 to 20 minutes), shape into round or oval loaves, place them either into floured *bannetons* or between folds of floured baker's linen, and cover with plastic. The dough can also be placed in loaf pans.

7. FINAL FERMENTATION: Approximately 1 to 1½ hours at 75°F.

8. BAKING: Transfer the risen loaves onto the loading conveyor or peel. Score the loaves as desired, presteam the oven, load the bread, and steam again. Bake at 450°F. Open the oven vents after the loaves show color, in order to finish the bake in a drying oven. If the breads are taking on too much color early in the bake (due to the presence of the honey), lower the oven temperature by 10° or 20°F. Loaves scaled at 1.5 pounds will bake in approximately 40 minutes.

1. Assorted Breads and a Couple of Pastries
Photo courtesy of King Arthur Flour

2. The author's bread stencil on Pain au Levain loaves

3. Baguettes, baked on the hearth with steam

4. Baguettes, baked on the hearth with no steam

5. Baguettes, baked on a sheet pan with steam

6. Baguettes, baked on perforated baguette screen with steam

7. Épis de blé, p. 82

8. Ciabatta, p. 105

9. Proper and improper scoring, p. 78

10. Oven spring and loaves of ciabatta, p. 23

11. Rolls made with Roasted Potato Bread dough and pan loaves made with baguette dough, pp. 117 and 103

12. Roasted Potato Bread made in the fendu style, p. 82

13. A six-pound ciabatta, p. 107

14. Bagels and Bialys, pp. 260 and 262

15. A resting loaf made with baguette dough, p. 101

16. A decorated plaque, p. 334

Five-Grain Bread with Pâte Fermentée

PRE-FERMENTED FLOUR: 30%

DOUGH YIELD | U.S.: About 29 loaves at 1.5 lb each | Metric: About 32 loaves at .68 kg each | Home: 3 medium loaves

OVERALL FORMULA

	U.S.	METRIC	HOME	BAKER'S %
Bread flour	20 lb	10 kg	2 lb	100%
Rye chops	1.6 lb	.8 kg	2.6 oz	8%
Flaxseeds	1.6 lb	.8 kg	2.6 oz	8%
Sunflower seeds	1.4 lb	.7 kg	2.2 oz	7%
Oats	1.4 lb	.7 kg	2.2 oz	7%
Water	17 lb	8.5 kg	1 lb, 11.2 oz	85%
Salt	.52 lb	.26 kg	.8 oz	2.6%
Yeast	.32 lb, fresh	.16 kg, fresh	.17 oz, instant dry	1.6%
TOTAL YIELD	**43.84 lb**	**21.92 kg**	**4 lb, 5.8 oz**	**219.2%**

SOAKER

Rye chops	1.6 lb	.8 kg	2.6 oz (1/2 cup)	26.7%
Flaxseeds	1.6 lb	.8 kg	2.6 oz (1/2 cup)	26.7%
Sunflower seeds	1.4 lb	.7 kg	2.2 oz (1/2 cup)	23.3%
Oats	1.4 lb	.7 kg	2.2 oz (5/8 cup)	23.3%
Water	7.5 lb	3.75 kg	12 oz (1 1/2 cups)	125%
TOTAL	**13.5 lb**	**6.75 kg**	**1 lb, 5.6 oz**	

PÂTE FERMENTÉE

Bread flour	6 lb	3 kg	9.6 oz (2 1/4 cups)	100%
Water	3.9 lb	1.95 kg	6.2 oz (3/4 cup)	65%
Salt	.12 lb	.06 kg	.2 oz (1 tsp)	2%
Yeast	.012 lb, fresh	.006 kg, fresh	(1/8 tsp, instant dry)	.2%
TOTAL	**10.032 lb**	**5.016 kg**	**1 lb**	

FINAL DOUGH

Bread flour	14 lb	7 kg	1 lb, 6.4 oz (5 cups)
Water	5.6 lb	2.8 kg	9 oz (1 1/8 cups)
Salt	.4 lb	.2 kg	.6 oz (1 T)
Yeast	.308 lb, fresh	.154 kg, fresh	.17 oz, instant dry (1 1/2 tsp)
Soaker	13.5 lb	6.75 kg	1 lb, 5.6 oz (all of above)
Pâte fermentée	10.032 lb	5.016 kg	1 lb (all of above)
TOTAL	**43.84 lb**	**21.92 kg**	**4 lb, 5.8 oz**

Fragrant and full of flavor, this multigrain bread is a pleasure to make, a pleasure to look at with all the soaker grains studding the loaf, and a pleasure to eat—a bread that is at once flavorful yet light. As a variation, toast the sunflower seeds rather than soaking them with the other grains, and notice the deep nuttiness that pervades the loaf.

1. SOAKER: Prepare the soaker by measuring the grains into a bowl and pouring the water over them. Stir to incorporate, then cover the bowl with a sheet of plastic. In hot weather, the dough's overall salt can be used to prevent enzymatic activity from commencing. Make the soaker at least 4 hours before mixing the final dough so the grains have enough time to absorb the water and soften. If rye chops are not available, cracked rye can be used, but use boiling water in the soaker.

2. PÂTE FERMENTÉE: Disperse the yeast in the water, add the flour and salt, and mix just until smooth. Cover the bowl with plastic and let stand for 12 to 16 hours at about 70°F. Alternatively, remove a portion from a previous mix for use as *pâte fermentée*. In this case, refer to "Preparing the Pre-Ferment," page 96, for correct handling of the pre-ferment.

3. MIXING: Place all the ingredients, including the soaker but not the *pâte fermentée*, in the mixing bowl. In a spiral mixer, mix on first speed for 3 minutes in order to incorporate the ingredients. As the dough is coming together, add the *pâte fermentée* in chunks. If necessary, correct the hydration by adding water or flour in small amounts. Turn the mixer to second speed and mix for 3 to 3½ minutes. The dough should be somewhat loose, but with definite dough strength and gluten development. Desired dough temperature: 75°F.

4. BULK FERMENTATION: 2 hours.

5. FOLDING: Fold the dough after 1 hour of bulk fermentation.

6. DIVIDING AND SHAPING: Divide the dough into 1.5-pound pieces (or make rolls with smaller pieces). Preshape lightly into rounds and place on a lightly floured work surface, seams up. Cover the rounds with plastic. When the dough has relaxed sufficiently (10 to 20 minutes), shape into round or oval loaves, place them either into floured *bannetons* or on lightly floured baker's linen, and cover with plastic. The dough can also be baked in loaf pans.

7. FINAL FERMENTATION: Approximately 1 to 1½ hours at 75°F.

8. BAKING: Transfer the risen loaves onto the loading conveyor or peel. Score the loaves as desired, presteam the oven, load the bread, and steam again. Bake at 460°F. Open the oven vents after the loaves show color, in order to finish the bake in a drying oven. Lower the oven temperature by 10° or 20°F if the loaves color too strongly. Loaves scaled at 1.5 pounds will bake in approximately 40 minutes.

Sunflower Seed Bread with Pâte Fermentée

PRE-FERMENTED FLOUR: 20%

DOUGH YIELD | U.S.: About 30 loaves at 1.5 lb each | Metric: About 33 loaves at .68 kg each | Home: 3 medium loaves

OVERALL FORMULA

	U.S.	METRIC	HOME	BAKER'S %
Bread flour	20 lb	10 kg	2 lb	100%
Rye chops	4 lb	2 kg	6.4 oz	20%
Sunflower seeds	4 lb	2 kg	6.4 oz	20%
Water	16 lb	8 kg	1 lb, 9.6 oz	80%
Salt	.46 lb	.23 kg	.7 oz	2.3%
Yeast	.3 lb, fresh	.15 kg, fresh	.17 oz, instant dry	1.5%
Malt syrup	.3 lb	.15 kg	.5 oz	1.5%
TOTAL YIELD	**45.06 lb**	**22.53 kg**	**4 lb, 7.8 oz**	**225.3%**

SOAKER

Rye chops	4 lb	2 kg	6.4 oz (1 3/8 cups)	100%
Water	5 lb	2.5 kg	8 oz (1 cup)	125%
TOTAL	**9 lb**	**4.5 kg**	**14.4 oz**	

PÂTE FERMENTÉE

Bread flour	4 lb	2 kg	6.4 oz (1 1/2 cups)	100%
Water	2.6 lb	1.3 kg	4.2 oz (1/2 cup)	65%
Salt	.08 lb	.04 kg	.1 oz (1/2 tsp)	2%
Yeast	.008 lb, fresh	.004 kg, fresh	(1/8 tsp, instant dry)	.2%
TOTAL	**6.688 lb**	**3.344 kg**	**10.7 oz**	

FINAL DOUGH

Bread flour	16 lb	8 kg	1 lb, 9.6 oz (5 3/4 cups)
Water	8.4 lb	4.2 kg	13.4 oz (1 5/8 cups)
Salt	.38 lb	.19 kg	.6 oz (1 T)
Yeast	.292 lb, fresh	.146 kg, fresh	.17 oz, instant dry (1 1/2 tsp)
Malt syrup	.3 lb	.15 kg	.5 oz (2 tsp)
Sunflower seeds	4 lb	2 kg	6.4 oz (1 3/8 cups)
Soaker	9 lb	4.5 kg	14.4 oz (all of above)
Pâte fermentée	6.688 lb	3.344 kg	10.7 oz (all of above)
TOTAL	**45.06 lb**	**22.53 kg**	**4 lb, 7.8 oz**

This traditional German bread's name is *Sonnenblumenbrot* (*Sonnen* = sun; *Blumen* = flower; *Brot* = bread). Hearty and aromatic, it is particularly delightful with hard cheeses, peanut butter, various jams and preserves, or just toasted with butter. Malt syrup is thick and flavorful and adds just a wisp of sweetness to the loaf. If unavailable, good honey will do in its place.

1. SOAKER: Pour water over the rye chops and stir to incorporate. Cover the bowl with a sheet of plastic. In hot weather, the dough's overall salt can be used to prevent enzymatic activity from commencing. Make the soaker at least 4 hours before mixing the final dough so the grains have enough time to absorb the water and soften. If rye chops are not available, cracked rye can be used. In this case, use boiled water for the soaker to ensure that the cracked rye softens sufficiently. While making the soaker, toast the sunflower seeds, about 10 minutes in a 350°F oven, until they are fragrant.

2. PÂTE FERMENTÉE: Disperse the yeast in the water, add the flour and salt, and mix until just smooth. Cover the bowl with plastic and let stand for 12 to 16 hours at about 70°F. Alternatively, remove a portion from a previous mix for use as *pâte fermentée.* In this case, refer to "Preparing the Pre-Ferment," page 96, for correct handling of the pre-ferment.

3. MIXING: Place all the ingredients, including the soaker and the toasted sunflower seeds, but not the *pâte fermentée,* in the mixing bowl. In a spiral mixer, mix on first speed for 3 minutes in order to incorporate the ingredients. As the dough is coming together, add the *pâte fermentée* in chunks. If necessary, correct the hydration by adding water or flour in small amounts. Turn the mixer to second speed and mix for 3 to 3½ minutes. The dough should be somewhat loose, but with definite dough strength and gluten development. Desired dough temperature: 75°F.

4. BULK FERMENTATION: 2 hours.

5. FOLDING: Fold the dough after 1 hour of bulk fermentation.

6. DIVIDING AND SHAPING: Divide the dough into 1.5-pound pieces (or make rolls with smaller pieces). Preshape lightly into rounds and place on a lightly floured work surface, seams up. Cover the rounds with plastic. When the dough has relaxed sufficiently (10 to 20 minutes), shape it into tight round loaves. Dip the top side of each loaf into a dampened cloth, then into a sheet pan of raw sunflower seeds (don't dip the outer surface of the bread into the toasted seeds, since they will be vigorously toasted in the oven). Place the loaves in floured *bannetons* or onto lightly floured baker's linen, top side up, and cover with plastic.

7. FINAL FERMENTATION: Approximately 1 to 1½ hours at 75°F.

8. BAKING: Transfer the risen loaves onto the loading conveyor or peel. Because the loaves are topped with sunflower seeds, scoring is a little difficult. A few quick strokes with a straight razor blade or some snips with scissors are sufficient. Presteam the oven, load the bread, and steam again. Bake at 460°F. Open the oven vents after the loaves show color, in order to finish the bake in a drying oven. The malt syrup contributes color along with flavor, and the oven temperature can be lowered by 10° or 20°F if the loaves color too quickly. Loaves scaled at 1.5 pounds will bake in approximately 40 minutes.

Golden Raisin and Walnut Bread

PRE-FERMENTED FLOUR: 25%

DOUGH YIELD | U.S.: About 27 loaves at 1.5 lb each | Metric: About 30 loaves at .68 kg each | Home: 3 medium loaves

OVERALL FORMULA

	U.S.	METRIC	HOME	BAKER'S %
Bread flour	**16 lb**	**8 kg**	**1 lb, 9.6 oz**	**80%**
Whole-wheat flour	**4 lb**	**2 kg**	**6.4 oz**	**20%**
Water	**14.4 lb**	**7.2 kg**	**1 lb, 7 oz**	**72%**
Salt	**.4 lb**	**.2 kg**	**.6 oz**	**2%**
Yeast	**.24 lb, fresh**	**.12 kg, fresh**	**.13 oz, instant dry**	**1.2%**
Golden raisins	**3.2 lb**	**1.6 kg**	**5.1 oz**	**16%**
Walnuts	**3.2 lb**	**1.6 kg**	**5.1 oz**	**16%**
TOTAL YIELD	**41.44 lb**	**20.72 kg**	**4 lb, 1.9 oz**	**207.2%**

STIFF BIGA

	U.S.	METRIC	HOME	BAKER'S %
Bread flour	2.5 lb	1.25 kg	4 oz (7/8 cup)	50%
Whole-wheat flour	2.5 lb	1.25 kg	4 oz (7/8 cup)	50%
Water	3.1 lb	1.55 kg	5 oz (5/8 cup)	62%
Yeast	.01 lb, fresh	.005 kg, fresh	(1/8 tsp, instant dry)	.2%
TOTAL	**8.11 lb**	**4.055 kg**	**13 oz**	

FINAL DOUGH

	U.S.	METRIC	HOME
Bread flour	13.5 lb	6.75 kg	1 lb, 5.6 oz (5 cups)
Whole-wheat flour	1.5 lb	.75 kg	2.4 oz (1/2 cup)
Water	11.3 lb	5.65 kg	1 lb, 2 oz (2 1/4 cups)
Salt	.4 lb	.2 kg	.6 oz (1 T)
Yeast	.23 lb, fresh	.115 kg, fresh	.13 oz, instant dry (1 1/4 tsp)
Biga	8.11 lb	4.055 kg	13 oz (all of above)
Walnuts	3.2 lb	1.6 kg	5.1 oz (1 1/4 cups)
Golden raisins	3.2 lb	1.6 kg	5.1 oz (1 cup, packed)
TOTAL	**41.44 lb**	**20.72 kg**	**4 lb, 1.9 oz**

The bite of walnuts in this bread is nicely rounded by the concentrated sweetness of golden raisins, which also give a lovely random flecking of color to the bread's crumb. Adjusting the proportion of whole-wheat flour gives a correspondingly more or less whole-grain flavor to the bread. If adjustments with the whole wheat are made, pay careful attention to the hydration—slightly more water may be needed as the percentage of whole-wheat flour increases.

1. BIGA: Mix the bread flour, whole-wheat flour, water, and yeast on first speed until evenly incorporated. The biga will be stiff, but a small addition of water may be necessary depending on the absorption of the whole-wheat flour. Cover the bowl with plastic to prevent a crust from forming, and leave at about 70°F for 12 to 16 hours.

2. MIXING: Place all the ingredients in the mixing bowl, with the exception of the biga, the walnuts, and the golden raisins. In a spiral mixer, mix on first speed for 3 minutes in order to incorporate the ingredients. As the dough is coming together, add the biga in chunks. If necessary, correct the hydration by adding water or flour in small amounts. Turn the mixer to second speed and mix for another 3 minutes. The dough should be of medium consistency, but with perceptible dough strength and gluten development. Add the walnuts and golden raisins and mix on first speed just until they are evenly incorporated. Desired dough temperature: 75°F.

3. BULK FERMENTATION: 2 hours.

4. FOLDING: Fold the dough after 1 hour of bulk fermentation.

5. DIVIDING AND SHAPING: Divide the dough into 1.5-pound pieces (or make rolls with smaller pieces). Preshape lightly into rounds and place on a lightly floured work surface, seams up. Cover the rounds with plastic. When the dough has relaxed sufficiently (10 to 20 minutes), shape it into tight round or oval loaves. Place the loaves into floured *bannetons* or on lightly floured baker's linen and cover with plastic.

6. FINAL FERMENTATION: Approximately 1 to 1½ hours at 75°F.

7. BAKING: Invert the risen loaves onto the loading conveyor or peel. Score the loaves with the desired pattern using a straight *lame.* Presteam the oven, load the bread, and steam again. Bake at 460°F. Open the oven vents after the loaves show color, in order to finish the bake in a drying oven. The sugars in the raisins will add color to the dough, so the oven temperature can be lowered by 10° or 20°F after about 20 minutes of baking. Loaves scaled at 1.5 pounds will bake in approximately 40 minutes.

Semolina (Durum) Bread

PRE-FERMENTED FLOUR: 40%

DOUGH YIELD | U.S.: About 22 loaves at 1.5 lb each | Metric: About 25 loaves at .68 kg each | Home: 2 large loaves

OVERALL FORMULA

	U.S.	METRIC	HOME	BAKER'S %
Durum flour	10 lb	5 kg	1 lb	50%
Bread flour	10 lb	5 kg	1 lb	50%
Water	12.4 lb	6.2 kg	1 lb, 3.8 oz	62%
Salt	.36 lb	.18 kg	.6 oz	1.8%
Yeast	.24 lb, fresh	.12 kg, fresh	.13 oz, instant dry	1.2%
Sugar	.4 lb	.2 kg	.6 oz	2%
Extra-virgin olive oil	1 lb	.5 kg	1.6 oz	5%
TOTAL YIELD	**34.4 lb**	**17.2 kg**	**3 lb, 4 oz**	**172%**

SPONGE

	U.S.	METRIC	HOME	BAKER'S %
Durum flour	4 lb	2 kg	6.4 oz (1½ cups)	50%
Bread flour	4 lb	2 kg	6.4 oz (1½ cups)	50%
Water	5.6 lb	2.8 kg	9 oz (1⅛ cups)	70%
Yeast	.24 lb, fresh	.12 kg, fresh	.13 oz (1¼ tsp)	3%
Sugar	.4 lb	.2 kg	.6 oz (½ tsp)	5%
TOTAL	**14.24 lb**	**7.12 kg**	**1 lb, 6.5 oz**	

FINAL DOUGH

	U.S.	METRIC	HOME
Durum flour	6 lb	3 kg	9.6 oz (2⅛ cups)
Bread flour	6 lb	3 kg	9.6 oz (2¼ cups)
Water	6.8 lb	3.4 kg	10.8 oz (1⅜ cups)
Salt	.36 lb	.18 kg	.6 oz (1 T)
Extra-virgin olive oil	1 lb	.5 kg	1.6 oz (3 T)
Sponge	14.24 lb	7.12 kg	1 lb, 6.5 oz (all of above)
TOTAL	**34.4 lb**	**17.2 kg**	**3 lb, 4 oz**

1. **SPONGE:** Mix the durum flour, bread flour, water, yeast, and sugar on first speed until evenly incorporated. The sponge will be fairly loose. Since the ripening is accomplished in a short time, a sponge temperature of 78° to 80°F is required. The sponge is ripe after about 1¼ hours, when it is on the verge of collapse.

2. **MIXING:** Add all of the ingredients, including the sponge, to the mixing bowl. In a spiral mixer, mix on first speed for 3 minutes in

The sponge in this bread is unusual: It is an old-fashioned type of sponge, once common in Austria and England, known as a "flying sponge." I assume that it is "flying" because all the yeast is used in it, and the duration of ripening is usually not much more than 1 hour. It may be, though, that the bakers in the shops of old, having much less to rely on in terms of mechanical equipment compared with the bakers of today, were the ones who were flying! In any case, although a flying sponge might not have all the virtues of a long and gradually fermenting sponge, it does impart a lightness and comparative depth of flour flavor to finished bread.

order to incorporate the ingredients. Correct the dough consistency as necessary. Turn the mixer to second speed and mix for another 2½ to 3 minutes. The dough should be of medium consistency, but with perceptible dough strength and gluten development. Desired dough temperature: 76°F.

3. BULK FERMENTATION: 1½ hours.

4. FOLDING: Fold the dough after 45 minutes of bulk fermentation.

5. DIVIDING AND SHAPING: Divide the dough into 1.5-pound pieces (or make rolls with smaller pieces). Preshape lightly into rounds and place on a lightly floured work surface, seams up. Cover the rounds with plastic. When the dough has relaxed sufficiently (10 to 20 minutes), shape it into tight round or oval loaves. For a variation, the top of the loaves can be pressed into a damp cloth and then into a tray of raw sesame seeds. Place the loaves into floured *bannetons* or on lightly floured baker's linen and cover with plastic.

6. FINAL FERMENTATION: Approximately 1 to 1¼ hours at 75°F.

7. BAKING: Invert the risen loaves onto the loading conveyor or peel. Score the loaves as desired. Presteam the oven, load the bread, and steam again. Bake at 460°F. Open the oven vents after the loaves show color, in order to finish the bake in a drying oven. Loaves scaled at 1.5 pounds will bake in 35 to 40 minutes.

SEMOLINA BREAD STICKS: Cut individual dough pieces at 1.33 ounces (38 g) (with a 36-part divider, dough weight per press is 3 pounds (1.36 kg)). Relax the dough, covered with plastic, for 10 or 15 minutes, then roll the individual pieces to about 16 inches long (shorter bread sticks, weighing less, can of course also be scaled). Once rolled, the bread sticks can be left plain, or rolled into a damp cloth and then into a tray of raw sesame seeds or fine semolina. An alternative method for making bread sticks is to take the desired weight of dough and press it into a flat rectangle. Using a pizza roller or sharp knife, individual bread sticks can be cut off the main bulk of dough. This is possibly the quickest method, but take care that the bread sticks are as close as possible to being equal in weight so that they bake uniformly. Whatever method is chosen, allow the shaped bread sticks to rest for 15 to 20 minutes, then bake at 380°F for about 20 minutes, until evenly browned and crisp. They will keep well for several days in an airtight container, and can be recrisped by warming for a few minutes at 350°F.

Semolina (Durum) Bread with a Whole-Grain Soaker

PRE-FERMENTED FLOUR: 40%

DOUGH YIELD | U.S.: About 27 loaves at 1.5 lb each | Metric: About 30 loaves at .68 kg each | Home: 3 medium loaves

OVERALL FORMULA

	U.S.	METRIC	HOME	BAKER'S %
Durum flour	10 lb	5 kg	1 lb	50%
Bread flour	10 lb	5 kg	1 lb	50%
Coarse cornmeal	1.6 lb	.8 kg	2.6 oz	8%
Millet	1.2 lb	.6 kg	1.9 oz	6%
Sesame seeds	1.2 lb	.6 kg	1.9 oz	6%
Water	15.8 lb	7.9 kg	1 lb, 9.3 oz	79%
Salt	.44 lb	.22 kg	.7 oz	2.2%
Yeast	.34 lb, fresh	.17 kg, fresh	.17 oz, instant dry	1.7%
TOTAL YIELD	**40.58 lb**	**20.29 kg**	**4 lb, .6 oz**	**202.9%**

SOAKER

	U.S.	METRIC	HOME	BAKER'S %
Coarse cornmeal	1.6 lb	.8 kg	2.6 oz (5/8 cup)	40%
Millet	1.2 lb	.6 kg	1.9 oz (3/8 cup)	30%
Sesame seeds	1.2 lb	.6 kg	1.9 oz (3/8 cup)	30%
Water, boiling	5 lb	2.5 kg	8 oz (1 cup)	125%
TOTAL	**9 lb**	**4.5 kg**	**14.4 oz**	

SPONGE

	U.S.	METRIC	HOME	BAKER'S %
Durum flour	4 lb	2 kg	6.4 oz (1 1/2 cups)	50%
Bread flour	4 lb	2 kg	6.4 oz (1 1/2 cups)	50%
Water	5.6 lb	2.8 kg	9 oz (1 1/8 cups)	70%
Yeast	.34 lb, fresh	.17 kg, fresh	.17 oz (1 1/2 tsp)	4.3%
TOTAL	**13.94 lb**	**6.97 kg**	**1 lb, 6.2 oz**	

FINAL DOUGH

	U.S.	METRIC	HOME
Durum flour	6 lb	3 kg	9.6 oz (2 1/8 cups)
Bread flour	6 lb	3 kg	9.6 oz (2 1/8 cups)
Water	5.2 lb	2.6 kg	8.3 oz (1 cup)
Salt	.44 lb	.22 kg	.7 oz (1 T + 1/2 tsp)
Soaker	9 lb	4.5 kg	14.4 oz (all of above)
Sponge	13.94 lb	6.97 kg	1 lb, 6.2 oz (all of above)
TOTAL	**40.58 lb**	**20.29 kg**	**4 lb, .6 oz**

Here is another semolina bread, this one made with a grain-and-seed soaker. Like the preceding bread, it incorporates a flying sponge. The yeast percentage is slightly higher to accommodate the presence of the soaker, but the sugar is eliminated in this formula; as a result, the sponge ripens in just about the same time as in the preceding semolina bread.

1. SOAKER: At least 4 hours before mixing the final dough, pour boiling water over the soaker grains. Cover the soaker with plastic to prevent evaporation, and let stand at room temperature.

2. SPONGE: Mix the durum flour, bread flour, water, and yeast on first speed until evenly incorporated. The sponge will be fairly loose. Since the ripening is accomplished in a short time, a sponge temperature of 78° to 80°F is required. The sponge is ripe after about 1¼ hours, when it will be on the verge of collapse.

3. MIXING: Place all the ingredients in the mixing bowl, including the soaker and sponge. In a spiral mixing bowl, mix on first speed for 3 minutes in order to incorporate the ingredients. Check the dough consistency and make corrections as necessary. Turn the mixer to second speed and mix for about 3 minutes. The dough should be of medium consistency, with a resisting tug when pulled on. Desired dough temperature: 76°F.

4. BULK FERMENTATION: 1½ hours.

5. FOLDING: Fold the dough after 45 minutes of bulk fermentation.

6. DIVIDING AND SHAPING: Divide the dough into 1.5-pound pieces (or make rolls with smaller pieces). Preshape lightly into rounds and place on a lightly floured work surface, seams up. Cover the rounds with plastic. When the dough has relaxed sufficiently (10 to 20 minutes), shape it into tight round or oval loaves. As in the preceding formula for Semolina Bread, the top of the loaves can be pressed into a damp cloth and then into a tray of raw sesame seeds. Place the loaves into floured *bannetons* or on lightly floured baker's linen and cover with plastic.

7. FINAL FERMENTATION: Approximately 1 to 1¼ hours at 75°F.

8. BAKING: Invert the risen loaves onto the loading conveyor or peel. Score the loaves as desired. Presteam the oven, load the bread, and steam again. Bake in a 460°F oven. Open the oven vents after the loaves show color, in order to finish the bake in a drying oven. Loaves scaled at 1.5 pounds will bake in approximately 40 minutes.

Corn Bread

PRE-FERMENTED FLOUR: 25%

DOUGH YIELD | U.S.: About 22 loaves at 1.5 lb each | Metric: About 25 loaves at .68 kg each | Home: 2 large loaves

OVERALL FORMULA

	U.S.	Metric	Home	Baker's %
Bread flour	15 lb	7.5 kg	1 lb, 8 oz	75%
Fine cornmeal	5 lb	2.5 kg	8 oz	25%
Water	12.6 lb	6.3 kg	1 lb, 4.2 oz	63%
Salt	.4 lb	.2 kg	.6 oz	2%
Yeast	.3 lb, fresh	.15 kg, fresh	.17 oz, instant dry	1.5%
Extra-virgin olive oil	1 lb	.5 kg	1.6 oz	5%
TOTAL YIELD	**34.3 lb**	**17.15 kg**	**3 lb, 6.6 oz**	**171.5%**

POOLISH

	U.S.	Metric	Home	Baker's %
Bread flour	5 lb	2.5 kg	8 oz (1¾ cups)	100%
Water	5 lb	2.5 kg	8 oz (1 cup)	100%
Yeast	.01 lb, fresh	.005 kg, fresh	(⅛ tsp, instant dry)	.2%
TOTAL	**10.01 lb**	**5.005 kg**	**1 lb**	

FINAL DOUGH

	U.S.	Metric	Home
Bread flour	10 lb	5 kg	1 lb (3⅝ cups)
Fine cornmeal	5 lb	2.5 kg	8 oz (¼ cup)
Water	7.6 lb	3.8 kg	12.2 oz (1½ cups)
Salt	.4 lb	.2 kg	.6 oz (1 T)
Yeast	.29 lb, fresh	.145 kg, fresh	.17 oz, instant dry (1½ tsp)
Extra-virgin olive oil	1 lb	.5 kg	1.6 oz (3 T)
Poolish	10.01 lb	5.005 kg	1 lb (all of above)
TOTAL	**34.3 lb**	**17.15 kg**	**3 lb, 6.6 oz**

1. **POOLISH:** Disperse the yeast in the water, add the flour, and mix until smooth. Cover the bowl with plastic and let stand for 12 to 16 hours at about 70°F.

2. **SOAKING AND MIXING:** Add the cornmeal to the mixing bowl and pour the dough water over it. Allow it to soak for about 15 minutes. This will begin softening the cornmeal, and mixing and handling quality will improve. Add the remaining ingredients to the mixing bowl, including the poolish. In a spiral mixer, mix on first

Corn has been a staple grain for thousands of years among the native peoples of the Americas and, for the past five hundred years, throughout Europe. It is no wonder that it found its way into bread making; during times of wheat shortages, many different grains were used to extend precious wheat flour and fill the bellies of the laboring peasants (a huge proportion of whom consumed little more than bread). Nutritionally, however, corn is deficient when eaten on its own, and can cause the niacin-deficiency disease pellagra (known in Switzerland as *Maiserkrankheit*, or "maize-eater's illness"). Interestingly, when corn is processed with lime, as in the making of traditional nixtamal for tortillas in Mexico, niacin is released and the corn becomes highly nutritious. The corn bread produced from this formula has a tight crumb, a golden crumb color, a somewhat dull crust color, and a unique aroma and sweetness provided by the corn.

speed for 3 minutes in order to incorporate the ingredients. The absorption of the cornmeal can vary considerably (particularly with medium or coarse cornmeal), so it is important to check the dough carefully while it is on first speed and make corrections as necessary. The dough should be of medium consistency once the ingredients are incorporated. Turn the mixer to second speed and mix for 3 to 3½ minutes. Cornmeal tends to have a puncturing effect on gluten; nevertheless, mix until there is a moderate gluten development. Desired dough temperature: 76°F.

3. **BULK FERMENTATION:** 1½ hours.

4. **FOLDING:** Fold the dough after 45 minutes of bulk fermentation.

5. **DIVIDING AND SHAPING:** Divide the dough into 1.5-pound pieces (or make rolls with smaller pieces). Preshape lightly into rounds and place on a lightly floured work surface, seams up. Cover the rounds with plastic. When the dough has relaxed sufficiently (10 to 20 minutes), shape it into tight round or oval loaves. Place the loaves into floured *bannetons* or onto lightly floured baker's linen and cover with plastic.

6. **FINAL FERMENTATION:** Approximately 1 to 1¼ hours at 75°F.

7. **BAKING:** Invert the risen loaves onto the loading conveyor or peel. Score the loaves as desired. Presteam the oven, load the bread, and steam again. Bake in a 460°F oven. Open the oven vents after the loaves show color, in order to finish the bake in a drying oven. Loaves scaled at 1.5 pounds will bake in approximately 40 minutes.

Beer Bread with Roasted Barley

PRE-FERMENTED FLOUR: 30%

DOUGH YIELD | U.S.: About 23 loaves at 1.5 lb each | Metric: About 25 loaves at .68 kg each | Home: 2 large loaves

OVERALL FORMULA

	U.S.	METRIC	HOME	BAKER'S %
Bread flour	16 lb	8 kg	1 lb, 9.6 oz	80%
Whole-wheat flour	4 lb	2 kg	6.4 oz	20%
Water	6.8 lb	3.4 kg	10.9 oz	34%
Beer	6.8 lb	3.4 kg	10.9 oz	34%
Salt	.4 lb	.2 kg	.6 oz	2%
Yeast	.24 lb, fresh	.12 kg, fresh	.13 oz, instant dry	1.2%
Malted barley	1 lb	.5 kg	1.6 oz	5%
TOTAL YIELD	**35.24 lb**	**17.62 kg**	**3 lb, 8.1 oz**	**176.2%**

POOLISH

Bread flour	6 lb	3 kg	9.6 oz (2¼ cups)	100%
Water	6 lb	3 kg	9.6 oz (1¼ cups)	100%
Yeast	.012 lb, fresh	.006 kg, fresh	(⅛ tsp, instant dry)	.2%
TOTAL	**12.012 lb**	**6.006 kg**	**1 lb, 3.2 oz**	

FINAL DOUGH

Bread flour	10 lb	5 kg	1 lb (3⅝ cups)
Whole-wheat flour	4 lb	2 kg	6.4 oz (1½ cups)
Water	.8 lb	.4 kg	1.3 oz (⅛ cup)
Beer	6.8 lb	3.4 kg	10.9 oz (1⅜ cups)
Salt	.4 lb	.2 kg	.6 oz (1 T)
Yeast	.228 lb, fresh	.114 kg, fresh	.13 oz, instant dry (1¼ tsp)
Malted barley	1 lb	.5 kg	1.6 oz (¼ cup)
Poolish	12.012 lb	6.006 kg	1 lb, 3.2 oz (all of above)
TOTAL	**35.24 lb**	**17.62 kg**	**3 lb, 8.1 oz**

The process of malting involves soaking barley until it sprouts, drying it, and finally grinding it (this is the procedure when malted barley is used at mills and added to wheat flour to

1. POOLISH: Disperse the yeast in the water, add the flour, and mix until smooth. Cover the bowl with plastic and let stand for 12 to 16 hours at about 70°F.

2. PREPARING THE BARLEY: Place the barley on a sheet pan and roast at 350°F, shaking the pan occasionally, for 4 or 5 minutes. This step does two things: It brings out the full nutty flavor of the correct amylase enzyme deficiencies). The soaking makes the barley sweet tasting, and that subtle sweetness comes through in the finished bread in this formula. Malted barley is easy to find at beer-brewing shops, but it is almost always still in its husk. While this is fine when making beer, it obviously is not when using the barley for bread. If husked malted barley is unavailable, unmalted barley can be roasted and used instead.

Working in Germany in the mid-1970s, I was taught a folk expression: "Beer is liquid bread." How true this is, considering the ingredients used for each pursuit. And for centuries the baker obtained his yeast from the brewer—skimming the foam from top-fermenting ales, and the sediment from bottom-fermenting lagers. *Bierbrot*—beer bread—was a daily part of production during my time in Germany. The bread had a hint of sweetness from the beer, along with a subtle bite from the strong southern German brew. Twenty years later, when I was a member of Baking Team USA, beer bread was one of the breads made in Paris at the Coupe du Monde de la Boulangerie (the World Cup of Baking), and it met with great approval. The beer bread detailed here is something of an amalgamation of the two, an unusual specialty bread with a lively, robust flavor.

barley, and it deactivates any enzymes that might otherwise interfere with dough fermentation. Take care to avoid overroasting, which would impart a bitter flavor to the barley. Once the barley has cooled, grind it to the desired degree of coarseness. It should be fairly fine since it will not be softened in a soaker.

3. MIXING: Place all the ingredients in the mixing bowl, including the ground barley and the poolish. When computing the desired dough temperature, mix the beer with the water and cool or warm them accordingly. In a spiral mixer, mix on first speed for 3 minutes in order to incorporate the ingredients. Make corrections to dough consistency as necessary, seeking a dough of moderately loose hydration. Turn the mixer to second speed and mix for 3 minutes. Desired dough temperature: 75°F.

4. BULK FERMENTATION: 2 hours.

5. FOLDING: Fold the dough after 1 hour of bulk fermentation.

6. DIVIDING AND SHAPING: Divide the dough into 1.5-pound pieces (or make rolls with smaller pieces). Preshape lightly into rounds and place on a lightly floured work surface, seams up. Cover the rounds with plastic. When the dough has relaxed sufficiently (10 to 20 minutes), shape it into tight round or oval loaves. Place the loaves into floured *bannetons* or onto lightly floured baker's linen and cover with plastic.

7. FINAL FERMENTATION: Approximately 1 to 1¼ hours at 75°F.

8. BAKING: Invert the risen loaves onto the loading conveyor or peel. Score the loaves as desired. Presteam the oven, load the bread, and steam again. Bake in a 460°F oven. Open the oven vents after the loaves show color, in order to finish the bake in a drying oven. Loaves scaled at 1.5 pounds will bake in approximately 40 minutes.

LEVAIN BREADS

5

The poet is not a "little god." No, he is not a "little god." He is not picked out by a mystical destiny in preference to those who follow other crafts and professions. I have often maintained that the best poet is he who prepares our daily bread: the nearest baker, who does not imagine himself to be a god. He does his majestic and unpretentious work of kneading the dough, consigning it to the oven, baking it in golden colors, and handing us our daily bread as a duty of fellowship. And if the poet succeeds in achieving this simple consciousness, this too will be transformed into an element in an immense activity . . . the handing over of mankind's products: bread, truth, wine, dreams. —PABLO NERUDA, NOBEL ADDRESS, 1971

The art of leavening bread solely by developing the latent characteristics present in grain has been practiced for thousands of years. Our early bread-baking ancestors learned that by skillful and patient fermentation of the flour, thriving cultures of microorganisms could be induced to take up residence in a little bowl of flour paste, and the resulting sourdough culture (levain) could then be used thousands of times—year after year after year—to make bread that was not only light in texture, due to the yeast in the culture, but delicious as well, thanks mostly to the presence of various strains of lactobacilli that contributed to the development of flavor.

For hundreds of years the yeast that was a by-product of the beer-brewing trade was also used by bakers, but for many bakers it was either difficult to procure or cost-prohibitive, so a healthy levain was highly prized.

In central, northern, and eastern Europe, rye grain flourished, tolerating the mediocre soils, cold winters, and humid summers. Rye sourdough cultures naturally found a home here, and along with them all styles of strong-flavored rye breads. In other parts of Europe, such as France, Spain, and Italy, wheat flour grew readily, and the prevailing sourdough cultures were generated from the fermentation of white flour (or whole wheat, or a combination of the two). The levain breads of these regions, too, were mostly based on white and whole-wheat flour, although rye was by no means nonexistent.

Flour Choice

The recommended white flour in the formulas (and the flour of choice for all the levain builds) is winter-wheat bread flour of medium strength— 11.5 to 12 percent protein, and with an ash content of about .5 percent. Stronger flours are not necessary, and with few exceptions high-gluten flours should be avoided. In doughs that have lots of heavy grains to hold up, high-gluten flour might be beneficial, but for the most part, bread work-up and flavor are better with lower-protein flour. Spring wheat with the same protein and ash content can substitute for the winter wheat.

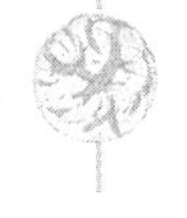

There are two general types of white-flour levain cultures that predominate today: a liquid-style culture and a stiff one. Liquid-levain cultures are usually maintained with a 100 or 125 percent hydration, while stiff levains are in the range of 50 to 60 percent hydration (detailed instructions for making both of these levains begin on page 358). Either of these two may begin its life with all or part rye flour in its initial builds, and even after it has been developed and is in the perpetuation stage of its life, there may be some rye included in its feedings; yet the cultures are overwhelmingly based on white flour. As it may be impractical to perpetuate both a stiff and a liquid culture, it can be helpful to know how to convert one to the other and back again (see page 362 for a description of the technique). With that skill, the baker has the ability to make a greater range of breads.

The breads offered in this chapter present a wide range of flavor characteristics. There are a few styles of everyday *pains au levain*—sourdough breads—as well as several breads that include additional ingredients such as olives and roasted garlic (it is my hope that every baker will learn the subtle art of fermentation—the truest skill of the baker—before exploring bread formulas whose ingredients mask the taste of fermented flour). One aspect of the breads in this section is worth noting: These breads can be mixed and, after suitable fermentation, divided, shaped, proofed, and baked; alternatively, the final fermentation can take place in a walk-in, a refrigerator, or a retarder-proofer, and the bake delayed for as much as 24 hours. This technique not only can aid substantially in structuring a bakery's production schedule, but it also offers enormous possibilities for changing the flavor and aroma characteristics of a bread. One characteristic of levain breads that ferment overnight in a retarder is an increased development of acidity, primarily acetic acid. Some people find the extra acidity tasty, while others prefer the more subdued flavor notes of breads that don't retard overnight. It is up to the baker to decide what flavor profiles best suit the tastes of his clientele and himself.

Building the Culture (also known as "Elaborating")

When we have a bowl of mature culture—either liquid or stiff—weighing a pound or so, and we need to build it up to several pounds, or dozens of pounds, in order to mix dough several hours later, how do we do that? Let's make a few assumptions in order to illustrate the technique. Let's assume we are maintaining a liquid-levain culture at 125 percent hydration, and that we have 1 pound of it, and that we need a total of 15 pounds for bread production (and that in order to perpetuate our culture we will return 1 pound to our bowl once the building is done, so in fact we need 16 pounds total).

We know that regardless of how much mature culture is in our bowl—be it 1 pound or 1 ton—the culture is always comprised of 225 units: 100 units of flour and 125 units of water (hence, the culture is 125 percent hydration). We also know that from the 1 pound presently in the bowl, we need to build another 15 pounds in order to arrive at 16 total pounds. Can we just give it one feeding and let it ripen at its own rate? In a sense the answer is yes, we can do that. It's asking a lot, however, for the microorganisms in our bowl to take in all that food and water at one sitting—after all, we humans could survive if we ate breakfast, lunch, and dinner all at once and nothing else till the next day, but we probably wouldn't feel too good on that sort of eating regimen—and neither would our culture if we bombarded it with such a hefty meal. Therefore, let's do our building in two stages: The first build will bring the culture to half the total desired weight (that is, up to 8 pounds), and the second build will bring it the rest of the way (to 16 pounds). Since we are starting with 1 pound of ripe culture in the bowl, we need to add a total of 7 pounds of flour and water for the first feeding. Here's how: We take what we need—7 pounds—and divide it by the total number of flour/water units in the feeding, that is, 225. The answer tells us what one of those 225 units weighs: $7 \div 225 = .031111$, which we will just slightly round up, because it is better to make a little too much culture than not enough. We will call the weight of one unit .0312 pound. We now take this factor and multiply it by 100 to find out how much flour to feed, and by 125 to find out how much water to feed:

Production Notes for the Formulas in This Chapter

Preparing the Levain Culture. At least 8 hours, or up to 16 hours before the final dough is mixed, the final build of the levain culture should be made. The culture is then left at room temperature, covered with plastic until ripe and ready to mix into bread dough. As mentioned in "Building the Culture" above, it is important to always ripen more culture than is necessary for the production at hand, in order to save a portion and perpetuate it. With liquid-levain cultures, ripeness is indicated by a mildly acidic

.0312 X 100 = 3.12 lb flour

.0312 X 125 = 3.9 lb water

These total 7.02 pounds, and along with the 1 pound of mature culture that we mix the flour and water into, we now have 8.02 pounds after the first build. Stir everything together until smooth, cover, and let it sit for several hours at room temperature until it is ripe (lots of wispy bubbles will form on the surface, and the mixture will have a pleasing sweet and tangy aroma). This could take 6 to 14 hours, depending on the vigor of the original 1 pound of culture. Once ripe, the half-built culture is ready for its second meal.

We now have to take our 8.02 pounds of ripe culture and increase it to 16 pounds. We therefore need a total of 7.98 pounds. That figure is divided by 225 (the number of units of flour and water in the culture), and the answer tells us what one unit will weigh: 7.98 ÷ 225 = .03546. Again we round up, and we'll call the unit weight .0355 pound. We again multiply this unit factor by 100 to find the weight of the flour in this second build, and then by 125 to determine the weight of the water:

.0355 X 100 = 3.55 lb flour

.0355 X 125 = 4.44 lb water

When we add these into the 8.02 pounds of ripe culture from the first build, we now have:

3.55 lb flour

4.44 lb water

8.02 lb ripe culture

16.01 lb total

We let this second feeding ripen for several hours until we see the same signs of ripeness that we saw in the first build. Once ripe, we remove 1 pound of the culture to our bowl in order to perpetuate it, and use the remaining 15 pounds for bread production.

This building principle is the same regardless of what kind of culture is being maintained. The only difference is the number of flour/water units that combine in the culture. If, for example, we maintain a stiff culture of 50 percent hydration, there are 50 units of water for each 100 units of flour, so we divide the required pounds needed for a build by 150 to find out the weight of 1 unit for that particular build. Multiplying that unit weight times 100 tells the needed flour weight for the build, and multiplying by 50 gives the weight of the water. One rule doesn't vary: Always build more culture than you require for the bread production at hand, so that you can save a bit when it's ripe and perpetuate your precious culture.

aroma and a subtle sweetness, as well as by numerous small bubbles, somewhat like soap bubbles, that partially cover the surface. It should have a pleasing tang when tasted, acidic but not aggressively so. With stiff-textured cultures (50 to 60 percent hydration), ripeness is indicated by a domed surface. When the culture has domed and has just barely begun to recede in the center, it is a sign that full ripeness has been achieved. Since many levain breads are leavened solely by the yeasts in the sourdough, it is of the highest importance that the final dough is mixed when the culture is at its prime level of maturity: Poor volume, poor luster to the crust, and deficient eating quality will result if the levain build is either too young or too ripe when it is added to the final mix.

During warm months, or with especially active cultures, ripening may occur in as little as 6 to 8 hours. If bread production isn't practical so few hours after the final build, some adjustments are possible. The baker can:

- **USE A SMALLER PORTION OF MATURE CULTURE FOR THE BUILD.** Fewer mature microorganisms will be available, and ripening will take longer.
- **USE COLDER WATER FOR THE FINAL BUILD AND KEEP THE FINAL BUILD IN A SLIGHTLY COOLER ENVIRONMENT.** This will slow down the rate of activity. But do not refrigerate a just-fed build: It must always ripen before it is chilled.
- **USE A PORTION OF THE DOUGH'S OVERALL SALT IN THE FINAL BUILD.** By adding up to 2 percent salt (maximum), the activity of the microorganisms will be significantly slowed. Even as little as .2 percent salt added will have a slowing effect. This can be a strategically valuable technique.

Preparing the Soaker. A few of the formulas in this chapter use soakers. The soaking makes hard grains palatable and reduces their tendency to break the developing gluten network during mixing; it also reduces their tendency to rob moisture from the dough once it has finished mixing. Cold soakers are made by simply pouring water over the grains, mixing everything together, and covering the bowl or bucket with plastic to prevent evaporation. Hot soakers are made when any of the soaker grains are particularly hard and won't soften sufficiently in cold water. In this case, bring the water to the boil and pour it over the grains. Stir and cover, as for a cold soaker. Salt is sometimes incorporated into the soaker, often the entire amount of overall dough salt, in order to lessen enzymatic activity that might otherwise develop, with the potential of bringing some off flavors to the soaker. It is recommended that the soaker be made when the final levain build is made. Both can then be left at room temperature until the time of the final mix.

Mixing the Final Dough. After removing a small portion of the ripe levain in order to perpetuate the culture, all the ingredients are placed in the mixing bowl. (There are some exceptions to this: Ingredients such as raisins or olives are incorporated at the end of the mix, and when a dough is mixed using the autolyse technique, the salt and the levain culture, in the case of stiff-textured levain, are left out. There is a full discussion of the autolyse technique on page 9.) In a spiral mixer, mix on first speed for about 3 minutes to thoroughly incorporate the ingredients. (Approximate mixing times for other types of mixers are given on page 11.) Check the dough's hydration and make corrections as necessary. It is also a good practice to taste for salt at this time to be certain it has not been inadvertently left out. Turn the mixer to second speed and mix for approximately 3 minutes, until a moderate gluten development has been achieved (combined, the first and second speeds total approximately 900 to 1,000 revolutions). Full gluten development in the mixer would certainly mean overoxidizing the carotenoid pigments and loss of both the wheaty flavor of the flour and the creamy color we see in well-made breads. Rather than mix fully, effective folding of the dough during bulk fermentation will complete the process of building dough strength, with no loss of color or flavor.

There are a few exceptions to the 3-minute mix on second speed: First, when mixing doughs with soakers, another 30 to 60 seconds of mixing may be necessary, since the dough develops a bit more slowly in the presence of soaker grains; second, when using the autolyse technique, only 1½ to 2 minutes of second-speed mixing will be necessary. The dough develops miraculously well during the autolyse, in spite of the lack of mechanical action, and surprisingly little time is needed on second speed to finish the mix. The dough will, in fact, break down rather quickly if overmixed.

Since flour absorption rates can vary significantly from season to season, and since soakers lose sometimes more and sometimes less water to evaporation, it isn't possible to be precisely exact about water quantities in the formulas. It should be noted, however, that looser doughs tend to ferment better, have better volume, and better flavor. For the most part, the doughs in this chapter should have a moderately loose feel to them. The formula's hydration percentage will serve as a guide initially; your hands and experience will ultimately be the best guide.

Bulk Fermentation and Folding. The formulas in this chapter that are completely naturally leavened, with no addition of baker's yeast, require a bulk fermentation of 2 to 3 hours. The number of folds required is determined by the length of their bulk fermentation as well as by how much dough strength was developed during the mix. The gentler the mixing, the more folds necessary to develop proper dough strength. Suffice it to say that no dough should ferment at room temperature for more than 1½ hours without being folded. A dough that goes too long without folding will have an excess buildup of carbon dioxide gas, which can interfere with the yeast's metabolism; one that is folded too frequently becomes too strong, which results in reduced extensibility and volume. As a general guideline, 1 or 2 folds are appropriate for all the breads in this chapter; again, length of bulk fermentation and degree of dough development during dough mixing determine the correct number of folds (a more complete discussion of folding begins on page 15).

Some of the formulas in this section use baker's yeast along with the levain. These doughs require less bulk fermentation than the naturally leavened doughs. One hour is sufficient, and 2 hours is a practical maximum duration. The baker's yeast accelerates the dough's maturity, and the dough will not support a longer bulk fermentation; in fact, beyond 2 hours, there is the risk of the dough becoming overaged, resulting in bread that lacks color and has a lusterless personality.

Dividing and Shaping. In days gone by, it was not uncommon to buy loaves of levain bread that weighed in excess of a dozen pounds. What a marvelous sight that must have been! Nowadays, it's more typical to see bread in the vicinity of a couple of pounds. The breads in this chapter can be appropriately scaled at 1.5 to 2.5 pounds, although larger or slightly smaller weights can also be chosen (the *miche* formulas on pages 164 and 167 seem to come into their own at weights up to 5 pounds or so). Once divided, the dough pieces are preshaped into rounds and placed, seams up, on a floured work surface. Cover them with plastic to prevent crusting, and leave for 15 to 20 minutes, that is, until they are sufficiently relaxed and can be given their final shaping. Most all the breads in this section are suitable in either round or oval shape. Once shaped, place the loaves, seams up, in floured *bannetons*, or with seams either up or down between folds of baker's linen. Cover the shaped loaves with plastic once again. Rolls can be made with many of the breads in this chapter, but it is not recommended that rolls retard overnight before baking. The crust will be extra thick and overly dominate the eating quality. Once shaped, rolls can be placed on sheet pans that have been sprinkled with coarse cornmeal or semolina, and later baked either on the sheet pans or directly on the hearth or baking stone.

Final Fermentation. Naturally leavened breads that are baked the same day as they are formed normally require 2 to 3 hours of proofing at about 75°F before the bake. It can be difficult at first to determine the perfect degree of proofing in naturally leavened breads. As you feel the outside of the loaf with your fingers, try to sense what is going on inside (just as doctors in former times tried to ascertain what was going on inside a patient by feeling his or her outside). The dough should feel light, somewhat loose, somewhat weak. Take heart: If the mixing, folding, and final shaping were done well, and if the hearth or stone is hot and the steam plentiful, that seemingly weak dough will spring exuberantly in the chamber of the oven.

Breads that are intended to retard overnight have different needs. Since fermentation will continue during refrigeration, the bread can't be left at room temperature for too long. If the dough is cool and the fermentation sluggish, the bread can receive upwards of 1 hour of floor time before retarding. During warm months, or with especially vigorous cultures, the bread might be better if the loaves are retarded as soon as they are formed. Experience will be the best guide; unless you work in an environment that is consistent in both temperature and humidity throughout the year, expect that there will be seasonal swings in the needs of the bread. The length of time the bread remains in the retarder will in part determine the best temperature. For breads that retard for up to about 8 hours, a retarder temperature of about 50°F should suffice. As the retarding time increases, the temperature of the retarder correspondingly decreases. Breads retarding for 16 hours need a retarder temperature closer to 40°F (home refrigerators should be about 40°F, and if making any of these breads at home, expect to retard them overnight). After 20 to 24 hours of refrigeration, dough begins to become quite acidic, regardless of the temperature of the retarder.

Last, breads that have a portion of baker's yeast along with the levain require much less time for their final fermentation. At 75° to 78°F, usually 60 to 90 minutes is sufficient, with more time required as the percentage of yeast decreases.

Steaming and Baking. The proofed loaves are transferred to the loading conveyor, seams down, and slashed with a razor. The oven is then steamed (it's always best to load bread into a moist oven) and the bread loaded. Once loaded, steam the oven again. About 8 seconds of total steam should suffice. Often, though, if the dough is a little sluggish or a bit underrisen, I steam again once the first 2 steamings have subsided. This keeps the bread moister a little longer so it can expand more before a crust begins to set on its surface. Never give a third steaming to bread that is at all overrisen: Because the surface stays moister longer, the bread will tend to flatten out. Once the bread begins to show color, the benefits of the steam are past, and the oven vents can be opened so the bread can finish the bake in a drying oven. Generally, oven temperatures of about 460°F are appropriate, and there is no need to reduce the temperature unless the bread is taking on too much color. This may be the case if there are any sweeteners in the dough (honey, raisins, and so on). Bake times given for the individual bread formulas are for round loaves weighing 1.5 pounds. Oval loaves tend to bake slightly quicker. When baking large loaves of 3, 5, or more pounds, the oven temperature should be lowered to about 420°F after about 15 minutes. These loaves require a lengthy bake, and in a very hot oven they would burn long before being properly baked.

How to bake bread that has been retarded overnight? Some people feel that breads should never go from the retarder directly into the oven, the theory being they have to come to room temperature before baking. I have found this to be untrue. If the bread is fully risen when it leaves the retarder, allowing it to come to room temperature before baking is a sure way to get flat bread. After all, when we look at things from the perspective of a hot oven of 460°F or more, there is not that much difference between bread temperature of 40° and 70°F. I would say, therefore, that once again the needs of the bread should dictate our actions. When it's ready, bake it.

Eating. Bad bread should be eaten warm, even hot. The heat helps to mask the defects. Good bread does not begin to taste like itself until it has had ample time to cool. In fact, naturally leavened breads in general taste better a few or even several hours after they have cooled. The crumb firms up and the flavors come together. And for days the bread is good to eat. It is true that the lovely contrast between crust and crumb becomes muted as the bread ages, but other parts of its personality begin to develop. Old bread does not necessarily mean stale bread.

Last Notes: A small portion of baker's yeast—up to .2 percent—can be added to a levain dough without any noticeable changes in the bread's sourdough characteristics. This small amount of yeast will have a slight impact on fermentation and loaf volume. On the other hand, some of the formulas contain yeast in the 1 to 1.25 percent range. When using this amount of yeast, bulk fermentation time can be substantially reduced, a factor that might benefit the baker's production schedule. Breads made with this amount of baker's yeast will of course be less acidic than the same dough made with no added yeast. Flavor characteristics can be adjusted by reducing the amount of yeast used, but remember to increase the length of bulk fermentation as the proportion of fresh yeast is reduced, and also to expect a longer final proofing before the bake.

The weight of the mature culture used in the levain build is not included in the final dough total or in the overall formula total yield, since it is presupposed that the baker will remove that portion prior to the final mix.

Vermont Sourdough

PRE-FERMENTED FLOUR: 15%

DOUGH YIELD | U.S.: About 22 loaves at 1.5 lb each | Metric: About 24 loaves at .68 kg each | Home: 2 large loaves

OVERALL FORMULA

	U.S.	METRIC	HOME	BAKER'S %
Bread flour	18 lb	9 kg	1 lb, 12.8 oz	90%
Whole-rye flour	2 lb	1 kg	3.2 oz	10%
Water	13 lb	6.5 kg	1 lb, 4.8 oz	65%
Salt	.38 lb	.19 kg	.6 oz	1.9%
TOTAL YIELD	**33.38 lb**	**16.69 kg**	**3 lb, 5.4 oz**	**166.9%**

LIQUID-LEVAIN BUILD

	U.S.	METRIC	HOME	BAKER'S %
Bread flour	3 lb	1.5 kg	4.8 oz (1 cup)	100%
Water	3.76 lb	1.88 kg	6 oz (3/4 cup)	125%
Mature culture (liquid)	.6 lb	.3 kg	1 oz (2 T)	20%
TOTAL	**7.36 lb**	**3.68 kg**	**11.8 oz**	

FINAL DOUGH

	U.S.	METRIC	HOME
Bread flour	15 lb	7.5 kg	1 lb, 8 oz (5 1/2 cups)
Whole-rye flour	2 lb	1 kg	3.2 oz (7/8 cup)
Water	9.24 lb	4.62 kg	14.8 oz (1 7/8 cups)
Salt	.38 lb	.19 kg	.6 oz (1 T)
Liquid levain	6.76 lb	3.38 kg	10.8 oz (all less 2 T)
TOTAL	**33.38 lb**	**16.69 kg**	**3 lb, 5.4 oz**

This is an excellent "everyday bread." Variations of this basic *pain au levain*–style bread are found all across the country. We make this bread daily at the King Arthur Flour Bakery, and since the levain culture resides in Vermont, and thus so too the steadily toiling microorganisms that give the bread its distinctive aroma and taste, and since my mother tongue is English, I prefer to simply call this bread Vermont Sourdough.

1. **LIQUID LEVAIN:** Make the final build 12 to 16 hours before the final mix, and let stand in a covered container at about 70°F.

2. **MIXING:** Add all the ingredients to the mixing bowl, including the levain, but not the salt. In a spiral mixer, mix on first speed just until the ingredients are incorporated into a shaggy mass. Correct the hydration as necessary. Cover the bowl with plastic and let stand for an autolyse phase of 20 to 60 minutes. At the end of the autolyse, sprinkle the salt over the surface of the dough, and finish mixing on second speed for 1½ to 2 minutes. The dough should have a medium consistency. Desired dough temperature: 76°F.

3. **BULK FERMENTATION:** 2½ hours.

4. **FOLDING:** Fold the dough either once (after 1¼ hours) or twice (at 50-minute intervals), depending on dough strength.

5. **DIVIDING AND SHAPING:** Divide the dough into 1.5-pound pieces; shape round or oblong.

6. **FINAL FERMENTATION:** Approximately 2 to 2½ hours at 76°F (alternatively, retard for up to 8 hours at 50°F, or up to 18 hours at about 42°F).

7. **BAKING:** With normal steam, 460°F for 40 to 45 minutes. More often than not, this bread is retarded before the bake. The result is a loaf with moderate tanginess and a sturdy crust that conveys a lot of bread flavor.

Vermont Sourdough with Whole Wheat

PRE-FERMENTED FLOUR: 15%

DOUGH YIELD | U.S.: About 22 loaves at 1.5 lb each | Metric: About 24 loaves at .68 kg each | Home: 2 large loaves

OVERALL FORMULA

	U.S.	METRIC	HOME	BAKER'S %
Bread flour	18 lb	9 kg	1 lb, 12.8 oz	90%
Whole-wheat flour	2 lb	1 kg	3.2 oz	10%
Water	13 lb	6.5 kg	1 lb, 4.8 oz	65%
Salt	.38 lb	.19 kg	.6 oz	1.9%
TOTAL YIELD	33.38 lb	16.69 kg	3 lb, 5.4 oz	166.9%

LIQUID-LEVAIN BUILD

Bread flour	3 lb	1.5 kg	4.8 oz (1 cup)	100%
Water	3.75 lb	1.88 kg	6 oz (3/4 cup)	125%
Mature culture (liquid)	.6 lb	.3 kg	1 oz (2 T)	20%
TOTAL	**7.35 lb**	**3.68 kg**	**11.8 oz**	

FINAL DOUGH

Bread flour	15 lb	7.5 kg	1 lb, 8 oz (5 1/2 cups)
Whole-wheat flour	2 lb	1 kg	3.2 oz (3/4 cup)
Water	9.25 lb	4.62 kg	14.8 oz (1 7/8 cups)
Salt	.38 lb	.19 kg	.6 oz (1 T)
Liquid levain	6.75 lb	3.38 kg	10.8 oz (all less 2 T)
TOTAL	**33.38 lb**	**16.69 kg**	**3 lb, 5.4 oz**

Using whole-wheat flour in lieu of rye seems like a trivial substitution, yet even though there is only 10 percent whole-wheat flour in the entire formula, the difference is distinct, enough to warrant giving this bread its own formula.

1. **LIQUID LEVAIN:** Make the final build 12 to 16 hours before the final mix, and let stand in a covered container at about 70°F.

2. **MIXING:** Add all the ingredients to the mixing bowl, including the levain, but not the salt. In a spiral mixer, mix on first speed just until the ingredients are incorporated into a shaggy mass. Correct the hydration as necessary; the dough should have a medium consistency. Cover the bowl with plastic and let stand for an autolyse phase of 20 to 60 minutes. At the end of the autolyse, sprinkle the salt over the surface of the dough, and finish mixing on second speed for 1½ to 2 minutes. Desired dough temperature: 76°F.

3. **BULK FERMENTATION:** 2½ hours.

4. **FOLDING:** Fold the dough either once (after 1¼ hours) or twice (at 50-minute intervals), depending on dough strength.

5. **DIVIDING AND SHAPING:** Divide the dough into 1.5-pound pieces; shape round or oblong.

6. **FINAL FERMENTATION:** Approximately 2 to 2½ hours at 76°F (alternatively, retard for up to 8 hours at 50°F, or up to 18 hours at about 42°F).

7. **BAKING:** With normal steam, 460°F for 40 to 45 minutes. Like the Vermont Sourdough with rye flour, this whole-wheat variation is often retarded before baking, resulting in a crusty loaf with a medium level of acidity.

Vermont Sourdough with Increased Whole Grain

PRE-FERMENTED FLOUR: 20%

DOUGH YIELD | U.S.: About 22 loaves at 1.5 lb each | Metric: About 24 loaves at .68 kg each | Home: 2 large loaves

OVERALL FORMULA

	U.S.	METRIC	HOME	BAKER'S %
Bread flour	17 lb	8.5 kg	11.2 oz	85%
Whole-rye flour	3 lb	1.5 kg	4.8 oz	15%
Water	13 lb	6.5 kg	1 lb, 4.8 oz	65%
Salt	.38 lb	.19 kg	.6 oz	1.9%
TOTAL YIELD	**33.38 lb**	**16.69 kg**	**3 lb, 5.4 oz**	**166.9%**

LIQUID-LEVAIN BUILD

Bread flour	4 lb	2 kg	3.2 oz (3/4 cups)	100%
Water	5 lb	2.5 kg	4 oz (1/2 cup)	125%
Mature culture (liquid)	.8 lb	.4 kg	.7 oz (1 1/2 T)	20%
TOTAL	**9.8 lb**	**4.9 kg**	**7.9 oz**	

FINAL DOUGH

Bread flour	13 lb	6.5 kg	8 oz (5 1/2 cups)
Whole-rye flour	3 lb	1.5 kg	4.8 oz (1 1/4 cups)
Water	8 lb	4 kg	.8 oz (2 7/8 cups)
Liquid levain	9 lb	4.5 kg	7.2 oz (all less 1 1/2 T)
Salt	.38 lb	.19 kg	.6 oz (1 T)
TOTAL	**33.38 lb**	**16.69 kg**	**3 lb, 5.4 oz**

There are two small changes in this formula compared to the Vermont Sourdough on page 153—an increase in pre-fermented flour from 15 to 20 percent, and an increase in whole-grain flour from 10 to 15 percent—yet the effect on the dough is surprisingly large. The whole-rye flour offers considerable fermentable sugars and minerals to the yeasts in the levain culture, and

1. **LIQUID LEVAIN:** Make the final build 12 to 16 hours before the final mix, and let stand in a covered container at about 70°F.

2. **MIXING:** Add all the ingredients to the mixing bowl, including the levain, but not the salt. In a spiral mixer, mix on first speed just until the ingredients are incorporated into a shaggy mass. Correct the hydration as necessary; the dough should have a medium consistency. Cover the bowl with plastic and let stand for an autolyse phase of 20 to 60 minutes. At the end of the autolyse, sprinkle the salt over the surface of the dough, and finish mixing on second speed for 1½ to 2 minutes. Desired dough temperature: 76°F.

this, combined with the increased proportion of ripe culture in the dough, produces a bread that is more acidic than the preceding ones. From a flavor perspective, this bread has a sharper tang and more of a whole-grain taste. Another effect of the increased acidity is a reduced extensibility, due to the acidity's tightening effect on the gluten structure. Therefore, loaf volume will not be as great with this bread as in the two preceding ones. One fold might be preferable to 2 for this dough, as a second fold might bring too much strength to the dough. The whole-rye flour can be replaced with either medium-rye flour or whole-wheat flour. When mixing the dough, check the hydration carefully. Rye is quite absorbent, and a bit of extra water might need to be added to achieve a dough of medium consistency.

3. **BULK FERMENTATION:** 2½ hours.

4. **FOLDING:** Fold the dough once, after 1¼ hours.

5. **DIVIDING AND SHAPING:** Divide the dough into 1.5-pound pieces; shape round or oblong.

6. **FINAL FERMENTATION:** Approximately 2 to 2½ hours at 76°F (alternatively, retard for up to 8 hours at 50°F, or up to 18 hours at about 42°F).

7. **BAKING:** With normal steam, 460°F for 40 to 45 minutes.

Pain au Levain (Sourdough Bread)

PRE-FERMENTED FLOUR: 15.5%

DOUGH YIELD | U.S.: About 22 loaves at 1.5 lb each | Metric: About 24 loaves at .68 kg each | Home: 2 large loaves

OVERALL FORMULA

	U.S.	METRIC	HOME	BAKER'S %
Bread flour	19 lb	9.5 kg	1 lb, 14.4 oz	95%
Medium rye flour	1 lb	.5 kg	1.6 oz	5%
Water	13 lb	6.5 kg	1 lb, 4.8 oz	65%
Salt	.36 lb	.18 kg	.6 oz	1.8%
TOTAL YIELD	**33.36 lb**	**16.68 kg**	**3 lb, 5.4 oz**	**166.8%**

LEVAIN BUILD

	U.S.	METRIC	HOME	BAKER'S %
Bread flour	2.9 lb	1.45 kg	4.6 oz (1 cup)	93.5%
Medium rye flour	.2 lb	.1 kg	.3 oz (1/8 cup)	6.5%
Water	1.86 lb	.93 kg	3 oz (3/8 cup)	60%
Mature culture (stiff)	.62 lb	.31 kg	1 oz (2 T)	20%
TOTAL	**5.58 lb**	**2.79 kg**	**8.9 oz**	

FINAL DOUGH

	U.S.	METRIC	HOME
Bread flour	16.1 lb	8.05 kg	1 lb, 9.8 oz (5 7/8 cups)
Medium rye flour	.8 lb	.4 kg	1.3 oz (3/8 cup)
Water	11.14 lb	5.57 kg	1 lb, 1.8 oz (2 1/4 cups)
Salt	.36 lb	.18 kg	.6 oz (1 T)
Levain	4.96 lb	2.48 kg	7.9 oz (all less 2 T)
TOTAL	**33.36 lb**	**16.68 kg**	**3 lb, 5.4 oz**

1. **STIFF-TEXTURED LEVAIN:** Make the final build approximately 12 hours before the final mix, and let stand in a covered container at about 70°F. During hot weather, or if the levain will ripen for longer than 12 hours, the flour in the levain build can be salted at 1.8 percent to slow its activity.

2. **MIXING:** Add all the ingredients to the mixing bowl except the salt and the levain. In a spiral mixer, mix on first speed just until the ingredients are incorporated into a shaggy mass. Correct the hydration as necessary. Cover the bowl with plastic and let stand for an autolyse phase of 20 to 60 minutes. At the end of the auto-

This bread is so emphatically French that it retains its French name here. A stiff-textured levain is used to generate the fermentation. When baked the same day it is mixed, the bread has a delicate flavor, an open cell structure, and a beautiful russet crust. Retarding overnight is not recommended, as many of the more graceful and delicate characteristics of the bread will be lost during the long cold time in refrigeration.

lyse, sprinkle the salt over the surface of the dough, cut the levain into fist-sized chunks and place on top of the dough, and finish mixing on second speed for 1½ to 2 minutes. The dough should be supple, with a medium consistency. Desired dough temperature: 76°F.

3. **BULK FERMENTATION:** 2½ hours.

4. **FOLDING:** Fold the dough twice, at 50-minute intervals.

5. **DIVIDING AND SHAPING:** Divide the dough into 1.5-pound pieces; shape round or oblong.

6. **FINAL FERMENTATION:** Approximately 2 to 2½ hours at 76°F.

7. **BAKING:** With normal steam, 440°F for 40 to 45 minutes.

Pain au Levain with Whole-Wheat Flour

PRE-FERMENTED FLOUR: 15.5%

DOUGH YIELD | U.S.: About 22 loaves at 1.5 lb each | Metric: About 25 loaves at .68 kg each | Home: 2 large loaves

OVERALL FORMULA

	U.S.	METRIC	HOME	BAKER'S %
Bread flour	15 lb	7.5 kg	1 lb, 8 oz	75%
Whole-wheat flour	4 lb	2 kg	6.4 oz	20%
Medium rye flour	1 lb	.5 kg	1.6 oz	5%
Water	13.6 lb	6.8 kg	1 lb, 5.8 oz	68%
Salt	.36 lb	.18 kg	.6 oz	1.8%
TOTAL YIELD	**33.96 lb**	**16.98 kg**	**3 lb, 6.4 oz**	**169.8%**

LEVAIN BUILD

	U.S.	METRIC	HOME	BAKER'S %
Bread flour	2.9 lb	1.45 kg	4.6 oz (1 cup)	93.5%
Medium rye flour	.2 lb	.1 kg	.3 oz (1/8 cup)	6.5%
Water	1.86 lb	.93 kg	3 oz (3/8 cup)	60%
Mature culture (stiff)	.62 lb	.31 kg	1 oz (2 T)	20%
TOTAL	**5.58 lb**	**2.79 kg**	**8.9 oz**	

FINAL DOUGH

	U.S.	METRIC	HOME
Bread flour	12.1 lb	6.05 kg	1 lb, 3.4 oz (4 1/2 cups)
Medium rye flour	.8 lb	.4 kg	1.3 oz (3/8 cup)
Whole-wheat flour	4 lb	2 kg	6.4 oz (1 1/2 cups)
Water	11.74 lb	5.87 kg	1 lb, 2.8 oz (2 3/8 cups)
Salt	.36 lb	.18 kg	.6 oz (1 T)
Levain	4.96 lb	2.48 kg	7.9 oz (all less 2 T)
TOTAL	**33.96 lb**	**16.98 kg**	**3 lb, 6.4 oz**

1. **STIFF-TEXTURED LEVAIN:** Make the final build approximately 12 hours before the final mix. During hot weather, or if the levain will ripen for longer than 12 hours, the flour in the levain build can be salted at 1.8 percent to slow its activity.

2. **MIXING:** Add all the ingredients to the mixing bowl except the salt and levain. In a spiral mixer, mix on first speed just until the ingredients are incorporated into a shaggy mass. Correct the hydration as necessary; the addition of a bit more water may be necessary depending on the absorption of the whole-wheat and rye

The addition of whole-wheat flour to this *pain au levain* brings the percentage of whole-wheat and rye flours up to 25 percent, and this has quite a perceptible effect on the bread's flavor. The volume may be slightly smaller, and cell structure slightly less open, yet the bread has a clean flavor and a balanced acidity that will make it compatible with a wide range of foods.

flours. The consistency of the dough should be medium—neither dry nor overly moist. Cover the bowl with plastic and let stand for an autolyse phase of 20 to 60 minutes. At the end of the autolyse, sprinkle the salt over the surface of the dough, cut the levain into fist-sized chunks and place on top of the dough, and finish mixing on second speed for 1½ to 2 minutes. Desired dough temperature: 76°F.

3. **BULK FERMENTATION:** 2½ hours.

4. **FOLDING:** Fold the dough twice, at 50-minute intervals.

5. **DIVIDING AND SHAPING:** Divide the dough into 1.5-pound pieces; shape round or oblong.

6. **FINAL FERMENTATION:** Approximately 2 to 2½ hours at 76°F (alternatively, retard for up to 8 hours at 50°F, or up to 18 hours at about 42°F).

7. **BAKING:** With normal steam, 440°F for 40 to 45 minutes.

Pain au Levain with Mixed Sourdough Starters

PRE-FERMENTED FLOUR: 16%

DOUGH YIELD | U.S.: About 22 loaves at 1.5 lb each | Metric: About 25 loaves at .68 kg each | Home: 2 large loaves

OVERALL FORMULA

	U.S.	METRIC	HOME	BAKER'S %
Bread flour	16.8 lb	8.4 kg	1 lb, 10.9 oz	84%
Whole-rye flour	1.6 lb	.8 kg	2.6 oz	8%
Whole-wheat flour	1.6 lb	.8 kg	2.6 oz	8%
Water	13.6 lb	6.8 kg	1 lb, 5.8 oz	68%
Salt	.36 lb	.18 kg	.6 oz	1.8%
TOTAL YIELD	**33.96 lb**	**16.98 kg**	**3 lb, 6.5 oz**	**169.8%**

LIQUID-LEVAIN BUILD

	U.S.	METRIC	HOME	BAKER'S %
Bread flour	1.6 lb	.8 kg	2.6 oz (5/8 cup)	100%
Water	2 lb	1 kg	3.2 oz (3/8 cup)	125%
Mature culture (liquid)	.32 lb	.16 kg	.5 oz (1 T)	20%
TOTAL	**3.92 lb**	**1.96 kg**	**6.3 oz**	

RYE SOURDOUGH BUILD

	U.S.	METRIC	HOME	BAKER'S %
Whole-rye flour	1.6 lb	.8 kg	2.6 oz (3/4 cup)	100%
Water	1.32 lb	.66 kg	2.1 oz (1/4 cup)	83%
Mature culture	.08 lb	.04 kg	.1 oz (1 tsp)	5%
TOTAL	**3 lb**	**1.5 kg**	**4.8 oz**	

FINAL DOUGH

	U.S.	METRIC	HOME
Bread flour	15.2 lb	7.6 kg	1 lb, 8.3 oz (5 1/2 cups)
Whole-wheat flour	1.6 lb	.8 kg	2.7 oz (5/8 cup)
Water	10.28 lb	5.14 kg	1 lb, .4 oz (2 cups)
Salt	.36 lb	.18 kg	.6 oz (1 T)
Liquid levain	3.6 lb	1.8 kg	5.8 oz (all less 1 T)
Rye sourdough	2.92 lb	1.46 kg	4.7 oz (all less 1 tsp)
TOTAL	**33.96 lb**	**16.98 kg**	**3 lb, 6.5 oz**

This *pain au levain* incorporates two starters: a sourdough rye and a liquid levain. Each contributes different flavor characteristics to produce a full-flavored bread, in spite of the relatively low percentage of pre-fermented flour.

1. **LIQUID LEVAIN:** Make the final build approximately 12 hours before the final mix.

2. **RYE SOURDOUGH:** Disperse the mature culture into the water, add the rye flour, and mix thoroughly. Sprinkle a light layer of rye flour on top of the paste, cover, and let stand at about 70°F for 12 to 16 hours, or until the sourdough has domed but not collapsed.

3. **MIXING:** Add all the ingredients to the mixing bowl except the salt. In a spiral mixer, mix on first speed just until the ingredients are incorporated into a shaggy mass. Cover the bowl with plastic and let stand for an autolyse phase of 20 to 60 minutes. At the end of the autolyse, sprinkle the salt over the surface of the dough, and finish mixing on second speed for 1½ to 2 minutes. Desired dough temperature: 76°F.

4. **BULK FERMENTATION:** 2½ hours.

5. **FOLDING:** Fold the dough twice, at 50-minute intervals.

6. **DIVIDING AND SHAPING:** Divide the dough into 1.5-pound pieces; shape round or oblong.

7. **FINAL FERMENTATION:** Approximately 2 to 2½ hours at 76°F (alternatively, retard for up to 8 hours at 50°F, or up to 18 hours at about 42°F).

8. **BAKING:** With normal steam, 460°F for about 40 to 45 minutes.

Miche, Pointe-à-Callière

PRE-FERMENTED FLOUR: 20%

DOUGH YIELD | U.S.: About 7 loaves at 5 lb each | Metric: About 8 loaves at 2.25 kg each | Home: 1 very large loaf

OVERALL FORMULA

	U.S.	METRIC	HOME	BAKER'S %
High-extraction whole-wheat flour	20 lb	10 kg	2 lb	100%
Water	16.4 lb	8.2 kg	1 lb, 10.2 oz	82%
Salt	.36 lb	.18 kg	.6 oz	1.8%
TOTAL YIELD	**36.76 lb**	**18.38 kg**	**3 lb, 10.8 oz**	**183.8%**

LEVAIN BUILD

	U.S.	METRIC	HOME	BAKER'S %
High-extraction whole-wheat flour	4 lb	2 kg	6.4 oz (1½ cups)	100%
Water	2.4 lb	1.2 kg	3.8 oz (½ cup)	60%
Mature culture (stiff)	.8 lb	.4 kg	1.3 oz (3 T)	20%
TOTAL	**7.2 lb**	**3.6 kg**	**11.5 oz**	

FINAL DOUGH

	U.S.	METRIC	HOME
High-extraction whole-wheat flour	16 lb	8 kg	1 lb, 9.6 oz (5½ cups)
Water	14 lb	7 kg	1 lb, 6.4 oz (2¾ cups)
Salt	.36 lb	.18 kg	.6 oz (1 T)
Levain	6.4 lb	3.2 kg	10.2 oz (all less 3 T)
TOTAL	**36.76 lb**	**18.38 kg**	**3 lb, 10.8 oz**

1. **STIFF-TEXTURED LEVAIN:** Make the final build approximately 12 hours before the final mix, and let stand in a covered container at about 70°F. During hot weather, or if the levain will ripen for longer than 12 hours, the flour in the levain build can be salted at 1.8 percent to slow its activity.

2. **MIXING:** Add all the ingredients to the mixing bowl except the salt and the levain. In a spiral mixer, mix on first speed just until the ingredients are incorporated into a shaggy mass. Cover the bowl with plastic and let stand for an autolyse phase of 20 to 60 minutes. At the end of the autolyse, sprinkle the salt over the surface of the dough, cut the levain into fist-sized chunks and place them on top of the dough, and finish mixing on second speed for

I originally tasted this remarkable bread from the hands of bread-master James MacGuire of Montreal. James developed this bread as an authentic rendition of the type of bread typically eaten by the early European settlers of Canada (Pointe à Callière was the site of Montreal's original settlement, on the banks of the St. Lawrence River). I offer it here with very slight modification. The dough is quite soft, and is meant to be. The baked loaves are large, somewhat flat in appearance, with large interior air holes, a chewy crumb, and an excellent keeping quality. I use a high-extraction flour with an ash content of about .92 percent. Some of the bran and most of the germ have been removed before milling, and in the bag the flour looks like a light whole wheat. (*Extraction* is a term that denotes the degree of milling. If all the bran and germ are removed, about 75 percent of the wheat berry remains, and when it is ground into white flour, that flour is considered 75 percent extraction.) If high-extraction whole-wheat flour is unavailable, the flour proportions in this formula can be changed: Use a blend of 85 to 90 percent complete whole-wheat flour (that is, 100 percent extraction) and for the remaining portion use white bread flour.

2 to 2½ minutes. The dough will be quite loose, and the gluten network should be only moderately developed. Desired dough temperature: 76°F.

3. BULK FERMENTATION: 2½ hours.

4. FOLDING: Fold the dough twice, at 50-minute intervals. Use the folds as a last opportunity to bring strength to the dough. Because of the wet nature of the dough, be sure to have ample dusting flour on the work surface when the dough is turned out for folding and dividing. If the bread has been mixed in a small stand mixer, a third fold may be necessary to help maximize dough strength. In that case, fold at 40-minute intervals.

5. DIVIDING AND SHAPING: Scale the dough pieces at 5 pounds each. Lightly preshape, allow the dough to relax, and give it a gentle final rounding. Place the loaves, seams up, on well-floured baker's linen or proofing baskets. Having the seams up during the final proofing encourages the loaves to have a low profile after the bake, a characteristic of this bread. After shaping, the loaves should be covered to prevent crusting from air currents. Due to the wet nature of the dough, however, it is best if nothing touches the exposed side. In the professional bakery, leaving the bread on a rack with a vinyl cover works best. At home, covering the loaf with a large bowl or even a cardboard box will do nicely.

6. FINAL FERMENTATION: Approximately 2 to 2½ hours at 76°F. This bread does not favor overnight fermentation.

7. BAKING: With normal steam, 440°F for about 60 minutes. Reduce the oven temperature to 420°F after 15 minutes. Due to the high water content, the bread requires a long and full bake. Cool thoroughly on racks, wrap in baker's linen, and let the bread's flavors meld for at least 12 hours before slicing. It is a great joy to see the eating quality of this bread transform over the course of several days—the flour's wheat flavor intensifies and the bread's acidity increases slightly as the loaf ages.

Mixed-Flour Miche

PRE-FERMENTED FLOUR: 20%

DOUGH YIELD | U.S.: About 7 loaves at 5 lb each | Metric: About 8 loaves at 2.25 kg each | Home: 1 very large loaf

OVERALL FORMULA

	U.S.	METRIC	HOME	BAKER'S %
High-extraction whole-wheat flour	12 lb	6 kg	1 lb, 3.2 oz	60%
Whole-rye flour	4 lb	2 kg	6.4 oz	20%
Bread flour	4 lb	2 kg	6.4 oz	20%
Water	16.6 lb	8.3 kg	1 lb, 10.6 oz	83%
Salt	.36 lb	.18 kg	.6 oz	1.8%
TOTAL YIELD	**36.96 lb**	**18.48 kg**	**3 lb, 11.2 oz**	**184.8%**

LEVAIN BUILD

	U.S.	METRIC	HOME	BAKER'S %
High-extraction whole-wheat flour	2 lb	1 kg	3.2 oz (3/4 cup)	50%
Whole-rye flour	2 lb	1 kg	3.2 oz (7/8 cup)	50%
Water	2.8 lb	1.4 kg	4.5 oz (1/2 cup)	70%
Mature culture (stiff)	.8 lb	.4 kg	1.3 oz (3 T)	20%
TOTAL	**7.6 lb**	**3.8 kg**	**12.2 oz**	

FINAL DOUGH

	U.S.	METRIC	HOME
High-extraction whole-wheat flour	10 lb	5 kg	1 lb (3 1/2 cups)
Whole-rye flour	2 lb	1 kg	3.2 oz (7/8 cup)
Bread flour	4 lb	2 kg	6.4 oz (1 1/2 cups)
Water	13.8 lb	6.9 kg	1 lb, 6.1 oz (2 3/4 cups)
Salt	.36 lb	.18 kg	.6 oz (1 T)
Levain	6.8 lb	3.4 kg	10.9 oz (all less 3 T)
TOTAL	**36.96 lb**	**18.48 kg**	**3 lb, 11.2 oz**

1. **STIFF-TEXTURED LEVAIN:** Make the final build approximately 12 hours before the final mix, and let stand in a covered container at about 70°F. During hot weather, or if the levain will ripen for longer than 12 hours, the flour in the levain build can be salted at 1.8 percent to slow its activity.

2. **MIXING:** Add all the ingredients to the mixing bowl except the salt and the levain. In a spiral mixer, mix on first speed just until

This *miche* has some characteristics similar to the preceding one—the dough is fairly loose, the loaves are large, the cross section of the sliced loaf is rather flat, the crumb is attractively open, and the keeping quality is excellent. The present bread, like the preceding *miche*, is similar to the type of large, naturally fermented whole-grain loaves that were common on country tables for centuries throughout many parts of Europe. The flavor is different in the present loaf, due to the inclusion of some whole rye and the exchange of some white flour for part of the high-extraction wheat used in the previous formula. Whole-rye flour is preferred for its full flavor, but if unobtainable, medium rye can be substituted. If high-extraction whole-wheat flour can't be found, complete whole-wheat flour (that is, 100 percent extraction) can be substituted.

the ingredients are incorporated into a shaggy mass. Cover the bowl with plastic and let stand for an autolyse phase of 20 to 60 minutes. At the end of the autolyse, sprinkle the salt over the surface of the dough, cut the levain into fist-sized chunks and place them on top of the dough, and finish mixing on second speed for 2 to 2½ minutes. The dough will be wet, and the gluten network should be only moderately developed. Desired dough temperature: 76°F.

3. BULK FERMENTATION: 2½ hours.

4. FOLDING: Fold the dough twice, at 50-minute intervals. If the bread has been mixed in a small stand mixer, a third fold may be necessary to help maximize dough strength. In that case, fold at 40-minute intervals.

5. DIVIDING AND SHAPING: Scale the dough pieces at 5 pounds each. Lightly preshape, allow the dough to relax 5 to 10 minutes, and give it a gentle final rounding. Place the loaves, seams up, on well-floured baker's linen or proofing baskets. Having the seams up encourages the loaves to have a low profile after the bake, a characteristic of this bread. Protect the bread from air currents either by proofing it on racks fitted with vinyl covers or, for the home baker, by covering the loaf with a large bowl or cardboard box.

6. FINAL FERMENTATION: Approximately 2 to 2½ hours at 76°F. This bread does not favor overnight fermentation.

7. BAKING: With normal steam, 440°F for about 60 minutes. Reduce the oven temperature to 420°F after 15 minutes. Due to the high water content, this bread requires a long and full bake. Cool thoroughly on racks, wrap in baker's linen, and resist the (understandable) temptation to cut into the loaf until it has rested for 12 hours, allowing the flavors and the crumb to set.

Whole-Wheat Levain

PRE-FERMENTED FLOUR: 15%

DOUGH YIELD | U.S.: About 22 loaves at 1.5 lb each | Metric: About 25 loaves at .68 kg each | Home: 2 large loaves

OVERALL FORMULA

	U.S.	METRIC	HOME	BAKER'S %
Whole-wheat flour	10 lb	5 kg	1 lb	50%
Bread flour	10 lb	5 kg	1 lb	50%
Water	13.8 lb	6.9 kg	1 lb, 6.1 oz	69%
Salt	.36 lb	.18 kg	.6 oz	1.8%
TOTAL YIELD	34.16 lb	17.08 kg	3 lb, 6.7 oz	170.8%

LIQUID-LEVAIN BUILD

	U.S.	METRIC	HOME	BAKER'S %
Whole-wheat flour	3 lb	1.5 kg	4.8 oz (1 1/8 cups)	100%
Water	3 lb	1.5 kg	4.8 oz (5/8 cup)	100%
Mature culture (liquid)	.6 lb	.3 kg	1 oz (2 T)	20%
TOTAL	6.6 lb	3.3 kg	10.6 oz	

FINAL DOUGH

	U.S.	METRIC	HOME
Whole-wheat flour	7 lb	3.5 kg	11.2 oz (2 1/2 cups)
Bread flour	10 lb	5 kg	1 lb (4 1/2 cups)
Water	10.8 lb	5.4 kg	1 lb, 1.3 oz (2 1/8 cups)
Salt	.36 lb	.18 kg	.6 oz (1 T)
Levain	6 lb	3 kg	9.6 oz (all less 2 T)
TOTAL	34.16 lb	17.08 kg	3 lb, 6.7 oz

The pre-ferment used in this bread is essentially a poolish (100 percent hydration), with natural sourdough starter used in lieu of baker's yeast. The protease enzyme degrades flour protein, and is quite active in a liquid environment such as the loose-textured starter used here. This results in a dough with high extensibility, which in turn helps give the bread a reduced elasticity, good volume, and a lightness that it would otherwise lack.

1. **WHOLE-WHEAT POOLISH:** Approximately 12 to 14 hours before the final mix, make the poolish by dispersing the mature culture in the water and mixing in the whole-wheat flour. Let stand in a covered container at about 70°F.

2. **MIXING:** Add all the ingredients to the mixing bowl. In a spiral mixer, mix on first speed for 3 minutes to incorporate all the ingredients. Correct the hydration as necessary. The dough should be of medium looseness. Finish the mix on second speed for 2 to 2½ minutes. The gluten network should be only moderately developed. Desired dough temperature: 76°F.

3. **BULK FERMENTATION:** 2½ hours.

4. FOLDING: Fold the dough twice, at 50-minute intervals.

5. DIVIDING AND SHAPING: Divide the dough into 1.5-pound pieces; shape round or oblong.

6. FINAL FERMENTATION: Approximately 2 to 2½ hours at 76°F (alternatively, retard for up to 8 hours at 50°F, or up to 18 hours at about 42°F).

7. BAKING: With normal steam, 460°F for 40 to 45 minutes.

Whole-Wheat Multigrain

PRE-FERMENTED FLOUR: 12%

DOUGH YIELD | U.S.: About 26 loaves at 1.5 lb each | Metric: About 29 loaves at .68 kg each | Home: 2 large loaves

OVERALL FORMULA

	U.S.	METRIC	HOME	BAKER'S %
Bread flour	10 lb	5 kg	1 lb	50%
Whole-wheat flour	10 lb	5 kg	1 lb	50%
Grains, assorted	3.6 lb	1.8 kg	5.8 oz	18%
Water	15 lb	7.5 kg	1 lb, 8 oz	75%
Salt	.44 lb	.22 kg	.7 oz	2.2%
Yeast	.2 lb, fresh	.1 kg, fresh	.1 oz, instant dry	1%
Honey	.6 lb	.3 kg	1 oz	3%
TOTAL YIELD	**39.84 lb**	**19.92 kg**	**3 lb, 15.6 oz**	**199.2%**

LIQUID-LEVAIN BUILD

	U.S.	METRIC	HOME	BAKER'S %
Bread flour	2.4 lb	1.2 kg	3.8 oz (7/8 cup)	100%
Water	3 lb	1.5 kg	4.8 oz (5/8 cup)	125%
Mature culture (liquid)	.48 lb	.24 kg	.8 oz (1½ T)	20%
TOTAL	**5.88 lb**	**2.94 kg**	**9.4 oz**	

SOAKER

	U.S.	METRIC	HOME	BAKER'S %
Grains (see headnote)	3.6 lb	1.8 kg	5.8 oz (1 3/8 cups)	100%
Water	4.32 lb	2.16 kg	6.9 oz (7/8 cup)	120%
TOTAL	**7.92 lb**	**3.96 kg**	**12.7 oz**	

FINAL DOUGH

Bread flour	7.6 lb	3.8 kg	12.2 oz (2¾ cups)
Whole-wheat flour	10 lb	5 kg	1 lb (4⅜ cups)
Water	7.68 lb	3.84 kg	12.3 oz (1½ cups)
Salt	.44 lb	.22 kg	.7 oz (1 T + ½ tsp)
Yeast	.2 lb, fresh	.1 kg, fresh	.1 oz, instant dry (1 tsp)
Honey	.6 lb	.3 kg	1 oz (1 T + 1 tsp)
Soaker	7.92 lb	3.96 kg	12.7 oz (all of above)
Liquid levain	5.4 lb	2.7 kg	8.6 oz (all less 1½ T)
TOTAL	**39.84 lb**	**19.92 kg**	**3 lb, 15.6 oz**

Soaked grains bring an added wheat flavor to this bread, and the honey contributes a mild sweet note. Bulk fermentation is only 1 to 2 hours because of the inclusion of baker's yeast, so the bread is suffused with wheat flavor but has little acidity. It is possible to buy grain blends from any number of ingredient suppliers, or you can make your own. Among the various grains and seeds suitable for the soaker are oats, millet, coarse cornmeal, cracked wheat or rye, flaxseeds, barley, sunflower seeds, and sesame seeds. These can be used in whatever combination is desired.

1. **LIQUID LEVAIN:** Make the final build 12 to 16 hours before the final mix, and let stand in a covered container at about 70°F.

2. **SOAKER:** Pour water over the grain blend, mix thoroughly, and cover with plastic to prevent evaporation. If particularly coarse grains are used, such as cracked wheat or rye, millet, coarse cornmeal, or barley, first boil the water and then pour it over the grains. Some or all of the dough's salt can be included in the soaker to inhibit enzymatic activity. Make the soaker right after the final build of the levain, cover the container with plastic, and let stand at room temperature.

3. **MIXING:** Add all the ingredients to the mixing bowl. In a spiral mixer, mix on first speed for 3 minutes. Check the hydration, adding water if necessary to achieve a dough of medium looseness. Turn the mixer to second speed and mix for 2½ to 3½ minutes. The dough should have a moderate gluten development. Desired dough temperature: 76°F.

4. **BULK FERMENTATION:** 1 to 2 hours.

5. **FOLDING:** If the bulk fermentation will last 2 hours, fold after 1 hour.

6. **DIVIDING AND SHAPING:** Divide the dough into 1.5-pound pieces; shape round or oblong.

7. **FINAL FERMENTATION:** Approximately 1 hour at 76°F.

8. **BAKING:** With normal steam, 460°F for 40 to 45 minutes. The oven temperature can be lowered by 15° to 20°F partway through the bake if the bread is taking on color too quickly.

Semolina Bread

PRE-FERMENTED FLOUR: 15%

DOUGH YIELD | U.S.: About 23 loaves at 1.5 lb each | Metric: About 25 loaves at .68 kg each | Home: 2 large loaves

OVERALL FORMULA

	U.S.	METRIC	HOME	BAKER'S %
Bread flour	**8 lb**	**4 kg**	**12.8 oz**	**40%**
Durum flour	**12 lb**	**6 kg**	**1 lb, 3.2 oz**	**60%**
Water	**13.4 lb**	**6.7 kg**	**1 lb, 5.4 oz**	**67%**
Salt	**.4 lb**	**.2 kg**	**.6 oz**	**2%**
Sesame seeds, toasted	**1 lb**	**.5 kg**	**1.6 oz**	**5%**
TOTAL YIELD	**34.8 lb**	**17.4 kg**	**3 lb, 7.6 oz**	**174%**

LIQUID-LEVAIN BUILD

	U.S.	METRIC	HOME	BAKER'S %
Bread flour	3 lb	1.5 kg	4.8 oz (1⅛ cups)	100%
Water	3.75 lb	1.875 kg	6 oz (¾ cup)	125%
Mature culture (liquid)	.6 lb	.3 kg	1 oz (2 T)	20%
TOTAL	**7.35 lb**	**3.675 kg**	**11.8 oz**	

FINAL DOUGH

	U.S.	METRIC	HOME
Bread flour	5 lb	2.5 kg	8 oz (1⅞ cups)
Durum flour	12 lb	6 kg	1 lb, 3.2 oz (4¼ cups)
Water	9.65 lb	4.825 kg	15.4 oz (2 cups)
Salt	.4 lb	.2 kg	.6 oz (1 T)
Sesame seeds, toasted (see headnote)	1 lb	.5 kg	1.6 oz (⅜ cup)
Liquid levain	6.75 lb	3.375 kg	10.8 oz (all less 2 T)
TOTAL	**34.8 lb**	**17.4 kg**	**3 lb, 7.6 oz**

1. LIQUID LEVAIN: Make the final build 12 to 16 hours before the final mix and let stand in a covered container at about 70°F.

2. MIXING: Add all the ingredients to the mixing bowl. In a spiral mixer, mix on first speed for 3 minutes. Correct the hydration as necessary, keeping the dough just slightly drier than normal. Turn the mixer to second speed and mix for 2 to 2½ minutes. Durum flour, in spite of its high protein level, has a tendency to break down in the mixer. Keep a good eye on the dough as it mixes—it

A high percentage of durum flour gives this bread a soft golden color, quite attractive to behold. Lightly toasting the sesame seeds for 5 or 6 minutes at 380°F and mixing them in with the dough adds a pronounced nuttiness to the flavor of the bread, but they are an optional ingredient and can be left out of the dough entirely. Sesame seeds can also be used to coat the outer surface of the bread by pressing the top of the loaf in a wet cloth once it has been shaped, then pressing it into a tray of raw sesame seeds.

will develop in the bowl more quickly than a dough made with all white flour, but it has little tolerance for excess mixing and will quickly unknit. If the dough's surface begins to look shiny, as if it is beginning to release water, it is entering the danger zone—turn off the mixer at once! Desired dough temperature: 76°F.

3. **BULK FERMENTATION:** 2 hours.

4. **FOLDING:** Fold the dough once, after 1 hour.

5. **DIVIDING AND SHAPING:** Divide the dough into 1.5-pound pieces; shape round or oblong.

6. **FINAL FERMENTATION:** Approximately 2 hours at 76°F (alternatively, retard for up to 8 hours at 50°F, or up to 18 hours at about 42°F).

7. **BAKING:** With normal steam, 460°F for 40 to 45 minutes.

Golden Raisin Bread

PRE-FERMENTED FLOUR: 15%

DOUGH YIELD | U.S.: About 27 loaves at 1.5 lb each | Metric: About 30 loaves at .68 kg each | Home: 2 large loaves

OVERALL FORMULA

	U.S.	METRIC	HOME	BAKER'S %
Bread flour	16 lb	8 kg	1 lb, 9.6 oz	80%
Whole-wheat flour	4 lb	2 kg	6.4 oz	20%
Water	13.8 lb	6.9 kg	1 lb, 6.1 oz	69%
Salt	.4 lb	.2 kg	.6 oz	2%
Yeast	.2 lb, fresh	.1 kg, fresh	.1 oz, instant dry	1%
Oats, rolled	2 lb	1 kg	3.2 oz	10%
Golden raisins	5 lb	2.5 kg	8 oz	25%
TOTAL YIELD	**41.4 lb**	**20.7 kg**	**4 lb, 2 oz**	**207%**

LIQUID-LEVAIN BUILD

	U.S.	METRIC	HOME	BAKER'S %
Bread flour	3 lb	1.5 kg	4.8 oz (1⅛ cups)	100%
Water	3.75 lb	1.875 kg	6 oz (¾ cup)	125%
Mature culture (liquid)	.6 lb	.3 kg	1 oz (2 T)	20%
TOTAL	**7.35 lb**	**3.675 kg**	**11.8 oz**	

FINAL DOUGH

Bread flour	13 lb	6.5 kg	1 lb, 4.8 oz ($4\frac{3}{4}$ cups)
Whole-wheat flour	4 lb	2 kg	6.4 oz ($1\frac{1}{2}$ cups)
Water	10.05 lb	5.025 kg	1 lb, .1 oz (2 cups)
Salt	.4 lb	.2 kg	.6 oz (1 T)
Yeast	.2 lb, fresh	.1 kg, fresh	.1 oz, instant dry (1 tsp)
Oats, rolled	2 lb	1 kg	3.2 oz (1 cup)
Golden raisins	5 lb	2.5 kg	8 oz ($1\frac{5}{8}$ cups)
Liquid levain	6.75 lb	3.375 kg	10.8 oz (all less 2 T)
TOTAL	**41.4 lb**	**20.7 kg**	**4 lb, 2 oz**

Little nuggets of sweet raisins, flecks of oats, some whole wheat, and a gentle acidity combine to make a tasty loaf.

1. **LIQUID LEVAIN:** Make the final build 12 to 16 hours before the final mix and let stand in a covered container at about 70°F.

2. **MIXING:** Add the oats and water to the mixing bowl and let the oats soak for a few minutes. Add the remaining ingredients with the exception of the raisins. In a spiral mixer, mix on first speed for 3 minutes, correcting the hydration as necessary—the absorption of the oats may require the addition of more water, and the dough should be slightly on the soft side (once the raisins are added, they will have a slight drying effect on the dough's consistency). Turn the mixer to second speed and mix for $2\frac{1}{2}$ to 3 minutes, until the dough has a moderate gluten development. Add the golden raisins and mix on first speed just until they are evenly incorporated. Desired dough temperature: 76°F.

3. **BULK FERMENTATION:** 1 to 2 hours.

4. **FOLDING:** If the bulk fermentation is 2 hours, fold the dough after 1 hour.

5. **DIVIDING AND SHAPING:** Divide the dough into 1.5-pound pieces; shape round or oblong.

6. **FINAL FERMENTATION:** Approximately 1 hour at 76°F.

7. **BAKING:** With normal steam, 460°F for 40 to 45 minutes. Lower the oven temperature to 430°F after 15 minutes to prevent the sugars in the raisins from darkening the dough too much.

Five-Grain Levain

PRE-FERMENTED FLOUR: 25%

DOUGH YIELD | U.S.: About 31 loaves at 1.5 lb each | Metric: About 34 loaves at .68 kg each | Home: 3 medium loaves

OVERALL FORMULA

	U.S.	METRIC	HOME	BAKER'S %
High-gluten flour	10 lb	5 kg	1 lb	50%
Bread flour	5 lb	2.5 kg	8 oz	25%
Whole-wheat flour	5 lb	2.5 kg	8 oz	25%
Cracked rye	1.84 lb	.92 kg	2.9 oz	9.2%
Flaxseeds	1.84 lb	.92 kg	2.9 oz	9.2%
Sunflower seeds	1.54 lb	.77 kg	2.5 oz	7.7%
Oats	1.54 lb	.77 kg	2.5 oz	7.7%
Water	19.6 lb	9.8 kg	1 lb, 15.4 oz	98%
Salt	.5 lb	.25 kg	.8 oz	2.5%
Yeast	.16 lb, fresh	.08 kg, fresh	.1 oz, instant dry	.8%
TOTAL YIELD	**47.02 lb**	**23.51 kg**	**4 lb, 11.1 oz**	**235.1%**

LIQUID-LEVAIN BUILD

	U.S.	METRIC	HOME	BAKER'S %
Bread flour	5 lb	2.5 kg	8 oz (1 7/8 cups)	100%
Water	6.26 lb	3.13 kg	10 oz (1 1/4 cups)	125%
Mature culture (liquid)	1 lb	.5 kg	1.6 oz (3 T)	20%
TOTAL	**12.26 lb**	**6.13 kg**	**1 lb, 3.6 oz**	

SOAKER

	U.S.	METRIC	HOME	BAKER'S %
Cracked rye	1.84 lb	.92 kg	2.9 oz (5/8 cup)	27.2%
Flaxseeds	1.84 lb	.92 kg	2.9 oz (5/8 cup)	27.2%
Sunflower seeds	1.54 lb	.77 kg	2.5 oz (1/2 cup)	22.8%
Oats	1.54 lb	.77 kg	2.5 oz (3/4 cup)	22.8%
Water, boiling	8.12 lb	4.06 kg	13 oz (1 5/8 cups)	120%
Salt	.136 lb	.068 kg	.2 oz (1 tsp)	2%
TOTAL	**15.02 lb**	**7.508 kg**	**1 lb, 8 oz**	

FINAL DOUGH

High-gluten flour	10 lb	5 kg	1 lb (4 3/8 cups)
Whole-wheat flour	5 lb	2.5 kg	8 oz (1 3/4 cups)
Water	5.22 lb	2.61 kg	8.4 oz (1 cup)
Salt	.364 lb	.182 kg	.6 oz (1 T)
Yeast	.16 lb, fresh	.08 kg, fresh	.1 oz, instant dry (1 tsp)
Soaker	15.02 lb	7.508 kg	1 lb, 8 oz (all of above)
Liquid levain	11.26 lb	5.63 kg	1 lb, 2 oz (all less 3 T)
TOTAL	**47.02 lb**	**23.51 kg**	**4 lb, 11.1 oz**

This is one of the most delectable breads I have ever eaten. It has a high percentage of whole grains and a solid level of acidity, yet it is surprisingly light. What appears to be a misprint—98 percent hydration—is in fact correct. The grains in the soaker take in a great deal of the overall dough water, and once mixed, the bread has a moderately loose texture. The percentage of salt appears high at first glance as well, but it is necessary to add salt to the soaker grains as well as to the flour.

1. **LIQUID LEVAIN:** Make the final build 12 to 16 hours before the final mix and let stand in a covered container at about 70°F.

2. **SOAKER:** Pour the boiling water over the grain blend and salt, mix thoroughly, and cover with plastic to prevent evaporation. Make the soaker at the same time as the final build of the levain and let stand at room temperature. If grains that don't require a hot soaker are used (such as rye chops in lieu of the cracked rye listed here), a cold soaker can be made. In that case, the grains in the soaker will absorb less water, and therefore it's likely that slightly less water will be needed in the final dough.

3. **MIXING:** Add all the ingredients to the mixing bowl. In a spiral mixer, mix on first speed for 3 minutes, adjusting the hydration as necessary. Mix on second speed for 3 to 3½ minutes. The dough should have a moderate gluten development. Desired dough temperature: 76°F.

4. **BULK FERMENTATION:** 1 to 1½ hours.

5. **FOLDING:** If the bulk fermentation will last 1½ hours, fold after 45 minutes.

6. **DIVIDING AND SHAPING:** Divide the dough into 1.5-pound pieces; shape round or oblong. Large loaves of several pounds are also a beautiful sight. And good rolls can be made from this dough.

7. **FINAL FERMENTATION:** Approximately 1 hour at 76°F. (The dough can be retarded for several hours or overnight, in which case the bulk fermentation should be 2 hours with 1 fold, and the yeast should be left out of the mix.)

8. **BAKING:** With normal steam, 460°F for 40 to 45 minutes. There is a great deal of water retention in this bread, so be sure to bake it thoroughly.

Sourdough Seed Bread

PRE-FERMENTED FLOUR: 15%

DOUGH YIELD | U.S.: About 27 loaves at 1.5 lb each | Metric: About 29 loaves at .68 kg each | Home: 2 large loaves

OVERALL FORMULA

	U.S.	METRIC	HOME	BAKER'S %
Bread flour	**18.4 lb**	**9.2 kg**	**1 lb, 13.4 oz**	**92%**
Whole-rye flour	**1.6 lb**	**.8 kg**	**2.6 oz**	**8%**
Sunflower seeds, toasted	**2.4 lb**	**1.2 kg**	**3.8 oz**	**12%**
Sesame seeds, toasted	**1.2 lb**	**.6 kg**	**1.9 oz**	**6%**
Flaxseeds	**1.4 lb**	**.7 kg**	**2.2 oz**	**7%**
Water	**15 lb**	**7.5 kg**	**1 lb, 8 oz**	**75%**
Salt	**.46 lb**	**.23 kg**	**.7 oz**	**2.3%**
TOTAL YIELD	**40.46 lb**	**20.23 kg**	**4 lb, .6 oz**	**202.3%**

LIQUID-LEVAIN BUILD

Bread flour	3 lb	1.5 kg	4.8 oz (1⅛ cups)	100%
Water	3.76 lb	1.88 kg	6 oz (¾ cup)	125%
Mature culture (liquid)	.6 lb	.3 kg	1 oz (2 T)	20%
TOTAL	**7.36 lb**	**3.68 kg**	**11.8 oz**	

SOAKER

Flaxseeds	1.4 lb	.7 kg	2.2 oz (⅜ cup)	100%
Water	4.2 lb	2.1 kg	6.7 oz (¾ cup)	300%
TOTAL	**5.6 lb**	**2.8 kg**	**8.9 oz**	

FINAL DOUGH

Bread flour	15.4 lb	7.7 kg	1 lb, 8.6 oz (5⅝ cups)
Whole-rye flour	1.6 lb	.8 kg	2.6 oz (⅝ cup)
Sunflower seeds, toasted (see headnote)	2.4 lb	1.2 kg	3.8 oz (⅞ cup)
Sesame seeds, toasted (see headnote)	1.2 lb	.6 kg	1.9 oz (⅜ cup)
Water	7.04 lb	3.52 kg	11.3 oz (1⅜ cups)
Salt	.46 lb	.23 kg	.7 oz (1 T + ½ tsp)
Soaker	5.6 lb	2.8 kg	8.9 oz (all of above)
Liquid levain	6.76 lb	3.38 kg	10.8 oz (all less 2 T)
TOTAL	**40.46 lb**	**20.23 kg**	**4 lb, .6 oz**

homework pg

This is another delicious grain bread, quite different from the preceding one. The sunflower seeds and sesame seeds are toasted for 5 or 6 minutes at 380°F prior to the mix, and they add a nuttiness to the flavor profile. The flax provides taste, color, and, not insignificantly, nutrition. This version is naturally leavened and favors an overnight fermentation. It can, however, be baked the day it is mixed, in which case a couple of hours or so of final proofing at room temperature will be required. Alternatively, up to 1 percent or so of baker's yeast can be added to the dough; this will speed up fermentation and bring the bread from the oven much more quickly, but slightly at the expense of the fullest flavor, which is best developed in this bread through natural leavening and long fermentation.

1. **LIQUID LEVAIN:** Make the final build 12 to 16 hours before the final mix and let stand in a covered container at about 70°F.

2. **SOAKER:** Make a cold soaker with the flaxseeds and water at the time the last levain build is made. Cover with plastic and let stand.

3. **MIXING:** Add all the ingredients to the mixing bowl. In a spiral mixer, mix on first speed for 3 minutes, adjusting the hydration as necessary. Mix on second speed for another 3 minutes or so. The dough should have a moderate gluten development. Desired dough temperature: 76°F.

4. **BULK FERMENTATION:** 2½ hours.

5. **FOLDING:** Fold once after 1¼ hours or, if the dough seems to need more strength, fold twice at 50-minute intervals.

6. **DIVIDING AND SHAPING:** Divide the dough into 1.5-pound pieces; shape round or oblong. Alternatively, pan loaves can be made. These too can be retarded overnight, but they will most likely require some floor time (that is, time to warm up a bit at room temperature) before they bake, since the metal pans get quite cold once refrigerated and this slows the bread's rise.

7. **FINAL FERMENTATION:** Up to 8 hours at 50°F, or up to 18 hours at 42°F.

8. **BAKING:** With normal steam, 460°F for 40 to 45 minutes.

time will not be on your side with sourdough

5grain p176
final fermentation-yeast
7-8h → 50°f
18h → 42°f
* NC favors Lactic

yeast is the most expensive → cost wise

2 organic acids
* Lactic favors warm temp
Acetic - favors cooler temp.

Com. yeast → oven spring increased
↓
Levain - Levure (mixed ferment

when it jumps from 1-4 w/i 12hrs its ready to use

Olive Levain

PRE-FERMENTED FLOUR: 18%

DOUGH YIELD | U.S.: About 25 loaves at 1.5 lb each | Metric: About 27 loaves at .68 kg each | Home: 2 large loaves

OVERALL FORMULA

	U.S.	METRIC	HOME	BAKER'S %
Bread flour	18 lb	9 kg	1 lb, 12.8 oz	90%
Whole-wheat flour	2 lb	1 kg	3.2 oz	10%
Water	12.6 lb	6.3 kg	1 lb, 4.2 oz	63%
Salt	.3 lb	.15 kg	.5 oz	1.5%
Olives, pitted	5 lb	2.5 kg	8 oz	25%
TOTAL YIELD	**37.9 lb**	**18.95 kg**	**3 lb, 12.7 oz**	**189.5%**

LIQUID-LEVAIN BUILD

Bread flour	3.6 lb	1.8 kg	5.8 oz (1 3/8 cups)	100%
Water	4.5 lb	2.25 kg	7.2 oz (7/8 cup)	125%
Mature culture (liquid)	.72 lb	.36 kg	1.2 oz (2 T + 1 tsp)	20%
TOTAL	**8.82 lb**	**4.41 kg**	**14.2 oz**	

FINAL DOUGH

Bread flour	14.4 lb	7.2 kg	1 lb, 7 oz (5 1/4 cups)
Whole-wheat flour	2 lb	1 kg	3.2 oz (3/4 cup)
Water	8.1 lb	4.05 kg	13 oz (1 5/8 cups)
Salt	.3 lb	.15 kg	.5 oz (2 1/2 tsp)
Liquid levain	8.1 lb	4.05 kg	13 oz (all less 2 T + 1 tsp)
Olives, pitted (see headnote)	5 lb	2.5 kg	8 oz (1 1/2 cups, packed)
TOTAL	**37.9 lb**	**18.95 kg**	**3 lb, 12.7 oz**

The olives really let their presence be known in this bread, and there are enough in each loaf that it would be hard to take a slice and not have the intense flavor of olives expanding in your mouth. The olives are drained, pitted if necessary (note that even olives that come "pitted" very often contain pits), and laid onto towels to dry for sev-

1. **LIQUID LEVAIN:** Make the final build 12 to 16 hours before the final mix and let stand in a covered container at about 70°F.

2. **MIXING:** Add all the ingredients to the mixing bowl, with the exception of the olives. In a spiral mixer, mix on first speed for 3 minutes, adjusting the hydration as necessary. Mix on second speed for approximately 3 minutes more. The dough should have a moderate gluten development. Add the olives and mix on first speed just until they are evenly incorporated. Desired dough temperature: 76°F.

eral hours or overnight. If they still seem moist, lay more towels on top and gently press to extract more of their liquid. Sliced olives or whole olives can be used. If the pieces are too small, however, which they often are when the olives are sliced, they tend to get a little lost in the dough and also might stain the dough a purple color.

The ingredient cost goes up dramatically when "high-octane" ingredients like olives are added to breads. The overall percentage of olives can be somewhat lowered, to about 22 percent, and the bread will still retain a discernible olive flavor.

The percentage of salt in the formula—1.5 percent—looks unusually low. This, of course, is because the olives contribute saltiness. If we were to add 1.8 or 2 percent salt, the bread would be too salty.

3. BULK FERMENTATION: 2½ hours.

4. FOLDING: Fold once after 1¼ hours or, if the dough seems to need more strength, fold twice at 50-minute intervals.

5. DIVIDING AND SHAPING: Divide the dough into 1.5-pound pieces; shape round or oblong.

6. FINAL FERMENTATION: The full character of Olive Levain seems to develop if the dough is retarded before baking. Therefore, retard for up to 8 hours at 50°F, or up to 18 hours at 42°F.

7. BAKING: With normal steam, 460°F for 40 to 45 minutes.

OLIVE FOUGASSE: A pleasant variation is to use Olive Levain dough to make fougasse. Take pieces weighing between 1 and 2 pounds, roll them flat, and brush the top surface with extra-virgin olive oil. Let rest for about 1 hour (because of the absence of baker's yeast, the dough requires a comparatively long rest before the bake). Before baking, the fougasse is cut with a knife or pizza wheel (illustrations for a traditionally shaped fougasse are on page 280). Bake at about 450°F, with steam at the outset. By nature, fougasse is crusty—this enhances the eating quality while at the same time reducing the shelf life—so be certain the bake is full.

Cheese Bread

PRE-FERMENTED FLOUR: 18%

DOUGH YIELD | U.S.: About 25 loaves at 1.5 lb each | Metric: About 27 loaves at .68 kg each | Home: 2 large loaves

OVERALL FORMULA

	U.S.	METRIC	HOME	BAKER'S %
Bread flour	20 lb	10 kg	2 lb	100%
Water	12 lb	6 kg	1 lb, 3.2 oz	60%
Olive oil	1 lb	.5 kg	1.6 oz	5%
Salt	.3 lb	.15 kg	.5 oz	1.5%
Yeast	.2 lb, fresh	.1 kg, fresh	.1 oz, instant dry	1%
Parmesan cheese, half grated, half cubed	4 lb	2 kg	6.4 oz	20%
TOTAL YIELD	**37.5 lb**	**18.75 kg**	**3 lb, 11.8 oz**	**187.5%**

STIFF-LEVAIN BUILD

	U.S.	METRIC	HOME	BAKER'S %
Bread flour	3.6 lb	1.8 kg	5.8 oz (1 3/8 cups)	100%
Water	2.16 lb	1.08 kg	3.5 oz (1/2 cup)	60%
Mature culture (stiff)	.72 lb	.36 kg	1.2 oz (2 T + 1 tsp)	20%
TOTAL	**6.48 lb**	**3.24 kg**	**10.5 oz**	

FINAL DOUGH

	U.S.	METRIC	HOME
Bread flour	16.4 lb	8.2 kg	1 lb, 10.2 oz (6 cups)
Water	9.84 lb	4.92 kg	15.7 oz (2 cups)
Olive oil	1 lb	.5 kg	1.6 oz (3 T + 2 tsp)
Salt	.3 lb	.15 kg	.5 oz (2 1/2 tsp)
Yeast	.2 lb	.1 kg	.1 oz, instant dry (1 tsp)
Levain	5.76 lb	2.88 kg	9.3 oz (all less 2 T + 1 tsp)
Parmesan cheese, half grated, half cubed	4 lb	2 kg	6.4 oz (1 5/8 cups)
TOTAL	**37.5 lb**	**18.75 kg**	**3 lb, 11.8 oz**

1. **STIFF LEVAIN:** Make the final build approximately 12 hours before the final mix and let stand in a covered container at about 70°F. During hot weather, or if the levain will ripen for longer than 12 hours, the flour in the levain build can be salted at 1.8 percent to slow its activity.

2. **MIXING:** Add all the ingredients to the mixing bowl, with the exception of the cheese. In a spiral mixer, mix on first speed for 3 min-

This is another strongly flavored bread, good with all sorts of soups and salads, and the quality of the cheese used will have a definitive effect on the bread flavor. Parmesan is the cheese of choice, although less-expensive types, such as Asiago, can be used in combination. The bread can be baked the day it is mixed, or retarded for up to 18 hours. If it will be retarded, use only half the yeast at most.

utes, adjusting the hydration as necessary. The dough should be slightly on the stiff side at this point. Once the cheese is incorporated, it will have a looser feel. Mix on second speed for approximately 3 minutes more, to a moderate gluten development. Add the cheese and mix on first speed just until evenly incorporated. Avoid overmixing. Desired dough temperature: 76°F.

3. **BULK FERMENTATION:** 2½ hours.

4. **FOLDING:** Fold once after 1¼ hours or, if the dough seems to need more strength, fold twice at 50-minute intervals.

5. **DIVIDING AND SHAPING:** Divide the dough into 1.5-pound pieces; shape round or oblong.

6. **FINAL FERMENTATION:** 1 to 1½ hours at 76°F. Alternatively, retard the dough for up to 8 hours at 50°F, or up to 18 hours at 42°F.

7. **BAKING:** With normal steam, 460°F for 40 to 45 minutes. Lower the oven temperaure to 440°F after 15 minutes to avoid excess darkening due to the cheese.

Normandy Apple Bread

PRE-FERMENTED FLOUR: 18%

DOUGH YIELD | U.S.: About 24 loaves at 1.5 lb each | Metric: About 27 loaves at .68 kg each | Home: 2 large loaves

OVERALL FORMULA

	U.S.	METRIC	HOME	BAKER'S %
Bread flour	18 lb	9 kg	1 lb, 12.8 oz	90%
Whole-wheat flour	2 lb	1 kg	3.2 oz	10%
Water	6.8 lb	3.4 kg	10.9 oz	34%
Apple cider	6.8 lb	3.4 kg	10.9 oz	34%
Salt	.4 lb	.2 kg	.6 oz	2%
Yeast	.2 lb, fresh	.1 kg, fresh	.1 oz, instant dry	1%
Apples, dried	3 lb	1.5 kg	4.8 oz	15%
TOTAL YIELD	37.2 lb	18.6 kg	3 lb, 11.3 oz	186%

STIFF-LEVAIN BUILD

Bread flour	3.6 lb	1.8 kg	5.8 oz (1⅜ cups)	100%
Water	2.16 lb	1.08 kg	3.5 oz (½ cup)	60%
Mature culture (stiff)	.72 lb	.36 kg	1.2 oz (2 T + 1 tsp)	20%
TOTAL	6.48 lb	3.24 kg	10.5 oz	

FINAL DOUGH

Bread flour	14.4 lb	7.2 kg	1 lb, 7 oz (5¼ cups)
Whole-wheat flour	2 lb	1 kg	3.2 oz (¾ cup)
Water	4.64 lb	2.32 kg	7.4 oz (1 cup)
Apple cider	6.8 lb	3.4 kg	10.9 oz (1¼ cups)
Salt	.4 lb	.2 kg	.6 oz (1 T)
Yeast	.2 lb, fresh	.1 kg, fresh	.1 oz, instant dry (1 tsp)
Levain	5.76 lb	2.88 kg	9.3 oz (all less 2 T + 1 tsp)
Apples, peeled, cored, sliced or cubed, and dried (see headnote)	3 lb	1.5 kg	4.8 oz (1⅝ cups)
TOTAL	**37.2 lb**	**18.6 kg**	**3 lb, 11.3 oz**

It's quite natural that an apple-growing region such as Normandy, France, would develop a bread that incorporates apples. This dough has not only dried apples, but apple cider as well. It is a good way to use up cider that has gone slightly off. The apples should be dried in the oven at 250°F until they feel leathery. This intensifies their flavor and at the same time prevents them from releasing excess moisture into the dough. Use unpasteurized and unfiltered cider if available, for its superior flavor.

1. **STIFF LEVAIN:** Make the final build approximately 12 hours before the final mix and let stand in a covered container at about 70°F. During hot weather, or if the levain will ripen for longer than 12 hours, the flour in the levain build can be salted at 1.8 percent to slow its activity.

2. **MIXING:** Add all the ingredients to the mixing bowl, including the apple cider, but not the dried apples. In a spiral mixer, mix on first speed for 3 minutes, adjusting the hydration as necessary to achieve a dough of medium consistency. Mix on second speed for approximately 3 minutes more, to a moderate gluten development. Add the dried apples and mix on first speed just until they are evenly incorporated. Desired dough temperature: 76°F.

3. **BULK FERMENTATION:** 1 to 2 hours.

4. **FOLDING:** If the bulk fermentation lasts 2 hours, fold after 1 hour. No folds are needed if the dough ferments for just 1 hour.

5. **DIVIDING AND SHAPING:** Divide the dough into 1.5-pound pieces; shape round or oblong. Rolls can be made too.

6. **FINAL FERMENTATION:** 1 to 1½ hours at 76°F.

7. **BAKING:** With normal steam, 450°F for about 40 minutes. Lower the oven temperature to 420°F after 15 minutes to avoid excess darkening from the sugars in the apples and cider.

Roasted Garlic Levain

PRE-FERMENTED FLOUR: 20%

DOUGH YIELD | U.S.: About 23 loaves at 1.5 lb each | Metric: About 26 loaves at .68 kg each | Home: 2 large loaves

OVERALL FORMULA

	U.S.	METRIC	HOME	BAKER'S %
Bread flour	18 lb	9 kg	1 lb, 12.8 oz	90%
Whole-wheat flour	2 lb	1 kg	3.2 oz	10%
Water	13 lb	6.5 kg	1 lb, 4.8 oz	65%
Olive oil	1 lb	.5 kg	1.6 oz	5%
Salt	.4 lb	.2 kg	.6 oz	2%
Yeast	.2 lb, fresh	.1 kg, fresh	.1 oz, instant dry	1%
Garlic, roasted	.7 lb	.35 kg	1.1 oz	3.5%
TOTAL YIELD	**35.3 lb**	**17.65 kg**	**3 lb, 8.2 oz**	**176.5%**

STIFF-LEVAIN BUILD

Bread flour	4 lb	2 kg	6.4 oz (1½ cups)	100%
Water	2.4 lb	1.2 kg	3.8 oz (½ cup)	60%
Mature culture (stiff)	.8 lb	.4 kg	1.3 oz (2 T + 1 tsp)	20%
TOTAL	**7.2 lb**	**3.6 kg**	**11.5 oz**	

FINAL DOUGH

Bread flour	14 lb	7 kg	1 lb, 6.4 oz (5⅛ cups)
Whole-wheat flour	2 lb	1 kg	3.2 oz (¾ cup)
Water	10.6 lb	5.3 kg	1 lb, 1 oz (2⅛ cups)
Olive oil	1 lb	.5 kg	1.6 oz (¼ cup)
Salt	.4 lb	.2 kg	.6 oz (1 T)
Yeast	.2 lb, fresh	.1 kg, fresh	.1 oz, instant dry (1 tsp)
Levain	6.4 lb	3.2 kg	10.2 oz (all less 2 T + 1 tsp)
Garlic, roasted (see headnote)	.7 lb	.35 kg	1.1 oz (½ bulb)
TOTAL	**35.3 lb**	**17.65 kg**	**3 lb, 8.2 oz**

1. STIFF LEVAIN: Make the final build approximately 12 hours before the final mix and let stand in a covered container at about 70°F. During hot weather, or if the levain will ripen for longer than 12 hours, the flour in the levain build can be salted at 1.8 percent to slow its activity.

Roasting the garlic softens the flavor and provides a mellow smoothness that pervades this loaf. Pre-fermenting 20 percent of the flour adds another flavor dimension, one that complements rather than competes with the garlic. To prepare the garlic, slice ½ inch off the top of the bulbs, place in a baking pan, sprinkle a bit of olive oil over the exposed cloves to keep them moist, cover with aluminum foil, and roast in the oven (at 350° to 400°F) until the cloves are very soft, about 40 minutes. Once cooled and removed from their skins, a quick mashing is all that is necessary. In the mixer they will merge with the dough. If a bit of a clove stays intact even after the rigors of the mix, it will not in any way impair the eating quality. The bread is a special treat when brushed with olive oil and grilled, or simply toasted and buttered. Rolled thin, brushed with olive oil, sprinkled lightly with coarse salt, and baked hot and quick, it makes an exceptional fougasse.

2. MIXING: Add all the ingredients to the mixing bowl, including the garlic. In a spiral mixer, mix on first speed for 3 minutes, adjusting the hydration as necessary to achieve a dough of medium consistency. Mix on second speed for approximately 3 minutes more, to a moderate gluten development. Desired dough temperature: 76°F.

3. BULK FERMENTATION: 1 to 2 hours.

4. FOLDING: If the bulk fermentation lasts 2 hours, fold after 1 hour. No folds are needed if the dough ferments only 1 hour.

5. DIVIDING AND SHAPING: Divide the dough into 1.5-pound pieces; shape round or oblong. Tasty rolls can be made as well.

6. FINAL FERMENTATION: 1 to 1½ hours at 76°F.

7. BAKING: With normal steam, 460°F for 40 to 45 minutes.

Roasted Hazelnut and Prune Bread

PRE-FERMENTED FLOUR: 20%

DOUGH YIELD | U.S.: About 26 loaves at 1.5 lb each | Metric: About 29 loaves at .68 kg each | Home: 2 large loaves

OVERALL FORMULA

	U.S.	METRIC	HOME	BAKER'S %
Bread flour	15 lb	7.5 kg	1 lb, 8 oz	75%
Whole-wheat flour	5 lb	2.5 kg	8 oz	25%
Water	13.2 lb	6.6 kg	1 lb, 5.1 oz	66%
Butter, soft	1 lb	.5 kg	1.6 oz	5%
Salt	.4 lb	.2 kg	.6 oz	2%
Yeast	.3 lb, fresh	.15 kg, fresh	.17 oz, instant dry	1.5%
Hazelnuts, roasted and skinned	2.5 lb	1.25 kg	4 oz	12.5%
Dried prunes, coarsely chopped	2.5 lb	1.25 kg	4 oz	12.5%
TOTAL YIELD	**39.9 lb**	**19.95 kg**	**3 lb, 15.5 oz**	**199.5%**

STIFF-LEVAIN BUILD

	U.S.	METRIC	HOME	BAKER'S %
Bread flour	4 lb	2 kg	6.4 oz (1½ cups)	100%
Water	2.4 lb	1.2 kg	3.8 oz (½ cup)	60%
Mature culture (stiff)	.8 lb	.4 kg	1.3 oz (2 T + 1 tsp)	20%
TOTAL	**7.2 lb**	**3.6 kg**	**11.5 oz**	

FINAL DOUGH

	U.S.	METRIC	HOME
Bread flour	11 lb	5.5 kg	1 lb, 1.6 oz (4 cups)
Whole-wheat flour	5 lb	2.5 kg	8 oz (1⅞ cups)
Water	10.8 lb	5.4 kg	1 lb, 1.3 oz (2⅛ cups)
Butter, soft	1 lb	.5 kg	1.6 oz (3 T)
Salt	.4 lb	.2 kg	.6 oz (1 T)
Yeast	.3 lb, fresh	.15 kg, fresh	.17 oz, instant dry (1½ tsp)
Levain	6.4 lb	3.2 kg	10.2 oz (all less 2 T + 1 tsp)
Hazelnuts, roasted and skinned (see headnote)	2.5 lb	1.25 kg	4 oz (⅞ cup)
Dried prunes, coarsely chopped	2.5 lb	1.25 kg	4 oz (⅝ cup)
TOTAL	**39.9 lb**	**19.95 kg**	**3 lb, 15.5 oz**

The concentrated crunch of the roasted nuts and the intense sweetness of the dried fruit balance each other in this bread. The combination of flavors and textures makes a bread that is easy to enjoy. The hazelnuts should be thoroughly roasted. Whole nuts are baked at 350° to 400°F on sheet pans for 8 to 12 minutes. Once cool enough to handle, their skins should readily come off when rubbed between your hands, and the nuts themselves should have a brownish hue. The interior portion of a loaf of bread never gets above 212°F, so the nuts will not continue to roast as the bread bakes (except those nuts that are exposed on the surface). Therefore, take the time to get a full roasting so the nuts can impart all of their delicious flavor to the bread. The prunes should be chopped coarsely before using.

1. **STIFF LEVAIN:** Make the final build approximately 12 hours before the final mix and let stand in a covered container at about 70°F. During hot weather, or if the levain will ripen for longer than 12 hours, the flour in the levain build can be salted at 1.8 percent to slow its activity.

2. **MIXING:** Add all the ingredients to the mixing bowl, with the exception of the hazelnuts and prunes. In a spiral mixer, mix on first speed for 3 minutes, adjusting the hydration as necessary. The nuts and the prunes will take some moisture from the dough once incorporated, so the dough should be slightly on the loose side at this point of the mix. Turn the mixer to second speed and mix for approximately 3 minutes more, to a moderate gluten development. Add the nuts and fruit and mix on first speed just until they are evenly incorporated into the dough. Desired dough temperature: 76°F.

3. **BULK FERMENTATION:** 1 to 1½ hours.

4. **FOLDING:** If the bulk fermentation lasts 1½ hours, fold after 45 minutes. No folds are needed if the dough ferments only 1 hour.

5. **DIVIDING AND SHAPING:** Divide the dough into 1.5-pound pieces; shape round or oblong. Rolls or pan loaves can be made as well.

6. **FINAL FERMENTATION:** About 1 hour at 76°F.

7. **BAKING:** With normal steam, 460°F for 40 to 45 minutes. Lower the oven temperature to 420°F after 15 minutes to avoid excessive browning due to the prunes.

SOURDOUGH RYE BREADS

6

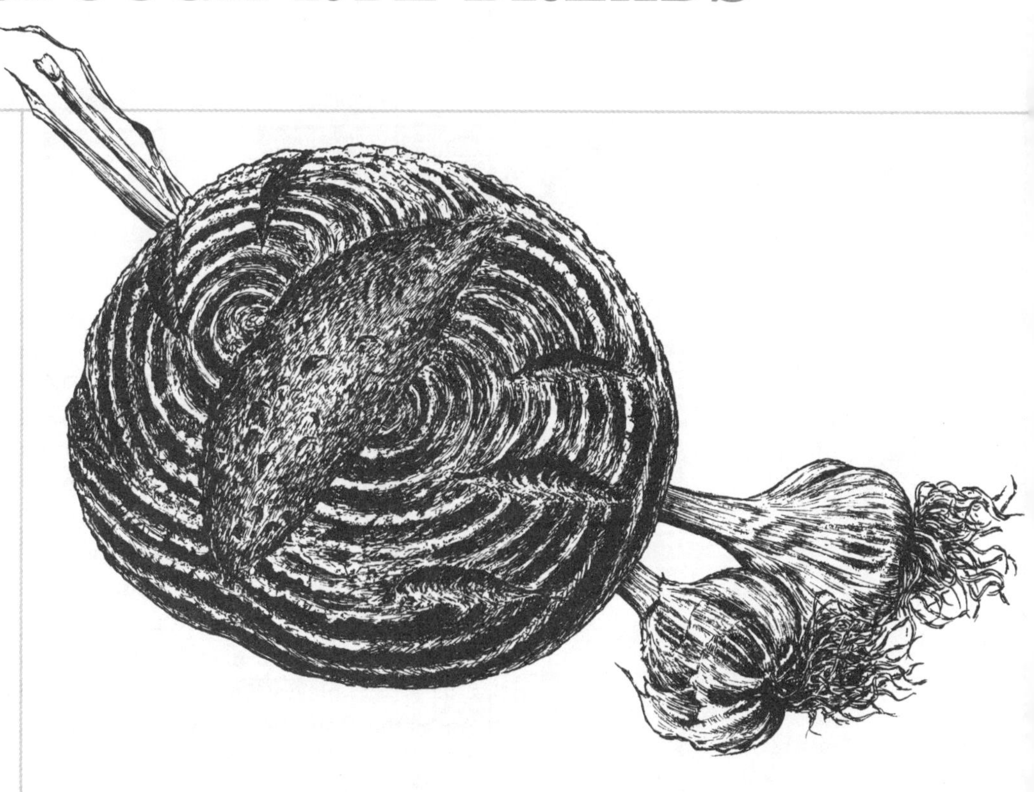

Bread is revered in Hungary, perhaps as in no other place in the world, and country folks still call it "life." As a child, if I dropped a slice of bread, I had to kiss it before eating it. It's interesting to note that [my mother] got her starter from her mother in 1921, when she married my father, just as her mother must have gotten it when she married my grandfather. So the bread we ate had a micro part of the past centuries. —GEORGE LANG, FROM *THE CUSINE OF HUNGARY*

Rye breads represent an area of great potential for the baker. They have fine flavor, excellent keeping quality, and good versatility with foods. At the same time, the nature of rye flour is distinctly different from that of wheat, and there are special production requirements that pertain only to rye. Understanding these technical aspects is important.

The growing culture of rye, the characteristics of pentosans, and the need to acidify rye flour with sourdough in order to deter the "starch attack" are explained beginning on page 47. I won't reiterate that material here, but I will explain some of the other unique traits of rye doughs. We should keep in mind that when the percentage of rye flour in a formula is low, and we are making what is essentially a white bread with the addition of some rye, these traits have less impact on the bread. It is when the rye flour constitutes 50 percent or more of the overall dough flour that these characteristics have the biggest impact, and that impact continues to increase as the proportion of rye increases.

Production Notes for the Formulas in this Chapter

Preparing the Sourdough. The sourdough is prepared by dispersing the mature culture into the water, adding the flour, and mixing by hand or machine until the flour is thoroughly incorporated. The consistency should be fairly stiff, but loose enough to allow it to "breathe." Sprinkle rye flour on top and cover the bowl with baker's linen or plastic. The sourdough will ripen in 14 to 16 hours at about 70°F (the three-phase Detmolder breads are an exception; refer to the 90 percent formula on page 200 for a detailed explanation). Adjust ripening times based on ambient temperature and humidity. The ripe sourdough should be domed, with a pleasingly acidic tang. If the sourdough has collapsed, the room it ripened in is too warm or the length of ripening is too long. If it appears not to have matured at all, the room temperature is too cool or ripening time should be lengthened.

Preparing the Soaker. Several of these breads contain soakers. Soaking some hard grains several hours in advance of mixing makes it easier to incorporate them into the dough, and the finished bread will be more palatable. Cold soakers are prepared by pouring water over the grains, mixing, and then covering the container tightly with plastic to prevent evaporation. Hot soakers (used for particularly hard grains such as cracked rye that won't soften sufficiently without precooking) are made by first bringing the water to the point of boil, then pouring it over the grains and covering the container tightly with plastic. It is common to see some or all of the overall dough salt used in soakers. The presence of salt reduces the level of enzymatic activity (particularly the enzyme amylase). In the sourdough and final dough, enzymatic activity is necessary, but an excess of enzymatic activity adds off flavors to the soaker, and therefore salt is often added. Although soakers need only a few hours of standing before use, it is generally easier to make them at the same time the sourdough is mixed, and to let them stand at room temperature until mixing the final dough.

Mixing the Final Dough. After removing a small portion of the ripe sourdough in order to perpetuate the culture, all the ingredients are placed in the mixing bowl (some exceptions, such as walnuts or raisins, are noted in the individual formula sections). Once the ingredients have come together, carefully check the dough consistency and add water or flour as necessary. Rye flour has a higher absorption capacity than wheat flour, and as the proportion of rye increases, there is a corresponding increase in dough hydration. Rye doughs should be fairly loose textured, so be cautious and stingy about adding flour. Looser doughs bring out the full robust flavor of rye more thoroughly than dry doughs, which ferment with difficulty and tend to have poor volume (another aspect of rye bread is the economic one, underscored by a saying among German bakers: "Water makes the baker rich"). As the percentage of rye flour increases, mixing should become gentler in order to prevent the fragile pentosans from releasing water and causing a pasty dough to form. Mixing guidelines can only be approximate, and depend on the type of mixer (oblique, spiral, planetary, stand, and so on) and the rpms in each speed. In general, for a spiral mixer with 100 rpms in first speed and 200 rpms in second, the following times can be used as a guide (see page 11 for approximate mixing times for other styles of mixers):

- **DOUGHS WITH UP TO 50 PERCENT RYE FLOUR:** First speed for 3 minutes, second speed for 3 to 4 minutes. Perceptible gluten development of the white flour should be noted when the dough is tugged. The desired dough temperature for these doughs is 78° to 80°F.

- **DOUGHS WITH 50 TO 70 PERCENT RYE FLOUR:** First speed for 3 minutes, second speed for approximately 2 minutes. There should be slight gluten development. The desired dough temperature is 80°F.

- **DOUGHS WITH 70 TO 90 PERCENT RYE FLOUR:** First speed for 4 minutes, second speed for 1½ to 2 minutes. The rye flour is dominant here, and very little dough strength will be evident. The desired dough temperature is 82°F.

- **DOUGHS WITH 100 PERCENT RYE FLOUR:** The intention with these doughs is simply to mix a smooth paste. Ten minutes of mixing on first speed is adequate. There will be no gluten development. The desired dough temperature is 84° to 85°F.

Bulk Fermentation. Bulk fermentation time decreases as the rye percentage increases. One reason for this is that in rye breads there is little of the gas-trapping properties present in wheat gluten, so lengthy bulk fermentation will not improve dough volume and crumb structure. Further, there is little need to have a lengthy fermentation in order to develop flavor in rye breads. The incorporation of nicely ripened sourdough into the dough injects it with substantial flavor. Lengthy bulk fermentation has the tendency to overacidify the dough, resulting in bread with an unpleasantly sour flavor. Therefore, as the percentage of rye in a formula increases, there is a corresponding decrease in fermentation time. Bulk fermentation requirements (approximate) for the doughs are as follows: Sixty minutes for doughs with rye content up to 40 percent; 45 to 60 minutes for doughs with 40 to 60 percent rye; 30 minutes for doughs with 60 to 80 percent rye; 10 to 20 minutes for doughs with 90 to 100 percent rye. Dough folding is not required for any of the formulas in this section.

Dividing and Shaping. Rye breads can be baked in loaf pans, although hearth baking tends to bring out the fullest flavor (100 percent rye breads require panning, for obvious reasons). Scale the dough into appropriate weights, usually 1.5 to 2.5 pounds. After preshaping, the dough pieces rest, seams up, on a floured work surface, covered with plastic to prevent a skin forming on the surface. A fairly short rest of 5 to 10 minutes is sufficient for the bench rest. The final shaping is generally round or oblong, and the shaped loaves can then be placed, seams up, in floured *bannetons*, or between folds of baker's linen, seams down. As the proportion of rye increases, *bannetons* become more useful, for they provide lateral support for the fragile loaves. Once shaped, the loaves are again covered with plastic to prevent a skin from forming on the surface. Rolls can be made with many of the breads described in this chapter, although as the percentage of rye flour increases, so too does the density of the bread. Above 50 percent rye flour, rolls tend to be dense and have a thick crust, and larger dough weights are recommended. Rolls can be placed on sheet pans sprinkled with coarse cornmeal or semolina, and baked either on the sheet pans or directly on the hearth or baking stone.

Final Fermentation. Fifty to 60 minutes is usually sufficient for the final proofing of the breads, at temperatures between 78° and 84°F. Breads leavened only by sourdough will require more proofing time. In general, breads should be loaded into the oven when 85 to 90 percent risen. Breads that receive a completely full rise tend to collapse in the oven.

Steaming and Baking. The proofed loaves are slashed with a straight blade prior to steaming the oven. As rye percentage increases, however, so too does the fragility of the bread. A dough docker is commonly used in place of the razor for doughs with 80 percent or more rye flour. This tool, a rolling cylinder from which dozens of 2-inch-long steel or plastic spikes protrude, is rolled over the surface of the proofed bread. The numerous small holes provide openings for expansion of the bread, without creating the same sort of weak areas in the surface that a blade does. The oven is filled with steam prior to loading the bread, then steamed again once loaded. Six to 10 seconds of total steam should be adequate.

Thorough steaming encourages strong oven spring and optimum bread volume. For breads with up to 50 percent rye flour, open the oven vents once the bread begins to color, usually after about 15 minutes. As the percentage of rye increases, the vents are opened progressively earlier. At 90 percent rye, the vents are opened and the steam expelled after only 5 minutes of baking. The reason for such early venting is as follows: Once the bread has gotten the benefits of oven spring, it is necessary to dry the surface of the loaf by opening the vents in order to encourage the firming, particularly the lateral firming, of the bread. If the steam remains in the baking chamber too long, the surface of the bread will remain moist, and the loaves will tend to flatten. Again: The steam gives spring to the bread, and the venting dries the bread so it can rise upward rather than flatten outward.

Rye breads favor a hot initial oven temperature and a gradually receding temperature as the baking proceeds. The initial high heat encourages optimum oven spring and loaf volume, and the receding oven temperature ensures that the bread is thoroughly baked. (An unusual technique is employed at industrial bakeries in Germany in baking a rye bread called Berliner Country Bread. The initial baking takes place at exceptionally high temperatures—upwards of 800°F (430°C)! After at most 5 minutes, the breads are transferred to different hearths set at normal baking temperatures, where they finish baking. The fierce initial heat causes the bread to spring to maximum volume, overcoming the low loaf volume that results from the poor gas-retention property of rye doughs.) The specific bake temperatures and bake times for the individual breads in this section are based on 1.5-pound round loaves (with the exception of breads baked in pullman pans). Of course, scale weights can be heavier or lighter for all the breads; adjust baking times accordingly when baking larger or smaller loaves. Further, times may vary depending on oven type and bread shape—round loaves take longer to bake than oblong loaves due to their higher proportion of crumb to crust—and the bake times given should be considered guidelines. In every case, a bold, full bake encourages maximum bread flavor.

Eating. Breads with up to 60 percent rye flour should be eaten in the same way as wheat-based breads: cooled thoroughly and then enjoyed. But as the percentage of rye increases, the bread requires more rest time before eating. A full 24 hours of resting allows the crumb to stabilize and firm up; the rest period also helps the flavors to develop fully. In the case of *Vollkornbrot*, made with 100 percent rye, 48 hours to as much as 72 hours of resting before eating is recommended. After the bake, the breads are left to cool, then wrapped in baker's linen or put into tubs, which are then covered with baker's linen to allow them to breathe. Breads of this nature should be sliced thinly, and they pair beautifully with cheeses, cured fish and meat, or simply butter and jam. As a rule, sandwiches made with these breads are open face, since a double thickness of these compact and concentrated breads can be a bit too much of a workout for the jaw.

A Final Note. In the final dough and overall formula sections of each formula, the total yield does not include the weight of the mature rye culture used in the sourdough phase, as it is expected that the baker will have removed it prior to mixing the final dough.

Ripe Sourdough

Preparation of a rye sourdough simply involves taking a small portion of ripe culture, dispersing it in water, and adding rye flour. The ingredients are then mixed thoroughly by hand or machine, and finally the mixture is sprinkled with a thin layer of rye flour (this layer of flour provides an environmental barrier and protects the flour/water paste from drying as it ripens). A covering of baker's linen or plastic as an added measure to prevent drying completes the procedure. The microorganisms that are in the ripe culture acidify the flour. Gas production is a natural by-product of this biological activity, and as the hours go on and the sourdough ripens, there is a distinct increase in volume. When ripened, the sourdough should be domed, with islands of rye (from the sprinkled flour) interspersed with shiny areas of sourdough. If the surface of the sourdough is collapsed and concave, it is an indication that it has overripened and that cooler temperatures and/or less ripening time is necessary. The taste of the sourdough should be distinctly aromatic and tangy. Before putting the sourdough in the mixer and mixing the final dough, a small portion of the ripe sourdough must be removed in order to perpetuate the culture. Failure to do this will mean the sourdough culture has been lost, and a new one must be begun. A good precaution is for the baker to leave a clean bowl in clear sight and close proximity to the ripening sourdough. When he or she goes to mix the next day, this visual reminder should be sufficient to prevent the loss of the precious culture.

40 Percent Caraway Rye

PRE-FERMENTED FLOUR: 40%

DOUGH YIELD | U.S.: About 23 loaves at 1.5 lb each | Metric: About 25 loaves at .68 kg each | Home: 2 large loaves

OVERALL FORMULA

	U.S.	METRIC	HOME	BAKER'S %
High-gluten flour	12 lb	6 kg	1 lb, 3.2 oz	60%
Whole-rye flour	8 lb	4 kg	12.8 oz	40%
Water	13.6 lb	6.8 kg	1 lb, 5.8 oz	68%
Caraway seeds	.35 lb	.175 kg	.6 oz	1.75%
Salt	.36 lb	.18 kg	.6 oz	1.8%
Yeast	.25 lb, fresh	.125 kg, fresh	.13 oz, instant dry	1.25%
TOTAL YIELD	**34.56 lb**	**17.28 kg**	**3 lb, 7.1 oz**	**172.8%**

SOURDOUGH

Whole-rye flour	8 lb	4 kg	12.8 oz (3½ cups)	100%
Water	6.64 lb	3.32 kg	10.6 oz (1⅜ cups)	83%
Mature sourdough culture	.4 lb	.2 kg	.6 oz (2 T)	5%
TOTAL	**15.04 lb**	**7.52 kg**	**1 lb, 8 oz**	

FINAL DOUGH

High-gluten flour	12 lb	6 kg	1 lb, 3.2 oz (4⅜ cups)
Water	6.96 lb	3.48 kg	11.2 oz (1½ cups)
Caraway seeds	.35 lb	.175 kg	.6 oz (2½ T)
Salt	.36 lb	.18 kg	.6 oz (1 T)
Yeast	.25 lb, fresh	.125 kg, fresh	.13 oz, instant dry (1 tsp)
Sourdough	14.64 lb	7.32 kg	1 lb, 7.4 oz (all of above minus 2 T)
TOTAL	**34.56 lb**	**17.28 kg**	**3 lb, 7.1 oz**

1. **SOURDOUGH:** Prepare the sourdough and ripen for 14 to 16 hours at 70°F.

2. **MIXING:** Add all the ingredients to the mixing bowl. In a spiral mixer, mix for 3 minutes on first speed, and 3 to 4 minutes on second, until a strong gluten development is achieved. Desired dough temperature: 78° to 80°F.

3. **BULK FERMENTATION:** 1 hour.

This rye bread combines a reasonably light texture with an agreeably hearty rye flavor. Whole-rye flour is used, and all of it is acidified, imparting a moderate tang to the finished taste. The 60 percent of white flour in the formula contributes to the bread's lightness, and it's a good, everyday kind of rye bread, particularly suited to palates that are not used to the more robust rye breads comprised of 80, 90, and even 100 percent rye. Medium rye flour in place of whole rye flour brings a loaf with slightly less rye flavor, but it is an acceptable substitute.

4. DIVIDING AND SHAPING: Divide the dough into 1.5-pound pieces; shape round or oblong.

5. FINAL FERMENTATION: 50 to 60 minutes at 78° to 80°F.

6. BAKING: With normal steam, 460°F for 15 minutes, then lower the oven temperature to 440°F and bake for 20 to 25 minutes.

VARIATION: Tasty rolls can be made from this dough as well. It is easiest to bake them on sheet pans that have been sprinkled with cornmeal or coarse semolina. Bake time for a 3-ounce round roll is 20 to 24 minutes. Alternatively, *Salzstangerl,* or salt sticks (a common sight in Austrian and German bakeries), can be made by shaping the rolls into fingers, pressing the top side into a damp cloth, and then into a tray of caraway and coarse salt mixed together. Proof and bake these rolls with the salt/caraway side up on the sheet pan.

Whole-Rye and Whole-Wheat Bread

PRE-FERMENTED FLOUR: 25%

DOUGH YIELD | U.S.: About 22 loaves at 1.5 lb each | Metric: About 25 loaves at .68 kg each | Home: 2 large loaves

OVERALL FORMULA

	U.S.	METRIC	HOME	BAKER'S %
High-gluten flour	**10 lb**	**5 kg**	**1 lb**	**50%**
Whole-rye flour	**5 lb**	**2.5 kg**	**8 oz**	**25%**
Whole-wheat flour	**5 lb**	**2.5 kg**	**8 oz**	**25%**
Water	**13.6 lb**	**6.8 kg**	**1 lb, 5.8 oz**	**68%**
Salt	**.36 lb**	**.18 kg**	**.6 oz**	**1.8%**
Yeast	**.25 lb, fresh**	**.125 kg, fresh**	**.13 oz, instant dry**	**1.25%**
TOTAL YIELD	**34.21 lb**	**17.105 kg**	**3 lb, 6.5 oz**	**171.05%**

SOURDOUGH

Whole-rye flour	5 lb	2.5 kg	8 oz (2 1/8 cups)	100%
Water	4.15 lb	2.08 kg	6.6 oz (7/8 cup)	83%
Mature sourdough culture	.25 lb	.125 kg	.4 oz (1 T + 1 tsp)	5%
TOTAL	**9.4 lb**	**4.705 kg**	**15 oz**	

FINAL DOUGH

High-gluten flour	10 lb	5 kg	1 lb (3⅝ cups)
Whole-wheat flour	5 lb	2.5 kg	8 oz (1¾ cups)
Water	9.45 lb	4.72 kg	15.2 oz (1⅞ cups)
Salt	.36 lb	.18 kg	.6 oz (1 T)
Yeast	.25 lb, fresh	.125 kg, fresh	.13 oz, instant dry (1 tsp)
Sourdough	9.15 lb	4.58 kg	14.6 oz (all of above minus 1 T + 1 tsp)
TOTAL	**34.21 lb**	**17.105 kg**	**3 lb, 6.5 oz**

The presence of whole-wheat flour in this bread adds a flavor note that would be lacking if all white flour were used. The whole-wheat flour also makes the loaf somewhat denser. At the same time, the combination of the whole wheat along with the acidified rye makes a bread with good moisture retention and good keeping qualities.

1. **SOURDOUGH:** Prepare the sourdough and ripen for 14 to 16 hours at 70°F.

2. **MIXING:** Add all the ingredients to the mixing bowl. In a spiral mixer, mix for 3 minutes on first speed, and 3 minutes on second. The bran particles in the whole-wheat flour have a slight puncturing effect on the developing gluten network, so an additional 15 to 30 seconds of mixing on second speed may be necessary for proper dough development. Desired dough temperature: 78° to 80°F.

3. **BULK FERMENTATION:** 1 hour.

4. **DIVIDING AND SHAPING:** Divide the dough into 1.5-pound pieces; shape round or oblong.

5. **FINAL FERMENTATION:** 50 to 60 minutes at 78° to 80°F.

6. **BAKING:** With normal steam, 460°F for 15 minutes, then lower the oven temperature to 440°F and bake for 20 to 25 minutes.

Light Rye Bread

PRE-FERMENTED FLOUR: 15%

DOUGH YIELD | U.S.: About 22 loaves at 1.5 lb each | Metric: About 25 loaves at .68 kg each | Home: 2 large loaves

OVERALL FORMULA

	U.S.	METRIC	HOME	BAKER'S %
High-gluten flour	17 lb	8.5 kg	1 lb, 11.2 oz	85%
Medium rye flour	3 lb	1.5 kg	4.8 oz	15%
Water	13.2 lb	6.6 kg	1 lb, 5.1 oz	66%
Caraway seeds	.35 lb	.175 kg	.6 oz	1.75%
Salt	.4 lb	.2 kg	.6 oz	2%
Yeast	.3 lb, fresh	1.5 kg, fresh	.16 oz, instant dry	1.5%
TOTAL YIELD	**34.25 lb**	**17.125 kg**	**3 lb, 6.5 oz**	**171.25%**

SOURDOUGH

Medium rye flour	3 lb	1.5 kg	4.8 oz (1⅛ cups)	100%
Water	2.4 lb	1.2 kg	3.8 oz (½ cup)	80%
Mature sourdough culture	.15 lb	.075 kg	.2 oz (2 tsp)	5%
TOTAL	**5.55 lb**	**2.775 kg**	**8.8 oz**	

FINAL DOUGH

High-gluten flour	17 lb	8.5 kg	1 lb, 11.2 oz (6⅛ cups)
Water	10.8 lb	5.4 kg	1 lb, 1.3 oz (2⅛ cups)
Caraway seeds	.35 lb	.175 kg	.6 oz (2½ T)
Salt	.4 lb	.2 kg	.6 oz (1 T)
Yeast	.3 lb, fresh	.15 kg, fresh	.16 oz, instant dry (1½ tsp)
Sourdough	5.4 lb	2.7 kg	8.6 oz (all of above minus 2 tsp)
TOTAL	**34.25 lb**	**17.125 kg**	**3 lb, 6.5 oz**

1. **SOURDOUGH:** Prepare the sourdough and ripen for 14 to 16 hours at 70°F.

2. **MIXING:** Add all the ingredients to the mixing bowl. In a spiral mixer, mix for 3 minutes on first speed and 3 to 4 minutes on second, until a strong gluten development is achieved. Desired dough temperature: 78° to 80°F.

3. **BULK FERMENTATION:** 1 hour.

This light, mildly acidic bread is similar to what is commonly referred to as Jewish rye bread. Whole dark rye may be substituted for the medium rye in the formula. In this case, a little more water may be needed in the sourdough phase. The bread will also have a slightly more pronounced flavor. White rye flour is commonly used in this style of bread; it is, however, almost devoid of flavor, so medium or whole rye is a better choice.

4. DIVIDING AND SHAPING: Divide the dough into 1.5-pound pieces; shape oblong.

5. FINAL FERMENTATION: 50 to 60 minutes at 78° to 80°F.

6. BAKING: With normal steam, 460°F for 15 minutes, then lower the oven temperature to 440°F and bake for 20 to 25 minutes. Just before loading, score the loaves by making 3 or 4 cuts across the surface, perpendicular to the length of the loaf.

CARAWAY SEED VARIATION: Caraway seeds can be added in one of two ways to the top of the loaf. One method is to take the shaped loaf and press the top surface into a damp cloth and then into a sheet pan that contains a bed of caraway seeds. This method is speedy and suitable for bulk production; however, it does coat the surface with quite a lot of seeds. Another method is to press the top of the shaped loaf into a damp cloth (or to use a mister to moisten the surface) and then to sprinkle caraway seeds onto the moistened surface.

Sourdough Rye with Walnuts

PRE-FERMENTED FLOUR: 30%

DOUGH YIELD | U.S.: About 26 loaves at 1.5 lb each | Metric: About 28 loaves at .68 kg each | Home: 2 large loaves

OVERALL FORMULA

	U.S.	METRIC	HOME	BAKER'S %
Whole-rye flour	**10 lb**	**5 kg**	**1 lb**	**50%**
High-gluten flour	**10 lb**	**5 kg**	**1 lb**	**50%**
Water	**13.6 lb**	**6.8 kg**	**1 lb, 5.8 oz**	**68%**
Salt	**.36 lb**	**.18 kg**	**.6 oz**	**1.8%**
Yeast	**.3 lb, fresh**	**.15 kg, fresh**	**.16 oz, instant dry**	**1.5%**
Walnuts	**5 lb**	**2.5 kg**	**8 oz**	**25%**
TOTAL YIELD	**39.26 lb**	**19.63 kg**	**3 lb, 14.6 oz**	**196.3%**

SOURDOUGH

	U.S.	METRIC	HOME	BAKER'S %
Whole-rye flour	6 lb	3 kg	9.6 oz (2 5/8 cups)	100%
Water	4.98 lb	2.49 kg	8 oz (1 cup)	83%
Mature sourdough culture	.3 lb	.15 kg	.5 oz (1 T + 2 tsp)	5%
TOTAL	**11.28 lb**	**5.64 kg**	**1 lb, 2.1 oz**	

FINAL DOUGH

High-gluten flour	10 lb	5 kg	1 lb (3⅝ cups)
Whole-rye flour	4 lb	2 kg	6.4 oz (1¾ cups)
Water	8.62 lb	4.31 kg	13.8 oz (1¾ cups)
Salt	.36 lb	.18 kg	.6 oz (1 T)
Yeast	.3 lb, fresh	.15 kg, fresh	.16 oz, instant dry (1½ tsp)
Sourdough	10.98 lb	5.49 kg	1 lb, 1.6 oz (all of above minus 1 T, 2 tsp)
Walnuts	5 lb	2.5 kg	8 oz (2 cups)
TOTAL	**39.26 lb**	**19.63 kg**	**3 lb, 14.6 oz**

The rich flavor of walnuts combines with the full-bodied flavor of rye to make an excellent bread, one that pairs especially well with goat cheese.

1. **SOURDOUGH:** Prepare the sourdough and ripen for 14 to 16 hours at 70°F.

2. **MIXING:** Add all the ingredients except the walnuts to the mixing bowl. In a spiral mixer, mix for 3 minutes on first speed, and 3 to 4 minutes on second. A moderate gluten development should be noted. Add the walnuts and mix on first speed just until they are uniformly dispersed in the dough. Desired dough temperature: 78° to 80°F.

3. **BULK FERMENTATION:** 1 hour.

4. **DIVIDING AND SHAPING:** Divide the dough into 1.5-pound pieces; shape round or oblong.

5. **FINAL FERMENTATION:** 50 to 60 minutes at 78° to 80°F.

6. **BAKING:** With normal steam, 460°F for 15 minutes, then lower the oven temperature to 440°F and bake for 20 to 25 minutes.

The Detmolder Method of Rye Bread Production

The Detmolder method of making sourdough rye bread, developed in Germany, is a fascinating and highly effective technique that represents the highest expression of the baker's skill. It develops the latent potential of a mature rye culture through a series of builds before the mixing of the final dough. Rye sourdough cultures possess three distinct characteristics—yeast, acetic acid, and lactic acid—and each aspect thrives under different conditions of moistness (hydration), temperature, and duration of ripening. In the Detmolder system, the sourdough is built up in three phases, each favoring the development of one aspect of the sourdough. Paying careful attention to the time and temperature requirements of each phase is necessary in order to obtain the highest-quality results.

The first, or "freshening," phase encourages the development of the yeast cells of the sourdough. The yeast microorganisms present in sourdough thrive under moist conditions at an average temperature, and these conditions are supplied with a high-hydration paste (150 percent hydration) that matures for 5 to 6 hours at about 78°F.

Once the yeast phase has been properly developed, more rye flour and water are added to it. This second build is called the "basic sour" phase. Proper development requires a rather stiff-textured paste (60 to 65 percent hydration). The ripening temperature for this phase is 73°F to 80° and ripening time is 15 to 24 hours (lower temperatures require longer ripening times, and higher temperatures require shorter ripening times). During this phase, the acetic acid potential of the sour is developed, which will eventally impart a prominent sour tang to the bread.

After full ripening of the basic sour, more rye flour and water are added to make the "full sour." This phase develops the lactic acid, which will provide a smooth and mild acidity to the finished bread. Lactic acid development is favored by moist and warm conditions, and in this phase we have mixed a paste of 100 percent hydration and a ripening temperature of about 85°F. Note that ripening is accomplished in a relatively short period of time, 3 to 4 hours. Once the lactic development is complete, the full potential of the sourdough has been developed, and the final dough is ready to mix. Before mixing together the ingredients of the final dough, the baker removes a portion of the ripe sourdough in order to perpetuate the culture.

The building process began with less than 50 grams of culture more than 24 hours earlier, and has been expanded to produce a final dough of more than 18 kilograms. That represents an expansion factor of 360, and the finished loaves are indeed a testament to the wonder of nature, the health of the culture, and—not least—the expertise of the baker.

The precision required for the three-phase method is unlike anything else in bread production. It also is very labor-intensive, and other Detmolder methods simplify the process: For example, there is a one-phase method, as well as a two-phase. Although these breads don't have quite the ultimate flavor complexity of breads made with the three-phase technique, they are of excellent quality and fit more easily into many production schedules.

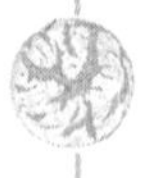

Long Trail Rye Bread

As the pH of a dough decreases, there is a corresponding increase in acidity. Other than the flavor provided by the acidity, it contributes another distinct benefit: Keeping quality improves. Historically, rural people throughout Europe baked just once every three or four weeks. The large loaves kept well partially because of their size (often more than 12 pounds), but mostly because of their sourdough characteristic.

I had an interesting experience with well-aged sourdough bread in the late 1970s. I had a one-month vacation during the summer, but was short on funds, so decided I would do something that was inexpensive: I decided to hike the Long Trail. The Long Trail winds its way through Vermont, beginning in the south at the Massachusetts border, and follows the Green Mountains for 275 miles until it ends at the Canadian border. It isn't feasible to carry enough food for the entire hike, so I did what many hikers do: I loaded boxes with preweighed provisions and sent them to myself to post offices that were near the Trail, with a note on the outside saying "Please Hold for Long Trail Hiker." Each week or so I would come to a road crossing and walk or hitch into town, retrieve my food parcel, load my pack, and return to the forest. In each of the food boxes there were a couple of loaves of naturally leavened 90 percent rye bread made with the three-stage building method. By the time I picked up my last box of provisions, the bread was five weeks old. It had been kept wrapped in aluminum foil at room temperature in the height of summer—by no means the best of storage conditions. In spite of this, those last loaves had a crisp tang, a moist crumb, delicious flavor, and not a hint of mold.

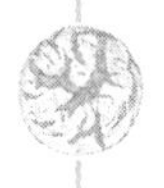

Three-Stage 90 Percent Sourdough Rye

PRE-FERMENTED FLOUR: 37.8%

DOUGH YIELD | U.S.: About 24 loaves at 1.5 lb each | Metric: About 26 loaves at .68 kg each | Home: 2 large loaves

OVERALL FORMULA

	U.S.	METRIC	HOME	BAKER'S %
Whole-rye flour	7.56 lb	3.78 kg	12.1 oz	37.8%
Medium rye flour	10.44 lb	5.22 kg	1 lb, .7 oz	52.2%
High-gluten flour	2 lb	1 kg	3.2 oz	10%
Water	15.78 lb	7.89 kg	1 lb, 9.2 oz	78.9%
Salt	.36 lb	.18 kg	.6 oz	1.8%
Yeast (optional; see headnote)	.16 lb, fresh	.08 kg, fresh	.1 oz, instant dry	.8%
TOTAL YIELD	36.3 lb	18.15 kg	3 lb, 9.9 oz	181.5%

FRESHENING

Whole-rye flour	.16 lb	.08 kg	.3 oz (1½ T)	100%
Water	.24 lb	.12 kg	.4 oz (1 T)	150%
Mature rye culture	.08 lb	.04 kg	.1 oz (1 tsp)	50%
TOTAL	**.48 lb**	**.24 kg**	**.8 oz**	

BASIC SOUR

Whole-rye flour	2 lb	1 kg	3.2 oz (⅞ cup)	100%
Water	1.56 lb	.78 kg	2.5 oz (⅜ cup)	78%
Freshening sour	.48 lb	.24 kg	.8 oz (all of above)	24%
TOTAL	**4.04 lb**	**2.02 kg**	**6.5 oz**	

FULL SOUR

Whole-rye flour	5.4 lb	2.7 kg	8.6 oz (2¼ cups)	100%
Water	5.4 lb	2.7 kg	8.6 oz (1 cup)	100%
Basic sour	4.04 lb	2.02 kg	6.5 oz (all of above)	74.8%
TOTAL	**14.84 lb**	**7.42 kg**	**1 lb, 7.7 oz**	

FINAL DOUGH

Medium rye flour	10.44 lb	5.22 kg	1 lb, .7 oz (4⅛ cups)
High-gluten flour	2 lb	1 kg	3.2 oz (¾ cup)
Water	8.58 lb	4.29 kg	13.7 oz (1¾ cups)
Salt	.36 lb	.18 kg	.6 oz (1 T)
Yeast (optional; see headnote)	.16 lb, fresh	.08 kg, fresh	.1 oz, instant dry (1 tsp)
Full sour	14.76 lb	7.38 kg	1 lb, 7.6 oz (all of above minus 1 tsp)
TOTAL	**36.3 lb**	**18.15 kg**	**3 lb, 9.9 oz**

1. **FRESHENING:** The mature culture is dispersed in water and the whole-rye flour mixed thoroughly into it. The temperature of this loose paste should be 77° to 79°F. Ripen the paste for 5 to 6 hours. During this phase, the yeast potential of the sourdough is developed.

2. **BASIC SOUR:** Mix the freshening paste into the water and then add the flour. The temperature of the basic sour should be 73° to 80°F, and the ripening time will be 15 to 24 hours (the longer the ripening time, the cooler the temperature, and vice versa). Typically, this phase is left to ripen overnight. This is the stiff phase, and if need be, a small portion of water can be added, depending on the

Baker's yeast is not an absolutely necessary addition to this dough. If your rye culture is well maintained, and the three steps in the building process follow the time and temperature needs of each individual phase, the existing yeast population within the culture should be sufficient to leaven the bread without the inclusion of commercial yeast. Final fermentation may take a bit longer if the bread is leavened only by the sourdough, and the baked loaves may be slightly denser. Nevertheless, the bread will be a tribute to the health and vigor of the sourdough culture that engendered such delicious results.

absorption rate of the flour. During this stage, the acetic properties of the sourdough are developed.

3. FULL SOUR: Disperse the basic sour into the water and mix in the flour. The temperature should be about 85°F, and ripening should last 3 to 4 hours. Add more water as needed to obtain a paste of medium looseness. This is a looser build than the preceding one, during which the lactic character of the dough is developed.

4. MIXING: After removing a small portion of the mature sourdough, put the sourdough and all the final dough ingredients into the mixer (the yeast is optional). In a spiral mixer, mix on first speed for approximately 4 minutes, then on second for 1 to 1½ minutes. The dough will be sticky, but avoid any inclination to add flour. There will be no perceptible gluten development. Desired dough temperature: 82° to 84°F.

5. BULK FERMENTATION: 10 to 20 minutes. Due to the high degree of souring that has occurred during the 3 development phases, very little bulk fermentation time is required before dividing the dough.

6. DIVIDING AND SHAPING: Divide the dough into 1.5- or 2.5-pound pieces; shape round.

7. FINAL FERMENTATION: About 1 hour at 82°F.

8. BAKING: Score the loaves with a dough docker. Bake with normal steam (open the oven vents after 5 minutes to extract moisture and allow the sides of the breads to begin firming), at 480° to 490°F for 10 minutes, then lower the oven temperature to 410°F and bake for 40 to 50 minutes for a 1.5-pound loaf, about 1 hour for a loaf scaled at 2.5 pounds. Once baked, leave the loaves on cooling racks and, when fully cooled, put into tubs or wrap in baker's linen. Let stand for at least 24 hours before slicing in order to stabilize the crumb.

Three-Stage 80 Percent Sourdough Rye

PRE-FERMENTED FLOUR: 37.8%

DOUGH YIELD | U.S.: About 24 loaves at 1.5 lb each | Metric: About 26 loaves at .68 kg each | Home: 2 large loaves

OVERALL FORMULA

	U.S.	METRIC	HOME	BAKER'S %
Medium rye flour	**16 lb**	**8 kg**	**1 lb, 9.6 oz**	**80%**
High-gluten flour	**4 lb**	**2 kg**	**6.4 oz**	**20%**
Water	**15.6 lb**	**7.8 kg**	**1 lb, 9 oz**	**78%**
Salt	**.36 lb**	**.18 kg**	**.6 oz**	**1.8%**
Yeast	**.16 lb, fresh**	**.08 kg, fresh**	**.1 oz, instant dry**	**.8%**
TOTAL YIELD	**36.12 lb**	**18.06 kg**	**3 lb, 9.7 oz**	**180.6%**

FRESHENING

Medium rye flour	.16 lb	.08 kg	.3 oz (1½ T)	100%
Water	.24 lb	.12 kg	.4 oz (1 T)	150%
Mature rye culture	.08 lb	.04 kg	.1 oz (1 tsp)	50%
TOTAL	**.48 lb**	**.24 kg**	**.8 oz**	

BASIC SOUR

Medium rye flour	2 lb	1 kg	3.2 oz (¾ cup)	100%
Water	1.52 lb	.76 kg	2.4 oz (¼ cup)	76%
Freshening sour	.48 lb	.24 kg	.8 oz (all of above)	24%
TOTAL	**4 lb**	**2 kg**	**6.4 oz**	

FULL SOUR

Medium rye flour	5.4 lb	2.7 kg	8.6 oz (2¾ cups)	100%
Water	5.4 lb	2.7 kg	8.6 oz (1⅛ cups)	100%
Basic sour	4 lb	2 kg	6.4 oz (all of above)	74.1%
TOTAL	**14.8 lb**	**7.4 kg**	**1 lb, 7.6 oz**	

FINAL DOUGH

Medium rye flour	8.44 lb	4.22 kg	13.5 oz (3⅜ cups)
High-gluten flour	4 lb	2 kg	6.4 oz (1½ cups)
Water	8.44 lb	4.22 kg	13.5 oz (1¾ cups)
Salt	.36 lb	.18 kg	.6 oz (1 T)
Yeast	.16 lb, fresh	.08 kg, fresh	.1 oz, instant dry (1 tsp)
Full sour	14.72 lb	7.36 kg	1 lb, 7.5 oz (all of above minus 1 tsp)
TOTAL	**36.12 lb**	**18.06 kg**	**3 lb, 9.8 oz**

This three-phase rye is slightly lighter than the 90 percent rye in the preceding formula, yet still quite robust. Observe the time and temperature requirements for the three build phases. Small adjustments in water quantities may be necessary, depending on the absorption rate of the rye flour used.

1. **FRESHENING:** The mature culture is dispersed in water and the medium rye flour mixed thoroughly into it. The temperature of this loose paste should be 77° to 79°F. Ripen the paste for 5 to 6 hours. During this phase, the yeast potential of the sourdough is developed.

2. **BASIC SOUR:** Mix the freshening paste into the water and then add the flour. The temperature of the basic sour should be 73° to 80°F, and the ripening time will be 15 to 24 hours (the longer the ripening time, the cooler the temperature, and vice versa). Typically, this phase is left to ripen overnight. This is the stiff phase, and if need be, a small portion of water can be added, depending on the absorption rate of the flour. During this stage, the acetic properties of the sourdough are developed.

3. **FULL SOUR:** Disperse the basic sour into the water and mix in the flour. The temperature should be about 85°F, and ripening should last 3 to 4 hours. Add more water as needed to obtain a paste of medium looseness. This is a looser build than the preceding one, during which the lactic character of the dough is developed.

4. **MIXING:** After removing a small portion of the mature sourdough, place the sourdough and all the final dough ingredients in the mixing bowl (the yeast is optional). In a spiral mixer, mix on first speed for approximately 4 minutes, then on second for 1 to 1½ minutes. The dough will be sticky, but avoid any inclination to add flour. There will be no perceptible gluten development. Desired dough temperature: 82° to 84°F.

5. **BULK FERMENTATION:** 10 to 20 minutes. Due to the high degree of souring that has occurred during the 3 development phases, very little bulk fermentation time is required before dividing the dough.

6. **DIVIDING AND SHAPING:** Divide the dough into 1.5- or 2.5-pound pieces; shape round.

7. **FINAL FERMENTATION:** About 1 hour at 82°F.

8. **BAKING:** Score the loaves with a dough docker. Bake with normal steam (open the oven vents after 5 minutes to extract moisture and allow the sides of the breads to begin firming), at 480° to 490°F for 10 minutes, then lower the oven temperature to 410°F and bake for 40 to 50 minutes for a 1.5-pound loaf, about 1 hour for a loaf scaled at 2.5 pounds. Once baked, leave the loaves on cooling racks and, when fully cooled, put into tubs or wrap in baker's linen. Let stand for at least 24 hours before slicing in order to stabilize the crumb.

Three-Stage 70 Percent Sourdough Rye

PRE-FERMENTED FLOUR: 35%

DOUGH YIELD | U.S.: About 23 loaves at 1.5 lb each | Metric: About 26 loaves at .68 kg each | Home: 2 large loaves

OVERALL FORMULA

	U.S.	METRIC	HOME	BAKER'S %
Medium rye flour	14 lb	7 kg	1 lb, 6.4 oz	70%
High-gluten flour	6 lb	3 kg	9.6 oz	30%
Water	15 lb	7.5 kg	1 lb, 8 oz	75%
Salt	.36 lb	.18 kg	.6 oz	1.8%
Yeast	.2 lb, fresh	.1 kg, fresh	.1 oz, instant dry	1%
TOTAL YIELD	**35.56 lb**	**17.78 kg**	**3 lb, 8.7 oz**	**177.8%**

FRESHENING

	U.S.	METRIC	HOME	BAKER'S %
Medium rye flour	.16 lb	.08 kg	.3 oz (1½ T)	100%
Water	.24 lb	.12 kg	.4 oz (1 T)	150%
Mature rye culture	.08 lb	.04 kg	.1 oz (1 tsp)	50%
TOTAL	**.48 lb**	**.24 kg**	**.8 oz**	

BASIC SOUR

	U.S.	METRIC	HOME	BAKER'S %
Medium rye flour	2 lb	1 kg	3.2 oz (¾ cup)	100%
Water	1.52 lb	.76 kg	2.4 oz (¼ cup)	76%
Freshening	.48 lb	.24 kg	.8 oz (all of above)	24%
TOTAL	**4 lb**	**2 kg**	**6.4 oz**	

FULL SOUR

	U.S.	METRIC	HOME	BAKER'S %
Medium rye flour	4.84 lb	2.42 kg	7.7 oz (⅞ cup)	100%
Water	4.84 lb	2.42 kg	7.7 oz (1 cup)	100%
Basic sour	4 lb	2 kg	6.4 oz (all of above)	82.6%
TOTAL	**13.68 lb**	**6.84 kg**	**1 lb, 5.8 oz**	

FINAL DOUGH

	U.S.	METRIC	HOME
Medium rye flour	7 lb	3.5 kg	11.2 oz (2¾ cups)
High-gluten flour	6 lb	3 kg	9.6 oz (2¼ cups)
Water	8.4 lb	4.2 kg	13.4 oz (⅝ cups)
Salt	.36 lb	.18 kg	.6 oz (1 T)
Yeast	.2 lb, fresh	.1 kg, fresh	.1 oz, instant dry (1 tsp)
Full sour	13.6 lb	6.8 kg	1 lb, 5.7 oz (all of above minus 1 tsp)
TOTAL	**35.56 lb**	**17.78 kg**	**3 lb, 8.6 oz**

With 70 percent rye, this bread is somewhat lighter still than the two preceding Detmolder ryes. The extra white flour makes shaping a bit easier, and the finished loaves should have more volume. Observe the time and temperature requirements for the three build phases. Small adjustments in water quantities may be necessary, depending on the absorption rate of the rye flour used.

1. **FRESHENING:** The mature culture is dispersed in water and the medium rye flour mixed thoroughly into it. The temperature of this loose paste should be 77° to 79°F. Ripen the paste for 5 to 6 hours. During this phase, the yeast potential of the sourdough is developed.

2. **BASIC SOUR:** Mix the freshening paste into the water and then add the flour. The temperature of the basic sour should be 73° to 80°F, and the ripening time will be 15 to 24 hours (the longer the ripening time, the cooler the temperature, and vice versa). Typically, this phase is left to ripen overnight. This is the stiff phase, and if need be, a small portion of water can be added, depending on the absorption rate of the flour. During this stage, the acetic properties of the sourdough are developed.

3. **FULL SOUR:** Disperse the basic sour into the water and mix in the flour. The temperature should be about 85°F, and ripening should last 3 to 4 hours. Add more water as needed to obtain a paste of medium looseness. This is a looser build than the preceding one, during which the lactic character of the dough is developed.

4. **MIXING:** After removing a small portion of the mature sourdough, place the sourdough and all the final dough ingredients in the mixing bowl (the yeast is optional). In a spiral mixer, mix on first speed for approximately 4 minutes, then on second for 1 to 1½ minutes. The dough will be sticky, but avoid any inclination to add flour. There will be no perceptible gluten development. Desired dough temperature: 82° to 84°F.

5. **BULK FERMENTATION:** 10 to 20 minutes. Due to the high degree of souring that has occurred during the 3 development phases, very little bulk fermentation time is required before dividing the dough.

6. **DIVIDING AND SHAPING:** Divide the dough into 1.5- or 2.5-pound pieces; shape round.

7. **FINAL FERMENTATION:** About 1 hour at 82°F.

8. **BAKING:** Score the loaves with a dough docker. Bake with normal steam (open the oven vents after 5 minutes to extract moisture and allow the sides of the breads to begin firming), at 480° to 490°F for 10 minutes, then lower the oven temperature to 410°F and bake for 40 to 50 minutes for a 1.5-pound loaf, about 1 hour for a loaf scaled at 2.5 pounds. Once baked, leave the loaves on cooling racks and, when fully cooled, put into tubs or wrap in baker's linen. Let stand for at least 24 hours before slicing in order to stabilize the crumb.

Sourdough Rye with Raisins and Walnuts

PRE-FERMENTED FLOUR: 30%

DOUGH YIELD | U.S.: About 26 loaves at 1.5 lb each | Metric: About 28 loaves at .68 kg each | Home: 2 large loaves

OVERALL FORMULA

	U.S.	METRIC	HOME	BAKER'S %
High-gluten flour	13 lb	6.5 kg	1 lb, 4.8 oz	65%
Medium rye flour	7 lb	3.5 kg	11.2 oz	35%
Water	13.6 lb	6.8 kg	1 lb, 5.8 oz	68%
Salt	.36 lb	.18 kg	.6 oz	1.8%
Yeast	.3 lb, fresh	.15 kg, fresh	.16 oz, instant dry	1.5%
Raisins	2.5 lb	1.25 kg	4 oz	12.5%
Walnuts	2.5 lb	1.25 kg	4 oz	12.5%
TOTAL YIELD	**39.26 lb**	**19.63 kg**	**3 lb, 14.6 oz**	**196.3%**

SOURDOUGH

Medium rye flour	6 lb	3 kg	9.6 oz (2 3/8 cups)	100%
Water	4.8 lb	2.4 kg	7.7 oz (1 cup)	80%
Mature sourdough culture	.3 lb	.15 kg	.5 oz (1 T + 2 tsp)	5%
TOTAL	**11.1 lb**	**5.55 kg**	**1 lb, 1.8 oz**	

FINAL DOUGH

High-gluten flour	13 lb	6.5 kg	1 lb, 4.8 oz (4 3/4 cups)
Medium rye flour	1 lb	.5 kg	1.6 oz (3/8 cup)
Water	8.8 lb	4.4 kg	14.1 oz (1 3/4 cups)
Salt	.36 lb	.18 kg	.6 oz (1 T)
Yeast	.3 lb, fresh	.15 kg, fresh	.16 oz, instant dry (1 1/2 tsp)
Sourdough	10.8 lb	5.4 kg	1 lb, 1.3 oz (all of above minus 1 T, 2 tsp)
Raisins	2.5 lb	1.25 kg	4 oz (3/4 cup)
Walnuts	2.5 lb	1.25 kg	4 oz (1 cup)
TOTAL	**39.26 lb**	**19.63 kg**	**3 lb, 14.6 oz**

This rye bread has a light texture, and the raisins and walnuts give it a delightful flavor.

1. SOURDOUGH: Prepare the sourdough and ripen for 14 to 16 hours at 70°F.

2. MIXING: Add all the ingredients except the raisins and walnuts to the mixing bowl. In a spiral mixer, mix for 3 minutes on first speed and about 3 minutes on second, achieving a well-developed gluten structure. Add the raisins and walnuts and mix on first speed just until they are uniformly dispersed in the dough. Desired dough temperature: 78° to 80°F.

3. BULK FERMENTATION: 1 hour.

4. DIVIDING AND SHAPING: Divide the dough into 1.5-pound pieces; shape round or oblong.

5. FINAL FERMENTATION: 50 to 60 minutes at 78° to 80°F.

6. BAKING: With normal steam, 460°F for 15 minutes, then lower the oven temperature to 430°F and bake for 20 to 25 minutes. The raisins will cause the dough to darken, so the bake is finished at 430°F. If the bottoms of the breads are coloring too quickly, transfer the breads to sheet pans to finish the bake.

VARIATIONS: A sweeter version of this bread can be made by eliminating the walnuts entirely and increasing the percentage of raisins to 22 to 25 percent. In this case, lower the oven temperature to 420°F after 15 or 20 minutes to prevent too much coloration from the sugars in the raisins. Another variation replaces the raisins used in the original formula with 22 to 25 percent currants.

66 Percent Sourdough Rye

PRE-FERMENTED FLOUR: 40%

DOUGH YIELD | U.S.: About 23 loaves at 1.5 lb each | Metric: About 26 loaves at .68 kg each | Home: 2 large loaves

OVERALL FORMULA

	U.S.	METRIC	HOME	BAKER'S %
Medium rye flour	13.2 lb	6.6 kg	1 lb, 5.1 oz	66%
High-gluten flour	6.8 lb	3.4 kg	10.9 oz	34%
Water	15 lb	7.5 kg	1 lb, 8 oz	75%
Salt	.36 lb	.18 kg	.6 oz	1.8%
Yeast	.2 lb, fresh	.1 kg, fresh	.1 oz, instant dry	1%
TOTAL YIELD	35.56 lb	17.78 kg	3 lb, 8.7 oz	177.8%

SOURDOUGH

Medium rye flour	8 lb	4 kg	12.8 oz (3½ cups)	100%
Water	6.4 lb	3.2 kg	10.2 oz (1¼ cups)	80%
Mature sourdough culture	.4 lb	.2 kg	.6 oz (2 T)	5%
TOTAL	14.8 lb	7.4 kg	1 lb, 7.6 oz	

FINAL DOUGH

Medium rye flour	5.2 lb	2.6 kg	8.3 oz (1⅛ cups)
High-gluten flour	6.8 lb	3.4 kg	10.9 oz (2½ cups)
Water	8.6 lb	4.3 kg	13.8 oz (1¾ cups)
Salt	.36 lb	.18 kg	.6 oz (1 T)
Yeast	.2 lb, fresh	.1 kg, fresh	.1 oz, instant dry (1 tsp)
Sourdough	14.4 lb	7.2 kg	1 lb, 7 oz (all of above minus 2 T)
TOTAL	35.56 lb	17.78 kg	3 lb, 8.7 oz

This rye bread, made with 66 percent rye flour, has full flavor and good keeping quality. The medium rye makes a loaf somewhat lighter than if whole rye were used. The degree of sour flavor can be adjusted by lowering the percentage of rye flour used in the sourdough phase. In that case, be

1. SOURDOUGH: Prepare the sourdough and ripen for 14 to 16 hours at 70°F.

2. MIXING: Add all the ingredients to the mixing bowl. In a spiral mixer, mix for 3 minutes on first speed and about 2 minutes on second. When the dough is tugged, you should be able to feel a bit of gluten strength from the 34 percent white flour, but the overall dough strength will not be much. Desired dough temperature: 80°F.

3. BULK FERMENTATION: 30 to 45 minutes.

sure the final dough-ingredient weights are properly adjusted as well. As the percentage of rye flour increases in a dough, rolls become more difficult to make, because the dense texture of the dough makes rolls with too high a proportion of crust. Sixty-six percent rye flour may be at about the upper limit for roll production.

4. DIVIDING AND SHAPING: Divide the dough into 1.5-pound pieces; shape round or oblong.

5. FINAL FERMENTATION: 50 to 60 minutes at 80°F.

6. BAKING: With normal steam, 460°F for 15 minutes, then lower the oven temperature to 440°F and bake for 30 to 40 minutes. The baked bread should rest for up to 24 hours before slicing in order to improve its eating quality.

Flaxseed Bread

PRE-FERMENTED FLOUR: 40%

DOUGH YIELD | U.S.: About 25 loaves at 1.5 lb each | Metric: About 27 loaves at .68 kg each | Home: 2 large loaves

OVERALL FORMULA

	U.S.	METRIC	HOME	BAKER'S %
Medium rye flour	12 lb	6 kg	1 lb, 3.2 oz	60%
High-gluten flour	8 lb	4 kg	12.8 oz	40%
Flaxseeds	2 lb	1 kg	3.2 oz	10%
Water	15 lb	7.5 kg	1 lb, 8 oz	75%
Salt	.36 lb	.18 kg	.6 oz	1.8%
Yeast	.3 lb, fresh	.15 kg, fresh	.16 oz, instant dry	1.5%
TOTAL YIELD	**37.66 lb**	**18.83 kg**	**3 lb, 12 oz**	**188.3%**

SOURDOUGH

Medium rye flour	8 lb	4 kg	12.8 oz (3¼ cups)	100%
Water	6.4 lb	3.2 kg	10.2 oz (1¼ cups)	80%
Mature sourdough culture	.4 lb	.2 kg	.6 oz (2 T)	5%
TOTAL	**14.8 lb**	**7.4 kg**	**1 lb, 7.6 oz**	

SOAKER

Flaxseeds	2 lb	1 kg	3.2 oz (⅝ cup)	100%
Water	6 lb	3 kg	9.6 oz (1¼ cups)	300%
TOTAL	**8 lb**	**4 kg**	**12.8 oz**	

FINAL DOUGH

Medium rye flour	4 lb	2 kg	6.4 oz (1⅝ cups)
High-gluten flour	8 lb	4 kg	12.8 oz (3 cups)
Water	2.6 lb	1.3 kg	4.2 oz (½ cup)
Salt	.36 lb	.18 kg	.6 oz (1 T)
Yeast	.3 lb, fresh	.15 kg, fresh	.16 oz, instant dry (1½ tsp)
Soaker	8 lb	4 kg	12.8 oz (all of above)
Sourdough	14.4 lb	7.2 kg	1 lb, 7 oz (all of above minus 2 T)
TOTAL	**37.66 lb**	**18.83 kg**	**3 lb, 12 oz**

Flax is a uniquely valuable plant. Not only are the seeds highly nutritious, the plant is also the source for linen and linseed oil, and in the days before vinyl flooring, linoleum was produced from it.

Flaxseed Bread, or *Leinsamenbrot,* is a trustworthy and tasty loaf common in Germany. The presence of the flaxseeds gives the crumb a nice mottled aspect, the rye contributes a fine tang, and the soaker gives the bread excellent keeping quality. The combination of flavors makes a delicious loaf.

1. **SOURDOUGH:** Prepare the sourdough and ripen for 14 to 16 hours at 70°F.

2. **SOAKER:** Pour cold water over the flaxseeds. Cover with plastic to prevent evaporation.

3. **MIXING:** Add all the ingredients to the mixing bowl. In a spiral mixer, mix for 3 minutes on first speed and about 3 minutes on second. The 40 percent white flour will give the dough a perceptible but not overly strong gluten development. Desired dough temperature: 80°F.

4. **BULK FERMENTATION:** 30 to 45 minutes.

5. **DIVIDING AND SHAPING:** Divide the dough into 1.5- or 2-pound pieces; shape round or oblong.

6. **FINAL FERMENTATION:** 50 to 60 minutes at 80°F.

7. **BAKING:** With normal steam, 460°F for 15 minutes, then lower the oven temperature to 440°F and bake for 30 to 35 minutes for a 1.5-pound loaf, 40 to 45 minutes for a loaf scaled at 2 pounds. For the best eating quality, cover the cooled loaves with baker's linen and let stand at room temperature for at least several hours or up to 24 hours before slicing. Sesame seeds are commonly added to *Leinsamenbrot:* Once shaped, the tops of the loaves are pressed into a damp cloth and then into a pan of raw sesame seeds. Alternatively, the seeds can be sprinkled onto the moistened surface of the loaves.

80 Percent Sourdough Rye with a Rye-Flour Soaker

PRE-FERMENTED FLOUR: 35%

DOUGH YIELD | U.S.: About 24 loaves at 1.5 lb each | Metric: About 26 loaves at .68 kg each | Home: 2 large loaves

OVERALL FORMULA

	U.S.	METRIC	HOME	BAKER'S %
Whole-rye flour	16 lb	8 kg	1 lb, 9.6 oz	80%
High-gluten flour	4 lb	2 kg	6.4 oz	20%
Water	15.6 lb	7.8 kg	1 lb, 9 oz	78%
Salt	.36 lb	.18 kg	.6 oz	1.8%
Yeast	.3 lb, fresh	.15 kg, fresh	.16 oz, instant dry	1.5%
TOTAL YIELD	**36.26 lb**	**18.13 kg**	**3 lb, 9.8 oz**	**181.3%**

SOURDOUGH

	U.S.	METRIC	HOME	BAKER'S %
Whole-rye flour	7 lb	3.5 kg	11.2 oz (3 cups)	100%
Water	5.8 lb	2.9 kg	9.3 oz (1 1/8 cups)	83%
Mature sourdough culture	.35 lb	.175 kg	.6 oz (2 T)	5%
TOTAL	**13.15 lb**	**6.575 kg**	**1 lb, 5.1 oz**	

SOAKER

	U.S.	METRIC	HOME	BAKER'S %
Whole-rye flour	4 lb	2 kg	6.4 oz (1 3/4 cups)	100%
Water, boiling	4 lb	2 kg	6.4 oz (3/4 cup)	100%
TOTAL	**8 lb**	**4 kg**	**12.8 oz**	

FINAL DOUGH

	U.S.	METRIC	HOME
Whole-rye flour	5 lb	2.5 kg	8 oz (2 1/8 cups)
High-gluten flour	4 lb	2 kg	6.4 oz (1 1/2 cups)
Water	5.8 lb	2.9 kg	9.3 oz (1 1/8 cups)
Salt	.36 lb	.18 kg	.6 oz (1 T)
Yeast	.3 lb, fresh	.15 kg, fresh	.16 oz, instant dry (1 1/2 tsp)
Soaker	8 lb	4 kg	12.8 oz (all of above)
Sourdough	12.8 lb	6.4 kg	1 lb, 4.5 oz (all of above minus 1 1/2 T)
TOTAL	**36.26 lb**	**18.13 kg**	**3 lb, 9.8 oz**

Particularly notable in this bread is the hot rye-flour soaker. This initial heating gelatinizes the rye starch and gives the bread an unusually smooth eating quality; the soaker also contributes to the bread's excellent keeping quality.

1. SOURDOUGH: Prepare the sourdough and ripen for 14 to 16 hours at 70°F.

2. SOAKER: Make the soaker by pouring the boiling water over the rye. Cover with plastic right away to prevent evaporation. The soaker can be made at the same time as the sourdough and kept at room temperature until mixing the final dough.

3. MIXING: Add all the ingredients to the mixing bowl (including the soaker, which will have absorbed all the water and be quite thick). In a spiral mixer, mix on first speed for 3 minutes. The dough should be moderately loose textured, and sticky. Turn the mixer to second speed and mix for approximately 2 minutes. With only 20 percent white flour, there will be little in the way of gluten development. Desired dough temperature: 82°F.

4. BULK FERMENTATION: 30 minutes.

5. DIVIDING AND SHAPING: Divide the dough into 1.5- or 2.5-pound pieces; shape round or oblong.

6. FINAL FERMENTATION: 50 to 60 minutes at 82°F.

7. BAKING: With normal steam, 470°F for 15 minutes, then lower the oven temperature to 430°F and bake for 35 to 40 minutes for a 1.5-pound loaf, 45 to 50 minutes for a loaf scaled at 2.5 pounds. After the bake, cool the loaves and then wrap in baker's linen and let stand for 24 hours before slicing, in order to stabilize the texture of the crumb.

70 Percent Rye with a Rye Soaker and Whole-Wheat Flour

PRE-FERMENTED FLOUR: 35%

DOUGH YIELD | U.S.: About 8 pullman loaves at 4.5 lb each | Metric: About 9 pullman loaves at 2.05 kg each | Home: 1 pullman loaf

OVERALL FORMULA

	U.S.	METRIC	HOME	BAKER'S %
Medium rye flour	**7 lb**	**3.5 kg**	**11.2 oz**	**35%**
Whole-wheat flour	**6 lb**	**3 kg**	**9.6 oz**	**30%**
Rye chops	**7 lb**	**3.5 kg**	**11.2 oz**	**35%**
Water	**15.6 lb**	**7.8 kg**	**1 lb, 9 oz**	**78%**
Salt	**.36 lb**	**.18 kg**	**.6 oz**	**1.8%**
Yeast	**.3 lb, fresh**	**.15 kg, fresh**	**.16 oz, instant dry**	**1.5%**
TOTAL YIELD	**36.26 lb**	**18.13 kg**	**3 lb, 9.8 oz**	**181.3%**

SOURDOUGH

Medium rye flour	7 lb	3.5 kg	11.2 oz (2¾ cups)	100%
Water	5.6 lb	2.8 kg	9 oz (1⅛ cups)	80%
Mature sourdough culture	.35 lb	.175 kg	.6 oz (2 T)	5%
TOTAL	**12.95 lb**	**6.475 kg**	**1 lb, 4.8 oz**	

SOAKER

Rye chops	7 lb	3.5 kg	11.2 oz (2½ cups)	100%
Water	7 lb	3.5 kg	11.2 oz (1⅜ cups)	100%
Salt	.14 lb	.07 kg	.2 oz (1 tsp)	2%
TOTAL	**14.14 lb**	**7.07 kg**	**1 lb, 6.6 oz**	

FINAL DOUGH

Whole-wheat flour	6 lb	3 kg	9.6 oz (2¼ cups)
Water	3 lb	1.5 kg	4.8 oz (⅝ cup)
Salt	.22 lb	.11 kg	.4 oz (2 tsp)
Yeast	.3 lb, fresh	.15 kg, fresh	.16 oz, instant dry (1½ tsp)
Soaker	14.14 lb	7.07 kg	1 lb, 6.6 oz (all of above)
Sourdough	12.6 lb	6.3 kg	1 lb, 4.2 oz (all of above minus 2 T)
TOTAL	**36.26 lb**	**18.13 kg**	**3 lb, 9.8 oz**

The whole-wheat flour, along with the soaked rye chops, contributes to the depth of flavor of this bread. Chops, as the name suggests, are milled by chopping rather than grinding the grain; both rye and wheat chops are available, and both add a great deal of texture to breads. If the rye chops called for in the formula are unavailable, cracked rye is a suitable substitute. It does not absorb water as readily as the chops, however, and if using them, first boil the water. The method described calls for dough pieces of 4.5 pounds that are baked in uncovered pullman pans (this weight fits a pullman pan with the dimensions 13 by 3³/₄ by 3³/₄ inches); in Germany these loaves are also shaped into large rounds weighing as much as 11 pounds. Prepare the pullman pans by lightly oiling them and then coating them with pumpernickel rye meal or whole-rye flour. This method of preparing the pans is typical for long-baking, high-rye-flour breads, and helps prevent the dough from sticking to the pan. For other types of pan loaves, just oiling the pan is sufficient.

1. **SOURDOUGH:** Prepare the sourdough and ripen for 14 to 16 hours at 70°F.

2. **SOAKER:** Make the soaker by pouring cold water over the rye chops and salt. Cover with plastic to prevent evaporation. If using cracked rye, prepare a hot soaker using boiling water.

3. **MIXING:** Add all the ingredients to the mixing bowl, including the soaker. In a spiral mixer, mix on first speed for 3 minutes in order to incorporate all the ingredients. The dough should be dense and sticky, with medium looseness. Finish the mix on second speed for approximately 2 minutes. Desired dough temperature: 82°F.

4. **BULK FERMENTATION:** 30 minutes.

5. **DIVIDING AND SHAPING:** Divide the dough into 4.5-pound pieces. Shape the dough pieces into logs and place them in the prepared pullman pans (see headnote). Sprinkle a thin layer of whole-rye flour or pumpernickel meal over the top. They do not need a lid. Cover the loaves with plastic to prevent a crust from forming.

6. **FINAL FERMENTATION:** 50 to 60 minutes at 82°F.

7. **BAKING:** With normal steam, 480°F for 15 minutes, then lower the oven temperature to 410°F and bake for approximately 1 hour. The proofed loaves do not require scoring of any kind. After about 1 hour, remove the bread from the pans in order to firm up the side walls, and finish the bake on sheet pans. The bread should be wrapped in baker's linen after it cools and allowed to stand for at least 24 hours before slicing.

Vollkornbrot (whole grain bread)

germanfot 8 loaves @ 1.5 lb each

PRE-FERMENTED FLOUR: 41%

DOUGH YIELD | U.S.: About 8 pullman loaves at 4.5 lb each | Metric: About 9 pullman loaves at 2.05 kg each | Home: 1 pullman loaf

OVERALL FORMULA

	U.S.	METRIC	HOME	BAKER'S %
Rye meal	13.68 lb	6.84 kg	1 lb, 5.9 oz	68.4%
Rye chops	6.32 lb	3.16 kg	10.1 oz	31.6%
Sunflower seeds	1.1 lb	.55 kg	1.8 oz	5.5%
Water	16.42 lb	8.21 kg	1 lb, 10.3 oz	82.1%
Salt	.4 lb	.2 kg	.6 oz	2%
Yeast	.36 lb, fresh	.18 kg, fresh	.19 oz, instant dry	1.8%
TOTAL YIELD	**38.28 lb**	**19.14 kg**	**3 lb, 12.9 oz**	**191.4%**

SOURDOUGH

		– lbs –				
Rye meal	8.22 lb	3.05	4.11 kg		13.2 oz (3⅝ cups)	100%
Water	8.22 lb	3.05	4.11 kg	48.8 oz	13.2 oz (⅝ cup)	100%
Mature sourdough culture	.41 lb	.15	.206 kg		.7 oz (2 T + 1 tsp)	5%
TOTAL	**16.85 lb**		**8.426 kg**		**1 lb, 11.1 oz**	

*

SOAKER

Rye chops	6.32 lb	2.34	3.16 kg		10.1 oz (2¼ cups)	100%
Water	6.32 lb	2.34	3.16 kg	37.44 oz	10.1 oz (1¼ cups)	100%
TOTAL	**12.64 lb**		**6.32 kg**		**1 lb, 4.2 oz**	

Dee

FINAL DOUGH

Rye meal	5.46 lb	2.02	2.73 kg		8.7 oz (2⅜ cups)
Water	1.88 lb	.70	.94 kg	11.2 oz	3 oz (⅜ cup)
Salt	.4 lb	.15	.2 kg		.6 oz (1 T)
Yeast	.36 lb, fresh	.13	.18 kg, fresh		.19 oz, instant dry (1¾ tsp)
Sunflower seeds Dee	1.1 lb	.41	.55 kg		1.8 oz (⅜ cup)
Soaker	12.64 lb	4.68	6.32 kg		1 lb, 4.2 oz (all of above)
Sourdough	16.44 lb	6.08	8.22 kg		1 lb, 10.4 oz (all of above minus 2 T + 1 tsp)
TOTAL	**38.28 lb**		**19.14 kg**		**3 lb, 12.9 oz**

*

This excellent bread seems to defy reality—over and over, people say, "It's not possible to make bread with 100 percent rye." Then we make it, and after a suitable rest, we slice it thinly, eat it, and marvel at its outstanding flavor. It keeps for weeks wrapped in plastic and refrigerated. It is a wonderful accompaniment to smoked fish, cured meats, aged cheeses, preserves, or just a simple spreading of butter.

1. **SOURDOUGH:** Prepare the sourdough and ripen for 14 to 16 hours at 70°F.

2. **SOAKER:** Make the soaker by pouring cold water over the rye chops. Cover with plastic to prevent evaporation. Some or all of the dough's overall salt can be added during hot weather.

3. **MIXING:** Add all the ingredients to the mixing bowl, including the sourdough and soaker. In a spiral mixer, mix on first speed only, for 10 minutes. Desired dough temperature: 84° to 85°F.

4. **BULK FERMENTATION:** 10 to 20 minutes.

5. **DIVIDING AND SHAPING:** Divide the dough into 4.5-pound pieces. Shape the pieces into logs, and place in pullman pans that have been lightly oiled and then coated with rye meal or whole-rye flour. Sprinkle a thin layer of whole-rye flour or pumpernickel meal over the top. They do not need a lid. Cover the loaves with plastic to prevent a crust from forming.

6. **FINAL FERMENTATION:** 50 to 60 minutes at 82°F.

7. **BAKING:** With normal steam, 470°F for 15 minutes, then lower the oven temperature to 380°F and bake for approximately 1¼ hours more. The proofed loaves do not require scoring of any kind. Fifteen minutes before the end of the bake, remove the bread from the pans, and finish the bake on sheet pans in order to firm up the side walls. Because of the high water-retention properties of breads such as this one, a full bake is imperative. The bread should be wrapped in baker's linen after it cools and left to stand for at least 24 to 48 hours before slicing. A 72-hour wait before slicing is not excessive.

Vollkornbrot with Flaxseeds

PRE-FERMENTED FLOUR: 38%

DOUGH YIELD | U.S.: About 8 pullman loaves at 4.5 lb each | Metric: About 9 pullman loaves at 2.05 kg each | Home: 1 pullman loaf

OVERALL FORMULA

	U.S.	METRIC	HOME	BAKER'S %
Rye meal	**13.68 lb**	**6.84 kg**	**1 lb, 5.9 oz**	**68.4%**
Rye chops	**6.32 lb**	**3.16 kg**	**10.1 oz**	**31.6%**
Flaxseeds	**1.1 lb**	**.55 kg**	**1.8 oz**	**5.5%**
Water	**17 lb**	**8.5 kg**	**1 lb, 11.2 oz**	**85%**
Salt	**.4 lb**	**.2 kg**	**.6 oz**	**2%**
Yeast	**.36 lb, fresh**	**.18 kg, fresh**	**.19 oz, instant dry**	**1.8%**
TOTAL YIELD	**38.86 lb**	**19.43 kg**	**3 lb, 13.8 oz**	**194.3%**

SOURDOUGH

	U.S.	METRIC	HOME	BAKER'S %
Rye meal	7.6 lb	3.8 kg	12.2 oz (3¼ cups)	100%
Water	7.6 lb	3.8 kg	12.2 oz (1½ cups)	100%
Mature sourdough culture	.38 lb	.19 kg	.6 oz (2 T)	5%
TOTAL	**15.58 lb**	**7.79 kg**	**1 lb, 9 oz**	

RYE-CHOPS SOAKER

	U.S.	METRIC	HOME	BAKER'S %
Rye chops	6.32 lb	3.16 kg	10.1 oz (2¼ cups)	100%
Water	6.32 lb	3.16 kg	10.1 oz (1¼ cups)	100%
TOTAL	**12.64 lb**	**6.32 kg**	**1 lb, 4.2 oz**	

FLAXSEED SOAKER

	U.S.	METRIC	HOME	BAKER'S %
Flaxseeds	1.1 lb	.55 kg	1.8 oz (⅜ cup)	100%
Water	2.75 lb	1.375 kg	4.4 oz (½ cup)	250%
TOTAL	**3.85 lb**	**1.925 kg**	**6.2 oz**	

FINAL DOUGH

	U.S.	METRIC	HOME
Rye meal	6.08 lb	3.04 kg	9.7 oz (2⅝ cups)
Water	.33 lb	.165 kg	.5 oz (1 T)
Salt	.4 lb	.2 kg	.6 oz (1 T)
Yeast	.36 lb, fresh	.18 kg, fresh	.19 oz, instant dry (1¾ tsp)
Rye-chops soaker	12.64 lb	6.32 kg	1 lb, 4.2 oz (all of above)
Flaxseed soaker	3.85 lb	1.925 kg	6.2 oz (all of above)
Sourdough	15.2 lb	7.6 kg	1 lb, 8.4 oz (all of above minus 2 T)
TOTAL	**38.86 lb**	**19.43 kg**	**3 lb, 13.8 oz**

In this formula, flaxseeds have been used in place of sunflower seeds, which gives a subtle change in visual and eating quality. Due to the absorption of the flaxseeds, this dough has a slightly higher hydration than the preceding *Vollkornbrot*.

1. **SOURDOUGH:** Prepare the sourdough and ripen it for 14 to 16 hours at 70°F.

2. **SOAKERS:** Both soakers are made by pouring cold water over the rye chops on the one hand, and the flaxseeds on the other. Cover each with plastic to prevent evaporation. Some or all of the dough's salt can be added to the rye soaker during hot weather.

3. **MIXING:** Add all the ingredients to the mixing bowl, including the sourdough and the soakers. In a spiral mixer, mix on first speed only, for 10 minutes. Desired dough temperature: 84° to 85°F.

4. **BULK FERMENTATION:** 10 to 20 minutes.

5. **DIVIDING AND SHAPING:** Divide the dough into 4.5-pound pieces. Shape the pieces into logs and place them in pullman pans that have been lightly oiled and then coated with rye meal or whole-rye flour. Sprinkle a thin layer of whole-rye flour or pumpernickel meal over the top. They do not need a lid. Cover the loaves with plastic to prevent a crust from forming.

6. **FINAL FERMENTATION:** 50 to 60 minutes at 82°F.

7. **BAKING:** With normal steam, 470°F for 15 minutes, then lower the oven temperature to 380°F and bake for approximately 1¼ hours more. The proofed loaves do not require scoring of any kind. Fifteen minutes before the end of the bake, remove the bread from the pans and finish the bake on sheet pans in order to firm up the side walls. Because of the high water-retention properties of breads such as this one, a full bake is imperative. The bread should be wrapped in baker's linen after it cools and left for at least 24 to 48 hours before slicing.

Horst Bandel

The bakery I owned in Vermont was primarily a retail store, but it was also intentionally a place where people could spend an hour with a pastry and a cup of coffee, visiting with a friend, or spending (not wasting) an unhurried bit of their day in whatever way they wished. Many of the regulars were well known, not only by name, but also by the baked goods they liked.

One such customer, a local minister, bought the same type of bread two or three times a week, and when he was seen striding toward the door, often his bread was bagged before he had even entered. He rarely spoke beyond the simple words needed to convey his order. In he came with his black garments, white collar, and stern demeanor, bought his bread and left. This went on for many months, and then one fine day he asked to speak with me. As I went to the front, I wondered if there was some defect in his usual bread. I was surprised by his request. His daughter was marrying, and he was assembling and decorating the cake. However, his home oven wasn't large enough for the cakes, and he asked if I would bake several large cake layers for him, as well as sell him marzipan for decorating the cake. Although as a rule I did not sell unfinished products, I decided to comply with his request. He was, after all, a regular customer, and more significantly, he was speaking!

A month later, he returned and showed me photos of the cake he had made for his daughter. I commented on how clean and appealing it looked, how skillful the marzipan decorations.

"Where did you learn to do work like that?" I asked.

"My family owned a bakery for 150 years in Germany. As a young man, I became an apprentice, and then a journeyman. As I was preparing to take over the family business as the *meister,* the Nazis came to power and my family fled for America. I became a minister and have not baked since."

I was intrigued by his story, and we spent several minutes chatting about life, about baking. Then he told me this:

"We used a wood-fired oven for all our baking. After we finished baking the day's bread, we would bake a black pumpernickel. It went into the oven last of all, and baked overnight in the lingering heat of the oven. Next morning, we would pull it from the oven, dark, dense, and fragrant. Would you like me to show you how to make that bread?" The time that elapsed between the last word of his question and my response of *"Yes!"* was so small that it defied measuring.

Beginning the following Monday, the minister Horst Bandel began to come to the bakery once a week. Now, however, he was no longer dressed in the tight black clothes in which I was long accustomed to seeing him. Instead, it was loose pants and a T-shirt. Everything about him seemed looser now: His manner was relaxed and smiling, there was a youthful spring in his legs. Each week, we shared a couple of hours at the bench, and each week we made a few different things—his style of marzipan roses, little dough figures like those he made in his family's bakery, his Christmas stollen. And each week, we made the black pumpernickel of his youth. Once it was consigned to the oven, he would leave, an arm enclosing a bag full of baked goods. When I returned to the bakery early the next morning, I would have the distinct and vivid pleasure of removing the pumpernickel from the oven and being almost overcome with the intensity of the aroma.

Horst came each Monday for a couple of months. Then one Saturday morning I received a call from him: His daughter was returning to college, and he was going to drive her. He would not be able to come on Monday—was I all right alone with the bake? I told him I was, and knew somehow that this was also his way of telling me it was time for my independence. We did not bake again together afterwards. Eventually, Horst left Vermont for the coal country of Pennsylvania, seeking a needier flock. I have continued to make this bread over these many years, and always think of Horst when I do. I think he would accept his bread being enjoyed more widely, and so I take the liberty of providing here the formula for Horst Bandel's Black Pumpernickel.

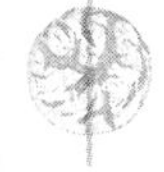

Horst Bandel's Black Pumpernickel

PRE-FERMENTED FLOUR: 28%

DOUGH YIELD | U.S.: About 9 pullman loaves at 4.4 lb each | Metric: About 10 pullman loaves at 1.98 kgs each | Home: 1 pullman loaf

OVERALL FORMULA

	U.S.	METRIC	HOME	BAKER'S %
Rye meal	6 lb	3 kg	9.6 oz	30%
Rye berries	4 lb	2 kg	6.4 oz	20%
Rye chops	5 lb	2.5 kg	8 oz	25%
High-gluten flour	5 lb	2.5 kg	8 oz	25%
Old bread	4 lb	2 kg	6.4 oz	20%
Water	14 lb	7 kg	1 lb, 6.4 oz	70%
Salt	.4 lb	.2 kg	.6 oz	2%
Yeast	.4 lb, fresh	.2 kg, fresh	.21 oz, instant dry	2%
Molasses, blackstrap	.8 lb	.4 kg	1.3 oz	4%
TOTAL YIELD	**39.6 lb**	**19.8 kg**	**3 lb, 14.9 oz**	**198%**

SOURDOUGH

Rye meal	6 lb	3 kg	9.6 oz (2⅝ cups)	100%
Water	6 lb	3 kg	9.6 oz (1¼ cups)	100%
Mature sourdough culture	.3 lb	.15 kg	.5 oz (1 T + 1 tsp)	5%
TOTAL	**12.3 lb**	**6.15 kg**	**1 lb, 3.7 oz**	

RYE-BERRY SOAKER

Rye berries	4 lb	2 kg	6.4 oz (1 cup)	100%
Water	As needed			
TOTAL	**4 lb**	**2 kg**	**6.4 oz**	

OLD-BREAD SOAKER

Old bread	4 lb	2 kg	6.4 oz (3⅝ cups)
Water	As needed		
TOTAL	**4 lb**	**2 kg**	**6.4 oz**

FINAL DOUGH

High-gluten flour	5 lb	2.5 kg	8 oz (1¾ cups)
Rye chops	5 lb	2.5 kg	8 oz (1¾ cups)
Water	8 lb	4 kg	12.8 oz (1⅝ cups)

Salt	.4 lb	.2 kg	.6 oz (1 T)
Yeast	.4 lb, fresh	.2 kg, fresh	.21 oz, instant dry (2 tsp)
Molasses	.8 lb	.4 kg	1.3 oz (1½ T)
Rye-berry soaker (not including absorbed water)	4 lb	2 kg	6.4 oz (all of above)
Old bread soaker (not including absorbed water)	4 lb	2 kg	6.4 oz (all of above)
Sourdough	12 lb	6 kg	1 lb, 3.2 oz (all of above minus 1 T + 1 tsp)
TOTAL	**39.6 lb**	**19.8 kg**	**3 lb, 14.9 oz**

Old bread has been used by bakers in Europe for centuries. When faced with the choice of throwing away the day's leftovers or reusing them, the choice was simple. The practice of soaking old bread and then adding it into a new batch not only makes economic sense, it also gives a rich depth of flavor to the new breads. Far from being expended, the old bread contains much that is still fermentable, and is a worthy addition to many different breads. Using old bread in new bread is so widely practiced in Germany that there are laws on the books there regulating the maximum amount of old bread the baker can add to a new batch of dough.

Traditionally, this style of bread is baked in covered pans overnight in the receding heat of a wood-fired oven. It can also be loaded at the end of the day's bake in other kinds of ovens and removed the next day—if the oven loses sufficient heat overnight. Many of the more substantial modern ovens (some steam tube ovens, for example) retain too much heat and can't be used to produce this kind

1. **SOURDOUGH:** Prepare the sourdough and ripen it for 14 to 16 hours at 70°F. Substitute whole-rye flour or pumpernickel if rye meal is unavailable.

2. **RYE-BERRY SOAKER:** Soak whole rye berries overnight. The next day, boil them in about 3 times their volume of water until they are soft and pliable, about an hour or so. To save on fuel, I prefer to cover them thoroughly with water in a hotel pan and put them in the oven, which cooks them well without having to use the stovetop. Once the berries are soft and pliable, strain them and set aside. Discard any remaining cooking liquid.

3. **OLD-BREAD SOAKER:** Using either a portion of the previous pumpernickel bake, or some other type of leftover bread (preferably a strong dark bread), soak the bread, crusts and all, in hot water and let stand for at least 4 hours. Squeeze out as much moisture as possible and reserve the water for use as needed in the final dough. For deeper flavor in the finished bread, slice old bread, lay it on sheet pans, bake again until dry and dark, and use that bread in the old-bread soaker.

4. **MIXING:** Add all the ingredients to the bowl, including the sourdough and both of the soakers, but do not add any of the final dough water reserved from squeezing the liquid from the old-bread soaker. The rye berries and old bread absorb varying amounts of water during their cooking and soaking, so wait until the dough comes together before adding any additional liquid. It is quite possible that no additional dough water will be required. The dough should be of medium consistency but not wet, and it will be slightly sticky. Add high-gluten flour as needed if the mix is on the wet side. Mix on first speed only, for 10 minutes. Desired dough temperature: 82° to 84°F.

5. **BULK FERMENTATION:** 30 minutes.

of bread. More's the pity. The good news is that cyclothermic-style ovens, rotary ovens, and even home ovens can be used. Experimentation may be necessary before the parameters of the bake time are established; once they are, the baker can be confident of consistently producing one of the most remarkable breads in the world.

The hydration of this formula seems to be low at first glance. The rye berries and old bread add lots of moisture that does not appear in the overall formula's water figure, and when all are combined, the dough is amply moist.

Blackstrap molasses is used in this formula to provide a slight bitter note and deeper color. If unavailable, leave it out entirely. Don't add sweet molasses, which would not balance well with the other flavors in the bread.

6. DIVIDING AND SHAPING: Divide the dough into 4.4-pound pieces. Shape the pieces into logs and place them in pullman pans that have been lightly oiled and then coated with rye meal or whole-rye flour. The lids should also be oiled and coated with rye meal or whole-rye flour. This prevents the bread from sticking to the pan during the long bake. Slide the lids onto the tops of the pans.

7. FINAL FERMENTATION: 50 to 60 minutes at 82°F.

8. BAKING: When the dough is approximately ¾ inch from the top of the pan, it is sufficiently risen. Since the bread bakes for 12 to 16 hours, it is of vital importance that the oven temperature gradually recedes throughout the bake. The speed at which it recedes will partially determine the length of the bake. In any event, the bread should be loaded into an oven that is in the 350° to 375°F range. Ideally, it will stay in that range for upwards of an hour, then begin to decrease. In a commercial hearth deck oven that has moderate heat retention, the oven can be turned off. In the home oven, try lowering the oven temperature to 275°F after an hour, and then turning the oven off 3 or 4 hours later. Since there are so many variations in oven design, experimentation may be necessary until you find the baking method most suitable for your oven. You will know when this bread is baked: The aroma will fill the entire room. Due to the lengthy bake, a great amount of the natural sugars in the dough will have caramelized, and these will contribute greatly, not only to the aroma, but also to the deep, almost black, color of the baked bread. Remove the bread from the pans and let it cool completely. Resist any urge to slice it; it should rest at minimum for 24 hours, wrapped in baker's linen, before the knife reveals the bread's inner self.

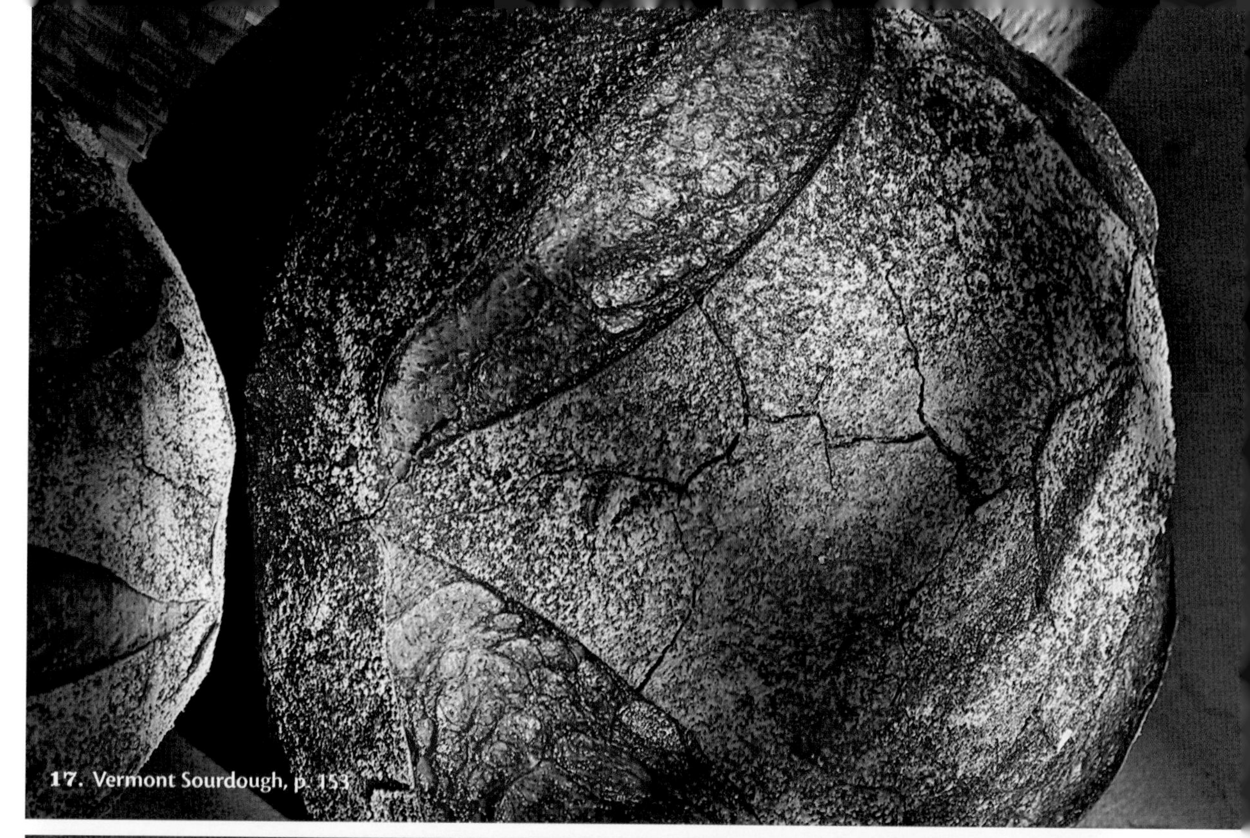

17. Vermont Sourdough, p. 153

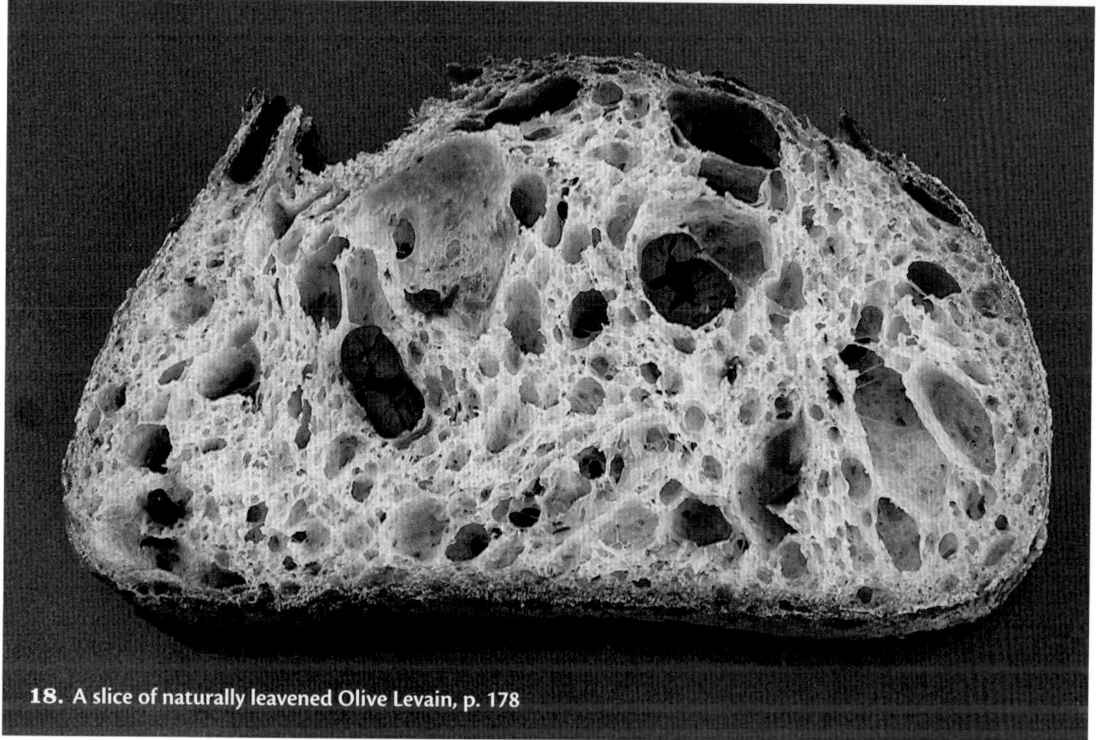

18. A slice of naturally leavened Olive Levain, p. 178

19. Baguettes with Poolish, p. 101

20. Naturally leavened Sourdough Seed Bread, p. 176

21. Assorted Rye Breads from Chapter 6

22. Different styles of Brioche, p. 253

23. A five-strand wreath, p. 302

24. An oval platter, made with Light and Dark Yeasted Decorative Dough, p. 321

25. Two-kilo loaves of Miche, Pointe-à-Callière, p. 164

26. Three-stage 90 Percent Sourdough Rye, p. 201

27. Fougasse, p. 278

28. A triple-decker Challah, p. 240

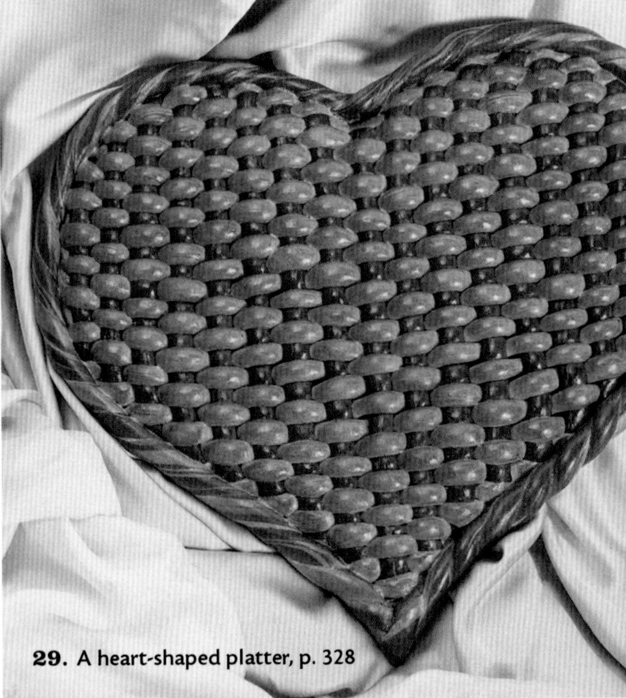

29. A heart-shaped platter, p. 328

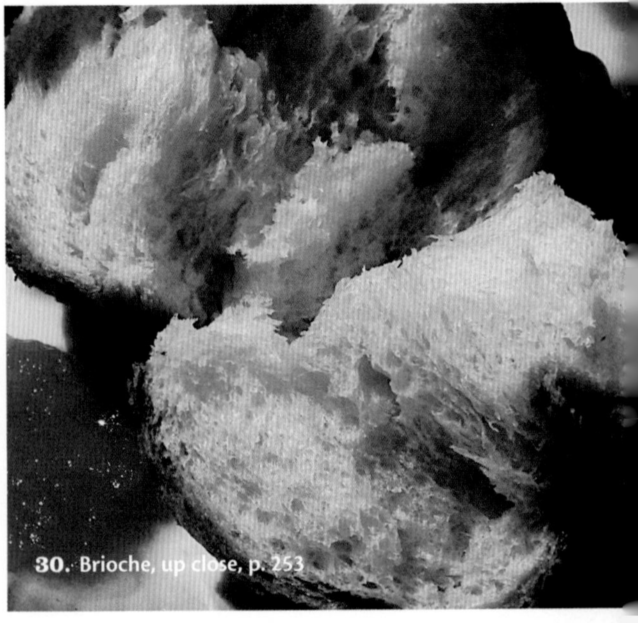

30. Brioche, up close, p. 253

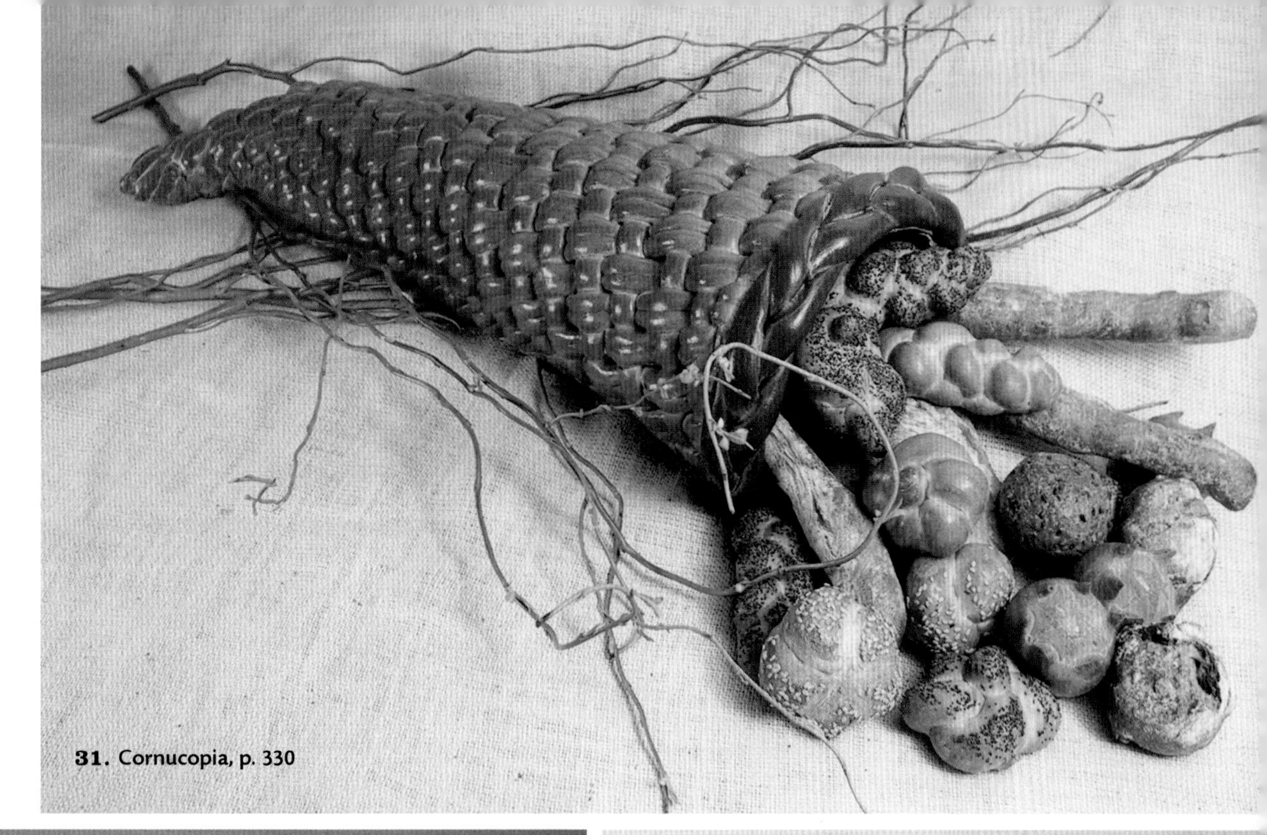
31. Cornucopia, p. 330

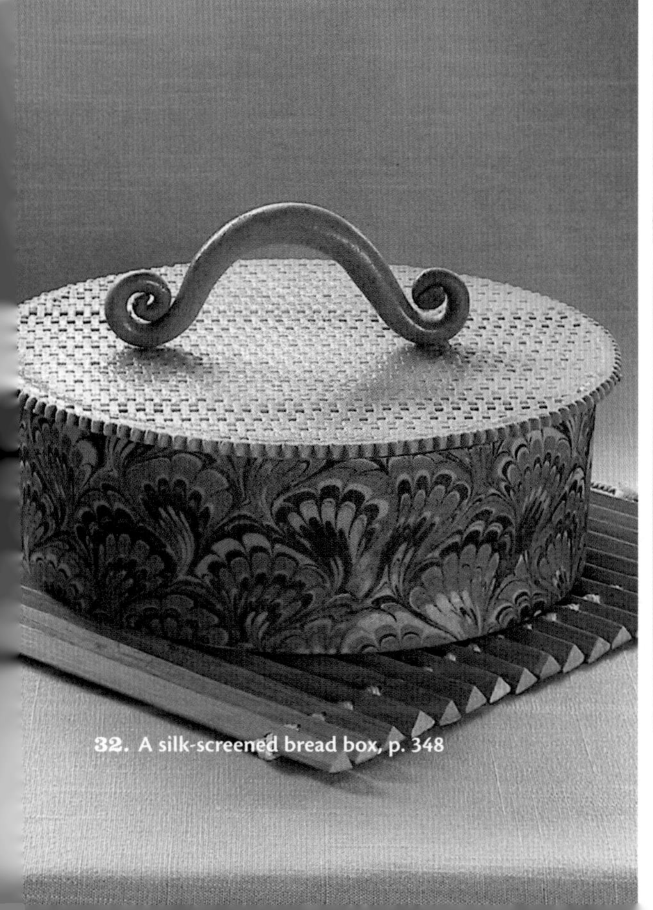
32. A silk-screened bread box, p. 348

33. A woven basket with "lace cloth" liner, p. 345

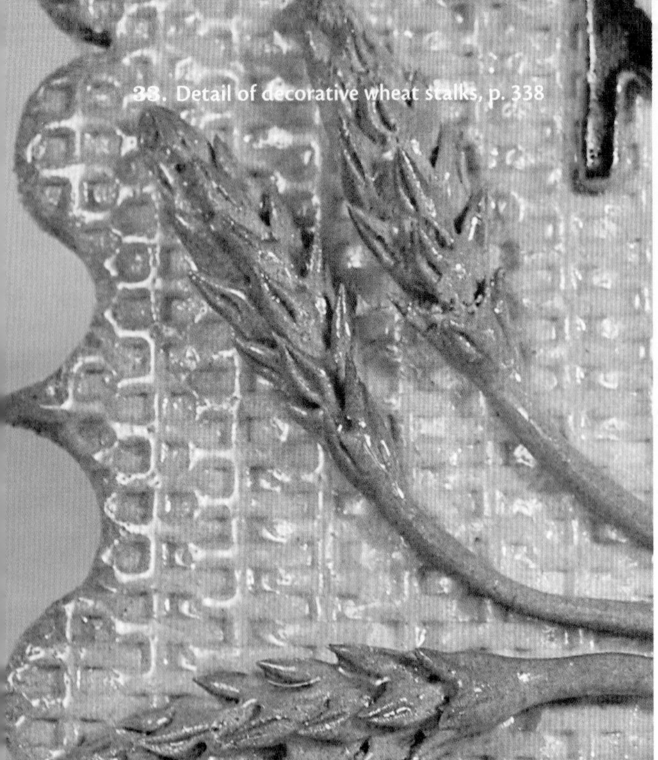

33. Detail of decorative wheat stalks, p. 338

35. Detail of decorative roses, p. 339

34. Good advice for all (a pâte morte plaque), techniques from Chapter 10

Black Bread

PRE-FERMENTED FLOUR: 35%

DOUGH YIELD | U.S.: About 24 loaves at 1.5 lb each | Metric: About 27 loaves at .68 kg each | Home: 2 large loaves

OVERALL FORMULA

	U.S.	METRIC	HOME	BAKER'S %
Medium rye flour	12 lb	6 kg	1 lb, 3.2 oz	60%
High-gluten flour	8 lb	4 kg	12.8 oz	40%
Old bread	1.6 lb	.8 kg	2.6 oz	8%
Coffee	.48 lb	.24 kg	.8 oz	2.4%
Oil	.48 lb	.24 kg	.8 oz	2.4%
Water	13.6 lb	6.8 kg	1 lb, 5.8 oz	68%
Salt	.36 lb	.18 kg	.6 oz	1.8%
Yeast	.3 lb, fresh	.15 kg, fresh	.19 oz, instant dry	1.5%
TOTAL YIELD	**36.82 lb**	**18.41 kg**	**3 lb, 10.7 oz**	**184.1%**

SOURDOUGH

Medium rye flour	7 lb	3.5 kg	11.2 oz (2¾ cups)	100%
Water	5.6 lb	2.8 kg	9 oz (1⅛ cups)	80%
Mature sourdough culture	.35 lb	.175 kg	.6 oz (2 T)	5%
TOTAL	**12.95 lb**	**6.475 kg**	**1 lb, 4.8 oz**	

OLD-BREAD SOAKER

Old bread	1.6 lb	.8 kg	2.6 oz (1½ cups)	100%
Coffee, ground	.48 lb	.24 kg	.8 oz (6 T)	30%
Vegetable oil	.48 lb	.24 kg	.8 oz (2 T)	30%
Water, hot	8 lb	4 kg	12.8 oz (1⅝ cups)	500%
TOTAL	**10.56 lb**	**5.28 kg**	**1 lb, 1 oz**	

FINAL DOUGH

Medium rye flour	5 lb	2.5 kg	8 oz (2 cups)
High-gluten flour	8 lb	4 kg	12.8 oz (2⅞ cups)
Salt	.36 lb	.18 kg	.6 oz (1 T)
Yeast	.3 lb, fresh	.15 kg, fresh	.19 oz, instant dry (1¾ tsp)
Old-bread soaker	10.56 lb	5.28 kg	1 lb, 1 oz (all of above)
Sourdough	12.6 lb	6.3 kg	1 lb, 4.2 oz (all of above minus 2 T)
TOTAL	**36.82 lb**	**18.41 kg**	**3 lb, 10.8 oz**

There are two ways in which old bread is incorporated into a fresh batch of dough: It can be soaked, with the crust, until thoroughly moistened and then added, or it can be sliced and baked again before the soaking. In this formula, the old bread is sliced, then returned to the oven on sheet pans and baked until it is a deep, dark brown, but take care not to blacken it as it will taste bitter. It adds a potent toasty flavor when soaked and incorporated into the new dough. The ground coffee also adds its own bite to the bread. The result is a bread that is quite black, without any hint of the sweetness that molasses often brings to dark breads.

1. **SOURDOUGH:** Prepare the sourdough and ripen it for 14 to 16 hours at 70°F.

2. **OLD-BREAD SOAKER:** Put the rebaked old bread in a dough bucket or large bowl. Pour the hot water over it. Add the ground coffee and oil and stir thoroughly with a spoon until the coffee is dissolved and the bread is completely moistened. Cover with a lid or plastic. It is most efficient to make the bread soaker at the same time that the sourdough is prepared, and to then let it stand at room temperature until mixing time.

3. **MIXING:** Add all the ingredients to the mixing bowl. Note that all the dough water is used in the sourdough and the soaker, and no additional water is added. Some of the soaker water may need to be warmed or cooled when computing the desired dough temperature. In a spiral mixer, mix for 3 minutes on first speed, then about 3 minutes on second. The 40 percent white flour will give the dough a perceptible, but not overly strong, gluten development. Desired dough temperature: 80°F.

4. **BULK FERMENTATION:** 30 to 45 minutes.

5. **DIVIDING AND SHAPING:** Divide the dough into 1.5- or 2-pound pieces; shape round or oblong.

6. **FINAL FERMENTATION:** 50 to 60 minutes at 80°F.

7. **BAKING:** With normal steam, 460°F for 15 minutes, then lower the oven temperature to 440°F and bake for 30 to 35 minutes for a 1.5-pound loaf, 5 to 10 minutes more for a 2-pound loaf.

VARIATION: Charnushka seeds (also known as nigella or black caraway) can be added to the tops of the loaves. They provide a taste that goes nicely with the strength of the bread's flavor. To apply once the bread has been shaped, moisten the surface and sprinkle the seeds over the top, or press the surface into a damp cloth and then into a tray of the seeds.

Five-Grain Sourdough with Rye Sourdough

PRE-FERMENTED FLOUR: 25%

DOUGH YIELD | U.S.: About 31 loaves at 1.5 lb each | Metric: About 35 loaves at .68 kg each | Home: 3 medium loaves

OVERALL FORMULA

	U.S.	METRIC	HOME	BAKER'S %
Whole-rye flour	5 lb	2.5 kg	8 oz	25%
High-gluten flour	15 lb	7.5 kg	1 lb, 8 oz	75%
Flaxseeds	1.8 lb	.9 kg	2.9 oz	9%
Cracked rye	1.8 lb	.9 kg	2.9 oz	9%
Sunflower seeds	1.5 lb	.75 kg	2.4 oz	7.5%
Oats	1.5 lb	.75 kg	2.4 oz	7.5%
Honey	.3 lb	.15 kg	.5 oz	1.5%
Water	19.8 lb	9.9 kg	1 lb, 14.4 oz	99%
Salt	.44 lb	.22 kg	.7 oz	2.2%
Yeast	.36 lb, fresh	.18 kg, fresh	.19 oz, instant dry	1.8%
TOTAL YIELD	**47.5 lb**	**23.75 kg**	**4 lb, 10.4 oz**	**237.5%**

RYE SOURDOUGH

	U.S.	METRIC	HOME	BAKER'S %
Whole-rye flour	5 lb	2.5 kg	8 oz (1 3/4 cups)	100%
Water	4.15 lb	2.075 kg	6.7 oz (7/8 cup)	83%
Mature sourdough culture	.25 lb	.125 kg	.4 oz (1 T + 1 tsp)	5%
TOTAL	**9.4 lb**	**4.7 kg**	**15.1 oz**	

HOT SOAKER

	U.S.	METRIC	HOME	BAKER'S %
Flaxseeds	1.8 lb	.9 kg	2.9 oz (1/2 cup)	27.3%
Cracked rye	1.8 lb	.9 kg	2.9 oz (5/8 cup)	27.3%
Sunflower seeds	1.5 lb	.75 kg	2.4 oz (1/2 cup)	22.7%
Oats	1.5 lb	.75 kg	2.4 oz (3/4 cup)	22.7%
Salt	.44 lb	.22 kg	.7 oz (3 1/2 tsp)	6.7%
Water, boiling	8.25 lb	4.125 kg	13.2 oz (1 5/8 cups)	125%
TOTAL	**15.29 lb**	**7.645 kg**	**1 lb, 8.5 oz**	

FINAL DOUGH

	U.S.	METRIC	HOME
High-gluten flour	15 lb	7.5 kg	1 lb, 8 oz (5 1/2 cups)
Water	7.4 lb	3.7 kg	10.5 oz (1 3/8 cups)
Yeast	.36 lb, fresh	.18 kg, fresh	.19 oz, instant dry (1 3/4 tsp)
Honey	.3 lb	.15 kg	.5 oz (2 tsp)
Soaker	15.29 lb	7.645 kg	1 lb, 8.5 oz (all of above)
Sourdough	9.15 lb	4.575 kg	14.7 oz (all of above minus 1 T + 1 tsp)
TOTAL	**47.5 lb**	**23.75 kg**	**4 lb, 10.4 oz**

Although this bread has a full 75 percent white flour, when eaten it has a delicious whole-grain taste, thanks to both the soaker and the sourdough. The white flour provides a strong structure that gives the finished bread a surprising lightness—and with 33 percent of the flour weight being heavy grains, you might not expect such an open texture to the finished loaves. This bread also has excellent keeping quality, due in part to the high moisture retention of both the soaker and the sourdough. Cracked rye is called for in the formula, and since it does not soften easily with cold water, boiling water is used to make the soaker. Rye chops can be used in lieu of the cracked rye, in which case a cold soaker can be prepared. Grains absorb more water when a soaker is hot, however, so if making a cold soaker check the hydration carefully when mixing the final dough. At first glance, there appears to be too much salt in the formula. However, the 2.2 percent salt in the overall formula is based on the combined weight of the rye and white flour. The soaked grains, too, need an addition of salt, and the total amount used in the formula is therefore in balance.

1. **SOURDOUGH:** Prepare the sourdough and ripen it for 14 to 16 hours at 70°F.

2. **SOAKER:** Prepare the soaker at the same time the sourdough is made. Boil the water in a covered pot to avoid loss of moisture, then pour the grains and salt into the water and stir until everything is moistened. Cover the pot with plastic and let stand at room temperature. The boiling water will activate the enzymes in the grains, so the salt is added to this soaker to inhibit excess enzymatic activity.

3. **MIXING:** Add all the ingredients to the mixing bowl. In a spiral mixer, mix for 3 minutes on first speed, checking the hydration once the ingredients are incorporated. The dough should be moderately loose and somewhat sticky. Turn the mixer to second speed and mix for 3 to 4 minutes. In spite of the soaker and sourdough, a reasonable amount of gluten development should be noted when the dough is tugged. Desired dough temperature: 78°F.

4. **BULK FERMENTATION:** 1 hour, with no folds.

5. **DIVIDING AND SHAPING:** Divide into 1.5- or 2-pound pieces; shape round or oblong. Shaping gives the baker a final opportunity to strengthen the dough. Shape these loaves tightly, but avoid tearing the outer surface. It's a big effort for the bread to lift all those grains; good shaping brings strength back into the loaves so that when baked they have good volume and crumb texture.

6. **FINAL FERMENTATION:** 50 to 60 minutes at 80°F.

7. **BAKING:** With normal steam, 460°F for 15 minutes, then lower the oven temperature to 440°F and bake for about 30 minutes for a 1.5-pound loaf, 8 to 10 minutes more for a 2-pound loaf. The honey in the dough might cause it to color too quickly, particularly on the bottom of the loaves. The oven temperature can be lowered further, or the loaves can finish the bake on sheet pans to protect them from excess coloring.

Sunflower Seed Bread with Rye Sourdough

PRE-FERMENTED FLOUR: 20%

DOUGH YIELD | U.S.: About 27 loaves at 1.5 lb each | Metric: About 30 loaves at .68 kg each | Home: 2 large loaves

OVERALL FORMULA

	U.S.	METRIC	HOME	BAKER'S %
Medium rye flour	4 lb	2 kg	6.4 oz	20%
Bread flour	12.66 lb	6.33 kg	1 lb, 4.3 oz	63.3%
Rye chops	3.34 lb	1.67 kg	5.3 oz	16.7%
Sunflower seeds, toasted	4 lb	2 kg	6.4 oz	20%
Water	16 lb	8 kg	1 lb, 9.6 oz	80%
Malt syrup	.3 lb	.15 kg	.5 oz	1.5%
Salt	.42 lb	.21 kg	.7 oz	2.1%
Yeast	.3 lb, fresh	.15 kg, fresh	.16 oz, instant dry	1.5%
TOTAL YIELD	**41.02 lb**	**20.51 kg**	**4 lb, 1.4 oz**	**205.1%**

SOURDOUGH

Medium rye flour	4 lb	2 kg	6.4 oz (1⅝ cups)	100%
Water	3.2 lb	1.6 kg	5.1 oz (⅝ cup)	80%
Mature sourdough culture	.2 lb	.1 kg	.3 oz (1 T)	5%
TOTAL	**7.4 lb**	**3.7 kg**	**11.8 oz**	

SOAKER

Rye chops	3.34 lb	1.67 kg	5.3 oz (1⅛ cups)	100%
Water	3.34 lb	1.67 kg	5.3 oz (⅝ cup)	100%
TOTAL	**6.68 lb**	**3.34 kg**	**10.6 oz**	

FINAL DOUGH

Bread flour	12.66 lb	6.33 kg	1 lb, 4.3 oz (4⅝ cups)
Sunflower seeds, toasted	4 lb	2 kg	6.4 oz (1⅜ cups)
Water	9.46 lb	4.73 kg	15.2 oz (2 cups)
Salt	.42 lb	.21 kg	.7 oz (3½ tsp)
Yeast	.3 lb, fresh	.15 kg, fresh	.16 oz, instant dry (1½ tsp)
Malt syrup	.3 lb	.15 kg	.5 oz (2 tsp)
Soaker	6.68 lb	3.34 kg	10.6 oz (all of above)
Sourdough	7.2 lb	3.6 kg	11.5 oz (all of above minus 1 T)
TOTAL	**41.02 lb**	**20.51 kg**	**4 lb, 1.4 oz**

This is another flavorful whole-grain bread, but at the same time it retains a lightness of texture. My preference is to toast the sunflower seeds that go into the dough and to add raw sunflower seeds to the surface of the dough when shaping. The toasted ones in the interior add a nutty quality to the taste. The raw ones on the bread's surface toast during the bake, furthering the nutty flavor.

1. **SOURDOUGH:** Prepare the sourdough and ripen it for 14 to 16 hours at 70°F.

2. **SOAKER:** Stir the rye chops into the water and cover with plastic. Prepare at the same time the sourdough is made. Cracked rye can be substituted, in which case boiling water should be used. Some or all of the dough's salt can be added to inhibit enzymatic activity.

3. **MIXING:** Add all the ingredients to the mixing bowl, including the toasted sunflower seeds. In a spiral mixer, mix for 3 minutes on first speed, checking the hydration once the ingredients are incorporated. The dough should be moderately loose and somewhat sticky. Turn the mixer to second speed and mix for about 3 more minutes. The dough should have some "muscle" when tugged, and should offer resistance to the tug. Desired dough temperature: 78°F.

4. **BULK FERMENTATION:** 1 hour, with no folds.

5. **DIVIDING AND SHAPING:** Divide the dough into 1.5-pound pieces; shape round or oblong.

6. **FINAL FERMENTATION:** 50 to 60 minutes at 80°F.

7. **BAKING:** With normal steam, 460°F for 15 minutes, then lower the oven temperature to 440°F and bake for about 30 minutes. If the loaves are coloring too quickly due to the malt syrup, either lower the oven temperature another 10°F or finish the bake on sheet pans to protect the bottom of the bread from excess coloring.

STRAIGHT DOUGHS

7

No booksellers, no books
No books, no learning
No learning, no knowledge
No knowledge, no wisdom
No wisdom, no ethics
No ethics, no conscience
No conscience, no community
No community, no bread.

—THE TALMUD

Straight doughs are simply doughs in which all the ingredients are mixed at once. None of the flour is prefermented; in other words, there is no sourdough or levain build, nor is there any sort of sponge, and no *pâte fermentée*, biga, or poolish is used. This saves time of course, but it also means the breads lack the benefits of pre-ferments.

Many straight-dough breads are bland, insipid, and boring: bread that serves little purpose other than holding some meat or sopping up soup. Fortunately, some very respectable breads can be made with the straight-dough method.

There is a correlation between the amount of time that elapses between the mixing and baking of a bread and the resulting flavor and keeping quality of that bread. If a bread is mixed, risen, shaped, and baked all within, say, a three-hour period, it will tend to lack flavor and keeping quality. The same ingredients, but with less yeast and more time between mixing and baking, will yield a bread that is far superior to the hastily made one. One reason that breads with pre-ferments tend to taste good and keep well is because of the lengthy pre-fermentation of a portion of the bread's flour. With many straight doughs, there is a simple and effective technique that can be used as a means of improving both flavor and keeping quality: bulk fermentation of the dough. In this method, the desired dough temperature is a couple of degrees lower, and once mixed, the dough receives a short rising at room temperature (30 to 60 minutes is sufficient), then it's degassed, covered well with plastic, and refrigerated. It is then degassed 2 or 3 times over the next few hours. The next day, it is ready to be divided, shaped, and baked. Another benefit to this technique is that, in a production setting, the baker has dough to work up at the outset of the workday, and the loaves can bake early, freeing up oven space for the later batches of dough. For the home baker, too, this method can work well: The dough can be mixed the day before baking and left to mature in the refrigerator overnight. Little time or effort is then required the next day to shape, proof, and bake. Several of the breads in this chapter can be handled in this fashion, and a note is made to that effect in the individual formulas that follow.

French Bread

DOUGH YIELD | U.S.: About 39 baguettes at .875 lb each | Metric: About 43 baguettes at .4 kg each | Home: 4 baguettes

	U.S.	METRIC	HOME	BAKER'S %
Bread flour	20 lb	10 kg	2 lb (7¼ cups)	100%
Water	14 lb	7 kg	1 lb, 6.4 oz (2¾ cups)	70%
Salt	.36 lb	.18 kg	.6 oz (1 T)	1.8%
Yeast	.25 lb, fresh	.125 kg, fresh	.13 oz, instant dry (1¼ tsp)	1.25%
TOTAL YIELD	**34.61 lb**	**17.305 kg**	**3 lb, 7.1 oz**	**173.05%**

French bread made in the straight-dough style can be remarkably good. Although I freely confess to being a poolish kind of guy—I love the fragrant nuttiness of a ripe poolish, the aroma and flavor of a well-made poolish baguette—I find that when good flour is used to make straight-dough French bread, and when the flour is treated well and handled with care and patience, the resulting bread, with the flour's intrinsic characteristics coaxed to prominence, can stand confidently alongside French bread made with a pre-ferment. The mixing with this style of French bread is gentle, and gluten development is light. Dough strength is developed through 2 or 3 folds and a long bulk fermentation.

1. **MIXING:** Place all the ingredients in the mixing bowl. In a spiral mixer, mix on first speed for about 3 minutes in order to incorporate the ingredients thoroughly. Check for hydration and make corrections as necessary. With hydration of 70 percent, the dough should be fairly loose textured. After the incorporation phase of mixing is complete, keep the mixer on first speed for another 3 minutes, then finish by mixing on second speed for about 1 minute. Gluten development should be evident, but by no means should the dough feel strong. Desired dough temperature: 76°F.

2. **BULK FERMENTATION:** 2½ to 3 hours.

3. **FOLDING:** Two folds are generally sufficient (if the dough has been mixed very lightly, a third fold, evenly spaced between the other two, can be added). If the dough ferments for 2½ hours, fold at 50-minute intervals. If bulk fermentation is for 3 hours, fold at 1-hour intervals. Don't underestimate the ability of folding to increase dough strength. Remember that the dough has not been highly developed in the bowl and, depending on the relative development of the dough during mixing, use the folds appropriately—with more or less vigor in your folding motions—to increase dough strength to the desired extent.

4. **DIVIDING AND SHAPING:** Divide the dough into 12- to 16-ounce pieces for baguettes. Preshape into rounds and place, seams up, on a lightly floured work surface. Cover the dough with plastic to prevent a skin from forming. Once the dough is sufficiently relaxed (15 to 20 minutes), shape into baguettes. Place them between folds of baker's linen, leaving ample space for the bread to rise without touching its neighbor. Cover with baker's linen and plastic so that air currents don't crust the surface.

5. FINAL FERMENTATION: 1½ to 2 hours at about 76°F.

6. BAKING: With normal steam, 460°F for 24 to 26 minutes for baguettes, depending on dough weight.

Oatmeal Bread

DOUGH YIELD | U.S.: About 27 loaves at 1.5 lb each | Metric: About 30 loaves at .68 kg each | Home: 2 large loaves

	U.S.	METRIC	HOME	BAKER'S %
High-gluten flour	15 lb	7.5 kg	1 lb, 8 oz (5½ cups)	75%
Whole-wheat flour	5 lb	2.5 kg	8 oz (1⅞ cups)	25%
Rolled oats	3.3 lb	1.65 kg	5.3 oz (1⅝ cups)	16.5%
Water	12.5 lb	6.25 kg	1 lb, 4 oz (2½ cups)	62.5%
Milk	2.2 lb	1.1 kg	3.5 oz (½ cup)	11%
Honey	1.5 lb	.75 kg	2.4 oz (3 T)	7.5%
Vegetable oil	1.5 lb	.75 kg	2.4 oz (5½ T)	7.5%
Salt	.44 lb	.22 kg	.7 oz (3½ tsp)	2.2%
Yeast	.34 lb, fresh	.17 kg, fresh	.18 oz, instant dry (1½ tsp)	1.7%
TOTAL YIELD	**41.78 lb**	**20.89 kg**	**4 lb, 2.5 oz**	**208.9%**

1. MIXING: Place the oats in the mixing bowl. Add the water and turn the machine on for a moment to wet all the oats. Let stand for 15 or 20 minutes to soften. Add all the remaining ingredients to the bowl. In a spiral mixer, mix on first speed for 3 minutes in order to incorporate the ingredients thoroughly. The dough consistency should be moderately loose, with a slight tackiness from the honey. Turn the mixer to second speed and mix for 3 to 3½ minutes, until a moderate gluten development has been achieved. Desired dough temperature: 76°F.

2. BULK FERMENTATION: 2 hours (or overnight retarding).

3. FOLDING: Fold the dough once, after 1 hour.

4. DIVIDING AND SHAPING: If the dough is going to be shaped into pan loaves, the dimensions of the pan will determine the dough weight. For a loaf pan measuring 8 by 4 by 2½ inches, about 18 ounces of dough will make a good fit. Larger commercial strap

I have made this bread for years and years. I love its light texture, mild sweetness, clean flavor, and food friendliness. It's a yummy bread for sandwiches, morning toast, or as a simple treat with butter and jam. High-gluten is a good choice for the white-flour portion of the dough—the extra strength helps lift the heavy oats and honey, and yields a lighter loaf. (If you do not have high-gluten flour, you can substitute a good-quality bread flour.) This dough lends itself well to the technique of retarding the bulk dough after the mix, as described at the beginning of this chapter.

pans with dimensions of 9 by 5 by 2¾ inches will take 1.5 pounds of dough. Freestanding loaves that will be baked directly on the hearth or baking stone can be divided into any weight. Tasty rolls of about 3 ounces each can also be made with the dough. Divide into desired weights and preshape the dough lightly into rounds. Place the dough pieces on a lightly floured work surface, seams up. Cover the rounds with plastic. Once the dough is sufficiently relaxed, shape into blunt cylinders for pan loaves; for round loaves or rolls, shape accordingly. A nice finish for the bread or rolls is made by dipping the top of the dough into a damp cloth (or misting the surface) and then pressing the moistened surface into a tray of oatmeal. Cover the loaves with baker's linen and plastic so that air currents don't crust the surface.

5. FINAL FERMENTATION: 1 to 1½ hours at about 76°F.

6. BAKING: With normal steam, 460°F. The milk, honey, and oil contribute a lot to bread coloring; therefore, lower the temperature by 20° to 30°F after 15 minutes to finish the bake in a receding oven. Eighteen-ounce loaves baked in loaf pans will take 30 to 32 minutes to bake, while loaves in larger strap pans will take 36 to 40 minutes.

Oatmeal Bread with Cinnamon and Raisins

DOUGH YIELD | U.S.: About 32 loaves at 1.5 lb each | Metric: About 36 loaves at .68 kg each | Home: 3 medium loaves

	U.S.	METRIC	HOME	BAKER'S %
High-gluten flour	15 lb	7.5 kg	1 lb, 8 oz (5½ cups)	75%
Whole-wheat flour	5 lb	2.5 kg	8 oz (1⅞ cups)	25%
Rolled oats	3.3 lb	1.65 kg	5.3 oz (1⅝ cups)	16.5%
Water	12.5 lb	6.25 kg	1 lb, 4 oz (2½ cups)	62.5%
Milk	2.2 lb	1.1 kg	3.5 oz (⅜ cup)	11%
Honey	1.5 lb	.75 kg	2.4 oz (3 T)	7.5%
Vegetable oil	1.5 lb	.75 kg	2.4 oz (5½ T)	7.5%
Salt	.44 lb	.22 kg	.7 oz (1 T + ½ tsp)	2.2%
Yeast	.7 lb, fresh	.35 kg, fresh	.37 oz, instant dry (1¼ T)	3.5%
Cinnamon, ground	.3 lb	.15 kg	.5 oz (2 T)	1.5%
Raisins, soaked and drained (see headnote)	6.6 lb	3.3 kg	10.6 oz (2⅛ cups)	33%
TOTAL YIELD	**49.04 lb**	**24.52 kg**	**4 lb, 13.8 oz**	**245.2%**

1. **MIXING:** Place the oats in the mixing bowl. Add the water and turn the machine on for a moment to moisten all the oats. Let stand for 15 or 20 minutes to soften. Add all the remaining ingredients except the raisins to the bowl. In a spiral mixer, mix on first speed for 3 minutes in order to incorporate the ingredients thoroughly. The dough consistency should be moderately loose, with a slight tackiness from the honey. Turn the mixer to second speed and mix for 3 to 3½ minutes, until a moderate gluten development has been achieved. Add the drained raisins and mix on first speed only, just until the raisins are thoroughly incorporated. Desired dough temperature: 76°F.

2. **BULK FERMENTATION:** 2 hours (or overnight retarding).

3. **FOLDING:** Fold the dough once, after 1 hour.

4. **DIVIDING AND SHAPING:** If the dough is going to be shaped into pan loaves, the dimensions of the pan will determine dough weight. For a loaf pan measuring 8 by 4 by 2½ inches, about 18 ounces of dough will make a good fit. Larger commercial strap pans with dimensions of 9 by 5 by 2¾ inches will take 1.5 pounds

By adding cinnamon and raisins to the Oatmeal Bread formula that precedes this one, two significant things happen: First, the spice of the cinnamon and the sweetness of the raisins change the flavor markedly. Second, the cinnamon (specifically the chemical compound *cinnamic aldehyde*) greatly impairs the yeast's activity, so a higher percentage of yeast is necessary to overcome it. (Tree-bark spices in general, such as mace, allspice, nutmeg, and cinnamon, have compounds that inhibit yeast activity when used in appreciable amounts.) In the present formula, the 3.5 percent yeast used is notable, and is directly related to the effect of the cinnamon in the dough. An alternative method of making the bread is to roll scaled-out dough pieces to a rectangular shape, egg wash the surface, sprinkle on cinnamon (and sugar if desired), then spread on the raisins, roll the dough up, and place in loaf pans. When using the cinnamon in this fashion—sprinkling it onto the dough rather than incorporating it into the dough—the yeast is not impeded, and the percentage of yeast in the formula can be reduced to 1.75 to 2 percent. The raisins should be soaked in warm water for at least 30 minutes before mixing (or overnight if more convenient), and well drained prior to the mix. If not soaked first, those on the surface tend to burn.

of dough. Freestanding loaves can be made too, but keep in mind that when baking directly on the hearth or baking stone, the bread will color quite quickly due to the raisins, and therefore finishing the bake on sheet pans may be necessary. Rolls can also be made with the dough.

Divide the dough into the desired weights and preshape lightly into rounds. Place the dough pieces on a lightly floured work surface, seams up. Cover the rounds with plastic. Once the dough is sufficiently relaxed (10 to 15 minutes), shape into blunt cylinders in order to make pan loaves. For round loaves or rolls, shape accordingly. A nice finish for the bread or rolls is made by dipping the top of the dough into a damp cloth (or misting the surface) and then pressing the moistened surface into a tray of oatmeal. Cover the loaves with baker's linen and plastic so that air currents don't crust the surface.

5. FINAL FERMENTATION: 1½ hours or more at about 76°F.

6. BAKING: With normal steam, 450°F. The raisins particularly, but also the milk, honey, and oil, contribute a lot to bread coloring; therefore, lower the temperature by 20° to 30°F after 15 minutes to finish the bake in a receding oven. Eighteen-ounce loaves baked in loaf pans will take 30 to 35 minutes to bake, with 1.5-pound loaves in the larger strap pans taking closer to 40 to 45 minutes.

Five-Grain Bread

DOUGH YIELD | U.S.: About 33 loaves at 1.5 lb each | Metric: About 37 loaves at .68 kg each | Home: 3 medium loaves

OVERALL FORMULA

	U.S.	METRIC	HOME	BAKER'S %
High-gluten flour	10 lb	5 kg	1 lb	50%
Whole-wheat flour	8 lb	4 kg	12.8 oz	40%
Whole-rye flour	2 lb	1 kg	3.2 oz	10%
Rolled oats	2.4 lb	1.2 kg	3.8 oz	12%
Flaxseeds	2.4 lb	1.2 kg	3.8 oz	12%
Wheat bran	1.6 lb	.8 kg	2.6 oz	8%
Cornmeal	1.6 lb	.8 kg	2.6 oz	8%
Water	18 lb	9 kg	1 lb, 12.8 oz	90%
Vegetable oil	1 lb	.5 kg	1.6 oz	5%
Eggs	2.4 lb	1.2 kg	3.8 oz	12%
Salt	.56 lb	.28 kg	.9 oz	2.8%
Yeast	.5 lb, fresh	.25 kg, fresh	.26 oz, instant dry	2.5%
TOTAL YIELD	**50.46 lb**	**25.23 kg**	**5 lb, 2 oz**	**252.3%**

SOAKER

Rolled oats	2.4 lb	1.2 kg	3.8 oz (1 1/8 cups)	30%
Flaxseeds	2.4 lb	1.2 kg	3.8 oz (3/4 cup)	30%
Wheat bran	1.6 lb	.8 kg	2.6 oz (1 1/2 cups)	20%
Cornmeal	1.6 lb	.8 kg	2.6 oz (5/8 cup)	20%
Water	10 lb	5 kg	1 lb (2 cups)	125%
TOTAL	**18 lb**	**9 kg**	**1 lb, 12.8 oz**	

FINAL DOUGH

High-gluten flour	10 lb	5 kg	1 lb (3 5/8 cups)
Whole-wheat flour	8 lb	4 kg	12.8 oz (2 7/8 cups)
Whole-rye flour	2 lb	1 kg	3.2 oz (7/8 cup)
Water	8 lb	4 kg	12.8 oz (1 5/8 cups)
Vegetable oil	1 lb	.5 kg	1.6 oz (3 T + 2 tsp)
Eggs	2.4 lb	1.2 kg	3.8 oz (2 eggs)
Salt	.56 lb	.28 kg	.9 oz (1 1/2 T)
Yeast	.5 lb, fresh	.25 kg, fresh	.8 oz, instant dry (2 1/4 tsp)
Soaker	18 lb	9 kg	1 lb, 12.8 oz (all of above)
TOTAL	**50.46 lb**	**25.23 kg**	**5 lb, 2 oz**

Here is another hearty grain bread, flecked with color, high in fiber, great in taste. The grains total 40 percent of the flour weight, and contribute significantly to flavor and nutrition. They also hold quite a lot of moisture, which helps to extend the fresh life of the bread. Grain types and percentages in the soaker can be altered, as long as the overall hydration remains balanced. If the dough is refrigerated overnight (which it seems to favor), be sure to degas it 2 or 3 times as it cools.

1. **SOAKER:** Prepare a cold soaker by stirring the rolled oats, flaxseeds, wheat bran, and cornmeal into the soaker water. Cover the bowl with plastic to prevent moisture loss. In particularly hot weather, some or all of the dough salt can be added to the grains to deter enzymatic activity from commencing.

2. **MIXING:** Place all the ingredients in the mixing bowl, including the soaker. In a spiral mixer, mix on first speed for 3 minutes in order to incorporate the ingredients thoroughly. The dough should have a medium consistency. Turn the mixer to second speed and mix for 3 to 3½ minutes, until the gluten network has been fairly well developed. Desired dough temperature: 76°F.

3. **BULK FERMENTATION:** 2 hours (or overnight retarding).

4. **FOLDING:** Fold the dough once, after 1 hour.

5. **DIVIDING AND SHAPING:** Divide the dough into 1.5-pound pieces (or make rolls with smaller pieces). Preshape lightly into rounds and place on a lightly floured work surface, seams up. Cover the rounds with plastic. When the dough has relaxed sufficiently, shape it into tight round or oval loaves. Place the loaves in floured *bannetons* and cover with baker's linen and plastic.

6. **FINAL FERMENTATION:** 1 to 1½ hours at about 76°F.

7. **BAKING:** With normal steam, 460°F. Although there are no raisins or other sweeteners in the bread, the eggs and oil contribute color, so the oven may need to be lowered by 10° to 20°F partway through the bake. Loaves scaled at 1.5 pounds will take approximately 40 minutes to bake, with round loaves taking slightly longer than oblong ones.

Challah

DOUGH YIELD | U.S.: About 30 braids at 1.125 lb each | Metric: About 33 braids at .51 kg each | Home: 3 braids

	U.S.	METRIC	HOME	BAKER'S %
Bread flour	13.4 lb	6.7 kg	1 lb, 5.4 oz (4⅞ cups)	67%
High-gluten flour	6.6 lb	3.3 kg	10.6 oz (2⅜ cups)	33%
Sugar	1.6 lb	.8 kg	2.6 oz (5 T)	8%
Yolks	1.5 lb	.75 kg	2.4 oz (4 yolks)	7.5%
Whole eggs	2.8 lb	1.4 kg	4.5 oz (2 eggs)	14%
Vegetable oil	1.5 lb	.75 kg	2.4 oz (5½ T)	7.5%
Water	6.4 lb	3.2 kg	10.2 oz (1¼ cups)	32%
Salt	.38 lb	.19 kg	.6 oz (1 T)	1.9%
Yeast	.6 lb, fresh	.3 kg, fresh	.32 oz, instant dry (2¾ tsp)	3%
TOTAL YIELD	**34.78 lb**	**17.39 kg**	**3 lb, 7 oz**	**173.9%**

1. **MIXING:** Place all the ingredients in the mixing bowl. In a spiral mixer, mix on first speed for 3 minutes until all the ingredients are thoroughly incorporated, then on second for approximately 3 minutes. The goal is to develop a strong gluten network. The dough will be comparatively stiff, which is appropriate for braiding. The desired dough temperature is 78° to 80°F.

2. **BULK FERMENTATION:** 2 hours. The dough can also rise overnight. In this case, lower the desired dough temperature to 75°F, and after 1 hour of bulk fermentation, degas the dough, cover it well with plastic, and refrigerate. Degas twice more over the next few hours. A colder dough temperature makes it easier to form strands. The dough can be divided and shaped straight from refrigeration.

3. **FOLDING:** The dough is quite strong coming off the mixer, so a true strength-inducing fold is not necessary. Instead, degas the dough once by gently pressing out the built up fermentation gases after 1 hour of fermentation.

4. **DIVIDING AND SHAPING:** Divide the dough into appropriate-sized pieces. Preshape round and let rest on an unfloured work surface, covered with plastic. When relaxed enough to be elongated without tearing, usually 10 to 15 minutes, roll out the strands and form the braids. Once braided, proof the loaves covered with baker's linen and a sheet of plastic to prevent the formation of a skin. If using a proof box with humidity, set the controls low enough to

Challah is a classic braided egg bread of European origin. It is wonderfully versatile, and can be formed into innumerable braids and rolls, seeded or not, or baked in loaf pans, braided or not. It keeps well due to the substantial amount of eggs and oil in the dough. Old challah makes delectable French toast. The challah described here is the same as that used for the braiding exercises in Chapter 9.

prevent excess humidity from causing the individual strands to merge together.

5. FINAL FERMENTATION: 1½ to 2 hours at about 76°F.

6. BAKING: Before baking, thoroughly egg wash the surface of the loaves. If desired, sprinkle poppy or sesame seeds on top. Bake without steam at 380°F. Baking time is determined by the size of the loaves. Pan loaves will take longer to bake than freestanding loaves. A braid weighing 18 ounces (1.125 pounds) should bake in about 30 minutes. If the oven has vents, they should remain open throughout the bake.

VARIATION: A tasty variation is to make bread sticks with the challah dough. Cut individual dough pieces at 1.33 ounces (38 g)—with a 36-part divider, dough weight per press is 3 pounds, or 1.36 kg. Relax the dough, covered with plastic, for 10 or 15 minutes, then roll the individual pieces to about 16 inches long. Once rolled, the bread sticks can be left plain, or rolled into a damp cloth and then into a tray of sesame or poppy seeds. An alternative method for making bread sticks is to take the desired weight of dough and press it into a flat rectangle. Using a pizza roller or sharp knife, individual bread sticks can be cut off the main bulk of dough. This is possibly the quickest method, but take care that the bread sticks are as close as possible to being equal in weight so that they bake uniformly. Whatever method is chosen, allow the shaped bread sticks to rest for 15 to 20 minutes, then bake at 380°F for about 20 minutes, or until evenly brown and crisp. They will keep well for several days in an airtight container, and can be recrisped by warming for a few minutes at 350°F.

Berne Brot

DOUGH YIELD | U.S.: About 33 braids at 1.125 lb each | Metric: About 33 braids at .51 kg each | Home: 3 braids

	U.S.	METRIC	HOME	BAKER'S %
Bread flour	15 lb	7.5 kg	1 lb, 8 oz (5½ cups)	75%
High-gluten flour	5 lb	2.5 kg	8 oz (1⅞ cups)	25%
Milk	9 lb	4.5 kg	14.4 oz (1¾ cups)	45%
Yolks	.5 lb	.25 kg	.8 oz (2 yolks)	2.5%
Whole eggs	2.66 lb	1.33 kg	4.3 oz (2 eggs)	13.3%
Butter, soft	3 lb	1.5 kg	4.8 oz (9½ T)	15%
Sugar	1.1 lb	.55 kg	1.8 oz (3½ T)	5.5%
Salt	.4 lb	.2 kg	.6 oz (1 T)	2%
Yeast	.44 lb, fresh	.22 kg, fresh	.23 oz, instant dry (2 tsp)	2.2%
TOTAL YIELD	**37.1 lb**	**18.55 kg**	**3 lb, 10.9 oz**	**185.5%**

Berne Brot is a braided Swiss bread from the city of Berne. Although visually it is similar to challah, it is actually quite different: Instead of vegetable oil, Berne Brot has butter, and in place of water, it has milk. This richness is very evident in the eating: The bread is tender and moist, with a thin, leathery crust and delicate pale gold crumb. The butter, eggs, and milk help it keep well; leftover bread makes excellent French toast. This is another dough that lends itself to overnight retarding in bulk form. In this case, the desired dough temperature is 75° to 78°F. After mixing, bulk ferment at room temperature for 1 hour, then place the dough in the retarder or refrigerator. The dough should be degassed twice during the first 4 to 6 hours of refrigeration. The benefits of overnight retarding are improved dough texture and keeping quality. A colder dough temperature also makes it easier to form strands.

1. **MIXING:** Place all the ingredients in the mixing bowl. In a spiral mixer, mix on first speed for 3 minutes until all the ingredients are thoroughly incorporated, then on second speed for approximately 3 minutes more. The goal is to develop a strong gluten network. The dough will be comparatively stiff, although slightly looser than challah dough. The desired dough temperature is 78° to 80°F.

2. **BULK FERMENTATION:** 2 hours.

3. **FOLDING:** Fold the dough once, after 1 hour of fermentation.

4. **DIVIDING AND SHAPING:** Divide the dough into appropriate-sized pieces. Preshape round and let rest on an unfloured work surface, covered with plastic. When relaxed enough to be elongated without tearing, usually 10 to 15 minutes, roll out the strands and form the braids. Once braided, proof the loaves, covered with baker's linen and a sheet of plastic to prevent the formation of a skin. If using a proof box with humidity, set the controls low enough to prevent excess humidity from causing the individual strands to merge together.

5. **FINAL FERMENTATION:** 1½ to 2 hours at about 76°F.

6. **BAKING:** Before baking, thoroughly egg wash the surface of the Berne Brot. If desired, sprinkle poppy or sesame seeds on top. Bake without steam at 375°F. Baking time is determined by the size of the loaves. A braid weighing 18 ounces (1.125 pounds) should bake in about 30 to 35 minutes. If the oven has vents, they should remain open throughout the bake.

Pullman Bread

DOUGH YIELD | U.S.: About 15 pullman loaves at 2.25 lb each | Metric: About 17 pullman loaves at 1 kg each | Home: 1 pullman loaf with dough left over for 1 small loaf

	U.S.	METRIC	HOME	BAKER'S %
Bread flour	20 lb	10 kg	2 lb (7¼ cups)	100%
Milk powder	1 lb	.5 kg	1.6 oz (5 T)	5%
Sugar	.5 lb	.25 kg	.8 oz (1½ T)	2.5%
Butter, soft	1 lb	.5 kg	1.6 oz (3 T)	5%
Water	12 lb	6 kg	1 lb, 3.2 oz (2⅜ cups)	60%
Salt	.36 lb	.18 kg	.6 oz (1 T)	1.8%
Yeast	.5 lb, fresh	.25 kg, fresh	.26 oz, instant dry (2¼ tsp)	2.5%
TOTAL YIELD	**35.36 lb**	**17.68 kg**	**3 lb, 8.1 oz**	**176.8%**

Pullman bread is so called because of its former use on long-distance Pullman trains in the United States. In France it is known as *pain de mie,* or "bread of crumb," since it is characterized by having comparatively little crust. It lends itself well to regular toast, French toast, and canapés. The bread is normally baked in rectangular straight-sided pullman pans. Any covered loaf pans can be used, however, for example round cylindrical pans and fluted loaf pans. The powdered milk and the butter give a soft crumb texture to the loaf, and an easy-going eating quality.

1. **MIXING:** Place all the ingredients in the mixing bowl. In a spiral mixer, mix on first speed for 3 minutes until all the ingredients are thoroughly incorporated, then on second for 3 to 3½ minutes more. The dough consistency should be medium. The goal is to develop a fairly strong gluten network. Desired dough temperature is 78° to 80°F.

2. **BULK FERMENTATION:** 2 hours.

3. **FOLDING:** Fold the dough once, after 1 hour of fermentation.

4. **DIVIDING AND SHAPING:** Divide the dough into appropriate-sized pieces. For pullman pans that measure 13 by 3¾ by 3¾ inches, the dough weight is 2.25 pounds. Oil the pans and lids. Preshape round and let rest on an unfloured work surface, covered with plastic. After 10 to 15 minutes, when the dough is sufficiently relaxed, shape the loaves into long cylinders with no tapers at the ends. Place in the pullman pans; the dough should come about halfway up the sides. Slide the lids on and proof the loaves at about 76°F.

5. **FINAL FERMENTATION:** 1 to 1½ hours at about 76°F.

6. **BAKING:** When the dough is about ½ inch from the top of the pan, check that the lids are fully closed and load the bread into a 400°F oven. Since the pans are covered, there is no need to steam the oven. Bake the 2.25-pound loaves for 40 to 45 minutes. Remove a loaf from the oven to check doneness: The bread should have an even golden color all around, and the crust should be evenly firm. Remove the breads from the pans as soon as they are unloaded. If the loaves remain in the pans, they will sweat from condensation.

Semolina Bread with a Soaker and Fennel Seed

DOUGH YIELD | U.S.: About 27 loaves at 1.5 lb each | Metric: About 30 loaves at .68 kg each | Home: 3 medium loaves

OVERALL FORMULA

	U.S.	METRIC	HOME	BAKER'S %
Durum flour	12 lb	6 kg	1 lb, 3.2 oz	60%
Bread flour	8 lb	4 kg	12.8 oz	40%
Millet	1.6 lb	.8 kg	2.6 oz	8%
Wheat flakes	1.6 lb	.8 kg	2.6 oz	8%
Coarse cornmeal	.8 lb	.4 kg	1.3 oz	4%
Fennel seeds	.3 lb	.15 kg	.5 oz	1.5%
Water	16.4 lb	8.2 kg	1 lb, 10.2 oz	82%
Salt	.44 lb	.22 kg	.7 oz	2.2%
Yeast	.36 lb, fresh	.18 kg, fresh	.19 oz, instant dry	1.8%
TOTAL YIELD	**41.5 lb**	**20.75 kg**	**4 lb, 2.1 oz**	**207.5%**

SOAKER

	U.S.	METRIC	HOME	BAKER'S %
Millet	1.6 lb	.8 kg	2.6 oz (1/2 cup)	40%
Wheat flakes	1.6 lb	.8 kg	2.6 oz (7/8 cup)	40%
Coarse cornmeal	.8 lb	.4 kg	1.3 oz (1/4 cup)	20%
Water, hot	5 lb	2.5 kg	8 oz (1 cup)	125%
TOTAL	**9 lb**	**4.5 kg**	**14.5 oz**	

FINAL DOUGH

	U.S.	METRIC	HOME
Durum flour	12 lb	6 kg	1 lb, 3.2 oz (4 1/4 cups)
Bread flour	8 lb	4 kg	12.8 oz (2 7/8 cups)
Fennel seeds	.3 lb	.15 kg	.5 oz (2 T)
Water	11.4 lb	5.7 kg	1 lb, 2.2 oz (2 1/4 cups)
Salt	.44 lb	.22 kg	.7 oz (3 1/2 tsp)
Yeast	.36 lb, fresh	.18 kg, fresh	.19 oz, instant dry (1 3/4 tsp)
Soaker	9 lb	4.5 kg	14.5 oz (all of above)
TOTAL	**41.5 lb**	**20.75 kg**	**4 lb, 2.1 oz**

1. **SOAKER:** Prepare a hot soaker by stirring the millet, wheat flakes, and cornmeal into the soaker water. Cover the bowl with plastic to prevent moisture loss. In particularly hot weather, some or all of the dough salt can be added to the grains to deter enzymatic activity.

Durum wheat has more protein than any other kind of wheat; the *quality* of the protein for bread making, however, is not as good as the protein in hard winter or hard spring wheat. Durum has a tendency to break down in the mixer if even slightly overmixed. It is advisable, therefore, to slightly undermix the dough, and make folds on the bench if it is necessary to increase dough strength. Durum is typically milled into semolina, which is quite coarse and sandy textured, or into durum flour, which has more of a floury feel. Semolina tends to have somewhat of a puncturing effect on the developing gluten network of the dough as it mixes, unlike the softer durum flour. For bread making (and when making pasta too, for that matter), I find that durum is incorporated more easily into the dough and makes a nicer finished loaf. The soaker in the present formula gives a deeper body to the bread, as well as better moisture retention, so the loaf stays fresher a little longer. The fennel seeds contribute a distinct flavor that complements the other ingredients in the dough. A light toasting of the seeds adds even more flavor.

2. MIXING: Place all the ingredients in the mixing bowl, including the soaker and the fennel seeds. In a spiral mixer, mix on first speed for 3 minutes in order to incorporate the ingredients thoroughly. The dough should have a medium consistency. Turn the mixer to second speed and mix for about 2½ minutes more, until the gluten network has been fairly well developed. Keep a close eye on the dough as it mixes, and be careful not to overmix (if the dough goes from matte to shiny and from firm to sticky, it has been overmixed). Desired dough temperature: 76°F.

3. BULK FERMENTATION: 2 hours (or overnight retarding).

4. FOLDING: Fold the dough once, after 1 hour.

5. DIVIDING AND SHAPING: Divide the dough into 1.5-pound pieces (or make rolls with smaller pieces). Preshape lightly into rounds and place on a lightly floured work surface, seams up. Cover the rounds with plastic. When the dough has relaxed sufficiently (10 to 20 minutes), shape it into tight round or oval loaves. Place the loaves in floured *bannetons* and cover with baker's linen and plastic. Fennel seeds can be added to the tops of the loaves by first misting the top surface of the bread (or pressing the top into a damp cloth) and then sprinkling on the seeds. Be sparing, though; the seeds have a potent flavor and will dominate if used in excess.

6. FINAL FERMENTATION: About 1 hour at 76°F.

7. BAKING: With normal steam, 460°F. Loaves scaled at 1.5 pounds will take approximately 40 minutes to bake, with round loaves taking slightly longer than oblong ones.

Whole Wheat with Pecans and Golden Raisins

DOUGH YIELD | U.S.: About 26 loaves at 1.5 lb each | Metric: About 29 loaves at .68 kg each | Home: 2 large loaves

	U.S.	METRIC	HOME	BAKER'S %
Whole-wheat flour	10 lb	5 kg	1 lb (3⅝ cups)	50%
Bread flour	10 lb	5 kg	1 lb (3⅝ cups)	50%
Water	13.6 lb	6.8 kg	1 lb, 5.8 oz (2¾ cups)	68%
Salt	.4 lb	.2 kg	.6 oz (1 T)	2%
Yeast	.3 lb, fresh	.15 kg, fresh	.16 oz, instant dry (1½ tsp)	1.5%
Golden raisins, soaked and drained (see headnote)	3 lb	1.5 kg	4.8 oz (1 cup)	15%
Pecans	3 lb	1.5 kg	4.8 oz (1⅜ cups)	15%
TOTAL YIELD	**40.3 lb**	**20.15 kg**	**4 lb, .2 oz**	**201.5%**

Wheat flavored, sweet flavored, and nutty, the ingredients in this bread combine in a balanced and flavorful way. Peanut butter is a happy addition between a couple of slices, and the flavors are even more intensified when the bread is toasted. Pour warm water over the golden raisins and let them sit for up to 30 minutes to soften. Drain the raisins well before the mix. This step can be done just before mixing, or a day ahead. The pecans can be roasted prior to mixing, but keep the roasting light—overroasting makes them bitter.

1. **MIXING:** Add all the ingredients except the raisins and pecans to the mixing bowl. In a spiral mixer, mix on first speed for 3 minutes in order to incorporate the ingredients thoroughly. The dough consistency should be moderately loose. Turn the mixer to second speed and mix for about 3 minutes more, until a moderately strong gluten development has been achieved. Add the drained raisins and pecans, and mix on first speed only, just until the raisins and nuts are thoroughly incorporated. Desired dough temperature: 76°F.

2. **BULK FERMENTATION:** 2 hours (or overnight retarding).

3. **FOLDING:** Fold the dough once, after 1 hour.

4. **DIVIDING AND SHAPING:** The dough can be made into pan loaves, round or oblong loaves, or rolls. (If making pan loaves, the dimensions of the pan will determine dough weight. For a loaf pan measuring 8 by 4 by 2½ inches, about 18 ounces of dough will make a good fit. Larger commercial strap pans with dimensions of 9 by 5 by 2¾ inches will take 1.5 pounds of dough.) Divide the dough into the desired weights and preshape lightly into rounds. Place the dough pieces on a lightly floured work surface, seams up. Cover the rounds with plastic and let rest 10 to 20 minutes, until relaxed. Shape into blunt cylinders for pan loaves. For round or oblong loaves or rolls, shape accordingly. Cover the loaves with baker's linen and plastic so that air currents don't crust the surface.

5. **FINAL FERMENTATION:** 1 to 1½ hours at 76°F.

6. BAKING: With normal steam, 450°F. The raisins will contribute a lot of color, so lower the oven temperature by about 15°F after 20 minutes to finish the bake in a receding oven. Eighteen-ounce loaves baked in loaf pans will take 30 to 35 minutes to bake, with 1.5-pound loaves in the larger strap pans taking closer to 40 minutes. Freestanding loaves weighing 1.5 pounds will bake in about 40 minutes, with round loaves taking slightly longer than oblong ones.

Hazelnut and Fig Bread with Fennel Seeds and Rosemary

DOUGH YIELD | U.S.: About 27 loaves at 1.5 lb each | Metric: About 29 loaves at .68 kg each | Home: 2 large loaves

	U.S.	METRIC	HOME	BAKER'S %
Whole-wheat flour	10 lb	5 kg	1 lb (3⅝ cups)	50%
Bread flour	10 lb	5 kg	1 lb (3⅝ cups)	50%
Water	13.6 lb	6.8 kg	1 lb, 5.8 oz (2¼ cups)	68%
Salt	.4 lb	.2 kg	.6 oz (1 T)	2%
Yeast	.3 lb, fresh	.15 kg, fresh	.16 oz, instant dry (1½ tsp)	1.5%
Fennel seeds	.3 lb	.15 kg	.5 oz (2 T)	1.5%
Rosemary	.1 lb	.05 kg	.2 oz (2 T or leaves of 4 sprigs)	.5%
Hazelnuts, roasted and skinned (see headnote)	3 lb	1.5 kg	4.8 oz (1 cup)	15%
Dried figs	3 lb	1.5 kg	4.8 oz (1 cup)	15%
TOTAL YIELD	**40.7 lb**	**20.35 kg**	**4 lb, 9 oz**	**203.5%**

1. MIXING: Add all the ingredients except the hazelnuts and figs to the mixing bowl; the fennel seeds and rosemary can go in at the outset. In a spiral mixer, mix on first speed for 3 minutes in order to incorporate the ingredients thoroughly. The dough consistency should be moderately loose. Turn the mixer to second speed and mix for about 3 minutes more, until a moderately strong gluten development has been achieved. Add the hazelnuts and figs (either chop the figs or leave them whole, but in either case remove the hard nub of the stem before adding them to the dough), and mix on first speed just until the nuts and figs are thoroughly incorporated. Desired dough temperature: 76°F.

2. BULK FERMENTATION: 2 hours.

Although on the face of it, the ingredients in this formula are similar to those in the preceding Whole Wheat with Pecans and Golden Raisins, the figs and roasted hazelnuts will add quite a different flavor note. The fennel seeds and rosemary further heighten the flavors—this bread is loaded. The hazelnuts should be roasted until they begin to darken slightly in color, about 12 to 14 minutes at 375°F should be sufficient. Shaking the baking pan a couple of times helps even out the roasting. When the cooled nuts are rubbed vigorously between your hands, most of the papery skins should fall away from the nut.

3. FOLDING: Fold the dough once, after 1 hour.

4. DIVIDING AND SHAPING: Divide the dough into 1.5-pound pieces (or make rolls of about 3 ounces). Preshape lightly into rounds and place on a lightly floured work surface, seams up. Cover the rounds with plastic. When the dough has relaxed sufficiently, shape it into tight round or oval loaves. Place the loaves in floured *bannetons* and cover with baker's linen and plastic.

5. FINAL FERMENTATION: 1to 1½ hours at 76°F.

6. BAKING: With normal steam, 450°F. The figs will contribute a lot to the bread coloring, particularly if they have been chopped; therefore, lower the temperature by about 15°F after 20 minutes. Loaves weighing 1.5 pounds will bake in about 40 minutes, with round loaves taking slightly longer than oblong ones.

Un-kneaded, Six-Fold French Bread

DOUGH YIELD | U.S.: About 5 baguettes at 12 oz | Metric: About 4 baguettes at .4 kg | Home: About 5 baguettes at 12 oz

	U.S.	METRIC	HOME	BAKER'S %
Bread flour	2.28 lb	1 kg	8¼ cups	100%
Water	1.66 lb	.73 kg	3⅜ cups	73%
Salt	.05 lb	.02 kg	3½ tsp	2%
Yeast	.02 lb, fresh	.01 kg, fresh	1—1¼ tsp	1%
TOTAL YIELD	**4 LB**	**1.76 KG**	**4 LB**	**176 %**

For this formula we are going to take our normal methods of mixing and leave them on the shelf for the time being. This bread is fascinating for its unique production technique: the dough is un-kneaded—simply brought together with a few strokes of a plastic bowl scraper—and folded every 30 minutes for 3½ hours. The combination of a lengthy bulk fermentation along with the frequent foldings yields a dough that has very agreeable lightness, a beautiful creamy crumb color, and an internal structure of large, random holes. Although this dough can be made on a large scale, it's probably more suitable for the home bake, and the formula is therefore written for a small yield. The dough also makes an excellent pizza crust. Feeling adventurous? Try 75% hydration.

1. MIXING: Place all the ingredients into the mixer. With a rounded plastic bowl scraper, bring the ingredients together into a shaggy mass. Do this by running the scraper down the inside wall of the bowl and bringing the ingredients up from the bottom of the bowl and folding them on top of the ingredients that were on top of the bowl. Rotate the bowl about 20% with each stroke, so you are always working on a different portion of the dough. There is no need to empty the contents onto the work table. Cover the bowl with a sheet of plastic. Desired dough temperature is 75°F. When doing the calculations to figure the water temperature (see page 382 for a discussion of desired dough temperature), remember that there is virtually no friction generated by mixing in this fashion.

2. BULK FERMENTATION: 3½ hours.

3. FOLDING: Set a timer for 30 minutes. When it goes off, use the plastic scraper to mix the dough 20 strokes in the same manner as the initial mixing. Use fair vigor, but avoid tearing the dough. Reset the timer and continue giving 20 strokes with the scraper each time it goes off. The folding is done a total of 6 times.

4. DIVIDING AND SHAPING: Divide the dough into 12 to 14 ounce pieces (for baking on a small pizza stone, scale down accordingly). Pre-shape gently into rounds or blunt cylinders and let the divided pieces rest on a lightly floured bench, covered with plastic. Allow the dough to relax for about 15 minutes, until it can be shaped with no tearing. Use your gentlest hand to shape. The shaped baguettes should have sufficient tautness to ensure good volume when baked, but strive to shape as delicately as possible in order to retain lots of air pockets within the dough. Sift flour lightly onto a length of baker's linen and lay the baguettes onto it with their seams up. A slight crust will form on the surface that is in contact with the linen (the eventual top side of the loaf), and this will help give better definition to the cuts once the loaves are scored. The slight sheen of flour on the bread's surface also gives it a nice rustic appearance.

5. FINAL FERMENTATION: 1 to 1½ hours at 75°F.

6. BAKING: Carefully invert the baguettes so the seams are on the bottom and transfer them to the peel. Score the bread. In the home oven, just steam the oven once, as soon as the bread is loaded (see page 27). Bake at 460°F for 24 to 26 minutes, depending upon dough weight.

Toast Bread

DOUGH YIELD | U.S.: About 15 pullman loaves at 2.19 lb each | Metric: About 17 pullman loaves at 1 kg each | Home: 1 pullman loaf with dough left over for a small loaf

	U.S.	METRIC	HOME	BAKER'S %
High-gluten flour	10 lb	5 kg	1 lb (3⅝ cups)	50%
Bread flour	10 lb	5 kg	1 lb (3⅝ cups)	50%
Water	13.2 lb	6.6 kg	1 lb, 5.1 oz (2⅝ cups)	66%
Sugar	.2 lb	.1 kg	.3 oz (2 tsp)	1%
Butter, soft	.4 lb	.2 kg	.6 oz (1 T)	2%
Malt powder	.02 lb	.01 kg	.03 oz (⅜ tsp)	.1%
Salt	.4 lb	.2 kg	.6 oz (1 T)	2%
Yeast	.32 lb, fresh	.16 kg, fresh	.17 oz, instant dry (1½ tsp)	1.6%
TOTAL YIELD	**34.54 lb**	**17.27 kg**	**3 lb, 6.8 oz**	**172.7%**

This is an English-style pullman bread, and while its uses are broader than its name implies, it seems to fulfill its character most fully when toasted. The quantities of sugar, butter, and malt powder in the dough are almost insignificantly small, yet in the aggregate they make the bread something other than "just plain white." If malt powder is unavailable, malt syrup can be substituted at about 5 times the weight of the powder; or, it can be left out entirely without greatly changing the bread's handling characteristics or flavor. The pullman pans used measure 13 by 3¾ by 3¾ inches. Alternatively, commercial strap pans, measuring 9 by 5 by 2¾ inches, can be used and hold 1.5 pounds of dough, and loaf pans measuring 8 by 4 by 2½ inches can also be used and will hold between 1 pound and 1.125 pounds (18 ounces) of dough.

1. **MIXING:** Add all the ingredients to the mixing bowl. In a spiral mixer, mix on first speed for 3 minutes in order to incorporate the ingredients thoroughly. The dough consistency should be medium. Turn the mixer to second speed and mix for about 3 minutes more, until a fairly strong gluten development has been achieved. Desired dough temperature: 76°F.

2. **BULK FERMENTATION:** 2 hours.

3. **FOLDING:** Fold the dough once, after 1 hour.

4. **DIVIDING AND SHAPING:** Divide the dough into appropriate-sized pieces, depending on the pan size in which they will bake. Preshape lightly into rounds and place on a lightly floured work surface, seams up. Cover the rounds with plastic. When the dough has relaxed sufficiently (10 to 20 minutes), shape it into tight cylinders. Place the dough in the loaf pans and cover with baker's linen and plastic.

5. **FINAL FERMENTATION:** 1 to 1½ hours at 76°F.

6. **BAKING:** With normal steam, 430°F. Large pullmans will bake in 40 to 45 minutes. Smaller loaves will take between 30 and 36 minutes, depending on dough weight. Thump the bottom of the loaves when you think they are done, and listen for a pronounced hollow sound.

MISCELLANEOUS BREADS

8

A journeyman baker had to be strong to do the work and dumb to embrace a profession that more often than not broke his health, left him both infirm and impecunious, or killed him prematurely. They were highly susceptible to a startling array of serious maladies . . . ranging from a chronic bronchial cold to pleurisy, pneumonia, asthma, emphysema, and tuberculosis. Strenuous toil produced hernias, ulcers, and varicose veins. The stress and strain of arduous exertion performed through every night and part of every day was said to have generated grave "nervous" disorders. Their work made bakery workers characteristically "misanthropic," "morose," and "very unstable." Those who remained in the bakery were said to die typically between the ages of forty and fifty as a result of exhaustion, disease, or dissipation. . . .

—STEVEN KAPLAN, FROM *THE BAKERS OF PARIS AND THE BREAD QUESTION: 1700–1775*

In this section, we will look at breads and doughs that either defy categorization or are unusual in some unique way. Brioche, bread sticks, pizza, pretzels, flat breads, fougasse, and some other tasty baked goods have a long history, but somehow they don't fit neatly into typical bread categories. The breads in this chapter are an interesting hodgepodge of flavors, tastes, and textures.

There are some other differences between this chapter and the other bread chapters. For one, we will dispense here with the practice of basing each formula on 20 pounds or 10 kilograms of flour. Since many of the items in this chapter are savory, the instructions for assembling and cooking various vegetable preparations are included. A third focus is on the special equipment needed for many of the products.

Bobby, Dee, Emily

Brioche

DOUGH YIELD | U.S.: 13.69 lb | Metric: 6.845 kg | Home: 3 lb, 5.7 oz

	U.S.	METRIC	HOME	BAKER'S %
Bread flour	4.62 lb	2.31 kg	1 lb, 2.4 oz (4¼ cups)	77%
High-gluten flour	1.38 lb	.69 kg	5.6 oz (1¼ cups)	23%
Water, cold	.58 lb	.29 kg	2.2 oz (¼ cup)	9.6%
Eggs, cold	2.94 lb	1.47 kg	11.8 oz (6 eggs)	49%
Salt	.15 lb	.075 kg	.6 oz (1 T)	2.5%
Sugar	.72 lb	.36 kg	2.9 oz (6 T)	12%
Yeast	.3 lb, fresh	.15 kg, fresh	.16 oz, instant dry (1½ tsp)	5%
Butter, cold	3 lb	1.5 kg	12 oz (1½ cups)	50%
TOTAL YIELD	**13.69 lb**	**6.845 kg**	**3 lb, 5.7 oz**	**228.1%**

Brioche seems to defy reality. With all that butter—50 percent of the flour weight is butter in this formula—it should be earthbound and heavy; yet when properly made, it is ethereal and light, feathery, delicate, subtle, and delectable. It seems, too, to somehow defy classification. Is it bread? Not really. Pastry? Not quite that either. It must be some other thing all of its own. To just file it under *viennoiserie*—lightly sweetened yeast goods—seems to dishonor its uniqueness somehow. In the *Iliad* and the *Odyssey,* Homer portrays characters that, from all external appearances, are human, yet they are actually gods from Mt. Olympus. In the same way, brioche is not quite bread and not quite pastry, but some semi-divine thing all of its own. Brioche dough is wonderfully versatile: It can be shaped into the traditional *tête* and *grande tête* shapes; it can be fashioned into loaves or freestanding

There are a few rules to abide by in mixing brioche, and adhering to them goes a long way toward achieving consistency in results:

1. **ALL INGREDIENTS MUST BE COLD:** The overall mix time for brioche is long—15 minutes or more—and quite a lot of friction will be developed in the mixer. If made with cold ingredients, the dough will remain cool enough to incorporate the butter without becoming oily. Several hours before mixing, then, refrigerate *all* the ingredients; even the water, which comes from the tap at 60°F or more in summer, should be refrigerated so it will be about 40°F. During particularly hot weather, it may even be beneficial (although not always practical) to refrigerate the mixing bowl and dough hook.

2. **MIXING:** Place all the ingredients except the cold butter in the mixing bowl. Begin the mix on first speed until the ingredients are incorporated, then turn the mixer to second speed. Mix until the dough is strong and tough, 5 to 7 minutes in a spiral mixer.

Meanwhile, take the cold butter and beat it with a rolling pin until it is pliable. To test for pliability, press your index finger into the butter before pounding with the pin, and notice how firm and cold it is—you can barely make an indentation. Now, pound the butter flat with the rolling pin (preferably not a ball-bearing pin) along its entire length and press your finger into the surface again. In just a few seconds, the butter will have gone from completely hard to pliable (but still quite cold).

When all the butter is ready, and the dough is strong, add the butter bit by bit while the machine continues to mix. There is no need to wait for one addition of butter to be incorporated before braids; it serves as the base for a variety of coffee cakes; it makes superb French toast; and it can even be treated as puff pastry and laminated for delicious brioche *feuilleté.*

adding the next portion. Once all the butter is in, the dough will be a bit confused, a little uncertain how to react to all that butter, and it will break. Soon enough, it will sort things out and begin to become smooth and satiny. The amount of time it mixes once the butter is incorporated will vary, depending on the mixer. Generally, you can expect the dough to mix for 8 or 10 minutes once the butter is added. Mix until the dough "sheets" fully. To test for sheeting, take a piece of dough about the size of an apricot. Holding it in both hands, gently and gradually begin to stretch the dough out. When it is sheeting fully, you will be able to coax it out into a thin, almost transparent, sheet. This means the dough is mixed. (And if you find yourself covered with goose bumps, you are not alone. I always marvel at the dough at this point—with all that butter, how can it do that? It seems to be ignoring some fundamental law of physics.) Transfer the dough into a lightly floured dough bucket or container, tuck plastic around the dough so that no air can enter, and let stand at room temperature for 1 hour. Fold the velvety dough, place it back in the dough bucket or container, cover again with plastic, and refrigerate. Degas 2 or 3 times over the next several hours. It is best to make the dough 1 day ahead and chill it thoroughly before using it. Unless you are baking in a food competition and facing time constraints, let the dough chill overnight and use it the next day.

3. DIVIDING AND SHAPING: Various shapes can be made with brioche, and the size of the baking mold will determine the dough weight. Traditional *tête* brioche weights range from 1¾ ounces to 2¼ ounces, while a *grande tête* weighs between 12 and 16 ounces. Loaf brioches such as Brioche Nanterre are scaled at between 10 and 14 ounces, depending on the size of the loaf pan. Larger pullman loaves can be made as well. Generally, the dough should fill the mold or loaf pan to about 50 percent of capacity when first placed in it. When proofed, the mold should be about 85 percent full, and during the bake the dough should fill the mold completely.

4. BAKING: Once proofed, brush the brioche with egg wash (with the exception of pullman loaves baked with the lid on). Because of the high proportion of eggs, butter, and sugar in the dough, a moderate oven is indicated. Bake at about 380°F. Bake times will of course vary with the weight and shape of the dough. The butter will contribute abundantly to the crust color, so it is important to bake fully: The finished brioche should have a rich and deeply golden crust and an unforgettably fragrant aroma. If underbaked, there will not be sufficient structure to hold the brioche up, and it will cave in and collapse, a woeful and avoidable sight.

Sesame Bread Sticks

DOUGH YIELD | U.S.: 72 bread sticks at 1.33 oz each | Metric: 72 bread sticks at .038 kg each | Home: 24 br

	U.S.	METRIC	HOME	BAKER'S
Bread flour	3.54 lb	1.61 kg	1 lb, 2.9 oz (4¼ cups)	100%
Water	1.98 lb	.9 kg	10.6 oz (1⅜ cups)	56%
Olive oil	.21 lb	.097 kg	1.1 oz (1 T + 1 tsp)	6%
Malt syrup	.12 lb	.048 kg	.6 oz (¾ tsp)	3%
Salt	.06 lb	.029 kg	.3 oz (½ T)	1.8%
Yeast	.09 lb, fresh	.04 kg, fresh	.05 oz (½ tsp)	2.5%
Sesame seeds, as needed				
TOTAL YIELD	**6 lb**	**2.724 kg**	**1 lb, 15.6 oz**	**169.3%**

These bread sticks are crunchy from a thorough bake and nutty from the sesame seeds, and their flavor is rounded out by the olive oil and malt syrup. Like all bread sticks, they will keep for several days in an airtight container.

1. MIXING: For large-scale production of bread sticks (50 dozen or more), a full-sized spiral mixer can be used. For smaller quantities (3 to 24 dozen), a small spiral mixer or 20- to 30-quart planetary mixer works well. Place all the ingredients except the sesame seeds in the mixing bowl. In a planetary-style mixer, mix on first speed until the ingredients are incorporated, about 3 minutes. The dough should be of medium consistency. Turn the mixer to second speed and mix for another 4 or 5 minutes, to a moderate gluten development. Desired dough temperature: 76°F.

2. BULK FERMENTATION: 1 hour.

3. DIVIDING AND SHAPING: If using a 36-part dough divider, divide the dough into 2 pieces weighing 3 pounds (1.36 kg) each. If scaling the bread sticks individually, divide the dough into 1.33-ounce portions. Let the divided pieces rest on a lightly floured work surface, covered with plastic, for 10 to 15 minutes. Roll the pieces, trying to keep an even dimension along the length, to 14 to 16 inches long. Roll each piece over a moistened cloth, then roll in a tray of sesame seeds to coat. Transfer the individual bread sticks to sheet pans. Alternatively, the dough can be pressed on a floured bench into a flat rectangle and cut into thin strips with a pizza wheel.

4. BAKING: The bread sticks can be baked right away with no further proofing. Bake at 380°F for approximately 20 minutes, or until golden brown. These and the following grissini should have a crunch when baked that permeates right through to the center of the bread stick. If they are doughy, return them to a 350°F oven until completely baked. Once cool, the bread sticks can be stored in airtight containers for up to 5 days.

…sini at 1.33 oz each | Metric: 72 grissini at .038 kg each | Home: 24 grissini

		METRIC	HOME	BAKER'S %
	…b	1.52 kg	1 lb, 1.9 oz (4⅛ cups)	100%
	…b	.79 kg	9.3 oz (1⅛ cups)	52%
		.182 kg	2.1 oz (5 T)	12%
		.152 kg	1.8 oz (3½ T)	10%
Salt	.07 lb	.03 kg	.4 oz (2 tsp)	2%
Yeast	.1 lb, fresh	.046 kg, fresh	.05 oz, instant dry (½ tsp)	3%
TOTAL YIELD	**6 lb**	**2.72 kg**	**1 lb, 15.6 oz**	**179%**

These Italian bread sticks are richer than the preceding Sesame Bread Sticks, due to the higher percentage of olive oil in the dough and the inclusion of butter. Adding roasted garlic or grated Parmesan cheese to the dough (as detailed below) are two ways they can be varied. Other variations for this versatile dough are the addition of ground black pepper, sesame seeds, or a mixture of sesame, poppy, and fennel seeds.

1. **MIXING:** For large-scale production of grissini (50 dozen or more), a full-sized spiral mixer can be used. For smaller quantities (3 to 24 dozen), a small spiral mixer or 20- to 30-quart planetary mixer works well. Place all the ingredients in the mixing bowl. In a planetary-style mixer, mix on first speed until the ingredients are incorporated, about 3 minutes. The dough should be of medium consistency. Turn the mixer to second speed and mix for another 4 or 5 minutes, to a moderate gluten development. Desired dough temperature: 76°F.

2. **BULK FERMENTATION:** 1 hour.

3. **DIVIDING AND SHAPING:** If using a 36-part dough divider, divide the dough into 2 pieces weighing 3 pounds (1.36 kg) each. If scaling the bread sticks individually, divide the dough into 1.33-ounce portions. Let the divided pieces rest on a lightly floured work surface, covered with plastic, for about 10 to 15 minutes. Roll or stretch the pieces, trying to keep an even dimension along the length, to 14 to 16 inches long. Before transferring to baking sheets, the individual bread sticks can be rolled in a tray of fine semolina if desired; this adds a bit of texture to the taste. An alternative means of dividing the dough is to press it into a flat rectangle on a floured bench and cut it into thin strips with a pizza wheel.

4. **BAKING:** By the time the bread sticks have been divided, they can be baked right away with no further proofing. Bake at 380°F for about 20 minutes, or until golden brown. Once cool, the bread sticks can be stored in airtight containers for up to 5 days.

ROASTED GARLIC GRISSINI: For the 6-pound (2.72-kg) batch size, 3 bulbs of garlic are needed; the home-sized batch of 2 pounds requires 1 bulb. To prepare the garlic, cut about ½ inch off the top of whole bulbs, and place the bulbs right side up on a baking sheet. There is no need to peel the bulbs. Sprinkle a light coat of olive oil on the exposed cloves. Cover the baking sheet with aluminum foil and bake at about 350°F until the garlic is soft, about 45 minutes. Remove the garlic from its husk by squeezing the individual cloves. Add the garlic to the dough at the beginning of the mix.

CHEESE GRISSINI: For this variation, use good-quality Parmesan or Gruyère cheese. The 6-pound (2.72-kg) batch size needs .34 pound of cheese (10 percent of the flour weight); the 2-pound batch requires 1.8 ounces. Add the grated cheese at the beginning of the mix. Alternatively, roll the stretched bread sticks in a bed of grated cheese and ground black pepper.

Soft Butter Rolls

DOUGH YIELD | U.S.: 72 rolls at 1.33 oz each | Metric: 72 rolls at .038 kg each | Home: 24 rolls

	U.S.	METRIC	HOME	BAKER'S %
Bread flour	3.3 lb	1.5 kg	1 lb, 1.6 oz (4 cups)	100%
Water	1.52 lb	.69 kg	8.1 oz (1 cup)	46%
Eggs	.33 lb	.15 kg	1.8 oz (1 egg)	10%
Butter, soft	.26 lb	.12 kg	1.4 oz (3 T)	8%
Sugar	.2 lb	.09 kg	1.1 oz (2 T)	6%
Dry milk (powdered milk)	.17 lb	.075 kg	.9 oz (3 T)	5%
Salt	.07 lb	.03 kg	.4 oz (2 tsp)	2%
Yeast	.17 lb, fresh	.075 kg, fresh	.09 oz, instant dry (1 tsp)	5%
TOTAL YIELD	**6.02 lb**	**2.73 kg**	**1 lb, 15.4 oz**	**182%**

These soft butter rolls go down real easy. It's true that they are versatile, fun to make, use high-quality ingredients, and how often does someone show up at a picnic with homemade hamburger rolls?

1. MIXING: Place all the ingredients in the mixing bowl. In a planetary-style mixer, mix on first speed until the ingredients are incorporated, about 3 minutes (for production of 50 dozen or more, a full-sized spiral mixer can be used). The dough should be of medium consistency. Turn the mixer to second speed and mix for about 5 more minutes, until the gluten network is moderately developed. Desired dough temperature: 76°F.

2. BULK FERMENTATION: 1 hour.

3. DIVIDING AND SHAPING: If using a 36-part dough divider, divide the dough into 2 pieces weighing 3 pounds (1.36 kg) each. Don't round or preshape the dough. If hand scaling, divide the dough into 1.33-ounce portions, trying to cut pieces that are square. Place the dough pieces on a sheet pan lined with parchment paper so that the sides of the individual pieces almost touch—during the bake they will join, and there will be a minimum of crust. Allow the dough to proof fully, until they are quite light to the touch.

4. BAKING: Just before the bake, brush the top of the rolls with melted butter. Bake at 400°F for 15 to 18 minutes, or until the tops are golden. The sides and center should remain soft and pliable. Brush again with butter when the rolls are removed from the oven.

LITTLE CLOVERLEAF ROLLS: Once the dough has been divided into 1.33-ounce pieces, divide each piece into thirds—no need to use the scale for this, just eyeball it. Lightly round the little pieces and place them in groups of 3 into greased muffin cups. Proof until light to the touch, brush with melted butter, bake at 400°F for about 15 minutes, and brush once again as they come out of the oven.

BRAIDS: Little 1-strand braids or rolls can be made with the dough, using the patterns illustrated on page 295.

HAMBURGER ROLLS: Divide the dough into 2.25-ounce pieces. Preshape round. Let the rounds relax for about 5 minutes under a sheet of plastic. Lightly flour the work surface and, with a rolling pin, roll each piece into a disk about 3½ inches in diameter. Proof on sheet pans lined with parchment paper, and cover with plastic to prevent a crust from forming. When risen and light to the touch, bake at 400°F for about 20 minutes; the crust should be golden but the rolls should be soft when gently squeezed. Brush the rolls with melted butter while they are still hot. A variation on this is to sprinkle grated Parmesan cheese on top of the rolls just before the bake.

CINNAMON-RAISIN BREAD: Divide the dough into appropriate sizes depending on the dimensions of your loaf pans. Pans measuring 9 by 5 by 2¾ inches can take 1.125 pounds (18 ounces) of dough. Scale the dough pieces at about 14 ounces for pans measuring 8 by 4 by 2½ inches. Roll the dough into flat rectangles about as long as the loaf pans being used. Brush the surface with melted butter and then sprinkle on a layer of cinnamon sugar. On top of that, sprinkle dark or golden raisins that have been soaked in warm water for 30 minutes and then well drained. Roll up the dough into tight cylinders. Place the loaves in the pans, seams down. Proof under plastic, until well risen and light to the touch, and brush with melted butter just before the bake. Bake at 400°F for 30 to 35 minutes. Brush again with butter when the loaves are removed from the oven.

Bagels

DOUGH YIELD | U.S.: About 64 bagels at 4 oz each | Metric: About 76 bagels at .113 kg each | Home: 13 bagels

	U.S.	METRIC	HOME	BAKER'S %
High-gluten flour	10 lb	5 kg	2 lb (7½ cups)	100%
Water	5.8 lb	2.9 kg	1 lb, 2.6 oz (2⅜ cups)	58%
Diastatic malt powder	.05 lb	.025 kg	.2 oz (2 tsp)	.5%
Salt	.2 lb	.1 kg	.6 oz (1 T)	2%
Yeast	.13 lb, fresh	.065 kg, fresh	.07 oz, instant dry (¾ tsp)	1.3%
Malt syrup, as needed for boiling				
TOTAL YIELD	**16.18 lb**	**8.09 kg**	**3 lb, 3.5 oz**	**161.8%**

Good bagels are one of the tastiest baked treats you could ask for. Repeat: *good* bagels. And while most people don't often have access to really well-made bagels, when we have them, we tend to remember both the bagels and where we got them. Like most baked goods, bagels have a few needs in their production, and they require a little special equipment, but there is nothing out of the ordinary, and nothing that is cost prohibitive.

Most all the bagels sold today are extruded, that is, the dough is forced through tubes and mechanically cut to size. This process pumps out the bagels at high speed—thousands per hour—but is very strenuous for the dough. For a chewy bagel, one that takes a while to get through, hand forming and boiling, rather than extruding and steaming, give the best results.

Another change that has gradually permeated the bagel industry has been the increasing tendency to make bagels perceptibly sweet,

SPECIAL EQUIPMENT REQUIRED FOR THE BAGELS DETAILED HERE:

A kettle large enough to hold several bagels during the boiling stage.

A strainer with a handle to remove the bagels from the kettle.

A large bowl full of ice water to cool the bagels after the water bath.

A sufficient number of bagel boards. These are constructed out of wood cut to 5 by 24 by 1 inch, with one side covered with baker's linen (cut the linen to 6 by 25 inches, pull it tight across the 5-inch width, and staple it around the sides).

1. MIXING: Add all the ingredients except the malt syrup to the mixing bowl. In a spiral mixer, mix on first speed for 3 minutes in order to incorporate all the ingredients. Bagel dough is quite stiff. Depending on the flour's absorption, slightly more water may need to be added, but be sure the dough remains stiff. Turn the mixer to second speed and mix for an additional 3 minutes. A stand mixer or planetary mixer will require 5 to 6 minutes on second speed. The dough should be tough, strong, and well developed. Desired dough temperature: 76°F.

2. BULK FERMENTATION: 1 hour.

3. DIVIDING AND SHAPING: Divide the dough into 4-ounce pieces that are more or less square. Flatten them one by one, and roll them up into tight cylinders. Roll each dough piece 10 to 11 inches long, with no taper at the ends (illustration A). Shape the dough into a bagel like the old-timers did: Wrap it around the broadest part of your hand. The ends should overlap slightly on your palm (B). Roll your hand back and forth on the bench in order to seal the 2 ends together (C). Place the finished bagels (D) on sheet pans that have been sprinkled with cornmeal or semolina. Refrigerate the bagels for at least 6 hours or overnight, covered with plastic.

and to flavor them so extravagantly that they barely seem to be a bread product any longer. You will notice that there is no sugar in the dough in this formula. This is typical of traditional bagels, which were offered only as plain, poppy, or sesame, and sometimes salt and onion. For those who can't conceive of an unsweetened bagel, I would first urge that you try making bagels the old-fashioned way. If your tastes have become accustomed to today's style of bagels, the addition of perhaps 2 to 3 percent sugar in the present formula would not negatively impact the flavor or handling characteristics of the dough. My thanks to Rick Coppedge, an excellent baker from New York, for his technical help with bagels.

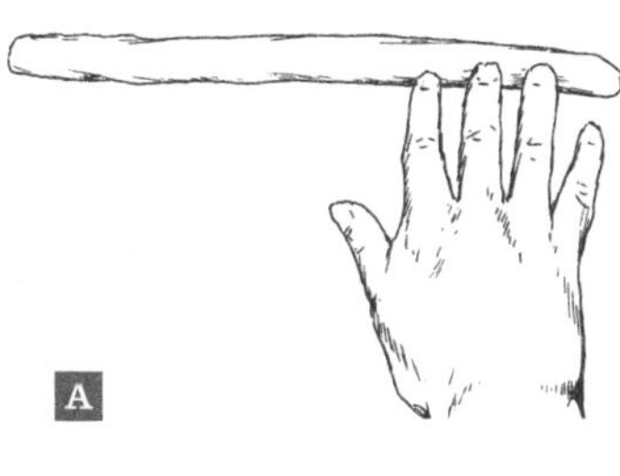

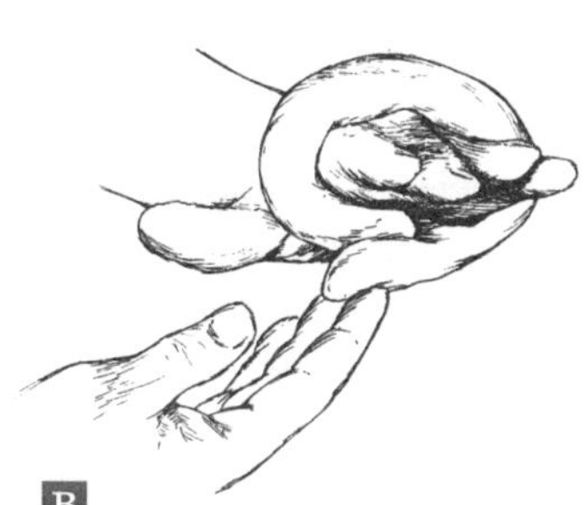

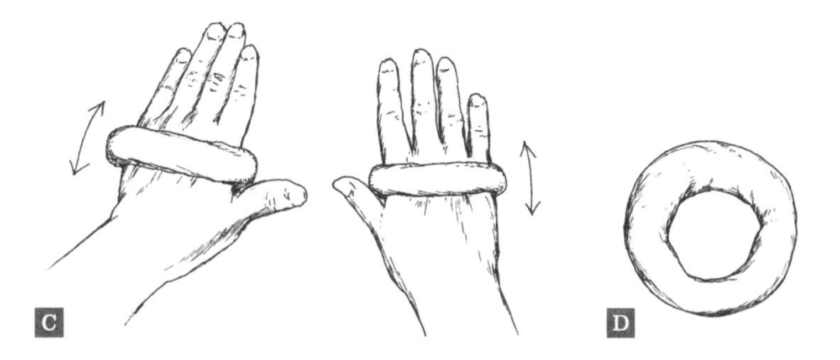

Forming bagels

4. Prior to boiling the bagels, take the linen-covered bagel boards and submerge them in water—they will be placed directly onto the hearth of the oven or baking stone, and will last much longer if they are soaked beforehand.

5. **BOILING:** Bring a large kettle of water to the boil. Add malt syrup before it comes to the boil—enough syrup to make the water the color of strong tea. The malt syrup will slightly permeate the dough, and once in the oven the bagels will take on a rich color and a good shine. The boiling also reactivates the yeast, which is sluggish from its long refrigeration, and pregelatinizes the starch on the surface of the bagels, which contributes to their chewiness.

6. When the water is boiling, take the bagels out from refrigeration. Put several into the kettle (keep the heat on, and add as many as can comfortably fit without lowering the temperature of the kettle too much), and leave for about 45 seconds. They will puff considerably and float.

7. Remove the bagels from the water and place in the bowl of ice water.

8. Once the bagels have chilled for 3 or 4 minutes, place 4 or 5 onto the soaked boards. If you want seeded bagels, press one side into a tray of sesame seeds, poppy seeds, or the seeds of your choice, then put them on the boards, seeded side down. For salted bagels, a light sprinkling of coarse salt is all that is needed.

9. Bake the bagels at 500°F. Put the bagel boards into the oven, directly onto the hearth or preheated baking stone. After 3 or 4 minutes, when the tops of the bagels have begun to dry out, flip the boards so the bagels are now directly on the hearth or stone. Bake until golden, 15 to 18 minutes in all. Make sure some cream cheese is close by.

Bialys

DOUGH YIELD | U.S.: 72 bialys at 3 oz each | Metric: 72 bialys at .085 kg each | Home: 12 bialys

	U.S.	METRIC	HOME	BAKER'S %
High-gluten flour	8.38 lb	3.81 kg	1 lb, 6.4 oz (5 1/8 cups)	100%
Water	4.86 lb	2.21 kg	13 oz (1 5/8 cups)	58%
Salt	.16 lb	.073 kg	.4 oz (2 tsp)	1.9%
Yeast	.13 lb, fresh	.061 kg, fresh	.07 oz, instant dry (3/4 tsp)	1.6%
Onion filling, as needed				
TOTAL YIELD	**13.53 lb**	**6.154 kg**	**2 lb, 3.9 oz**	**161.5%**

I have heard bialys described as "bagels without the holes." With bad press like that, it's unlikely that people will go out of their way to find one. Bialys, originally made by Jewish bakers in Bialystok, Poland, came to New York about one hundred years ago. For many of the years I owned a bakery in southern Vermont, we made bialys each Saturday, and I can't remember a time that there was ever an unsold bialy at the end of the day. They are delightful little rolls, with just a whisper of onion flavor permeating the dough. The dough is stretched out just before baking, leaving a thin indentation in the center that is surrounded by a circular ridge of dough, and is finished with a dollop of onion filling placed into the central cavity. With a hot oven and a quick bake, the result is a chewy and delicious treat.

1. ONION FILLING: Grind or finely chop some onions (1 medium onion is plenty for a dozen bialys). Add some fresh white bread crumbs, about 10 percent of the weight of the onions. Place in a covered container and let them visit, in the refrigerator or at room temperature, for a couple of hours. The onion mix can also be made a day or more ahead. Refrigerate until needed.

2. MIXING: Bialy dough is quite stiff. Place all the dough ingredients in the mixing bowl. In a planetary mixer, mix on first speed for about 3 minutes to incorporate the ingredients. Turn the mixer to second speed, and mix for an additional 5 to 6 minutes, until the gluten is well developed. Desired dough temperature: 76°F.

3. BULK FERMENTATION: 2 hours, with a fold after 1 hour.

4. DIVIDING AND SHAPING: Divide the dough into 3-ounce pieces—in a 36-part divider, the press weight is 6.75 pounds (3.06 kg). Round the dough tightly (illustration A). Place, seams down, on sheet pans sprinkled with 1/4 inch of flour. Place in a draft-free location, or cover with baker's linen and then a sheet of plastic. Proof the rolls fully, about 1 1/2 hours.

5. FILLING AND BAKING: Pick up a roll and press both thumbs into the center of it, creating a hollow (illustration B). Rotate the roll, keeping both thumbs deep in the dough as you do so, and stretch the hollow outward as the roll rotates (C). The bialy should have a circular wall of dough that surrounds a thin membrane in the center. The center indentation should be about 1 1/2 inches in diameter. Place the bialy on a baker's peel or loading conveyor. When all the rolls have been shaped, put 1 rounded teaspoon of the onion filling in the central cavity (D). Bake at 480°F for 8 to 10 minutes. The bialys should be nicely browned, but the outer wall of dough should be moist and supple and not dried out. The fragrance of the onions will mingle alluringly with the rich smell of baked dough as you go get some butter. Try one warm; I think you will be a believer.

VARIATIONS: Use chopped garlic in place of (or along with) the onions. Poppy or sesame seeds, alone or mixed together, can also be sprinkled onto the bialys before baking.

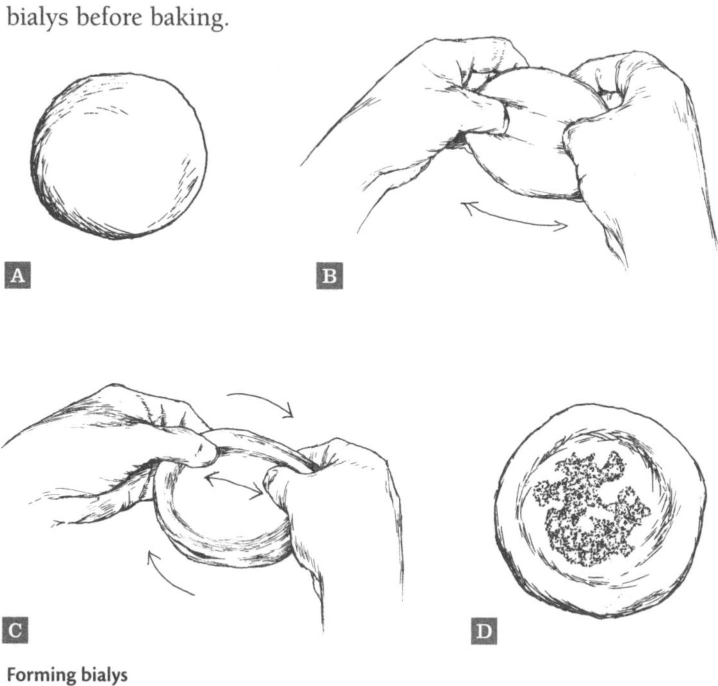

Forming bialys

Irish Soda Bread

DOUGH YIELD | U.S.: 10 loaves at 2.25 lb each | Metric: 10 loaves at 1 kg each | Home: 1 large loaf

	U.S.	METRIC	HOME	BAKER'S %
Whole-wheat pastry flour	5.63 lb	2.5 kg	5.3 oz (1¹/₄ cups)	50%
Wheat flakes, ground	2.82 lb	1.26 kg	2.6 oz (⁵/₈ cup)	25%
White pastry flour	2.81 lb	1.25 kg	2.6 oz (⁵/₈ cup)	25%
Milk powder	.47 lb	.21 kg	.4 oz (1 T + 1 tsp)	4.2%
Sugar	.09 lb	.04 kg	.1 oz (¹/₂ tsp)	.8%
Salt	.17 lb	.08 kg	.15 oz (³/₄ tsp)	1.5%
Baking soda	.28 lb	.13 kg	.12 oz (1¹/₂ tsp)	2.5%
Baking powder	.09 lb	.04 kg	.04 oz (¹/₂ tsp)	.8%
Buttermilk	10.14 lb	4.50 kg	9.25 oz (1 cup + 2 T)	90%
TOTAL YIELD	**22.51 lb**	**10 kg**	**1 lb, 4.6 oz**	**199.8%**

Years ago I lived in Ireland, and for several months worked at a bakery in Dublin. One of the things we made each day was Irish soda bread. Each morning, shortly after four o'clock, a van would pull up, and out would come a groggy and cranky delivery boy, wheeling fresh buttermilk into the bakery in steel milk cans that were about as tall as he was. The delivery boy was dark and gloomy; this only intensified the silvery brightness of the shining milk cans. By then, another baker and myself would have mixed the ingredients for the baking powder, and it would be in a long wooden mixing trough along with the rest of the dry ingredients. We would then hoist up one of the canisters of buttermilk and pour it into the trough. Then we would each stand at one end of the trough and begin mixing—not just with our hands; these were large batches, and we'd

1. **MIXING:** Before making the actual mix, process the wheat flakes in a food processor until they are broken down. Don't turn them into powder, though—they should still have a coarse texture. If you live in Ireland, mix the dough by hand if using less than 5 Imperial gallons of buttermilk. In North America, hand mixing is still preferred for its gentleness, but using any kind of mixer is acceptable as long as it is used minimally, and only on first speed. In either case, place all the dry ingredients in the mixing bowl and whisk them around for a few seconds so they are somewhat dispersed. Then pour over the buttermilk. Mix swiftly but lightly, just until the dough comes together. It should be quite moist, but not runny. Add more buttermilk if necessary and mix lightly to incorporate.

2. **DIVIDING AND SHAPING:** Flour the work surface, turn out the dough, and sprinkle a light dusting of pastry flour over the top of the dough to facilitate dividing. Divide the dough into 2.25-pound portions (the Home recipe yields 1 loaf weighing 1 pound, 6 ounces). To shape, cup both hands at the base of the dough and, with swift strokes, rotate the dough as you rapidly bring your hands (palms up) together and then apart, always at the base of the dough. This will bring the dough into a round cohesion while remaining gentle and not toughening it. Don't expect the kind of structure sought in a loaf of white yeasted dough; simply bring the soda bread to roundness, tightening it only enough to eliminate any large air pockets inside the dough. Flatten the rounded piece

literally be up to our elbows. The boss was emphatic about how gently the bread had to be handled, and once scaled, we had to shape it with the lightest touch possible. Then it was right to the oven, and a good hot one it was. Once baked, the loaf had a pungent aroma of fragrant wheat meal and tangy buttermilk, full of flavor and fat from those green-pastured cows.

I've made Irish soda bread pretty much every year since returning to the United States, always around St. Patrick's Day. And admittedly it isn't quite the same. True buttermilk is virtually unobtainable here, and what we see most commonly is free of fat and stuffed with stabilizers and gums. Substituting about 20 percent sour cream or yogurt for an equal weight of buttermilk will add body to the bread—just whisk the sour cream or yogurt into the buttermilk until the liquid is smooth. Irish whole-meal flour is only rarely found (although that is changing now and it is becoming more available; if you are able to obtain it, substitute it for the combination of whole-wheat flour and whole-wheat flakes). Fortunately, we can simulate Irish flour by processing wheat flakes in a food processor and adding them to the dough along with the whole-wheat flour. Whole-wheat pastry flour can be used in lieu of whole-wheat bread flour in the interest of tender results. In a way, I'm glad we can't quite duplicate the bread here; like the Guinness, it's somehow right that soda bread can't simply cross the ocean and still be as good as it is in Ireland herself.

of dough slightly, flour the surface thoroughly but not thickly with pastry flour, and then transfer it to a sheet pan lined with parchment paper. Check that the dough is still round, and flour the top again if need be. Now, use a plastic or metal dough cutter and divide the dough into 4 equal sections, north, south, east, and west. Don't cut right through to the bottom, but do go down about 80 percent of the way.

3. **BAKING:** Place the soda bread in a 475°F oven for 15 minutes, then lower the oven temperature to 450°F and bake for an additional 20 minutes or so (the Home loaf, being lighter, will need only about another 15 minutes baking time). It should brown nicely and have somewhat of a thin crust on top and bottom, but some "give" when the loaf is pressed in its very center. If the cut parts are quite pale, it is an indication that the bread is not done yet. Irish soda bread is best eaten the day it is made. It does toast well, however, and is particularly good, toasted or not, with butter or marmalade. A pot of strong tea helps the soda bread to keep on going down, and the soda bread helps keep the tea flowing.

Traditional English Hot Cross Buns

DOUGH YIELD | U.S.: 144 buns at 2.7 oz each | Metric: 144 buns at .077 kg each | Home: 12 buns

OVERALL FORMULA

	U.S.	METRIC	HOME	BAKER'S %
Bread flour	10 lb	4.55 kg	13.3 oz	100%
Milk	5 lb	2.275 kg	6.7 oz	50%
Butter, soft	1.5 lb	.683 kg	2 oz	15%
Eggs	1 lb	.455 kg	1.3 oz	10%
Sugar	1.75 lb	.796 kg	2.3 oz	17.5%
Salt	.08 lb	.036 kg	.1 oz	.8%
Allspice, ground*	.08 lb	.036 kg	.1 oz	.8%
Yeast	.5 lb, fresh	.228 kg, fresh	.26 oz, instant dry	5%
Dried currants	3 lb	1.365 kg	4 oz	30%
Candied lemon or orange peel (finely chopped)	1 lb	.455 kg	1.3 oz (1/4 cup, packed)	10%
TOTAL YIELD	**23.91 lb**	**10.879 kg**	**1 lb, 15.4 oz**	**239.1%**

SPONGE

	U.S.	METRIC	HOME	BAKER'S %
Bread flour	1 lb	.455 kg	1.3 oz (1/4 cup)	100%
Milk	5 lb	2.275 kg	6.7 oz (7/8 cup)	500%
Sugar	.25 lb	.114 kg	.3 oz (1/2 T)	25%
Yeast	.5 lb, fresh	.228 kg, fresh	.26 oz, instant dry (2 1/4 tsp)	50%
TOTAL	**6.75 lb**	**3.072 kg**	**8.6 oz**	

FINAL DOUGH

	U.S.	METRIC	HOME
Bread flour	9 lb	4.095 kg	12 oz (2 3/4 cups)
Butter, soft	1.5 lb	.683 kg	2 oz (4 T)
Eggs	1 lb	.455 kg	1.3 oz (1 egg)
Sugar	1.5 lb	.682 kg	2 oz (1/4 cup)
Salt	.08 lb	.036 kg	.1 oz (1/2 tsp)
Allspice, ground*	.08 lb	.036 kg	.1 oz (1/2 T)
Sponge	6.75 lb	3.072 kg	8.6 oz (all of above)
Dried currants	3 lb	1.365 kg	4 oz (3/4 cup)
Candied lemon or orange peel, finely chopped	1 lb	.455 kg	1.3 oz (1/4 cup, packed)
TOTAL	**23.91 lb**	**10.879 kg**	**1 lb, 15.4 oz**

CROSSING PASTE (or Royal Icing)

Butter, melted	.25 lb	1.14 kg	4 oz (1/2 cup)
Milk	.19 lb	.086 kg	3 oz (3/8 cup)
Vanilla	.5 oz	.014 kg	.5 oz (1 T)
Sugar	.25 lb	.114 kg	4 oz (1/2 cup)
Lemon peel, grated	1	1	1
Egg, large, beaten	1/2	1/2	1/2
Flour, sifted	.5 lb	.227 kg	8 oz (1 7/8 cup)

SIMPLE SYRUP

Sugar	1 lb	.5 kg	4 oz (8 T)
Water	1 lb	.5 kg	4 oz (1/2 cup)
TOTAL	**2 lb**	**1 kg**	**8 oz**

*Depending on the freshness of the allspice, slightly more or less may be needed.

*Soak raisins in alcohol to plump up.

These hot cross buns are rolls of substance, lightly sweetened, but not to the extent that the sweetness overpowers the spice or the fruit. The crossing paste is piped on just before the bake, and becomes integrated to the bun itself, unlike the sweet white icing that is generally seen in North America, which is piped on after the buns have cooled. Once baked, the buns are quickly brushed, while good and hot, with simple syrup. This gives them a lustrous appearance, contributes slightly to the balanced sweetness, and helps extend the shelf life of the buns. In all, this is a fine product, and an excellent one in any baker's Easter repertoire.

1. SPONGE: Disperse the yeast in the milk, add the flour and sugar, and, using a whip or wire whisk if mixing by hand, mix just until smooth. The sponge will be very thin. Desired temperature: 80°F. Cover with plastic and let stand for 30 to 40 minutes, when the sponge will have risen to about 3 or 4 times its original height. It should be quite light, and in spite of the minimal amount of flour in it, there should be an unusual but quite evident structure to it. Give it a little jiggle to check.

2. MIXING: Small quantities of up to 12 dozen buns can be mixed in a 20-quart planetary mixer or small spiral mixer. Stand mixers can mix up to 2 dozen buns. Place the final dough flour in the mixing bowl, add the soft butter, and mix just until the butter is dispersed. Add the eggs, sugar, salt, and allspice and mix them all together. Next, add the sponge. Mix on first speed for about 3 minutes until everything is thoroughly combined. Turn the mixer to second speed and mix for about 3 minutes. Strong gluten is not the goal of this mix, but enough dough development is necessary so that there is sufficient strength to lift the fruits and butter (combined, these are a considerable weight in the dough). When a moderate gluten development has been achieved, add the currants and diced peel. Mix until these are evenly distributed throughout the dough. Desired dough temperature: 78°F.

3. BULK FERMENTATION: 1 hour, with a light fold after 30 minutes.

4. DIVIDING AND SHAPING: If using a 36-part dough divider, weigh off 4 presses weighing 6 pounds each. If dividing by hand, cut the dough into 2.7-ounce pieces. Round the pieces well, and place them on sheet pans in an even configuration. Cover the trays of buns with a sheet of plastic to prevent crusting on the surface.

5. FINAL FERMENTATION: About 1 hour at 76°F.

6. CROSSING PASTE: While the buns proof, make the crossing paste. In a saucepan, melt the butter with the sugar and heat until the sugar is dissolved. Add the milk, vanilla, grated lemon peel, and beaten egg. Whisk all these together, and then add the sifted flour (cake, pastry, or all-purpose flour all work fine). Using a round tip with a 1/4 to 3/8-inch diameter, fill a piping bag with the paste. When the buns are finally proofed (approximately 1 hour), pipe lines in one direction on each of them, transecting the top of each bun. When all the lines have been piped in one direction, rotate the baking sheet 90 degrees and pipe lines again, so that the lines form an even cross (the cross, by thhe way, is an ancient Celtic representation of the four seasons).

7. SIMPLE SYRUP: Prepare the simple syrup by combining the sugar and water in a pot. Bring to a full boil, stirring once or twice so the sugar won't burn on the bottom of the pot. The syrup can be brushed while still hot onto the buns, or it can be made days ahead and kept refrigerated.

8. BAKING: Bake the buns at 440°F for 14 to 16 minutes. They will show some browning on the surface, but still have some softness and give when squeezed. As soon as they are removed from the oven, brush them with the simple syrup. The buns are best when eaten fresh, but day-old buns can be reheated successfully, covered in aluminum foil, and heated for about 6 minutes at 350°F.

Pretzels

DOUGH YIELD | U.S.: 72 pretzels at 3 oz each | Metric: 72 pretzels at .085 kg each | Home: 12 pretzels

OVERALL FORMULA

	U.S.	METRIC	HOME	BAKER'S %
Bread flour	7.94 lb	3.61 kg	1 lb, 5.2 oz	100%
Water	4.76 lb	2.17 kg	12.7 oz	60%
Salt	.16 lb	.072 kg	.4 oz	2%
Yeast	.16 lb, fresh	.072 kg, fresh	.08 oz, instant dry	2%
Butter, soft*	.4 lb	.18 kg	1.1 oz	5%
Diastatic malt powder	.08 lb	.036 kg	.2 oz	1%
TOTAL YIELD	**13.5 lb**	**6.14 kg**	**2 lb, 3.7 oz**	**170%**

PÂTE FERMENTÉE

	U.S.	METRIC	HOME	BAKER'S %
Bread flour	1.59 lb	.72 kg	4.2 oz (1 cup)	100%
Water	1.03 lb	.47 kg	2.7 oz (3/8 cup)	65%
Salt	.032 lb	.014 kg	.08 oz (3/4 tsp)	2%
Yeast	.003 lb, fresh	.001 kg, fresh	.002 oz, instant dry (a small pinch)	.2%
TOTAL	**2.655 lb**	**1.205 kg**	**7 oz**	

FINAL DOUGH

	U.S.	METRIC	HOME
Bread flour	6.35 lb	2.89 kg	1 lb, 1 oz (3 7/8 cups)
Water	3.73 lb	1.7 kg	10 oz (1 1/4 cups)
Salt	.128 lb	.058 kg	.3 oz (1/2 T)
Yeast	.157 lb, fresh	.071 kg, fresh	.08 oz, instant dry (3/4 tsp)
Butter, soft*	.4 lb	.18 kg	1.1 oz (2 T)
Diastatic malt powder	.08 lb	.036 kg	.2 oz (2 tsp)
Pâte fermentée	2.655 lb	1.205 kg	7 oz (all of above)
TOTAL	**10 lb**	**4.531 kg**	**2 lb, 3.7 oz**

*The butter in the dough can be replaced with either shortening or lard.

SOME SPECIAL EQUIPMENT IS NEEDED FOR PRETZEL MAKING:

Plastic gloves that go well up the forearm, the kind used for washing dishes.

A heavy wire screen (about the gauge of a cooling rack) with two handles, and a second wire screen, without handles, that fits on top of the first, for dipping the pretzels.

A stainless-steel tank, large enough to hold the screens and deep enough so the pretzels can be completely submerged.

I had to beg and beg for my first baking job. The owner didn't want me because I had no experience. I didn't give up. The other bakers were Frenchmen and Germans, and I, so the owner told me, couldn't possibly bake because I was American. I persisted. Wearing down her resistance was no easy task, but eventually I succeeded, and got hired to make the pretzels. Although this was the lowliest position in the bakery, I couldn't have been happier. I rolled them out by the dozens; I made hundreds each day, thousands each week, tens of thousands within a few short months. It was a great early education for my hands: Slack doughs, dry doughs, young doughs, old doughs—my hands got to feel all the variables, and begin to learn the effect of subtle changes in the dough. Never have I regretted those pretzel days.

Pretzels are the preeminent symbol of baking in Germany, and they date back hundreds of years. The story of their origin is that they were given to children who had successfully completed their prayers: The pretzel's shape, with its interlocking twist of dough, is meant to suggest the arms folded in prayer. During medieval times, merchants hung an object or carving outside their door that would let passersby—a great number of whom were illiterate—know what sort of shop was within. The pretzel

A stainless-steel spoon to stir the sodium hydroxide pellets into the water

Sodium hydroxide (lye) pellets, mixed slowly and carefully in the dipping tank, at the rate of 4 ounces lye (by weight) to 1 gallon cold water (this is a 3 percent solution).

1. PÂTE FERMENTÉE: Disperse the yeast in the water, add the flour and salt, and mix until just smooth. The *pâte fermentée* should have the consistency of finished bread dough. Cover the bowl with plastic and let stand for 12 to 16 hours at about 70°F. When ripe, the *pâte fermentée* will be domed and just beginning to recede in the center.

2. MIXING: If production is 9 dozen pretzels or fewer, a small spiral mixer or 20-quart planetary mixer can be used. Add all the ingredients to the mixing bowl except the *pâte fermentée.* In a planetary-type mixer, mix on first speed for 3 minutes in order to incorporate the ingredients. As the dough is coming together, add the *pâte fermentée* in chunks. The dough will be fairly stiff. Turn the mixer to second speed and mix for an additional 5 to 6 minutes until the dough has moderately strong gluten development. Desired dough temperature: 75°F.

3. BULK FERMENTATION: Two hours.

4. FOLDING: Fold the dough once, after 1 hour of bulk fermentation.

5. DIVIDING AND SHAPING: If using a 36-part dough divider, weigh off 2 presses at 6.75 pounds. If dividing by hand, strive to cut squarish pieces at 3 ounces each. Roll the dough pieces up into blunt cylinders. Use the heel of your hand to get a tight seam on the bottom edge. Let the dough relax for a few minutes under a sheet of plastic.

To shape the pretzels, roll the cylinder to about 16 inches long. The center should be perceptibly thicker than the ends. Do leave a small bulb of dough at each end, however; the finished pretzel looks nicer with those bulbs. Pick up the dough by the ends and, with a quick motion, twirl it in such a way that it twists around itself twice. This motion is done in the air, and as soon as the second twist has occurred, quickly lay the thick part of the pretzel down, still holding the ends in each hand. Take the ends and press them into the dough at each side. The little bulbs of dough at the ends should just be barely outside the body of dough. The illustrations on the next page show the shaping process in detail.

became the symbol for the baker in Germany, and to this day, wooden or iron pretzels still hang above the baker's door in hundreds of shops throughout the country.

Pretzels are unique in that just before baking they are first dipped in a solution of sodium hydroxide (lye) and water. They are then quickly slashed with a blade, coarse salt is sprinkled on, and into the oven they go. The lye dissipates in the oven, leaving a very thin, shiny crust and an appealing brownness. It is of the utmost importance that gloves and even eye protection are worn when dipping pretzels, as lye is quite corrosive. Long-sleeved shirts are also advised, unless the gloves fit well up above the wrist. Finally, the dipping tank that holds the lye pellets and water must be made of stainless steel.

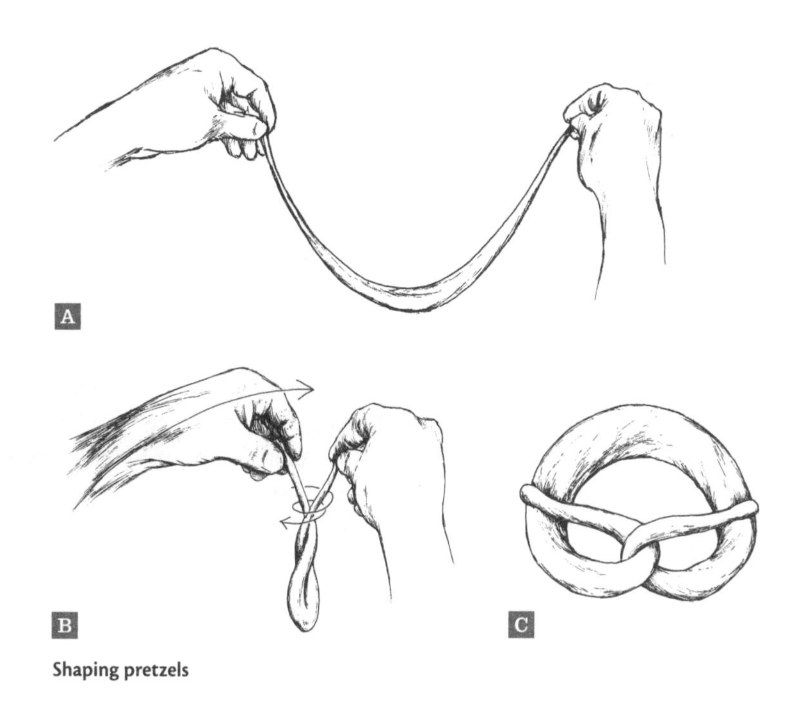

Shaping pretzels

The motion of forming pretzels, like so many other hand motions in baking, requires some practice and attentiveness before it becomes second nature. Another, albeit slower, method of forming the pretzel is to lay it down on the bench with the thicker part away from you, like an upside-down letter *U*. Take the two ends and twist them twice around each other. Then bring the ends onto the sides of the body of dough and press them into it. Whichever method is used, the shaped pretzel should look like the one in illustration C. Lightly oil the wire dipping screen with the handles and place the shaped pretzels on it. If more pretzels are being made than can fit on the screen, the extras can go onto boards or sheet pans lined with baker's linen.

6. FINAL FERMENTATION: Let the pretzels proof until about 75 percent risen, 30 to 45 minutes. Refrigerate them for 30 minutes to allow formation of a skin. This makes them more durable for the dipping to come. The pretzels can also be retarded overnight. In this case, refrigerate after 20 minutes of final fermentation.

7. DIPPING: The dipping tank should be filled with the lye solution. Take the screen with the chilled pretzels and place the slightly smaller screen (without the handles) over the pretzels. This will ensure that the pretzels remain submerged and do not float to the top. Wearing gloves and protection for the eyes, slowly lower the screens to the bottom of the dipping tank, completely submerging the pretzels. Leave the pretzels in the solution for about 5 seconds, then raise the screen and let them drain. Using a *lame,* make one quick slash along the top, thickest, part of the pretzel. Sprinkle coarse salt lightly over the slashed area.

8. BAKING: Transfer the dipped pretzels to a baker's peel and load them immediately into a 450°F oven, with the oven vents open. They will brown nicely and bake in 14 to 16 minutes. The lye dissipates completely in the oven, and the warm pretzel is left to be enjoyed either plain, or with mustard and meat or cheese. In Germany, beer is close at hand.

Note: If several rounds of pretzels have to bake, you can use flat perforated sheet pans. Once dipped, carefully transfer them to the sheet pans and bake. While they bake, more pretzels can be dipped, transferred to screens, and loaded into the oven.

Flat Breads

The remaining recipes in this chapter are for flat breads of one type or another. Flat breads have been an important food of virtually every culture on earth since antiquity, whether the tortilla of Mexico, paratha of India, the focaccia of Italy, or the moo shoo pancake of China. Some are yeasted, while others are not. Some are filled, some topped, and some are plain breads used to scoop up other foods. Some are cooked on hot ungreased griddles (probably the earliest form of bread cooking), while others are baked. The variety is matched only by the versatility.

Pizza Dough

DOUGH YIELD | U.S.: 10 crusts at 1 lb each | Metric: 10 crusts at .454 kg each | Home: 2 crusts

OVERALL FORMULA

	U.S.	METRIC	HOME	BAKER'S %
Bread flour	**5.68 lb**	**2.58 kg**	**1 lb, 2.2 oz**	**100%**
Water	**3.86 lb**	**1.75 kg**	**12.4 oz**	**68%**
Salt	**.1 lb**	**.046 kg**	**.3 oz**	**1.8%**
Yeast	**.07 lb, fresh**	**.034 kg, fresh**	**.04 oz, instant dry**	**1.3%**
Extra-virgin olive oil	**.29 lb**	**.13 kg**	**.9 oz**	**5%**
TOTAL YIELD	**10 lb**	**4.54 kg**	**1 lb, 15.8 oz**	**176.1%**

BIGA

	U.S.	METRIC	HOME	BAKER'S %
Bread flour	1.14 lb	.52 kg	3.6 oz (7/8 cup)	100%
Water	.68 lb	.31 kg	2.2 oz (1/4 cup)	60%
Yeast	.002 lb, fresh	.001 kg, fresh	.001 oz (a small pinch)	.2%
TOTAL	**1.822 lb**	**.831 kg**	**5.8 oz**	

FINAL DOUGH

	U.S.	METRIC	HOME
Bread flour	4.54 lb	2.06 kg	14.6 oz (3 3/8 cups)
Water	3.18 lb	1.44 kg	10.2 oz (1 1/4 cups)
Salt	.1 lb	.046 kg	.3 oz (1/2 T)
Yeast	.068 lb	.033 kg	.04 oz (1/2 tsp)
Extra-virgin olive oil	.29 lb	.13 kg	.9 oz (2 T)
Biga	1.822 lb	.831 kg	5.8 oz (all of above)
TOTAL	**10 lb**	**4.54 kg**	**1 lb, 15.8 oz**

I might be biased. For many years, flour has been the predominant factor in my work life: sponges and doughs, mixing, kneading, shaping; flour, flour, flour. After all this, it doesn't seem odd to me that I think pizza is mostly about the crust. Well-made toppings are easy enough to make (as long as the more-is-better philosophy doesn't result in a mass of lavalike cheese in a molten, tongue-searing puddle). Fresh ingredients for the top, and not too many of them, a hot, hot oven, and a quick and lively bake—these are all important. (The best pizza I have ever eaten was baked in a wood-fired Québec-style clay oven in Norwich, Vermont. A Bosnian immigrant named Milos built and tended the fire, made the toppings for a dozen pizzas, and handled the bake—about 2 minutes per pizza. My meager contributions consisted of making the dough for the crusts and helping as much as I possibly could with the eating!) It's the crust that is most often elusive. Just as it is really no secret that the best pizzas bake in just a few minutes, it is also no secret that the best pizza dough is one that has all the benefits of slow fermentation and enough moisture so that the baked crust is crisp and brown, with a light, open-textured chewiness. One common technique used to lengthen and slow down fermentation is to retard the dough (many pizza makers divide the dough into pizza-sized weights and retard them that way).

1. BIGA: Disperse the yeast in the water, add the flour, and mix until just smooth. The biga should be stiff and dense. Cover the bowl with plastic and let stand for 12 to 16 hours at about 70°F. When ripe, the biga will be domed and just beginning to recede in the center.

2. MIXING: Add all the ingredients to the mixing bowl except the biga and the olive oil. For production of 20 crusts or fewer, a small spiral mixer or 20-quart planetary mixer works well. In a planetary-type mixer, mix on first speed for 3 minutes in order to incorporate the ingredients. As the dough is coming together, add the biga in chunks. If necessary, correct the hydration by adding water or flour in small amounts. The dough should be of medium consistency at this point. Turn the mixer to second speed and begin drizzling in the olive oil. Mix on second speed for 5 to 6 minutes until the dough has some supple body to it. The olive oil will coat and lubricate the gluten strands, slowing their development, so the extra mixing time is beneficial. The dough will not be highly developed at the end of the mix, but nevertheless it should have perceptible gluten development when tugged. Desired dough temperature: 75°F.

3. BULK FERMENTATION: 2 hours.

4. FOLDING: Fold the dough once, after 1 hour of bulk fermentation.

5. DIVIDING AND SHAPING: Divide the dough into 1-pound pieces. Round lightly, place on a floured work surface with the seams down, sprinkle a light coating of flour over the tops, and cover with plastic. Let the dough relax for about 20 minutes. When the dough is sufficiently relaxed and will stretch without tearing, begin stretching it between both hands. Rotate the dough as you stretch it so the thickness remains roughly equal. As the dough gets thinner, your fingers can easily puncture it, so make your hands into fists to finish the stretching. Eventually, the dough should be about 16 inches in diameter and quite thin, except for a bulbous rim about 1 inch wide all around.

6. FINAL FERMENTATION: Once shaped, there is no need to let the dough proof. It can bake right away. Transfer the pizza to a peel onto which coarse cornmeal or semolina has been sprinkled. Spread over the toppings of your choice. Leave the rim of the crust free of toppings.

A second method, and the one employed in the present formula, is to make a biga the day before the final dough is mixed. The biga then injects the final dough with all the fragrance and flavors of its gentle fermentation.

7. BAKING: Except in a wood-fired oven, it is almost impossible to have an oven that is too hot for pizza. Ideally, the temperature soars to over 700°F, ensuring a quick, searing bake (if you are able to bake at these temperatures, there is no need to cook the toppings—the oven will do that). Needless to say, neither standard hearth bread ovens nor home ovens can reach this realm of heat. Nevertheless, very good pizza can be made at lower temperatures, better pizza, certainly, than is available from a standard pizza chain. The best we can do is to crank up our oven to the highest possible temperature. If baking in a home oven, a preheated baking stone is essential. Quickly slide the pizza into the hottest part of the oven. If more than one pizza is being made, stretch the dough for the second one and assemble it while the first bakes. If pizzas are going to be baked over the course of a few hours, refrigerate some of the dough once it has been divided to prevent it from becoming overaged.

Pissaladière

DOUGH YIELD | U.S.: 10 crusts at 1 lb each | Metric: 10 crusts at .454 kg each | Home: 2 crusts

OVERALL FORMULA

	U.S.	METRIC	HOME	BAKER'S %
Bread flour	**4.64 lb**	**2.1 kg**	**14.8 oz**	**80%**
Whole-wheat flour	**1.16 lb**	**.523 kg**	**3.7 oz**	**20%**
Water	**3.77 lb**	**1.7 kg**	**12 oz**	**65%**
Salt	**.1 lb**	**.047 kg**	**.3 oz**	**1.8%**
Yeast	**.09 lb, fresh**	**.039 kg, fresh**	**.05 oz, instant dry**	**1.5%**
Extra-virgin olive oil	**.29 lb**	**.131 kg**	**.9 oz**	**5%**
TOTAL YIELD	**10.05 lb**	**4.54 kg**	**1 lb, 15.8 oz**	**173.3%**

PÂTE FERMENTÉE

Bread flour	1.16 lb	.52 kg	3.7 oz (7/8 cup)	100%
Water	.75 lb	.34 kg	2.4 oz (1/4 cup)	65%
Salt	.02 lb	.01 kg	.07 oz (1/4 tsp)	2%
Yeast	.002 lb, fresh	.001 kg, fresh	.001 oz, instant dry (a small pinch)	.2%
TOTAL	**1.932 lb**	**.871 kg**	**6.2 oz**	

FINAL DOUGH

Bread flour	3.48 lb	1.58 kg	11.1 oz (2½ cups)
Whole-wheat flour	1.16 lb	.523 kg	3.7 oz (⅞ cup)
Water	3.02 lb	1.36 kg	9.6 oz (1¼ cups)
Salt	.08 lb	.037 kg	.2 oz (1 tsp)
Yeast	.088 lb, fresh	.038 kg, fresh	.05 oz, instant dry (½ tsp)
Extra-virgin olive oil	.29 lb	.131 kg	.9 oz (2 T)
Pâte fermentée	1.932 lb	.871 kg	6.2 oz (all of above)
TOTAL	**10.05 lb**	**4.54 kg**	**1 lb, 15.8 oz**

TOPPING

3 medium onions, thinly sliced
2 cloves garlic, minced
3 tablespoons olive oil
1 teaspoon fresh thyme, minced, or more to taste
Salt and pepper, to taste
2 ounces good-quality anchovies
3 ounces niçoise olives, pitted

1. **PREPARING THE TOPPING:** Sauté the onions and garlic in the olive oil over medium low heat for 25 to 30 minutes, or until they are very soft and have begun to brown. Add the thyme, salt, and pepper. Set aside to cool. Slice the anchovies in half lengthwise (if using salt-cured anchovies, rinse them well and remove the backbone with your thumb). Pit the olives if necessary. Refrigerate the topping ingredients until ready to use.

2. **PÂTE FERMENTÉE:** Disperse the yeast in the water, add the flour and salt, and mix until just smooth. The *pâte fermentée* will have the consistency of finished bread dough. Cover the bowl with plastic and let stand for 12 to 16 hours at about 70°F. When ripe, the *pâte fermentée* will be domed and just beginning to recede in the center.

3. **MIXING:** Add all the ingredients to the mixing bowl except the *pâte fermentée* and the olive oil. For production of 20 crusts or fewer, a small spiral mixer or 20-quart planetary mixer works well. In a planetary-type mixer, mix on first speed for 3 minutes in order to incorporate the ingredients. As the dough is coming together, add the *pâte fermentée* in chunks. If necessary, correct the hydration by adding water or flour in small amounts. The dough should be of medium consistency at this point. Turn the mixer to second speed and begin drizzling in the olive oil. Mix on second speed for

We are now in the south of France, and will stay there for this and the two following recipes. Pissaladière is the pizza of Provence, replete with onions cooked long and slow, fresh herbs, anchovies, and pungent black niçoise olives. The present formula is made with a portion of whole-wheat flour, which gives a bit more body to the crust; and with a *pâte fermentée* for added flavor and crust quality. A well-ripened French bread dough, with some extra-virgin olive oil beaten in (about .5 ounces of oil per 1 pound of dough), can be used as a substitute for the dough detailed here.

5 to 6 minutes until the dough has moderate gluten development. Desired dough temperature: 75°F.

4. BULK FERMENTATION: 2 hours.

5. FOLDING: Fold the dough once, after 1 hour of bulk fermentation.

6. DIVIDING AND SHAPING: Divide the dough into 1-pound pieces. Round lightly, place on a floured work surface, seams down, and cover with plastic. Let the dough relax for about 20 minutes. Begin to either stretch the dough by hand, or use a rolling pin to flatten and stretch it. During the stretching, you may want to let the dough relax for a couple of minutes and then return to it. Pissaladière is usually shaped into a rectangle. With a 1-pound dough piece, roll the dough to about ¼ inch thick, with dimensions of about 12 by 16 inches. Transfer the dough to a baker's peel that has been sprinkled with coarse cornmeal or semolina.

7. ADD THE TOPPING: Spread the onion mixture evenly onto the dough, leaving a rim of about 1 inch wide around the entire perimeter of the dough. Place the anchovies in a lattice pattern on top of the onions. Then place 1 olive in each of the sections formed by the anchovies.

8. FINAL FERMENTATION: After the toppings have been added, let the dough rise for about 20 minutes.

9. BAKING: Bake the pissaladière at the hottest setting of your oven, at least 500°F. In the home oven, bake on a thoroughly preheated baking stone. In any event, avoid baking on a sheet pan: The goal is instant strong heat for the dough, and the buffer of a sheet pan delays the heating of the dough significantly, resulting in a serious loss of eating quality.

Fougasse with Olives

DOUGH YIELD | U.S.: 10 fougasses at 1 lb each | Metric: 10 fougasses at .454 kg each | Home: 2 fougasses

OVERALL FORMULA

	U.S.	METRIC	HOME	BAKER'S %
Bread flour	**4.89 lb**	**2.21 kg**	**15.6 oz**	**90%**
Whole-wheat flour	**.54 lb**	**.25 kg**	**1.7 oz**	**10%**
Water	**3.69 lb**	**1.67 kg**	**11.8 oz**	**68%**
Salt	**.08 lb**	**.037 kg**	**.3 oz**	**1.5%**
Yeast	**.1 lb, fresh**	**.044 kg, fresh**	**.05 oz, instant dry**	**1.8%**
Extra-virgin olive oil	**.27 lb**	**.123 kg**	**.9 oz**	**5%**
Niçoise olives, pitted	**.43 lb**	**.197 kg**	**1.4 oz**	**8%**
TOTAL YIELD	**10 lb**	**4.531 kg**	**1 lb, 15.8 oz**	**184.3%**

PÂTE FERMENTÉE

Bread flour	1.36 lb	.62 kg	4.3 oz (1 cup)	100%
Water	.88 lb	.4 kg	2.8 oz (3/8 cup)	65%
Salt	.027 lb	.012 kg	.09 oz (1/2 tsp)	2%
Yeast	.003 lb, fresh	.001 kg, fresh	.002 oz, instant dry (a small pinch)	.2%
TOTAL	**2.27 lb**	**1.033 kg**	**7.2 oz**	

FINAL DOUGH

Bread flour	3.53 lb	1.59 kg	11.3 oz (4 1/4 cups)
Whole-wheat flour	.54 lb	.25 kg	1.7 oz (3/8 cup)
Water	2.81 lb	1.27 kg	9 oz (1 1/8 cups)
Salt	.053 lb	.025 kg	.2 oz (1 tsp)
Yeast	.097 lb, fresh	.043 kg, fresh	.05 oz, instant dry (1/2 tsp)
Extra-virgin olive oil	.27 lb	.123 kg	.9 oz (2 T)
Niçoise olives, pitted	.43 lb	.197 kg	1.4 oz (1/4 cup)
Pâte fermentée	2.27 lb	1.033 kg	7.2 oz (all of above)
TOTAL	**10 lb**	**4.531 kg**	**1 lb, 15.8 oz**

1. **PÂTE FERMENTÉE:** Disperse the yeast in the water, add the flour and salt, and mix until just smooth. The *pâte fermentée* will have the consistency of finished bread dough. Cover the bowl with plastic and let stand for 12 to 16 hours at about 70°F. When ripe, the *pâte fermentée* will be domed and just beginning to recede in the center.

2. **MIXING:** Add all the ingredients to the mixing bowl except the *pâte fermentée*, the olives, and the olive oil. For production of 20

In Latin, the word *focus* means "the fireplace in a house, hearth": the central focal point of the home. The French *fougasse* as well as the Italian *focaccia* also have connections to the hearth: The Latin words *focacius panis* mean "bread cooked under the coals of the hearth"; it's a short etymological step from here to both *fougasse* and *focaccia.* Fougasse is another regional specialty from Provence, a dense, crusty loaf with an unusual shape and a pronounced flavor. One reason it tastes so good is because of its high proportion of crust to crumb; this is also why it doesn't have long keeping quality, and is best eaten while fresh. Note that there is what appears to be a reduced percentage of salt (1.5 percent) in this olive fougasse, and in the variation with anchovies that follows. Because of the saltiness of these two ingredients, less salt is needed in the dough.

pounds of fougasses or fewer, a small spiral mixer or 20-quart planetary mixer works well. In a planetary-type mixer, mix on first speed for 3 minutes in order to incorporate the ingredients. As the dough is coming together, add the *pâte fermentée* in chunks. If necessary, correct the hydration by adding water or flour in small amounts. The dough should be of medium consistency at this point. Turn the mixer to second speed and begin drizzling in the olive oil. Mix on second speed for 5 to 6 minutes until the dough has moderate gluten development.

Add the pitted olives and mix on first speed just until they are evenly incorporated. In a planetary mixer, as opposed to a spiral mixer, it is a more difficult and lengthy process to add ingredients at the end of a mix, such as the olives in the present case. If it takes too long to incorporate them, the olives will break apart and the dough will take on an unpleasant purplish hue. Here is a technique that can help: Once the dough has been fully mixed and it is time to add the olives, pull the dough away from the hook, creating an opening in the center of the dough. Pour about one-third of the olives into this opening, then turn on the mixer. The olives, rather than just smearing around the outside of the bowl, will be incorporated from the inside outward. After 20 or 30 seconds, turn off the mixer and again pull the dough away from the hook, creating another opening. Pour half the remaining olives into the opening and turn the mixer on once more. Do this a third time, adding the remaining olives, and mix until the olives have been evenly mixed into the dough. The desired dough temperature is 76°F.

3. BULK FERMENTATION: 2 hours.

4. FOLDING: Fold the dough once, after 1 hour of bulk fermentation.

5. DIVIDING AND SHAPING: Divide the dough into 1-pound pieces. Round lightly, place on a floured bench with the seams down, and cover with plastic. Let the dough relax for about 20 minutes. When sufficiently relaxed, use a rolling pin to flatten the dough into an oval shape.

6. FINAL FERMENTATION: About 1 hour at 76°F.

7. BAKING: When the fougasse has risen, the final shaping occurs. Pick up the dough and stretch it gently so that it is about half again as long as it was. Now, shape it into a long triangle with a base about half the length of the height. Next, using a pizza wheel

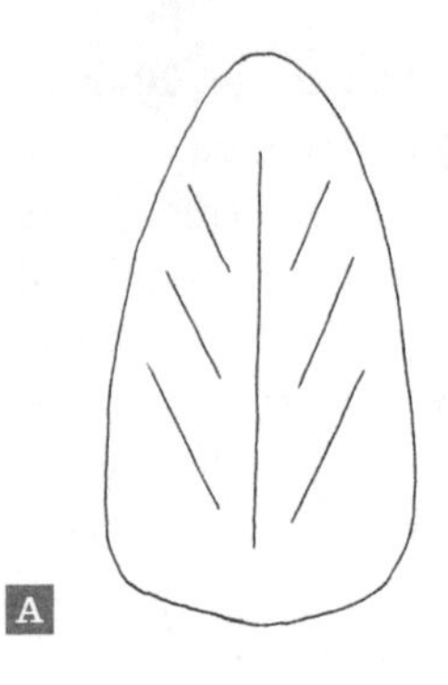

or a paring knife, cut several diagonal slices into the dough, as in illustration A at left. Now stretch the dough some more, so the cuts open, as in illustration B. Transfer the fougasse to a loading conveyor or a baker's peel sprinkled with coarse cornmeal or semolina, and load it into a 450°F oven. In a home oven, bake on a fully preheated baking stone. Steam the oven just before the load, and again once the fougasses are in. Bake for about 20 minutes, until the breads are richly colored and crusty, but still have some "give" when squeezed. Open the oven vents halfway through the bake.

VARIATION: I took along a fly rod and fly-tying materials on a visit to Haute Provence some years ago, and spent a delightful day fishing in a briskly flowing mountain river. I had stopped in a bakery in Digne les Bains early in the day, and bought an anchovy fougasse for lunch. To this day, I have vivid recollections of that glistening fougasse, eaten high on a bank along the river.

To make an anchovy fougasse, substitute an equal weight of anchovies for the niçoise olives. If using salt anchovies (these are the most flavorful, but require cleaning), they must first be soaked to remove the excess salt, then filleted by running your thumb down the backbone and removing the bone. Chop the anchovies finely and add them to the dough toward the end of the mix. Proceed as for the olive fougasse.

Focaccia

YIELD | 2 focaccias

Focaccia, like pizza, is a traditional rustic food made with whatever ingredients are at hand (whatever is seasonal is not only most readily available, it is usually the cheapest too). It may be flat or raised. It may have oil and herbs in the dough, or the dough may be plain, with ingredients spread on top. A simple focaccia may have just a splash of olive oil and a sprinkling of fresh rosemary and coarse salt. A popular one from Florence (where focaccia is called *schiacciata*) is

DOUGH

2 pounds (900 g) ciabatta dough (page 105), bulk fermented at least 1½ hours
4 tablespoons extra-virgin olive oil

OPTIONAL TOPPINGS

Onions , thinly sliced
Garlic, thinly sliced
Eggplant, thinly sliced
Potatoes, thinly sliced
Mushrooms, thinly sliced
Fennel, thinly sliced
Cured meats, thinly sliced
Grated cheese

topped with grapes and fennel seeds. Cheeses, meats, fruits, vegetables, oils, and herbs—combine them tastefully, and use a well-made dough, and you have one of the more pleasant baked products to eat out of hand.

Lightly sauté the vegetables first so they won't scorch during baking. Season the toppings with salt and pepper, red pepper flakes, fresh herbs, and so on, to taste. When putting the topping on the dough, apply it so it covers the dough evenly, but avoid using an excessive amount of topping, which not only weighs the dough down, but also makes it difficult to identify the individual elements of the topping. Cheeses such as Parmesan and mozzarella add great flavor, but again they should be spread thoroughly but not thickly over the dough.

I like the foccacia described here because the dough is light but has a great crust. I like it because it so readily accommodates so many toppings. And I like it because it allows me to use a dough that I have at hand—in this case, ciabatta dough. Although it can be made free form—the dough stretched flat, toppings put on, and baked on the hearth—my preference is to bake it in a cake pan. I think this not only enhances the flavor of the dough, but it also gives the focaccia a much better keeping quality. It can also be a good method from a selling perspective: It is easy to take a baked focaccia and divide it into 6 or 8 reliably even portions for sale, or simply to put the baked focaccias on cake circles and sell them whole.

1. DIVIDING AND SHAPING: Divide the dough into pieces weighing 1 pound. For each piece, you will need a 10-inch round cake pan. Lightly preshape the pieces into rounds and place them, seams down, on a floured work surface. Cover lightly with baker's linen or plastic. Pour 2 tablespoons of good-quality extra-virgin olive oil into each of the cake pans and swirl it around to coat the sides and bottom. After a 20-minute rest, begin to stretch the dough into a disk, trying to keep it evenly thick. Do this either by hand or with a rolling pin. If the dough is reluctant to stretch fully, let it rest for a few more minutes. When the dough is fully 10 inches in diameter, place it in the oiled pans. Add the toppings.

2. BAKING: Once the dough has fully risen (the final fermentation usually takes about 1½ hours at room temperature), bake it in a 450°F oven for about 20 minutes. When the focaccias are done, the tops will be richly colored, and the dough will have pulled in slightly from the sides of the pans. I like to remove one from the pan when I think it's done, just to check and be sure. The entire side and bottom should be brown, fragrant, and crusty thanks to the good olive oil that was spread in the pans. Within, the dough will have some give and softness, a sign that it is baked but not dried out. The bright crust and lovely dough, combined with the flavors of the topping, will be irresistible.

Aloo Paratha

YIELD | 8 paratha, each about 7 inches in diameter

These delectable filled flat breads originated in India. Filled with potatoes, herbs, and spices, they are a fine accompaniment to milder foods. A friend and former student, Maneet Chauhan, grew up eating and making these and a great variety of other flat breads in her native India. My thanks to Maneet for her patience and clarity in teaching me how to make Aloo Paratha.

Have on hand flour to work up the breads, a rolling pin, the ghee (or vegetable oil), a brush to brush the surface of the breads as they cook, and either an Indian *tava* (a handleless iron griddle for cooking breads) or a 10-inch heavy-bottomed skillet. A pair of tongs is also helpful to flip the breads.

DOUGH

2⅜ cups (10.6 oz/300 g) whole-wheat flour*
Heaping ½ tsp (3 g) salt
About 1 cup (7.9 oz/225 g) water

FILLING

1 lb potatoes
1 tsp cumin seeds, toasted
1 tsp coriander seeds, toasted and ground
2 tsp grated fresh ginger
1 T + 1 tsp finely chopped green chilies
½ cup chopped fresh cilantro
Salt to taste
2 T mustard oil**

About ¼ cup ghee (Indian clarified butter), for brushing

*In India, the flour of choice for making flat breads is chapati flour, a very finely ground and sifted whole-wheat flour. The whole-wheat flour available in the United States is coarser, but it can be used in place of the chapati flour either by sifting it through a fine sieve, or by combining whole-wheat flour with unbleached bread flour in a ratio of 2 parts whole-wheat to 1 part white flour.

**Mustard oil can be made by toasting 1 tablespoon black mustard seeds in a dry skillet until they start to pop. Grind them in a mortar, put into a small bowl, and pour over 2 tablespoons vegetable oil.

Note: There will be filling left over after making the eight paratha. It makes a flavorful addition to egg dishes, or it can be afrozen for future use.

1. **TO MAKE THE DOUGH:** Mix together the dough ingredients and knead either by hand for 10 to 15 minutes, or in a mixer for about 5 minutes on medium speed. The dough should be fairly soft. Put the dough in a bowl and cover it with a sheet of plastic for at least 30 minutes. The dough can also be made a day ahead, wrapped, and refrigerated. In this case, allow it to stand at room temperature for about 30 minutes before proceeding with assembly.

2. **TO MAKE THE FILLING:** Boil the potatoes in their jackets. When done, peel and grate. Mix the grated potatoes with the cumin, coriander, ginger, chilies, cilantro, salt, and mustard oil. (The filling can be made a day ahead and refrigerated in a covered container.)

3. Divide the dough and the filling into 8 equal portions. Make balls with the dough.

4. Take a ball of dough and press into the center of it with your thumbs to make a bowl shape. Fill the opening with the potato stuffing. Pinch the opening well to seal the filling. Take your time with this step; if the opening isn't completely sealed, the filling will come out. Repeat with the remaining balls of dough.

5. Flour your hands. Pick up one of the pouches of dough and begin to flatten it out by patting it between the hands. Flour the bench and use the rolling pin to roll the dough to about 7 inches in diameter. The goal is to distribute the filling as evenly as possible across the entire flat surface of the dough. As you roll the dough pieces, try to sense how the filling inside is spreading. Repeat the rolling with the remaining pouches.

6. Heat the *tava* or skillet over medium heat. When drops of water bounce off the surface it is hot enough to begin (if the water stays put and only slowly evaporates, the surface is too cool; if the water turns to steam instantly, the surface is too hot). Put one of the paratha onto the *tava* or in the skillet and cook it for about 2 minutes, or until brown spots appear on the bottom of the dough. Flip the dough over with the tongs or your fingers and cook the other side for a minute or so. While it cooks, lightly but thoroughly brush ghee or oil onto the cooked side. Flip the dough again so that the oiled side is again in contact with the pan, and cook for 30 seconds. While it cooks, brush ghee or oil onto the top side of the dough. Flip the dough once more and finish cooking for another 30 seconds.

7. Remove the paratha and keep warm and pliable by wrapping in a clean dish towel. Continue cooking the remaining pieces. The paratha can be eaten as soon as they are cooked, or they can be cooked ahead of time and reheated in a preheated 300°F oven for 8 to 10 minutes, wrapped loosely in aluminum foil.

Focaccia con Formaggio

YIELD | 1 focaccia

This cheese-filled focaccia is quick to prepare, and a delightful accompaniment to a meal. The flavors are simple and clean, so it is a good supporting player to many other foods.

INGREDIENTS

24 oz (340 g) French bread dough (page 101) or ciabatta dough (page 105)
3/4 cup (6 oz/170 g) ricotta cheese
Extra-virgin olive oil, for brushing
Coarse salt and pepper to taste
1 T fennel seeds, toasted
About 1/2 cup (2 oz/60 g) grated Parmesan cheese (optional)

1. Divide the dough into two 12-ounce pieces. Roll out one piece to at most 1/8 inch thick. It can be circular or rectangular. Transfer it to an inverted sheet pan lined with parchment paper.

2. Spread on the ricotta cheese in a thin, even layer. Leave a rim of about 1/2 inch all around the edges of the dough. Brush or drizzle olive oil liberally over the ricotta. Sprinkle with some coarse salt and pepper, then with the fennel seeds. If you are using it, add the Parmesan cheese now.

3. Roll out the second piece of dough, again no more than 1/8 inch thick. Form into the same shape as the first piece. Place it on top of the first piece and carefully seal the edges all around. Brush the top of the dough lightly with oil. Make a few slits with a knife through the top layer in order to vent steam while the focaccia bakes. Sprinkle coarse salt very lightly on top, if desired.

4. Transfer the focaccia, still on the parchment paper, to a baker's peel. Load it into a 475°F oven, paper and all, so it bakes on the hearth or a preheated baking stone. Bake for about 10 minutes, or until the dough is golden. Remove from the oven and divide into wedges or strips. The focaccia is best eaten warm, but can be reheated covered in aluminum foil for about 8 minutes at 350°F.

BRAIDING TECHNIQUES

9

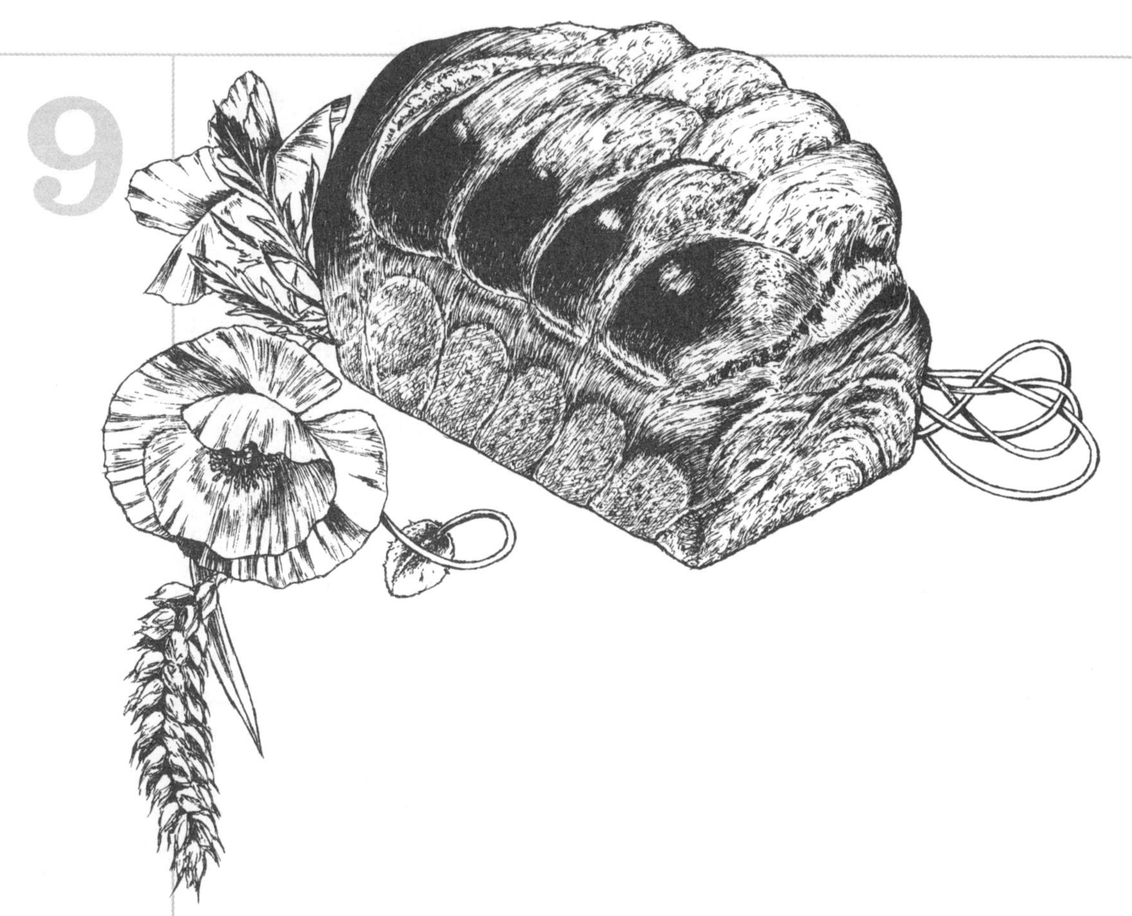

Better bread with water than cake with trouble.

—RUSSIAN PROVERB

My early attempts at braiding took place before I got a job in a bakery. I'd hate to see one of those tortured homemade loaves now. I am sure my recollection is accurate: The strands all had a mind of their own. Some were thick as a rolling pin, others looked like pasta, and still others had a complete identity crisis, being overly bulging and anorexically attenuated at the same time.

But I'm sure I was delighted with these attempts; after all, I had succeeded in getting all the strands (most of them anyway) to stay put, even if it was through force and not skill.

When I finally did get my first job in a bakery, I was hired initially to make German soft pretzels, which I gladly did, by the thousands. Before many days had gone by, Susanne, my boss, asked if I would like to make challah on Fridays, a request to which I eagerly and instantly assented. Then soon enough she asked me to make a braided loaf of Swiss origin on Saturdays. I was on my way, and very happy with the opportunity to focus twice weekly on making braids—2-strand, 3-strand, 4-strand, and even double-decker loaves. But I couldn't imagine the good fortune soon to come my way.

One day, Susanne brought in an old technical German baker's manual, entirely devoted to braiding techniques. My eyes widened as I looked through page after page of precise, immaculate braids. How could anyone work with such skill and accuracy? These breads were perfect in every way, certainly requiring a dexterity I could never hope to attain. Perhaps my boss saw the feverish excitement on my face. Perhaps she sensed something I didn't quite understand at the time. In any case, she offered to spend some time each week translating the manual so I could learn these fabulous methods.

And so we did. Susanne would translate in her strong German accent, "First strand *up,* fourth strand *over,* sixth strand *down,*" and I would follow along. What a wonderful endeavor: separate and chaotic lengths of dough, patiently tamed and coaxed into harmonious braided loaves. What I didn't realize at the time was that the act of rolling pretzel dough hundreds of times each day, which seemingly was quite different work from braiding, had slowly given my hands an understanding about the vagaries of dough, and this would prove to be an enormous benefit as I immersed myself in braiding.

In order to give a day off to the woman who worked the counter all week, Susanne asked me if I would be willing to be the counterperson on Mondays after my bake day was over. At the time, the bakery was in a small location on a side street. There wasn't too much business on Monday afternoons, and I was happy to work the counter. So for the next few months, until Susanne moved her bakery to a prominent building she bought in the center of Main Street, I spent Monday afternoons waiting on customers—and making braids. It was a great way to practice, to work out the finer points, and to acquire enough proficiency to begin making larger decorative items—braided flowers and animals, wreaths, and intricate lattice weavings. If there was one source of frustration, it was that I couldn't concentrate only on the braids, but also had to help the occasional customer. After all, wasn't it rather insensitive for a customer to come in just when I was trying to fashion sixty strands of dough into a cornucopia? Such impertinence!

Why braid? Why go to the trouble at all? Why not simply take a chunk of dough and stuff it into a loaf pan and avoid the cumbersome task of rolling out all those strands? We are fortunate, as humans, to have an urge—irrepressible!—to take something that is good and make it better, to take something pleasing and make it more so, to create beauty in any way we can. And this, I think, is why a braided loaf provides both baker and eater with more gratification than the same weight of dough baked in a pan. There is an immense delight in taking a number of discordant strands of dough and bringing them into a harmony. The beauty of shape, the symmetry of form, the rapport between hand and dough—these have always given braiding a special satisfaction to me. I hope some of that satisfaction finds its way into your hands as well.

Tips for Braiding

From a technical perspective, there are a number of points relative to braiding that must be abided. Although in the lessons that follow we will look at only a few of the hundreds of possible braiding patterns, the rules that apply to one pattern tend to apply to all. As with so many aspects of baking, an effort made to keep the small things accurate brings the highest results in the finished work. In the list that follows, what may appear to be a small detail will in fact have an impact on the end result.

- The dough used for braid work is generally on the stiff side. The strands made from softer doughs have a tendency to merge together. By using comparatively stiff doughs, there is a sovereign independence to each strand, and each strand rises distinct from its neighbor.

- Certain doughs used for braiding are fully yeasted, for example the challah and Berne Brot in Chapter 7. Other doughs, such as the Lattice Dough from Chapter 10, have a reduced percentage of yeast. And some braids are made from unyeasted dough. All three methods have appropriate application. For eating purposes, the braids made with a full yeast percentage are most suitable. The keeping quality of finished bread tends to increase as yeast percentage is reduced. Challah is an excellent dough for braiding, and was used for all the braids shown in the illustrations in this chapter.

- Fully yeasted doughs can be mixed up to 1 day before braiding. The mixed dough receives full gluten relaxation during the hours under refrigeration, which makes braiding easier. The long, slow fermentation improves keeping quality. And last, if the braids are intended for sale, by mixing a day before and retarding the dough in bulk, production time is saved the following day, since mixing and fermentation were completed the day before.

- The thought of braiding several strands of dough can be a bit daunting. A lot can be learned by practicing with Play-Doh, or even shoelaces, where the pressure of yeast is absent. In studying the braiding diagrams, it becomes clear that once a pattern is established, that pattern continues throughout the braiding process.

- If the dough is divided in a 36-part divider, slightly round each piece so that the pieces are the same shape when you begin rolling out the strands. If the dough is hand divided, strive to cut the dough into evenly sized rectangles, with any scrap placed on top of the body of the rectangle. Form the strand by folding the long edge of the rectangle over the scrap and tightly rolling the dough piece into a rope. If a dough molder is used, allow the dough to rest after going through the molder, then extend the relaxed strands to their finished length.

- There is no difference in technique between rolling out one strand of dough to make a roll and rolling out several dozen for a large display piece. Here is the method: Using one hand, lay your palm in the center of the dough. Your shoulder should be above the dough so that the strength of shoulder and back contribute to the rolling. Pressing down, roll the dough back and forth on an unfloured bench several times until you meet resistance in the dough. You should have a sort of dog-bone shape, with the center narrow and each end bulbous. Now, place both hands side by side at the center of the strand, with your index fingers touching each other. Continue to roll, but now the pressure (still mostly from the shoulders and back, which should remain above the work) will be both downward *and* outward. If the dough is sliding along the bench and not rolling, either there is a residue of flour on the bench, or, more likely, the downward and outer pressure of your hands is insufficient.

Once your hands have reached the ends of the dough, look at the strand. In all likelihood, it will require more lengthening, so return both hands to the center, again with both index fingers touching, and repeat the rolling out. You may need to repeat these rollings several times, depending on the resistance of the dough to stretching, and on the required length of the strand. Often, there is asymmetry to the strand. In this case, don't continue to return both hands to the center and roll outward, but instead place your hands on the areas that need work and carefully lengthen those areas, with the ultimate goal of rolling the strand to a symmetrical shape. If an area is encountered where the strand is too thin, in every case avoid any further lengthening in that area.

During the entire rolling process, the palm should be mostly in contact with the dough. If the fingers are used, lumps and bumps will result in the shape of the strand. The smoothness of the palm helps ensure a smooth evenness to the rolled strand. An added bonus to rolling lots and lots of strands is the subtle massage the palm receives from the action. Bakers who make a lot of braids seem to have an elevated feeling of goodwill!

- Quite a bit of vigor is required to roll out the strands. Strong downward and outward pressure helps to roll the strand as quickly as possible. This in turn helps to prevent the dough from being overworked. Overworked strands usually become too dry, and often have interior gas bubbles that make for irregular braids.

- For symmetry in the finished work, it is very important that each strand be rolled out so that its shape and length is as similar as possible to all the other strands. Often, particularly when rolling out long strands (such as in a lattice, where the strands might be 4 feet in length or more), it is preferable to roll out the individual strands only partway. Once the last strand has been rolled, return to the first and roll again to the finished length. Keep in mind that as you are rolling, when you meet the dough's resistance, you must let it rest—it will simply rip if you try to continue the rolling.

- Since the dough is on the stiff side, keeping rolled strands under plastic prevents dehydration. If the dough becomes so dry that it simply will not roll into shape, swiping the bench with a barely dampened towel will give some traction to the dough and permit elongation. Caution must be exercised here, though; if there is even the slightest amount of excess moisture, the surface of the strands will become pasty and stick together in the finished braid.

- Rolling the full-length strands in a light (almost invisible) coating of flour before assembly helps keep the individual strands separate, and so improves the definition of the finished braid. You should avoid even the smallest excess of dusting flour on the bench during rolling, however. Extra flour will cause the dough to slide aimlessly around the bench, refusing to roll out.

- After rolling out the strands and placing them in the correct position, put a weight of some kind onto the joined ends of the strands before beginning the braiding. This helps to prevent the strands from unraveling as you make the braid.

- Each braid requires a certain minimum number of strands in order to accomplish its pattern. In most cases, however, increasing above that minimum is possible. For example, the 5-strand braid in the illustration on page 303 can be made with 6, 7, 8, or any number of strands. There is, of course, a practical limit to the number of strands that looks appropriate for each of the braids. The 3-strand braid in the illustration on page 299 is an example of a pattern that cannot be made with more or fewer strands.

- One of the major defects of some braids, beyond the poor shaping of the individual strands, is excessive pulling during assembly. As the braid is being formed, only a light, gentle placement of the strands is necessary. If a strand is pulled beyond its natural ability to stretch, it will eventually pull back, distorting the finished loaf.

- Keep a little bit of space between the strands as they are laid into position. There must be room between them to accommodate the bread as it rises. If the initial braid is made too tightly, the pressure exerted by the rising of the dough and by the final expansion in the oven will result in a distorted loaf, often with unsightly bursting as the dough seeks room to expand.

- When finishing the braid, both ends must be well sealed. What may seem to be somewhat of an indelicate squeezing together of the ends of the strands is necessary to ensure that they don't pop open during the bake, disfiguring the loaf. Also, if there are any strands that seem too long when finishing the loaf, simply cut them off and place them on the bottom of the loaf if it is for sale, or discard them if you are making a display piece. Look carefully at the finished loaf. Often the 2 ends will have a different aspect. With a few quick strokes, manipulate the ends, and the entire length of the loaf, so that there is an even symmetry throughout. Lines should be parallel from end to end. Some open spaces should be evident, suggesting the braid was made loosely enough to allow for expansion during the rise and for maintaining an even shape during the bake.

- Unless made with unyeasted doughs such as *pâte morte,* braids are egg washed before going into the oven, and never require steam. The coating of egg wash should be thin but thorough. Take care that all surfaces are evenly washed. Missed spots are pale and lusterless, surrounded by shine, and will draw the eye to them.

- Frequently, braided loaves are topped with poppy or sesame seeds. This can be done in one of two ways. First, as soon as the loaf is braided, apply a thin, even coat of egg wash and then invert the loaf into a tray of seeds, or sprinkle seeds over the surface. Alternatively, wait until the bread is almost ready to bake, then egg wash it and sprinkle seeds on top. In this latter method, do not attempt to invert the bread into the seeds; it will be too fragile for such treatment, since its rise is almost complete.

- A complete rise is not recommended before loading the oven. The strands on a braid that is 100 percent risen will almost certainly merge. A rise of about 85 percent will enable the strands to expand individually, and the baked loaves will be full, open, and attractive.

- When making larger pieces such as platters and cornucopias, a good method is to refrigerate the unbaked piece for an hour or more (overnight is acceptable, unless the yeast percentage is too high). This enables the dough to attain a relaxed equilibrium, minimizing the danger of distortion in the oven. Unless they are exposed to air currents while under refrigeration, the loaves can be left uncovered. This helps the individual strands remain distinct.
- Large display pieces must be cooled on wire racks. If they remain on the baking sheet, moisture will not be able to escape, and they will be subject to early mold. Since these pieces often have a shelf life of a year or more, it is sad to see mold creeping along the bottom when the cause of it is easily avoided (the voice of experience is speaking here).
- Egg wash is usually enough to give a vivid natural shine to the braids. Oftentimes, the baker may want to use varnish on display pieces to enhance the shine. A precaution: If the entire piece is enclosed by varnish, there is no way inner moisture can escape, and mold will result, so leave the bottom unvarnished.

Challah

DOUGH YIELD | U.S.: 34.78 lb | Metric: 17.39 kg | Home: 3 lb, 7 oz

	U.S.	METRIC	HOME	BAKER'S %
Bread flour	13.4 lb	6.7 kg	1 lb, 5.4 oz ($4\frac{7}{8}$ cups)	67%
High-gluten flour	6.6 lb	3.3 kg	10.6 oz ($2\frac{3}{8}$ cups)	33%
Sugar	1.6 lb	.8 kg	2.6 oz (5 T)	8%
Yolks	1.5 lb	.75 kg	2.4 oz (4 yolks)	7.5%
Whole eggs	2.8 lb	1.4 kg.	4.5 oz (2 eggs)	14%
Vegetable oil	1.5 lb	.75 kg	2.4 oz ($5\frac{1}{2}$ T)	7.5%
Water	6.4 lb	3.2 kg	10.2 oz ($1\frac{1}{4}$ cups)	32%
Salt	.38 lb	.19 kg	.6 oz (1 T)	1.9%
Yeast	.6 lb, fresh	.3 kg, fresh	.32 oz, instant dry ($2\frac{3}{4}$ tsp)	3%
TOTAL YIELD	**34.78 lb**	**17.39 kg**	**3 lb, 7 oz**	**173.9%**

1. **MIXING:** Place all the ingredients in a mixing bowl. In a spiral mixer, mix on first speed for 3 minutes until all the ingredients are thoroughly incorporated, then on second speed for about 3 min-

utes. In a planetary-style or stand mixer, mix on first speed for about 3 minutes to incorporate all the ingredients, then on second speed for 5 to 6 minutes. The goal is to develop a strong gluten network. The dough will be comparatively stiff, which is appropriate for braiding. The desired dough temperature is 78° to 80°F.

2. **BULK FERMENTATION:** 2 hours.

3. **FOLDING:** Fold the dough once, after 1 hour of fermentation.

4. **DIVIDING AND SHAPING:** Divide the dough into appropriate-sized pieces. Preshape round, and rest on an unfloured work surface, covered with plastic. When sufficiently relaxed (10 to 20 minutes), roll out the strands and form the braids. Once braided, proof the loaves, covered with baker's linen and a sheet of plastic to prevent the formation of a skin. If using a proof box with humidity, set the controls low enough to prevent excess humidity from causing the individual strands to merge together.

5. **FINAL FERMENTATION:** 1½ to 2 hours at about 76°F.

6. **BAKING:** Before baking, thoroughly egg wash the loaves. If desired, sprinkle poppy or sesame seeds on top. Bake without steam at 380°F. Baking time is determined by the size of the loaves. Pan loaves will take longer to bake than will freestanding loaves. A braid weighing 18 ounces should bake in about 30 minutes. If the oven has vents, they should remain open throughout the bake.

Note: The challah dough can be retarded overnight in bulk form. In this case, the desired dough temperature is 75° to 78°F. After mixing, bulk ferment at room temperature for 1 hour, then place the dough in the retarder or refrigerator. The dough should be degassed twice during the first 4 to 6 hours of refrigeration. The benefits of overnight retarding are improved dough texture and keeping quality. Colder dough temperature also makes it easier to form strands.

ONE-STRAND ROLLS

METHOD ONE

1. Roll the dough piece, with a slight taper, to about 10 inches long for a 3-ounce piece. Place the larger end on the right (illustration A).

2. Pick up the dough piece and bring the larger end over the smaller end, leaving an opening in the center. Only a small portion of the smaller end should extend from the bottom (B).

3. Take the larger end behind and under the smaller end; bring it up through the opening (C).

4. Bring the large end back toward the rear of the dough piece and join it to the smaller tag end of dough. Smear them together so they don't separate during the rise and bake. The 3 segments of dough should be of similar thickness (D).

METHOD TWO

1. Roll out the dough piece, with no taper, to about 16 inches long for a 3-ounce piece. Overlap the dough so that just a small tag of dough shows on the bottom part of the strand. There should be an opening in the center (illustration A).

2. Pick up the dough piece, take the long top end, and bring it behind the lower part of the dough. Bring it up through the center opening (B).

3. Repeat step 2, again bringing the long end of dough behind and up through the opening in the center (C).

4. Repeat step 2 again, pulling the end of the strand up so that a small bulb of dough pops up in the center of the roll (D). Smear the small tag end of dough underneath the roll to seal it.

METHOD THREE

1. Roll out the dough piece, with no taper, to about 14 inches long for a 3-ounce piece. Form the dough into the shape of the number 6, as in illustration A.

2. Twist the bottom portion of the dough over to create a sort of figure-8 pattern (B).

3. Take the long tag end of dough, bring it under the lower portion of the figure 8, and then up through the opening (C). A small bulb of dough should come out of the openings at each end of the dough (D).

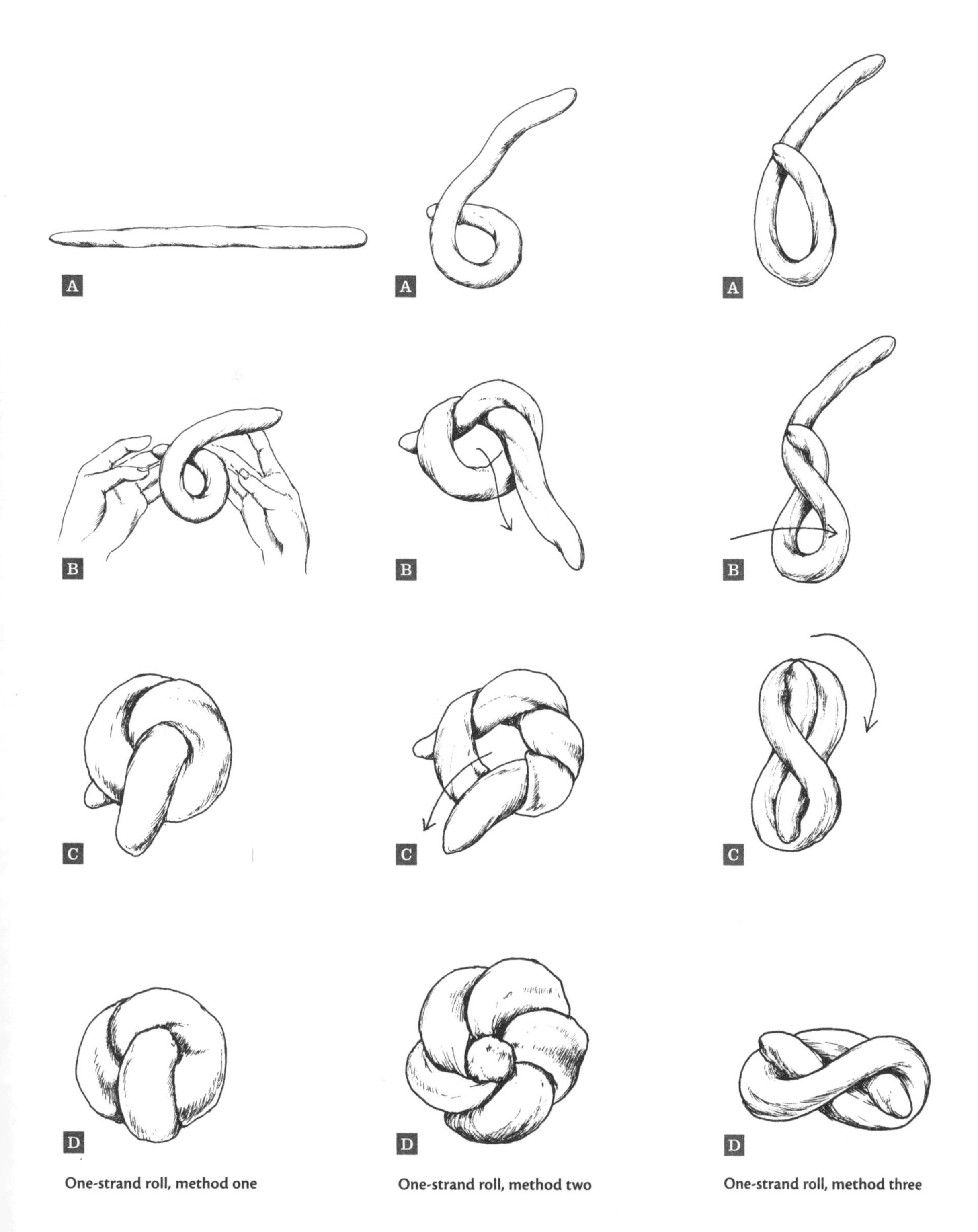

One-strand roll, method one

One-strand roll, method two

One-strand roll, method three

TWO-STRAND BRAID

METHOD ONE

1. Roll out each strand to the desired length, with no taper. Place 1 strand atop the other so that a long X shape results (illustration A).

2. Pick up the 2 ends of the bottom piece of dough, cross them over the top dough piece, and place them back on the work surface (B).

3. Continue this process, taking the 2 bottom ends and crossing them over the top until all the dough has been used. You now have a 2-strand rope of dough (C). This can be used as a border for a display piece, or the ends can be enclosed to make a ring shape, or the rope can be coiled up into a rosette shape as in illustration D. It can also be used as the top layer of a tiered braid.

METHOD TWO

1. Roll out both strands of dough so that they have tapered ends. Place one down in a north-south orientation, and place the other at right angles on top, in an east-west orientation (illustration A).

2. Bring south upward to north and north down to south, with south passing to the left of north as they cross (B).

3. Cross east over the top of west, reversing their position (C). Continue this process until all the dough is used.

4. Finish the loaf by pressing together the strands at the bottom end of the loaf. There should be a distinct taper to the loaf, from top to bottom, so that it makes a nice teardrop shape (D).

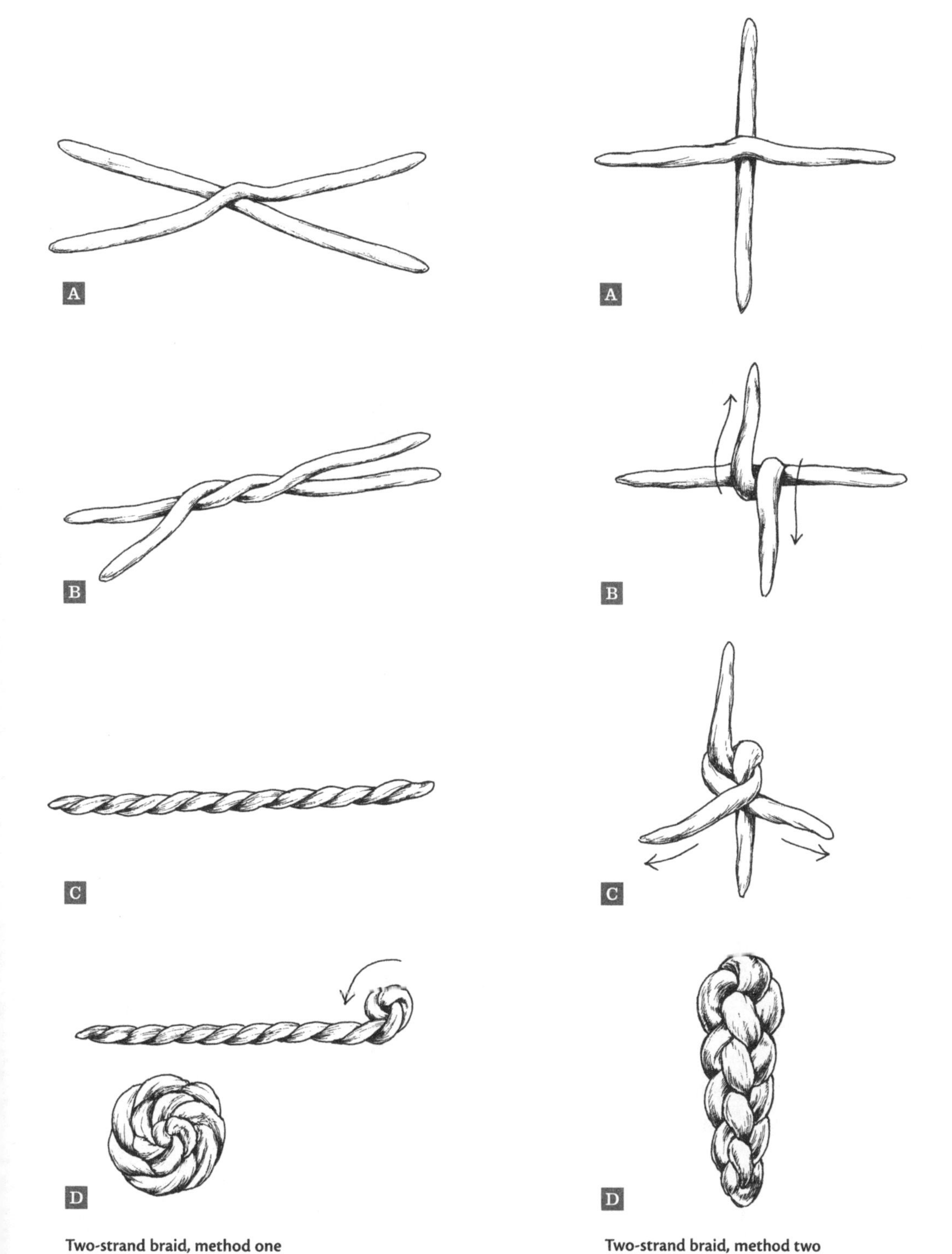

Two-strand braid, method one

Two-strand braid, method two

THREE-STRAND BRAID

METHOD ONE

1. Roll the strands with a slight taper at the ends. Join the ends farthest from you, and spread out the strands so they are evenly spaced from one another (illustration A).

2. Cross the outer left strand over the middle strand, placing it on the work surface inside and adjacent to the right-hand strand (B).

3. Place the outer right strand over the middle strand and place it alongside the left-hand strand (C).

4. Continue with this process, crossing the outer left strand over the middle strand, then the outer right over the new middle strand, until all the dough is used. Seam the edges and adjust the loaf so it has a symmetrical aspect (D).

METHOD TWO

In a production setting, when a large number of loaves are required, this is the quickest braiding technique.

1. Roll the strands to an equal length, with a slight taper at the ends (illustration A).

2. Instead of joining the strands at one end, begin to braid in the center of the loaf by taking the left strand, crossing it over the middle strand, and laying it to the inside of the right strand (B).

3. Place the outer right strand over the middle strand and place it alongside the left strand (C).

4. Continue in this fashion until all the dough is used (D).

5. Flip the entire braid over so that the unbraided strands are closer to you (E).

6. Continue braiding, first taking the right strand over the middle strand and placing it to the inside of the left strand, and proceeding until all the dough is used (F).

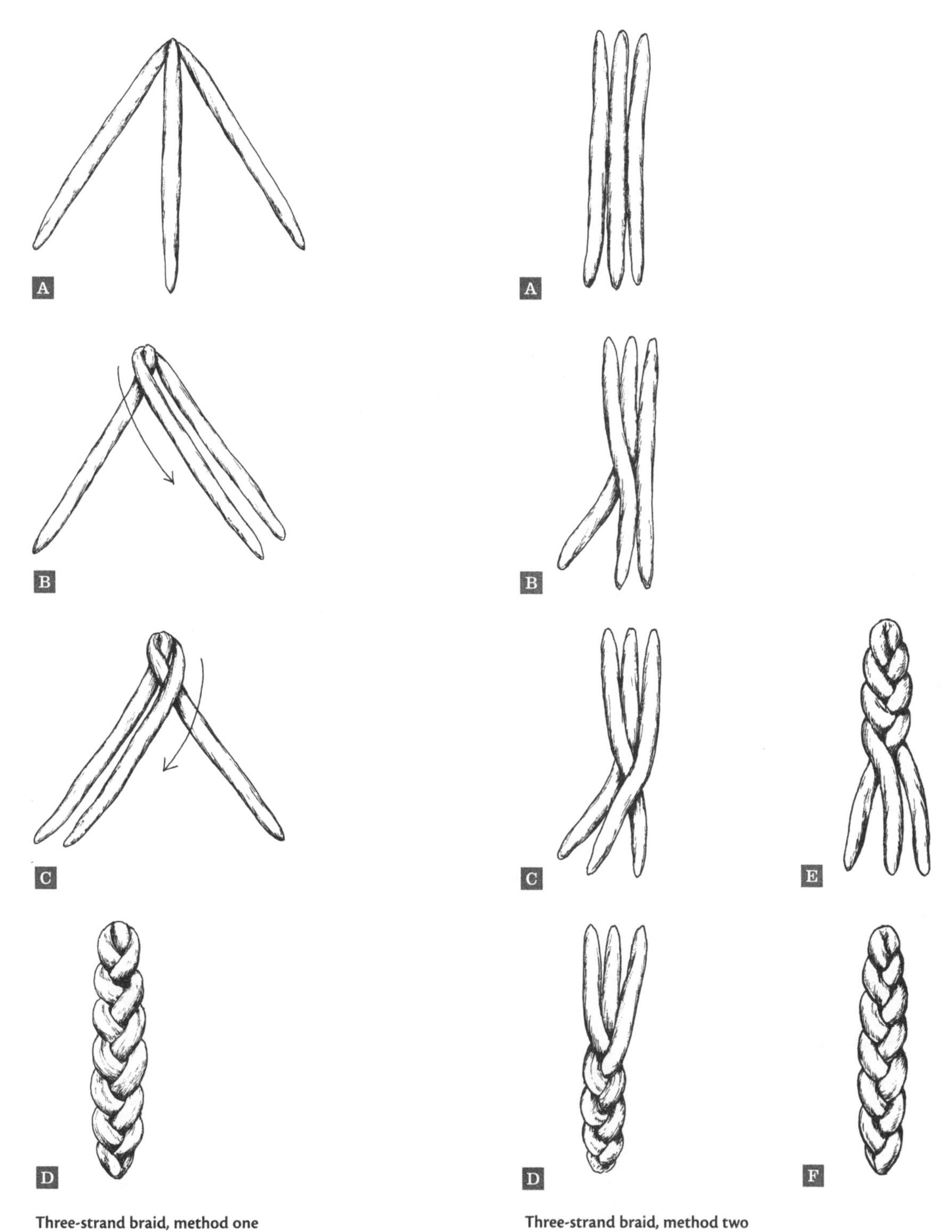

Three-strand braid, method one

Three-strand braid, method two

FOUR-STRAND BRAID

This braid is excellent as a finished loaf. It can also be used as a border for decorative work, as a handle for a dough basket, as a wreath, and so on.

METHOD ONE

1. Roll the strands with slightly tapering ends and evenly space them on the work surface, with 2 strands on the left and 2 on the right (A).

2. Lift strand 3, then bring strand 1 under 3 to the outside, facing up and away. Return strand 3 to its original place (B).

3. Bring strand 4 over strand 3 and to the outside of strand 2, facing up and away (C).

4. Bring strand 1 over strand 3 and place on the inside of strand 2 (D).

5. Bring strand 2 over strand 1 and to the outside of strand 3, facing up and away (E).

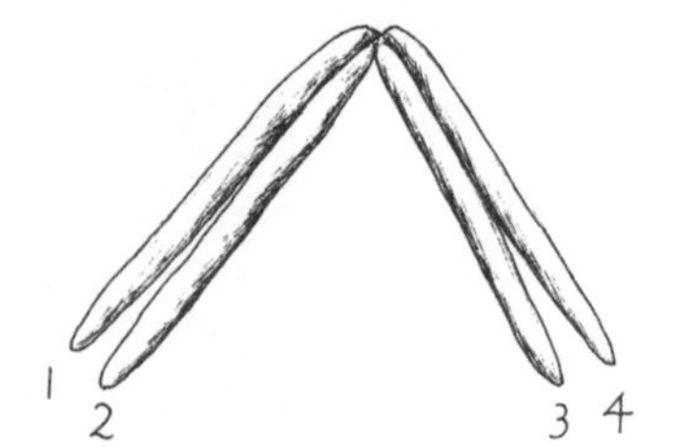

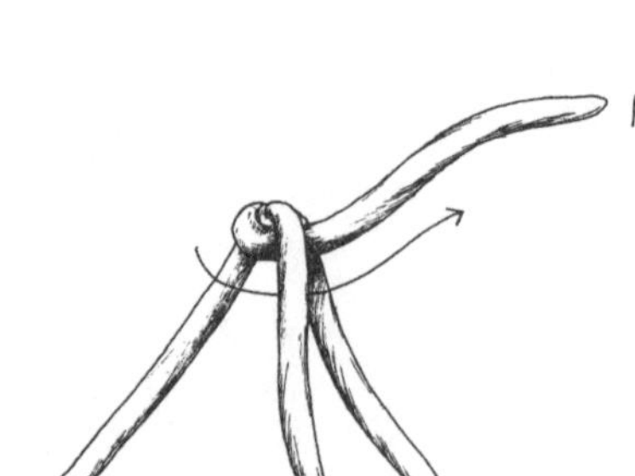

6. Bring strand 4 over strand 1 and place on the inside of strand 3 (F).

7. Continue the pattern until all the dough is used. Manipulate the finished loaf into an even shape (G).

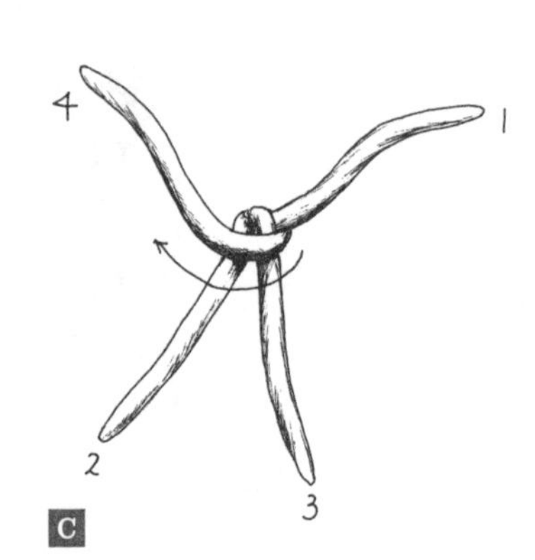

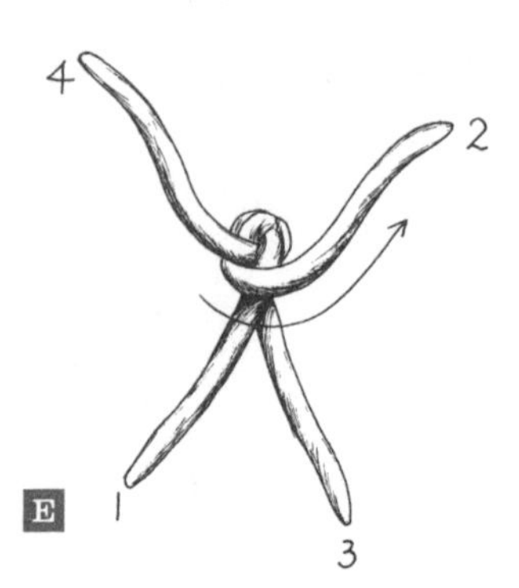

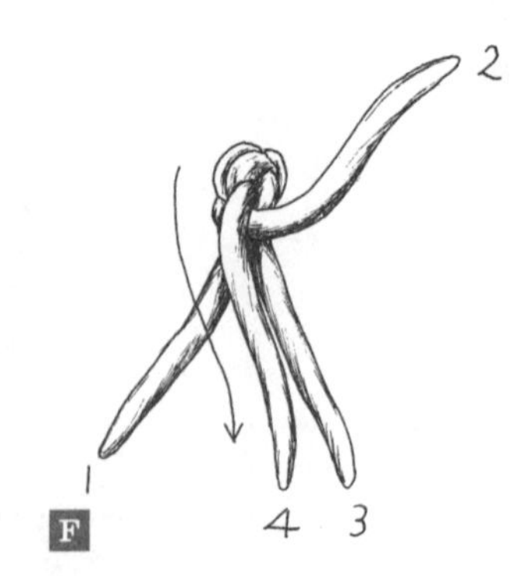

Four-strand braid, method one

METHOD TWO

This style of braiding produces a flat braid that is not necessarily best suited for sliced bread. It works very well when used as the base for a tiered braid.

1. Roll the strands with slightly tapering ends and evenly space them on the work surface, with 2 strands on the left and 2 on the right (A).

2. Bring strand 4 over strand 3 and place it inside strand 2 (B).

3. Lift strand 2 and bring strand 1 under it, over strand 4, and place to the inside of strand 3. Return strand 2 to the outside of strand 4 (C).

4. Bring strand 3 over strand 1 and place it inside strand 4 (D).

5. Lift strand 4 and bring strand 2 under it, over strand 3 and to the inside of strand 1. Return strand 4 to the outside of strand 3 (E).

6. Repeat this pattern until all the dough has been used. Contour the finished loaf so that it is evenly tapered (F).

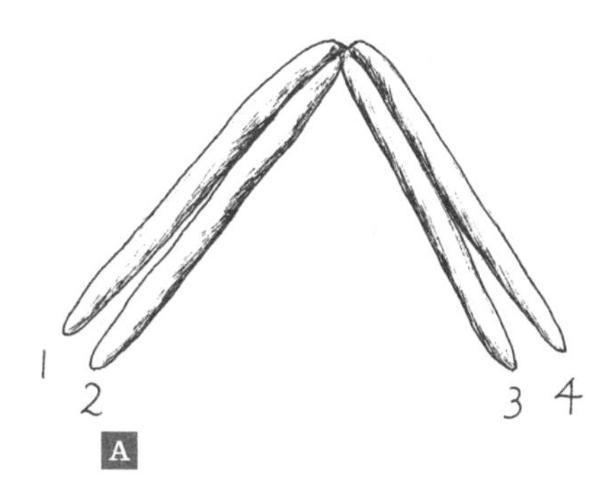

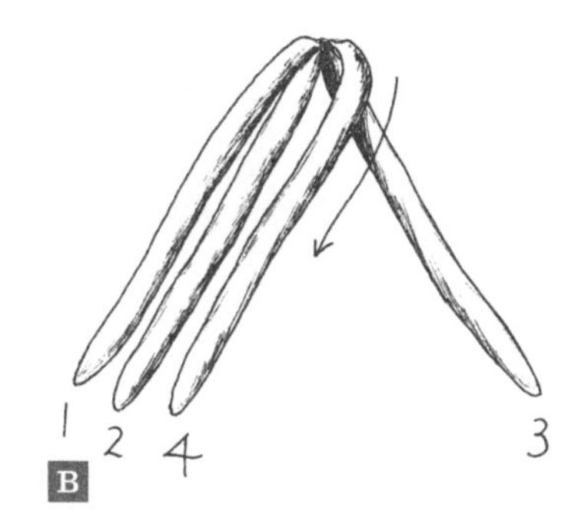

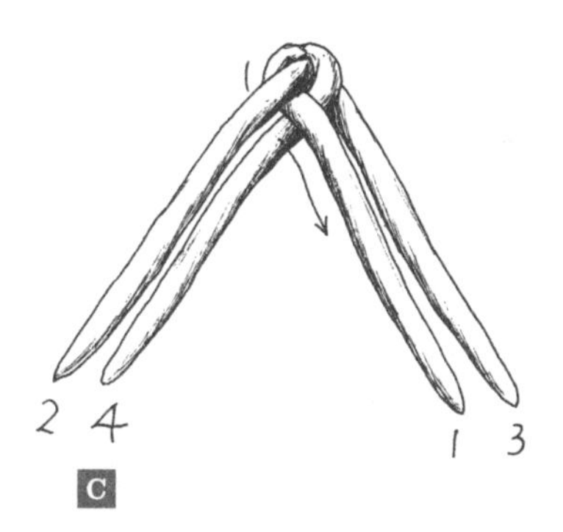

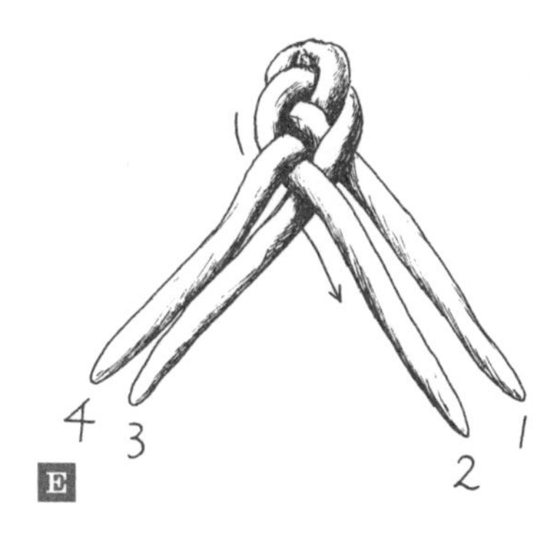

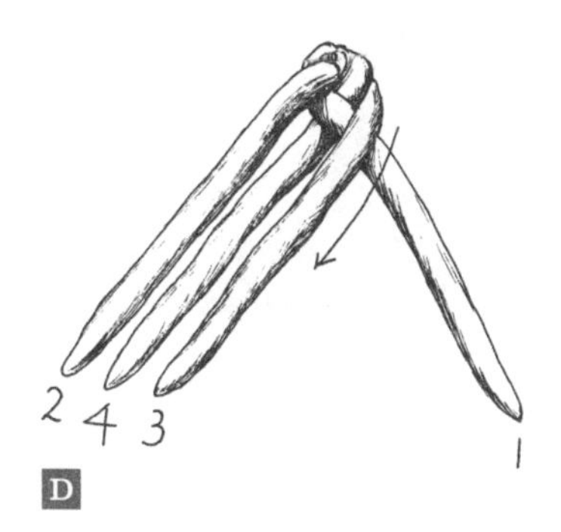

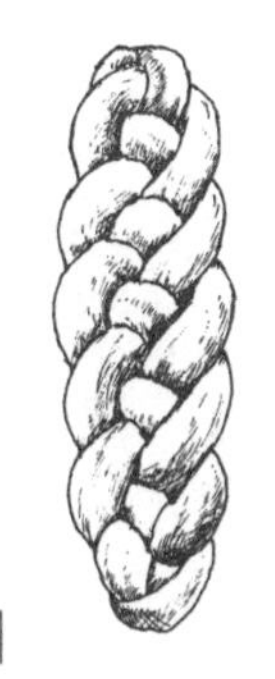

Four-strand braid, method two

FIVE-STRAND BRAID

This braid is beautiful to behold with its spiral top, and well worth the effort required to learn the braiding technique. It is an unusual loaf for two reasons. First, when finished it is lying on its side and must be turned upright to have the correct aspect. Second, unlike other braids where an even number of strands is distributed to each side at the beginning of the braiding process (or as close to even as possible, when using an odd number of strands), with this braid, regardless of the number of strands used, there are always 2 on one side and the remainder on the other side at the beginning.

1. The strands are rolled with a slight taper at the ends. Place them on the bench with 2 strands on the left and 3 on the right (illustration A).

2. Lift strands 1 and 5. Bring strand 5 over and to the outside of strand 2 (B).

3. Place strand 1 to the inside of strand 2 (C).

4. Twist strands 1 and 2. Place strand 1 inside and parallel to strand 5. Place strand 2 inside and parallel to strand 3 (D).

5. Bring strand 4 across and place between strands 5 and 1 (E).

6. Bring strand 5 to the inside of strand 2 (F).

7. Twist strands 5 and 1, placing strand 5 to the inside of strand 4, and strand 1 to the inside of strand 2 (G).

8. Repeat this pattern until all the dough is used. Tuck the dough pieces together at the end of the braid (H).

9. Turn the loaf so that what was the right side is now on top. The top will have parallel strands of dough running at an angle to the length of the dough (I). Seam the other end of the loaf and gently bring an even symmetry to the finished loaf.

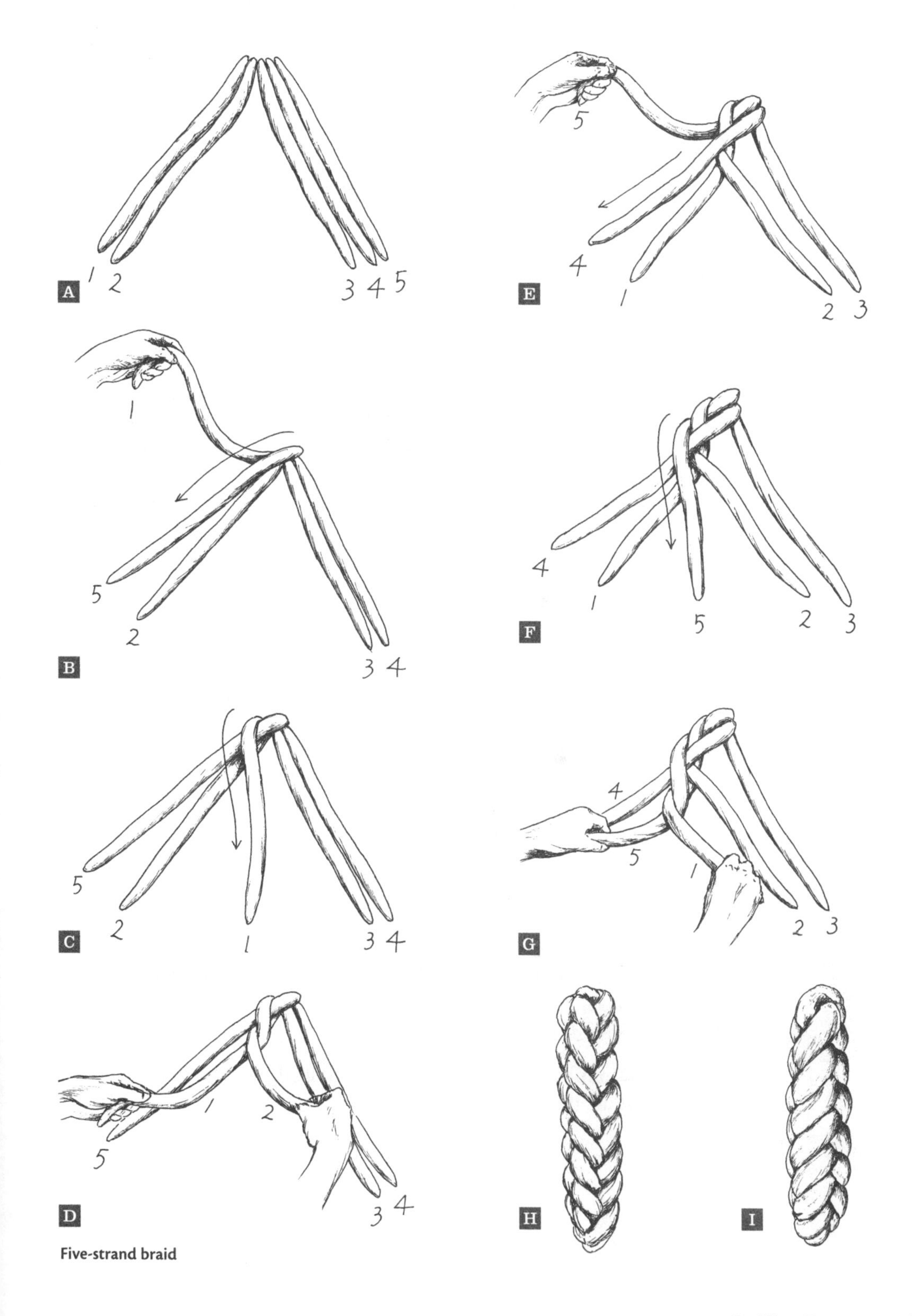

Five-strand braid

SIX-STRAND BRAID

METHOD ONE

This is one of the easiest braids to make, and a good choice when starting out. It also is very pleasing to look at. Like many of the other braids in this chapter, it may also be baked in a loaf pan.

1. Roll the strands with an even taper and place them on the bench with 3 strands on the left, 3 on the right (illustration A).

2. Bring strand 1 over to the inside, placing it alongside stand 4 (B).

3. Bring strand 6 over to the inside, placing it alongside strand 3 (C).

4. Continue the pattern, bringing the left outer strand to the inside and placing it alongside the innermost right strand, then bringing the outer right strand to the inside, placing it alongside the innermost left strand. Finish the braid by manipulating it so that it has a harmonious visual aspect (D).

METHOD TWO

This braid is characterized by its height, making it a good choice as a stand-alone loaf with nice-sized slices. Note the similarity in its construction to the first 4-strand braid illustrated on page 300.

1. Begin as for the preceding braid, with 2 groups of 3 strands evenly spaced to left and right (illustration A).

2. Lift strand 4. Swing strand 1 under strand 4 and bring to the top of the right side, facing up and away from the right-hand strands. Return strand 4 to its original place (B).

3. Bring strand 6 up and over to the far side of the left group of strands, facing up and away. Bring strand 1 over strand 6 and place alongside strand 3 (C).

4. Bring strand 2 up and over the far side of the right group of strands, facing up and away. Bring strand 6 over strand 2 and place alongside strand 4 (D).

5. Continue with this pattern until all the dough has been used. Adjust the shape (E).

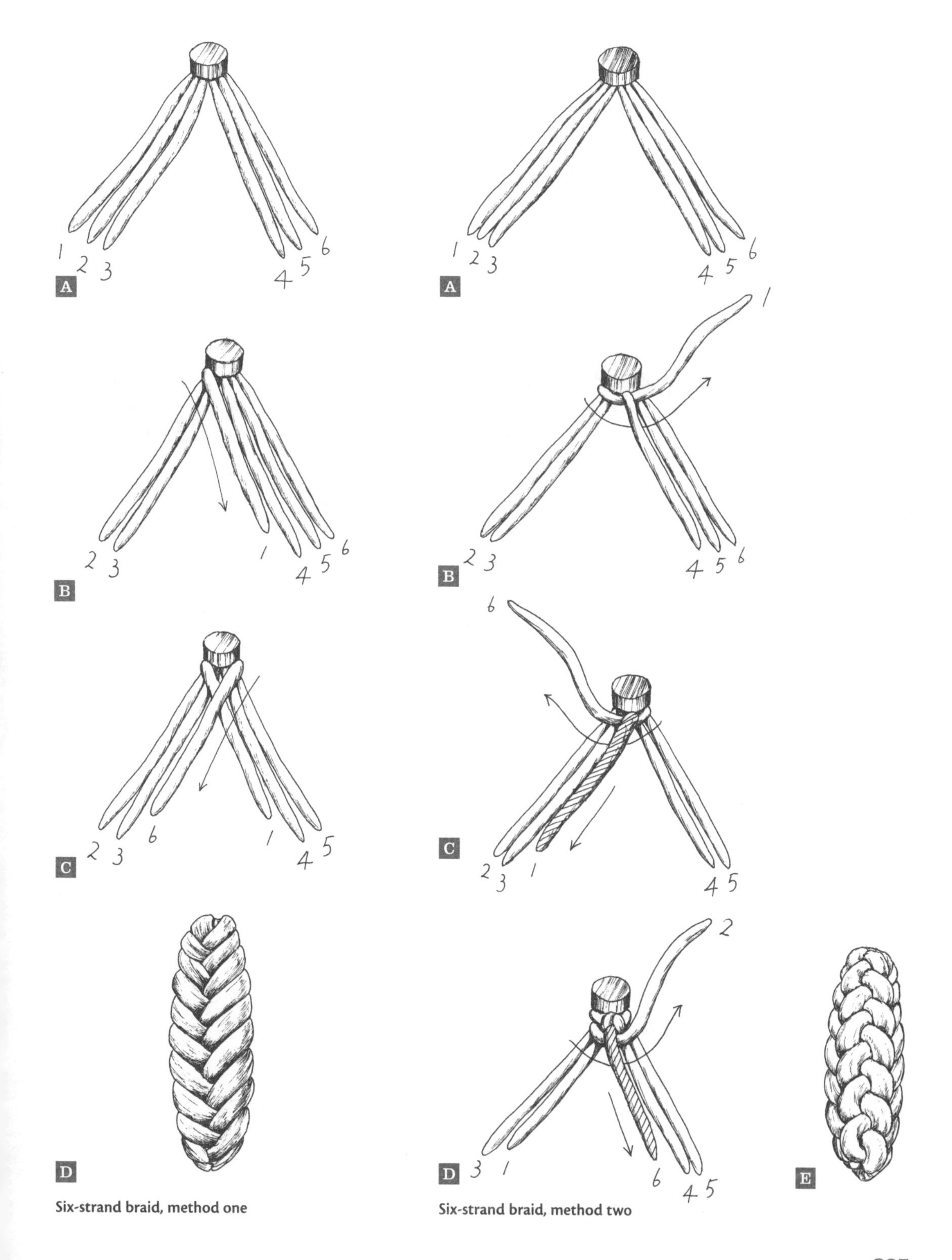

Six-strand braid, method one

Six-strand braid, method two

METHOD THREE: THE WINSTON KNOT

To make the Winston Knot, 2 groups made up of 3 strands each are interwoven to form the braid. Throughout the procedure, each group of 3 is treated as 1 unit and the strands within the unit are not separated.

1. Place 1 group of 3 strands in a north-south orientation. Place the second group of 3 strands over the first group in an east-west orientation (illustration A).

2. Take the group of strands labeled "1" in the illustration and, rotating them counterclockwise—but not turning them over—bring them over the top of the east-west strands and down alongside the strands labeled "2" as shown in illustration B. Throughout the exercise, the strands are rotated and not turned over, so the part that faces up at the beginning continues to face up throughout the procedure.

3. Lift strand group 2, bring group 4 under it, over group 1, and to the inside of group 3. Lay group 2 back down alongside group 1 (C).

4. Rotate strand group 3 over group 4; lay it down alongside group 1 (D).

5. Lift group 1, rotate group 2 under it and over group 3. Lay group 1 back down (E).

6. Rotate group 4 over group 2 and lay it alongside group 2 (F).

7. Bring the ends of all 4 groups together and pinch them into one unit (G). If any strands are sticking out, they can be cut off so that the pinched ends all meet together.

8. Take the pinched ends and flip them over to the center of the loaf and press gently. Now take the opposite end of the braid and flip it to the center, laying it over the pinched ends (H). Gently press. Now turn the entire braid over and there it is: the Winston Knot (I).

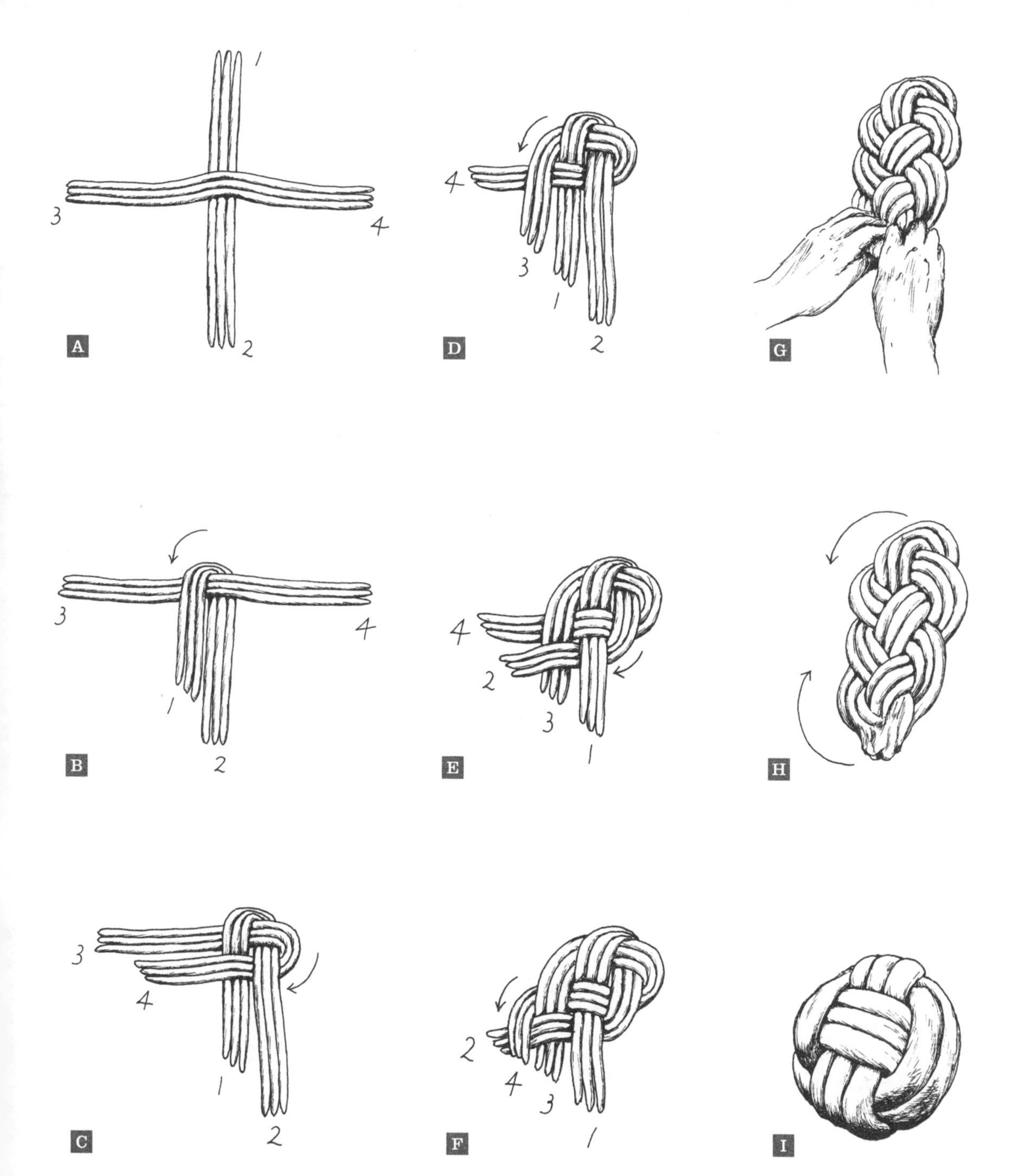

Six-strand braid, method three: The Winston Knot

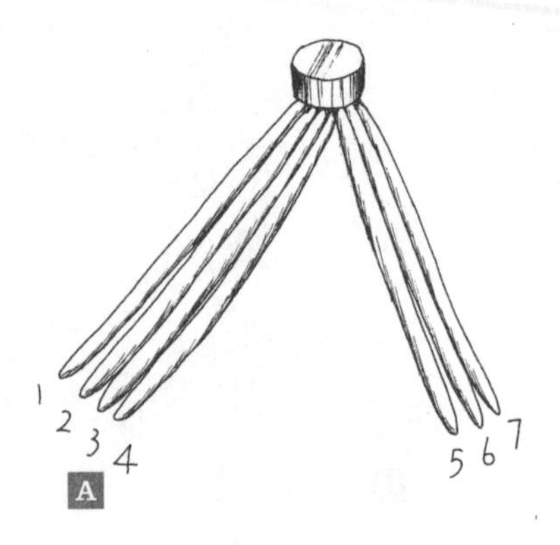

SEVEN-STRAND BRAID

This braid is quite flat when finished, and therefore doesn't look its best when made as a freestanding loaf. A better choice is to use this braid as a base for a tiered loaf. In that case, as few as 4 strands can be used to build the braid, or as many as 10 or 12. The correct number of strands to use is determined by the number of layers in the tiered braid and the weight of the individual layers. The triple-decker braid illustrated here uses this braiding technique for the base layer.

1. Roll the strands with an even taper and place on the work surface with 4 strands on the left, 3 on the right (illustration A).

2. Lift strand 2, bring strand 1 over strands 3 and 4, and place it alongside strand 5 (on the inside of the right-hand group of strands). Lay strand 2 back in its original position (B).

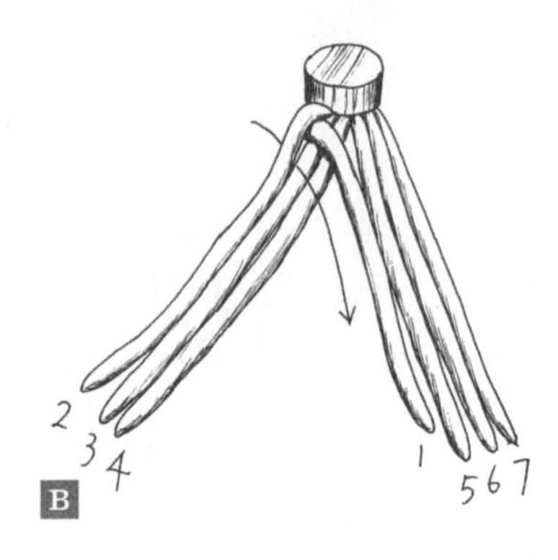

3. Lift strand 6, bring strand 7 over strands 5 and 1, and place it alongside strand 4 (on the inside of the left-hand group of strands). Return strand 6 to its original location (C).

4. Continue with this pattern, lifting the second strand from the outside and bringing the outer strand to rest on the inside of the opposite group, then replacing the lifted strand to its original location. Alternate left and then right. When all the dough has been used up, clean the ends of the dough pieces by pinching them together to form a sturdy seam. Adjust the finished braid so it has a symmetrical appearance (D).

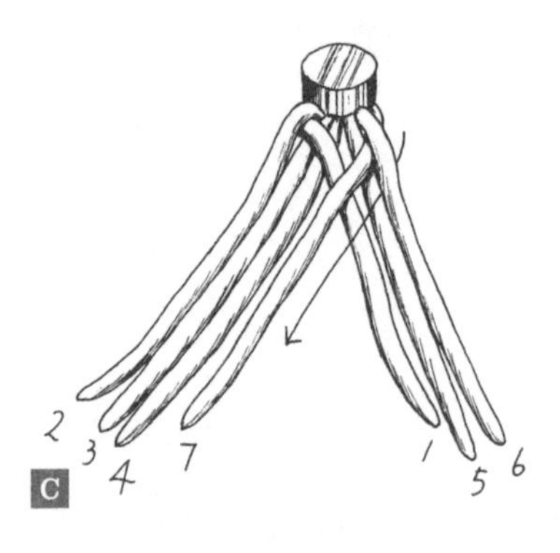

Seven-strand braid

TIERED BRAIDS

Tiered braids are wonderful for parties, festive functions, and weddings. They are impressive to look at with their 2- or 3-layer construction. A few aspects of this style of braiding can cause construction problems, so read the instructions carefully before beginning.

The ultimate size of a tiered braid is determined either by the size of the oven it is baked in or the size of available sheet pans. It is not feasible to bake these loaves directly on the hearth or on baking stones because the eggs, oil, and sugar in the dough can easily cause the bottom of the loaf to burn.

Egg wash can be made using whole eggs; alternatively, water can be added to the eggs (5 parts egg to 1 part water is a good ratio). A pinch of salt will extend the keeping quality of the egg wash. Thoroughly whisk the eggs (and water and salt if used), then strain through a sieve to separate out the larger bits of albumen.

DOUBLE-DECKER BRAID

Check the braid as it proofs; if the top braid shows any signs of sliding off, carefully reposition it to the center of the bottom braid. The longer the braid has proofed, the more fragile it will be and the more difficult to adjust the positions of the individual braids. Therefore, check the positions frequently and make adjustments as necessary. The dough weight used for this braid is 29.25 ounces. Once baked, the loaf will weigh about 1.5 pounds. This size fits comfortably on a standard-size sheet pan (24 by 16 inches).

1. Roll 3 strands of dough, each weighing 6.5 ounces. Bring a slight taper to the ends. Roll a second group of 3 strands, each weighing 3.25 ounces (illustration A).

2. Make a 3-strand braid with the 6.5-ounce strands in the usual fashion. Using the side of your hand or a thin rolling pin, make a slight indentation along the center of the braid, from one end to the other as shown in illustration B.

B

Tiered braid: Double-decker braid

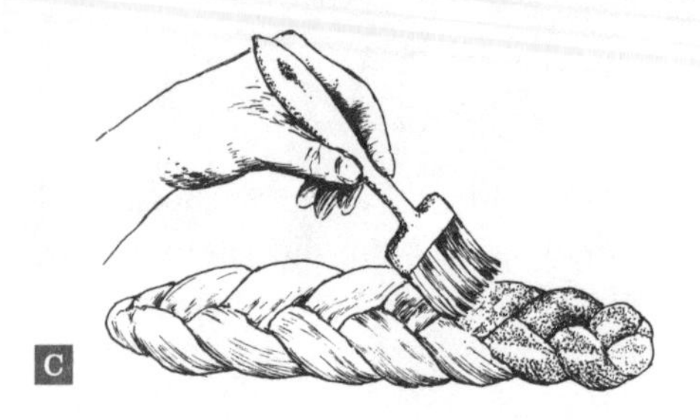

3. Lightly egg wash the braid (C).

4. Make a second 3-strand braid with the 3.25-ounce strands. It should be slightly shorter than the first braid, and proportionally narrower (D).

5. When the egg wash is tacky, apply the second braid to the top of the first one. Press lightly but thoroughly so the top braid adheres completely to the bottom braid (E).

TRIPLE-DECKER BRAID

Using the braiding techniques already described, a most impressive 3-story loaf can be made, an attainable challenge for the baker and a real treat for the eyes (not to mention the eating pleasure it affords). For this loaf, 3 separate braids are made. The first consists of 6 strands, each weighing 5 ounces. The second is also formed from 6 strands, but this time the weight of each strand is 2.5 ounces. Finally, a 3-strand braid forms the top; each of these strands weighs 2 ounces. In all, the weight of the unbaked braid is 3 pounds, 3 ounces. Baked weight is about 2 pounds, 10 ounces. Placed diagonally, this braid will fit on a full-sized sheet pan (24 by 16 inches).

1. First make the 6-strand braid with the 5-ounce strands, using the technique described on page 308 for the 7-strand braid. Since 6 and not 7 strands are used, begin by having 3 on the left side and 3 on the right. Once made, use a narrow rolling pin to create a slight furrow along the length of the braid. Egg wash the surface lightly.

2. Make the 6-strand braid using the 2.5-ounce strands. The braiding method used is the first 6-strand braid technique, described on page 304. The length should be just slightly shorter than the base-

Egg Wash

There are a couple of ways to use egg wash. One is to brush it on dough after forming it or just before loading it into the oven. In this case, it is the shine provided by the wash that we seek. A second use is as glue. When making tiered braids, it is essential that one braid is not put on top of a lower braid until the egg wash on the lower one is tacky. If it is applied when the wash is wet, the braid will almost certainly slide off during either proofing or baking. On the other hand, the egg wash will go from wet to tacky to dry, and if the second (or third) braid is put on after the wash has dried, again there is the risk of the upper braid sliding off. To check for proper tackiness, simply touch the surface of the dough with a finger. If it sticks, the egg wash is ready to hold the braid.

level braid. Use the rolling pin to slightly indent the center of this braid down its entire length. Lightly egg wash this layer.

3. Make the 3-strand braid in the usual fashion using the 2-ounce strands. Make this braid slightly shorter than the length of the middle layer.

4. To assemble the loaf, place the middle braid on top of the lower one when the egg wash is tacky. Press it thoroughly into place. It should be slightly shorter than the bottom braid, and centered both front to back and side to side.

5. When the egg wash on the middle braid is tacky, carefully apply the top braid to it, pressing thoroughly.

6. Check the loaf a few times during the final proofing to make sure the braids remain symmetrical. Gently reposition them if they are losing their balance.

TWO ADVANCED BRAIDING TECHNIQUES

HUNGARIAN BREAD RING

A wonderfully festive bread ring of Hungarian origin is made using 6 strands of dough for the inner ring and 1 larger strand to form the outer circle. I used to make this ring every weekend, partly for the simple enjoyment of seeing the random strands take on a lovely cohesive finished shape, and partly because customers loved buying them. Taken to a dinner, the ring would be passed and pieces torn from the whole as it circled the table. For more venerable celebrations such as weddings, the ring took on a more symbolic aspect, as the breaking of this bread has a rich uniting power. When made from challah dough or Yeasted Decorative Dough, the Hungarian Bread Ring can be hung on a wall, where it can grace a kitchen or other room for years. Here is the method of construction (note that the weights used below are sufficient for one ring baked on a standard 24-by-16-inch sheet pan):

1. Scale 6 dough pieces at 3 ounces and 1 piece at 14 ounces. Lightly round them and let stand to relax under a sheet of plastic. Once sufficiently relaxed (about 10 minutes), begin working the 14-ounce dough piece into a rope. Eventually it will be almost 4 feet long, so work it out gradually to its final length by repeating the rolling out and relaxing. Roll the six 3-ounce pieces to approximately 16 inches long, with a slight taper at the ends. Strive for a graceful, symmetrical shape (illustration A, page 312).

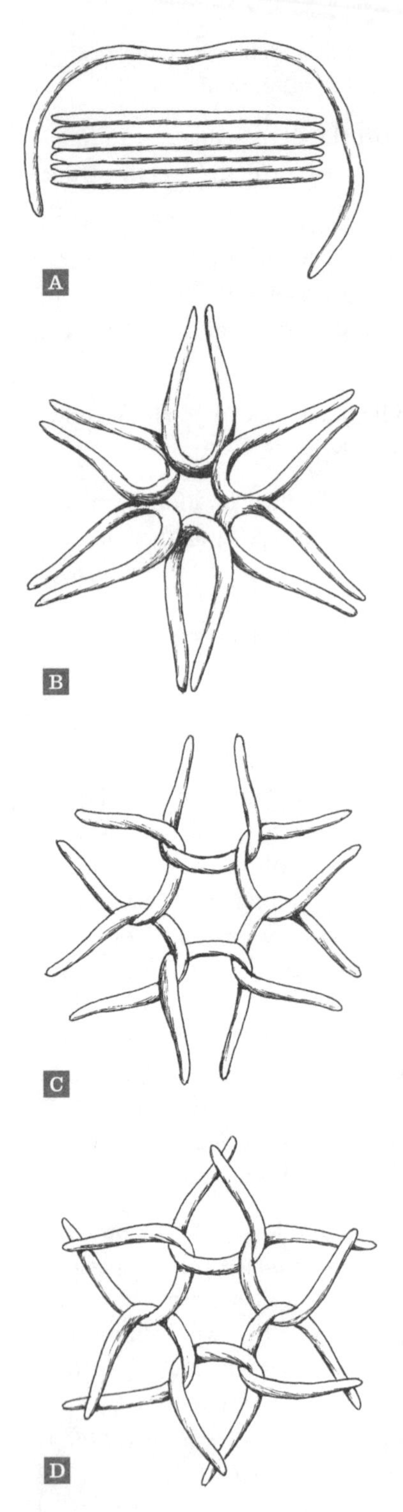

2. Lay out the 6 strands as in illustration B, so that the right shoulder of each strand is on top of the left shoulder of its neighbor. Throughout the braiding procedure, keep the strands an equal distance from each other. Take the time to align the strands after each step so that they remain in a symmetrical relationship with each other.

3. Entwine the right and left shoulder of each strand as in illustration C. Align the 6 linked strands evenly.

4. Overlap the ends of each strand as in illustration D. Note that in the illustration, the left portion overlaps the right portion in each strand. As long as all 6 are treated the same, the left can overlap the right, or the right can overlap the left.

5. Finish elongating the 14-ounce strand, taking care to keep the diameter the same along the entire length. Lay one end of this long strand at the point of overlap of one of the 3-ounce strands, as in illustration E. Now, lay the rest of the long strand at the same point of overlap of the other 5 strands. When it has come completely around the circumference, unite the 2 ends together. The seaming must be thorough, so that these ends do not open or separate. Refer to illustration F for an effective method of combining the ends of the long strand. Illustration G shows the proper placement of the outer ring. Make sure the outer strand is long enough so that you don't have to stretch it as you spread it around the circle of inner strands. Be patient (remember, the finished ring might be on someone's wall for a long time), and remove the strand and elongate it further if necessary. Once it is placed around the perimeter, it should be loose enough so that it will not shrink during proofing or baking.

6. Now, we will begin to lock the 6 inner strands to the outer ring, beginning with the strand that is at the point where the 2 ring ends are joined. Pick up the bottom portion of the overlapped strand, and bring it over the top of the outer ring, as in illustration H. Be sure that the seam of the outer ring is completely covered. Repeat with the remaining 5 strands, taking the bottom portion of the strand and bringing it over the top of the outer ring. Once all 6 strands have been completed in this way, step back and check for symmetry. Adjust the strands as necessary so the shapes of the 6 loops are as close to identical as possible and the overlapped ends of the individual strands are equally spaced around the circumference.

7. To finish the ring, join the ends of the inner strands together with a smearing motion, making sure the seam is under the outer ring.

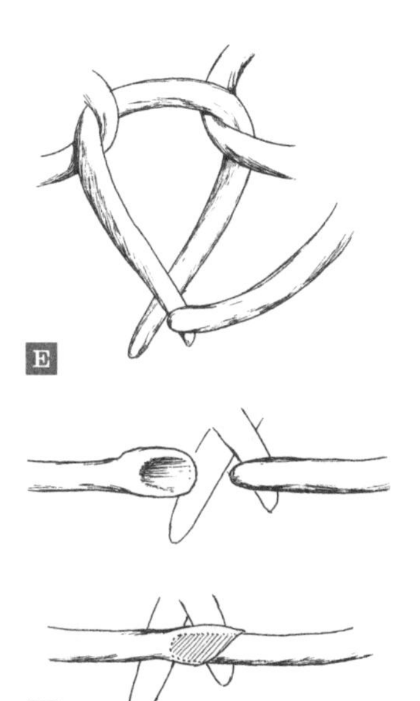

Tear off any bits of these ends that are too long so that the seam is tidy and not bulging from an excess of dough. Adjust the loop shapes and curve of the outer ring as necessary to achieve symmetry. If an imaginary line were drawn from one overlapped end across the ring to the other side, the line would hit the opposite overlapped end.

8. The bread ring has been fully shaped! Proof it under a length of baker's linen. When about 85 percent risen, carefully egg wash it. The brush can be used to make subtle adjustments to the shape of the loops or the outer ring. Take care to be thorough as you wash the ring. Bake in a 380°F oven until it has a rich color, 25 to 30 minutes. If it is to be eaten, remove earlier than if the ring will be used as a decoration. Cool on a wire screen. If you are going to hang the ring, allow it to dry for at least 24 hours so it will not sag.

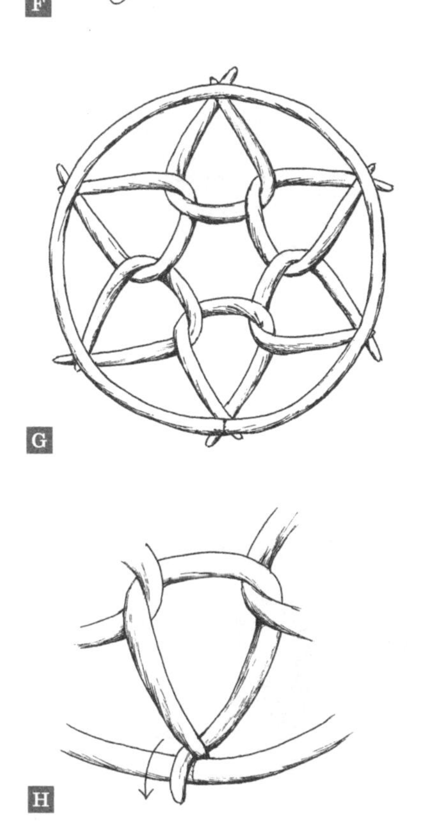

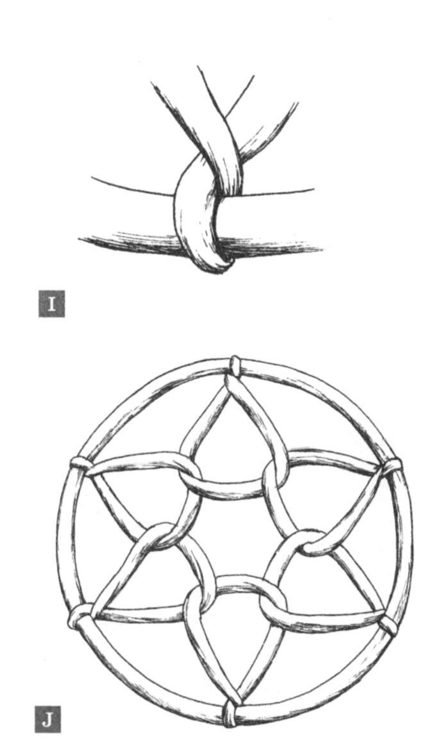

Hungarian bread ring

A SIX-POINT STAR

The Six-Point Star detailed below is made of 20 strands of dough. When working with this number of strands, speed in rolling and braiding the strands is a great benefit. Keep in mind, however, that to accomplish the work with consistency and high quality, speed must be subordinate to proficiency. That is, we first must gain the skills necessary to roll out numerous strands of dough to a common length and with an even taper. Once that ability is acquired, speed will naturally follow. Striving for speed before mastering accuracy results in sloppy work. Since Yeasted Decorative Dough (page 319) has considerably less yeast than challah, it may be a better dough to work with when learning how to make the Six-Point Star. Either dough will yield fine results, so if you are able to braid accurately and rapidly, challah is certainly a valid choice. The finished Six-Point Star is not only impressive to look at, it is quite

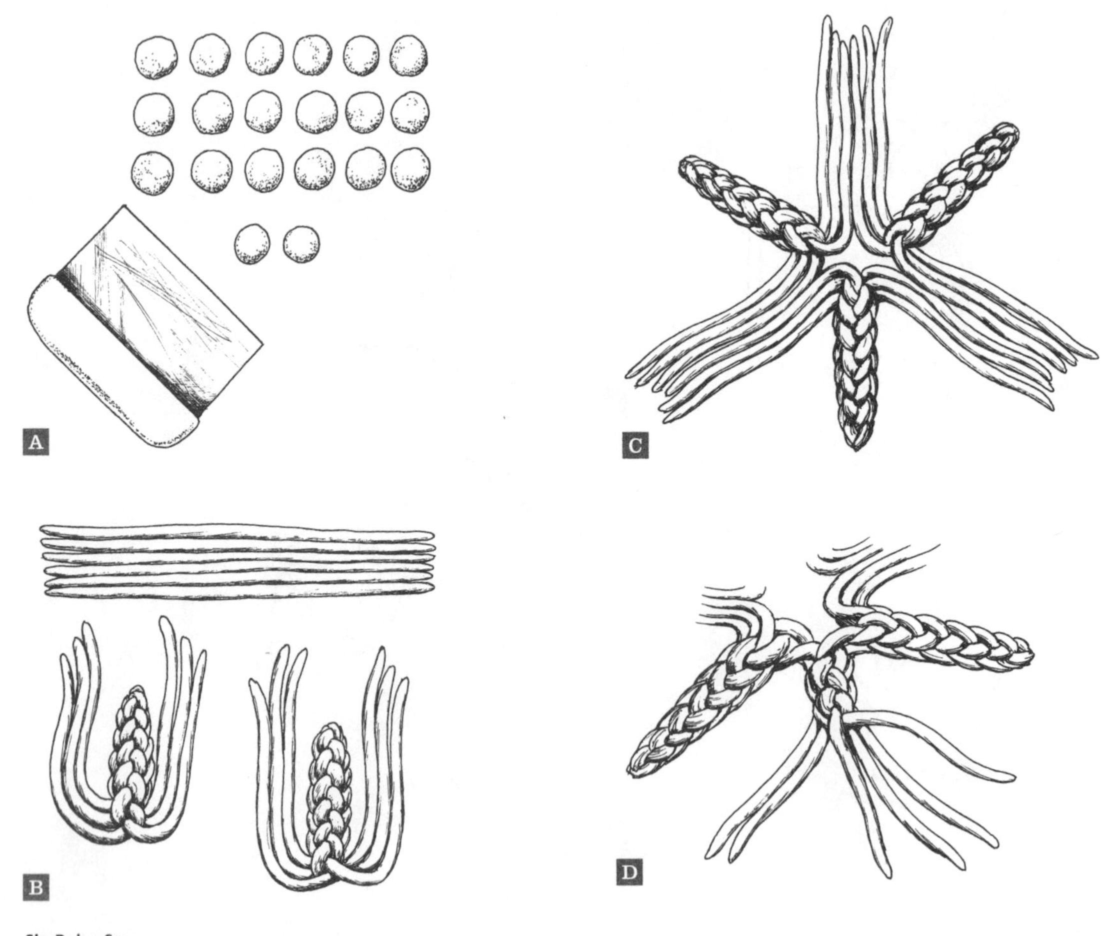

Six-Point Star

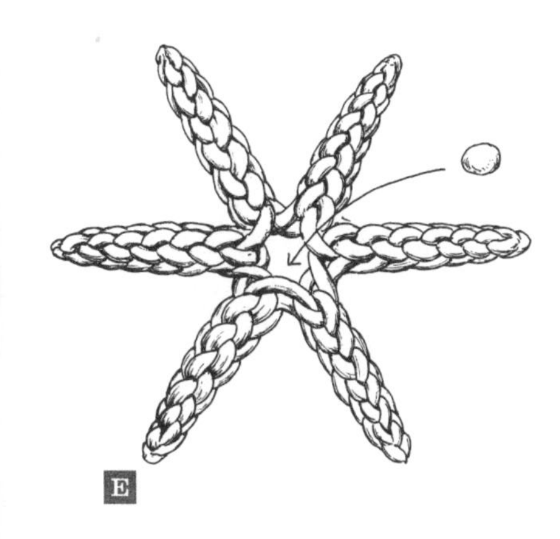

unlikely that anyone seeing the finished piece will be able to deduce how it was constructed. Like the Hungarian Bread Ring, it has excellent keeping quality, and careful attention to detail yields a result that will be enjoyed for a long time. The dough weights in this exercise are appropriate for a finished piece that will fit a standard sheet pan.

1. Scale 18 dough pieces weighing 1.75 ounces each. These pieces will be braided into the shape of a star. Lightly round them. Scale 2 more dough pieces, each weighing 1 ounce, and round these as well. These 2 pieces will be formed into a rosette to finish the star. Put all 20 pieces under a sheet of plastic and let them relax for 5 to 10 minutes.

2. Roll the first 18 strands to approximately 18 inches long with an even taper. Set them up in groups of 6. Take the first 6 and begin forming a 6-strand braid, using the technique for either of the 6-strand braids detailed on page 304 (the illustrations show the second technique). When the braid is half formed, put it aside. Repeat this procedure with the remaining 2 groups of 6 strands, stopping the braid when about half the length of the strands has been braided.

3. Position the 3 half-formed braids as shown in illustration C. Notice that half the unbraided strands are placed to the left of the finished portion of each braid, and half are placed to the right. In this way, 6 unbraided strands are adjacent to each other in 3 separate groups.

4. Even though the 6 unbraided strands come from 2 different half-braided loaves, we will treat them as 6 independent strands. Begin braiding one of the groups of 6 strands with the same pattern used to begin the braiding (illustration D). When the braid is finished, join the ends well, and braid the remaining 2 groups of 6 strands.

5. You now have 6 braids, all of which should be of equal length and taper. Transfer the piece with care to a sheet pan lined with parchment paper. Make adjustments to braid placement and taper as necessary. Check for even spacing and symmetry of the individual braids. If there is a hollow in the center of the star, lay in a small scrap piece of dough (see illustration E). Lightly egg wash the center of the star.

6. Roll the remaining 2 strands to approximately 14 inches long. Braid them into a 2-strand rope, as described in the first 2-strand

braid technique earlier on page 296. Put a weight on each of the ends and leave them in place for 3 or 4 minutes. (This step seems insignificant, but the rest period allows the dough to relax and lose its "memory.") Coil the joined strands into a rosette as in illustration F. Seam the outer edge well so it won't open during proofing or baking.

Six-Point Star (continued)

7. When the egg wash has become tacky and is able to function as glue, lay the 2-strand rosette in the center of the star (G). When the star has proofed about 85 percent, carefully egg wash the entire surface. Check for even spacing of the 6 individual braids. Bake at approximately 375°F until it is richly colored, about 30 minutes. Pay careful attention to the star as it bakes. If it takes on color too quickly, lower the oven temperature to 360°F. The bottom must show signs of darkening by the end of the bake. If the bottom is too pale, it is an indication that the center of the star has not baked. In this case, the extra internal moisture will significantly shorten the keeping quality. Cool the star on a wire screen for at least 6 hours. If left on the sheet pan, internal moisture can cause mold to form on the bottom of the star within a few days. There is no need to apply a spray varnish to these decorative pieces if the egg wash has been carefully applied. In fact, if the dough piece is completely sealed with varnish, it will not be able to breathe, and will almost certainly mold from within.

DECORATIVE AND DISPLAY PROJECTS

10

If I bear burdens
they begin to be remembered as
gifts, goods, a basket of bread
that hurts my shoulders but closes
me in fragrance. I can eat as I go.

—DENISE LEVERTOV, FROM "STEPPING WESTWARD"

In this chapter, we will examine several decorative techniques. The projects demonstrated all have excellent keeping quality: They will often last two or three years in a suitable environment. In the first part of the chapter, four decorative projects will be demonstrated, all made with a yeasted decorative dough. The projects in the second part of the chapter are fashioned from an unyeasted dough made with sugar syrup and rye flour.

The French call this type of dough *pâte morte,* literally "dead dough," because it is unyeasted. Yeast always keeps us on the edge, and clearly there are some benefits to making large decorative projects without the intrusion of it. Many projects benefit visually when made with yeasted dough, however, so we will work with both.

As we shall see, when working with 60 or more strands of dough, it's necessary to take certain precautions. One precaution is to use a minimum amount of yeast. In the formula below, a mere .4 percent yeast is called for. This enables us to get a gentle puffing from the yeast, adding to the quality of the baked piece, but the overall proportion is small enough to be comparatively easy to work with. Most of the projects made with Yeasted Decorative Dough use braiding techniques; mastery of the techniques detailed in the preceding chapter will be a great help with the more meticulous and demanding projects in this chapter. Note too that Dark Yeasted Decorative Dough uses the same proportions of ingredients as Yeasted Decorative Dough. The only difference is that 8 percent of the white flour is replaced with an equal weight of sifted cocoa powder. This addition of cocoa gives a rich chocolate-like hue to the finished work and provides an appealing visual contrast. Both doughs are made using the same method.

Light Yeasted Decorative Dough

DOUGH YIELD | U.S.: 7 lb, 8.58 oz | Metric: 3.428 kg | Home: 3 lb, 12.2 oz

	U.S.	METRIC	HOME	BAKER'S %
Bread flour	4 lb, 6.4 oz	2 kg	2 lb, 3.2 oz (8 cups)	100%
Milk powder	3.5 oz	100 g	1.75 oz (6 T)	5%
Sugar	3.2 oz	90 g	1.6 oz (3 T)	4.5%
Salt	1 oz	30 g	.5 oz (2½ tsp)	1.5%
Butter, soft	3.5 oz	100 g	1.75 oz (3½ T)	5%
Yeast	.28 oz, fresh	8 g, fresh	.01 oz, instant dry (⅛ tsp)	.4%
Water	2 lb, 6.7 oz	1.1 kg	1 lb, 3.35 oz (2⅜ cups)	55%
TOTAL YIELD	**7 lb, 8.58 oz**	**3.428 kg**	**3 lb, 12.2 oz**	**171.4%**

Dark Yeasted Decorative Dough

DOUGH YIELD | U.S.: 7 lb, 8.68 oz | Metric: 3.448 kg | Home: 3 lb, 12.2 oz

	U.S.	METRIC	HOME	BAKER'S %
Bread flour	4 lb	1.84 kg	2 lb (7¼ cups)	92%
Cocoa powder, sifted	6 oz	160 g	3 oz (⅞ cup)	8%
Milk powder	3.5 oz	100 g	1.75 oz (6 T)	5%
Sugar	3.2 oz	90 g	1.6 oz (3 T)	4.5%
Salt	1 oz	30 g	.5 oz (2½ tsp)	1.5%
Butter, soft	3.5 oz	100 g	1.75 oz (3½ T)	5%
Yeast	.28 oz, fresh	8 g, fresh	.01 oz, instant dry (⅛ tsp)	.4%
Water	2 lb, 7.2 oz	1.12 kg	1 lb, 3.6 oz (2⅞ cups)	56%
TOTAL YIELD	**7 lb, 8.68 oz**	**3.448 kg**	**3 lb, 12.2 oz**	**172.4%**

Add all the ingredients to the mixing bowl. In a spiral mixer, mix on first speed for approximately 3 minutes until all the ingredients are incorporated. Check the consistency and make adjustments as necessary. The dough should be quite stiff, but sufficiently hydrated to form a firm mass. Mix on second speed for an additional 3 minutes. In a planetary mixer, mix on first speed for approximately 3 minutes. When all the ingredients are incorporated and hydration is correct, turn the mixer to second speed and mix for approximately 5 minutes. The goal is a strongly developed gluten network. Desired dough temperature is 75°F or less.

Since the dough is so stiff, it is subject to rapid dehydration. Therefore, keep it well covered with a sheet of plastic at all times. While the stiff texture of the dough does make work-up somewhat more difficult, that same stiffness results in distinctness among all the strands, which, in a wetter dough, would tend to merge together and impair the appearance of the finished project. Fermentation is not the goal with these doughs, and a 15-minute bench rest is adequate before portioning the dough.

A last note: The first four projects detailed in this chapter are all sized to fit on a standard sheet pan, which measures 24 by 16 inches. Adjust the dough weights accordingly if larger or smaller pieces are required.

TOOLS

The tools required for these projects are few, but since the dough is on the dry side, and since yeast, however minimal, is a presence, you should have all the necessary tools at hand before dividing the dough into individual pieces. You will need:

A scale and bench knife for dividing the dough
Plastic sheets to cover the bulk dough and dough pieces
Dusting flour
A slightly dampened clean cloth (optional)
A sharp paring knife
A pizza wheel is handy if you have one
A stiff cardboard template appropriate to the project being made
A long palette knife, to free up the piece before transferring it to a sheet pan
One sheet pan lined with parchment paper
Egg wash and a soft brush
Refrigeration space to cool the piece for at least 1 hour before the bake

Making a Lattice Braid

Our first four projects with the Yeasted Decorative Dough begin with the making of a lattice, which is then finished in different ways. The weight of the individual strands of dough varies slightly among the projects, but the basic technique for making the lattice is the same.

Oval Platter with Four-Strand Rim

(color photograph 24)

For this project, we will use 32 long strands of light dough and 24 cross strands made with dark dough. The light-colored long strands weigh 2.25 ounces each (if you have access to a 36-part dough divider, weigh and divide a 5-pound press). The dark cross strands weigh 1.5 ounces each (the press weight for 36 pieces is 3 pounds, 6 ounces). Once the lattice is braided, an outer border is made with 4 strands of dark dough, each weighing 4.5 ounces. The final platter measures approximately 22 inches long by 15 inches wide, and a cardboard template with those dimensions should be cut before beginning the project.

1. Begin by scaling the 32 long strands. If dividing by hand, lightly round each piece. If using a dough divider, the pieces won't require rounding. In either case, place the pieces on an unfloured work surface, spaced closely together (but not touching one another) in chronological rows; that is, the first pieces rounded are at the beginning of the first row, and the last rounded piece is at the end of the last row. As the dough pieces relax, you will know which is the first to roll. Cover the dough pieces with plastic.

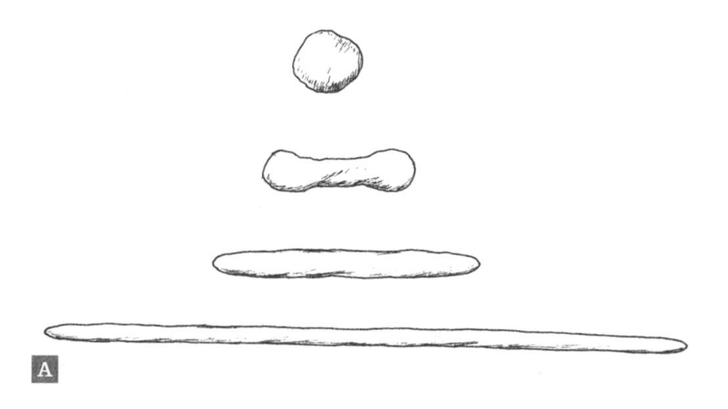

2. Since we will be working with dozens of strands of dough, it is highly recommended to roll them 2 at a time. After a short rest of 2 or 3 minutes, test the first 2 dough pieces to see if they are sufficiently relaxed to begin rolling. Place one hand on top of each piece, press down, and roll back and forth with vigor. The goal is to create a sort of dog-bone shape, narrow in the center and bulbous at each end (this is the same technique described for making strands for braiding beginning on page 288). If the dough refuses to lengthen, it needs more relaxing; replace it under the plastic sheet. If the pieces roll without resistance or tearing, continue to elongate them (A).

Once the "dog bone" is formed, take 1 dough piece, place your hands side by side with your index fingers touching in the center, press down, and roll. The correct motion is both back and forth (this is the visible part) and at the same time outward. The strength of the outward motion corresponds to the degree of relaxation of the dough. Elongate the dough until you have reached the extent of the dough's ability to stretch without tearing, roughly a foot long. The dough piece will not be at its full length. Don't expect it to be, and don't worry that it's not. The rolling will be done in 2 phases, and eventually the strands will be much longer. Above all, remain attentive to the dough. If it shows any signs of tearing, either it is insufficiently relaxed or hand pressure is too harsh. As you continue to work on the dough pieces, the degree of relaxation will increase, and the dough will become more malleable.

3. Once the first lengthening of all the strands is complete, return to the first piece. It will have relaxed enough to roll again, and this time you will be able to lengthen it fully to 26 to 28 inches long. Roll all the pieces to the same approximate length.

4. Once these light-colored strands are rolled out, the dark ones can be rolled. Since the dough weight is much less than that for the long strands, these dark strands will be proportionally shorter. Again make dog bones to begin, working with 2 dough pieces at a time, then elongate them one by one as you did for the light strands. Place the finished pieces off to one side, covered with plastic.

5. To begin the process of weaving the lattice, take 2 strands of the light dough and place them on the bench in front of you. Take a second pair of strands and lay it so that one end slightly overlaps the ends of the first pair (all of the light strands are laid out in an east-west orientation). Note in illustration B how the ends of each pair overlap slightly, and that the first pair is laid out on the *left side* of the bench, and the second pair on the *right side*. Continue this pattern until all 16 pairs (32 strands total) are laid out. Illustration C shows your progress to this point.

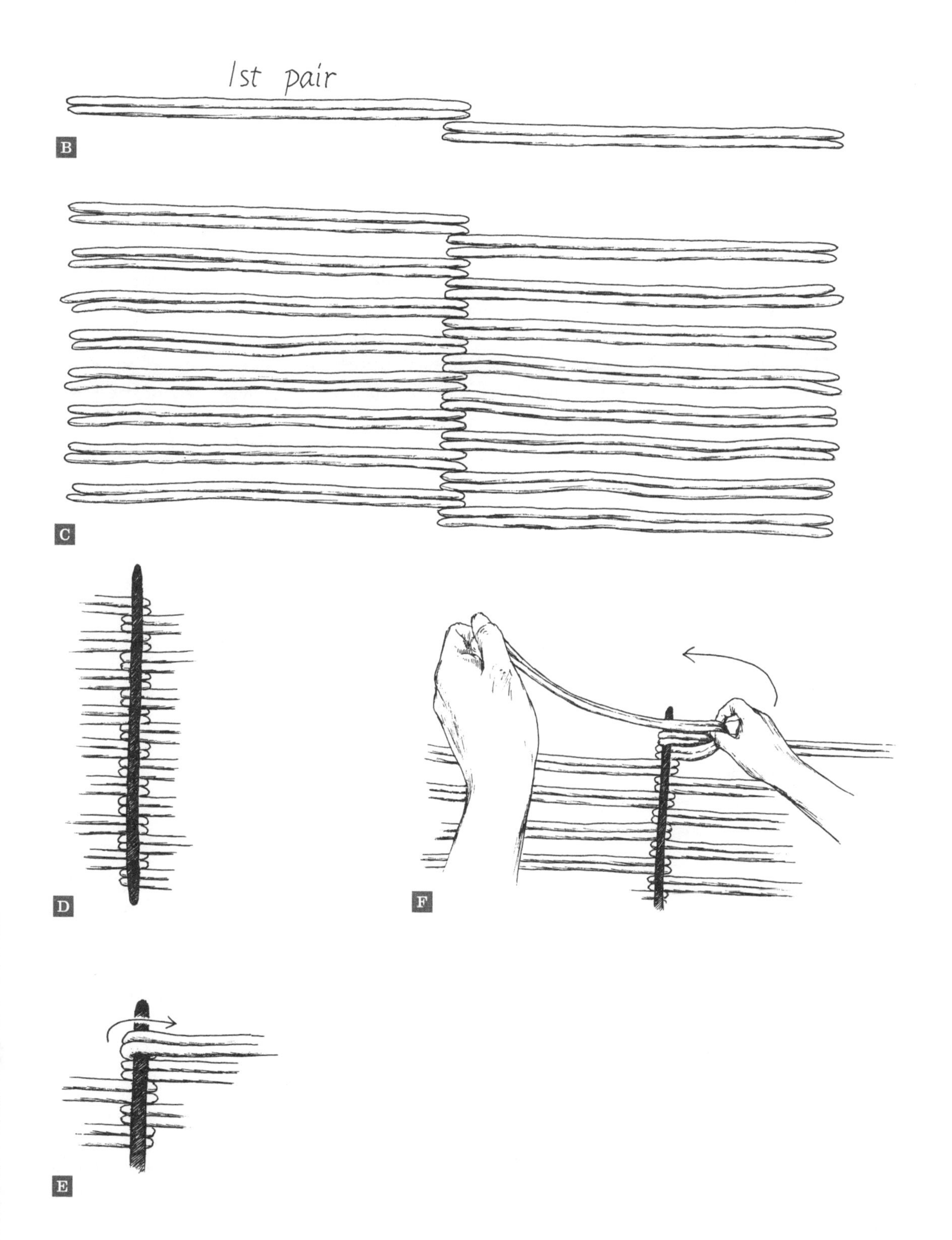
1st pair
B
C
D
F
E

6. Take one of the dark cross strands and lay it on top of the long strands at the point of overlap, as in illustration D on page 323. Now take the first pair of strands that were laid down, bring it from the left side over the top of the cross strand, and lay it on the bench on the right side, as in illustration E. Take the next pair of long strands from the right side, bring it over the cross strand and lay it on the bench on the left side, as in illustration F. Continue with this pattern until all 16 pairs of long strands have been brought to the opposite side. The cross strand should be in a straight line once the long strands have been brought over to their new positions; therefore, take care and place the strands in their new location without undue pulling. Throughout the entire weaving procedure, check frequently to be sure the cross strands remain straight. Use a light touch, and leave just a bit of air space in the weaving to allow for expansion as the dough rises and then bakes. If the weaving is excessively tight, the lack of room for expansion will cause the dough to twist and lose symmetry in the oven.

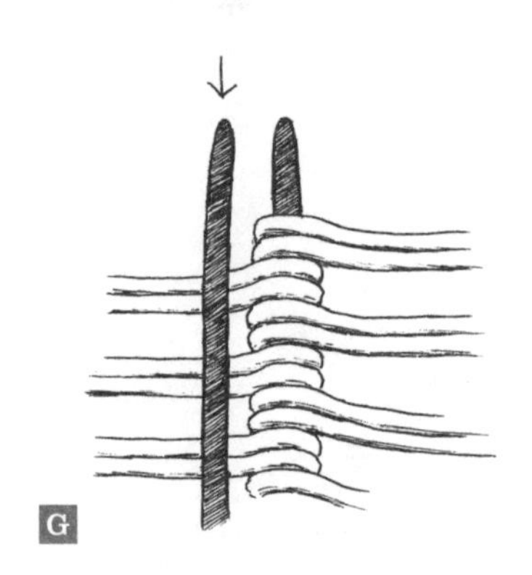

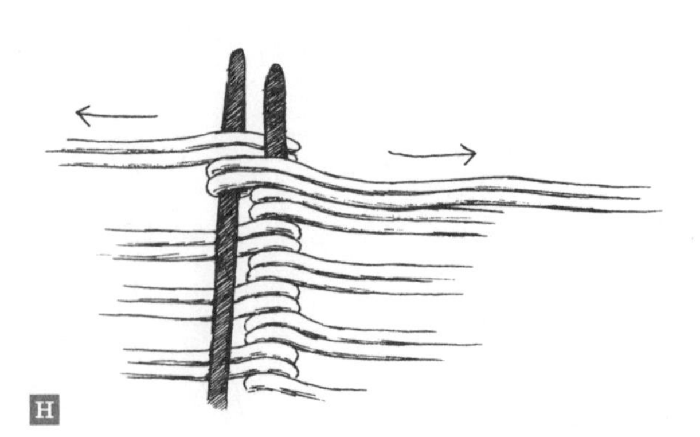

7. Take the second cross strand and place it parallel and to the left of the first strand, as in illustration G. Now, bring the long strands back over this second cross strand, beginning with the first pair and working to the other side. See illustration H. A third cross strand is now laid down and the process continues. Repeat the procedure until all the cross strands have been used.

8. Take the oval cardboard template and place it over the finished lattice. Next, take a sharp knife or pizza wheel and cut around the template. Once cut, pull away the scrap dough and remove the template. Run a large palette knife under the lattice to free up any areas that may be sticking to the bench. Once you are sure that the lattice is free, carefully slide your hands underneath it. Spread your

fingers absolutely as wide as you can, lift the lattice, and transfer it to the sheet pan lined with parchment. Some of the strands may have come free from the weaving as you transferred the piece, so take a moment and bring them back to their correct positions. Check the symmetry of the lattice, particularly the right-angle relationship between the long and the cross strands. The transferring of the lattice is always a nervous time. You can do it by yourself, with care and confidence. But if a trustworthy friend is close by, don't hesitate to ask for a bit of assistance for this step.

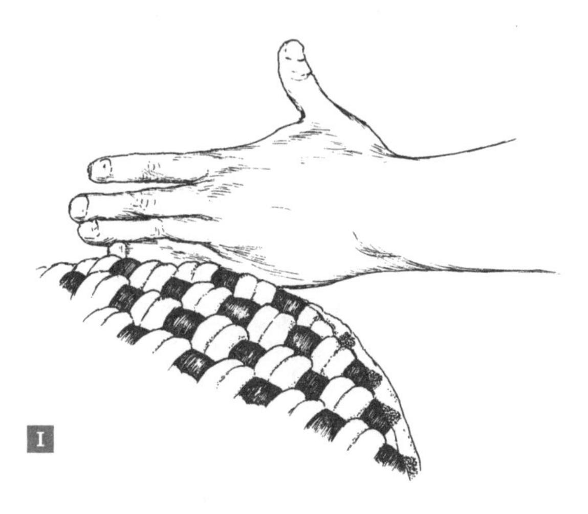

9. Using your thumb, the heel of your hand, or a small rolling pin, press around the perimeter of the lattice, flattening a rim ¾ inch wide, as in illustration I. Refrigerate the sheet pan while you prepare to make an outer border for the lattice.

10. The outer border is made from the four 4.5-ounce strands of dough. Roll these out, one by one, until you meet the dough's resistance, that is, until you have rolled it as long as possible without tearing it. Let the strands relax under a sheet of plastic until they can be rolled further. Continue to elongate the strands, stopping always when the dough is at the point of tearing and allowing it to relax again, until the strands are approximately 5 feet long. Place the ends together and lay a weight on the joined ends. Make a braid similar to the first 4-strand braid detailed on page 300. The length of the finished braid must be long enough to enclose the perimeter of the lattice, in this case about 4½ feet. Refer to the notes at the end of this section for tips on making braids with extra-long strands of dough.

J

K

11. Remove the lattice from refrigeration and lightly egg wash the flattened portion of the perimeter. Once the egg wash has become tacky and can function as glue, the 4-strand braid can be placed around the lattice. Illustration J shows the outer braid being placed at the edge of the lattice. Note that it is positioned precisely in the center, midway between the left and right ends of the lattice. Carefully wind the braid around the perimeter, laying it loosely around on the flattened base made earlier and avoiding pulling or stretching the braid. When the braid has returned to the starting position, lay the end down. Check the entire rim of the lattice to be sure the border braid has been evenly applied, making any necessary adjustments. When you are satisfied with its placement, cut off any excess dough from the end of the braid. Carefully interweave the 2 ends of the border braid. As much as possible, try to make this area of joining so smooth that no one can tell where the braid has begun. See illustration K. There is an important reason for beginning the border braid in the center of the lattice. Ideally, the 2 braided ends will remain intact during the bake, but that is not always the case. Sometimes one of the strands in the border braid pops up. If this happens, a simple dough flower or some decorative motif can be applied after the bake. People seeing the finished lattice will think that, as a special flourish, the baker placed a flower symmetrically at the edge. This same flower would look quite out of place if it were at some other point around the perimeter.

12. Once the border is on, the assembly of the platter is complete. Before baking, though, the work has to relax completely. Therefore, refrigerate it for a minimum of 1 hour. Since there is so little yeast in the dough, it can remain refrigerated for up to 24 hours with no ill effects. There is no need to cover the platter with plastic; in fact, by leaving it uncovered, the distinction of the individual strands is greater.

13. The platter bakes at approximately 360°F. Before loading it into the oven, carefully brush it with egg wash. Take enough time to be thorough, but avoid pools of egg in any of the creases. Bake time will be upwards of 1 hour. If the platter is taking on color too quickly, lower the oven temperature by 10°F. If the temperature is too high, or if the bake too long, the light strands will darken to the point that their color is indistinguishable from that of the dark strands. When you think the platter is fully baked, turn it over carefully. The bottom should have taken on color (although the seams may still be somewhat pale), indicating the piece is baked through.

When you are satisfied that the bake is done, transfer the platter to a wire cooling rack. Leave it for at least 12 hours in order to expel the internal moisture. If left overnight on a sheet pan, the bottom of the platter would sweat, and in all likelihood mold would form within a few days, completely spoiling all your hard work. If the platter was properly egg washed before the bake, there is no need to spray it with varnish or lacquer. It will keep its lovely shine for many months.

A Few Construction Notes: We've chosen to make the oval platter using paired long strands and single cross strands. This, of course, is an optional construction method, but one that has a couple of merits worth noting. First of all, it takes half the time to cross over the paired strands as it would if the strands were treated individually and not in pairs. By using paired strands, there is less risk of the dough dehydrating or overaging. When working with 60 strands, any time we can save that doesn't impair the finished project is time well saved. Aside from easier assembly, the combination of paired long strands and individual cross strands is visually interesting. The visual aspect of the platter is also enhanced by the use of dark dough for the cross strands.

The Decorative Dough used is comparatively dry. Although this is appropriate for this type of work, the dry condition of the dough can pose difficulties. If the strands seem to just slide along the bench and refuse to roll and lengthen, the cause is usually not enough downward pressure being exerted by the hands. There are times, however, when the dough will slide around regardless of the efforts exerted to roll it out. A lightly moistened cloth can be kept at hand in this event. Wipe it across the bench as needed; this will provide some traction and make the rolling much easier. Be careful not to overdo it: Too much water on the bench will make the surface of the strands pasty. Assembly in this case will be difficult, and the strands will tend to merge together and not stand out distinctly one from another.

Rolling and braiding the border can be a challenge, particularly since the individual strands are almost 5 feet long. When rolling strands of great length like these, one tip worth remembering is to work on the strand in sections rather than as one long unit. Use both hands to elongate the left half of it, then leave that area alone and work on the right half of the strand. Continue like this until you have sufficient length. As always, strive for an even diameter to the entire strand, with no significant lumps, bumps, or valleys down its length. Braiding these long strands can also be somewhat daunting. Here's a way to ease that difficult undertaking: After weighting down the strands at one end, double back a foot or so of the strands at the other end. This way, when you begin to braid, instead of trying to work with an unwieldy length of several feet, you will have effectively shortened the working length of the strands.

Heart-Shaped Platter with Marbleized Rim

(color photograph 29)

The construction of the heart-shaped platter begins almost identically to that of the oval platter. Before beginning the project, have a cut-out heart-shaped template on hand. For the present example, the template should measure 16 inches across at its widest point, and 12 inches through its center line, suitable for a standard sheet pan. As in the construction of the oval platter, the long horizontal strands for the heart are made with light decorative dough (but we will use them singly and not paired as we did for the oval platter), and the vertical cross strands with dark dough.

1. We begin by scaling the dough pieces that will become the rim of the heart. The rim is constructed of 2 strands of dough fashioned into a rope border. Each of the 2 strands consists of 1 light and 1 dark dough piece, which have been kneaded together. Divide 2 light and 2 dark pieces weighing 3.5 ounces each. Join the light pieces to the dark, and knead them until they are sufficiently marbleized. Note that they are not rolled to full length at this point. Once ready, wrap the 2 rim pieces in plastic and leave them until the heart has been woven and cut.

2. Now, divide 32 light strands and 22 dark strands, each weighing 1.75 ounces (press weight for a 36-part divider is 4 pounds). Begin by rolling the light strands 24 inches long. In all likelihood, the dough will show resistance to full elongation, and the strands will therefore be rolled out in 2 phases. Roll the strands only until you risk tearing the dough. Leave them in chronological order on the bench as you proceed. Once all 32 strands have been partially rolled, the first ones will be relaxed and can be extended to the full length. Now roll the 22 dark strands in the same manner, to about 16 inches long.

A

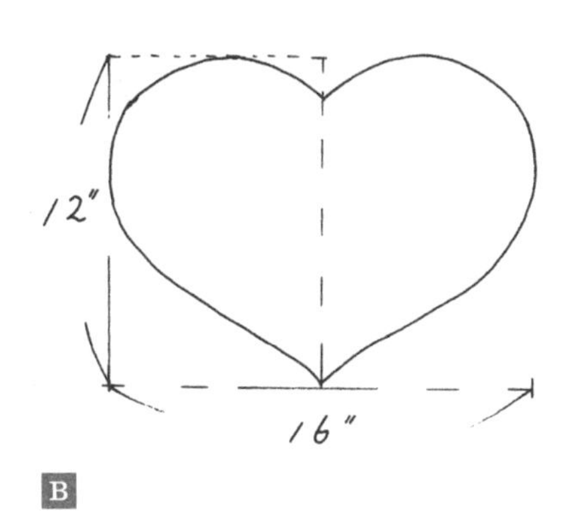

B

3. The lattice is woven in the same manner as the oval platter, so refer to those illustrations for a visual representation of the process. The only difference is that the light strands are not paired for the heart. Once woven, place the heart template over the lattice, being sure, in the interest of symmetry, that one of the cross strands is lined up in the center of the heart, so that it intersects both the lower point of the heart and the area where the 2 lobes of the heart meet. See illustration A. Carefully cut around the template (illustration B) using a sharp knife or pizza wheel. Remove the excess dough and the template, and carefully transfer the heart to a sheet pan lined with parchment paper. Now, press with your thumb around the entire perimeter of the heart, making a flat edge that will hold the rim. Refrigerate the heart as you make the border.

4. Roll the 2 marbleized border pieces to approximately 5 feet long. They should be evenly slender along their entire length, with no unsightly lumps and bumps. Fashion them into a 2-strand rope, as

in the first 2-strand braid detailed on page 296. Once the rope is formed, lay a weight on each end and allow the rope to relax for 5 minutes or so. This relaxation period is important, for it gives the strands time to lose their "memory." If the border were applied without this rest time, the braid would have a tendency to unravel, either during proofing or in the oven.

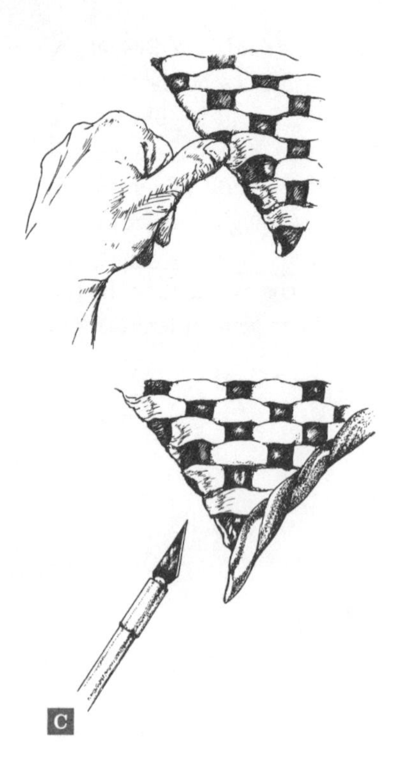

5. When the border rope has relaxed sufficiently (lift off one of the weights—if the rope stays more or less in place and doesn't unwind, it is ready to go), egg wash the flattened rim of the heart. When it is tacky enough to serve as glue, the border rope can be applied. Cut one end of the rope on a steep angle, as in illustration C. Place the cut end slightly below the bottom of the heart, again as in illustration C. Now work the rope around the perimeter of the heart, loosely, without stretching. Press the rope deeply into the area of the heart where the 2 lobes meet. Continue around until you have covered the entire heart. Cut the rope again, with an angle corresponding to, but opposite, the initial cut. Join the 2 ends together as seamlessly as possible. If the strands pop up during the bake, this area can be covered with a small cut-out heart.

6. Refrigerate the heart for at least 1 hour or up to 24 hours, so it relaxes completely before baking. Egg wash thoroughly and bake at 360°F. Observe the same baking precautions as for the oval platter. If necessary, lower the oven temperature by 10°F if the heart is taking on color too quickly. Once baked, transfer the heart to a wire cooling rack and leave for 12 hours or more to expel as much dough moisture as possible.

Like the oval platter, the heart will keep well for a long while. Again like the oval platter, the heart serves well as a serving tray. Put some of your nice loaves on it and bring to the table, honoring both your breads and your guests.

Cornucopia (color photograph 31)

A bakery speaks of bounty and abundance, honest flavors and honest work, and the cornucopia embodies and mirrors those qualities perfectly. Mounded full with its profusion of rolls and breads and *viennoiserie,* and prominently displayed in the shop window or on a counter, enticing customers with the skill of its construction and the alluring contents, the cornucopia is the apotheosis of the harvest and holiday season. There are many ways to construct this "horn of plenty." In its simplest form, a single coil of dough is wound around a conical form. That form may be fashioned from heavy poster board or, more elaborately, from chicken wire snipped, curved, and wired into the desired shape. Sometimes, branches with leaves or vines with grapes are applied to the outside of the finished shape. In the present example, the cornucopia is built from a woven lattice, as in the oval and heart platters. This form of construction is more complex and requires more dexterity than simply winding one coil of dough around a form, but the results are a pleasure to look at, and the long life expectancy of the finished piece makes the baker's efforts worthwhile.

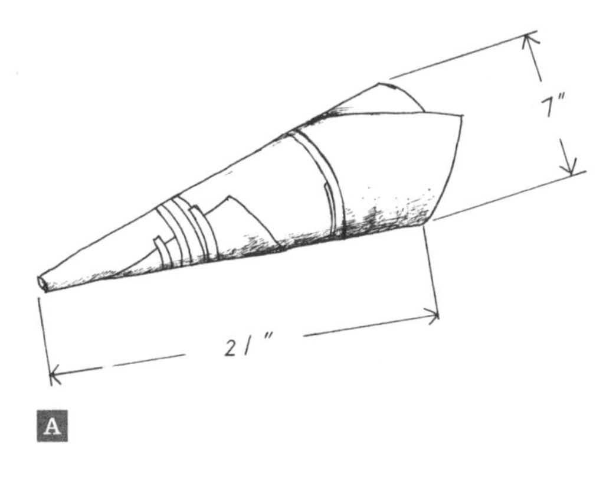

A

The lattice for our cornucopia is made using paired long strands and single cross strands. Since much of the focus will be on the baked goods spilling from the opening, light dough is used for both long and cross strands. The cornucopia itself will therefore be more subtle, which is desirable in this case. The finish will be a 3-strand braid made with dark dough, boldly encircling the mouth of the cornucopia.

1. The first step is to take a piece of heavy poster board and wind it into a cone shape. Tape it well, and then trim the opening with a sharp knife. Illustration A above shows how to fashion the cone. Stuff the cone with tightly wadded aluminum foil or newspaper so that the weight of the dough won't cause the cone to collapse in the oven. One word of caution: The cornucopia must fit into the oven! Be certain that the height of the poster board at the opening is low enough to be accommodated by the oven. For many bakers this will not pose a problem, but with a hearth-style deck oven, the diameter of the cone at its high point will be limited by the height of the deck.

2. The cornucopia in the present example is sized to fit a standard sheet pan. Begin by first weighing 3 pieces of dark dough for the rim, at 3 ounces each (if no dark dough is on hand, the rim can of course be constructed with light dough, which will result in a cornucopia with slightly less contrast between the body and the rim). Lightly round the 3 rim pieces, wrap them in plastic, and refrigerate while you proceed.

3. For the lattice itself, 68 strands of dough will be woven. Both the long as well as the cross strands weigh 2.5 ounces (press weight for a 36-part divider is 5 pounds, 10 ounces). Roll the strands in 2 phases, as in the two preceding projects. In all, 42 long strands, rolled to 36 inches, and 26 cross strands, rolled to 20 inches, are required. Build the lattice in the same manner as for the oval platter. The finished dimensions should be approximately 28 inches long by 18 inches wide.

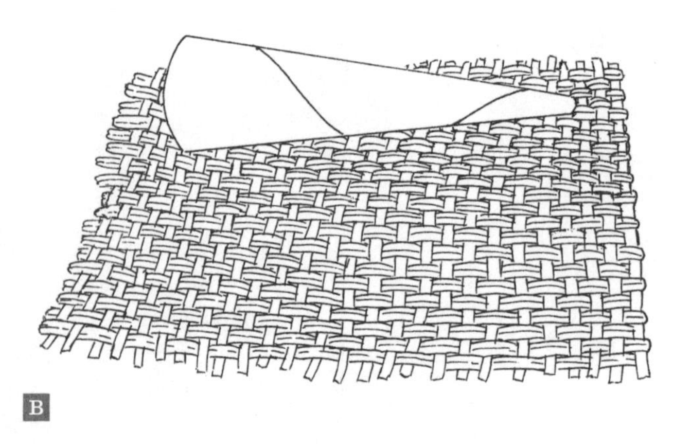

B

4. Once the lattice has been braided, trim it to remove the scrap around the perimeter. Lightly egg wash the surface, and when the egg has become tacky and will serve as glue, lay on the cone, as in illustration B. Note that the cone is placed parallel to the length of the lattice and close to the top edge. Now, slowly roll the cone toward you, pressing the dough into the cone as you do so (an extra pair of hands can be quite helpful here, so you may want to conscript a friend who happens to be close by). If any areas of dough are sagging and falling from the cone, unroll it and begin again. Remember though, that the egg wash is in a gluing phase, so

try to get a tight adherence of cone and dough with the first roll. When you have rolled the cone so that it is completely encircled with dough, take a sharp knife or pizza wheel and trim the dough where the edges join. A small bit of overlap is advised, so that a full, tight seam can be made at this joint.

5. Carefully lift the cornucopia onto a sheet pan lined with parchment paper, with the seam on the bottom—out of sight and unable to come apart. Check the entire piece for evenness and balance, making any adjustments as necessary. If a tag end of dough protrudes from the rear of the piece, it can be trimmed and curved to enhance the cornucopia's shape.

6. Now, it's time to work on the opening. First, trim the excess dough from the opening, leaving a rim of cardboard about ½ inch wide all around the mouth. Take the 3 strands of refrigerated dark dough and roll them to approximately 20 inches long. Make a standard braid with these 3 strands. Lightly egg wash the mouth of the cornucopia, and when the glue has become tacky, apply the braid so that the seam is on the bottom of the cornucopia. The braid should cover both the cardboard rim and the edge of the cornucopia, making a clean finish around the entire periphery. See illustration C for the correct orientation of this braid.

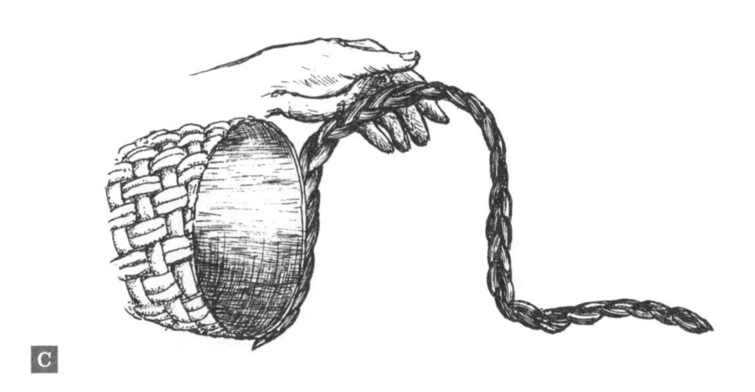

C

7. As with the previous projects, refrigerate the cornucopia for at least 1 hour to relax it. Egg wash the entire surface and bake at 360°F. It may be necessary to turn the piece from front to back once or twice during the bake if it is coloring unevenly. Lower the oven temperature by 10°F if the cornucopia is taking on color too quickly. Once baked, transfer it to a wire cooling rack to release its internal moisture for at least 12 hours.

Round Decorated Plaque (color photograph 16)

Our last project made using Light Yeasted Decorative Dough marks a departure from the previous projects, both in method of construction and thematic possibility. The round decorated plaque is like a framed picture, with an elaborate border enclosing a scene that can be as varied as the skills and imagination of the baker allow. In this example, we show a baker at the oven, a basket of baked loaves at his side. The outside diameter of the plaque in the present example is 16 inches, sufficient to fit a standard sheet pan. The construction is built once all the components are prepared.

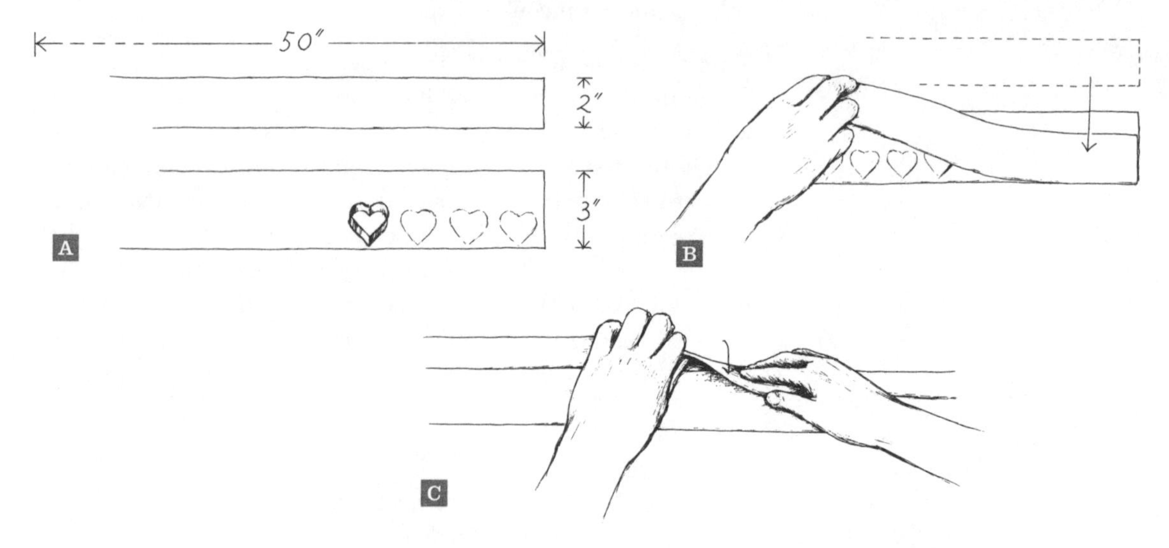

1. The first step is to make a 3-strand braid in the usual fashion. The strands weigh 4.5 ounces each. Roll them long and thin, even from end to end. The finished braid should be 38 inches long. Once formed, place it under a sheet of plastic to prevent it from drying out and refrigerate it.

2. Next, make the outer border. This consists of a 14-ounce dough piece that has been rolled to a flat strip and trimmed to a dimension of 3 by 50 inches. Using a leaf, oval, heart, or other small cutter, cut through the dough at the top edge. Leave an even, symmetrical interval between each cut.

3. Now, take a second 14-ounce piece of dough, roll it out, and trim it to 2 by 50 inches. Lay this piece over the cut piece previously rolled, placing it even with the bottom edge of the cut piece. There will be a 1-inch strip of dough protruding from the top of the 3-inch piece. Lightly egg wash this 1-inch strip. Fold it up and press

D

it into the top (2-inch) piece. Now turn this entire joined border over. The cuts made will be on top, backed by an underlying strip of dough. Carefully transfer this border piece to a sheet pan, cover it with plastic, and refrigerate. Refer to illustration C to see the progress to this point.

4. Next, roll out a sheet of dough, the center of the plaque, onto which you will later apply the baking scene: Take a piece of dough weighing about 1.5 pounds and roll it approximately ¼ inch thick and 14 inches in diameter. Place the dough on a sheet pan lined with a piece of parchment paper and rest it thoroughly under plastic. Once it is completely relaxed, about 20 minutes, place a 12-inch round on top of the dough (a cake pan or cake round works well for this) and carefully cut around the perimeter. Remove the excess dough. Cover the dough round with plastic and refrigerate.

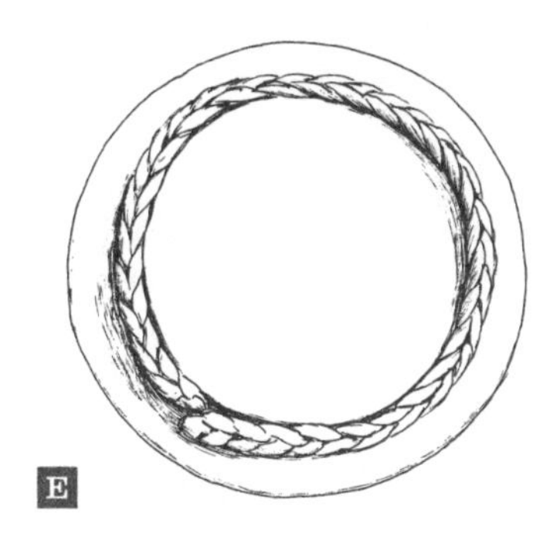

E

5. Now, take a 3-pound piece of dough, which will function as the base for the plaque. Roll this dough to an 18-inch round about ⅜ inch thick. Transfer to a sheet of parchment paper and onto an inverted sheet pan. Using a dough docker (lacking one, a fork will do), thoroughly dock the dough and let it rest, covered with plastic. Cut the relaxed dough to a 16-inch-diameter round. Transfer it from the back of the sheet pan by sliding the parchment paper onto the front side of a second sheet pan.

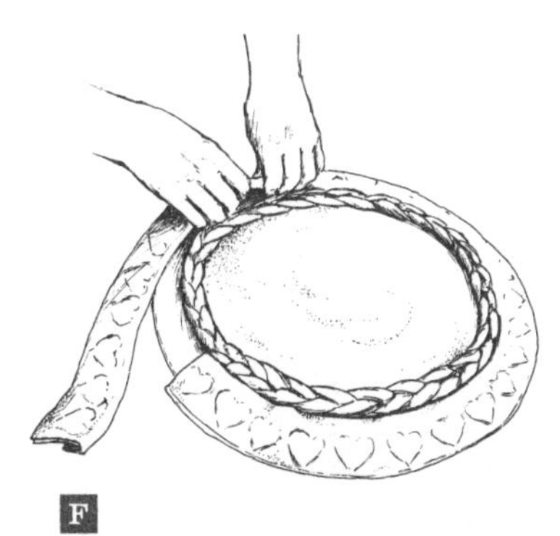

F

6. The construction of the plaque can now proceed:

- Egg wash the 16-inch base layer.
- Apply the 12-inch-round centerpiece. Make sure that it is centered on the base layer (illustration D).
- Apply the 3-strand braid so that about 75 percent of its width is on the centerpiece, with the remaining 25 percent on the base layer (illustration E).
- As shown in illustration F, loosely apply the outer border with its cut motif. The area where this border joins together can later be hidden with a decoration, so be sure the seam is positioned in a way that an applied decoration will not appear out of place. The seam should also line up with the seam of the 3-strand braid.
- Trim any dough that protrudes from the base layer.
- Apply the design of choice. Figures, lettering, and so on can be made from Light or Dark Yeasted Decorative Dough and *pâte morte,* alone or in combination.

- The finished plaque is now refrigerated for 1 hour at least. Prior to the bake, egg wash the surface. More than likely there will be a number of different textures to the plaque, so take the time to be thorough. Bake at 360°F for 15 minutes. Lower the oven temperature by 10°F and bake for another 45 minutes to 1 hour. If any parts of the plaque begin to take on too much color before the entire piece is fully baked, these parts can be covered with small metal cups or pieces of parchment paper to minimize further darkening. Once baked, transfer the plaque to a cooling rack for a minimum of 12 hours.

Pâte Morte

Pâte morte, or "dead dough," is a decorative medium that uses no baker's yeast and offers design possibilities that are limited only by the creative talents of the baker. Whether used to make delicate flowers, subtly browned at the edges from a quick bake; large decorative plaques commemorating an event or simply displayed alluringly in the bakery's front window; or long-lasting baskets lined with dough "cloth," *pâte morte* can be woven, rolled to paper thinness, pressed into molds, cut out into letters or numbers, fashioned into branches, or patterned with overlays of different colors to achieve varying textures—the technical possibilities are varied and offer great potential. The dough is made by first mixing a sugar syrup, which is then cooled and added to sifted flour.

Sugar Syrup for Pâte Morte

	U.S.	METRIC	HOME
Water	2 lb	1 kg	1 lb (2 cups)
Sugar	2 lb	1 kg	1 lb (2 cups)
Corn syrup	1 lb	.5 kg	.5 lb (1 3/8 cups)
TOTAL YIELD	**5 lb**	**2.5 kg**	**2.5 lb**

1. Bring the ingredients to the boil, stirring occasionally to avoid burning the sugar. Once the syrup boils, turn it off to avoid darkening it. Cover and allow it to cool before use. Refrigerated, the syrup keeps for weeks. Glucose can be substituted for the corn syrup.

Pâte Morte

	U.S.	METRIC	HOME	BAKER'S %
White rye flour, sifted	2 lb	1 kg	1 lb (4 cups)	100%
Sugar syrup, approximately	1.3 lb	.65 kg	10.4 oz (1 cup)	65%
TOTAL YIELD	**3.3 lb**	**1.65 kg**	**1 lb, 10.4 oz**	**165%**

1. Using a mixer with a paddle attachment, add the ingredients to the mixing bowl and mix until just smooth. Alternatively, mix the dough by hand until just smooth. Avoid overmixing, as this will cause the dough to bubble in the oven. It is often necessary to adjust the amount of syrup, depending on the relative dryness of the flour. Therefore, stay close to the mixer and check the dough consistency when it is about 90 percent mixed. The finished dough should be quite firm, but not at all crumbly. Once mixed, wrap the *pâte morte* in plastic.

Note the following special considerations:

- The dough must be on the stiff side so that the shaped pieces retain their distinction and don't merge together. Therefore, *thorough* covering of the unused dough with plastic is important to prevent dehydration.
- White rye is the flour of choice because of its low gluten content and fine particle size. Medium and whole rye are not suitable for fine work due to their granular nature.
- Ciril Hitz, a highly skilled Swiss pastry chef living in the United States, has developed an innovation: He uses about 25 percent light buckwheat flour to 75 percent white rye; the inclusion of buckwheat helps reduce the formation of surface bubbles on the pieces as they bake, and facilitates the rolling out of the dough.
- The dough accepts color readily. Caramel color can be added to the syrup to make a darker-hued dough. Swirling 2½ ounces of caramel color or coffee extract into 1.3 pounds of syrup yields a dough with a deep, rich tone. Other additions are cinnamon, chili powder, paprika, and ground turmeric, which give the dough varying shades of reddish or brick hues, or soft yellow in the case of turmeric. Cocoa can be used in lieu of caramel color. About 1.5 ounces of powder to 2 pounds of flour is a good amount to begin with; increase or decrease the powders to vary the shades. Don't use cayenne pepper!

- White flour with about 12 percent protein can be used all or partly in place of the rye. The gluten in white flour makes it more difficult to achieve fine, thin flower petals or leaves, but it can be a good choice when a whiter color is desired rather than the grayish cast of the all-rye dough. A portion of cake flour added along with the white flour enables the dough to be rolled thinner, with less shrinkage. *Pâte morte* made with white flour accepts dye readily.
- For fine work, such as fashioning flowers, branches, and leaves, it's best to use the dough within a few hours of mixing it. Even when wrapped and refrigerated, the dough slowly dehydrates, and as the dough gets older it becomes less suitable for these types of applications.
- When hot from the oven, the pieces have a matte tone. To give them a brilliant shine, use a fine paintbrush and carefully brush them with the sugar syrup. For intricate items like wheat stalks, where complete coverage is impractical, use the syrup simply to highlight the wheat and give an overall luster. Food-grade sprays can be used to achieve shine, although they are not always easy to come by. Coffee extract can also be brushed onto the pieces, either prior to, or just after the bake.

A Stalk of Wheat

1. To fashion a stalk of wheat from *pâte morte,* take a piece of dough about the size of a large grape. Roll it briskly between your palms into a sphere. Place the ball onto the bench, and begin to elongate about 50 percent of it into a thin rope. This portion of the dough

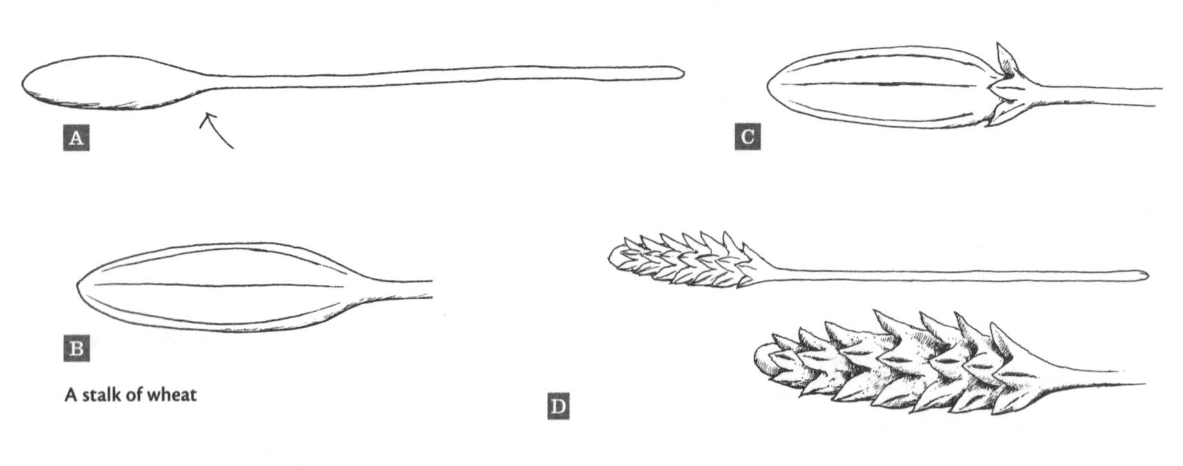

A stalk of wheat

will become the stalk; the other 50 percent, as yet unrolled, will become the head of the wheat. Since the dough is on the dry side to begin with, don't use dusting flour on the bench.

2. Once the stalk section has been rolled out, begin tapering the remaining part of the dough into an elongated oval shape. Illustration A shows the progress to this point. Notice that the stalk remains quite thin right up to the neck of the wheat, where it then opens abruptly into the shape of the head. Next, take a thin-bladed knife and scribe 3 lines down the entire length of the head. The first line is made right down the center, with the other 2 on the near and far shoulder. Refer to illustration B for the correct spacing of the lines.

3. A pair of scissors is used for the final step in fashioning the wheat stalk. Take a small snip of dough that bisects the middle of the 3 lines, close by the end of the wheat head where it tapers to the stalk. Take a second snip with the scissors, of the same size as the first, along the line on the far side of the dough. Then take a third snip in the same manner along the near side of the dough. Illustration C shows the progress to this point. Now return to the center line, and repeat the scissor cuts, first in the center, then on the far side, and finally on the near side, always aligning the scissors in the center of the scribed lines. Continue this pattern of snipping down the entire length of the dough. Illustration D shows the finished stalk of wheat and a close-up of the snipped kernels. Notice how the individual kernels are all bisected, just as they are in nature. It's true that if you make a large display piece, using dozens of finely crafted wheat stalks, all carefully snipped, most people viewing it will not notice your subtle efforts at all, and with a quick glance just pass by. Noble art museums are little different; after an hour or two of gazing at great art, people can be heard saying, "oh, not another Vermeer" as they stroll off to the café.

A Rose

Owning a bakery was a great opportunity for me, because I was able to pursue learning in a number of aspects of baking and pastry that might not have been lucrative on their own, but which contributed to product variety and ever-changing window and bakery counter displays. One month, there might be a display of pulled-sugar flowers on a poured-sugar base; the next month might be a chocolate display as a harbinger of a coming holiday;

and the next month might see a display of fine-filigreed royal icing. One year, I took a class in gum-paste flower production, and found this enjoyable and challenging medium great for small counter displays as well as for wedding cake decoration. I loved the thin, curling petals and artfully formed leaves. From start to finish it might take me an hour to make a complete rose, but I loved the results, and never saw the time spent as anything other than valuable and important. Shortly after learning the fundamentals of gum paste, I was asked to participate in an international competition sponsored by the Société Culinaire Philanthropique in New York City. I was happy to accept the invitation, and set to work trying to refine my skills. I was making an elaborate bread display, and found myself experimenting with flowers made from *pâte morte*. Soon, I was using gum-paste tools and techniques to make the flowers, and found that the results were more delicate and graceful than anything I had yet been able to do. Here is the method I used, and still use, for making a rose.

1. Take a piece of fresh *pâte morte* about the size of a golf ball and roll it into a cylinder ½ inch in diameter. Cut off a small nub the size of a cranberry, roll it into a sphere, and fashion it so that one end comes to a fine point and the other end remains bulbous and rounded. This will become the core of the rose; although it will eventually be hidden by the petals, the core will determine the final size and shape of the rose. Now cut twelve ½-inch sections from the cylinder. These will become the individual petals. Using the

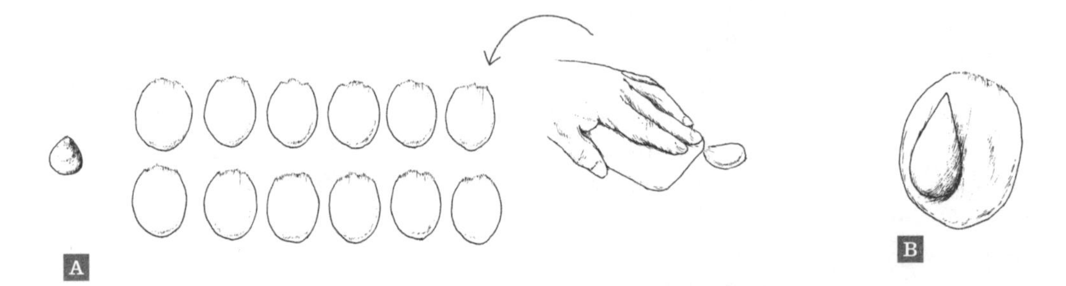

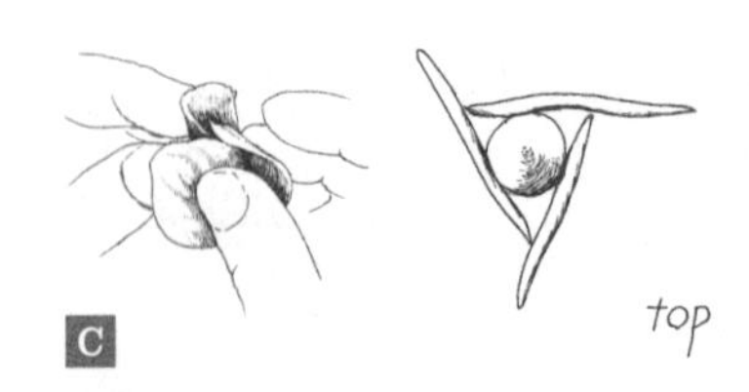

rounded corner edge of a plastic bowl scraper, flatten one side of each petal until it is rounded and quite thin. A few helpful hints: It's a bit easier to work on a steel table, although wood can be used if a steel table isn't available. A very thin layer of vegetable oil on the table helps make a thin petal. And using an artist's palette knife to remove the shaped petal from the table prevents the petal from ripping as it is lifted. Illustration A shows the progress to this point.

2. The next step is to make a 3-petal rosebud. Pick up the bulbous core in your left hand (for righties), with the point facing up. Take 1 petal and place it on the far side of the core, with about half the width of the petal exposed on the right side of the core, and with a small portion of the petal protruding above the core, as in illustration B. Take a second petal and place it so that one edge is snugly positioned on the right side of the core. This edge should also be touching the first petal, and the top of this second petal should be at the same height as the first one. Now, take a third petal and treat it just as you did the second petal, placing one edge against the second petal, tight to the core. Refer to illustration C. Wrap the right-hand portion of each petal in a clockwise motion (viewed from the top). Use your thumb to fold back the 3 petals so they take on a graceful appearance. The top edges should be very thin; if there are little irregularities or small tears, so much the better: The rose will be more lifelike if the petals look just a little rough. The opening at the top should be small, with the cone point recessed below the juncture of the 3 petals, and almost none of the point visible when viewed from above. Roll the base of the dough between both index fingers so that the petals and top portion of the dough take on a bulb shape. The excess dough on the bottom can be removed. It is too difficult to rework this scrap dough, and it should be discarded. Illustration D shows the completed bud.

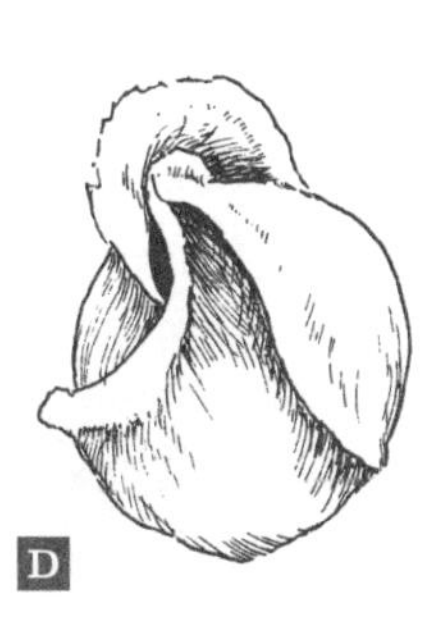

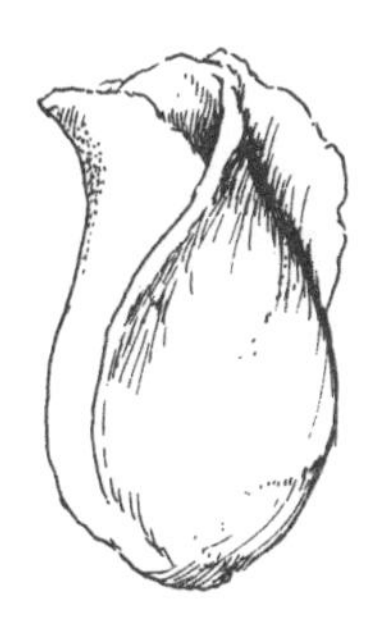
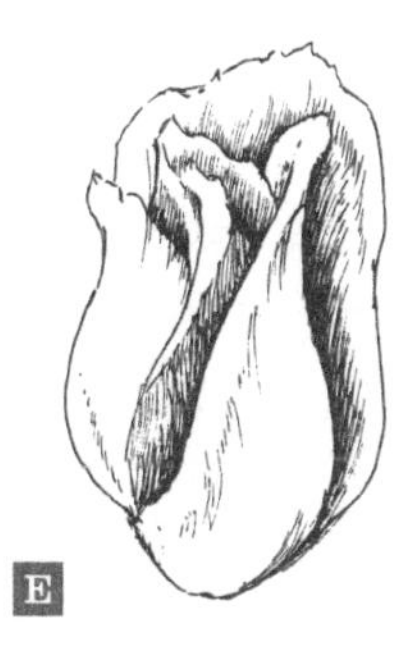

3. Now, a layer of petals is affixed to the bud. Hold the bud in your left hand and place a shaped petal on the far side of the bud, its height the same as the height of the bud petals. Gently curve the petal so that it contours with the shape of the bud. Take a second petal and tuck an edge inside the first petal, so that the first petal overlaps the second one by about one-third of its width. Refer to illustration E for visual details. Add a third and fourth petal to complete the second layer of the rose. Gracefully flare the petals, giving them a natural curve. Again, roll the base of the dough

F

between both index fingers, remove the excess dough from the base, and manipulate the rose into a bulbous shape.

4. A third layer is now added on, this one consisting of 5 petals. The technique is the same as for the second layer, but be sure to offset the first petal so that it originates at the space between 2 petals of the second layer, and is not placed directly behind a second-layer petal. Remove the excess dough from the base again, and manipulate the shape of the petals and base until you are satisfied that it is properly rose shaped. The rose is now full size (see illustration F), and ready for a calyx. Keep in mind that when making a number of roses, a considerable amount of time can be saved, and the results will be more interesting, if some of the roses are full sized, others are made with 1 outer layer after the 3 bud petals are affixed, and others are fashioned with only the 3 bud petals. In fact, a delicate bud can be made using just a small core and 1 wrapped and flared petal.

5. Roses have a calyx consisting of 5 sepals, or modified leaves, that rise upward from underneath the base of the flower. If you have a gum-paste calyx cutter, it works perfectly well with pâte morte. If you don't, you can eliminate the calyx altogether. Roll out a small piece of dough until it is thin and even. Cut out the calyx using the cutter. Notice how the outer edges of each leaf are rigidly cut, and how lifeless the shape is. Rub a little flour into one of your palms. Place the calyx in your palm, and using either a gum-paste ball tool or a pencil eraser, begin to flatten and flare each of the 5 sections. The edges should be thin and leaflike. With a small brush, wet the center of the calyx with water, then press it into the bottom of the

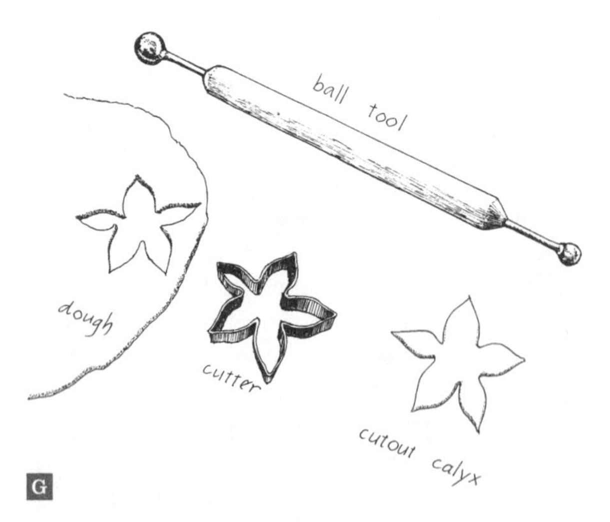

G

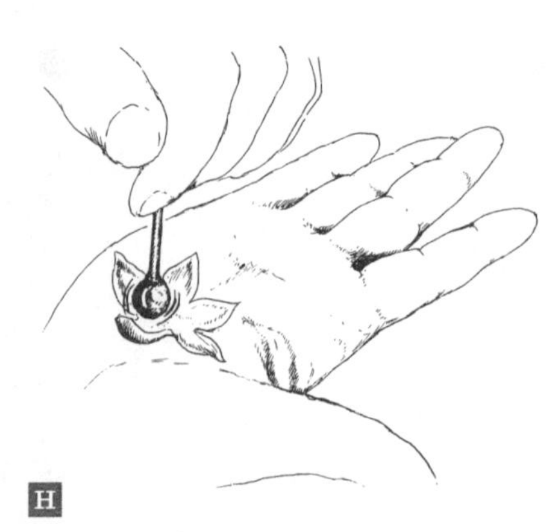

H

rose. Shape the 5 individual sepals upward around the base, so that each leaf is shaped slightly different from the others. Use a little more water if the calyx droops away from the base too much. Illustration G, H, and I show the calyx construction and application.

6. The last step in the production of the rose is the making of the leaves. Roll out another small piece of dough until it is thin. Cut leaf shapes either using a cutter or freehand with a paring or X-ACTO knife (see illustration J). They are then further thinned at the edges, either by placing the leaves under a strip of plastic and flattening the edges, or by pressing the individual leaves between the halves of metal or silicone leaf molds. Once shaped, use a fine knife to vein them (unless they've been pressed in molds). See illustration K. Then crinkle a sheet of aluminum foil and lay the leaves on it so that they take on randomly curled shapes. They will be baked on the foil in order to retain their distinct shapes. They will then be glued to the rose once everything is baked.

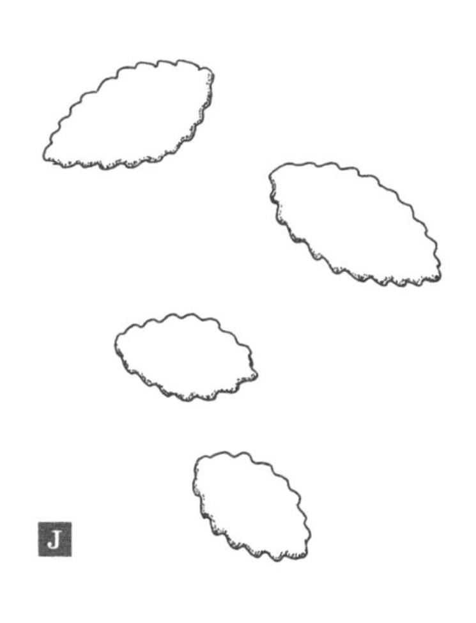

7. The roses and leaves can now be left to dry for a day or more, or baked right away. The main purpose of baking them is to firm them, but the oven has another, wonderful effect. The thin outer edges of the petals take on color fairly quickly, and this gives the rose a nice varied aspect, darker at the fringe of the petals, lighter as the dough thickens near the base. Oven temperature is not too important, but a close eye is, so that the rose and the petals don't take on too much color. Nevertheless, don't bake in an oven that is either too fierce or too timid.

8. The final step is the gluing of the leaves to the rose. Four or 5 leaves are plenty for 1 rose. Place them so they are coming up from the base of the rose or along a stalk at different angles. A glue gun is handy for the gluing, but a cooked-sugar glue can also be used. Whatever type of glue is used, a small bead at the base of the leaf is all that is needed. Apply it quickly to the rose or to the stalk, and hold the leaf onto the surface for a few seconds until the glue has hardened. Color photograph 35 shows finished roses and buds.

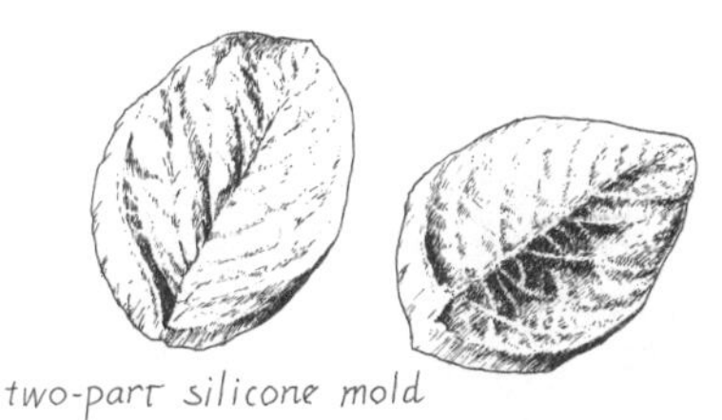

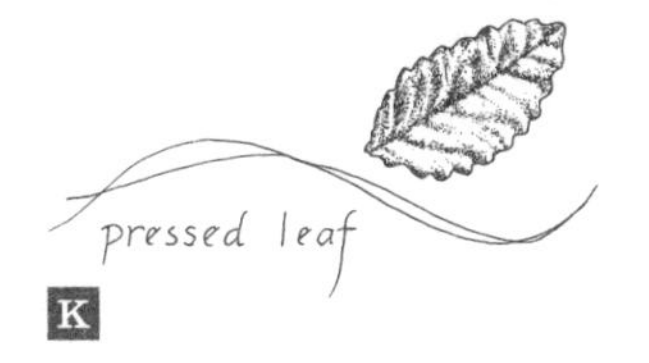

Cooking Sugar for Glue and Making Coffee Extract

An extremely durable glue can be made from cooked sugar, which can then be applied to leaves, branches, and handles for baskets; in fact, this food-grade glue can be used anywhere you need to affix segments of baked decorative dough. To make it, put 8 ounces of water into a small, heavy saucepan. Pour over it 1$^1/_2$ pounds of sugar (in other words, work with a ratio of 1 part water to 3 parts sugar). Begin cooking the sugar over medium heat, stirring occasionally to prevent the sugar from scorching on the bottom of the pot. It helps too to brush the sides of the pot with a clean brush dipped in water, in order to prevent possible recrystallization of the cooked sugar. Stir and wash the sides 3 or 4 times during the first 5 minutes or so. Once the sugar is boiling, don't stir or brush it anymore. Put a thermometer into the pot. As the sugar cooks, water will evaporate out of the mixture and the sugar will become visibly thicker. Eventually, it will change in color too, going from clear to whitish and eventually amber. Watch carefully, and once the sugar reaches about 316°F, remove the pot from the heat and immerse the bottom of the pot in a pan of cold water to prevent further cooking of the sugar.

The sugar is now ready to be used as glue. The need for caution is evident: 316°F makes boiling water seem cool by comparison. Using a toothpick or small palette knife, apply the glue at the junction of 2 pieces of dough. A small dab suffices for light objects, for example when gluing leaves to flowers. For larger, structural pieces, a larger bead is necessary to ensure a durable joining. The glue will thicken eventually and become difficult to work with (therefore, have everything ready ahead of time). It can be gently reheated until it is again fluid enough to work with. Cleaning a pot full of hard sugar might seem an insurmountable job, but in fact it is quite easy. All you need do is pour water over the congealed sugar and heat the contents to a rolling boil. This thins the sugar out enough so that it can be poured down the sink.

Isomalt, most commonly used for pulled-sugar work, is a brand of invert sugar that will not crystallize and is easier to work with than granulated sugar. It just needs to be heated until thoroughly melted, with no water added and no brushing of the sides of the pot, and it is ready to use. It is more tolerant of reheating than glue made with granulated sugar. Both of these glues can be a bit fussy, and a glue gun from the hardware store does an admirable job gluing pieces together. It is generally only in bread competitions that you would encounter a situation where everything must be edible, and of course in that situation a cooked-sugar glue is required.

A deeply colored paste can be made from espresso powder, which can then be painted onto branches or woven baskets to give a rich realism. Take a jar of instant espresso powder and pour it into a bowl. Fill the empty jar about two-thirds full with brewed espresso or strong coffee, and pour it over the powder. Whisk thoroughly to dissolve the coffee. Brush the resulting paste onto items made with *pâte morte* before baking, or while they are hot from the oven. In a pastry application, the coffee paste can be added to buttercream to make mocha flavoring. The coffee paste can be stored for several weeks in the refrigerator.

Branches

Branches are easily fashioned with *pâte morte*. Roll a piece of dough with a slight taper. The thicker end will be the base of the branch. With a sharp knife, cut through the dough to create smaller branches coming off the main stem. Carefully roll the cut edges to soften them; otherwise, the sharp line from the cut will give the branches an unnatural appearance. Depending on the size of the dough piece, a few or several smaller branches might be cut from the main stem. Make a few shallow snips with fine scissors to simulate thorns, if appropriate. Once the cutting and rolling is complete, place the branches on crinkled aluminum foil to set up. They are then baked on the aluminum foil and, once baked, they can be brushed with coffee extract while still hot. Flowers and leaves can be applied with cooked sugar or a glue gun once the branches are cool.

A Woven Bread Basket with a "Lace Cloth" Liner (color photograph 33)

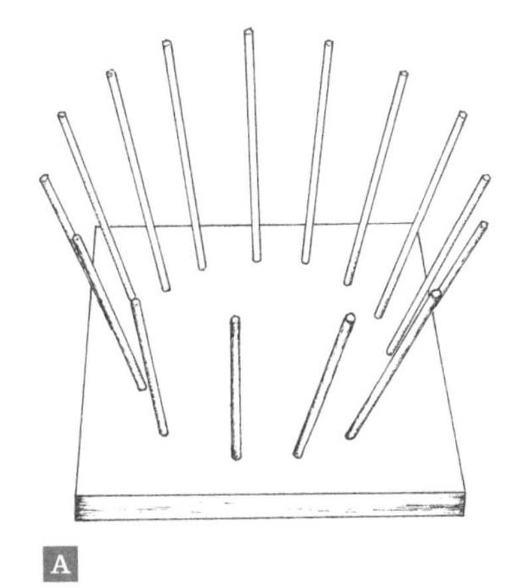

A

In order to make a woven bread basket, a sugar board is required —the same sort of board used to make baskets from pulled sugar. The base for the board is wood or plastic, and there are an odd number of holes bored into it, into which metal pegs are inserted. Some patterns make round baskets, some oval, and others square. Also, on some boards the pegs are vertical to the base, while on others the pegs flare outward. Illustration A shows a sugar board with the pegs inserted, ready to accept the weaving. For this project, coat the base and the pegs with a thin coating of butter or shortening so they can be removed easily from the woven basket after baking.

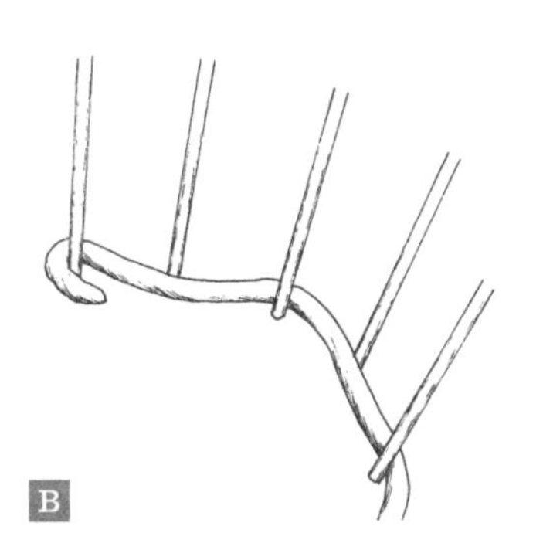

B

1. Roll out a rope of *pâte morte* no more than ¼ inch thick. It's easiest to work with a piece that is no more than 24 inches long. Take one end of the dough and loop it around a peg so that the tag end is inside the circle of pegs. Now, begin weaving the dough rope around the pegs, first to the inside of the adjacent peg, then to the outside of the next peg, and so on until all the dough is used. End by looping the dough around the inside of a peg in the same manner in which you started. Try to keep the dough evenly taut throughout the weaving; however, avoid pulling too hard or the dough may break. Illustration B shows the first loop and the weaving pattern, and illustration C shows the way the end loop is made.

2. Roll another piece of *pâte morte* to the same thickness as the first. Again, make a loop in one end, and this time loop the tag end right on top of the loop made when the first rope of dough was finished off. Weave the dough around the pegs the same way as with the first rope. Continue rolling out ropes and weaving them around the pegs until the basket is at the desired height. Once finished, check the basket for evenness and make any small corrections that are necessary.

3. Next, roll another rope of dough, this time making it slightly thinner than the metal pegs. Measure the height of the basket and cut a sufficient number of dough pegs—these will eventually replace the metal ones. Make sure they are straight and that the ends are just slightly tapered.

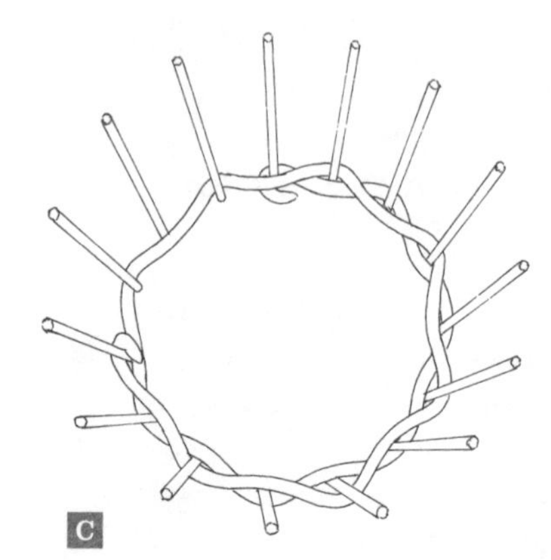

C

4. Dry the basket and the pegs for a day or two; this helps everything keep its shape in the oven. Leaving the basket on the sugarboard base, bake it and the pegs for 2 or 3 hours at 250°F (the pegs will be done after 2 hours). The objective is not to color the dough so much as to thoroughly dry it. Once baked, it is time to make the base.

5. Roll a piece of *pâte morte* about ¼ inch thick and large enough to cover the basket bottom (in this exercise, the base is 6 inches in diameter). Without removing the metal pegs, lift the basket off the base, place on the rolled-out dough, and gently press the pegs into the base to indent it. Use a sharp knife to cut the base, leaving as little dough protruding as possible. Return the basket to the oven and bake for another 1 to 2 hours to dry the base.

6. Once the base has dried and the basket cooled, remove the steel pegs and insert the baked dough pegs. If desired, the basket can be brushed with coffee extract while the basket is still hot. This helps to ensure even absorption.

D

7. The basket can be considered done at this point, ready to hold rolls or small breads. Further elaboration is also possible by adding a handle, a patterned dough cloth, or both.

8. If a handle is desired, it is best made at the same time as the basket. A 4-strand braid has been used for the basket shown in illustration D. The braid is made from the same *pâte morte* as the basket and pegs, and is laid to dry on a sheet pan. For the handle to fit the basket snugly, be sure that the length of the base of the handle, from outside edge to outside edge, is just slightly less than the inside diameter of the basket. After everything has been baked, the handle can be applied to the basket with either the sugar glue described on page 344, or with a glue gun.

9. Making a patterned dough cloth is fun, and also a challenge. The needed tools are a piece of patterned lace or other cloth with an open pattern (solid fabric can't be used), a lattice cutter (like a crimped pizza wheel) or some other implement to cut out the dough cloth, and a spray bottle. Also needed are some cocoa powder and some vodka.

10. Begin by making a *pâte morte* using regular sugar syrup but with bread flour in place of the rye. The dough should be stiff, about 65 percent hydration at most. (It is quite difficult to quantify exactly the correct consistency of the dough, since flour absorption rates vary so much. The dough must be stiff, but if it is too stiff, it may dehydrate and shred; on the other hand, if it is too loose, it also may shred. You may have to make 2 or 3 attempts before getting it just right.) Roll the dough into a thin sheet, $\frac{1}{16}$ inch thick at most. Be sure there is enough dusting flour under the sheet so that it does not stick to the bench. Next, use the lattice cutter to cut out the dough, remembering that it must be large enough to fit inside the basket and also drape over the top. Let the dough dry for 10 or 15 minutes.

Meanwhile, whisk some vodka into 2 tablespoons of cocoa powder, and slowly add more vodka until the paste becomes thin and completely free of lumps. Strain this liquid into the spray bottle. Adjust the nozzle so the spray comes out in a fine, even mist. If the color seems too pale, thin some more cocoa and add it. Next, place the piece of lace or other open-work cloth on top of the dough. Spritz the dough with the cocoa liquid, striving for an even coat. When satisfied that the coverage is adequate, carefully remove the lace. The open pattern of the lace will be visible on the dough. The vodka serves as a propellant and quickly dries, leaving the cocoa behind to color the dough.

Allow the dough to rest uncovered, in a draft-free place, for about 30 minutes. It should be flexible, but dry enough so that it won't rip once placed in the basket. After the rest period, gently lift up the dough piece and place it inside the basket. Allow it to drape naturally over the edge with beautiful folds. The dough lace is so thin that it will dry quite quickly, and there is no need to bake it. The basket is now complete; filled with breads and rolls, it is an impressive and very realistic piece of work.

A Silk-Screened Bread Box with a Patterned Lid (color photograph 32)

Our last decorative project employs a couple of new techniques, including the method used to silk screen a pattern onto the side wall of the bread box, and the patterning of the top of the box. The box here is 7 inches in diameter. To determine the length needed for the silk screen, multiply the diameter by π (pi, which equals 3.14): $7 \times 3.14 = 21.98$ inches for the length of the silk screen. To make the box, you will need a silk screen of suitable length, some cocoa paste, a flat-sided plastic dough scraper, a patterned rolling pin, and a couple of round rings, one that is 7 inches in diameter for the box perimeter and another that is 9 inches in diameter to cut the box lid.

1. Begin by rolling a piece of *pâte morte* about ¼ inch thick and somewhat larger than the finished size of the box lid. Use a grooved or basket-weave rolling pin, and beginning at the end nearest you, press the pin into the dough and begin to roll the pin away from you toward the other side of the dough. Take care to keep the pressure steady and even so that the depth of the impression is consistent. Cut out the lid using a ring an inch or so larger than the ring that will support the side of the box. The edge of the lid can be either smooth or (as in the photo) cut with a scalloped pastry cutter. Transfer the lid to an inverted sheet pan.

2. Next, take a piece of *pâte morte* and fashion it into a handle: Simply roll a piece of dough with tapered ends, roll the ends in a little, and curve the center of the dough. (Handles can also be made with dark or marbleized *pâte morte,* and can be shaped into small spheres, pointed as in a cupola, or fashioned in any variety of ways.) Lay the handle on a baking sheet lined with parchment paper.

3. To make the base of the box, roll another piece of dough to about ¼ inch. Take the 7-inch ring that will support the box side and place it over the dough. Carefully cut the dough from the outside of the ring. Once baked, the base should fit snugly into the bottom of the box. But shrinkage may be a factor, so it's a good idea to cut 2 or 3 bases, each slightly larger than the prior one, so that after the bake the best size can be used. If you wind up with a base that is just a bit too large, it can be sanded after baking until it fits snugly.

4. Finally, it's time for the silk screen. Roll another piece of *pâte morte,* this one long enough to become the circumference of the box, and about ⅛ inch thick. The dough piece for the box here was rolled 24 inches long (2 inches longer than the eventual size) so I could cut the ends cleanly. Don't trim the dough yet; that happens once the silk screen has been applied. Using a double boiler, melt 6 ounces of cocoa paste and stir it frequently until it is just melted. Lay the silk screen over the dough, and at one end pour the melted cocoa paste. Using the flat side of a plastic dough scraper (or the kind of squeegee tool used for silk-screen work), press firmly and draw the cocoa paste evenly along the length of the silk screen. Carefully lift the screen; the pattern should be cleanly and evenly applied. If it isn't, turn over the dough and try again, or roll another piece and repeat the process. Once satisfied with the results, trim the dough to the desired width (2½ inches in the box in the photo), and then trim one end of the dough so that it is at right angles to the length. Thoroughly grease the outside of the ring that will support the dough, and carefully wrap the dough, patterned side out, around the outside of the ring. Note where the ends overlap, remove the dough, trim the other end at right angles, and replace the dough on the outside of the ring. The 2 ends should meet cleanly.

5. All the components are now ready, but for best results, let the dough dry for at least 2 days. This helps to stabilize it so that when it is finally baked there is less danger of distortion. The bake itself is more a dehydration than an actual bake. Place the sheet pan in a low oven, about 250°F, for an hour or two. The side of the box should remain wrapped abound the greased ring for the entire bake. Check it frequently in case it slumps. If it does, just remove it and rewrap it around the ring. It can now finish drying for about 1 week at room temperature, at which point it should be strong enough to support the lid.

6. Let all the baked components cool thoroughly before assembling the box. Using either a glue gun or cooked sugar, apply a small bit to the handle and affix it to the center of the box. Then place the base in the bottom of the box and glue it at several points. That's all there is to the assembly. It can now be filled with any number of things, and with a little care in handling, it can be enjoyed for quite a long while.

A note on using cocoa paste: Leave the silk screen in a warm area before use, and be sure the cocoa paste is thoroughly melted and warm (no more than 120°F). This ensures a fluid flow once the paste is drawn along the screen. If the screen is cool, the cocoa paste might seize up, clogging the small holes in the screen rather than flowing smoothly through them onto the dough.

Pâte morte offers the baker innumerable possibilities for creative decorative work, and this section shows just a small fraction of what can be made. There are abundant methods beyond the few shown here that can expand the baker's expression. For example, molds made from either food-grade silicone or plaster of paris can be fashioned, into which the dough is pressed, removed, and baked prior to final assembly (I have used molds to make things as diverse as legs for miniature tables, ears of corn, and a bust of Beethoven). Wheelbarrows and roosters, baker's peels and Easter bunnies, tables and chairs, sleeping kittens—all can be made with the dough. Certain skills are of course required to become proficient with *pâte morte,* all attainable with perseverance; once these are acquired, only your imagination will determine the limits of potential for this interesting and rich aspect of baking.

Appendix

Developing and Perpetuating a Sourdough Culture

There is so much confusion and misinformation surrounding the topic of making a sourdough culture that, even after more than a quarter century of working with sourdough (or perhaps because of that quarter century), I find myself baffled and befuddled by much of what I read. Sometimes, it seems as if the baker has to be a scientist in a lab coat and mask surrounded by test tubes to make sourdough. Sometimes, it seems as if the only way to make sourdough is to wait until Capricorn is somewhere or another in the sky, the winds are lightly from the east, the moon is waxing, and a special type of crystal is bobbing above the bowl of flour and water as one incants secret chants. Oh the mysteries! The reality is, gratefully, between these two extremes. To make a viable and long-lived sourdough culture takes understanding, persistence, and an occasional bit of intuition, but it is not a terribly daunting endeavor.

There are two distinct phases involved in sourdough: The first is *developing* the culture, a process that generally takes 6 to 10 days; the second is *perpetuating* the culture, so that it can be successfully used in bread production for years. Developing a sourdough culture simply requires attracting yeasts and bacteria that will coexist, the wild yeasts providing *leavening* and the various strains of *Lactobacillus* providing *flavor.*

Wild yeasts live in abundance in the air, as well as on seeds, grains, fruits, and vegetables. The skin of grapes and other fruits contain wild yeast, as does the powdery film at the base of the outer leaves of cabbage. Flour also is a favorable environment for wild yeast; in fact, there are tens of thousands of yeast cells in a single gram of flour (a gram of commercial yeast, on the other hand, contains several billion yeast cells).

Sourdough and Alchemy

The suffusing aromas of a bakery filled with just-baked sourdough breads have an allure that brings us to a place of almost preconscious truth. It is tempting to simply stop in front of the fragrant loaves, disregarding all the work still around us: How perfectly the cupped hands form around the contours of the warm bread; how the subtle gradations of color draw the eye to pause and linger on the globe-like wholeness of each loaf. We feel as if we are in the presence of some long ancient mystery, ancient yet always renewed.

Bread baking has always brought me in touch with the ephemeral nature of life, and never more than when I am producing sourdough breads. I have often maintained that sourdough represents the true alchemy of the baker. When we create a sourdough culture from seemingly inert flour and water, and coax bread-friendly yeasts and bacteria to take up residence in our little bowl of fragile culture; when we keep the culture in harmonious balance for years, fresh and vigorous, constantly renewed, and bake with it again and again, it is easy to feel like an alchemist, and more: For rather than needless gold from base metals, the baker's alchemy is in the bringing together of ingredients that on their own cannot uphold life, and transforming them into nourishing, life-sustaining bread.

Once water is added to the flour, the life cycle of the incipient culture is begun. After 24 hours in a warm room, the flour-water paste will show signs of having risen. The evidence of rise indicates the presence of gas within the bowl; the presence of gas means that metabolism is under way—yes, there is life in the bowl: A little colony of microorganisms has begun taking up residence. At first, things are tentative and fragile, there is little strength, the culture is vulnerable to intrusion by non-bread-friendly yeasts and bacteria. Soon, a natural selection will take place, and if all goes well, beneficial strains of bacteria will dominate the culture. They will work to create an environment that favors their own perpetuation, the synergy between yeasts and bacteria sufficient to ward off the incursion of competing strains. The baker, by providing food and water in sufficient quantity, at proper intervals, and keeping the developing culture in a favorable temperature zone, does his or her part to aid in the growth of the sourdough. Soon, the culture is strong enough to make bread, and unfathomable flavors follow, almost as if by magic.

Regional uniqueness is a fortunate characteristic of sourdough bread. The ambient yeasts and bacteria in one area will naturally differ from those in another, and breads from different locations have a subtle distinctiveness of their own. Although there is a symbiotic stability between the yeasts and bacteria in a healthy culture, if a baker gets a knob of mature sourdough culture from another baker halfway around the world, it will lose some of its original characteristics once the recipient baker has refreshed and worked with the culture in his home environment (in this sense, the Vermont Sourdough in Chapter 5 would be erroneously named if it were made in another area; that formula and the same production method will make Kansas Sourdough or Finland Sourdough or Wherever Sourdough).

Notes on Sourdough

Methods are offered below for making three different styles of sourdough culture: white liquid levain, stiff-textured levain, and a rye culture. Before giving the actual methods for each type, a few considerations are in order:

- Occasionally grapes, potato water, grated onions, honey, and so on are added to flour and water during the initial phases of culture development. While these can provide an additional nutritional boost, they are not required for success. Good-quality flour will be sufficient to supply the needed nutrients to the culture.
- Bleached flour is never appropriate when developing or perpetuating sourdough. Vital nutrients necessary to sustain the microorganisms (not to mention the humans who later consume the bread) are lost in the bleaching process.
- High-gluten flour is not a good flour choice when beginning a culture. Being higher in protein, it contains proportionally less starch, and much of the nutrient supply for the microorganisms comes from the starch.
- Chlorinated water impedes fermentation and can be harmful during the fragile beginnings of culture development. Chlorine gas rapidly dissipates, however, and by keeping an open jug of water on the counter for several hours, most all the chlorine will dissipate. Filtered water and well water can, of course, be used to begin a culture.
- All or part rye flour is often used in the beginning stage of developing a culture that will eventually become all white. Rye is quite high in nutrients and fermentable sugars, and can help get

the culture off to a good start. Similarly, some bakers soak bran in water overnight before commencing their culture; the drained water is mixed with the flour, as it is nutrient rich from the bran.

- Yeast production is faster than the production of acidity during the early stages. This is why we see evidence of a rise in the culture after several hours, but taste little acidity. If correct feedings and temperature are maintained, acidity will become evident after a few days.

- The bacteria in sourdough cultures come mainly from the genus *Lactobacillus*. In young and developing cultures, homofermentative bacteria develop, producing lactic acid. Older cultures have more complex flavors than young ones, largely due to the presence of heterofermentative bacteria, which produce both lactic and acetic acid.

- The presence of both lactic and acetic acids, in balance, is most favorable in sourdough bread production. The lactic acid provides smoothness (somewhat akin to yogurt), while the acetic acid gives a pronounced sour bite (think vinegar). The development of lactic acid is favored in warm environments and loose dough conditions; acetic acids develop more readily in cool and stiff conditions. The baker can use that knowledge to impart desired flavors to his or her bread through manipulation of temperature and hydration.

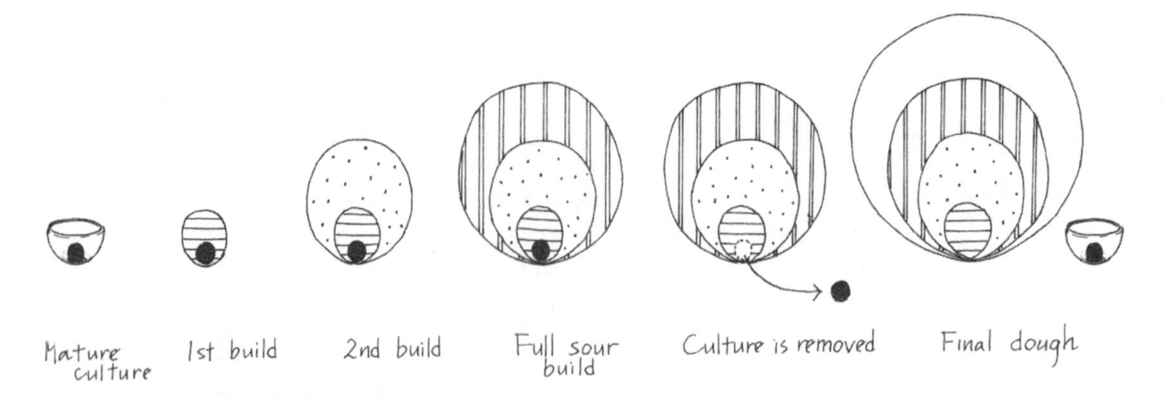

Building a culture and saving a portion

- Ideally, sourdough cultures should be refreshed daily and used to make bread daily (this is more proof that we live in a less-than-ideal world). "Refreshing" simply means feeding the culture with flour and water. In typical bread production, the sourdoughs are built in 1, 2, or 3 stages over a period of roughly 16 to 24 hours. Each build constitutes a refreshing, and when the baker removes a small portion of the ripe sourdough just before mixing the final dough, the removed sourdough is considered fully refreshed. One principle remains the same, whether the sourdough is developed using 1 build or 3 builds, and this principle is at the heart of sourdough bread production: Once the culture has been built and is at the point of maturity, a small portion must be removed and saved for future use.

- It's good practice to evaluate the maturity of the sourdough prior to each bread-making session. The signs of ripeness in a sourdough are similar to those of a yeasted pre-ferment. The rye or stiff white sourdough will be domed on the top, and just beginning to recede in the center. This is the time of perfect ripeness: The microorganisms have happily acidified the flour you fed them, and are now ready to make bread. If the culture is maintained in liquid form, look for evidence that the sourdough has not risen and then fallen from overripeness. If there is a "high-water mark" at the edges of the container and the culture has dropped, then it is overripe. The solution is to ripen the sourdough in a cooler environment, to let less time elapse between the building of the sourdough and the mixing of the bread, or to add a small percentage of salt in order to retard the activity of the wild yeast in the culture (see "Sourdough and Salt" on page 357).

- It is important to mention the effect of cold temperatures on a natural sourdough culture. According to Professor Raymond Calvel, "To maintain the viability of the culture, it is necessary to ensure that the temperature of the refrigeration chamber stays between 8° and 10°C (46.4° and 50°F) whenever the chef [mature culture] is retarded for periods of 48 hours or more. At lower temperatures, part of the flora of the culture may be destroyed, and consequently the taste of bread produced from this culture may be spoiled" (*The Taste of Bread*). Master Montreal baker James MacGuire adds: "Below 8°C it is usual for wild yeasts in the culture to be destroyed, while the acetic acid bacteria will continue to thrive."

- I remember once asking a respected yeast microbiologist if he thought sourdough rye breads generated from rye culture were superior to rye breads made using white culture. He responded that, as long as a culture has a balanced component of heterofermentative bacteria, it mattered not at all whether the bread was derived from rye or white culture. I suspect that from a laboratory perspective this is entirely true. From my empirical baker's perspective, having used rye and white culture for many years, I feel that rye breads are superior when mature rye culture is their foundation, perhaps because the microorganisms in the mature culture have a thorough familiarity with metabolizing rye flour.

- The words *sourdough* and *levain* are often used interchangeably in the United States. This, however, is not the case in Europe. In Germany, the word for sourdough is *Sauerteig,* and it always refers to a culture of rye flour and water. In France, the word for sourdough is *levain,* which refers to a culture that is made entirely, or almost so, of white flour. (The *desem* method of sourdough production, originally from Belgium, utilizes a whole-wheat culture, maintained in a cool environment, and almost always the bread is made without the addition of baker's yeast.) While outwardly these methods are different, there are a number of similarities between them. Most important is that each is a culture of naturally occurring yeasts and bacteria that have the capacity to both leaven bread and provide it with flavor. A German-style culture is made using all rye flour and water. A white levain culture may begin with a high percentage of rye flour, or with all white flour. In any case, it eventually is maintained with all or virtually all white flour. While a rye culture is almost always of comparatively stiff texture, a levain culture can be either loose or stiff (ranging in hydration between 50 and 125 percent). Whichever method is used, the principle is the same. The baker mixes a small paste or dough of flour and water, freshens it with new food and water on a consistent schedule, and develops a colony of microorganisms that ferment and multiply. In order to retain the purity of the culture, a small portion of ripe culture is removed before the mixing of the final dough. This portion is held back, uncontaminated by yeast, salt, or other additions to the final dough, and used to begin the next batch of bread.

Sourdough and Salt

German bakers employ a technique called *Salzsauer,* in which up to 2 percent of salt is included in the sourdough phase (as in other applications of baker's math, this means that there is 2 percent salt relative to the amount of flour in the sourdough). This allows the sourdough to remain viable for up to 48 hours before final dough mixing (I imagine the method was also used in order to enable the baker to have a day off in the days before refrigeration was universal in bakeries). The salt serves to retard the activity of the wild yeast in the culture, prolonging full ripening.

This method is not reserved just for rye breads, and can be used with similarly successful results when using nonrye cultures. During hotter months, I frequently use this technique, just to prevent a sourdough from overripening in the 16 hours between mixing it and then mixing the final dough. Is it detrimental to a culture to be in the presence of salt? From a baker's perspective (that is, empirical rather than strictly scientific), it is apparent that the wild yeast and bacteria in sourdough cultures are strains that are not averse to salt, since they continue to thrive when mixed into a salted bread dough. We can surmise, therefore, that no damage is done to a culture when salt is added to sourdough in order to slow the pace of its ripening. As for amounts, it would seem prudent to add salt to a sourdough in an amount that does not exceed the percent used in the overall formula, that is, 1.8 to 2 percent.

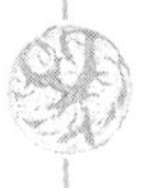

Below are detailed methods for developing three different styles of sourdough culture. All the sourdough breads in this book are generated from one of these three. It will be noted that at each feeding, a portion of the prior feed is thrown away. This is done so that the quantity of sourdough remains workable. At each feeding we are adding flour and water that weigh approximately the same as the culture we are adding it to, and if we didn't discard a portion of the culture, we would soon need a cement mixer to hold the contents of the culture.

The culture needs a certain mass in order to attract needed flora and build its strength. Although the weights given below can be reduced, it is recommended, even for home use, that the given weights be observed so the culture can get off to a vigorous start.

Developing a Liquid Levain Culture

DAY ONE. INITIAL MIX

	U.S.	METRIC	HOME	BAKER'S %
Whole-rye flour	.75 lb	300 g	4.8 oz (1½ cups)	100%
Water	.94 lb	375 g	6 oz (¾ cup)	125%
Honey	.03 lb (.5 oz)	10 g	.2 oz (1 tsp)	3.3%
TOTAL	**1.72 lb**	**685 g**	**11 oz**	

Mix the ingredients well, cover with plastic, and let stand in a warm area (75° to 80°F) for 24 hours. Medium rye flour can be used in place of whole rye, but avoid using white rye flour.

DAY TWO. TWO FEEDINGS

	U.S.	METRIC	HOME	BAKER'S %
Initial mix	.45 lb	200 g	5.5 oz (half of above)	111%
Whole-rye flour	.2 lb	90 g	1.2 oz (⅜ cup)	50%
White flour	.2 lb	90 g	1.2 oz (¼ cup)	50%
Water, 90°F	.5 lb	225 g	3 oz (⅜ cup)	125%
TOTAL	**1.35 lb**	**605 g**	**10.9 oz**	

Mix the ingredients well, cover with plastic, and let stand in a warm area (75° to 80°F). Ideally, the 2 feedings should be 12 hours apart. The white flour should be an unbleached bread flour with 11 to 12 percent protein.

DAYS THREE, FOUR, AND FIVE. TWO FEEDINGS

	U.S.	METRIC	HOME	BAKER'S %
Initial mix	.45 lb	200 g	5.5 oz (half of above)	111%
White flour	.4 lb	180 g	2.4 oz (1/2 cup)	100%
Water	.5 lb	225 g	3 oz (3/8 cup)	125%
TOTAL	**1.35 lb**	**605 g**	**10.9 oz**	

Mix the ingredients well, cover with plastic, and let stand in a warm area (75° to 80°F). Ideally, the 2 feedings should be 12 hours apart. By day six, the culture should have enough ripeness to be used for bread production. In order to continue developing strength and complexity (heterofermentative bacteria), however, it may be fed for 2 or 3 more days before beginning to use it. In that case, follow the same feeding schedule as for days three, four, and five.

Developing a Stiff Levain Culture

DAY ONE. INITIAL MIX

	U.S.	METRIC	HOME	BAKER'S %
Whole-rye flour	.65 lb	300 g	4 oz (1 cup)	50%
White flour	.65 lb	300 g	4 oz (1 cup)	50%
Water	.85 lb	390 g	5.6 oz (3/4 cup)	65%
TOTAL	**2.15 lb**	**990 g**	**13.6 oz**	

Mix the ingredients well, cover with plastic, and let stand in a warm area (75° to 80°F) for 24 hours. Medium rye can replace the whole rye, but avoid using white rye flour. The white flour should be an unbleached bread flour with 11 to 12 percent protein. Since rye flour has a higher absorption rate than white, the hydration will be 65 percent on day one. Note that from here on, it is reduced to 60 percent.

DAYS TWO, THREE, FOUR, AND FIVE. TWO FEEDINGS

	U.S.	METRIC	HOME	BAKER'S %
Initial mix	.65 lb	300 g	4.5 oz (one-third of above)	100%
White flour	.65 lb	300 g	4 oz (1 cup)	100%
Water	.39 lb	180 g	2.4 oz (less than 3/8 cup)	60%
TOTAL	**1.69 lb**	**780 g**	**10.9 oz**	

Mix the ingredients well, cover with plastic, and let stand in a warm area (75° to 80°F). Ideally, the 2 feedings should occur 12 hours apart. By day six, the culture should have enough ripeness to be used for bread production. In order to continue developing strength and complexity (heterofermentative bacteria), however, it may be fed for 2 or 3 more days before beginning to use it. In that case, follow the same feeding schedule as for days two, three, four, and five.

Developing a Sourdough Rye Culture

DAY ONE. INITIAL MIX

	U.S.	METRIC	HOME	BAKER'S %
Whole-rye flour	1 lb	450 g	6.4 oz (1¾ cups)	100%
Water	1 lb	450 g	6.4 oz (¾ cup)	100%
TOTAL	**2 lb**	**900 g**	**12.8 oz**	

Mix the ingredients to a smooth paste, cover with plastic, and let stand in a warm area (75° to 80°F) for 24 hours. Whole rye, preferably organic, is preferred when developing a rye culture, due to its full spectrum of nutrients, which will encourage a population of healthy and content microorganisms. If medium rye is used, the hydration can be reduced to approximately 90 percent. Avoid using white rye flour, as it is essentially devoid of beneficial nutrients.

DAY TWO. ONE FEEDING

	U.S.	METRIC	HOME	BAKER'S %
Initial mix	.5 lb	225 g	3.2 oz (one-quarter of above)	100%
Whole-rye flour	.5 lb	225 g	3.2 oz (⅞ cup)	100%
Water	.5 lb	225 g	3.2 oz (⅜ cup)	100%
TOTAL	**1.5 lb**	**675 g**	**9.6 oz**	

Mix the ingredients to a smooth paste, cover with plastic, and let stand in a warm area (75° to 80°F) for 24 hours.

DAYS THREE, FOUR, FIVE, AND SIX. TWO FEEDINGS

	U.S.	METRIC	HOME	BAKER'S %
Initial mix	.5 lb	225 g	3.2 oz (one-third of above)	100%
Whole-rye flour	.5 lb	225 g	3.2 oz (⅞ cup)	100%
Water	.5 lb	225 g	3.2 oz (⅜ cup)	100%
TOTAL	**1.5 lb**	**675 g**	**9.6 oz**	

Mix the ingredients to a smooth paste, cover with plastic, and let stand in a warm area (75° to 80°F). Feedings should be roughly 12 hours apart. On day seven, the culture can be used to make bread. It will have more vigor and flavor, however, if the feeding schedule is followed for 2 or 3 more days. A common practice among German bakers is to sprinkle the surface of the sourdough with rye flour when the culture has been refreshed. This provides a bit of a food source for the microorganisms within, and also acts as an environmental buffer, helping to prevent the culture from drying. When the sourdough has ripened and risen, the flour will look like islands on the surface.

Converting a Liquid Levain Culture to a Stiff-Textured Culture

It is rarely practical, or necessary, for the baker to develop and maintain 3 or more sourdough cultures. In my baking life, I find good use in the maintenance of just 2: a stiff rye sourdough and a white liquid levain. Yet there have been instances when I have come upon a formula for a bread, and I can't resist the urge to make it. Alas, it calls for a stiff white culture, and all I have is a liquid one. While I could reconfigure the formula in a way that allows me to use a liquid culture, it is really no great matter to transform a bit of liquid to stiff, and the resulting bread will probably be a little closer to the original intent if made with the stiff culture.

Let's suppose we want to convert a liquid culture to a stiff one of 60 percent hydration. Here is the method: The liquid culture that I maintain has a hydration of 125 percent. This means that in any given amount of culture, there are 125 units of water for each 100 units of flour. For visual ease, I will begin the conversion by taking 225 grams of the liquid culture. Those 225 grams consist of:

Flour	100 g
Water	125 g (125% hydration)
Total	225 g

In the 225 grams of liquid culture, 125 of those grams are water. I divide the 125 by 60 (the desired hydration for the stiff culture): 125 ÷ 60 = 2.08. The 2.08 represents the weight of 1 unit (either flour or water) in the new culture. I know that there will be 100 units of flour in the new culture, so now I multiply 2.08 × 100. This tells me that there will be 208 grams total flour in the 60 percent hydration culture. Since I already have 100 grams of flour in the initial liquid culture, I simply add 108 grams of flour: 100 g + 108 g = 208 g. So we have:

Flour	208 g
Water	125 g (60% hydration)
Total	333 g

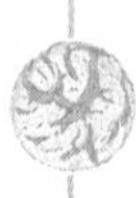

Rheological Testing and the Analysis of Flour

Rheology is defined as "the study of deformation and flow of matter"; expressed another way, rheology measures how substances break down. It may seem odd to intentionally mix a dough only to see how slowly or quickly it deforms, but in fact, by knowing the parameters of the dough as indicated in various tests, the baker or miller can make a number of educated deductions about how the flour might perform during baking. In this section, we will look at a number of tests performed at a lab on a sample of bread flour, discuss the various tests, and examine the specific information the tests provide that help to indicate flour performance in the bakery. Thom Leonard from Lawrence, Kansas, and Tod Bramble of the King Arthur Flour Company have both generously offered their expertise in this section of the book, and I would like to acknowledge and thank both for their efforts.

Anyone who has worked or observed in a bakery where there is an old-timer or two running around will attest to the marvelous knack they have. Years of skill in the hand have given them the ability to tell much about the nature of a given dough: whether it needs more or less water in the mix, whether it's young or old, how well or poorly it ferments, and the overall tolerance of the dough to the rigors it undergoes on the path from flour in the bag to bread being pulled from the oven. These bakers are involved in unscientific but very real rheological assessments. The scientific rheological tests discussed here are precise, interesting, and certainly have an application to the baker's daily life. While it's helpful to learn how to understand them, it should also be borne in mind that the information they provide is more of a suggestion than a guarantee of flour performance. The baker, in the bakery, with dough in the bowl or forming under his or her hands, is the final judge of how well or poorly a certain flour functions. Nevertheless, by interpreting rheological information about a flour before actually mixing it, the baker can (and does, as more and more bakers become fluent in rheological interpretations) make small adjustments—for example, an extra fold or two in a dough made with flour that has a low P/L value, or a small addition of malt because of a high Falling Number.

Amylase Activity and the Question of Malt

Cereal grains, such as wheat and rye, are concerned above all with the same thing all biological creatures are: perpetuating the species. The germ of the grain provides the initial source of nutrients, in the form of fats and minerals, that initiate the life cycle of the plant, and from the germ emanate both an embryonic root and an embryonic shoot. The endosperm is the plant's source of long-term nutrient storage, in the form of starch. Within the starch are found amylase enzymes, and when the grain is moistened, these enzymes convert the starch into sugars. Specifically, α-amlyase (alpha-amylase) begins breaking the long starch chains in the dough, after which β-amylase (beta-amylase) continues the breakdown. When the beta-amylase has finished its chore, it produces maltose, which the yeast then consumes as it proceeds with the business of fermentation. There is always a sufficient level of beta-amylase in flour, but often alpha-amylase levels are inadequate for proper dough fermentation. When the level of enzymatic activity is too low, fermentation is sluggish and the bread suffers accordingly. With too high a level of amylase activity, the rate of fermentation is excessive, and different problems ensue.

When grains are intact, the amylases are more or less inert; once they sprout, amylase activity increases dramatically. Sometimes, grain stays too long in the field before being harvested, or rains come during the last phase of growth. In both cases, there may be an elevated level of amylase activity in the grain, which in an extreme situation can spoil the flour (moist growing conditions in many parts of northern and central Europe very often result in rye flour that has an advanced level of amylase activity before harvest has even begun). The farmer, therefore, prefers to harvest while amylase levels in the grain are low. While this helps to ensure that the crop is undamaged, it also necessitates the addition of malt at the mill or in the bakery to correct deficiencies in amylase activity.

How does the baker determine whether or not to add malt to his flour before mixing? If the flour being used has malted barley as an ingredient listed on the bag, then the mill has added malt, and it is likely that no additional malt is needed. If the baker has access to a flour analysis (which by all rights he should), then reading the Falling Number will tell him whether additional malt is necessary. If the baker does need to add malt, it should be in the form of diastatic malt. This is malt that has active amylase enzymes. The enzymes have been deactivated in nondiastatic malt, and its only contribution to bread is in the form of flavor.

With breads that undergo a very long and slow fermentation, such as those kept in a retarder for several hours or overnight, the addition of malt may prove helpful. This is because the great length of the fermentation results in a considerable amount of the sugars in the flour being consumed by the yeast. When the bread finally gets to the oven, there are insufficient residual sugars in the dough to provide good crust color. By adding diastatic malt powder to the dough, more starch can be converted to sugar during fermentation, and therefore more residual sugars remain in the dough at the time of baking. When adding diastatic malt, bear in mind that more is not better, and an excess yields a gummy crumb. It is always better to start on the low end when adding malt, starting with perhaps .1 to .2 percent of the flour weight.

Here is our lab analysis, with the actual figures for the flour sample:

Moisture Level	13.65%
Protein Quantity (NIR)	11.72%
Ash Content (14% MB)	.445%
Falling Number	281 seconds
FARINOGRAPH (14% MB)	
Peak Time	4 minutes
Tolerance	10½ minutes
Absorption	61.6%
MTI (BU)	35

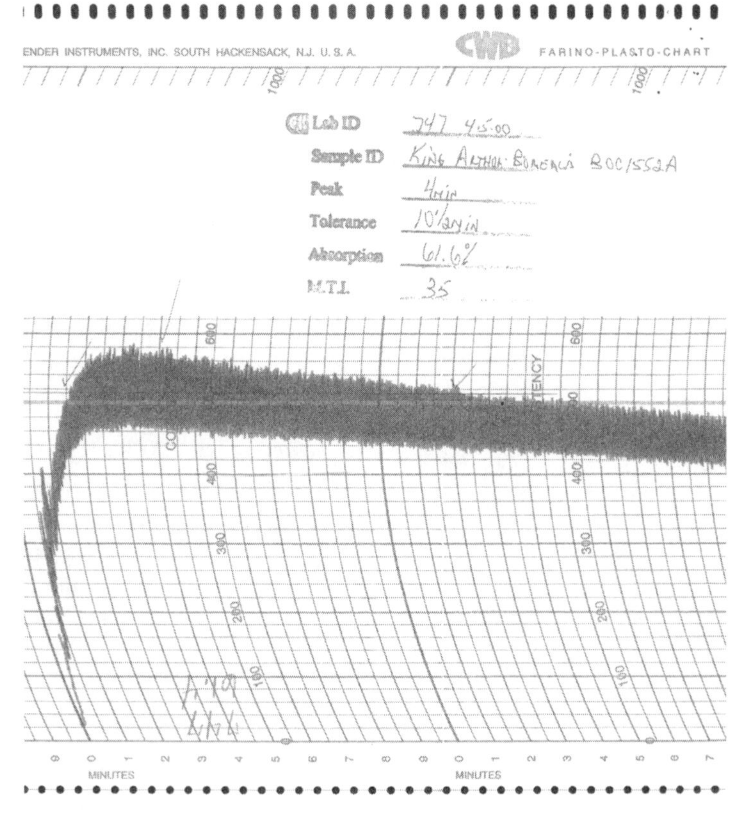

Farinogram

Moisture (13.65 Percent)

Since moisture levels naturally vary in grain samples depending on growing and harvesting conditions, as well as the age and storage method of the grain, all rheological tests in the United States are based on flour with a 14 percent moisture basis (MB). If an actual flour sample has more or less than 14 percent moisture, as does our present sample (13.65 percent), the test results are adjusted to reflect a 14 percent moisture level. We should note here that in Europe, tests are performed on flour with 0 percent moisture basis, so flours tested in Europe yield different figures than the same samples tested in the United States.

Protein Quantity (11.72 Percent)

As one would expect, soil fertility and available moisture during the growing season have a significant impact on flour protein, with rich soil and low moisture levels as harvest-time nears producing flour with higher protein levels. The quantity of protein in a flour sample is calculated from the nitrogen content of the flour. The most common method for determining protein quantity, in use for almost a century, is called the Kjeldahl method. A newer test, equally accurate, is known as the Near Infrared Reflectance, or NIR. An infrared beam infuses a flour sample, and an almost instant reading of the protein content is produced. In the present flour sample, the protein was determined using the NIR method.

Ash Content (.445 Percent)

The ash content is an indication of the mineral content of a given sample of flour. To perform the test, a 50-gram sample of flour is incinerated at 900°F; what remains is a charred little pile that is almost all minerals. The pile is weighed, and the result is expressed as a percentage of the original, unincinerated flour.

Ash content is important to the baker for several reasons. First, it indicates the degree of milling. The mineral (and protein) content of flour increases toward the periphery of the grain. A low ash content therefore suggests that the flour was milled from the heart of the endosperm (the source for patent flour). An increasing ash content suggests that the flour was milled from farther out on the endosperm.

Protein quality is quite different from protein quantity, and the baker generally prefers flour that is milled closer to the heart. Although the amount of protein there may be less than it is at the outside portion of the endosperm, the quality of that protein is often superior for bread baking (particularly the baking of free-standing hearth loaves). Second, as mineral content increases, the flour becomes darker. White flour that is milled closer to the periphery of the endosperm will be perceptibly darker than white flour milled from the heart of the endosperm. White breads made with high ash flour will have a distinctly gray cast. Third, minerals in flour assist in dough fermentation by providing nutrients for the yeast. Flour with a very low ash content, almost devoid of minerals, will ferment sluggishly. Flour with a high ash content, such as whole-wheat flour, will have a much higher rate of fermentation. Generally speaking, breads made with all or part white flour have the best characteristics when the flour has an ash content of about .45 to .55 percent.

It's interesting to note that in Europe, bakers purchase flour based neither on protein content nor on descriptive names, but solely on the basis of ash content. In Germany, for instance, a formula might call for Type 550 wheat flour, indicating flour with an ash content of .55 percent. The same flour in France would be sold as Type 55. Since Europeans test their flours based on a 0 percent moisture basis, and not 14 percent moisture as in North America, test results are different there than on the same flour tested in the United States. A sample of flour that showed a .46 percent test result for ash in the United States (14 percent MB) would test to .55 percent ash in Europe (0 percent MB), and be known as Type 550 (in Germany) or Type 55 (in France).

Falling Number (281 Seconds)

The Falling Number test measures the activity of the amylase enzymes in a sample of flour, which gives an indication of the diastatic ability of the flour. In the Falling Number test, a hot paste is made with 7 grams of flour and 25 grams of distilled water. This slurry is put into a glass cylinder, and a sort of ski pole–shaped device is placed on the paste. The length of time it takes for the ski pole to descend through the paste is timed, and the resulting number of seconds is the Falling Number value for that sample of flour. If there is a high level of amylase enzymes in the flour sample, the enzymes quickly begin to convert the starch into sugar and break down the viscous paste, and the ski pole falls through quickly, resulting in a low number. If, on the other hand, the enzyme level is low, the conversion of starch into sugar is slow, thus taking longer for the ski pole to break down the paste and descend, and the Falling Number is higher. Therefore, a low

Falling Number indicates a flour that is high in enzymes, and a high Falling Number indicates a flour low in enzymes. For the baker, a Falling Number between 225 and 300 indicates a flour with a reasonable level of enzymatic activity.

Typically, the enzyme level is corrected at the mill by the addition of amylase (although in some cases, for example with many organic flours, no corrections are made and it is up to the baker to make any adjustments deemed necessary). The amylase may come from one of two sources. One source is malted barley. To obtain this, barley (a cereal grain quite rich in amylase) is soaked and sprouted, which activates the amylases. Then the barley is dried and ground into powder, and this malted barley powder is added to the flour. A second source is fungal amylase, which is derived from the mold *Aspergillus oryzae*. This mold is grown in a liquid-nutrient slurry, and the mold excretes amylase, which is separated and dried. While both sources correct deficiencies in the flour sample's Falling Number, they act differently in the dough. Fungal amylase is deactivated at relatively low temperatures, while barley malt remains active at higher temperatures (and therefore continues to convert starch to sugar further into the bake). For this reason, millers tend to prefer fungal amylase, since there are fewer negative consequences in the bread if the flour has inadvertently been overmalted.

The Farinograph

The farinograph is more widely used than any other flour-testing apparatus in the United States, and gives a wide range of information about the potential baking quality of a given sample of flour. It measures the dough's resistance to breakdown, thereby assessing flour strength. Essentially, the farinograph is a miniature mixer, holding either 50 grams or 300 grams of flour, water jacketed for temperature control, with two mixing blades that generally are geared to 63 rpms. A dough is mixed, and the force required to turn the blades is measured and recorded on a grid. The curve that results as the dough first increases in strength and then begins to deteriorate is called a farinogram (see on page 365). The farinogram moves forward mechanically as the test proceeds, coinciding with the 1-minute intervals that are represented along the horizontal axis of the grid. What is known as "Brabender Units" are measured in increments of 5 units along the vertical axis. To explain the various measurements that the farinograph gauges, we will use the information from the flour sample lab analysis given earlier, which the photograph of the actual farinogram illustrates.

Water is added to the flour sample, mixing commences, and as resistance to mixing increases, the curve on the farinogram begins to rise on the chart. Readings are noted along the way, as the dough sample first increases in gluten strength and then begins to break down. The amount of water necessary to make a dough that results in the center of the curve rising to the 500 Brabender Unit line at the time of maximum gluten development (Peak Time), is called the Absorption. Typically, for bread flour the Absorption is between 60 and 65 percent (it is 61.6 percent in the present example). It is important to keep in mind that the Absorption percentage refers simply to the amount of water required for the test, and is not necessarily an indication of the correct hydration for that flour. Life in the bakery is different from life in the lab, and the baker may very well add more (sometimes much more) water to the flour than the amount used in the farinograph.

The Peak Time (4 minutes in the present sample) is the time necessary for the dough to reach its maximum gluten development, indicated by the curve reaching its highest point. Weaker flours will obviously reach their peak of development earlier than stronger flours. Bread flours with comparatively low-to-medium protein levels (11 to 12 percent) may have a Peak Time of 3½ minutes or so, while high-gluten flours, with 13 to 14 percent protein, may take 7 minutes or more to reach their Peak Time. We reiterate that when the curve reaches the Peak Time, it is centered on the 500 BU line.

The length of time the farinogram curve remains above the 500 BU line is called the Tolerance (it is also referred to as the Stability Time), and provides another indication of the flour's tolerance to mixing, with a higher figure indicating greater tolerance. Typical Tolerance values for bread flours range from 9 to about 14 minutes (our sample has a Tolerance of 10½ minutes).

A last measurement of flour strength provided by the farinograph is the Mixing Tolerance Index, or MTI. The difference in Brabender Units from the top of the curve at Peak Time to the top of the curve 5 minutes after Peak Time is measured, and this number is the Mixing Tolerance Index (the MTI in the present example is 35). Lower-gluten flours generally break down more quickly, resulting in higher MTI numbers. High-gluten flours generally have a higher resistance to breakdown, so the fall of the curve during the measured 5 minutes is less, which results in lower MTI readings. Normal readings are about 25 to 40. Flours with MTI readings of less than 25, that is, with a great resistance to breakdown, often yield breads with a gummy crumb.

The Chopin Alveograph

The Chopin alveograph is another instrument used to measure the relative strength and baking ability of flour. It is the most common instrument used in Europe for flour testing, while in the United States it is much less frequently used, although it is gaining slowly in popularity. Interestingly, in the United States it is most often used by the cracker industry, where flour extensibility is highly important, as it indicates how thinly a cracker dough can be extruded.

The testing apparatus consists of a mixer, water jacketed to keep the dough at 24°C, that mixes an unyeasted dough for 7 minutes. The dough consists of 125 cubic centimeters of water salinated at 2.5 percent, and 250 grams of flour (this is the standard dough used by the American Association of Cereal Chemists, although in Europe flour and water quantities may be different). A sheeting mechanism extrudes the mixed dough onto a plate, where it is then literally blown into a bubble by air pumped from a diaphragm at a calibrated rate. Last of all, a recording device called a manometer measures the changes the dough bubble undergoes onto a chart. Each flour sample is mixed once, the tests are performed 5 times, and the average value is used to evaluate the flour. The purpose of this somewhat strange setup is to measure the dough's resistance to rupturing as more and more air is blown into the bubble. Stronger doughs obviously can be blown up more than weaker ones before they pop, and different aspects of the test record various aspects of the dough's deformation. Taken as a whole, the alveograph gives the baker a sense of the balance between the extensibility and elasticity of a dough made with a certain flour. Page 371 shows our sample. The figures are as follows:

ALVEOGRAPH (14% MB)	
P	87.0
L	117.0
G	24.0
W	335.0
P/L	0.75
Starch Damage	8.69%

The P value (87.0) is measured in millimeters along the vertical axis of the chart. It is an indication of the dough's tensile strength (elasticity), or how much the blowing bubble resists expansion, with stronger doughs having higher readings.

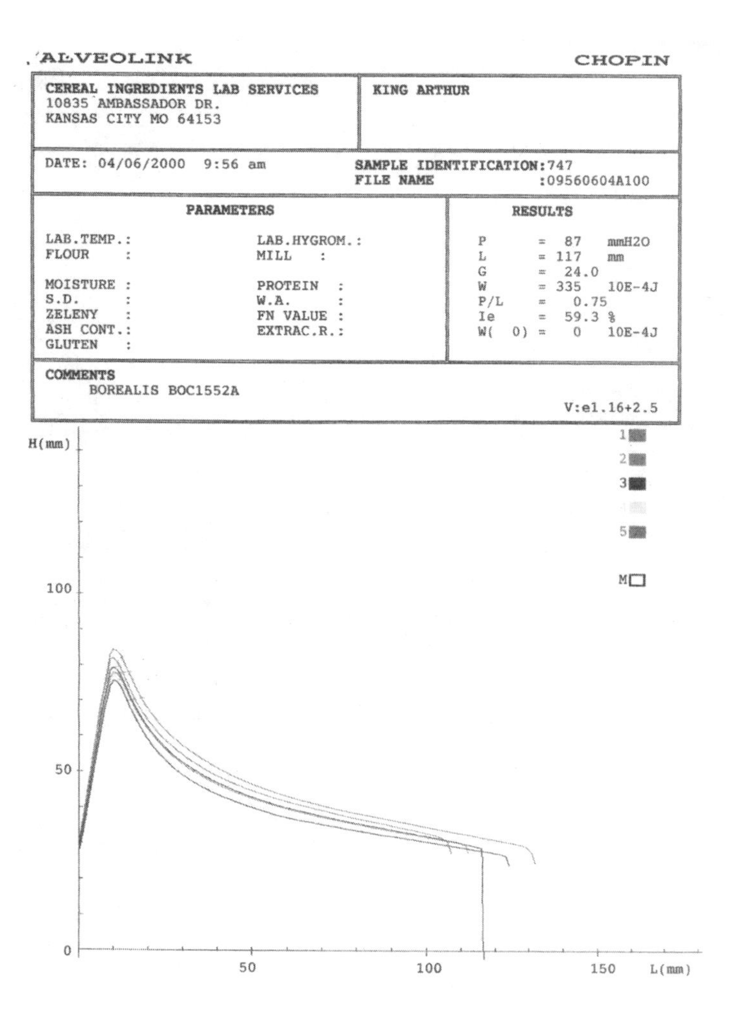

Alveogram

The L value (117.0) is measured in millimeters along the horizontal axis. The measurement is taken from the point where the curve of the alveogram begins, to the point along the baseline where the bubble ruptures. The L value denotes the extensibility of the flour.

The G value (24.0) is known as the "swelling index," and is measured by taking the square root of the volume of air needed to rupture the dough bubble. It provides an indication of relative loaf volume, as well as dough extensibility. Higher values indicate greater dough extensibility. Readings for bread flours are generally in the range of 21 to 25.

The area under the curve is multiplied by a factor of 6.54, and the result is the W value of the flour. The W value indicates the energy required to inflate the dough bubble to the point of rupture. There is a direct relationship between the baking strength of the flour sample and its W value. Typically, the W value ranges between about 45 and 400, with higher numbers indicating stronger flours. Bread flour W values are generally in the 250 to 375 range (335.0 in the present example).

A last measurement is the P/L value, which, along with the W value, is considered to be the most important indication of the flour's potential performance. The P/L value is a measurement of the relationship between the dough's extensibility and its elasticity. Obviously, both characteristics are essential in any flour, and it is the balanced proportion of both that distinguishes the best flour. Too much elasticity, indicated by a high P/L value, results in bread that is tight and compact, given to tearing, and which develops with difficulty. Too much extensibility, indicated by a low P/L value, is also undesirable, because the dough tends to be slack and sticky, and yields bread of poor volume, since it has difficulty retaining trapped carbon dioxide gases released during fermentation. For North American flours, a P/L value of between .65 and approximately 1.1 suggests a balanced flour (our sample has a P/L value of 0.75).

Starch Damage

When the wheat berry finally has been milled into flour, some of the starch molecules have invariably been damaged in the process. When starch damage is less than 10 percent (it is 8.69 percent in the present sample), there is typically no negative impact on flour performance. For a full discussion of starch damage, see page 39.

Conclusion

Again, we note that values and numbers and curves and figures scrawled by a machine onto gridded paper can give the baker some important and valuable information. But the baker's hands are the final arbiters of the dough, making their minute assessments during the mixing and shaping, scoring, and baking, and ultimately we must determine flour quality by evaluating the actual products of any particular flour.

Flour Additives

It is rare indeed to get a bag of flour that contains only flour. For decades, millers have been adding a variety of substances to flour for a variety of reasons.

Enrichment Additives

In the early twentieth century, nutritional deficiency diseases, such as pellagra, beriberi, and rickets, were comparatively common in the United States, particularly among poorer people. During the 1930s, extensive health surveys revealed the extent of the deficiencies among much of the population. In response, the government decided to add vitamins to a staple food that most Americans consumed daily. White flour was the obvious choice, and since then, the label on every bag of enriched flour lists its nutritional additives, which include thiamin, riboflavin, niacin, iron, and, optionally, calcium. In the late 1990s, the Food and Drug Administration mandated the addition of folic acid to enriched flour, to help prevent neural birth tube defects in fetuses. It is worth noting that mill feed, the 28 percent or so of the wheat berry that is removed (primarily the bran and germ) when whole grain is milled into white flour, and which is used primarily as livestock feed, contains most of the nutrients that are later chemically added back into the white flour to enrich it. While the use of enriched flour is not federally required, more than three-quarters of the states require white bread to be made with enriched flour. As a rule, none of these additives alters the color or flavor of bread, or affects the baking quality of the flour.

Chemical Additives

Natural aging, or oxidizing, of flour is a process that takes three to four weeks, and is essential to stabilize the baking quality of flour. Flour that is not sufficiently aged is called "green flour," and breads made with it are difficult indeed to work with (see "Oxidizing and Overoxidizing," page 7, for a fuller discussion). To avoid the time required to naturally age flour, a number of chemical additives have been used for almost a century in the United States to artificially mature it.

Flour that is chemically bleached requires virtually no aging, and in a mere day or two can be used for baking. At the same time, though, flour that is bleached has lost its component of carotenoid pigments, and aroma, flavor, and crumb color are irretrievably compromised. It is a common sight at many mills to see large tanker trucks pull in under a chute in order to receive a full load—many tons—of freshly milled flour. The flour is trucked to the bakery, pumped into a silo, and within days is used in bread doughs. This flour is either bleached and therefore artificially matured, or is simply used as green flour, with all the attendant consequences. When a baker becomes big enough to require silos, the choices are hard indeed, because natural aging is rarely practical. And, unquestionably, unbleached flour that has aged naturally is the preferred choice if bread quality is the baker's dominant criterion.

In order to bleach flour, a calibrated measure of benzoyl peroxide is released toward the end of the milling, the effect of which is to whiten and artificially oxidize it (in Canada, a maximum of 150 parts per million is permitted, while in the United States there is no legal maximum). Chlorine gas is also used as a bleaching agent, but generally only in the milling of cake flour. Not only does the chlorine whiten the flour, it also lowers the pH to about 4.8. Bleaching cake flour can in fact improve its performance, as the increased acidity helps improve the structure of the baked cake. In the United States (though not in Canada), there is no limit to the amount of benzoyl peroxide or chlorine gas that can be used.

Another approved maturing agent, permitted for use since 1962, is azodicarbonamide, or ADA. Also known as Maturox, ADA oxidizes what are known as the thiol groups of proteins in the flour, which in turn reduces mix-time requirements, increases dough strength, and somewhat reduces the effects of overmixing. It is activated quickly in doughs, which can be problematic for bakers who want a slower-acting impact from their chemical additives. A pronounced increase in loaf volume can be achieved with ADA, but if added too early in the production process (for example, when added to a pre-ferment), it can be used up before the bread is baked, and the extra loaf volume will not be achieved. All flour treated with ADA must be labeled as bleached.

Potassium bromate ($KbrO_3$) has been used as an artificial oxidant for nearly a century. It has a slow reaction time in doughs, coming into its own once the bread is in the oven, and making breads that have an almost supernatural volume. Banned in Europe, Canada, and Japan, bromate has been a regular additive to flour in the United States until quite recently. There is increasing evidence that potassium bromate is carcinogenic, and although not officially banned, it is used less and less as a flour treatment. In California, Proposition 65 requires that bread made with bromate carry a rather chilling label: "Warning: This product may contain a chemical deemed by the state of California to cause cancer or birth defects."

A last approved flour oxidant is ascorbic acid. It has an almost instantaneous tightening effect on bread dough, greatly increasing elasticity (anyone who has inadvertently added just a bit too much ascorbic acid to a baguette dough knows the difficulties ahead when the time comes for shaping: The dough is all elasticity and no extensibility). Like ADA and potassium bromate, ascorbic acid is an additive that is thought to improve loaf volume. Although it is an acid, it has no effect on the overall pH of flour. Further, since it dissipates entirely in the oven, it does not add vitamin C to bread. A small addition of ascorbic acid is common at the mill (usually 20 to 40 parts per million); in the shop, the baker may decide to add more. Depending on the source, ascorbic acid can have a greater or lesser tightening impact on dough. When first beginning to use it, caution is advised. Twenty ppm is a safe start; this is roughly ¼ teaspoon of ascorbic to a hundredweight of flour.

The function of additives is sometimes to strengthen and "improve" flour, and sometimes additives are used as "reducing agents" to intentionally weaken doughs by breaking the bonds between flour proteins. The main additive in this category in use in the United States is L-cysteine (an amino acid found in proteins, and a major source of which is human hair). Its effect on bread doughs is virtually opposite that of the oxidizing agents. L-cysteine reduces the dough's elasticity, and when used in no-time or short-time doughs, the dough's nearly instant extensibility enables the baker (or a machine) to work with it almost immediately, with little risk of tearing. It's common in bagel production, where high-protein, low-hydration doughs resist the stresses of the extruding machines unless tamed by L-cysteine; and in mass pizza production as well, where the addition of L-cysteine prevents pressed-out pizza doughs from shrinking back due to the elastic properties of the dough. It was frequently paired with potassium bromate before the latter fell into disfavor: The L-cysteine would weaken dough structure so machining could proceed without cumbersome floor time; later in the process, the bromate would kick in and strengthen the dough, ensuring lofty loaves.

Baker's Percentage

When working with a bread formula, the easiest method is to use what is known as baker's percentage, or baker's math. In using baker's percentage, each ingredient in a formula is expressed as a percentage of the flour weight, and the flour weight is always expressed as 100 percent. When using baker's percentage, each ingredient is weighed. This includes liquids, too. There are a number of good reasons for using baker's percentage in formulas. For one, since each ingredient is weighed, it enables us to work with precision using only one unit of measure. Second, it is quite easy to scale a formula up or down when working with baker's percentage. And last, it allows bakers to share a common language. This common language not only enables bakers to communicate with each other, but also allows them to assess a formula quickly simply by seeing the percentages used. In this discussion, we will convert a simple bread formula into percentages, transfer a formula from percentages to pounds, and learn to compute the formula conversion factor for scaling a recipe up or down.

Computing Percentages in a Formula

Here is a straightforward recipe for white bread:

Flour	75 lb
Water	49.5 lb
Salt	1.5 lb
Yeast	.9 lb

As mentioned above, when using baker's percentage, the flour is represented as 100 percent, and each of the other ingredients is expressed as a percentage of the flour's weight. We can start with the formula as follows:

Flour	75 lb	100%
Water	49.5 lb	?
Salt	1.5 lb	?
Yeast	.9 lb	?

To determine the percentage of the other ingredients, divide the weight of each ingredient by the weight of the flour, and then multiply the result (which is in decimal form) by 100 to convert it to a percent. For example, to calculate the percentage of water, divide the weight of the water by the weight of the flour and multiply by 100: 49.5 ÷ 75 = .66 × 100 = 66 percent. Following the same method, we arrive at the following values for the salt and yeast:

Flour	75 lb	100%	
Water	49.5 lb	66%	(49.5 ÷ 75 = .66 × 100 = 66%)
Salt	1.5 lb	2%	(1.5 ÷ 75 = .02 × 100 = 2%)
Yeast	.9 lb	1.2%	(.9 ÷ 75 = .012 × 100 = 1.2%)

It is worth noting that by simply looking at the percentages we can ascertain important things about this bread. For one thing, we know at a glance that the salt and yeast are within appropriate ranges. We can also see that the bread has a 66 percent hydration (hydration is defined as the percentage of liquid in a dough, again based on the flour weight). If gallon pitchers were used to measure the water, the formula would be cumbersome and much more difficult to assess. Using baker's percentage, we can infer that the ingredients in this dough are in balance, without even seeing the mixed dough.

Computing Pounds from Percentages

For our second example, let's assume that a baker colleague has given you his formula for ciabatta. However, it's not based on actual pounds but rather on the percentages for each ingredient:

Flour	100%
Water	73%
Salt	1.8%
Yeast	1.1%

You decide to make this dough using 50 pounds of flour. But how much do the other ingredients weigh?

Flour	100%	50 lb
Water	73%	?
Salt	1.8%	?
Yeast	1.1%	?

To obtain the weights of the remaining ingredients, first divide the percentage by 100 to obtain a decimal, then multiply the resulting decimal by the weight of the flour. For example, the water is calculated as 73 ÷ 100 = .73. Multiply .73 by the flour weight to obtain the weight of the water: .73 × 50 = 36.5 pounds. The entire formula looks like this:

Flour	100%	50 lb	
Water	73%	36.5 lb	(73 ÷ 100 = .73 × 50 = 36.5 lb)
Salt	1.8%	.9 lb	(1.8 ÷ 100 = .018 × 50 = .9 lb)
Yeast	1.1%	.55 lb	(1.1 ÷ 100 = .011 × 50 = .55 lb)

Resizing a Formula Using the Formula Conversion Factor

There are often times when we need to recalculate the size of a formula in order to make either more or less bread. By employing baker's math, this is quick, accurate, and easy. Let's assume that you use the formula below for French bread:

Flour	120 lb	100%
Water	78 lb	65%
Salt	2.4 lb	2%
Yeast	1.5 lb	1.25%
Total	201.9 lb	168.25%

How can you recalculate the formula to obtain 150 pounds of dough, retaining the percentages of the ingredients? The first step is to determine the formula conversion factor. To establish this, first add the percentages of the formula, which in this case total 168.25. (One way to visualize this is that regardless of the weight of the bread we are mixing—it could be 1 pound or 1 ton—there are always 168.25 units that combine to make up the dough. One hundred of those units are flour, 65 of the units are water, 2 units are salt, and 1.25 are the yeast.) Then divide the new desired dough weight by the sum of the percentages:

150 ÷ 168.25 = .8915 = formula conversion factor

By performing this simple calculation we know that each of the 168.25 units that make up the 150 pounds of dough weighs .8915 pound. It's better to have a little extra bread rather than not enough, so we round the conversion factor up to .892. The last step is to multiply the percentages of each ingredient by .892:

Flour	100%	(.892 × 100 = 89.2)	89.2 lb
Water	65%	(.892 × 65 = 57.98)	57.98 lb
Salt	2%	(.892 × 2 = 1.78)	1.78 lb
Yeast	1.25%	(.892 × 1.25 = 1.12)	1.12 lb
Total			150.08 lb

It's helpful to remember that when performing the calculations for the conversion factor, we always divide what we *need* (150 pounds in this case) by what we *have* (168.25 units in this case). The resulting number is the conversion factor, and it is then multiplied by the percentage of each ingredient.

Baker's Percentage and Pre-Ferments

There are a few considerations relating to baker's percentage when making bread with pre-ferments. The first is relatively simple: The pre-ferment is treated as any other ingredient. The second, figuring overall baker's percentage (Overall Formula), is slightly more complicated. Here is the final dough formula for French bread using a poolish:

FINAL DOUGH		
Flour	13.4 lb	100%
Water	6.4 lb	47.8%
Salt	.4 lb	3%
Yeast	.233 lb	1.7%
Poolish	13.217 lb	98.6%

Although there is accuracy to the percentages as they are expressed, there is also confusion. The 3 percent salt seems excessive, the 47.8 percent water seems far too little. As a whole, it is difficult to make any sense out of the formula by looking at the percentages. Of course, it is the presence of the poolish, comprised of equal weights flour and water, that makes the formula appear bewildering. When using pre-ferments, it is therefore a good idea to break the formula into its component parts, in this case overall formula, poolish, and last of all final dough—if those figures are desired. (In fact, the figures for the overall formula are by far the most important, followed by those for pre-ferments; figures for final dough generate more confusion than clarity, and it doesn't hurt to omit them altogether.) In any case, with the present formula, here is how we would represent those separate parts:

OVERALL FORMULA

Bread flour	20 lb	100%
Water	13 lb	65%
Salt	.4 lb	2%
Yeast	.25 lb	1.25%
Total	33.65 lb	168.25%

POOLISH

Bread flour	6.6 lb	100%
Water	6.6 lb	100%
Yeast	.017 lb	.25%
Total	13.217 lb	

FINAL DOUGH

Bread flour	13.4 lb	100%
Water	6.4 lb	47.8%
Salt	.4 lb	3%
Yeast	.233 lb	1.7%
Poolish	13.217 lb	98.6%
Total	33.65 lb	

Expressing the formula in this way gives an instant sense of the proportion of ingredients, one that would be completely lacking if the overall formula were omitted.

A final consideration for breads with pre-ferments concerns resizing of the formula. In the example used here, let's imagine we want to resize the above formula to make 50 pounds of bread. Knowing that the total of the percentages in the overall formula is 168.25 is not much help in computing the new weights for the poolish or final dough. The easiest way to proceed is to divide the new desired dough weight by the original dough weight: 50 ÷ 33.65 = 1.486. This tells us that we need to increase the weight of each ingredient by a factor of 1.486, which we do by multiplying the initial weight of each ingredient by that factor to obtain the new weight:

OVERALL FORMULA

	Initial Weight	× 1.486	
Bread flour	20 lb	29.72 lb	100%
Water	13 lb	19.32 lb	65%
Salt	.4 lb	.59 lb	2%
Yeast	.25 lb	.37 lb	1.25%
Total	33.65 lb	50 lb	168.25%

POOLISH

Bread flour	6.6 lb	9.81 lb	100%
Water	6.6 lb	9.81 lb	100%
Yeast	.017 lb	.025 lb	.25%
Total	13.217 lb	19.645 lb	

FINAL DOUGH

Bread flour	13.4 lb	19.91 lb	100%
Water	6.4 lb	9.51 lb	47.8%
Salt	.4 lb	.59 lb	3%
Yeast	.233 lb	.346 lb	1.7%
Poolish	13.217 lb	19.645 lb	98.6%
Total	33.65 lb	50.001 lb	

A Hypothetical Problem

At the beginning of mixing, a baker discovers that she has added 3 pounds too much water to the dough. The hydration should be 66 percent and now the dough is too wet. How much flour is needed to correct this and bring the hydration to 66 percent?

3 lb (extra water) ÷ 66 = .04545

.04545 × 100 = 4.5 lb flour needed

The 3 pounds of water is divided by 66 because there are 66 "units" in the extra water, and this calculation tells you the weight of one of those units. The result, .04545, is multiplied by 100, because the flour is represented by 100 units.

Desired Dough Temperature

One of the most important skills a baker must learn is the ability to accurately control dough temperature. The benefits are clear and immediate: more consistency in fermentation and in bread flavor, and more predictability in the overall production schedule. If a dough is coming off the machine at 65°F one day and 80°F the next, there will not be uniformity in the results. For the professional baker who is filling the oven over and over, accurate dough temperatures mean there will be no long gaps when the oven is burning fuel but empty; neither will there be times when more bread is risen and ready to bake than can fit into the oven. Because the home baker is always at a disadvantage—not able to mix doughs to the level of strength that the professional can, and lacking good steam—it is particularly important to do absolutely everything possible to benefit the doughs. By mixing doughs that are in the temperature zone that most favors *both* fermentation and flavor development, the home baker is well on the way to making consistently high-quality bread. After all, with something so emphatically alive as bread dough, we must do all we can to keep the billions of toiling microorganisms happy. And we do so by providing them a temperature that encourages good *gas* production from the yeast (for loaf volume), and at the same time good *flavor* development from the lactobacilli. For the most part, the temperature zone that works best, particularly for wheat-based breads, is 75° to 78°F.

Desired dough temperature is not an exact science, and there are numerous variables that can alter the results. It is, though, the best tool at the baker's disposal for consistently mixing doughs that stay within expected temperature parameters. The calculation of desired dough temperature involves taking into consideration several factors. These factors are the variables over which we have no control when we enter the bakeshop or kitchen and prepare to mix the dough: the air temperature, the temperature of the flour, the "friction factor" of the mixer, and the temperature of the pre-ferment, if any. After figuring these, it's easy and quick to compute the water temperature (the only variable over which we do have control).

Let's assume that we want a desired dough temperature of 76°F. With a straight dough we multiply 76 by 3, and if there is a pre-ferment we multiply it by 4. The result is the total temperature factor. Once this factor is determined, the known temperatures are subtracted from it, and the result is the correct temperature of the water for the dough. Here are two examples:

Desired dough temperature (DDT)	76°F	76°F
Multiplication factor	× 3 (straight dough)	× 4 (dough with pre-ferment)
Total temperature factor	228°F	304°F
Minus flour temperature	72°F	72°F
Minus room temperature	68°F	68°F
Minus pre-ferment temperature	n/a	70°F
Minus friction factor	26°F	26°F
Water temperature	62°F	68°F

For the straight dough, water at 62°F gives us a final dough temperature of approximately 76°F. With a pre-ferment, water at 68°F yields a dough temperature of 76°F.

What is this "friction factor," and how do we come up with its value for our mixer? As a dough spins, heat is generated by the friction caused by the action of the dough hook and bowl on the dough. In the course of the mix, a considerable amount of temperature increase is directly due to the friction being generated, enough so that we must consider it when we make the computations for desired dough temperature (in fact, for doughs that mix for 3 minutes on first speed and 3 or 4 minutes on second, the friction factor for most mixers is in the range of 24° to 28°F, quite a substantial temperature increase). Several factors affect the amount of friction generated during mixing, such as the type of mixer being used (stand, spiral, oblique, or planetary), the length of mix time, the mixing speeds used, and the quantity of dough in the bowl.

There are a couple of ways to establish the friction factor for a given mixer. The first is to wing it: Make the calculations for desired dough temperature and ascribe, say, 26°F as the friction factor, then mix the dough as you normally would. After the mix, take the dough temperature and see how accurate the actual temperature is compared to the desired temperature. If the dough is, for instance, 2°F cooler than anticipated, decrease the friction factor by 2°F, and the next time you mix use this lower figure when doing your calculations. The more scientific method used to determine the friction factor for a given mixer is first to make a trial dough. But for this dough, water (and not friction) is considered one of the variable factors, and we arbitrarily decide on a certain temperature for the water. We take the temperature of the dough after mixing and use the results to calculate the friction factor. It is important to mix the dough as you normally would, for instance, 3 minutes on first speed and 3 minutes on second. Once we arrive at the amount of friction generated by that mixer and those mix times, we use that friction factor whenever we compute desired dough temperature. Here are two examples:

Actual dough temperature (after mixing)	78°F	78°F
Multiplication factor	× 3 (straight dough)	× 4 (dough with pre-ferment)
Total temperature factor	234°F	312°F
Minus flour temperature	71°F	71°F
Minus room temperature	73°F	73°F
Minus water temperature	66°F	66°F
Minus pre-ferment temperature	n/a	78°F
Friction factor	24°F	24°F

A true story: On September 1 a couple of years ago, I was on the bread shift at the King Arthur Flour Bakery. The summer had been a hot one, and when I arrived in the early hours, the windows were all wide open. I took the temperature of the air, flour, and poolish, as the bread mixer does each morning (we know the friction factor and don't need to determine it each day), and calculated the water temperature for the French bread dough: I needed 34°F water. We keep large buckets of water in the retarder all summer, and I put some ice in a couple of them to bring the temperature down to the required 34°F. When I mixed the bread, the temperature came out at 75°F, just as I had wanted.

Four days later, I was again on the bread shift. Again the windows had been open wide overnight, but this time, the first early harbinger of fall had come down in the night on the winds from Canada. The bakery was chilly and cool—a delight! I took the temperatures of the air, flour, and poolish, and this time needed 96°F water for the French bread. I rubbed my eyes a couple of times, but put aside any incredulity and got that warm, warm water from the sink. Once mixed, I had French bread at 75°F. In the course of four days, the dough water had more than a 60°F change of temperature, and in both instances the final dough temperature came out where I wanted it—for which I could only thank those quick calculations that are the heart of desired dough temperature.

Computing Batch Cost

The ingredients that go into a loaf of bread are relatively inexpensive. Certainly, the ingredient cost of a loaf of lean dough, like a baguette or ciabatta, is astonishingly low. Of course, this changes quickly when we add cheese, olives, or other costly ingredients. Whether making breads that cost a dime or a dollar per pound of dough, it's important to know how to compute the batch cost for a given quantity of dough. Let's take the example of a batch of dough using the following weights:

Flour	100 lb
Water	66 lb
Salt	2 lb
Yeast	1.5 lb

Simple arithmetic tells us that dough yield is 169.5 pounds. Next, consider the cost per pound of our ingredients:

Flour	$.18 per pound
Water	$0.00
Salt	$.09 per pound
Yeast	$.56 per pound

Note that although water is considered to be free, it is still included in the dough weight. The next step is to compute the entire batch cost:

Flour	$.18 × 100 =	$18.00
Water		$0.00
Salt	$.09 × 2 =	$.18
Yeast	$.56 × 1.5 =	$.84
Batch cost		$19.02

It has cost $19.02 in ingredients to make 169.5 pounds of dough. To compute the cost of 1 pound of dough, divide the batch cost by the dough weight:

19.02 ÷ 169.5 = $.112

The batch cost is 11.2¢ per pound of dough.

Useful Conversions and Equivalencies

Temperature Conversion Formulas

To convert from Celsius to Fahrenheit:
Celsius temperature × 1.8 + 32.

To convert from Fahrenheit to Celsius:
Fahrenheit temperature – 32 × .555.

C°	F°	C°	F°	C°	F°
–5	23	24	75.2	195	383
–3	26.6	25	77	200	392
–1	30.2	26	78.8	205	401
0	32	27	80.6	210	410
1	33.8	28	82.4	215	419
3	37.4	29	84.2	220	428
5	41	30	86	225	437
7	44.6	31	87.8	230	446
10	50	32	89.6	235	455
12	53.6	33	91.4	240	464
15	59	35	95	245	473
18	64.4	175	347	250	482
20	68	180	356	255	491
22	71.6	185	365	260	500
23	73.4	190	374	265	509

Yeast Conversions, Fresh to Dry

Formulas using fresh yeast, also known as baker's yeast or compressed yeast, can be converted to dry yeast by using the following factor:

- **FROM FRESH YEAST TO ACTIVE DRY:** For each pound of fresh yeast, use .4 pound of active dry yeast (this yeast must be dissolved in water before incorporating it into dough). For each ounce of fresh yeast, use .4 ounce of active dry yeast.

- **FROM FRESH YEAST TO INSTANT YEAST:** For each pound of fresh yeast, use .33 pound dry yeast (this yeast can be included, without first dissolving it, with the other ingredients in the dough). For each ounce of fresh yeast, use .33 ounce of instant dry yeast.

Dry Yeast Conversions, Ounce to Tablespoons/Teaspoons

.1 oz = .9 tsp

.2 oz = 1.8 tsp

.3 oz = 2.7 tsp

.4 oz = 1 T + .6 tsp

.5 oz = 1 T + 1.5 tsp

.6 oz = 1 T + 2.4 tsp

.7 oz = 2 T + .3 tsp

.8 oz = 2 T + 1.2 tsp

.9 oz = 2 T + 2.1 tsp

1 oz = 3 T

Grams, Kilograms, Ounces, Pounds

Europeans have the advantage of using the precise metric system in baking. Writing, scaling, and interpreting formulas is always more cumbersome when using ounces, pounds, and quarts. Fortunately, more and more professional formulas are being written using metric measurements. A thorough working knowledge of the metric system is important. Below is a list of the most common conversions.

1 g = .035 oz

1 oz = 28.35 g

1 lb = 16 oz = 453.6 g

1000 g = 1 kg = 35.27 oz = 2 lb, 3¼ oz

1 fl oz = 29.57 mL
(Note that 1 fluid ounce weighs 1.043 ounces, and therefore a *pint* is *not* a pound the world around.)

1 liter = 1000 mL = 33.8 fl oz = 1.06 qt

1 qt = .95 liter

1 qt = 2 pints = 4 cups = 32 oz

TO CONVERT	TO	MULTIPLY BY
Ounces (oz)	Grams (g)	28.35
Grams (g)	Ounces (oz)	.035
Pounds (lb)	Kilograms (kg)	.45
Kilograms (kg)	Pounds (lb)	2.2
Fluid ounces (fl oz)	Milliliters (mL)	29.57
Quarts (qt)	Liters (L)	.946
Liters (L)	Quarts (qt)	1.1
Gallons (gal)	Liters (L)	3.785

Fractions and Decimals

To convert ounces into pounds, divide the ounces by 16:

5 oz ÷ 16 = .3125 lb   140 oz ÷ 16 = 8.75 lb

To convert pounds into ounces, multiply the portion of a pound by 16:

.68 lb × 16 = 10.88 oz

To convert 1.75 lb to pounds and ounces:

.75 lb × 16 = 12 oz   Therefore, 1.75 lb = 1 lb, 12 oz

To convert a fraction of an ounce into a decimal, divide the top portion of the fraction by the bottom portion:

¼ oz → 1 ÷ 4 = .25 oz

To convert the decimal portion of an ounce into a fraction, first represent the decimal as a fraction, then find the lowest common denominator. For example:

.5 oz = 5/10 = ½ oz

.75 oz = 75/100 = ¾ oz

Sample Proofing Schedule

Date:

Bread	Water Temp.	Dough Temp.	Finish Mix	Fold	Fold	Divide	Shape	Bake

Epilogue

The bread was there before I was, before any of us were; the foundations and fundamentals have been in place and intact for centuries. With an eager mind and willing hands, we enter into the baking life, with a sense of awe at what we see being made and how it comes to be made. We are most fortunate to have found work that is useful, stimulating, and fulfilling.

One challenge we face is to fashion a baking life that is sustainable. The work is good, too good to risk leaving it aside in a few short years. As a baker, it is easy to work ten hours a day, or twelve, or more. But the pace can't be sustained, and sooner or later a baker with that kind of regimen will be exhausted. It is rare that a baker gets rich from his or her work; in fact, I am sure most bakers enter the trade for reasons other than the promise of wealth. To know for ourselves how much of the world's prosperity we need, and to be content with it, allows for the possibility of happiness because the endless yearning for more and more ceases. When we have for part of our reward the respect of those who receive our baked goods, the integrity of providing nourishment and pleasure to others, and the awareness that our contributions of skill and labor add to the well-being of our community, we have already come a long way toward fashioning a sustainable lifestyle from baking.

We all have teachers, and collectively they have helped bring us along the continuum of baking to where we, as individual bakers, are today. If, at the end of our baking days, we have not attained the level of quality and workmanship of our teachers, then we have failed. If we end our careers at the same level of accomplishment as our teachers, we have achieved the status quo. When we surpass our teachers and bring the world of baking some small degree further, when we pass on to the next generation of bakers some part of our acquired abilities and leave the baking world a little better than it was when we entered it, then—*then*—we will have achieved positive evolution.

Bake, learn, share, teach, bake. Stand proudly on the shoulders of your teachers. Bake.

—Hartland, Vermont

Glossary

Absorption The ability of a flour to absorb water.

Acetic acid An acid in sourdough culture and sourdough bread. It develops best under cool and stiff dough conditions. Along with lactic acid, it provides the sour taste in sourdough bread.

Aldehydes Organic compounds that contribute to bread flavor and aroma.

Aleurone layer The outermost layer of the endosperm, generally removed with the rest of the bran prior to milling.

Alveograph Also known as the Chopin alveograph, a testing instrument that is used to measure the relative strength and baking ability of a sample of flour. It is more commonly used in Europe than in North America.

Amylases Enzymes present in cereal grains that convert starches into sugars and dextrins.

Ascorbic acid A flour oxidant, added either at the mill or by the baker, that increases dough elasticity and volume.

Ash The charred remains after a flour sample is incinerated; it consists mostly of minerals. The ash content is an indication not only of the mineral content of a flour sample, but also suggests what portion of the grain has been milled. Flour with a low ash content has been milled close to the center of the endosperm; whole-grain flour has the highest readings.

Autolyse A method for mixing certain wheat breads and sourdough breads, developed by Professor Raymond Calvel, in which the flour and water (and sometimes the pre-ferment) are mixed very lightly, after which the dough rests before the remaining ingredients are added and final mixing begins. Extensibility, dough volume, and potential improvement in aroma and flavor result from the autolyse technique.

Azodicarbonamide A chemical agent, added to white flour at the mill, that artificially oxidizes the flour and increases loaf volume. Not all flour is treated with azodicarbonamide.

Baker's percentage The standard method of calculating the proportion of ingredients in a bread dough. The flour is always considered 100 percent, and each of the other dough ingredients is expressed as a percentage of the flour weight.

Banneton A coiled or woven basket, generally round or oval shaped, sometimes lined with linen, used for the final proofing of bread.

Bâtard An oval-shaped loaf.

Benzoyl peroxide A bleaching agent added to white flour at the mill to chemically oxidize and whiten it. Not all flour is treated with benzoyl peroxide.

Biga An Italian term for pre-ferment, which can be either stiff or loose textured. It is made from flour, water, and a small portion of yeast.

Bleaching The process of adding benzoyl peroxide or chlorine gas to flour in order to chemically oxidize and whiten it.

Boule A round loaf.

Bran The outermost edible layer of the wheat kernel, consisting mainly of minerals and cellulose.

Bromate A chemical bread additive, considered carcinogenic, that artificially matures white flour and increases loaf volume.

Caramelization A combination of sugars and heat that contributes to the crust browning of bread. It occurs in the oven at surface temperatures between 300° and 400°F.

Chef In bread making, *chef* refers to a piece of ripe sourdough culture, kept aside before final dough mixing in order to perpetuate the culture.

Chlorine A gas added at the mill to artificially whiten flour. It is generally used in the milling of cake flour.

Clear flour Flour milled from the outer periphery of the endosperm.

Couche Linen used by bakers to hold bread during its final proofing.

Crumb The inner portion of a loaf of bread.

Desem A style of naturally leavened bread making using whole-wheat flour, of Flemish origin.

Dextrin A complex carbohydrate in flour starch that is related to glucose, and produced by amylase activity on the starch.

Diastatic malt Malt that has active amylase enzymes in it.

Durum One of the hard wheats, characterized by a high-protein level and golden color. Semolina and durum flour are milled from it.

Einkorn An ancient "one seed" wheat, first cultivated about twelve thousand years ago in the Fertile Crescent.

Elasticity The characteristic, found mostly in wheat doughs, that allows the dough to spring back after being stretched. It contributes significantly to volume and loaf structure. In wheat flour, glutenin contributes elasticity.

Emmer One of the first cultivated grains, an ancient wheat originally grown about twelve thousand years ago in the Fertile Crescent.

Endosperm The innermost, starchy portion of a cereal grain. The gluten-forming proteins in wheat flour are located in the endosperm.

Extensibility The ability of a dough to be extended or stretched. In wheat flour, the protein gliadin contributes extensibility.

Extraction rate The percentage of flour obtained (extracted) from grain; once the bran and germ are removed, the extraction rate is typically about 72 percent for white flour.

Falling Number test A test performed on a flour sample that measures its degree of amylase activity.

Farinograph A testing device that measures a bread's resistance to break down or collapse when made with a specific flour sample.

Fermentation In bread production, *fermentation* refers to the conversion, by yeast, of sugars into carbon dioxide, alcohol, heat, and organic acids.

Folding A technique, used to degas bread dough, that can also have the effect of strengthening the dough.

Fungal amylase An amylase derived from fungal sources, which is dried and added as a powder at the mill to correct enzymatic deficiencies in flour. It is often used instead of malted barley.

Germ The embryo of a cereal grain, from which the root and shoot of the new plant emerge; it comprises 2.5 to 3.5 percent of the kernel and is high in fats and vitamins.

Gliadin A flour protein that provides extensibility to dough; combined with glutenin, it forms gluten.

Gluten The combination of proteins that contribute, particularly in wheat flour, to dough elasticity, extensibility, and strength. Gluten's ability to trap gasses encourages loaf structure and volume.

Glutelin A protein found in certain cereal grains, such as wheat, rye, and barley, as well as in certain grasses, such as corn and rice.

Glutenin A protein, found mainly in wheat flour, that provides elasticity and strength; combined with gliadin, it forms gluten.

Green flour White flour that has not been sufficiently aged, either naturally or by the addition of chemical additives. Generally, lack of dough strength, gummy crumb, poor crust color, and poor volume result from the use of green flour.

Hard wheat One of the six classes of wheat that are high in protein and generally used in bread production.

Heterofermentative lactobacilli Naturally occurring bacteria in sourdough cultures that produce both lactic and acetic acid.

Homofermentative lactobacilli Naturally occurring bacteria in sourdough cultures (particularly young cultures) that produce mainly lactic acid.

Hydration The percentage of liquid ingredients in a bread dough in relation to its flour weight.

Hygroscopic Attracting and holding moisture; a characteristic, for example, of sugar and salt in a dough environment.

Kamut A grain, originally from Egypt, occasionally used in bread making.

Ketones Organic compounds that contribute to bread flavor and aroma.

Lactic acid An acid in sourdough culture and bread. In bread, it is responsible, along with acetic acid, for imparting a sour taste. It develops best in warm and moist dough conditions.

Lactobacilli In sourdough bread production, the strains of bacteria that produce mostly lactic and acetic acid and contribute to bread flavor and aroma.

Lame A slender piece of metal fitted with a razor blade, used for scoring bread.

L-cysteine A flour additive that weakens dough structure and increases extensibility, often used in no-time doughs.

Levain The French term for sourdough bread. It can also refer to the final stage of building before a dough is mixed.

Maillard browning A chemical reaction that requires proteins, sugars, heat, and moisture, and contributes to crust browning. It occurs when surface dough temperatures are between 212° and 350°F.

Malted barley Barley that has been soaked, sprouted, dried, then ground into a powder. Quite high in amylase enzymes, it is generally added to flour at the mill. The baker may also add malt powder or syrup to dough.

Miche A French term for a large, round loaf, originally often weighing in excess of 10 pounds; for centuries, it was the kind of bread typically eaten by people in Europe.

Nondiastatic malt Malt in which the natural amylase enzymes have been deactivated.

No-time dough Bread dough that receives no fermentation after mixing. It is usually chemically treated to weaken the gluten and allow it to be divided and shaped once mixing is finished.

Oblique mixer A style of bread mixer with two mixing arms that enter the mixing bowl at an angle and rotate as the mixing bowl spins; also known as a fork mixer.

Organic acids Acids produced by bacteria, particularly in doughs using pre-ferments, which provide flavor and aroma to bread.

Oven spring The rapid expansion in loaf volume that occurs during the first few minutes of baking.

Oxidation of dough The process of incorporating oxygen into a mixer by the action of the mixing arm. It helps strengthen gluten bonds, but an excess can cause artificial maturing of the dough and, eventually, dough breakdown.

Oxidation of flour A process, occurring after milling, that strengthens flour proteins. Natural oxidizing results from allowing flour to age for a few weeks after milling. Artificial oxidation is done at the mill by chemically treating the flour, making it bakeable without the need to age it naturally.

Pâte fermentée A pre-ferment, sometimes called simply "old dough." It can be prepared as a separate mixture, or taken from a batch of fully mixed dough for later use in another dough.

Patent flour White flour milled from the heart of the endosperm.

Peel A flat, long-handled shovel made of wood or metal used to unload bread from an oven. Lacking a conveyor-style loader, a peel is also used to load bread into an oven.

Pentosan A cereal gum that is a type of polysaccharide found in grain; pentosans are particularly high in rye.

Pericarp Literally the "fruit coat," the pericarp consists of several layers that surround individual cereal grains; it is part of the bran layer.

Phytic acid A substance in wheat bran that can interfere with the body's ability to absorb calcium and iron. In a sourdough environment, almost all phytic acid is neutralized, thereby increasing the nutritional value of the bread.

Planetary mixer A style of mixer, useful not only for bread doughs but also for pastry doughs, creams, and batters, with a fixed bowl and a mixing arm that enters the bowl vertically from above. Most heavy-duty, or stand-type, home mixers are planetary in design.

Poolish A type of pre-ferment made of equal weights of flour and water and a small portion of yeast, used in both bread and pastry production.

Pre-ferment A portion of a dough's overall ingredients that are mixed together and allowed to ferment before being added to the final dough mix.

Proofing A term denoting the rising of bread, either before or after loaf shaping.

Pullman bread Loaves baked in straight-sided loaf pans, often lidded to give an even crust around the entire surface and a square shape to the slices.

Pumpernickel A meal or coarse flour ground from the entire rye berry. It also refers to bread made using mostly or all pumpernickel meal and baked for 12 or more hours in a low oven. In the United States pumpernickel bread is usually artificially darkened by the use of caramel color.

Retarding The process of slowing fermentation by refrigerating bread dough or shaped loaves, often for 16 hours or more.

Rheology Technically, the study of the deformation and flow of matter. In bread making, *rheology* refers to the different tests performed on a flour sample that measure its relative strength and baking ability.

Sauerteig The German term for sourdough bread, generally referring to rye-based breads.

Soft wheat A class of wheat that is low in protein, generally used in pastry production.

Sourdough starter A culture of microorganisms, often perpetuated for many years (or generations), that contains wild yeasts and bacteria. A sourdough culture provides both leavening and flavor to bread.

Spelt flour A flour with good bread-making qualities, known as *Dinkel* in Germany and *farro* in Italy. It can be tolerated by people with certain bread allergies.

Spiral mixer A style of bread mixer that has one curved vertical mixing arm in the back, and a mixing bowl that rotates as the arm spins.

Sponge A general term for a pre-ferment, usually relatively loose textured.

Spring wheat A hard wheat (the source for high-gluten flour), planted in spring and harvested in late summer.

Starch The reserve of carbohydrates found in cereal grains. In wheat, it comprises approximately 72 percent of the overall kernel.

Starch, damaged Starch granules that have been damaged, primarily during the milling process, and are therefore susceptible to amylase activity and absorption of dough water.

Starch attack In rye bread, the breaking down of dough structure during the bake, caused by amylase activity that degrades the crumb after the commencement of starch gelatinization and crumb development. It is prevented by the use of sourdough, which inhibits excessive amylase activity.

Starch gelatinization The process that starch undergoes in the presence of heat and moisture that causes it to swell, gel, and set loaf structure.

Starch retrogradation The gradual giving up of moisture by starch after baking, which contributes to bread staling.

Starter A general term for a sourdough culture.

Straight dough A style of mixing, also known as "direct method," in which all the dough ingredients are mixed at once and no pre-ferments are used.

Straight flour Flour milled from the entire endosperm, without separation into clear or patent flours.

Strap pans Loaf pans commonly used in commercial bread production; three or more pans are connected into one unit by metal strapping.

Tempering The process of soaking grain at the mill prior to milling. It toughens the bran and facilitates the separation of the bran from the endosperm during milling.

Thermal Death Point (T.D.P.) The temperature at which yeast cells die, about 140°F.

Transfer peel A thin strip of wood used to transfer raw bread from linen *couches* to a loading conveyor or peel prior to the bake.

Triticale A cross of wheat and rye developed in Scotland in 1875.

Vollkornbrot Literally, "full-grain bread," it refers to a class of German-style breads that are made entirely or almost entirely with whole grains.

White whole wheat A hard wheat; the normal reddish pigment of the bran has been neutralized in white whole wheat, softening the bran's slightly bitter flavor and yielding a flour that is lighter in color than that milled from red wheat.

Winter wheat A hard wheat, planted in autumn and harvested the following year in late spring or early summer.

Yeast A single-celled fungus, of which there are thousands of different strains. In bread making, the metabolic action of yeast converts sugars to carbon dioxide gas and alcohol during the process of fermentation.

Bibliography

Alford, Jeffrey, and Naomi Duguid. *Flatbreads and Flavors*. New York: William Morrow, 1995.

Amendola, Joseph, and Donald Lundberg. *Understanding Baking*. New York: Van Nostrand Reinhold, 1992.

Banfield, Walter T. *Manna: A Comprehensive Treatise on Bread Manufacture*. London: Maclaren, 1947.

Bilheux, Roland, Alain Escoffier, Daniel Hervé, and Jean-Marie Pouradier. *Special and Decorative Breads*. Paris: Compagnie Internationale de Consultation Education et Media, and New York: Van Nostrand Reinhold, 1989.

Boily, Lise, and Jean François Blanchette. *The Bread Ovens of Quebec*. Ottawa, Canada: National Museums of Canada, 1979.

Calvel, Raymond. *The Secrets of the Parisian Baguette and French Bread*. Editions Jérôme Villette on behalf of the Union des Fabricants Français d'Equipements pour la Boulangerie et la Pâtisserie, 1998.

Calvel, Raymond, James MacGuire, and Ronald Wirtz. *The Taste of Bread*. Gaithersburg, Md.: Aspen Publishers, 2001.

Calvel, Raymond. *Une Vie, du Pain et des Miettes*. Paris, France: L'Amicale des Anciens Éléves et des Amis du Professeur Calvel, 2002.

Child, Julia, and Simone Beck. *Mastering the Art of French Cooking*. Vol. 2. New York: Alfred A. Knopf, 1979.

Collister, Linda, and Anthony Blake. *The Bread Book*. New York: The Lyons Press, 1993.

Consonni, Giancarlo, "Wheat and Corn." *Slow: The International Herald of Tastes,* July 2002, 82–87.

Corriher, Shirley. *Cookwise*. New York: William Morrow, 1997.

Couet, Alain, and Éric Kayser, with Bernard, Isabelle, and Valérie Ganachaud, Daniel Hervé, Léon Mégard, and Yves Saunier. *Special and Decorative Breads, Volume Two*. Paris: Compagnie Internationale de Consultation Education et Media, and New York: Van Nostrand Reinhold, 1990.

David, Elizabeth. *English Bread and Yeast Cookery.* Newton, Mass.: Biscuit Books, 1994.

Davis, Sharon P. *From Wheat to Flour.* Washington, D.C.: Millers' National Federation, and Englewood, Colo.: Wheat Foods Council, 1996.

Doose, Otto. *Rustikale Sauerteigbrote.* Stuttgart, Germany: Hugo Matthaes Druckerei, and Verlag GmbH, 1985.

Dupaigne, Bernard. *Le Pain.* Paris: La Courtille, 1979.

Dupaigne, Bernard. *The History of Bread.* New York: Harry N. Abrams, 1999.

Field, Carol. *The Italian Baker.* New York: Harper & Row, 1985.

Glezer, Maggie. *Artisan Baking Across America.* New York: Artisan, 2000.

Hoseney, R. Carl. *Principles of Cereal Science and Technology.* St. Paul, Minn.: American Association of Cereal Chemists, 1994.

Jacob, H. E. *Six Thousand Years of Bread: Its Holy and Unholy History.* New York: Lyons & Burford, Publishers, 1944.

Kaplan, Stephen Laurence. *The Bakers of Paris and the Bread Question, 1700–1775.* Durham, N.C.: Duke University Press, 1996.

Kline, L., and T. F. Sugihara. "Microorganisms of the San Francisco Sour Dough French Bread Process." *Applied Microbiology* (March 1971), 459–465.

L'École Lenôtre. *Les Pains et Viennoiseries de l'École Lenôtre.* France: *Éditions Jérôme Villette*, 1995.

Leonard, Thom. *The Bread Book.* Brookline, Mass.: East West Health Books, 1990.

McGee, Harold. *On Food and Cooking.* New York: Charles Scribner's Sons, Macmillan, 1984.

Mintz, Sidney W., and Daniela Schlettwein-Gsell. "Food Patterns in Agrarian Societies: The Core-Fringe-Legume Hypothesis." *Gastonomica, The Journal of Food and Culture* 1, no. 3 (2001), 41–52.

Pyler, E. J. *Baking Science & Technology.* Chicago: Siebel Publishing, 1973.

Rambali, Paul. *Boulangerie.* New York: Macmillan, 1994.

Richter, Victor F. A. *Vienna Bread and Continental Breads de Luxe.* London: Maclaren & Sons, Ltd.

Roussel, Philippe, and Hubert Chiron. *Les Pains Francais.* Levallois-Perret, France: Maé-Erti, 2004.

Scherber, Amy, and Toy Kim Dupree. *Amy's Bread.* New York: William Morrow, 1996.

Schünemann, Claus, and Günter Treu. *Baking, the Art and Science.* Calgary, Canada: Baker Tech, 1988.

Steffen, Franz-Josef. *Brotland Deutschland.* Bochum, Germany: Deutscher Bäcker-Verlag GmbH, 2000.

Steffen, Franz-Josef. *Flechten, Formen, Modellieren.* Bochum, Germany: Deutscher Bäcker-Verlag GmbH, 1986.

Sugihara, T. F., L. Kline, and L. B. McCready. "Nature of the San Francisco Sour Dough French Bread Process." *Baker's Digest* 44 (1970), 48–55.

Toussaint-Samat, Maguelonne. *A History of Food.* Cambridge, Mass.: Blackwell Publishers, 1996.

Wing, Daniel, and Alan Scott. *The Bread Builders.* White River Junction, Vt.: Chelsea Green Publishing, 1999.

Index

C

D

E

F

G

H

I

J

K

L

M

N

O

P

R

S

T

U

V

W

Y

JEFFERY HAMELMAN has been baking professionally for nearly thirty years. For half that time he owned a bakery in Vermont. He has served as a baking and pastry instructor at several culinary schools and has baked and taught in France, Germany, Canada, Ireland, Brazil, and Japan. In 1996, he was selected as Captain of Baking Team USA, the three-person team that represented the United States in Paris at the Coupe du Monde de la Boulangerie-the World Cup of Baking. In 1998, he became the 76th Certified Master Baker in the United States. He is Director of the Bakery and Baking Education Center at the King Arthur Flour Company in Norwich, Vermont. In this capacity, he teaches professional baking classes one week each month and bakes for three weeks each month in King Arthur's production bakery.

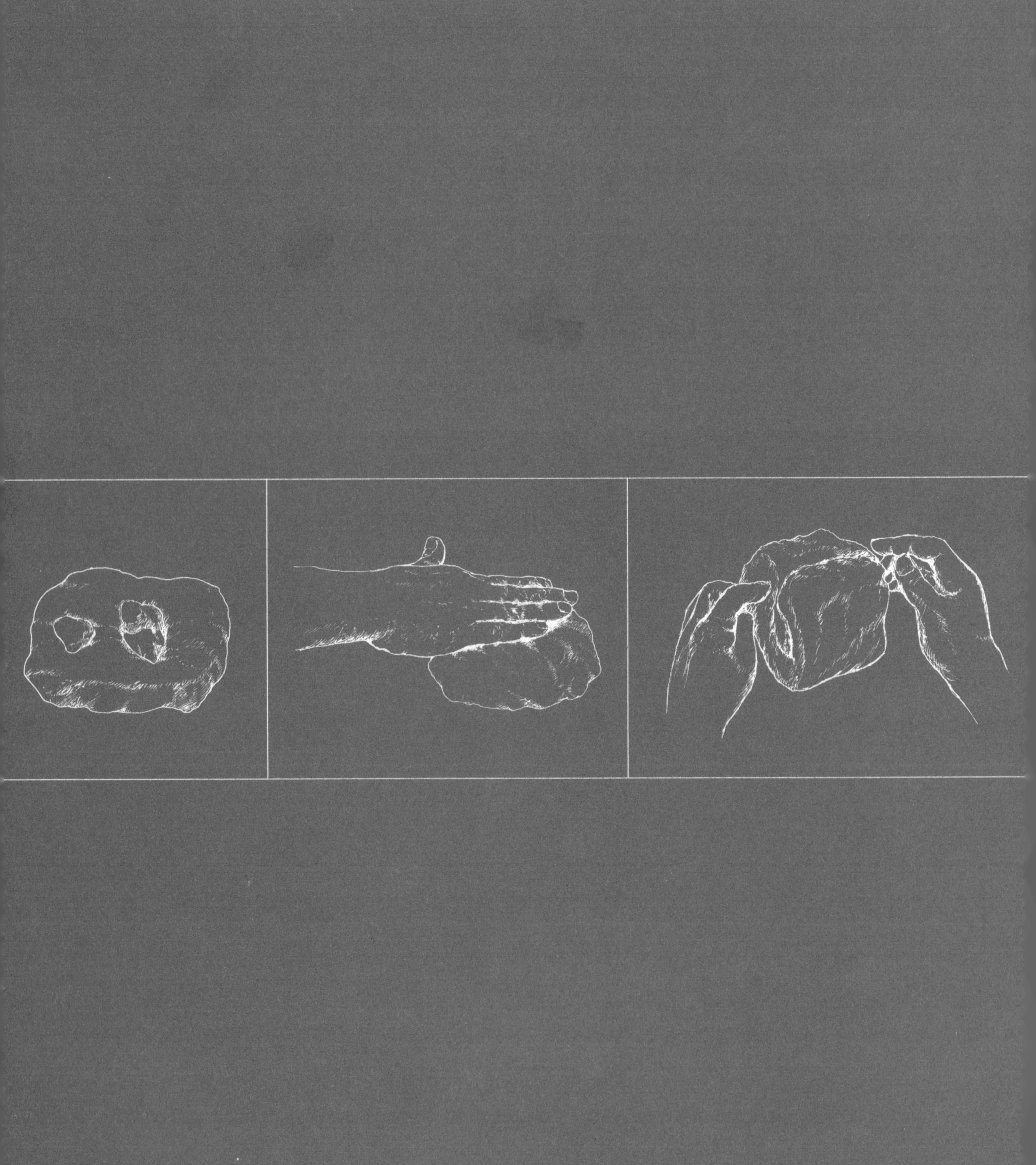